D0022826

POLICE ADMINISTRATION

MACMILLAN CRIMINAL JUSTICE SERIES

SECOND EDITION

POLICE ADMINISTRATION

Structures, Processes, and Behavior

CHARLES R. SWANSON
University of Georgia

LEONARD TERRITO
University of South Florida

ROBERT W. TAYLOR
University of Texas, Tyler

Macmillan Publishing Company
New York

Collier Macmillan Publishers
London

Copyright © 1988, Macmillan Publishing Company,
a division of Macmillan, Inc.

PRINTED IN THE UNITED STATES OF AMERICA

Earlier edition copyright © 1983 by Macmillan Publishing Co., Inc.

Macmillan Publishing Company
866 Third Avenue, New York, New York 10022

Collier Macmillan Canada, Inc.

Library of Congress Cataloging-in-Publication Data

Swanson, Charles R.,
  Police administration.

  (Macmillan criminal justice series)
  Includes bibliographies and index.
  1. Police administration.   I. Territo, Leonard.
II. Taylor, Robert W.   III. Title.   IV. Series.
HV7935.S95   1987   351.74   86–18186
ISBN 0–02–418530–2

Printing: 7   Year: 1 2 3

ISBN 0-02-418530-2

For Kittsu and Sherri

Preface

The publication of a book's first edition is, to some extent, a shot in the dark. Both the publisher and the authors hope that the book will meet with some degree of acceptance. If this happens and the work continues into a second edition, the authors must accept a different challenge: How to preserve the qualities that led readers to support the first edition while at the same time modifying the book's coverage. In planning the second edition we relied heavily on feedback from students, from professors who had used the first edition, and from reviewers such as Jack Greene, Temple University. It is not possible to satisfy each person who made the effort to advise us on what changes they believed were needed. Yet, it was our intention to consider all views respectfully before deciding on a course of action. We hope that we have done this.

Among the changes reflected in this edition are the addition of Bob Taylor as a coauthor, two new chapters "Concepts of Police Organizational Design" and "Information Systems and Applications," additional examples, diagrams, photographs, updated references, the reorganization of several chapters, and a major rewriting of Chapter 10, "Legal Aspects of Police Administration," to reflect changes in the law.

The three coauthors have been police officers and administrators. Collectively for over 55 years we have studied, practiced, researched, taught, and consulted on police administration. An inevitable by-product of these experiences is the development of certain perspectives. As these perspectives form the rationale for this book, it is important to the reader's understanding that they be stated plainly once again in this edition.

Most police administration books favor one view or another; the subtitle of this one, "Structures, Processes, and Behavior," effectively serves notice of our conviction that in healthy, achieving organizations the relative value of all three views is recognized and integrated. This book employs a public administration perspective and is interdisciplinary in content. It is intended for serious observers of police administration.

As such, the coverage is comprehensive and analytical, and it systematically draws upon empirical literature.

Sprinkled throughout are materials such as news clippings and vignettes from our own experiences—including failures, which are often most instructive, although dearly purchased—to illustrate points discussed in the narrative and to make them concrete. We have striven to make them timely and meaningful. We have tried to communicate not only any conclusions we may have reached but also any ambiguities we might feel. The reader should be aware of our bias that police administration is a complex and dynamic process; it is always—because of the stresses, strains, and influences of the larger society—in motion and in the process of becoming. Although not without its failures and unseemly sides, the notable theme of American police administration, contrary to the conventional wisdom, is its vitality and capacity for programmatic change.

Finally, the mention of a product or firm in this book is intended for illustrative purposes and does not necessarily constitute an endorsement or recommendation by the authors or the publisher.

Acknowledgments

Physically, writing a book is a solitary endeavor. However, as a process writing is highly interactive; anything that makes the transition from an idea to a published work requires extensive goodwill and support from many people. Although it is insufficient compensation for their gracious assistance, we wish to recognize here the individuals and organizations who helped to make this book a reality.

Don Slesnick, attorney at law, Miami Florida, and Janet E. Ferris, General Counsel, Florida Department of Law Enforcement, Tallahassee, Florida, wrote Chapter 10, "Legal Aspects of Police Administration." This is a major rewriting of the chapter in the first edition co-authored by Don Slesnick and Jack Call. While Jack's schedule precluded his being able to be part of the second edition, we appreciate his contribution to the first edition and feel fortunate to have Janet as part of the second edition. Hal Vetter, a friend for some 20 years, co-authored Chapter 8, "Stress and Police Personnel."

Maggie Deutsch, Chris Pfleger, Cindy Boyles, Linda Steed, Mike Copeland, Lucia Grimaldi, Gregg Gronlund, Robin Kester, Marian Pittman, Cecile Pulin, Lynn Humphrey, Dwayne Shumate, Kris Hill, Sophia Lenderman, and Jacqueline Maxfield provided typing and research assistance and made innumerable contributions.

Those who supplied photographs and written material and made suggestions about how to strengthen the book include: Charles Rinkevich and Peggy Hayward, Federal Law Enforcement Training Center, Glynco, Georgia; the Drug Enforcement Administration; Jim Campbell, East Carolina University; Chief John Kerns, Sacramento, California, Police Department; the U.S. Secret Service; Willie Ellison, Alcohol, Tobacco, and Firearms; Deputy Superintendent Jim Finley, Illinois State Police; Dr. Peter Nelligan, University of Texas at Tyler; Larry Gaines, Eastern Kentucky University; Drs. Walter Booth and Chris Hornick, Multidimensional Research Associates, Aurora, Colorado; Pat Karman, Ohio State University; Captain Lawrence Akley, St. Louis Metro Police Department; Chief Lee McGehee and Captain Glenn Whiteacre, Ocala, Florida, Police Department; the Maricopa, Arizona, Sheriff's Office; Inspector Vivian Edmonds and Commander Dorothy Knox, Detroit, Michigan, Police Department; Major Herman Ingram, Baltimore, Maryland, Police Department; Commissioner Morgan Elkins and Captain Dennis Goss, Kentucky State Police; Bobbie Cooksey, Criterion Inc., Dallas, Texas; the St. Paul, Minnesota, Police Department; Thomas J. Deakin and William Tafoya, Federal Bureau of Investigation; Ron Lynch, University of North Carolina; the Tigard, Oregon, Police Department; the California Highway Patrol; Dr. Zug Standing Bear, Valdosta State University; Norma Kane, Kansas City, Missouri, Police Department; San Diego, California, Police Department; Drs. Gary Sykes and Jerry Vito, University of Louisville; Chief Larry Robinson, Tyler, Texas, Police Department; Chief Jim Wetherington and Deputy Chief Sam Woodall, Columbus, Georgia, Police Department; Janice Lowenberg, U.S. Probation and Parole; the Texas Department of Public Safety; the Philadelphia Police Department; Sergeant Maurice McGough, St. Petersburgh, Florida, Police Department; National Tactical Officers Association; Assistant Chief Ken McLeod, Buckeye, Arizona, Police Department; Lt. James B. Bolger, Michigan State Police; Colonel Carroll D. Buracker, Fairfax County, Virginia, Police Department; Charles Tracy, Portland State University; Major Dave Sturtz, Ohio State Patrol; the National Consortium for Justice Information and Statistics, Sacramento, California; Commander Pat Shuck, U.S. Coast Guard; Chief Gary Latham, Flagstaff, Arizona Police Department; Sheriff Sherman Block and Undersheriff T. H. Von Minden, Los Angeles County, California, Sheriff's Office; Phoenix, Arizona, Police and Fire Departments; John Gillen, Lexicon, Inc., Simi Valley, California; Colonel James Frazier, Terror Counter-Action Office, Ft. Leavenworth, Kansas; Deputy Chief Troy McClain, Captain Terry Haucke, Dr. S. A. Somodevilla, and Sergeant Jody Thomas, Dallas, Texas, Police Department; Chief David Brehm, Wayzata, Minnesota, Police Department; Ernst Goudsmidt and Gary Bolen, ElectroCom Automation, Inc., Arlington, Texas; Ron Kazoroski, Florida Department of Law Enforcement; Mary Ann Wycoff, Police Foundation; Don Fish, Florida Police Benevolent Association; and, Captain Keith Bushey, Los Angeles, California, Police Department.

C. R. S.
L. T.
R. W. T.

Contents

1 Police Administration and Society

2 Politics and Police Administration: External Influences and Controls   23

3 Organizational Theory   49

4 Concepts of Police Organizational Design   101

5 Leadership   127

Interpersonal and Organizational Communication

Human Resource Management

Stress and Police Personnel

Labor Relations   291

Legal Aspects of Police Administration   333

11 Information Systems and Applications   365

12 Decision Making   399

13 Financial Management

14 Productivity and Evaluation of Police Services

15 Organizational Change

Police Administration

Police Administration and Society

Introduction

If the many different purposes of the American police service were narrowed to a single focus, what would emerge is the obligation to preserve the peace in a manner consistent with the freedoms secured by the Constitution.[1] It does not follow from this assertion that our police alone bear the responsibility for maintaining a peaceful society; that responsibility is shared by other elements of society, beginning with each individual and spreading to each institution and each level of government—local, state, and federal. However, because crime is an immediate threat to our respective communities, the police have a highly visible and perhaps even primary role in overcoming the threat and fear of crime.

The preservation of peace is more complex than simply preventing crimes, making arrests for violations of the law, recovering stolen property, and providing assistance in the prosecution of persons charged with acts of criminality. In all likelihood, the police only spend something on the order of 15 percent of their time enforcing the law. The most substantial portion of their time goes toward providing less glamorous services that are utterly essential to maintaining the public order and well-being. Illustrative of these services are providing directions to motorists, mediating conflicts, evacuating neighborhoods threatened or struck by natural disasters, and serving as a bridge between other social service agencies and persons who come to the attention of the police, such as the mentally disturbed.

The degree to which any society achieves some amount of public order through police action depends in part upon the price that society is willing to pay to obtain it. This price can be measured in the resources dedicated to the police function and in the extent to which citizens are willing to tolerate a reduction in the number, kinds, and extent of liberties they enjoy. In this regard, totalitarian and democratic governments reflect very different choices. This point underscores the fact that the American police service cannot be understood properly if it is examined alone, as an island in a lake. A more appropriate and persuasive analogy is that policing is like a sandbar in a river, subject to being changed continuously by the currents in which it is immersed. As a profoundly significant social institution, policing is subject to, and continuously shaped by, a multitude of forces at work in our larger society.

The year 1890—roughly one hundred years ago—is the date normally associated with the closing of the frontier and a milestone in our transition from a rural, agrarian society to one that is highly urbanized and industrialized. This period of time is a long one to have lived by current expectancies, but as a period of history, it is brief. Still, in this historically short time span, the changes that have taken place in this country are staggering.

Inevitably any attempt to highlight this period will have some deficits. However, the balance of this chapter does so to achieve two objectives: (1) to demonstrate the impact of social forces on policing and (2) to identify and set the stage for some of the content treated in subsequent chapters. These two objectives will be met by presenting material organized under the headings of (1) politics and administration, (2) police professionalization, (3) technology, (4) scrutiny of the police, (5) unionization, and (6) the economy.

Politics and Administration

Politics, stated simply, is the exercise of power. As such, it is value-free, its "goodness" or "badness" stemming from its application rather than from some inherent character. Although police executives can occasionally be heard avowing to "keep politics out of the department," this unqualified posture is unrealistic. Personal politics exist in every organization, and democratic control of the policing mechanism is fundamental to our society. However, policing and partisan party politics have had a long and not entirely healthy relationship in this country.

In New York City, at the middle of this past century, the approval of the ward's alderman was required before appointment to the police force, and the Tammany Hall corruption of the same period depended in part on the use of the police to coerce and collect graft and to control elections.[2] During this same time, the election of a new mayor—particularly if from a party different from the incumbent's—signaled the coming dismissal of the entire police force and the appointment of one controlled by the new mayor.

Later, at the turn of the century, our cities were staggering under the burden of machine politics, corruption, crime, poverty, and the exploitation of women and children by industry.[3] The federal government, too, was not without its woes, as illustrated by the somewhat later Tea Pot Dome scandal that stained Warren G. Harding's administration.

Central to the Reformation period of 1900–1926 was the need to arouse the public and establish a conceptual cornerstone. Steffens exposed the plight of such cities as St. Louis, Minneapolis, Pittsburgh, and Chicago in *The Shame of the Cities* (1906); novels such as Sinclair's *The Jungle* (1906) called attention to abuses in the meat-packing industry; and Churchill addressed political corruption in *Coniston* (1911). The conceptual cornerstone was supplied by Woodrow Wilson's 1887 essay calling for a separation of politics and administration.[4] However impractical that might now seem, it is important to understand that to the reformers "politics" meant "machine politics" and all the ills associated with it.[5]

With an aroused public and a conceptual touchstone, rapid strides were made. In 1906, the New York Bureau of Municipal Research was formed, and by 1910, the city manager movement was underway. In 1911, the Training School for Public Service was established in New York, and by 1914, the University of Michigan was offering a degree in municipal administration. Further serving to strengthen the reform movement—whose center was the desire to separate politics (in the worst sense) and administration—was the issuance in 1916 of a model city charter by the National Municipal League, which called for a strict separation of these two elements. Further crystallization of the politics-administration dichotomy is found in White's *Public Administration* (1926), in which he praised the 1924 city manager's code of neutrality that stipulated that "no city manager should take an active part in politics," and in Willoughby's *Principles of Public Administration* (1927).

These events combined to produce movement toward reducing corruption, waste, fraud, and abuse in government; the desire to create a professionally qualified cadre of people committed to careers in public service; the rise of the civil service; emphasis upon proper recruitment, selection, and training of public employees; the freeing of government from the influence of machine politics; and the development of new theories, techniques, and models related to organizations. In short, these events were not only historical milestones; they unleashed a process of improvement that is still in progress today.

Police Professionalization

The terms *profession* and *professional* are tossed around with great abandon and a conspicuous lack of definition. The general absence of attention to definition has produced endless and futile debates as to whether policing is in fact a profession. The term "profession" is derived from the Latin *pro* (forth) and *fateri* (confess), meaning to "announce a belief"; at its early use, the word referred to public or open avowals of faith.[6] Cogan notes that the earliest recorded use of the word "profession" as a learned vocation was in 1541 and that by 1576 the meaning had been generalized to mean any calling or occupation by which a person habitually earned his or her living.[7] By 1675, a refinement of the secular use of the term occurred when it was associated with the act of professing to be duly qualified.[8]

Roughly since 1920, much of the serious work on professions has centered on specifying what criteria must be met to constitute a profession. The result is not a single definition but rather a collection of similar definitions that usually approximate the following: (1) an organized body of theoretically grounded knowledge, (2) advanced study, (3) a code of ethics, (4) prestige, (5) standards of admission, (6) a professional association, and (7) a service ideal, which may also be stated alternatively as altruism.[9]

In 1960 Merton reduced the values that make up a profession to (1) knowing (systematic knowledge), (2) doing (technical skill and trained capacity), and (3) helping (the joining of knowing and doing).[10] Becker has reduced the argument further to the pithy observation that in a debate as to whether a particular type of work can be called a profession, if the work group is successful in getting itself called a profession, it is one.[11]

The rise of "professional" policing is associated initially with the paid, fulltime body of police that stemmed from England's Peelian Reform of 1829. Despite the existence of similar bodies in this country from 1845 onward, the genesis of American professional policing is associated with the initiatives of August Vollmer, who was chief of police in Berkeley, California, from 1902 to 1932.

Without detracting one bit from Vollmer's genius, note that his tenure as chief parallels closely the Reformation movement of 1900–1926, which, in addition to its politics-administration dichotomy concern, also had a heavy orientation toward good, progressive government. Carte summarizes the work of this giant by noting that:

> The image of professional policing as we know it today is largely the creation of one man, August Vollmer. Vollmer was a tireless crusader for the reform of policing through technology and higher personnel standards. Under his direction the Berkeley department became a model of professional policing—efficient, honest, scientific. He introduced into Berkeley a patrolwide police signal system, the first completely mobile patrol—first on bicycles, then in squad cars—modern records systems, beat analysis and modus operandi. The first scientific crime laboratory in the United States was set up in Berkeley in 1916,

August Vollmer, seated third from the left, at work in the Berkeley, California, Police Department about 1914. (Courtesy of the Berkeley Police Department.)

under the direction of a full-time forensic scientist. The first lie detector machine to be used in criminal investigation was built in the Berkeley department in 1921.

However, Vollmer's department was better known for the caliber of its personnel. He introduced formal police training in 1908, later encouraging his men to attend classes in police administration that were taught each summer at the University of California. Eventually he introduced psychological and intelligence testing into the recruitment process and actively recruited college students from the University, starting around 1919. This was the beginning of Berkeley's "college cops," who set the tone for the department throughout the 1920s and 30s and came to be accepted by police leaders as the ultimate model of efficient, modern policemen.[12]

The Pendleton Act of 1883 sought to eliminate the ills of the political spoils system in the federal government. Many states and local governments passed parallel legislation over the next thirty years, establishing civil service systems designed to protect government employees from political interference. Intuitively attractive, the application of these measures was questioned early by one observer of the police, Fosdick, who wrote in 1920:

> In its application to a police department civil service has serious limitations. In the endeavor to guard against abuse of authority, it frequently is carried to such extremes that rigidity takes the place of flexibility in administration, and initiative in effecting essential changes in personnel is crippled and destroyed. Too often . . . civil service is a bulwark for neglect and incompetence, and one of the prime causes of departmental disorganization. Too often does the attempt to protect the force against the capricious play of politics compromise the principle of responsible leadership, so that in trying to nullify the effects of incompetence and favoritism, we nullify capacity and intelligence too.
>
> As a result of this divided responsibility between police executives and civil service commissions, there are in most large departments many men whose continuance in office is a menace to the force and to the community, but who cannot be dismissed because the proof of incompetence or dishonesty does not satisfy the requirements of the civil service law.[13]

It is a matter of some irony that there is a basic tension between Vollmer's trained and educated "professional" police officer and the early administration of civil service acts. The reason was that Vollmer was highly concerned with competence and performance—his notion of merit—whereas the measure of merit for many of the initial years of civil service was simply the degree to which political influence was kept out of appointments and promotions.[14]

Of significant consequence to the very structure of police organizations was the continuing efforts during the Reformation period to separate politics and administration. One mechanism for doing so was to change the political structure; thus, in Los Angeles a council elected at large was substituted for the ward system.[15] Other reformers, persuaded that America was beseiged by crime and that the police were our first line of defense, saw the police as analogous to the military. A second mechanism, therefore, was giving chiefs expanded powers, large and competent staffs, and the capability to actually control their departments.[16] In many cities, the precincts had previously operated largely or totally autonomously, and this second mechanism required centralization, which meant consolidating or eliminating precincts, as in New York City and elsewhere,[17] a further blow to ward boss control. The military analogy was so potent that its logical extension—recruiting military officers as police commissioners or chiefs—became a common practice for some years. Illustrative of this practice was the appointment in 1923 in Philadelphia of Marine Corps General Smedley Butler as director of public safety.

The highly centralized military analogy model that became widely adopted and remains today as the dominant force of police organization is technically a bureaucratic structure, which has been subjected to a number of criticisms. At the time of its adoption in American policing, it may have been an essential part of promoting police professionalism. For whatever its weaknesses, it brought with it an emphasis upon discipline, inspections, improved record keeping, supervision, close-order drill, improved accountability, and other bits and pieces that contributed to the transformation of the police from semiorganized ruffians operating under the mantle of law into something entirely different.

Major interest in police professionalization was renewed during the 1950s and 1960s. During this time, the requirement of a high school diploma or a general equivalency degree became the minimum educational requirement for appointment. Character and background investigations became standard practice and increasingly more thorough. The use of the polygraph and psychological instruments to screen applicants became more widespread. Altogether, such factors signaled a shift from screening out the undesirable and hiring the rest to identifying and hiring those believed to be most able. At the state level, Police Office Standards and Training Commissions (POSTs) were created, often with the incentive of Law Enforcement Assistance Administration (LEAA) grants to initiate operations and to ensure that uniform minimum standards—including training—were met.

Training academies proliferated, and a few departments began to require a college

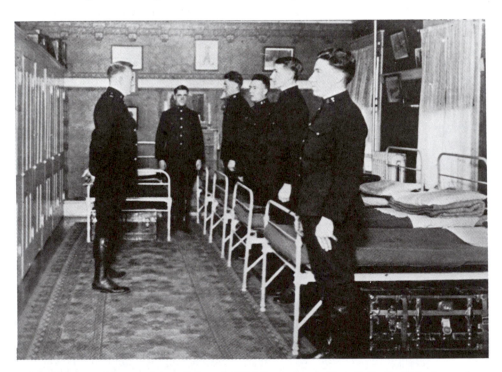

The military model at work in policing. A 1906 Pennsylvania State Police barracks inspection. (Courtesy of the Pennsylvania State Police.)

degree as an entry-level educational requirement. More numerous, however, were the departments that required a few college credits, such as six or twelve, and the departments that required as a condition of employment that officers agree to obtain a certain number of college hours within a specified time after appointment. Written promotional tests gained in prominence, although many rank-and-file members objected to them, favoring seniority instead. Even some chiefs complained that written tests interfered with their ability to promote the most able persons. The length of recruit academy curricula increased steadily, and social science subjects were introduced. From 1965 on, the number of junior colleges, colleges, and universities offering police administration or criminal justice degrees grew steadily, if not exponentially, due initially to the availability of "seed money" to start such programs from the Office of Law Enforcement Assistance (OLEA), LEAA's predecessor. Law Enforcement Education Program (LEEP) funds from LEAA were offered to induce and support the studies of students with career interests in criminal justice.

Further impetus to the movement to educate in-service officers and infuse college graduates into police departments was gained by providing incentive pay for college credits, which is a supplement above the regular salary based on the number of college credits earned. "Professionalization" of the police and "education" became virtually synonymous in the eyes of many observers. Illustratively, while conspicuously failing to define professionalization, the 1967 President's Commission on Law Enforcement and Administration of Justice nonetheless clearly equated professional and education.

Thus, despite a variety of practices designed to foster a higher caliber of personnel, the hallmark of 1950–1970—particularly after 1965—was the attempt to promote police professionalism through education. Education was seen as a means by which to improve community relations, which had suffered and contributed to the urban

San Francisco police recruits learning to type in a 1937 class. Note the traffic lights that were used as a training aid. The use of such training programs was a central strategy in early attempts to professionalize the police. (Courtesy of the San Francisco Archives.)

riots of 1965–1968; to reduce police use of violence; to promote more judicious use of police discretionary powers; and to provide an ideal of service that would serve as a counter to the problem of corruption.[18]

Technology

The term *technology* is often used interchangeably with *scientific,* as suggested by the phrase *high-technology industries.* The term is also appropriately employed to denote the means used to get the work of an organization done. In the police context, technology may refer to sophisticated equipment. The laser can be used by the police to develop fingerprints on objects found at the scene of a crime that could not be developed by less-advanced means such as the application of dusting powder. Technology may also refer to the methods or techniques of organizing and carrying out the work, such as the use of only a central police headquarters building as opposed to the use of a central headquarters supplemented by smaller precinct operations distributed geographically throughout the city, each with its own buildings.

It is convenient, if not appealing at times, to dismiss police departments as lumbering bureaucracies devoted to maintaining the status quo and utterly resistant to change. Whereas the police departments in this country are certainly overwhelmingly bureaucracies—a condition explored in greater detail in Chapters 3 and 4—the fact that they have not on the whole moved very far from the bureaucratic model does not make them inherently inept. News stories of the malfunctioning and occasional breakdowns of the "police bureaucracy" are noteworthy because they are the exceptions. Even when there are tragic consequences, these occasions divert attention from the massive numbers of routine and complex transactions that are handled by the police properly day in and day out. Moreover, to label the police as a bureaucracy scarcely differentiates them from virtually every other formal organization in the world. However, if the criticism is also understood to mean that the police have been resistant to the introduction of new scientific and work technologies, then the history of the police, certainly from 1900 onward, is an effective refutation of that view. The previously discussed innovations by August Vollmer illustrate this point.

In some instances the police have had new technologies forced upon them by Supreme Court decisions or by progressive mayors, city and county managers, city councils and county commissions. In other instances the police have actively advocated change. For example, police officials lobbied their state legislatures to obtain the enactment of statutes to establish the Police Officer Standards and Training Commissions (POSTs) mentioned earlier in this chapter. These statutes established minimum employment qualifications and provided for a basic course of entry-level training. In some states the passage of these statutes was accompanied by open conflict between associations that represented the interests of local units of government and those comprised of police officers. The former opposed passage of such legislation because police officers would have to be paid while they were "off attending school" and the latter supported the legislation because their vision was for a more professionalized police service. In yet other instances the impetus for new scientific and work technologies in police work came from new opportunities. Perhaps the most dramatic of these was the passage of the Omnibus Crime Control and Safe Streets Act of 1968, which created the grant-awarding Law Enforcement Assistance Administration (LEAA). Between creation of the LEAA in 1968 and its end some fifteen years

In 1954 with television still in its infancy, the New York Police Department was experimenting with it. Here Mayor Wagner and Commissioner Adams watch a mock lineup being broadcast from Police Headquarters to a police precinct. (Courtesy of the Library of Congress.)

later, criminal justice agencies, particularly the police, received massive amounts of money. Although some of these funds were allocated for basics such as cars and radios, significant portions of it went for innovations. Illustrative of the scientific and work technology innovations that occurred in policing subsequent to 1968 are:

1. Automatic vehicle monitoring (AVM) systems, which employ computer technology to show the actual location of each patrol vehicle and result in more rapid responses to calls for services and enhanced officer safety.[19]

2. Distribution of hidden video cameras and automatic police signaling devices at various locations to combat commercial robberies and burglaries.[20]

3. Development of quality-control measures designed to improve and maintain the performance of police laboratories analyzing evidence in criminal cases.[21]

4. Use of antifencing or ''sting'' operations in which police officers posed as businesspersons who purchased stolen property from thieves. The goals of such operations included the identification of actual fences or receivers of stolen property, the apprehension of violators, the recovery of property and the general disruption of stolen property markets. In just two years, when the technology was still developing and being tested, no less than sixty major operations were conducted in thirty-nine different jurisdictions nationally producing hundreds of significant arrests and the recovery of millions of dollars of property at a cost of only a fraction of its actual value.[22]

5. Introduction of computers to perform a variety of tasks, including the prepara-

tion of crime statistics, crime analysis, personnel scheduling, and record keeping.

6. Sensitivity to the needs of victims and witnesses, which grew during the mid-1970s into special programs such as court scheduling and case progress advisement, serving to improve the administration of justice by ensuring the cooperation of victims and witnesses.[23]

These, of course, are only a brief sampling; a much longer listing would include programs to divert juveniles from formal justice system processing,[24] crime prevention efforts, training police to intervene effectively in family crisis situations,[25] special weapons and tactics (SWAT) teams, the use of assessment centers in making hiring and promotional decisions, and the development of programs to assist police officers and their families deal with the special stresses associated with their work, and team policing.

Not all scientific or work technologies with which the police experiment or which they adopt are successful or remain in use. However, even those that fail or are abandoned often have significant value. For example, the Planning, Programming, Budgeting System (PPBS) discussed in Chapter 13 was virtually abandoned by the early 1970s without having ever having enjoyed widespread use in local government. Yet, PPBS was important because it created interest in how governments allocate

Members of the Columbia, Missouri, Special Tactics and Response (STAR) Team using hand signals to simulate a communications failure while training in a tear gas environment. (Courtesy of The Tactical Edge.)

and manage their resources. Currently the use of two scientific technologies by the police have sparked controversy: passive alcohol sensors and electric "stun guns."

The controversy around the use of passive alcohol sensors is summarized in the article "Flashlight Device Helps Detect Drunken Drivers." The sensor, which was developed by the Insurance Institute for Highway Safety, appears to be an ordinary flashlight, but in reality, contains a digital readout in its handle that displays the blood alcohol content of drivers in whose direction the device is aimed. Supported by the police and other groups committed to making the nation's streets and highways safer as an effective means of detecting drunk drivers, the surreptitious use of this new technology is regarded in some legal circles as the administration of a breath test by the police without having some prior probable cause. There is no question that the present use of the passive alcohol sensor by the police will be challenged vigorously in the courts.

Developed as a humane alternative to the use of physical or deadly force to gain control of violent subjects, electrical stun guns deliver a paralyzing shock that temporarily incapacitates the recipient. During the time the individual is incapacitated by the stun gun, police can apply handcuffs or other restraining devices on the subject.[26] Electrical stun guns, which may have the appearance of a police portable radio, can be activated by pressing one end against a person's body. They may also be in the form of the taser that fires darts attached to wires to deliver the electrical shock to the subject, which permits their use without the need to closely approach a violent subject. Critics of the stun gun maintain that these devices can encourage police brutality because they can inflict pain and leave little evidence of having been used. In 1986 New York City Police Officers were convicted on charges of torturing accused drug dealers with one of these devices, and a Deputy Sheriff in Bexar County, Texas, has been charged with the use of a stun gun during an interrogation of a suspect. In Baltimore, where the police do not use stun guns, the sale of stun guns to the public has been banned, and in Florida electrical guns are covered under that state's statute making it illegal to carry concealed weapons. Given the new limits placed by the Supreme Court on the use of deadly force by police officers, the continued use of electrical stun guns by the police seems assured, as does the continuing controversy and occasional abuse of this technology by individual police officers.

The Lion Alcolmeter. (Courtesy of Lion and the Insurance Institute for Highway Safety.)

BOX 1-1.

Flashlight Device Helps Detect Drunken Drivers

But Defense Attorneys in Virginia Town Don't Want the Sensor Used

The New York Times

CHARLOTTESVILLE, Va.—It all seemed routine. In a well-publicized program of checking motorists' sobriety at checkpoints, the police here beamed their flashlights into cars.

But while the drivers used the beam to help find their licenses, a device in the flashlight measured their breath for alcohol levels. A digital readout of the driver's blood-alcohol content glowed from a tiny screen in the flashlight's handle.

The Charlottesville drivers were unwitting participants in an experiment of the passive alcohol sensor, a device that helped to double arrests for drunken driving in the three weekends it was used last fall.

With the flashlight sensors, the police made 20 arrests for drunken driving for each 1,000 motorists who passed through the roadblocks. Without it, the arrest rate fell to slightly more than 11 arrests for every 1,000 motorists. An ensuing study showed that even with the sensor, more than three of every 10 legally intoxicated drivers went undetected. For that study, motorists were asked to submit to a voluntary breath test for research purposes only.

Robert Voas of the National Public Services Research Institute said the exercise showed that "police can be far more efficient and accurate in enforcing drunken driving laws." Voas called the sensor "the wave of the future," adding, "Up until now, we've required police to rely on their own natural senses and judgment—eyes, ears, nose—and asked them to determine rapidly whether a driver is drunk. From research, we know they miss a lot of people."

But since the use of the sensor was disclosed in June, defense lawyers in Charlottesville have objected to it both on legal and philosophical grounds.

"Virginia law says you don't have to give a breath test until you've been arrested," said Francis Lawrence, a local lawyer. "Now they're doing essentially a breath test as the first step—

without probable cause or reasonable suspicion."

The sensor used in Charlottesville was developed by the Insurance Institute for Highway Safety, a non-profit research institute financed by automobile insurance companies. The device utilizes an electrochemical fuel cell sensor that measures the alcohol level; a tiny pump in the butt of the flashlight draws the driver's breath over the sensor. When the device goes on the market later this year, it is expected to cost about $500, Voas said.

Ian S. Jones, a physicist who developed the sensor, said the device should be used only for screening suspected drunken drivers because the instrument has a margin of error of .05 percent. Thus, a driver registering a .10, the state's legal limit, could actually have a level ranging from .095 to .105. The margin of error increases if the sensor is held farther than the recommended 6 inches from the driver's mouth.

Jones said the device could help to limit the inconvenience of roadblocks to people who have not been drinking. Without the sensor, about 20 percent of the people who were stopped might have had a drink but were not legally impaired, he said. With the sensor, the number had dropped to about 8 percent, he said.

The Charlottesville police were in the middle of a yearlong pilot program involving sobriety checkpoints when the insurance institute asked the police to participate in the experiment. Except for a brief experiment with the sensors in Washington, D.C., last year, Charlottesville has been the only test site.

"It's a good piece of equipment that improves the accuracy and efficiency in detecting drunk drivers," said Lt. A. E. Rhodenhizer, director of the roadblock program for Charlottesville Police Department. "I don't have any doubt police around the country will really like them."

Before using the sensors at roadblocks, Rhodenhizer said he was advised by lawyers of the Department of Transportation that the device would survive court challenges.

According to Robert H. Reeder, general counsel of the Traffic Institute at Northwestern University, his organization concluded that the sensors would survive defense objections based upon precedent in a case involving dogs sniffing narcotics.

"In that case, the Supreme Court held that things open to view and to smell do not involve a search, and that you did not have to have probable cause to do it," Reeder said.

But Lawrence, the attorney who anticipates a court challenge to the sensors in Charlottesville, rejects that argument. "I seriously question whether the Supreme Court would conclude that the dogs were not doing a search if when you rolled down the car window, the police threw the dogs inside your car, which is exactly what they're doing here," he said.

Source. The Atlanta Constitution, *August 22, 1985, P. A-17.*

Scrutiny of the Police

In general, public organizations and private organizations can be differentiated on the basis of the following points:

1. their legal bases differ;
2. what constitutes "success" for public organizations is less clearly definable and measurable than it is for private enterprise. For example, the fact that the United States has not been attacked militarily by another country may be interpreted as "success" in our defense policy and programs. But how do we know if entirely too much defense capability has been purchased, diverting resources from domestic needs? Too, the absence of being attacked may have nothing to do with our defense posture because other governments never considered military action against this country;
3. public and private entities have different primary funding sources;[27]
4. the services provided by public agencies are generally of a more urgent or essential nature; and
5. traditionally, public agencies have been subject to closer scrutiny and formal criticisms than have their private counterparts.

There is no shortage of examples with which to illustrate the extent to which the police have been subject to scrutiny. Legislative committees at all three levels of government have held hearings on such subjects as organized crime, assaults on peace officers, and corruption. An early illustration of this type of review is the 1901 Fisk Committee, appointed by the California legislature to investigate corruption in San Francisco.[28] Another type of scrutiny by the police has been provided by a series of national commissions including the National Commission on Law Observance and Enforcement (1931); the President's Commission on Law Enforcement and Administration of Justice (1967); the National Advisory Commission on Civil Disorders (1968); the National Commission on the Causes and Prevention of Violence (1969); the National Commission on Criminal Justice Standards and Goals (1973) and the Commission on Accreditation for Law Enforcement Agencies (1982). Parallel to these national commissions have been state-level entities, such as the Missouri and Pennsylvania crime commissions, that also have urban counterparts such as the Chicago Crime Commission and the Citizens' Crime Commission of Greater Miami, Inc., in

Florida. Additionally, our cities have periodically appointed special investigative bodies, such as the Knapp Commission, which investigated police corruption in New York City during the mid-1970s.

Other types of scrutiny have come from the episodic use of civilian review boards to investigate complaints against the police, a practice advocated by the American Civil Liberties Union (ACLU) during the 1950s and 1960s;[29] periodic reports such as the Federal Bureau of Investigation's annual reported crime statistics in the *Uniform Crime Reports,* researchers working with and without grants to support their inquiry; and judicial review.

Significant judicial review of local police actions has been a somewhat recent practice.[30] However, during the period 1961–1969—a period frequently referred to as the "due process revolution"—the U.S. Supreme Court took an activist role, becoming quite literally givers of the law rather than interpreters of it. The Warren court's activist role in the piecemeal extension of the provisions of the Bill of Rights, via the due process clause of the Fourteenth Amendment, to criminal proceedings in the respective states may have been a policy decision.[31] Normally the Supreme Court will write opinions in about 115 cases during any particular term. During the 1938–1939 term, only 5 cases appear under the heading of criminal law; a scant three decades later, during the height of the due process revolution, about one quarter of each term's decisions related to criminal law.[32] The Supreme Court could scarcely have picked a worse period in which to undertake the unpopular role of policing the police; a burgeoning crime rate far outstripped population increases, and many politicians were campaigning on "law and order" platforms that all too often dissolved into rhetoric upon their election. The problem of crime increasingly came to the public's eye through the media. In sum, the high court acted to extend procedural safeguards to defendants in criminal cases precisely at a point in time when the public's fear of crime was high and there was great social pressure to do something about crime.

Fundamentally, the Supreme Court's role in the due process revolution was a response to a vacuum in which the police themselves had failed to provide the necessary leadership. The era of strong social activism by various special-interest groups was not yet at hand, and neither the state courts nor the legislatures had displayed any broad interest in reforming the criminal law. What institution was better positioned to undertake this responsibility? The Court may even have felt obligated by the inaction of others to do so. Therefore, it became the Warren court's lot to provide the reforms so genuinely needed but so unpopularly received. The high court did not move into this arena until after it had issued warnings that, to responsive and responsible leaders, would have been a mandate for reform.

Among the key decisions in the due process revolution were *Mapp* v. *Ohio, Gideon* v. *Wainwright, Escobedo* v. *Illinois,* and *Miranda* v. *Arizona.* For present purposes, the facts of these and related cases are less important than are their focus and effect. Their focus was upon the two vital areas of search and seizure and the right to counsel; their effect was to extend markedly the rights of defendants. The impact upon police work was staggering; the use of questionable and improper tactics was curbed, thereby creating the need for new procedures in such areas as interrogations, lineups, and seizure of physical evidence. In general, the reaction of the police to this whirlwind of due process decisions was one of wariness tinged with occasional outcries that they were being "handcuffed" and could not perform their jobs adequately.

Many people felt that the decisions went beyond seeking a fair trial in quest of a perfect one.

During the period of the due process revolution, the percentage of serious crimes cleared by arrest dropped from 26.7 percent in 1961 to 20.1 percent in 1969.[33] While it lacks scientific validity to state that the Supreme Court's due process revolution decisions caused decreased police effectiveness, these two factors are correlated, and in the minds of many people they are inexorably bound together. By the early 1970s, many police executives had come to recognize that, whereas the Supreme Court's decisions in the previous decade could be correlated with some indicators of reduced police effectiveness, these decisions also had the subtle effect of hastening the development of professional policing. This happened because the decisions forced the police to abandon the use of both improper tactics and at least some traditional approaches while virtually mandating continuous sophisticated training to implement innovative techniques and programs.

Unionization of Police Officers

The Historical Context

Nationally, the right of private sector employees to form unions and to bargain with their employers regarding the terms and conditions of the work relationship was established during the 1930s, but it was not until the 1960s that a similar right was established by many states for government employees. Yet concerted action by public employees has a considerably longer history.

In 1835 civilian employees of the Navy Department struck for shorter working hours and a general redress of grievances; within a year workers in the Philadelphia shipyard did the same thing and successfully obtained a ten-hour work day.[34] Shipyard workers in the Navy yard at Charlestown, Massachusetts, struck in 1852 over the length of the workday and the following year over wages.[35] Members of the Ithaca, New York, Police Department walked out in 1889 when their salaries were reduced from $12.00 to $9.00 per week.[36] The American Federation of Labor received a petition for a charter from a group of special police in Cleveland in 1897, and there was a major police strike in Cincinnati in 1918.[37] Other groups striking in 1918 included the normally staid London, England, police[38] and members of the Chicago Cubs and the Boston Red Sox during the World Series.[39] Unlike the Cincinnati police strike the preceding year, the Boston police strike of 1919 resulted in riots, looting, an estimated eight deaths, and at least twenty-one serious injuries.[40] Despite the fact that the strike was in part a product of Boston Police Commissioner Curtis' inflexibility and that the strikers had ample and genuine grounds on which to be aggrieved, public and official condemnation was swift in arriving. President Woodrow Wilson called the strike a crime against civilization,[41] and Massachusetts Governor Calvin Coolidge ensured his political future and earned a niche in labor history by declaring "There is no right to strike against the public safety by anybody, anywhere at anytime."[42] In the District of Columbia, police unions were banned and similar legislative acts were adopted quickly throughout this country. As a result, for all practical purposes the police labor movement was dead for the next forty years.

The reasons for withholding the right of government employees to organize and bargain are more complex than the trauma of the Boston police strike. In part, these reasons stem from philosophical ideas long prevalent in this nation, and in part, they are purely practical.[43] Traditional concepts of sovereignty asserted that government is, and should be, supreme and hence immune from contravening forces and pressures such as collective bargaining.[44] Related to sovereignty was the issue that to engage in collective bargaining was an illegal delegation of sovereign power.[45] This assertion maintained that only elected or appointed public officials could make public decisions and that to engage in bilateral negotiations was a compromise of the essential, unilateral, and total decision-making powers entrusted to officials.[46]

At a purely practical level, the unionization of police officers was objected to because labor's ultimate weapon was the strike and the police were seen as providers of essential services; if, as the Boston police had in 1919, they employed this tactic, grave injury to the public interest would presumably occur. Other practical reasons

An

Agreement

Between

the City of San Antonio

and

the San Antonio Police Officers'

Association

October 1, 1983–September 30, 1986

Cover of the 41 page labor contract between the City of San Antonio, Texas, and the union representing police officers in that city.

included the possibility of the police engaging in sympathy strikes, the potential for organized labor to have undue influence in government affairs, and the potential conflict of interest that unionized officers would have when policing industrial strikes.[47]

The Unionization of the Police

From 1959 through the 1970s, a number of events combined to foster public sector collective bargaining, although much of the ferment was during the 1960s. Significant among these forces were (1) the needs of labor organizations, which, having organized the private sector about as much as they could, turned their attention to the possibility of organizing public sector employees into unions with some relish; (2) the reduction of legal barriers that had sprung up following the ill-fated Boston Police Strike of 1919, the chief mechanisms for this reduction being the passage of state laws permitting public sector collective bargaining—a testimony to the political muscle of union leaders—and court decisions which struck down laws prohibiting union membership by public employees; (3) police frustration with the "war on crime," in which the police felt abandoned by the Supreme Court, through its decisions on due process and unappreciated by the public; (4) personnel practices in police agencies, including such acts as calling an officer back to duty in the middle of the night to sign a routine report and favoritism in work assignments; (5) salaries and benefits, which left the police trailing far behind those engaged in what the police saw as being less difficult and less dangerous occupations; (6) an increase in violence directed at the police, including a doubling of assaults on officers within a five-year period and the startling development of preplanned ambushes to kill officers who were lured to locations on bogus calls where they were attacked; and (7) the success of other groups, such as the demonstrators against the war in Vietnam who provided the police with an important object lesson: if groups of demonstrators could effect national policy, then groups of police officers working collectively could improve their salaries and working conditions.[48] In the chapter on labor relations, we return to these themes and develop them in greater detail because of their significance in the evolution of police collective bargaining.

The Economy

Economics refer to the ways in which goods and services are produced, distributed, and consumed in a society; as illustrated by the examples that follow, this force has had a pervasive influence on policing in this country. During colonial times in this country, police services were provided by citizens who were obliged from time to time to serve on the town watch. It was not until 1712 that Boston voted to pay watchmen for their toil.[49] This marked the beginning of the final shift from policing as everyone's responsibility to the rise of full-time paid police officers operating under the auspices of a specialized social institution. In Philadelphia, in 1833, a bequeath of a sum of money was provided from the estate of Stephen Girard to create a competent police force, and by the middle of the century most American cities had unified their night and day forces, which had previously operated separately.

The American Civil War of 1861–1865 was in part over slavery—a reprehensible institution that underpinned the economy of the South—and although it was the veterans turned bandits of that war who received the lion's share of attention, others turned their energy toward policing.

Money was among the issues involved in the Boston police strike of 1919, as it has been in many police strikes to the present. The Prohibition era resulted in high profits for organized crime and ample money to tempt and corrupt public officials, including the police; currently, the illegal importation, manufacturing, and distribution of drugs has produced similar problems, with key narcotics figures buying banks and corrupting key officials of the justice system of entire counties. The economic crash of 1929 and the years of the Great Depression that followed resulted in better educated people competing for police positions, particularly in urban areas, because of job scarcity, with many of these same people making careers of police service. Additionally, they often were effective recruiters in attracting similarly credentialed candidates for employment. On a less positive note, the reported funding of terrorist activities and groups by special Middle East interests has been associated with life and property loss throughout the world, creating significant problems for, and dangers to, the police.

The Law Enforcement Assistance Administration's activities clearly had significant economic impact on policing by making new scientific and work technologies available and affordable, including low-cost public domain programs or "software" such as Crime Analysis System Support (CASS) and Traffic Enforcement Software System (TESS) for use in police computer systems.

Since 1975, police agencies in various parts of the country have had to deal with budget reductions, sometimes as a result of the decay of the urban tax base and in other instances because of so-called "taxpayer revolts." In this regard, the economy has resulted in personnel cutbacks; reduced police services; the loss in some instances of a disproportionate number of minorities, who in many departments were the most numerous of the "last hired" and thus were the "first fired" as they lacked the seniority that would have ensured their jobs; reduced training; the loss of experienced officers to better paying industrial jobs; and an increased concern for productivity.

Complex Reality

In this chapter a series of headings such as politics and administration, police professionalization, technology, scrutiny of the police, unionization, and the economy have been used. These headings are useful because they allow us to isolate and focus upon important topics. However, the use of discrete headings also obscures a critically important fact: in the complex reality of daily living the material covered under the separate headings in this chapter ordinarily do not occur alone. Rather they occur in combinations that produce difficult circumstances for police leaders.

Summary

The role of the police is to maintain the peace within a carefully established framework of individual liberties. By devoting more resources to policing and reducing rights, we could be more effective in crime control; however, our system of government is incompatible with such a choice. Policing is an institution that does not stand alone;

it is part and parcel of the larger society it serves and is influenced by the forces of that larger society. For present purposes, the most significant of these forces have been (1) politics and administration, particularly the struggle to free policing from machine politics and the improvements resulting from the Reformation period of 1900–1926; (2) the attempts to professionalize the police from the early work of August Vollmer through the emphasis on education; (3) the application of new scientific and work technologies; (4) the continuing and varied scrutiny of the police by legislative committees, commissions, and particularly the U.S. Supreme Court; (5) the rise and impact of police unions from 1959 onward, especially during the late 1960s and early 1970s because of the needs of labor organizations, the reduction of legal barriers, and other forces; and (6) the many ways in which the economy has and continues to impact upon policing.

Discussion Questions

1. Whose responsibility is it for maintaining an orderly society?

2. What are the two key variables to determining the price of crime control?

3. With regard to the separation of politics and administration, what is its conceptual cornerstone?

4. Of what consequence to policing was the Reformation period of 1900–1926?

5. What were August Vollmer's contributions to American police professionalization?

6. Of what importance has technology been to American policing?

7. How are public and private organizations differentiated?

8. Of what consequence was the Boston police strike of 1919?

9. At least seven factors can be associated with the emergence of police unions since 1959. What are they?

10. What are five different illustrations of the impact of the economy on policing?

Notes

1. This section draws upon and extends material found in the National Advisory Commission of Criminal Justice Standards and Goals, *Police,* Russell W. Peterson, chairman (Washington, D.C.: U.S. Government Printing Office, 1973), p. 13.

2. Thomas A. Reppetto, *The Blue Parade* (New York: Free Press, 1978), pp. 41–42.

3. Alice B. Stone and Donald C. Stone, "Early Development of Education in Public Administration," in *American Public Administration: Past, Present, and Future,* ed. Frederick C. Mosher (University: University of Alabama Press, 1975), pp. 17–18. The themes in this and the subsequent paragraph are reflected in Stone and Stone's "Early Development," although they are ones sounded repeatedly in the literature. See Howard E. McCurdy, *Public Administration: A Synthesis* (Menlo Park, Calif.: Cummings, 1977), pp. 19–21; William L. Morrow, *Public Administration: Politics and the Political System* (New York: Random House, 1975), p. 25; Lynton K. Caldwell, "Public Administration and the Universities: A Half-Century of Development," *Public Administration Review,* 25 (March 1965), pp. 52–60.

4. Woodrow Wilson, "The Study of Administration," *Political Science Quarterly,* 2 (June 1887), pp. 197–222.

5. Edwin O. Stene, "The Politics-Administration Dichotomy," *Midwest Review of Public Administration,* 9 (April-July 1975), p. 84.

6. E. W. Roddenbury, "Achieving Professionalism," *Journal of Criminal Law, Criminology, and Police Science,* 44 (May 1953–1954), p. 109.

7. Morris L. Cogan, "Toward a Definition of Profession," *Harvard Educational Review,* 23 (Winter 1953), p. 34.

8. Everette Hughes, "Professions," in *The Professions in America,* ed. K. S. Lynn (Cambridge, Mass.: Riverside Press, 1965), pp. 1–14.

9. See, for example, Ernest Greenwood, "Attributes of a Profession," *Social Work,* 2:3 (July 1957), p. 45.

10. Robert K. Merton, "Some Thoughts on the Professions in American Society," address before the Brown University graduate convocation, Providence, Rhode Island, June 6, 1960.

11. Howard Becker, "The Nature of a Profession," in the Sixty-first Yearbook of the National Society for the Study of Education, 1962. Also Harold L. Wilensky, "The Professionalization of Everyone?" *The American Journal of Sociology,* 70:2 (September 1964), pp. 137–158.

12. Gene Edward Carte, "August Vollmer and the Origins of Police Professionalism," *Journal of Police Science and Administration,* 1:3 (September 1973), p. 274.

13. Raymond B. Fosdick, *American Police Systems* (Montclair, N.J.: A 1969 Patterson Smith Reprint of a Century Company Work), pp. 284–285.

14. *Ibid.,* p. 271.

15. Robert M. Fogelson, *Big-City Police* (Cambridge, Mass.: Harvard University Press, 1975), p. 76.

16. Extended treatment of this line of thinking is found in ibid., "The Military Analogy," pp. 40–66.

17. Ibid., p. 77.

18. James Q. Wilson, "The Police and Their Problems," *Public Policy,* 12 (1963), pp. 189–216.

19. Gilbert C. Larson and James W. Simon, *Evaluation of a Police Automatic Vehicle Monitoring (AVM) System* (Washington, D.C.: U.S. Government Printing Office, 1979).

20. Debra Whitcomb, *Focus on Robbery: The Hidden Camera Project* (Washington, D.C.: U.S. Government Printing Office, 1979).

21. Joseph L. Peterson et al., *Crime Laboratory Proficiency Testing Research Program* (Washington, D.C.: U.S. Government Printing Office, 1978).

22. James O. Golden, *What Happened? An Examination of Recently Terminated Anti-Fencing Operations* (Washington, D.C.: U.S. Government Printing Office, 1979).

23. Emilio C. Viano, *Victim/Witness Services: A Review of the Model* (Washington, D.C.: U.S. Government Printing Office, 1979).

24. Jack R. Shepherd and Dale M. Rothenberger, *Police Juvenile Diversion: An Alternative to Prosecution* (Washington, D.C.: U.S. Government Printing Office, 1980).

25. Patricia S. Anderson et al., *Family Crisis Intervention Programs* (Washington, D.C.: U.S. Government Printing Office, 1979).

26. The material on electrical stun guns was obtained in a December 31, 1985, interview with Lt. John Piehl, Largo, Florida, Police Department and from "Stun Gun Incident Raises Questions on Extent of Police Brutality," *The Atlanta Journal and Constitution,* May 12, 1985, A-27, Lawrence Kilman, "Law Enforcement's Latest Weapon Already A Source of Controversy," Athens (Georgia) *Banner-Herald,* May 1, 1985, p. 6, and " 'Stun Gun'—Police Feel a Backlash," *U.S. News & World Report,* May 13, 1985, p. 10. Also see Richard S. Michelson and William L. Shallow, "The Stun Gun," *Journal of California Law Enforcement,* 19:2 (1985), pp. 43–47.

27. There are, of course, quasi-private organizations, such as those in the aerospace industry, that depend heavily on government contracts and are subject also to considerable control.

See Murray Weidenbaum, *The Modern Public Sector* (New York: Basic Books, 1969), for an in-depth analysis of this point.

28. Fogelson, *Big-City Police,* pp. 9–10.
29. Ibid., p. 199.
30. Treatment of the Supreme Court's influence has been drawn from Thomas Phelps, Charles Swanson, and Kenneth Evens, *Introduction to Criminal Justice* (Santa Monica, Calif.: Goodyear, 1979), pp. 128–131.
31. In a legal sense, the Supreme Court opted for a piecemeal application when it rejected the "shorthand doctrine" (i.e., making a blanket a application of the federal bill of rights provisions binding on the states) in its consideration of *Hurtado* v. *California,* 110 U.S. 516 (1884); therefore, the statement should be read in the context that the activist role was a policy decision.
32. Fred P. Graham, *The Self-inflicted Wound* (New York: Macmillan, 1970), p. 37. For a recent look at the police and due process, see A. T. Quick, "Attitudinal Aspects of Police Compliance with Procedural Due Process," *American Journal of Criminal Law,* 6 (1978), pp. 25–56.
33. "Serious crime" has been used traditionally as an umbrella term encompassing criminal homicide, rape, robbery, burglary, larceny, auto theft, and aggravated assault; in 1978 arson was added to this list for crime-reporting purposes by the Federal Bureau of Investigation. The data cited are drawn from Federal Bureau of Investigation, *Uniform Crime Reports—1961* (Washington, D.C.: U.S. Government Printing Office, 1962), p. 85, and *Uniform Crime Reports—1969* (Washington, D.C.: U.S. Government Printing Office, 1970), p. 98.
34. David Ziskind, *One Thousand Strikes of Government Workers* (New York: Columbia University Press, 1940), pp. 24–25.
35. State of Massachusetts, Bureau of Labor Statistics, *Eleventh Annual Report,* 1880, p. 14.
36. Ziskind, *One Thousand Strikes,* p. 33; also John Burpo, *The Police Labor Movement* (Springfield, Ill.: Charles C Thomas, 1971), p. 3.
37. *The Evening Star* (Washington, D.C.), September 14, 1918, p. 10.
38. *The Sunday Star* (Washington, D.C.), September 1, 1918, p. 5.
39. *The Evening Star* (Washington, D.C.), September 10, 1918, p. 1.
40. Samuel Walker, *A Critical History of Police Reform* (Lexington, Mass.: Lexington Books, 1977), p. 117.
41. *The Evening Star* (Washington, D.C.), September 13, 1919, p. 5.
42. Walker, *A Critical History,* p. 117.
43. C. M. Rehmus, "Labor Relations in the Public Sector," Third World Congress, International Industrial Relations Association, in *Labor Relations Law in the Public Sector,* eds. Russell A. Smith, Harry T. Edwards, and R. Theodore Clark, Jr. (Indianapolis, Ind.: Bobbs-Merrill, 1974), p. 7.
44. Ibid., p. 7.
45. Ibid., p. 7.
46. Ibid., pp. 7–8.
47. K. Hanslowe, "The Emerging Law of Labor Relations in Public Employment," in *Labor Relations Law in the Public Sector,* p. 10.
48. These themes are identified and treated in depth in Hervey A. Juris and Peter Feuille, *Police Unionism* (Lexington, Mass.: Lexington Books, 1973).
49. William J. Bopp and Donald O. Shultz, *Principles of American Law Enforcement and Criminal Justice* (Springfield, Ill.: Charles C Thomas, 1974), p. 18.

Politics and
Police Administration:
External Influences
and Controls

*Terrifying are the weaknesses
of Power.*

GREEK PROVERB

Introduction

A discussion of the interplay between politics and the police often focuses exclusively upon the external influences and controls that are illegal and improper. However, the vast majority of influences and controls that impact upon law enforcement are both legal and proper.

This chapter provides an analysis of the major external influences and controls that emanate from the federal, state, and local levels of government and shows the profound effect that these agencies have upon the administration, operation, and policies of an agency. Numerous examples are produced to demonstrate the legal and proper way in which these external forces impact on a police department. Examples are also provided to show how they can illegally and unethically disrupt the mission, effectiveness, and morale of a police department. It is imperative that police administrators understand and be able to cope with the dynamic external political forces operating within their communities. The extent to which they can do this will significantly affect their ability to accomplish their law enforcement mission.

Our goal is to provide a perspective about politics and police that is informative, balanced, and realistic.

Police Accountability

The operations of the police, as with the operations of any other administrative agency that exercises governmental authority, must be subject to effective legislation and judicial review and control.[1]

Accountability of the police to other institutions conforms to the American notion of a system of checks and balances. There are, however, some questions about the actual means by which this accountability does occur and the degree to which it exists. It has been suggested that the degree of control over the police by political authority varies with the level of government at which the police functions take place. In this country, although cities and counties are legally creatures of the states under state constitutions, the states have traditionally divested themselves of much of their control over these jurisdictions and have allowed them to operate with considerable independence.[2] The existence of local autonomy has also been facilitated by the belief in home rule, which maintains that local government has the capability to manage its own affairs and that strong controls from the state capitol or the federal government are neither desirable nor consistent with American political philosophy. Nevertheless, the influences and controls being exerted upon local law enforcement from both the federal and state level have increased since the turbulent period of the 1960s.

Some argue that this is an encroachment of local hegemony and will eventually result in a significant shift of control and political power away from the local level. In reply, the proponents of this development argue that the traditionally strong local control of policing has resulted in a degree of parochialism that has retarded the growth of professionalism. They also maintain that the increased involvement in local law enforcement by the state and federal government has produced important qualitative improvements in such areas as personnel selection standards, training, crime laboratory capabilities, and labor-management relations, along with innovations such as crime prevention programs, which combine to improve the services delivered.

Federal Influence in Law Enforcement

Some authorities believe that trends occurring since the 1960s through the present have resulted in the partial nationalization of criminal justice. Up to the 1960s, it was safely said that criminal justice was almost completely the responsibility of state and local governments. Federal criminal statutes were limited in their coverage, federal assistance to local law enforcement was generally in the areas of training and the processing of evidence, and the Supreme Court concerned itself with only the most notorious violations of constitutional rights by state and local authorities.[3] This trend was reversed in no small measure by a series of opinions rendered by the U.S. Supreme Court under the strong leadership of Chief Justice Earl Warren, which greatly strengthened the rights of accused persons in criminal cases.

Supreme Court Decision Affecting Law Enforcement: 1961–1966

Several key decisions were made by a split vote of the Court and drew heavy criticism from law enforcement officers and others as hamstringing police in their struggle with lawlessness. These decisions included *Mapp* v. *Ohio* (1961), which banned the use of illegally seized evidence in criminal cases in the states by applying the Fourth Amendment guarantee against unreasonable searches and seizures; *Gideon* v. *Wainwright* (1963), which affirmed that equal protection under the Fourteenth Amendment requires that legal counsel be appointed for all indigent defendants in all criminal cases; *Escobedo* v. *Illinois* (1964), which affirmed that a suspect is entitled to confer with an attorney as soon as the focus of a police investigation of the suspect shifts from investigatory to accusatory; and *Miranda* v. *Arizona* (1966), which required police officers, before questioning suspects, to inform them of their constitutional right to remain silent, their right to an attorney, and their right to have an attorney appointed if they cannot afford to hire one. Although the suspect may knowingly waive these rights, the police cannot question anyone who, at any point, asks for a lawyer or indicates "in any manner" that he or she does not wish to be questioned.[4]

Objections by Law Enforcement Officials

Each of these decisions was attacked vehemently by a broad segment of the law enforcement community, which maintained that these rulings greatly reduced their crime fighting capability. Although it is difficult to assess fully and accurately the impact of these decisions on the incidence of crime, there is little doubt that they have profoundly affected the complexion of the entire process of administering justice.

The activism of the Warren court was reflected in the legislative and executive branches of the federal government. The catalysts for this activism resulted from the civil disorders sweeping through so many American cities[5] and a skyrocketing crime rate that would eventually emerge as a major issue during the 1968 presidential campaign.[6] These two factors—civil disorders and the rapidly increasing crime rate—brought into focus some of the glaring deficiencies that existed in the crime control mechanism at the local level. The concerns generated by these deficiencies gave impetus to the creation of the President's Commission on Law Enforcement and the Administration of Justice (1967). This was the first national commission to look at the problem of crime on a national level since the Wickersham Commission did so in 1931.

The final report produced two hundred recommendations that the commission believed could lead to a safer society. Those recommendations called for a greatly increased crime prevention and control effort on the part of the federal government, states, counties, cities, civic organizations, religious institutions, business groups, and individual citizens. The recommendations also called for basic changes in the operations of the police, schools, prosecutors, employment agencies, public defenders, social workers, prisons, housing authorities, and probation and parole officers.

History of Federal Legislation

Holten and Jones have traced the history of the federal legislation that eventually emanated from the sweeping recommendations of the commission report. The first in this series of enactments was the Omnibus Crime Control and Safe Street Act of 1968. This act made some sweeping changes in the federal criminal justice process, but its real importance lay in the assumption of a broad federal responsibility for encouraging change in the administration of justice at the state and local levels.[7] This legislation created the Law Enforcement Assistance Administration (LEAA) within the Department of Justice to channel federal grants-in-aid to the states for use in upgrading state or local criminal justice operations. Most of the funds were to go to the states as "block grants" to be employed by the states as they saw fit, subject to federal review and approval.[8] There was great concern and some suspicion among state and local officials that the acceptance of federal monies would eventually lead to federal control of local affairs. An often-heard adage during that time was "federal control follows federal money." Assurances that this would not occur were forthcoming from high offices in Washington. However, the record of federal, state, and local relations since the 1960s indicates that these fears were not groundless and once again supports the assumption that the acceptance of funding from any source generally brings with it varying degrees of control.

BOX 2-1.

Federal Judge Orders Local Police Files Turned Over to FBI

A federal judge has ruled that the Sarasota police department must turn over sensitive internal affairs files to U.S. Justice Department officials, but, at the same time, the judge took steps to make sure the files go no further.

The unprecedented decision means the FBI will be able to continue its probe into whether the police department is properly using federal money.

To carry out that investigation, the FBI had said, it must review the police internal affairs files which detail citizen complaints against policemen and the department's investigation of those complaints.

The police objected, and got a state court order supporting them, saying that material in the files is confidential and their self-policing program would be ruined if the confidentiality were breached.

In a 10-page opinion this week, U.S. District Judge W. Terrell Hodges ordered the files turned over to the FBI, but cautioned that the FBI and Justice Department can't disclose the information to anyone else.

In ruling on the case which is the first of its kind in the country, Hodges said, "The court is confronted with an apparent dilemma: The government has a legitimate right to the files but the defendants have a valid right-to-privacy

interest in those files which might be compromised after their delivery to the government."

What Hodges was referring to are two federal laws, the Freedom of Information Act and the Privacy Act, under which either the public or the subjects of internal affairs files could gain access to the sensitive material.

The judge, to deal with the potential problem, ruled that he will retain jurisdiction over the case to make sure the nondisclosure order is enforced.

"The defendants (the police department and city officials) do have a genuine privacy interest which should be protected if possible," Hodges said.

He added later there is no law that creates "an absolute right-to-privacy privilege against disclosure of a city's records to authorized governmental personnel as distinguished, perhaps, from members of the public generally."

The FBI first began reviewing city records last summer but police officers, whose names were in the internal affairs files as either investigative subjects or as witnesses, took the case to state court.

There, a judge ruled the city could not make the information available to the federal government.

Source: The Tampa Tribune, October 28, 1978, p. 6A.

Juvenile Justice and Delinquency Act: 1974

In 1974, Congress passed the Juvenile Justice and Delinquency Prevention Act, which established grants for projects in juvenile justice and set up the office of Juvenile Justice and Delinquency Prevention within LEAA. This act contains one condition that goes beyond requiring generalized plans for improvements in the juvenile justice system: states that receive funds under this act must abolish the use of detention in cases involving only so-called "status offenses" by juveniles. The failure of states to apply for the monies available led to a recent decision that states, to be eligible, must only show good faith in trying to move toward the realization of that goal. This situation illustrates the kinds of rules that the federal government can impose as a condition of obtaining funds.[9]

National Advisory Commission on Criminal Justice Stands and Goals: 1971

This commission was created to follow up on the work done by the President's Commission on Law Enforcement and the Administration of Justice. The end results of the Advisory Commission's work was published in a series of five volumes in 1973: *A National Strategy to Reduce Crime; Criminal Justice System; Police; Courts;* and *Community Crime Prevention*. The recommendations of the Advisory Commission report, as was the case for that of its predecessor, outlined highly specific recommendations for the improvement of the various components of the criminal justice system but gave a higher priority to the crime prevention aspects of crime control at the state and local level. The Advisory Commission recommended that the federal government should continue to provide monies through various grant and revenue sharing programs.

Civil Rights Act of 1964 and the Equal Employment Opportunity Act of 1972

The involvement of the federal government into the operations of local law enforcement has also occurred via two other pieces of important legislation, namely, the Civil Rights Act of 1964 and the Equal Employment Opportunity Act of 1972. There is little doubt that these two pieces of legislation have had a profound effect upon the personnel practices and policies of police departments in the areas of recruitment, training, job assignment, and promotion.

The Civil Rights Act of 1964 is divided into a number of titles, each dealing with a particular aspect of discrimination. The entire act touches on matters concerning voting rights, public accommodations, public education, establishment of the U.S. Commission on Civil Rights, discrimination in federally assisted programs, equal employment opportunity, and a number of procedural matters. Title VII of the Civil Rights Act of 1964 has been the main body of federal legislation in the area of fair employment. Prior to 1972, Title VII was directed primarily toward private employers with twenty-five or more employees, labor organizations with twenty-five or more members, and private employment agencies.[10] The essence of the substantive portion of Title VII provides that

It shall be an unlawful employment practice for an employer to (1) to fail or refuse to hire, or discharge any individual or otherwise to discriminate against any individual with respect to his compensation, terms, conditions, or privileges of employment, because of such individual's race, color, religion, sex, or national origin; (2) to limit, segregate, or classify his employees or applicants for employment in any way which would deprive or tend to deprive any individual of employment opportunity or otherwise adversely affect his status as an employee because of such individual's race, color, religion, sex, or national origin.[11]

In 1972 Congress expanded the coverage of title VII of the Civil Rights Act of 1964. On March 24, 1972, an amendment, known as the Equal Employment Opportunity Act, Title VII, was approved. It expanded coverage of Title VII to both public and private employers, including state and local governments, public and private educational institutions, labor organizations, and public and private employment agencies. In the case of government agencies, educational institutions, and labor organizations, the act applied to those organizations with twenty-five or more employees

BOX 2-2.

Fired Woman Trooper Will Appeal

Richmond, Va. (UPI)—

Virginia's first woman state trooper plans to ask the state police board Tuesday to reinstate her in the job she lost for refusing to take an out-of-town assignment on short notice.

Cheryl Petska, 31, was fired for insubordination Friday after she said she would not go on special duty in the strike-troubled Virginia coalfields because she was not given enough time to find a babysitter for her children.

Mrs. Petska's husband, Mark, works as an undercover state trooper and was scheduled to be away on assignment at the time. "This is abusive and unfair," Mrs. Petska's attorney Joseph Duvall said. "Everybody recognizes an emergency. But this was no emergency."

"The coal strikes have been going on for years, and as I understand it, some divisions already have their schedules (for special duty) up to 1980."

Mrs. Petska said she was told Friday to be at the coalfields Monday and "I thought the short notice was unjustified."

Duvall is filing a demand Tuesday for a hearing with the state superintendent in Richmond. If Mrs. Petska is not reinstated, he said, they will take the matter to court.

"I stood up for what is right and I'll stick behind that," the state trooper said.

Mrs. Petska said she believes she was fired because of mismanagement and "resentment by a majority of troopers who do not want women out in the field."

She sees the last-minute assignment to the coalfields 400 miles from her home in Fredericksburg as a kind of "test."

"There's been a test on me ever since I've been here the last two years," she said. "I've been through more because I'm the first woman."

"But after all this time, you get just a little bit annoyed that they resent you because you're a woman and not because you're not doing your job."

Mrs. Petska joined the force in October 1976. She said she hoped eventually to become an investigator.

The Virginia state police are under federal court order to recruit more women. Four of the state's 1,000 troopers are women.

Source: The Tampa Tribune, January 12, 1979, p. 6A.

during the first year after the date of enactment; thereafter, it applied to agencies with fifteen or more employees.[12]

Under the authority of Title VII as amended, the Equal Employment Opportunity Commission (EEOC) was designated as the regulatory agency with the function of setting standards and establishing guidelines for compliance with the requirements of the law. In 1970, the Equal Employment Opportunity Commission issued a set of Guidelines on Employee Selection Procedures that superseded and enlarged upon earlier guidelines on Employment Testing Procedures issued by the EEOC in 1966. These guidelines constitute the basic interpretation of the requirements of Title VII as it applies to state and local government, and it is these guidelines with which compliance must be shown by those involved in personnel practices. Many of the complaints filed with the Equal Employment Opportunity Commission and the cases that subsequently end up in court have arisen from personnel practices involving police and fire departments.[13]

The use of arrest and conviction records as a basis of employment discrimination also is subject to attack under equal opportunity laws. The EEOC has ruled that convictions may not be used in personnel selection unless the conviction is related directly to the work to be performed. Further, conviction records cannot be used as an absolute barrier to employment, but, rather, each conviction must be reviewed on the basis of its relevance to the job to be done.[14]

The Roles of State and Local Government in Law Enforcement

From the outset most Americans had a firm belief that the police should be controlled by local officials organized along municipal lines. For them, a national police, such as the Italian *carabinieri,* was inconceivable, and a state police, such as the German *polizei,* was undesirable.[15] However, the history of state and local relations in the area of law enforcement has often been a rocky and tumultuous one. Fogelson, for example, has noted that

> By the mid-nineteenth century, it was plain that for most police department's local control meant Democratic control. Hence the Republican leaders, who generally spoke for the upper middle and upper classes, demanded state control, arguing that it would remove the police from partisan politics and improve the quality of law enforcement. Their Democratic opponents countered that state control would merely shift the focus of political interference and plainly violate the principle of self-government. The issue erupted in one city after another, with the Republicans usually getting their way. They imposed state control of the police in New York City in 1857, Detroit in 1865, Cleveland in 1866, New Orleans in 1868, Cincinnati in 1877, Boston in 1885, and Omaha in 1887. They also established metropolitan police departments, with jurisdiction over the central city and adjacent territory, in New York City in 1857, Albany in 1865, and a few other places thereafter.
>
> Under these arrangements the state authorities appointed a board to manage, or at any rate to oversee, the big-city police. But the states did not contribute anything toward the upkeep of the police departments; nor, except in a few cases, did they authorize them to operate in the metropolitan area, much less throughout the entire state. Not until the early twentieth century did Pennsylvania, New York, and a few other states

from statewide constabularies; and these forces, which patrolled mainly in small towns and rural districts, supplemented rather than supplanted the municipal police. Thus despite these changes, the American police remained decentralized to a degree unheard of anywhere in Western Europe. By the late nineteenth century, moreover, state control was well on the wane. The Democrats attacked it at every opportunity; and in the face of mounting evidence that the state boards had neither removed the police from partisan politics nor improved the quality of law enforcement, the Republicans were hard pressed to defend it. The issue was soon resolved, usually when the Democrats took office. The state authorities not only abolished metropolitan policing in New York and Albany in 1870 but also reestablished local control in Cleveland in 1868, New York in 1870, New Orleans in 1877, Cincinnati in 1880, Detroit in 1891, and Omaha in 1897. By 1900 the big-city police were controlled by local officials and organized along municipal lines everywhere in urban American except for Boston, Baltimore, St. Louis, Kansas City, and a few other places.[16]

The type of direct takeover of local law enforcement by the states described by Fogelson will very likely not occur again or at least not on the grand scale of the 1800s. However, we may see some isolated cases. For example, several years ago some public officials in Georgia were urging the state to take over the administration of the Atlanta Police Department because of dramatic political upheavals that were affecting the morale and effectiveness of that department. A take-over by the state did not occur, but the political atmosphere was conducive to such a move.

Even if a state does not exercise its official political power to intervene in local police administration, it may be called upon to exercise its influence in less apparent ways, in which case the influence may not always be proper or appropriate:

Our department was going through a major reorganization and in the process was going to have to make about 50 promotions. One of the newly created positions was deputy chief. The only requirement for the position was that you had to have been a Major for one year. ''Ed Hawks'' had been a Major for about 8 months and he really wanted that deputy chief's position. Nobody believed that he even had a chance. He went to his cousin, who was close to the Governor, and talked to him. The Governor called the Mayor and expressed his ''confidence'' in what a great deputy chief Hawks would make. The mayor's son sat as a political appointee of the Governor on one of the most important state boards. So, the Mayor sat on the reorganization plan until the day after Ed Hawks had a year in grade as a Major—which meant that 50 promotions were held up for about four months—and then approved the implementation of the plan. . . . Hawks got promoted . . . crap like that is really demoralizing.

In a positive vein, the impact of the state on the affairs of local law enforcement is continuing via the imposition of preemployment and training standards as well as through various funding formulas tied to these standards. The first state to impose minimum standards of training for police officers was California, in 1959. This move was soon followed by the states of New York, Oklahoma, and Oregon. In 1970, the LEAA did make available discretionary grants to those states that wanted to implement minimum standards programs. By 1981, forty-eight states had employment and training requirements for all persons employed as law enforcement officers.[17] It must be noted, however, that much of the impetus for the implementation of minimum standards on a statewide basis came from the local law enforcement community. Requirements related to the minimum standards for employment as police officers are administered through state organizations, often termed Police Officers Standards

BOX 2-3.

City Hall Cooks Stir Up a Stew with the Police

By Raleigh Bryans

The late William B. Hartsfield, mayor of Atlanta for 23½ years, had a hangup about traffic enforcement.

As Hartsfield perceived it, a tough crackdown on speeding motorists during his first four-year term as mayor cost him reelection in 1941.

Resilient politician that he was, Hartsfield made a comeback. But never again, during another 19½ years as mayor, did he permit strict traffic law enforcement by city police.

"He permitted us to write only enough tickets to 'educate' people to traffic laws, and in election years—well, you don't write many tickets at all," recalls Clinton Chafin, the former Atlanta police officer who now is chief of Fulton County police.

Hartsfield's interference with traffic law enforcement is a classic example of politics at work on law enforcement. Police politics have always been around, and they have usually earned a bad name.

Long before Philadelphia Mayor Frank Rizzo, or Atlanta mayors Sam Massell and Maynard Jackson, City Hall politicians, not all of them mayors, overextended acceptable bounds of executive and political control of police. Nearly always, the end result has been a breakdown of professionalism in police departments and in the quality of law enforcement.

The terms of Massell and Jackson have spanned nearly a decade of Atlanta history. Since 1970, Atlanta police headquarters has been rocked repeatedly by questionable political interference, by public brawls and scandals involving superior officers or City Hall officials, and by recurring upheavals in command and secondary management posts.

There is no accurate way of measuring the impact this troubled decade has had on the morale and effectiveness of city police.

But the turmoil demonstrably has cost the city the talents of hundreds of men—Chafin is one example—who fled the force, either by resignations or early retirement, because they found the climate inhospitable or intolerable.

Nine-tenths of the men in the 122-member Fulton police force are former Atlanta police officers. The creation of the county force in 1975 gave men on the city force an escape hatch they fell over each other to take.

Turnover in the Atlanta force historically has been high, but the exodus of trained men this year has risen to 10 to 15 a month.

And even as the department trains and loses men, it has been handicapped in recruitment of new personnel by a protracted federal court contest between contending employee organizations about conflicting charges of race discrimination.

From a high of 1,415 officers in 1975, the force is now down to 1,112.

While crime rates here respond in partial degree to national trends, some observers have charged the chaos in the police bureau also may be contributing to the rise in crime.

Early in this decade, 25 years of relative stability ended in the Decatur Street headquarters of the Atlanta police. Herbert Jenkins, who had become chief in 1947, had achieved an outstanding reputation, nationally as well as locally, while serving under Hartsfield, then under Mayor Ivan Allan, Jr., and finally under Massell, under whom he was to complete his final two years as chief.

Jenkins fended off most efforts at unwanted City Hall meddling.

He lobbied into law the rule that the chief had full say about departmental promotions. He ran things without merit system rules that governed other city departments, but he also managed to run the police force without cronyism emanating from City Hall.

He did, that is, until his last two years. As he has chronicled in his autobiography, "Forty Years on the Force," Jenkins learned that times were changing as soon as Massell took office in 1970.

Massell promptly informed him that he wanted a virtually unknown lieutenant, John Inman, "moved upward" in the department's hierarchy. Inman's association with Seymour Zimmerman, a nightclub owner, drew criticism from Fulton County District Attorney Lewis

R. Slaton. Massell's brother Howard also had ties with the nightclub world.

Jenkins writes that Howard Massell "came by to see me at my office" and in the course of a conversation "told me that he had a keen interest in certain police matters."

In time, Inman, who had been hastily promoted to captain, "kept me informed of what Howard Massell suggested," Jenkins writes.

Jenkins did his time, resisting the manipulations of both Massells, and bowed out in March 1972.

To no one's surprise, Massell named Inman the new chief of police.

Inman made heads roll at police headquarters. During the summer of 1972, Inman broke Chafin successively from assistant chief to superintendent to captain. Chafin was the man Jenkins had trained for many years to become chief.

Inman downgraded or reassigned nearly every superior officer in the department who had been identified closely with Chafin, Jenkins or Mayor Allen, who chose not to seek re-election in 1969 but tried to head off Massell's election.

By the end of November, a Fulton County grand jury, having delved into a variety of provocative police department scandals, urged a review of all promotions and demotions made since the start of 1972.

"Vindictiveness has frequently been the basis for demotion and reassignment and . . . some promotions have been made on the basis of personal favoritism," the grand jury concluded.

The grand jury had taken a look into Howard Massell's association with known underworld figures and criticized the younger Massell for "control" of privilege licenses, such as liquor licenses, without taking sterner action against him.

Howard Massell, discredited with the public, moved from Atlanta to Miami in December. But by then, Inman no longer seemed to be responding to the dictates of Massell.

Starting in the fall of 1972 and for the next seven years, Inman embroiled himself in high-profile disputes with Mayor Massell, Maynard Jackson (both as vice-mayor and as mayor), and City Councilman Ira Jackson.

Inman stuck. And he stuck later when Massell's successor, Maynard Jackson, tried to oust him. Inman obtained a court ruling that his eight-year appointment was effectively as good as a contract.

During the period when Jackson was trying to fire him, Inman brought in seven heavily armed members of the police SWAT team to keep control of his office and prevent Chafin, the man Jackson was trying to install as chief, from assuming command. The "two chief" dispute rivaled Georgia's 1946 "two governor" dispute for headlines.

Inman also defied Mayor Jackson's effort to organize him out of office by superimposing a commissioner of public safety over the police chief. Inman was banished to a do nothing role while continuing to draw $35,000 a year in salary.

Inman soon faded into relative obscurity, superseded by A. Reginald Eaves, a political pal of Jackson.

Eaves became commissioner of public safety ("Superchief," the press called it) in August 1974 after a national search for experienced candidates. Jackson's appointment of Eaves, his chief of staff, was viewed by some as an attempt to politicize control of the police bureau in new directions.

Jackson was the city's first black mayor. He had commitments to the black community to abolish an image of police brutality and also to boost the numbers of black patrolmen and officers in the police bureau. In effect, he commissioned Eaves to carry out his mandates.

Within two weeks of Eaves' takeover, heads again rolled on Decatur Street, recalling the early days of the Inman regime. In one month, Eaves demoted six assistant police chiefs, six majors, 19 lieutenants and 57 sergeants. Fifteen other senior officers were transferred.

By February 1975, six months into his tenure as public safety commissioner, Eaves was causing waves of another sort. It was disclosed that one of his nephews had been hired on a CETA job without going through channels, and it was learned that Eaves' personal secretary had a criminal record. A national police intelligence group, the Law Enforcement Intelligence Unit, claiming it distrusted Eaves' intelligence chief, threw the city out of the intelligence network.

Jackson almost fired Eaves. He did not do so, apparently, because of black community support aroused by Eaves himself and by anti-Eaves statements from then-City Council President Wyche Fowler. Fowler, who is white, was made a symbol of an alleged white community effort to sack Eaves.

Eaves was to be sacked by Jackson, but that was much later, in March 1978. The basis for Eaves' dismissal arose in September 1975, however.

Oral examinations for promotion to sergeant and captain were held in the police bureau September 22 and November 21, 1975. Eaves promoted 21 blacks and seven whites to the rank of sergeant and seven blacks and two whites to the rank of captain.

No hint of irregularities in the testing surfaced at the time. Nor did the public know of anything improper when, almost a year later, four black policemen went to then-Chief Administrative Officer George Berry and charged Eaves had ordered copies of the test questions distributed in advance to members of the Afro-American Patrolmen's League.

Atlanta's "cheating scandal" did not surface until August 1977, two years after the events that caused it. Jackson, without saying so publicly, asked the city attorney to investigate the charge. In September, having received a 500-page city attorney's report, Jackson concluded cheating had occurred but that Eaves was not involved in it.

Under public pressure, Jackson in November named lawyers Felder Ward, Jr. and Randolph Thrower to head an independent investigation. The next February, Ward and Thrower issued a report implicating Eaves and many of his close bureau associates in the cheating scheme.

The Ward-Thrower report was Eaves' downfall, but not before another month of vacillation by Jackson in the face of a storm of political support in the black community for the embattled commissioner. Jackson fired Eaves and in time brought in a new command team, Commissioner Lee Brown and Police Chief George Napper.

Implicated with Eaves and others in the cheating scandal was Eldrin Bell, then the deputy police director. Bell, once the mayor's driver and security officer, weathered the scandal only to fall later in January of this year. Now, he's back to his old rank and the center of new controversy that still is unfolding.

Source: The Atlanta Journal and Constitution, September 23, 1979, P 1d.

and Training Commissions (POSTS), which generally operate under three broad mandates: (1) to establish minimum standards for employment in a state, county, or local law enforcement agency; (2) to articulate curricula of training for police officers; and (3) to conduct and encourage research designed to improve all aspects of law enforcement.[18]

In its assessment of the role of the states in criminal justice planning, in general the National Advisory Commission on Criminal Justice Standards and Goals suggested that the State Planning Agencies (SPAs) which were created by the Omnibus Crime Control and Safe Streets Act of 1968 as the state-level organizations through which federal funds were funneled from the LEAA, bear a special responsibility for the formation of minimum statewide standards.[19] However with the demise of LEAA in 1982 there has been a reduction or total dismantling of large state planning agencies.

Local Political Forces

The special dimension of police politics varies from community to community, but law enforcement activities are governed for the most part by the dominant values of the local political culture.

James Q. Wilson, in his now-classic study of the police in eight communities, identified three distinctly different styles of law enforcement, all of which were reflective of the political culture of the communities they serve. (1) The "watchman" style of law enforcement emphasizes order maintenance and is found in economically declining cities with traditional political machines. (2) The "legalistic style of law enforcement is found in cities with heterogeneous populations and reform-oriented, professional governments; law enforcement of both a reactive and proactive nature characterizes this style. (3) In the homogeneous suburban communities, the "service" style of law enforcement is oriented toward the needs of citizens.[20]

In Wilson's studies, these variations in the community political culture manifested themselves in a number of ways that subsequently affected both the qualitative and quantitative enforcement action taken by the police. Significant enforcement variations emerged in the areas of vice, juvenile offenses, order maintenance, and traffic enforcement. Numerous variations, linked to the community's political culture, also emerged in the police department's personnel entry standards, promotional policies, extent of specialization, and level of managerial skills. These, in turn, affected the overall operations of the department, which in turn impacted upon the citizen's perception and confidence in its police department.

As indicated earlier, there is an unfailing, consistent, and close relationship between the type of law enforcement a community has and its dominant political culture. This is not to suggest, however, that any community's political culture is unalterably fixed. In fact, the reform movements that have been a part of the American political scene throughout much of its history have corresponded with the emergence of new political cultures. Each new dominant political culture in time leaves its own unique mark upon the unit of government within its sphere of control.

Strong Mayor

To some extent, the type of local government that a community has will have impact on the way in which police chiefs are selected, the freedom they will enjoy in the performance of their status, and their tenure. For example, with a strong mayor form of government, the mayor is elected to office and serves as the chief executive of the city. The city council constitutes the chief legislative and policymaking body. The mayor nominates a candidate to serve as police chief, with majority approval needed from the city council. Once approved, the candidate assumes the position of police chief and serves at the discretion of the mayor.

Ideally, the person selected by the mayor as police chief should possess the full range of managerial and administrative skills necessary to operate the police department. However, to a great extent, the kind of persons selected to serve as police chief will be determined by the mayor's professional qualifications, philosophy about the role of law enforcement, and political commitments. If the mayor is endowed with sound business or public administration skills and also has a "good government" philosophy, then the chief of police will very likely be selected on the basis of professional abilities rather than extraneous political factors. Unfortunately, on too many occasions in the past, this appointment has been a method of repaying political favors. A classical case of the misuse of this appointing authority was illustrated by the Wickersham Commission in 1931:

> a few years ago the mayor of Indianapolis was called upon to introduce the police chief of that city to an assemblage of police chiefs during one of their conferences. In the

course of his introductory remarks, the mayor said "I know that my man is going to be a good chief because he has been my tailor for 20 years. He knows how to make good clothes; he ought to be a good chief."[21]

No big-city mayor would make this same choice today, but the choice will nevertheless still be a reflection of the mayor's personal value system, abilities, and the political environment of the community.

In the strong mayor form of local government, the tenure of the chief of police is often linked directly to the mayor, and the nature of the relationship is such that the chief is quite dependent upon the mayor for support and guidance on budgetary matters, enforcement practices, and a multitude of other areas essential to the overall success of the police department. If there is mutual respect between the police chief and the mayor, a strong professional and political bond will be formed. If the reverse holds true, however, significant antagonisms may begin to emerge. There are too many situations to enumerate positively or negatively that can affect the working relationship between a mayor and police chief. One finds that the important differences that do emerge are frequently those that evolve out of philosophical and ethical differences rather than questions of legality. These are differences that can occur in any form of government.

City Manager

There is no lack of supporters or detractors for every form of local government found in the United States. The proponents of the city manager form claim that it provides the most conducive atmosphere in which professional law enforcement can operate and minimizes external interference from outside controls.

The city manager more often than not is a professional administrator who is recruited for certain skills and training and appointed by the city council. A person with this background tends to make sincere efforts to select a competent individual to serve as police chief, since the manager's professional reputation is tied inextricably to the effective management of the city departments.

It is significant that city managers have sought qualified police chiefs and that they have in most instances based their selection on the professional qualifications of the candidate rather than political or other extraneous considerations that too often have governed appointments to this position in the past.[22] This does not mean that the city manager form of government removes the chief from local politics, but it does create more distance and insulation than exists in the one-to-one political relationship commonly found in the strong mayor form of government.

Tenure for Police Chiefs

There is little evidence to support the notion that any particular form of government necessarily provides greater job security to a police chief than an other. A study conducted several years ago in California showed that police chief's tenure in that state approximated three years before either being fired or resigning.[23,24]

Edward M. Davis, former chief of the Los Angeles Police Department, at the time of his acceptance speech for the presidency of the International Association of Chiefs of Police, made the following observation about the relationship of politics and the police and the absence of tenure and due process for police chiefs.

As I review the state of our profession throughout this nation, I have grown increasingly concerned about the plight of many police chiefs. In the vast majority of police departments, the agency's chief serves at the pleasure of a mayor or city manager. Because a great deal of politics can both be implied and involved where the police chief does not have some type of procedural due process, there is a very high turnover rate for police chiefs in America. Often the termination or appointment date for chiefs of police coincides with the political haymaking of mayoral elections. This part of politics in policing creates a great deal of insecurity on the part of many chiefs and inspires a reluctance to take any action which might be considered contrary to the desires of the local political machine. Politicians should not control the strings of local policing. Where this has been observed, the local enforcement agency has been prevented from bringing about a genuine sense of equal justice. By equal justice, I mean that the law should not be prostituted to satisfy political desires. The law must apply equally to paupers and kings. The potential for inequality of enforcement because of political interference will always be one of the strongest factors preventing us from achieving full professionalism. It is time, I think, to fully remove the cloak of politics from the administration of justice and provide some assurance of impartiality under the law.

Probably the best method of insuring impartiality in policing and preventing improper political interference is some kind of security for police chiefs. The head of a police agency must be permitted to exercise some freedom in managing his department. The most logical approach to this concept of due process is that the chief only be removed for cause and that it be necessary to prove that some malfeasance or misfeasance in office occurred. The process for removal of a chief should include a formal hearing before a duly constituted administrative tribunal and the chief should be given the opportunity to defend himself against the charges. If such a due process concept is not implemented by the employing municipality, the chief will be required to suffer through his stewardship with the knowledge that a politician can arbitrarily tell him what to do and fire him on the first occasion when he does not comply. Such political indulgences are, of course, destructive to the community because the chief is relegated to the status of a political pawn. The safety and security enjoyed by the community is seriously compromised.[25]

The issue of administrative due process for police chiefs was studied exhaustively in a report that revealed that 84 percent of all police chief executives responding to the survey indicated that the lack of protection from arbitrary and unjustified removal either affected or would affect their ability to fulfill their responsibilities objectively and independently.[26]

City Councils

The legally defined roles of city councils are fairly consistent throughout the United States; namely, they act as the chief legislative and policymaking body. Through its ordinance power, subject to constitutional and statutory provisions, including the city charter, the council carries out its legislative function; when within its authority, its enactments have the force of law and are binding upon both administration and electorate. In addition to legislative and policymaking functions, the council, in common with most legislative bodies, holds the purse strings and exercises control over appropriations.[27] Thus, the immediate impact of a council's actions on the operation of a law enforcement agency is considerable.

The record of involvement by council members and other elected officials in police operations to the detriment of both the efficiency and effectiveness of the police establishment is a well-established fact. One observer of this problem has noted that:

Local political leaders frequently promote more abuses of police power than they deter. In seeking favored treatment for a violator of the law or in exerting pressure for police assistance in the sale of tickets to a fund-raising dinner, the politician only encourages the type of behavior he is supposed to prevent. Although such political interference into police work is not as extensive as it once was, it still exists.[28]

James F. Ahern, former chief of the New Haven, Connecticut, Police Department, discusses this issue at length in his book *Police in Trouble*. He describes as follows the extent to which political forces negatively affected the New Haven Police Department and the course of action he took to nullify them.

There is nothing more degrading or demoralizing to a police department than the knowledge that every favor or promotion within it is controlled by hack politicians and outright criminals. And there is nothing more nearly universal. Five years ago, anyone with the most superficial knowledge of the workings of the New Haven Police Department could point to the political power behind every captain on the force. Every cop who wanted to get ahead had his "hook"—or, as they say in New York, his "rabbi." Everyone owed his success to a politician—from the Town Chairman on down—or to an influential underworld figure. Needless to say, in a situation like this there was no chance whatever of the department functioning in the public interest.

A day after I had taken office, I closed the second-story back door to the Mayor's office and issued a renewal of a long-standing and long-ignored departmental order prohibiting any police officer from seeing the Mayor without the authorization of the chief.

Given the incredible tangle of grimy politics that still existed in the lower levels of government and in the structures of the city's political parties, this action was largely symbolic. But as a gesture it was necessary. It would be immediately evident to everyone in the police department that if I would not permit the Mayor who had appointed me to influence departmental promotions or assignments, I certainly would allow no other politicians to influence them.

Mayor Lee was aware of the connections between politics and police and was himself capable of intervening in the affairs of the police department to advance cops whom he considered honest and effective who otherwise would have been buried. Riding home with the Mayor in a car one day, I showed him a draft of my order. He frowned slightly, nodded, and then approved.

But this order was only the opening shot in the war to end political interference in the police department. The far more substantive challenge was to make clear in every way possible, to every man in the department, that political influence of any kind was out. There was only one way to handle the problem, and it was somewhat heavy-handed. The men were made responsible for stopping interference themselves. They were warned that if politicians or underworld figures approached me with requests for promotions, transfers, or easy assignments for cops, the officers in question would be barred permanently from those positions.

The immediate reaction among the cops was total incredulity. Political maneuvering had been the basis for advancement in the department for so long that it was doubtful whether they believed there was another way to be promoted. I would not be surprised if they thought that promotions in the department would freeze until I resigned or retired. But they did believe me. And they did convey the message to their hooks. For the time being, political interference in the department all but stopped.[29]

To suggest that the experience of New Haven is typical of most communities would be an inaccurate generalization, but there is little doubt that the council's fiscal control over the police department's budget and its legislative powers make it a political force that is never taken lightly by chiefs of police. As a matter of fact, most police chiefs will go to great lengths to maintain the goodwill and support of their council members.

State Prosecutor

The prosecutor, state's attorney, or district attorney is the chief law enforcement officer under the statutes of some states. However, despite this designation, the state prosecutor does not have overall responsibility for the supervision of the police.[30] Even so, the prosecutor's enforcement policies, procedures for review of all arrests prior to their presentation in court, and overall supervision of the cases prepared by the police do have an observable effect upon police practices and enforcement policies. The initial contact of police officers with prosecutors occurs when the former brings a complaint to be charged. This encounter may be critical because it is an important point for making decisions about the disposition of the case and whether the complaint will be dismissed or reduced to a lesser offense. This discretionary power given the prosecuting attorney has tremendous influence on the ways in and extent to which certain laws are enforced or ignored. Police chiefs who perceive that the prosecutor consistently reduces or fails to vigorously enforce certain types of violations may very likely divert their enforcement efforts and resources elsewhere. Then, again, the chief may decide to "go public" and try to mobilize community support for enforcing the ignored violations. Very few police chiefs take this course of action, however, because it could result in a serious deterioration in the working relationship with the local prosecutor, a situation most would prefer to avoid.

The Judiciary

In its assessment of the relationships of the judiciary and the police, one governmental report noted that trial judges have acted as chief administrative officers of the criminal justice system, using their power to dismiss cases as a method of controlling the use of the criminal process. But, except in those rulings involving the admissibility of evidence, this has been done largely on an informal basis and has tended to be haphazard, often reflecting primarily the personal values of the individual trial judge.[31]

In contrast, the function of trial judges in excluding evidence that they determine to have been obtained illegally places them very explicitly in the role of controlling police practices. Trial judges have not viewed this role as making them responsible for developing appropriate police practices. However, many trial judges, when asked to explain their decisions, indicate that they have no more responsibility for explaining decisions to police than they have with regard to private litigants.[32]

Occasionally, judges will grant motions to suppress evidence to dismiss cases that they feel should not be prosecuted because the violation is too minor or for some other reason. Use of a motion to suppress evidence in this manner serves to confuse the standards that are supposed to guide the police and has a disturbing, if not demoralizing, effect on them.[33]

If judges consistently interject their personal biases into the judicial process and make it very clear to police that they will dismiss certain categories of violations, the police may discontinue enforcing that particular law. This, in turn, may put the police on a collision course with certain segments of the community that favor the rigorous enforcement of certain laws.

The following actual case illustrates this point.

A municipal judge decided that he was going to begin to dismiss all charges of public intoxication placed upon citizens by the police unless there were also companion charges such as disorderly conduct, resisting arrest, and so forth. The judge decided to implement this policy because he believed that incarcerating such offenders created an unnecessary backlog on the court docket, filled the jails with people who were basically not criminals, and essentially did nothing to rehabilitate the habitual drunk.

The bulk of individuals being arrested by the local police for public intoxication were arrested in the skid row section of the downtown area. Although the police rarely placed any additional charges on the persons arrested on skid row, they could have frequently added the charges of "vagrancy," "begging," and so forth. In this case, the police simply assumed that the judge did not want these types of individuals arrested and, therefore, stopped making arrests. This new enforcement policy had some rather interesting consequences that neither the police nor the judge fully anticipated.

Skolnick in commenting on police-judiciary relationships has noted that

When an appellate court rules that police may not in the future engage in certain enforcement activities, since these constitute a violation of the rule of law, the inclination of the police is typically not to feel *shame* but *indignation*. This response may be especially characteristic of "professional" police, who feel a special competence to decide, on

BOX 2-4.

North Franklin Policing Hit

By Ivan Hathaway, *Tribune Staff Writer*

Claiming that panhandlers are running rampant and "women have to walk out into the street to avoid being molested," a group of North Franklin Street merchants charged yesterday that police are not providing adequate protection.

The charge was leveled by a group of about 25 businessmen at a morning meeting at Todd's Restaurant, 208 E. Cass Street, which was attended by City Councilmen Joe Kotvas and Lee Duncan, Deputy Police Chief Allison Wainwright and Police Maj. J. W. Morton.

Making the strongest complaints was Harry Arkus, who told the city officials that customers entering stores on Franklin and its side streets have to make their way past panhandlers begging for money.

"These bums line the sidewalks, alienating customers. I've seen two women who had to walk out onto the street to avoid being molested," Arkus said.

One merchant told of being robbed in his store five times in recent years and of being mugged and robbed on the sidewalk only a week ago.

He said, referring to the most recent case, that had there been a policeman on the street the robber could have been caught.

Others complained of "drunks" being allowed to lie on the streets in front of their stores for 30 minutes or longer, saying that police response was slow.

Addressing Wainwright, Arkus said, "We see an officer walking the beat once in a while, and then we don't see him again for a few days and don't know where he is when we need him. We want to be protected."

Responding to the complaints, Wainright said police officials already were aware that downtown merchants "have a problem."

"The only answer to this problem you're having seems to be in assigning more officers to patrol the area. But we just don't have the men to do this," he said.

Source: The Tampa Tribune, January 16, 1973, p.1B.

BOX 2-5.

Police Crack Down on Panhandlers

By Ivan Hathaway, *Tribune Staff Writer*

A crackdown on "nuisance violations," aimed particularly at the growing number of panhandlers in the downtown area, has resulted in 10 arrests within a 24-hour period, Tampa police said yesterday.

Jail dockets indicated the 10 men were charged with "begging." They were held in lieu of $25 bond each.

The arrests came shortly after a meeting in which North Franklin Street merchants criticized the policing in their business area.

Col. Allison Wainwright, deputy chief of police, said the meeting did not bring about the crackdown, "though it may have been a contributing factor."

We've always been interested in protecting the downtown area. Because of a shortage of officers and the crime rate, we have not had the opportunity to enforce the ordinance as we would have liked to," Wainwright said.

But the panhandling has had a gradual increase and is now a major problem. People are being pushed around and verbally abused. Panhandlers are even approaching our plain-clothes detectives."

To cope with the problem, officers who had been assigned to other Tampa areas have been called in to patrol the "entire downtown area," and policemen are doubling up on their assignments, he said.

"It has been our experience that as soon as we apply enforcement in an area, we begin seeing results and the problem begins decreasing," Wainwright said.

The crackdown will continue "as long as possible," he said.

"With these additional men in the downtown area we have a hairline balance of manpower. We'll keep them there as long as we can. If a need for additional manpower arises in another part of the city, we will have to pull them out for reassignment," Wainwright said.

Source: The Tampa Tribune, January 18, 1973, p.4B.

their own, how to reduce criminality in the community. The police, for example, recognize the court's power to bar admission of illegally seized evidence if the police are discovered to have violated the constitutional rights of the defendant. They do not, however, feel morally blameworthy at having done so; nor do they even accept such injunctions with good grace and go about their business. On the contrary, the police typically view the court with hostility for having interfered with their capacities to practice their craft. Police tend to rest their *moral* position on the argument that the "independence" and social distance of the appellate judicary constitutes a type of government—by the courts—without the consent of the governed—the police. Thus, the police see the court's affirmation of principles of due process as, in effect, the creation of harsh "working conditions." From their point of view, the courts are failing to affirm democratic notions of the autonomy and freedom of the "worker." Their political superiors insist on "production" while their judicial superiors impede their capacity to "produce." Under such frustrating conditions, the appellate judicary inevitably comes to be seen as "traitor" to its responsibility to keep the community free from criminality.

Antagonism between the police and the judiciary is perhaps an inevitable outcome, therefore, of the different interests residing in the police as a specialized agency and the judiciary as a representative of wider community interests. Constitutional guarantees of due process of law do make the working life and conditions of the police more difficult. But if such guarantees did not exist, the police would of course engage in activities promoting self-serving ends, as does any agency when offered such freedom in a situation of conflicting goals. Every administrative agency tends to support policies permitting it to present itself favorably. Regulative bodies restricting such policies are inevitably viewed with hostility by the regulated. Indeed, when some hostility does not exist, the regulators may be assumed to have been "captured" by the regulated. If the police could, in this sense, "capture" the judiciary, the resulting system would truly be suggestive of a "police state."[34]

Judicial Review and Policymaking

Several years ago a series of recommendations was made by one government commission in an effort to reduce some of the antagonisms and misunderstandings occurring regularly between the American police and the judiciary. It was felt that, if these recommendations were followed, it would modify the current system of judicial control and make it consistent and, in fact, supportive of the objective of police policymaking:

(a) When a trial judge is confronted with a motion to suppress, he, and the appellate court which reviews the case, should request a showing of whether the conduct of the officer in the particular case did or did not conform to existing departmental policy. If not, the granting of such a motion would not require a reevaluation of departmental policy. However, it ought to cause the police administrator to ask whether a prosecution should, as a matter of policy, be brought when the officer violated departmental policy in getting the evidence.

If the departmental policy were followed, the judge would be given an opportunity to consider the action of the individual officer in the light of the overall departmental judgment as to what is proper policy. Hopefully, a judge would be reluctant to upset a departmental policy without giving the police administrator an opportunity to defend the reasons for the policy, including, where relevant, any police expertise which might bear upon the reasonableness of the policy. To do this will slow down the proceedings, will take judicial time and effort, but if judicial review of police policy is worthwhile at all, it would seem that it is worth doing properly.

(b) Trial judges in multijudge courts should develop appropriate formal or informal means to avoid disparity between individual trial judges in their decisions about the propriety of police policy. The Sentencing Council, created in the Eastern District of Michigan to minimize judicial disparity in sentencing, would seem to be a helpful model. This council uses a panel of judges to consider what is an appropriate sentence rather than leaving the decision entirely to a single judge. The panel serves to balance any substantially different views of individual judges, and results in a more consistent judicial standard. Again, this involves cost in judicial time.

(c) It seems obvious that judicial decisions, whenever possible, ought to be effectively communicated to the police department whose policy was an issue. Yet it is common in current practice for the police administrator to have to rely primarily upon the newspaper as a source of information about judicial decisions, even those involving an officer of his own department. One way of achieving effective communication might be through making the police officer commonly assigned by departments to regular duty in the courtroom responsible for reporting significant decisions to the police administrator. This would require a highly qualified, legally trained, court officer. In addition, trial judges would have to be willing to explain their decisions at least orally, if not in writing.

(d) If the exclusionary rule is to be a principal vehicle for influencing police policy (as distinguished from disciplining an individual officer who acts improperly), then it seems apparent that the appellate process must be accessible to the prosecution as well as the defense so that inconsistent or apparently erroneous trial court decisions can be challenged.

It is nonetheless often urged that allowing appeal in a particular case is unfair to the particular defendant. Moreover, where the authority to appeal does exist, prosecutors often limit appeals to cases involving serious crimes rather than systematically appealing all cases in which an important law enforcement policy is affected.[35]

Citizen Involvement

Citizen involvement in the policymaking process of law enforcement agencies is frequently met with considerable resistance from members of the law enforcement community. Many police administrators feel that their effectiveness rests on a high degree of autonomy. They view attempts to alter the way in which the law is enforced as efforts to negate the effectiveness of and to politicize the police. They argue further that during the last quarter-century law enforcement agencies have slowly, but surely, been successful in freeing themselves of partisan political interference and that public involvement by citizens will result in the police becoming instruments of pressure group politics and avowedly partisan to the most vocal and disruptive segments of society.[36]

One national commission took strong exception to this traditional posture of opposition to citizen involvement in the policymaking. The commission's argument was that

> In some areas of governmental activity, there is increasing utilization of citizen advisory committees as a way of involving members of the community in the policy making process. In some cases, the group may be advisory only, the governmental agency being free to accept or reject its advice. In other instances, the group is official and policies are cleared through the committee as a regular part of the policy making process. The advantages of both methods are that they serve as an inducement for the police administrator to articulate important policies, to formulate them, and to subject them to discussion in the advisory group. How effective this is depends upon the willingness of the group and the police administrator to confront the basic law enforcement policy issues rather than being preoccupied with the much easier questions of the mechanics of running the department. Where there is a commitment to exploring basic enforcement policy questions, the citizens' advisory group or policy making board has the advantage of involving the community in the decision making process, thus giving a broader base than would otherwise exist for the acceptance and support of enforcement policies.[37]

Citizen groups are varied and they have differentiated interests in police service. Chambers of commerce and service clubs generally promote police professionalism out of civic pride. Churches and church groups have historically campaigned against vice and corruption and recently have added an interest in civil liberty causes and police community relations.[38]

Chambers of Commerce and Service Clubs

One typically finds that the local chambers of commerce and service clubs are supportive of those efforts that lead toward efficient and clean government. Although such groups are characterized as being apolitical, they have and can exercise considerable influence. Their support for improving the quality of law enforcement in the community is frequently heard in the chambers of city hall and is demonstrated through various community projects intended to assist local law enforcement. Attuned police chiefs realize the benefit to be gained from the support of such groups, encourage personnel to become active members in these clubs, and frequently join one or two themselves. Support from these groups is not surprising when one considers that they are frequently comprised of men and women from the middle class, who are well educated and deeply involved in many aspects of community leadership.

There have been numerous instances where such groups have mobilized behind a police chief to get much needed budget increases for salaries, additional personnel, and equipment.

Churches

The religious leaders and congregation members of a community's church groups represent one of the most potentially powerful pressure groups in the community. Their influence can, and frequently does, extend into the voting booth, which assures a high degree of responsiveness from local elected officials. Church leaders and their congregations almost always find an open door and a receptive ear at the office of their local police chief when they present their concerns. The problems that are frequently of greatest concern to such groups are vice related, such as prostitution, massage parlors, X-rated theaters, and adult book stores. It is true that individual communities do impose different standards and have varying levels of tolerance, but, if the church leaders of a community mobilize and call upon their police chief to eradicate or reduce what they perceive to be a serious problem, there is a high probability that they will receive some positive response. And, if the police chief suggests that the police department cannot cope realistically with the problem because of limited personnel and resources, these very same church groups will likely begin applying pressure on the city officials to give the police chief the resources needed. Thus, the religious leaders of the community can be powerful allies of the police chief in certain types of enforcement efforts. On the other hand, this same pressure group may force the chief to redirect resources away from areas that may have a higher priority.

News Media

It is the responsibility of the police department and most especially its top leadership to establish and maintain a cordial association with all media representatives.[39] Both the electronic and print news media can be a powerful friend or a devastating antagonist of a local police department, and to a great extent this will be determined by the attitudes, policies, and working relationships among the editors, news directors, and police chief. When friction does occur between the police and the news media, as it invariably does in every community, it frequently emanates from the events surrounding a major crime or unusual occurrence. In the case of major crimes, for example, the police will often try not to release information that they believe would jeopardize the successful conclusion and prosecution of their investigation. The policy of the news media, on the other hand, is to inform the public. What exists is a clash of goals, both of which have their merits. If the representatives of the news media begin to believe that local law enforcement representatives are simply being arbitrary, uncooperative, or untruthful, their news stories will begin to reflect their dissatisfaction.

FIGURE 2-1. Col. Gerald L. Hough, Michigan State Police. [Courtesy of the Michigan State Police.]

They may accentuate stories that reflect negatively on the abilities of the police or fail to note reports that would reflect positively upon the police department.

The police chief and the police department should take every reasonable action to be certain that these occasional disagreements with the news media do not escalate into an unresolvable conflict.

News Media Policy in Practice

One department set forth the following policy statement for its officers to guide them in their working relations with the press:

The news media should be free at all times to record police activity. Thus police have nothing to hide. The constant scrutiny of both the news media and the community should be welcomed, as they can often be the best witnesses.

It is the newsman's right to have access to untainted information on all matters of public interest except when that information impedes operations of the police. For example, it is the duty of the police to protect the constitutional rights of all persons accused of crimes. Information may prejudice a suspect's right to a fair trial. Therefore, it must be withheld in the interests of justice until it is made part of the court's record and released by that court for public use.

In all instances except those involving juveniles, the identity of persons arrested and the nature of the offense charged should be disclosed. In some states, court decisions protect juveniles and prohibit the disclosure of any custody information by the police. Beyond the normal duties involved in an investigation, a department should have neither the authority nor the responsibility to ensure the privacy of persons who are temporarily subjected to publicity as victims of crimes.

The news photographer or television cameraman looks for unusual and human interest subject matter. His result may not always please the police; however, it is usually more appropriate to assist him rather than dissuade him.[40]

Such a policy sets the tone for the working relationship between the police and the media and, if followed, can significantly reduce the number of conflicts that could occur between these two groups.

Summary

Police departments, as is the case for all other administrative agencies, do not operate independently of external controls. These controls and influences are forthcoming from the federal, state, and local units of government, and in most instances they are both legal and proper. The extent to which these controls and influences impact upon a law enforcement agency depend in part upon national events and the unique political characteristics of each community.

In this chapter, we have not identified all the possible external sources of influence and control that could affect law enforcement agencies; instead we have identified those that are common to most law enforcement agencies and have traditionally exerted the greatest influence. Further, we have categorized them as those from the federal, state, and local level. For example, the impact of decisions made by the U.S. Supreme Court on local law enforcement is indisputable. The four decisions made between 1961 and 1966, *Mapp* v. *Ohio* (1961), *Gideon* v. *Wainwright* (1963), *Escobedo* v. *Illinois* (1964), and *Miranda* v. *Arizona* (1966), have profoundly altered police practices regarding search and seizure and interrogation. Further, few would argue with the fact that dramatic changes have occurred in the personnel practices of law enforcement agencies as a result of Equal Employment Opportunity Act of 1972. Thus, the influence and controls exerted from the federal level have been considerable, and the examples provided are not intended to be all encompassing but rather are used to illustrate this point.

The impact being exerted upon local law enforcement by the state has also increased dramatically since the 1970s. This has occurred primarily via legislation that imposes pre-employment and training standards upon local police agencies. There is no evidence to suggest that we will witness any significant additional intervention by the state except in those extraordinary cases where rampant malfeasance, misfeasance, or nonfeasance exist.

The greatest influence and controls over the day-to-day operation of a police department emanate from the local level, but these will be affected greatly by the dominant values and local political culture.

The principal government actors exerting influence and control over a law enforcement agency will be the mayor in the strong mayor form of government, city manager, city council, state prosecutor, and the trial judges. Since the strong mayor and city manager have hiring and firing authority over the police chief, it is safe to assume that they can, if they choose, exert considerable control and influence. The influence of city council is somewhat less direct but equally as formidable, since they contain the appropriations for the law enforcement agencies. The state attorneys can exert considerable influence and control upon a law enforcement agency because of the ultimate authority to review all arrests prior to their presentation in court and overall supervision of cases prepared by the police. Police chiefs who perceive that the prosecutor consistently reduces or fails to enforce certain types of violations vigorously may very likely direct their enforcement efforts and resources elsewhere.

Trial judges, on the other hand, have acted as a sort of chief administrative officer of the criminal justice system, using their power to dismiss cases as a method of controlling the use of the criminal process. In addition, if judges consistently interject their personal biases into the judicial process and make it clear to the police that they will dismiss certain categories of violations, the police may discontinue enforcing that particular law.

The nongovernmental groups discussed in this chapter that can exert varying degrees of control over law enforcement agencies were the chamber of commerce and service clubs, churches, and the media.

Although chambers of commerce and service clubs are viewed as apolitical, they have and can exert considerable influence. These are numerous instances in which such groups have mobilized behind a police chief to get much needed budget increases for salaries, additional personnel, and equipment.

The religious leaders and congregation members of a community church group represent one of the most potentially powerful pressure groups. Their interests usually involve matters related to morality, such as prostitution, massage parlors, X-rated theaters, and adult bookstores. If the church leaders of a community mobilize and call for action on these matters by the police chief, they will likely get quick response, even if the police chief believes that other law enforcement matters have a higher priority.

The news media can be a powerful friend or a devastating antagonist of a local police department, and to a great extent this will be determined by the attitudes, policies, and working relationships among the editor, news director, and police chief. A great deal can be done legitimately and intentionally by both the electronic and print media to make a law enforcement agency look very good in the eyes of the public or to seem quite ineffective. Thus, all things being equal, reasonable efforts should be taken by the police chief and other members of the department to be certain that occasional disagreements with the news media do not escalate into unresolvable conflicts. A carefully thought-out and documented media policy will go far in creating a harmonious working relationship between the law enforcement agency and media personnel.

At this point, it should be abundantly clear to the reader that police executives cannot merely be good administrators; they must also understand the art of politics. They must be sensitive to external forces that have an impact upon their agencies and whenever possible either draw upon them as positive resources or neutralize them if their objectives are illegal and destructive.

There has been an unfortunate tendency in police work to view politics of any kind as an evil phenomenon that has no place in law enforcement. Such a notion is naïve at best. Police executives who fail to understand or come to grips with these legitimate external political forces (mayors, city managers, city council members, churches, media, etc.) more often than not find themselves neutralized, under attack, or fired.

Discussion Questions

1. What four U.S. Supreme Court decisions were made between 1961 and 1966 that significantly affected the way local police departments conducted their criminal investigations?

2. What factors occurring during the 1960s brought into focus some of the glaring deficiencies that existed in the crime control mechanism at the local level?

3. What were some of the major recommendations of the President's Commission on Law Enforcement and Administration of Justice in 1967?

4. What was the major assumption of the Omnibus Crime Control and Safe Streets Act of 1968?

5. What resulted from the passage of the Juvenile Justice Delinquency Act of 1974?

6. What are the major features of the Civil Rights Act of 1964?

7. What are the major responsibilities of the Equal Employment Opportunity Commission?

8. What three styles of law enforcement were described by Wilson and what are their major features?

9. How are police chiefs selected under the ''strong mayor'' form of government and a city manager form of government?

10. Which form of government provides the greatest job security for a police chief?

Notes

1. The President's Commission on Law Enforcement and the Administration of Justice, *Task Force Report: The Police* (Washington, D.C.: U.S. Government Printing Office, 1967), p. 30.

2. A. E. Bent, *The Politics of Law Enforcement* (Lexington, Mass.: D.C. Heath, 1974), p. 63.

3. N. G. Holten and M. E. Jones, *The Systems of Criminal Justice* (Boston: Little, Brown, 1978), p. 416.

4. T. R. Dye, *Politics in States and Communities* (Englewood Cliffs, N.J.: Prentice-Hall, 1973), p. 214.

5. See the report of *The National Advisory Commission on Civil Disorders* (Kerner Report) (New York: Bantam Books, 1968) for a comprehensive analysis of the civil disorders occurring in American cities during the 1960s.

6. See Theodore H. White, *Making of the President 1968* (New York: Atheneum, 1969). The author traces the genesis and emergence of crime as a national political issue in his Chapter 7, entitled ''Appetite for Apocalypes: The Issue of Law-and-Order.''

7. Holten and Jones, *The Systems of Criminal Justice*, p. 417.

8. Dye, *Politics in States and Communities*, p. 219.

9. Holten and Jones, *The Systems of Criminal Justice*, pp. 418, 419.

10. L. Territo, C. R. Swanson, Jr., and N. C. Chamelin, *The Police Personnel Selection Process* (Indianapolis, Ind.: Bobbs-Merrill, 1977), p. 22.

11. P.L. 92–261, Section 703(a)(1)(2).

12. *Ibid.*

13. *Ibid.*

14. Equal Employment Opportunity Guidelines, Part 1607.

15. R. M. Fogelson, *Big-City Police* (Cambridge, Mass.: Harvard University Press, 1977), pp. 14, 15.

16. Ibid., p. 14.

17. Information provided by the National Association of State Directors of Law Enforcement Training, April 1981.

18. Ibid., p. 4.

19. The National Advisory Commission on Criminal Justice Standards and Goals, *A National Strategy to Reduce Crime* (Washington, D.C.: U.S. Government Printing Office, 1973), p. 149.

20. G. T. Cole, *Politics and the Administration of Justice* (Beverly Hills, Calif.: Sage Publications, 1973), p. 106.

21. The President's Commission on Law Enforcement, 3rd ed. *Task Force Report,* p. 127.

22. V. A. Leonard and H. W. Moore, *Police Organization and Management* (New York: McGraw-Hill, 1972), p. 21.

23. J. J. Norton and G. G. Cowart, "Assaulting the Politics/Administration Dichotomy," *Police Chief,* 45:11 (November 1978), p. 26.

24. For a comprehensive examination of the issue of selection, assessment, and retention of police chief executives, see the National Advisory Committee on Criminal Justice Standards and Goals, *Police Chief Executive* (Washington, D.C.: U.S. Government Printing Office, 1976).

25. E. M. Davis, "Tenure and Due Process for the Police Chief," *Police Chief,* 44:1 (January 1977), p. 8.

26. Norton and Cowart, "Assaulting the Politics/Administration Dichotomy," p. 27.

27. Leonard and Moore, *Police Organization and Management,* p. 15.

28. G. E. Berkley, M. W. Giles, J. W. Hackett, and N. C. Kassoff, *Introduction to Criminal Justice* (Boston: Holbrook Press, 1976), p. 216.

29. J. F. Ahern, *Police in Trouble* (New York: Hawthorn Books, 1972), pp. 96–98.

30. The President's Commission on Law Enforcement, *Task Force Report,* p. 30.

31. Ibid., p. 31.

32. Ibid., p. 31.

33. Ibid., p. 31.

34. J. H. Skolnick, *Justice Without Trial: Law Enforcement in Democratic Society* (New York: John Wiley, 1966), pp. 228–229.

35. The President's Commission on Law Enforcement, *Task Force Report,* pp. 32–33.

36. H. W. More, Jr., ed., *Critical Issues in Law Enforcement* (Cincinnati, Oh.: W. H. Anderson, 1972), p. 261.

37. The President's Commission on Law Enforcement, *Task Force Report,* p. 34.

38. Bent, *The Politics of Law Enforcement,* p. 72.

39. E. M. Davis, "Press Relations Guide for Peace Officers," *Police Chief,* 39:3 (March 1972), p. 67.

40. Ibid., pp. 66–68.

Theory and practice are inseparable.

DOUGLAS MCGREGOR

Organizational Theory

Introduction

Formal organizations can scarcely be conceived of as a recent innovation.[1] Alexander the Great and Caesar used them to conquer; the pharaohs employed them to build pyramids; the emperors of China constructed great irrigation systems with them; and the first popes created an organization to deliver religion on a worldwide basis.[2] The extent to which contemporary America is an organizational society is such that:

> We are born in organizations, educated by organizations, and spend most of our lives working for organizations. We spend much of our time . . . playing and praying in organizations. Most of us will die in an organization and when the time comes for burial, the largest organization of all—the state—must grant official permission.[3]

The basic rationale for the existence of organizations is that they do those things that people are unwilling or unable to do alone. Parsons notes that organizations are distinguished from other human groupings or social units in that to a much greater degree they are constructed and reconstructed to achieve specific goals; corporations, armies, hospitals, and police departments are included within this meaning, whereas families and friendship groups are not.[4] Schein defines an organization as:

49

the rational coordination of the activities of a number of people for the achievement of some common explicit purpose or goal, through division of labor and function, and through a hierarchy of authority and responsibility.[5]

Blau and Scott identify four different types of formal organizations by asking the question of *cui bono* or who benefits; (1) mutual benefit associations, such as police labor unions, where the primary beneficiary is the membership; (2) business concerns, such as International Business Machines, where the owners are the prime beneficiary; (3) service organizations, such as community mental health centers, where a specific client group is the prime beneficiary; and (4) commonweal organizations, such as the Department of Defense and police departments, where the beneficiary is the public-at-large.[6]

These four types of formal organizations each has its own central issues.[7] Mutual benefit associations, such as police unions, face the crucial problem of maintaining the internal democratic processes—providing for participation and control by their membership. For businesses, the central issue is maximizing profits in a competitive environment. Service organizations are faced with the conflict between administrative regulations and providing the services judged by the professional to be most appropriate. In the case of a community mental health center, an illustration is that, following a reduction in funding, a regulation is placed into effect that requires all clients to be treated in group sessions when the psychiatric social worker believes the only effective treatment for a particular client is to be seen individually. The core reason why police managers must have a working knowledge of organizational theory stems from the fact that police departments are commonweal organizations.

The key issue for a police department and other types of commonweal organizations is finding a way to accommodate pressures from two different sources, external and internal. The public, through its elected and appointed representatives, must and does have the means of controlling the ends served by its police department. This external democratic control feature also has the expectation that the internal workings of the police department will be bureaucratic, governed by the criterion of efficiency, and not also democratic. This is because democratic control by the members of a police department might be at the expense of lessening the police department's ability to affect the will of the community. Simultaneously, the large numbers of officers at the lower levels of the police department do not want to be treated like "cogs in a machine" and desire some voice in how the department operates. Thus, the challenge for police managers is how to maintain an organization that meets society's needs and the needs of the officers who work in it. This requires an understanding of such things as the different ways there are of organizing and the contrasting assumptions that various organizational forms make about the nature of people. Such knowledge is found within organizational theory.

This chapter consists of three major areas; each deals with different ways of thinking about how to organize work and work processes. Discussed more fully as they arise, the three major streams of thinking about work structures and processes to be treated are: (1) traditional organizational theory, upon which most police departments are based; (2) open systems theory, which represents a direct counterpoint to traditional theory; and (3) bridging theories, which to some greater or lesser degree show concern for the issues reflected both in traditional and open systems theories. Bridging theories do not fall neatly into either the traditional or the open systems category, yet reflect consideration of each, thus constituting a distinctly unique category.

Within each of the three major streams of thinking about work structures and processes there are illustrations of some of the specific techniques associated with various theorists as well as examples that are cast in a police context.

Traditional Organizational Theory

Traditional theory is associated with organizations described as mechanistic, closed systems, bureaucratic, and stable. This body of knowledge evolved over centuries and crystallized between 1900 and 1940. The three stems of traditional organizational theory are (1) scientific management, (2) the bureaucratic model, and (3) administrative or management theory.

Taylor: Scientific Management

The father of scientific management was Frederick W. Taylor (1856–1915), and the thrust of his thinking was to find the "one best way" to do work. In addition to its being a theory of work organization, Taylor's scientific management is a theory of motivation in its belief that employees will be guided in their actions by what is in their economic self-interest.

A Pennsylvanian born of Quaker-Puritan parents, Taylor was so discontent with the "evils" of waste and slothfulness that he applied the same careful analysis to

Frederick W. Taylor. (Courtesy of the Library of Congress.)

finding the best way of playing croquet and of taking a cross-country walk with the least fatigue that was to be the hallmark of his later work in factories.[8] From 1878 to 1890, Taylor worked at the Midvale Steel Company in Philadelphia, rising from the ranks of the laborers to chief engineer in just half of the time.[9] Taylor's experience at Midvale gave him insight into the twin problems of productivity and worker motivation. He saw workers as deliberately restricting productivity by ''natural soldiering'' and ''systematic soldiering.''

Natural soldiering came from the natural inclination of employees not to push themselves; systematic soldiering came from workers not wanting to produce so much as to see their quotas raised or other workers thrown out of their jobs.[10] To correct these deficiencies, Taylor called for a ''complete mental revolution''[11] on the part of both workers and managers, although it seems certain that he faulted management more for its failure to design jobs properly and to give workers the proper economic incentives to overcome soldiering than he did workers for not producing.[12]

Taylor's scientific management is only loosely a theory of organization because its focus was largely upon work at the bottom part of the organization rather than being a general model. Scientific management's method was to find the most physically and time efficient way to sequence tasks and then to use rigorous and extensive controls to enforce the standards.

Taylor's conversation with ''Schmidt'' illustrates this:

''Schmidt, are you a high-priced man?''

''Vell, I don't know vat you mean.''

''Oh yes, you do. What I want to know is whether you are a high-priced man or not.''

''Vell, I don't know vat you mean.''

''Oh, come now, you answer my questions. What I want to find out is whether you are a high-priced man or one of these cheap fellows here. What I want to find out is whether you want to earn $1.85 a day or whether you are satisfied with $1.15, just the same as all those cheap fellows are getting.''

''Did I vant $1.85 a day? Vas dot a high-priced man? Vell, yes, I vas a high-priced man.''

''Oh, you're aggravating me. Of course you want $1.85 a day—every one wants it! You know perfectly well that that has very little to do with your being a high-priced man. For goodness sake answer my questions, and don't waste any more of my time. Now come over here. You see that pile of pig iron?''

''Yes.''

''You see that car?''

''Yes.''

''Well, if you are a high-priced man, you will load that pig iron on that car tomorrow for $1.85. Now do wake up and answer my question. Tell me whether you are a high-priced man or not.''

''Vell—did I got $1.85 for loading dot pig iron on dot car tomorrow?''

''Yes, of course you do, and you get $1.85 for loading a pile like that every day right through the year. That is what a high-priced man does, and you know it just as well as I do.''

''Vell, dot's all right. I could load dot pig iron on the car tomorrow for $1.85, and I get it every day, don't I?''

''Certainly you do—certainly you do.''

''Vell, den, I vas a high priced-man.''

''Now, hold on, hold on. You know just as well as I do that a high-priced man has to do exactly as he's told from morning till night. You have seen this man here before, haven't you?''

"No, I never saw him."

"Well, if you are a high-priced man, you will do exactly as this man tells you tomorrow, from morning till night. When he tells you to pick up a pig and walk, you pick it up and you walk, and when he tells you to sit down and rest, you sit down. You do that right straight through the day. And what's more, no back talk. Now a high-priced man does just what he's told to do, and no back talk. Do you understand that? When this man tells you to walk, you walk; when he tells you to sit down, you sit down, and you don't talk back at him. Now you come on to work here tomorrow morning and I'll know before night whether you are really a high-priced man or not."[13]

Taylor also made other contributions including the concept of functional supervision, the exception principle, and integrating cost accounting into the planning process.

For Taylor, authority was based not upon position in a hierarchy but, rather, upon knowledge; functional supervision meant that people were responsible for directing certain tasks despite the fact this meant that the authority of the supervisor might cut across organizational lines.[14] The exception principle meant that routine matters should be handled by lower-level managers or by supervisors and that higher-level managers should only receive reports of deviations above or below standard performances.[15] The integration of cost accounting into the planning process became part of some budgeting practices treated in Chapter 13.

Despite the success of scientific management in raising productivity and cutting costs, "Taylorism" was attacked from a variety of quarters. Union leaders saw it as a threat to their movement because it seemed to reduce, if not eliminate, the importance of unions. The management of Bethlehem Steel ultimately abandoned task management, as Taylor liked to refer to his system, because they were uncomfortable with such an accurate appraisal of their performance[16] and some liberals saw it as an exploitation of workers. Upton Sinclair charged that Taylor had given workers a 61 percent increase in wages while getting a 362 percent increase in work.[17] Taylor replied to this charge by saying that employees worked no harder, only more efficiently. In hearings before the U.S. House of Representatives in 1912, Taylor's methods were attacked thoroughly and he died three years later a discouraged man.

Scientific management did not disappear with Taylor, however. There remained a core of people devoted to its practice, including Henry L. Gantt (1861–1919); Watlington Emerson (1853–1931), also a promoter of the staff concept; Frank (1868–1924) and Lillian (1878–1972) Gilbreth; and Morris Cooke (1872–1960), who in *Our Cities Awake* (1918) called for the application of scientific management in municipal government. Gantt gained a measure of immortality by developing a basic planning chart, which is illustrated in Figure 3-1, that remains in wide use today and still bears his name. Developed during the summer of 1917, while Gantt worked at the Frankford Arsenal, the Gantt chart contained the then revolutionary idea that the key factor in planning production was not quantity, but time.[18] Some international interest in scientific management also remained after Taylor's death; in 1918 France's Ministry of War called for the application of scientific management as did Lenin in an article in *Pravda*.[19] It is, of course, ironic that a Marxist society should call for the use of a management system based on the principle that economic self-interest guides the behavior of workers.

The fact that the period when scientific management was a dominant force has "come and gone" does not mean that it is all history. Many of the techniques associated with scientific management such as time and motion studies and work flow analysis (depicted in Figure 3-2) remain in use in what is generally called

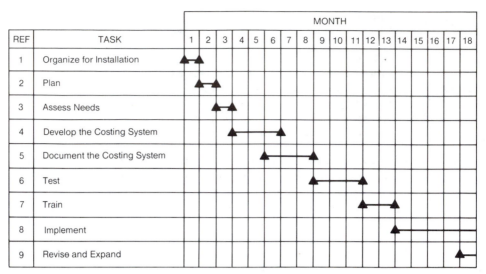

FIGURE 3-1. Gantt Chart for cost analysis system design and implementation in a police department. [Source: Kent John Chabotar, *Measuring the Costs of Police Services* (Washington, D.C.: U.S. Department of Justice, National Institute of Justice, 1982), p. 126.]

industrial engineering. Other modern successors to scientific management were developed during World War II to support of the war effort, and the refinement and more general application of these techniques is a post-1945 movement. The new techniques have alternatively been referred to as management science and operations research (OR), and their central orientation has been the application of quantitative and technical analysis to decision making.[20]

Weber: The Bureaucratic Model

In popular usage, bureaucracy has come to mean:

> the slowness, the ponderous, the routine, the complication of procedures, and the maladapted responses of "bureaucratic" organizations to the needs which they should satisfy and the frustrations which their members, clients, or subjects consequently endure.[21]

Organizational "breakdown" is far from the image of the ideal or pure bureaucracy developed by the towering German intellect Max Weber (1864–1920), the founder of modern sociology. For Weber, the choice was "only that between bureaucracy and dilettantism in the field of administration."[22] In this regard, Weber claimed that:

> Experience tends universally to show that the purely bureaucratic type of administrative organization—that is, the monocratic variety of the bureaucracy—is, from a purely technical point of view, capable of attaining the highest degree of efficiency and is in this sense formally the most rational known means of carrying out imperative control over human beings. It is superior to any other form in precision, in stability, in the stringency of its discipline, and in its reliability. It thus makes possible a particularly high degree of calculability of results for the heads of the organization and for those acting in relation

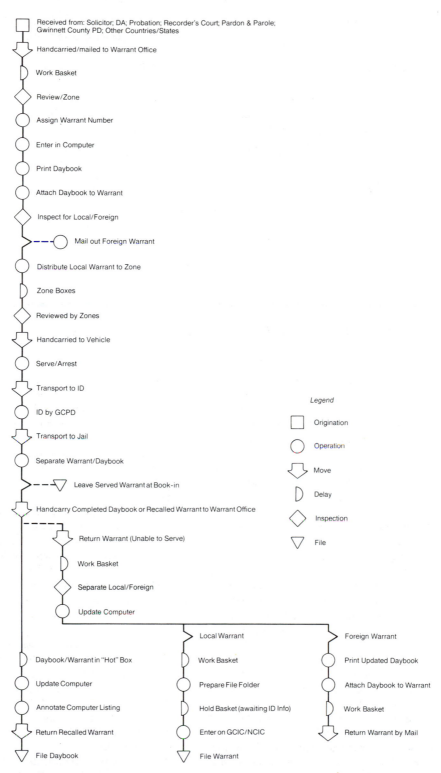

FIGURE 3-2. Analysis of Sheriff's Department criminal warrant work flow. [Source: Susan Reece and Charles Swanson, *Gwinnett County Sheriff's Department Workload and Staffing Analysis* (Athens: Vinson Institute of Government, University of Georgia; 1985).]

to it. It is finally superior both in intensive efficiency and in the scope of its operations, and is formally capable of application to all kinds of administrative tasks.[23]

The bureaucratic model of Weber included the following characteristics:

1. The organization of offices follows the principle of hierarchy; that is, each lower office is under the control and supervision of a higher one. There is a right of appeal and of statement of grievances from the lower to the higher.
2. Specified spheres of competence, meaning a division of labor, exist in each of which the authority and responsibility of every organizational member is identified.
3. Official functions are bound by a system of rational rules.
4. Administrative acts, decisions, and rules are recorded in writing.
5. The "rights" associated with a position are the property of the office and not of the officeholders.

BOX 3-1.

"Bureaucratic Breakdown" Leaves Man Dead

By LAURA WHITESIDE, *Tribune Staff Writer*

A judge's order to arrest an apparently suicidal man was carried out by Hillsborough County sheriffs deputies three days late—and only after the judge called a top sheriff's official—but by the time deputies showed up the man had committed suicide.

Circuit Judge Benjamin Sidwell said during an interview Wednesday, "A man's dead because of—whatever you want to call it—a bureaucratic breakdown."

Hillsborough Undersheriff John Kirk acknowledged that the order waited in the mailbox of a deputy who was out of town.

The dead man, James Trainor, Sr., died about eight hours before sheriff's deputies found him in his north Tampa apartment. He had drunk 10 to 12 ounces of insecticide, according to Hillsborough county Medical Examiner Peter Lardizabal.

Trainor's son and brother thought he was an alcoholic and was suicidal. They petitioned the court to have him treated because he wouldn't consent to treatment.

Sidwell took up the petition on April 14. Four days later, on April 18, he ordered that Trainor be arrested on April 21. He wanted to wait three days to have Trainor arrested so the man wouldn't have to spend the weekend in jail.

But Lt. Red Meighen, in charge of the warrants division of the sheriff's office, said the date on the warrant went unnoticed.

"I don't know how that was overlooked," Meighen said.

The deputy assigned to the north Tampa area where Trainor lived was on duty out of the state and, therefore, no action was taken on the order, Kirk said.

"They just put it in his box," Kirk said.

Meighen said the warrant was handled normally. Five employees in his office distribute warrant to the six deputies who cover assigned areas of the county.

"Those girls who put warrants in the boxes don't know when they (the deputies) are going to be out of town," he said.

When Trainor wasn't brought to the court Tuesday, April 22, Sidwell asked a mental health counselor to find out why. Sidwell said he thought it would be taken care of, but that Trainor still didn't show up two days later.

That's when Sidwell called Kirk.

Kirk recalled the phone call: "He asked me 'What does it take to get my papers served?' " Kirk said.

Kirk called the warrants division and deputies Wade Weatherman and Casey Wieleba. It was Wielba's mailbox the original order was left in and the order was still there when he returned from his mission out of town.

The deputies immediately went to Trainor's apartment near Dale Mabry Highway and Waters Avenue.

"We couldn't get an answer," two knocks on the door, Weatherman said. "He didn't have a car," and the deputies visited local liquor stores looking for him.

When they returned, Wieleba was able to see through a curtain a man lying on the living room couch. The apartment manager unlocked the door and the deputies found Trainor with a bottle of insecticide and a bottle of cola nearby.

"We called patrol and turned it over to them," Weatherman said.

In seeking the court's help, Trainor's son, James, Jr., said his father's problems were serious.

"My father told me that he had attempted to commit suicide," he said in the petition. "He is unable to function and I have reason to believe he is consuming as much as two quarts of alcohol per day."

Trainor had displayed "typical and classic alcoholic" tendencies during the past few months, said another son, Michael Trainor. "He got paranoid and would only go out at night. He walked around a lot.

"We were trying to get him under psychiatric care."

There was apparently one other precaution taken to keep Trainor from killing himself, but it, too, failed. According to Sheriff's Lt. Larry Terry, Trainor's family had asked a friend of Trainor's to stay with him until April 21, when the arrest order was to be carried out, but the friend moved away the following day.

Source: The Tampa Tribune, May 8, 1980, pp 1A and 13A.

Max Weber (Courtesy of the Library of Congress.)

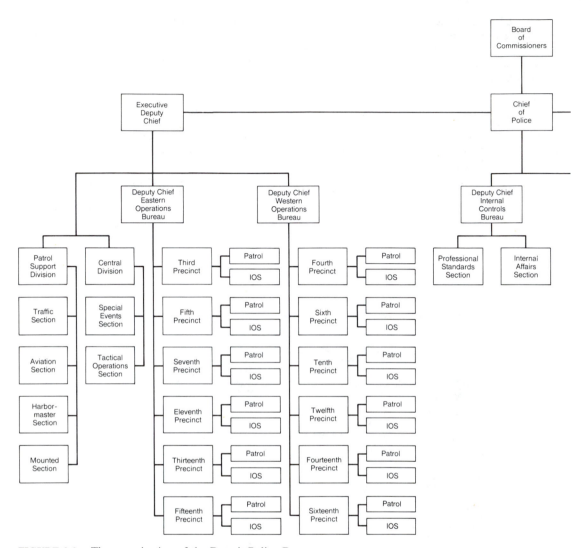

FIGURE 3-3. The organization of the Detroit Police Department.

6. Candidates are appointed on the basis of technical qualifications, and specialized training is necessary.

7. Organizational members do not own the means of production.[24]

Although not all of the characteristics of Weber's bureaucratic model can be revealed by an organizational chart, Figure 3-3 does depict two important features: (1) the principle of hierarchy and (2) a division of labor that results in specialization.

Weber's bureaucratic model rested on what he called rational-legal authority. This he contrasted to (1) traditional authority, which rested on an established belief in the sanctity of immemorial traditions and the legitimacy of the status of people exercising authority under those traditions, illustrated by kings or queens, and (2) charismatic authority, which stemmed from the exceptional sanctity, heroism, or exemplary character of an individual.[25]

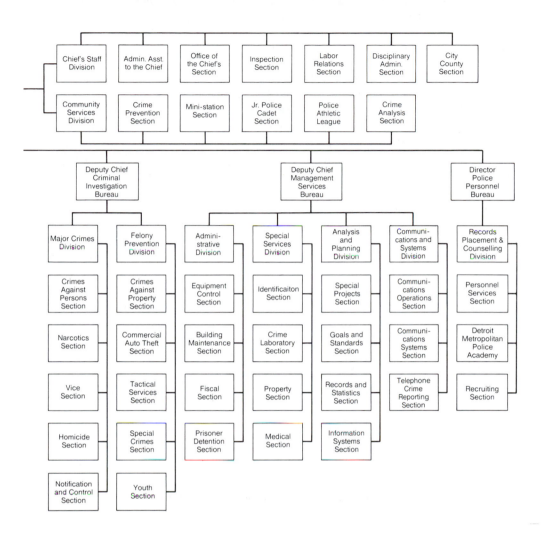

There are two dimensions to Weber's work that are often not considered. First, on the one hand, he considered bureaucracy as the most efficient form of organization, and, on the other hand, he feared that this very efficiency constituted a threat to individual freedom by its impersonal nature and oppressive routine.[26] Second, Weber deplored the career professional of moderate ambitions who craved security; this type of person Weber saw as lacking spontaneity and inventiveness, the modern-day "petty bureaucrat."[27]

As a closing note, Weber did not invent the bureaucratic model; it had existed for centuries. Thus, whereas Weber spawned the formal study of organizations, it scarcely seems fair to lay at his feet any real or fancied inadequacies of the model or its operation. Moreover, although it would be difficult to overstate Weber's contributions, it must be borne in mind that whereas while some people—such as Chester Barnard—read him in the original German,[28] his work was not translated into English and was not generally available until 1947, long after the bureaucratic model was well entrenched.

Administrative Theory

Administrative or management theory sought to identify generic or universal methods of administration. Its benchmark is the 1937 publication of Luther Gulick (1892–   ) and Lyndall Urwick's (1891–1983) edited *Papers on the Science of Administration*. In content, administrative theory is more compatible with the bureaucratic model than with scientific management because it concentrates upon broader principles. Administrative theory, also referred to as the principles approach, is distinguished from the bureaucratic model by its "how to" emphasis. At some risk of oversimplification, the principles both operationalize and reinforce features of the bureaucratic model. Consequently, because of the continuing pervasiveness of the bureaucratic model, the principles either explicitly or implicitly continue to play an important role in organizations, including police departments. The key contributors to this school are Henri Fayol (1841–1925), James Mooney (1884–1957) and Alan Reiley (1869–1947), and Gulick and Urwick.

Henri Fayol graduated as an engineer at the age of nineteen from France's National School of Mines at St. Etienne and began a forty-year career with the Commentary-Fourchambault Company.[29] His contributions are based on writings that were an outgrowth of his experiences as a manager. Fayol's fame rests chiefly on his *General and Industrial Management* (1916). The first English edition of this appeared in Great Britain in 1923, and although his "Administrative Theory of the State" appeared in *Papers on the Science of Administration*, his main work, *General and Industrial Management*, was not widely available in this country until 1949. Fayol's principles included:

1. A division of work, that is, specialization.
2. Authority, namely, the right to give orders and the power to extract obedience—whoever exercises authority has responsibility.
3. Discipline, in essence the obedience, application, energy and behavior, and outward marks of respect in accordance with the standing agreement between the firm and its employees.
4. Unity of command, with an employee's receiving orders from only one supervisor.
5. Unity of direction, with one head and one plan for a group of activities having the same objective—unity of command cannot exist without unity of direction.
6. Subordination of individual interest to the general interest—the interest of an individual or a group of employees does not prevail over the concerns of the firm.
7. Remuneration of personnel—to be fair to the employee and employer.
8. Centralization, a natural order of things—however centralization or decentralization is a question of proportion, finding the optimum degree for the particular concern.
9. Scalar chain, namely, the chain of superiors ranging from the ultimate authority to the lowest ranks, often referred to as the chain of command.
10. Order, that is, a place for everyone and everyone in his or her place.
11. Equity, namely, the combination of kindness and justice.
12. Stability of tenure of personnel, which allows employees to become familiar with their jobs and productive—a mediocre manager who stays is infinitely preferable to outstanding managers who come and go.

13. Initiative at all levels of the organization—this represents a great source of strength for business.

14. *Esprit de corps,* harmony, and union of personnel—these constitute a great strength, and efforts should be made to establish them.[30]

Fayol recognized that his scalar principle could produce disastrous consequences if it were followed strictly, since it would hamper swift action.[31] He therefore developed Fayol's gangplank, or horizontal bridge, discussed more fully in Chapter 6, as a means of combatting this issue. Fayol's belief that a mediocre manager who stays is better than outstanding ones who come and go has refound currency beginning in the late 1970s, as many city managers retreated from hiring police chiefs from outside the organization. Although it can be argued with some validity that this movement is due to the increased qualifications of internal candidates, it is also true that the frequent recruitment, screening, and selection of "portable" police managers has been an expensive, time consuming, and, at least occasionally in terms of results, disappointing process.

Mooney and Reiley's *Onward Industry* (1931) was generally consistent with the work of Fayol, as were the subsequent revisions of this publication, which appeared in 1939 and 1947 under the title of *The Principles of Organization.*[32]

In "Notes on the Theory of Organization," which was included in *Papers on the Science of Administration,* Gulick coined the most familiar and enduring acronym of administration, POSDCORB:

> *P*lanning, that is, working out in broad outline the things that need to be done and the methods for doing them to accomplish the purpose set for the enterprise;
>
> *O*rganizing, that is, the establishment of the formal structure of authority through which work subdivisions are arranged, defined and co-ordinated for the defined objective;
>
> *S*taffing, that is, the whole personnel function of bringing in and training the staff and maintaining favorable conditions of work;
>
> *D*irecting, that is, the continuous task of making decisions and embodying them in specific and general orders and instructions and serving as the leader of the enterprise;
>
> *Co*-ordinating, that is, the all important duty of interrelating the various parts of the work;
>
> *R*eporting, that is, keeping those to whom the executive is responsible informed as to what is going on, which thus includes keeping himself and his subordinates informed through records, research and inspection;
>
> *B*udgeting, with all that goes with budgeting in the form of fiscal planning, accounting and control.[33]

Gulick acknowledged that his POSDCORB was adapted from the functional analysis elaborated by Fayol in *General and Industrial Management.* Urwick's "Organization as a Technical Problem," which appeared in the *Papers on the Science of Administration,* also drew upon the work of another the Frenchman A. V. Graicunas, for his treatment of the span of control. Urwick asserted that:

> Students of administration have long recognized that, in practice, no human brain should attempt to supervise directly more than five, or at the most six individuals whose work is interrelated.[34]

Urwick, the Oxford-educated and military-career Englishman, also underscored management theory with his subsequent *Scientific Principles of Organization* (1938).

Critique of Traditional Theory

Scientific management is decried because of its "man as machine" orientation, and ample life is given to that argument by even a casual reading of the conversation between Taylor and the legendary Schmidt. On balance, although Taylor's emphasis was upon task, he was not totally indifferent to the human element arguing that:

> No system of management, however good, should be applied in a wooden way. The proper personal relations should always be maintained between the employers and men; and even the prejudices of the workmen should be considered in dealing with them.[35]

The bureaucratic model has no shortage of critics; the humanist Warren Bennis levels the following specific criticisms:

1. Bureaucracy does not adequately allow for the personal growth and development of mature personalities.
2. It develops conformity and "group think."
3. It does not take into account the "informal organization" and the emergent and unanticipated problems.
4. Its systems of control and authority are hopelessly outdated.
5. It has no adequate judicial process.
6. It does not possess adequate means for resolving differences and conflicts between ranks and, most particularly, between functional groups.
7. Communication and innovative ideas are thwarted or distorted due to hierarchical divisions.
8. The full human resources of bureaucracy are not utilized due to mistrust, fear or reprisals, and so on.
9. It cannot assimilate the influx of new technology . . . entering the organization.
10. It modifies the personality structure such that each man becomes and reflects the full, gray, conditioned "organization man."[36]

Herbert Simon has mounted the most precise criticisms of the principles approach. He writes:

> It is a fatal defect of the . . . principles of administration that, like proverbs, they occur in pairs. For almost every principle one can find an equally plausible and acceptable contradictory principle. Although the two principles of the pair will lead to exactly opposite organizational recommendations, there is nothing in the theory to indicate which is the proper one to apply.[37]

To illustrate his point, Simon notes that administrative efficiency is enhanced by keeping at a minimum the number of organizational levels through which a matter must pass before it is acted upon. Yet a narrow span of control, say, of five or six subordinates, produces a tall hierarchy. To some extent, Simon's criticism is blunted by invoking Fayol's exception principle and the gangplank, but in the main Simon's point that some of the principles contain logical contradictions is potent.

Less critical than both Bennis and Simon, Hage describes bureaucracy in mixed terms and specifically as having:[38]

1. High centralization
2. High formalization
3. High stratification
4. Low adaptiveness
5. Low job satisfaction
6. Low complexity
7. High production
8. High efficiency

In *Complex Organizations* (1972), Charles Perrow mounted a major and articulate defense of the bureaucratic model, concluding that:

> the extensive preoccupation with reforming, "humanizing," and decentralizing bureaucracies, while salutary, has served to obscure from organizational theorists the true nature of bureaucracy and has diverted us from assessing its impact on society. The impact on society in general is incalculably more important than the impact upon the members of a particular organization . . . bureaucracy is a form of organization superior to all others we know or can hope to afford in the near and middle future; the chances of doing away with it or changing it are probably non-existent in the west in this century. Thus it is crucial to understand it and appreciate it.[39]

Relatedly, in *The Case for Bureaucracy* (1985), Charles Goodsell notes that denunciations of the "common hate object" are fashionable, appealing, and make us feel good; they invite no retaliation or disagreement since almost everybody agrees that bureaucracy is bad . . . but fashionable contentions are not necessarily solid ones.[40] Goodsell observes that:

> the attacks are almost always made in the tone of unremitting dogmatism. They are usually unqualified in portraying wicked behavior and inadequate outcomes. The pessimistic picture presented seems unbroken. The absolutism itself, it would seem, cannot help but strain our credulity. How can we believe that all public bureaucracies, all of the time, are inefficient, dysfunctional, rigid, obstructionist, secretive, oligarchic, conservative, undemocratic, imperialist, oppressive, alienating, and discriminatory? How could any single human creation be so universally terrible in so many ways?[41]

Purely deductive models critical of bureaucracy abound, but they are—in the words of Alvin Gouldner—"a theoretical tapestry devoid of the plainest empirical trimmings."[42] Goodsell elaborates on this theme by observing that when empirical study is taken, single cases illustrating the conclusions desired are selected, and by concentrating on the problems, disorders, and dysfunctions of bureaucracy, rather than on what is working well, academics confirm both their own diagnoses and demonstrate the need for their own solutions.[43] Interestingly, Goodsell is able to muster a number of empirical studies that reveal positive evaluations of bureaucracies, including the police, by members of the public who have had direct contact with them; in general, these favorable evaluations are at least at the two-thirds level and many go beyond the 75 percent level.[44]

Despite philosophical criticisms and practical difficulties with the stems of traditional theory, in its entirety it must be appreciated for having formed the basic fund of knowledge on which the overwhelming majority of organizations in the world rest. Knowledge of traditional theory remains as an essential part of education and training for police leaders.

Open Systems Theory

Organizations described as flexible, adaptive, and organic are associated with open systems theory. This line of thought began its development in the late 1920s and is comprised of three major divisions: (1) human relations, (2) behavioral systems, and (3) open systems theory.

Human Relations

The human relations school developed in reaction to the mechanistic orientation of traditional organizational theory, which was viewed as neglecting or ignoring the human element.

MAYO: THE HAWTHORNE STUDIES

In 1927, a series of experiments, which were to last five years, began near Chicago at the Western Electric Company's Hawthorne plant.[45] This work was guided by Elton Mayo (1880–1949), a professor in the Harvard School of Business, and his associates, Fritz Roethlisberger (1898–1974) and William Dickson (1904–).[46] From the perspective of organizational theory, the major contribution of the Hawthorne experiments is the view that organizations are social systems. Two research efforts, the telephone relay assembly study and the telephone switchboard wiring study,[47] were especially important to the development of the human relations school.

In the first study, five women assembling telephone relays were put into a special room and were subjected to varying physical work conditions.[48] Even when the conditions changed unfavorably, production increased. Mayo and his associates were puzzled by these results. Ultimately, they decided that (1) when the experimenters took over many of the supervisory functions, it became less strict and less formal; (2) the women behaved differently from what was expected because they were receiving attention, creating the famous "Hawthorne effect"; and (3) by placing the women together in the relay assembling test room, the researchers had provided the opportunity for them to become a closely knit group.[49] Based on these observations, the researchers concluded that an important influence on productivity was the interpersonal relations and spirit of cooperation that had developed among the women and between the women and their supervisors. The influence of these "human relations" was believed to be every bit as important as physical work conditions and financial incentives.[50]

In the telephone switchboard wiring study, fourteen men were put on a reasonable piece rate; that is, without physically straining themselves, they could earn more if they produced more. The assumption was that the workers would behave as rational economic actors and produce more since it was in their own best interest. To insulate these men from the "systematic soldiering" they knew to exist among the plant's employees, the researchers also placed these workers in a special room. The workers' output did not increase. The values of the informal group appeared to be more powerful than the allure of financial betterment:

1. Don't be a "rate buster" and produce too much.
2. If you turn out too little work, you are a "chisler."
3. Don't be a "squealer" to supervisors.
4. Don't be officious; if you are an inspector, don't act like one.[51]

Taken together, the relay assembly study and the switchboard wiring study raise an important question: Why did one group respond so favorably and the other not? The answer is that, in the relay assembly study, the values of the workers and the supervisors were mutually supportive, whereas in the switchboard wiring study, the objectives of the company and the informal group conflicted. The harder question is: Why was there mutuality in one situation and not the other? The basis of mutuality has already been discussed; the conflict is more difficult to account for, but it may have been the interplay of some things we know and some things we must speculate about:

1. The researchers did not involve themselves in the supervision of the switchboard wiring room workers as they had with the relay assembly room employees.[52] The wiring room workers and their supervisor developed a spirit of cooperation, but it was one in which the supervisor was coopted by the informal group, which was suspicious of what would happen if output actually increased.[53]
2. The way in which the subjects for both studies were selected is suspect and may have influenced the findings. The relay assembly women were experienced operators known to be friendly with each other and "willing and cooperative" participants, whereas the men were designated by the foreman.[54]
3. The relay assembly-room workers were women and the switchboard wiring study employees were men. This difference in sexuality may have influenced the character of the responses. The studies were going on during the Depression; the women may have tried to hold onto their jobs by pleasing their supervisors, while the men restricted their output so there would be work to do and nobody would lose his job. In this context, both groups of employees can be seen as rational economic actors.

As a result of the Hawthorne studies, it was concluded that (1) the level of production is set by social norms, not by physiological capacities; (2) often workers do not react as individuals, but as members of a group; (3) the rewards and sanctions of the group significantly affect the behavior of workers and limit the impact of economic incentive plans; and (4) leadership has an important role in setting and enforcing group norms, and there is a difference between formal and informal leadership.[55]

When workers react as members of an informal group, they become susceptible to the values of that group. Thus, the informal group can be a powerful force in supporting or opposing police programs. Illustratively, a number of police unions started as an unorganized, informal group of dissatisfied officers. Although many factors contribute to the enduring problem of police corruption, such as disillusionment and temptation, an informal group that supports taking payoffs makes it more difficult to identify and prosecute "bad cops." In 1972, the Knapp Commission, investigating corruption in the New York City Police Department, distinguished between "meat-eaters" (those who overtly pursued opportunities to personally profit from their police powers) and "grass-eaters" (those who simply accepted the payoffs that the happen-stances of police work brought their way).[56] The behavior of the grass-eaters can be interpreted within the framework of the power that informal groups have. The Knapp Commission was told that one strong force that encouraged grass-eaters to accept relatively petty graft was their feeling of loyalty to their fellow officers. By accepting payoff money an officer could prove that he was one of the boys and could be trusted.

The foregoing discussion should not be interpreted to mean that informal groups always, or even frequently, engage in troublesome or unethical behavior, but rather as an illustration of the potency that such groups have. Astute police administrators are always alert for opportunities to tap the energy of informal groups to support departmental goals and programs.

As might be expected, the collision between the human relations school, fathered by Mayo's Hawthorne studies, and traditional organizational theory sent theorists and researchers in the various disciplines off into new and different directions. From among these at least three major themes are identifiable: (1) inquiries into what motivates workers, including the work of Maslow and Herzberg, which will be dis-cussed shortly; (2) leadership, the subject of Chapter 5; and (3) work on organizations as behavioral systems, covered later in this chapter. As a concluding note, the term *human relations* has been used in law enforcement with two entirely different meanings. Particularly from the mid-1960s to the early 1970s, the term was used as a label for training that was basically race relations; when used in describing the major content areas of more recent police management seminars, its use denotes a block of instruction relating to individual and group relationships in the tradition of the Hawthorne studies.

MASLOW: THE NEED HIERARCHY

Abraham Maslow (1908–1970) was a psychologist who developed the need hierar-chy to explain individual motivation. This model appeared first in a 1943 article[57] and later received extended coverage in Maslow's *Motivation and Personality* (1954).

Figure 3-4 depicts the need hierarchy. In Maslow's scheme, there were five categories of human needs:

1. Physiological or basic needs, such as food, shelter, and water.
2. Safety needs, including the desires to be physically safe, to have a savings account for financial security, and to be safe in one's job, knowing that you will not be arbitrarily fired.
3. Belongingness and love needs, such as the acceptance of one's work group in the police department and the affection of one's spouse, children, and parents.
4. Esteem needs, including the desire for a stable, fairly based, and positive evaluation of one's self as evidenced by compliments, commendations, promo-tions, and other cues.
5. Self-actualization needs, such as the want to test one's self-potential and gain a sense of fulfillment.[58]

The need hierarchy is arranged, like the rungs on a ladder, from the lower-order to the higher-order needs. A person does not move from one level to the next higher one until the majority of the needs at the level one is at are met. Once those needs are met, they cease to motivate a person, and the needs at the next level of

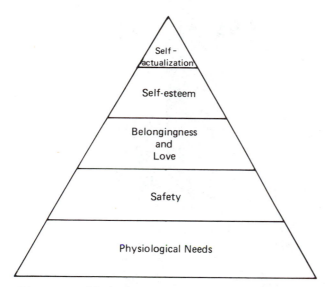

FIGURE 3-4. Maslow's need hierarchy.

the hierarchy predominate. To illustrate this, one does not attempt to self-actualize until one has feelings of self-confidence, worth, strength, capability, adequacy and mastery;[59] these feelings are only generated with the meeting of the esteem needs. Conversely, if people's esteem needs are unmet, they feel inferior, helpless, discouraged, and unworthwhile and are unable to move to the self-actualization level and test themselves.

It is important to understanding the need hierarchy that the character of something does necessarily not determine what need is met but, rather, to what use it is put; money can be used to buy food and satisfy a basic need, or it can be put in a savings account to satisfy safety needs. Too, any progress up the hierarchy can be reversed; the police officer who is fired or is given a lengthy suspension may be thrust into a financial situation in which the physiological needs will predominate. Police agencies that are managed professionally attempt to make appropriate use of theoretical constructs. For example, the fourth level of Maslow's need hierarchy is self-esteem, which includes the need for recognition as evidenced by compliments and commendations. Faced with a significant automobile theft problem in their state, Ohio state patrol officials wanted to develop a strategy that would have an impact upon the problem. One of the programs they developed was the Blue Max award.[60] In the Blue Max program each time a state trooper arrested a suspect in a stolen car he or she received a lightning bolt decal to place on the side of his or her patrol car. When a trooper made his or her fifth apprehension in a year, he was given his own car for the rest of the year with a special license that read ''ACE.'' At the end of the year the trooper who had made the most apprehensions received the coveted Blue Max award and was given a car reserved only for his use during the next year. In the first ten months in which the Blue Max program was operated, arrests of car thieves was up 49 percent as compared to the entire prior twelve months. The Blue Max program demonstrates the utility of theory and how meeting organizational goals and individual goals can be compatible.

The Blue Max medal and its presentation at an awards ceremony.
(Courtesy of the Ohio State Patrol.)

HERZBERG: MOTIVATION-HYGIENE THEORY

Because of their focus, neither the need hierarchy nor motivation-hygiene are
organizational theories in the larger sense; they are included here because they are
part of a stream of connected thinking. Motivation-hygiene theory developed from
research conducted by Frederick Herzberg (1923–), Bernard Mausner, and Barbara
Snyderman on job attitudes at eleven work sites in the Pittsburgh area and reported
on in *The Motivation to Work* (1959). The major statement of the theory, which
evolved out of this earlier research, is found in Herzberg's *Work and the Nature of
Man* (1966).

Herzberg saw two sets of variables operating in the work setting: (1) hygiene
factors, which he later came to call maintenance factors, and (2) motivators. Table
3-1 identifies Herzberg's hygiene factors and motivators. The hygiene factors relate
to the work environment; the motivators relate to the work itself. Herzberg borrowed
the term "hygiene" from the health care field and used it to refer to factors that if
not treated properly could lead to a deterioration in performance, creating an "unhealthy" organization. Hygiene factors that are not treated properly are a source of
dissatisfaction. However, even if all of them are provided, a police department does
not have motivated officers, just ones who are not dissatisfied. Hygiene factors and
motivators operate independently of each other; the police manager can motivate
subordinates if they are somewhat dissatisfied with their salaries. However, the greater

TABLE 3-1 Herzberg's Motivation-Hygiene Theory

Hygiene factors	Motivators
Supervisory practices	Achievement
Policies and administration	Recognition for accomplishments
Working conditions	Challenging work
Interpersonal relationships with subordinates, peers, and superiors	Increased responsibility
Status	Advancement possibilities
Effect of the job on personal life	Opportunity for personal growth and development
Job security	
Money	

From Frederick Herzberg, *Work and the Nature of Man* (Cleveland: World, 1966), pp. 95–96.

the level of dissatisfaction, the more difficult it becomes to employ the motivators successfully.

Note that police managers have more control over motivators than they do over basic hygiene factors; certain policies, such as automatically placing an officer involved in a shooting incident on suspension, may be mandated by the city administrator; working conditions may be lessened if the city council refuses to buy air-conditioned cars; the chief of police has little control over the status given the officer's job by society; and a chief cannot appropriate the money for higher salaries or improved fringe benefits.

In their leadership roles, police managers can try to influence, but they do not control such matters. It is over those hygiene factors that police managers do exercise control that they can do a considerable amount of good in reducing dissatisfaction and facilitating the use of the motivators or they can cause considerable unhappiness:

> The commander in charge of the uniformed division of a 100-officer department suddenly announced that officers were going to be placed on permanent shifts. Surprised and angered by this move, the officers and their wives mobilized to oppose the plan, and after a mass meeting with the commander, the plan was abandoned. The legacy of this incident was a period of barely subdued hostility, distrust, and low morale in the police department.

The nature of police work is in and of itself challenging, and some motivational effect is thus naturally occurring. Police managers can build on this by varying assignments appropriately. Measures that employ various of the other motivators include an established and active commendation system, the creation of field training officer and master patrol officer designations, an annual police awards banquet, an active staff development program, and a career system with various tracks, as discussed in Chapter 7.

As a concluding comment, Maslow's need hierarchy and Herzberg's motivation-hygiene theory can be interrelated; the physiological, safety, and belongingness and love needs of Maslow correspond to Herzberg's hygiene factors; the top two levels of the need hierarchy—esteem and self-actualization—correlate with Herzberg's motivators.

Behavioral Systems Theory

By 1960, human relations in the tradition of the Hawthorne studies lacked vitality. Its successor, which traces its ancestry to that 1927–1932 period, was behavioral systems theory. The theorists associated with this school saw organizations as being composed of interrelated behaviors and were concerned with making organizations more democratic and participative. Behavioral systems theory is basically a post-1950 development; many of the people involved in this movement are also described in other ways. For example, Argyris, Likert, Bennis, Maslow, Herzberg, and McGregor are often referred to as organizational humanists and in one way or another are tied to organizational development, a concept treated later in this section.

LEWIN: GROUP DYNAMICS

Kurt Lewin (1890–1947) was a psychologist who fled from Germany in the early 1930s.[61] His interests were diverse and included leadership; force-field analysis, a technique sometimes used in decision making; change; and group dynamics. Lewin's force-field analysis is illustrated in Figure 3-5. In force-field analysis driving forces

FIGURE 3-5. The Use of Force-Field Analysis Regarding The Decision to Adopt A New Police Promotional Ordinance

Driving Forces	Restraining Forces
Minority officers discontent with lack of minority promotions	Majority and some minority officers support present promotional system
Several discrimination complaints filed by minority officers	
Minority employees association formed and their attorney had presented plan which would grant preferential treatment to minorities temporarily	Elected and appointed officials willing to initiate change, but wanted the fullest and fairest competition to insure public confidence in those selected for leadership positions
	Majority officers association took no official policy stand but association's President appeared before Council to oppose changing the current promotional process
Elected and appointed community officials want to respond to legitimate employee and community concerns	Ill-considered change could splinter the department badly along racial lines
Possibility of litigation and court intervention	50 majority employees alleged prepared to get $5,000 second mortgages on their homes to raise $250,000 for filing a cross suit
	Officers with seniority and/or higher education opposed to reducing the importance of these factors in any new police promotional ordinance
Litigation could result in adverse publicity, damaging the city's progressive reputation and economic development	

push for some new condition or state, and restraining forces serve to resist the change or perpetuate things as they are. In using force-field analysis, if there are exactly opposing, driving and restraining forces, the arrows of these opposing forces meet at the zero or balance line. In some instances, there might not be an exactly opposite force, in which case an arrow is simply drawn, as in Figure 3-5, to the balance line. After all entries are made and the situation is summarized, the relative power of the driving and restraining forces must be subjectively evaluated. In this regard, the zero or balance line should be regarded as a spring that will be moved in one direction or another, suggesting the action that needs to be taken or the decision that needs to be made.

Lewin is also regarded as the father of the behavioral system school and founded the Research Center for Group Dynamics at the Massachusetts Institute of Technology.[62] In the same year as Lewin died, one of his followers, Leland Bradford, established a human relations effort at Bethel, Maine.[63] This undertaking was later to be called the National Training Laboratories for Group Development, which earlier focused on stranger T-group or sensitivity training, a method whereby behavior is changed by strangers in a group sharing their honest opinions of each other. The popularity of T-groups was greatest during the 1950s; its present use is diminished in large measure because some organizations that tried it were troubled by its occasional volatility and the fact that not all changes were positive:

> A division manager at one big company was described by a source familiar with his case as ''a ferocious guy—brilliant but a thoroughgoing autocrat—whom everyone agreed was just what the division needed, because it was a tough, competitive business.'' Deciding to smooth over his rough edges, the company sent him to sensitivity training, where he found out exactly what people thought of him. ''So he stopped being a beast,'' says the source, ''and his effectiveness fell apart.'' The reason he'd been so good was that he didn't realize what a beast he was. Eventually, they put in a new manager.[64]

HOMANS: EXTERNAL AND INTERNAL SYSTEMS

As a contemporary of Lewin's, the work of George Homans (1910–) is in the tradition of group dynamics. In *The Human Group* (1950), he advanced the idea that groups have both an internal and an external system.[65] The internal system is comprised of factors that arise within the group itself, such as the feelings that members of a group develop about each other during the life of the group. In contrast, the external system consists of variables in the larger environment in which the group exists, such as the administrative policies and supervisory practices to which the group is subject. Homans saw these two systems as being in a state of interaction and influencing each other.

For example, the decision of a chief of police to suspend an officer for three days without pay because of an accident while involved in a high-speed chase might result in a group of officers who saw the suspension as being unfair agreeing among themselves not to write any traffic citations during that time. This interaction brings the formal organization of the external system into conflict with the informal organization of the internal system. The formal sanction of the external system is countered with the informal sanction of reducing the city's revenue by the internal system.

Both Lewin and Homans have ties to the human relations school. Homans, for instance, drew upon the switchboard wiring room study to illustrate his concept of internal and external systems. Analytically, his work falls into the behavioral systems category and foreshadowed the dynamic interaction theme of open systems theory.

Argyris: Immaturity-Maturity Theory and the Mix Model

Chris Argyris (1923–) is a critic of the mechanistic model of organization and a leading proponent of more open and participative organizations. In *Personality and Organization: The Conflict Between System and the Individual* (1957), he states a theory of immaturity versus maturity. Argyris believes that, as one moves from infancy toward adulthood in years of age, the healthy individual also advances from immaturity to maturity. The elements of the personality that are changed during this process are summarized in Table 3-2. Simultaneously, Argyris views formal organizations as having certain properties that do not facilitate the growth into a mature state:

1. Specialization reduces the use of initiative by requiring the individuals to use only a few of their skills doing unchallenging tasks.
2. The chain of command leaves people with little control over their work environment and makes them dependent upon and passive toward superiors.
3. The unity-of-direction principle means that the objectives of the work unit are controlled by the leader. If the goals do not consider the employees, then ideal conditions for psychological failure are set.
4. The narrow span of control principle will tend to increase the subordinate's feelings of dependence, submissiveness, and passivity.[66]

The needs of a healthy, mature individual and the properties of formal organizations therefore come into conflict; the ensuing response by the individual may take any of several forms:

1. The employee may leave the organization only to find that other organizations are similar to the one left.
2. To achieve the highest level of control over one's self permitted by the organization, the person may climb as far as possible up the organizational hierarchy.
3. The worker may defend his or her self-concept by the use of defensive mechanisms such as daydreaming, rationalizing lower accomplishments, developing psychosomatic illnesses, or becoming aggressive and hostile, attacking and blaming what is frustrating personally.

TABLE 3-2 Argyris's Immaturity-Maturity Changes

Infancy-Immaturity ⟶	Adulthood-Maturity
Passive ⟶	Self-initiative
Dependent ⟶	Relatively independent
Behaving in a few ways ⟶	Capable of behaving many ways
Erratic, shallow, quickly changed interests ⟶	Deeper interests
Short time perspective ⟶	Much longer time perspective
Subordinate position in the family ⟶	Aspirations of equality or superordinate position relative to peers
Lack of self-awareness ⟶	Self-awareness and self-control

Data from p. 50 in *Personality and Organization: The Conflict Between System and the Individual* by Chris Argyris. Copyright © 1957 by Harper & Row Publishers, Inc. Reprinted by permission of the publisher.

4. The individual may decide to stay in spite of the conflict and adapt by lowering his or her work standards and becoming apathetic and disinterested.

5. Informal groups may be created to oppose the formal organization.

6. The employee may do nothing and remain frustrated, creating even more tension.[67]

In 1964 Argyris published *Integrating the Individual and the Organization*. The purpose of it was to present his thinking about how organizations could deal with the problem he had identified in *Personality and Organization: The Conflict Between System and the Individual*. Argyris doubted that it was possible to have a relationship between the individual and the organization that allowed the simultaneous maximizing of the values of both.[68] He did believe that it was possible to reduce the unintended, nonproductive, side consequences of formal organizations and to free more of the energies of the individual for productive purposes; Argyris's mix model was the way in which this was to be done;[69] it is basically an attempt to "mix" or accommodate the interests of the individual and the organization. The mix model favors neither people nor the organization. For example, Argyris saw the organization as having legitimate needs that were not people centered. He also believed that organizations cannot always provide challenging work. The fact, however, that some work was not challenging was viewed by Argyris as an asset to the individual and the organization: the unchallenging work provided some recovery time—for the individual and allowed the organization's routine tasks to get done.[70]

McGregor: Theory X and Theory Y

Douglas McGregor (1904–1964) believed that:

> Every managerial act rests on assumptions, generalizations, and hypotheses—that is to say, on theory. Our assumptions are frequently implicit, sometimes quite unconscious, often conflicting; nevertheless, they determine our predictions that if we do A, B will occur. Theory and practice are inseparable.[71]

In common practice, managerial acts, without explicit examination of theoretical assumptions, leads at times to remarkable inconsistencies in managerial behavior:

> A manager, for example, states that he delegates to his subordinates. When asked, he expresses assumptions such as, "People need to learn to take responsibility," or, "Those closer to the situation can make the best decision." However, he has arranged to obtain a constant flow of detailed information about the behavior of his subordinates, and he uses this information to police their behavior and to "second-guess" their decisions. He says, "I am held responsible, so I need to know what is going on." He sees no inconsistency in his behavior, nor does he recognize some other assumptions which are implicit: "People can't be trusted," or, "They can't really make as good decisions as I can."
> With one hand, and in accord with certain assumptions, he delegates; with the other, and in line with other assumptions, he takes actions which have the effect of nullifying his delegation. Not only does he fail to recognize the inconsistencies involved, but if faced with them he is likely to deny them.[72]

In *The Human Side of Enterprise* (1960), McGregor stated two different sets of assumptions that managers make about people:

Theory X:

1. The average human has an inherent dislike of work and will avoid it if possible.
2. Most people must be coerced, controlled, directed, and threatened with punishment to get them to put forth adequate effort toward the achievement of organizational objectives.
3. The average human prefers to be directed, wishes to avoid responsibility, has relatively little ambition, and wants security above all.

Theory Y:

1. The expenditure of physical and mental effort in work is as natural as play or rest.
2. External control and the threat of punishment are not the only means for bringing about effort toward organizational objectives. People will exercise self-direction and self-control in the service of objectives to which they are committed.
3. Commitment to objectives is a function of the rewards associated with their achievement.
4. The average human learns, under proper conditions, not only to accept but to seek responsibility.
5. The capacity to exercise a relatively high degree of imagination, ingenuity, and creativity in the solution of organizational problems is widely, not narrowly, distributed in the population.
6. Under the conditions of modern organizational life, the intellectual potentialities of the average human are only partially utilized.[73]

American police departments have historically been dominated by theory X assumptions. Even police departments with progressive national images may be experienced as tightly controlling environments by the people who actually work in them:

> The person leading a training session with about thirty-five managers of a West Coast police department observed that we often react to organizations as though they were living, breathing things. The managers agreed with this and noted the use of such phrases as "the department promoted me this year" and "the department hired me in 1975." They also understood that in fact someone, not the police department, had made those decisions. The managers were then divided into five groups and asked to make a list of what they thought the police department would say about them if it could talk. When the groups reported back, they identified a total of forty-two statements, some of which were duplicates of each other. These managers, all of whom were college graduates and many of whom held advanced degrees, indicated the police department would say such things as "They are idiots"; "They don't have any sense"; "Watch them or they'll screw up royally." All of the statements reported had a theory X character to them.

Theory X assumptions are readily recognized as being those that underpin traditional organizational theory. For example, we can relate a narrow span of control to theory X's first two propositions. In contrast, theory Y is formed by a set of views that are supportive of Argyris's mix model; they postulate that the interests of the individual and the organization need not be conflictual but can be integrated for mutual benefit. The principal task of management in a theory X police department is control, whereas in a theory Y department it is supporting subordinates by given them the resources to do their jobs and creating an environment where they can be self-controlling, mature, contributing, and self-actualizing.

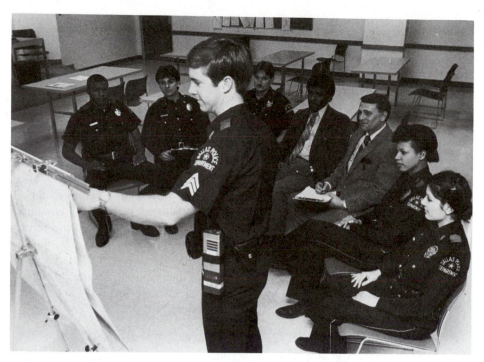

A quality circle at work in the Dallas Police Department. (Courtesy of the Dallas Police Department.)

The use of quality circles (QCs) or employee participation groups (EPGs) is one practice consistent with theory Y that is beginning to be used in police departments. Widely used in Japanese industries and such American corporations as 3M, Union Carbide, Chrysler, and Lockheed, these procedures have been credited with achieving numerous productivity and product improvements while also enjoying the support of both management and labor.[74]

Quality circles are small groups of people, roughly between five to ten with seven being regarded as ideal, who perform the same type of work, such as uniformed patrol, training, or robbery investigation. This group or QC voluntarily agrees to meet at least once a week during regular duty hours for an hour to identify, discuss, analyze, and solve specific work-related problems that the group members have identified as being important. As practiced in the Dallas Police Department, QCs also:

1. Are based on the premise that all members are of equal importance in making contributions.
2. Use sergeants as leaders because they can "blend" in with the group, being more readily perceived as equals than are higher ranks.
3. Provide formal training to the group leader and members in analytical techniques such as problem identification, data gathering, decision making, and making presentations.
4. Have access to needed information and the use of experts in areas such as budgeting and systems analysis.
5. Are assigned a facilitator—a top-level manager—to serve as a "go-between" and cut through "red tape" on behalf of the QC.

6. Receive the support of management to adopt all reasonable recommendations.

7. Implement the solution they recommend to, and is approved by, management.

QCs can be a valuable tool for police departments. Because circle members must cost out their solutions, a greater awareness is created with respect to how a department's resources are used. The QCs' emphasis on improvement results in creative solutions that are cost-effective. Each participating officer's knowledge of the department and its operating environment is enhanced and officers develop new skills such as problem identification, planning, and decision making. Although certain topics are considered beyond the legitimate scope of a QC's inquiry—such as personalities and matters of law—the available range of topics is broad. QC's also reduce the potential for dissatisfaction and conflict by providing a forum to air concerns and devise solutions, which has the additional benefit of improving communication both horizontally, among peers, and vertically, up and down the chain of command. On the down side, if police administrators create QCs as a façade of participation, officers quickly become disillusioned and withdraw. Moreover, QC leaders and facilitators must be properly trained in interpersonal and group dynamics and must themselves be genuinely committed to the process or else meetings of the group may devolve into classical, unproductive "gripe" sessions.

LIKERT: SYSTEMS 1, 2, 3 AND 4 AND THE LINKPIN

The work of Rensis Likert (1903–1981) is compatible with McGregor's theory X and theory Y in that fundamentally it contrasts traditional and democratic or participative management. In *New Patterns of Management* (1961), Likert identified four different management systems or climates: (1) exploitive authoritative, (2) benevolent authoritative, (3) consultative, and (4) participative group. In a subsequent publication, *The Human Organization* (1967), Likert extended and refined his notions of management systems, dropping the earlier designations and calling them system 1, system 2, system 3, and system 4, respectively. A partial description of these systems is given in Table 3-3.

Basically, Likert's system 1 reflects the content of McGregor's theory X, whereas system 4 incorporates the assumption of theory Y; system 2 and system 3 form part of a continuum in contrast to the simple opposites of McGregor's theory X and theory Y. Likert argues that system 2 management concepts predominate in the literature and that these conceptual tools do not fit a system 4 management style, which he believes most people prefer.[75]

Assuming some linkage between what Likert saw as predominating in the literature and actual practice, one would expect to find most people reporting their organization to be a system 2 environment. In a study of 18 different-sized local police departments in 15 different states throughout the country, Swanson and Talarico asked 629 uniformed police officers actually assigned to field duties what type of management climate their department had.[76] Some 16.6 percent of the officers reported a system 1; 42.9 percent a system 2; 35.9 percent a system 3; and only 4.6 percent a system 4. These data, then, provide some support for Likert's assertion.

Likert also contributes to the management literature by contrasting between the man-to-man and linkpin patterns of organization, depicted in Figure 3-6.[77] The man-to-man pattern is found in traditional organizations; the type of interaction characteristically is superior to subordinate, most often on an individual basis, and relies heavily on the use of positional authority. The linkpin pattern is found in the democratically

TABLE 3-3 Likert's Organizational and Performance Characteristics of Different Management Systems

Organizational variable	System 1	System 2	System 3	System 4
1. Leadership processes used:				Complete confidence and trust in all matters.
Extent to which superiors have confidence and trust in subordinates	Have no confidence and trust in subordinates	Have condescending confidence and trust, such as master has to servant	Substantial but not complete confidence and trust; still wishes to keep control of decisions	Subordinates feel completely free to discuss things about the job with their superior.
Extent to which superiors behave so that subordinates feel free to discuss important things about their jobs with their immediate superior	Subordinates do not feel at all free to discuss things about the job with their superior	Subordinates do not feel very free to discuss things about the job with their superior	Subordinates feel rather free to discuss things about the job with their superior	
Extent to which immediate superior in solving job problems generally tries to get subordinates' ideas and opinions and make constructive use of them	Seldom gets ideas and opinions of subordinates in solving job problems	Sometimes gets ideas and opinions of subordinates in solving job problems	Usually gets ideas and opinions and usually tries to make constructive use of them	Always gets ideas and opinions and always tries to make constructive use of them

From *The Human Organization* by Rensis Likert. Copyright © 1967 McGraw-Hill Book Company. Used with permission of McGraw-Hill Book Company.

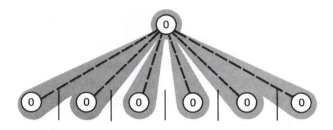

The Man-to-Man Pattern

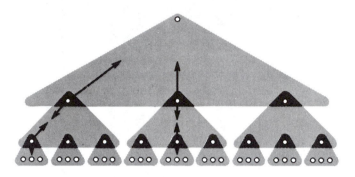

The Linkpin Pattern

FIGURE 3-6. Likert's man-to-man and linkpin patterns. [From *The Human Organization* by Rensis Likert. Copyright © 1967 McGraw-Hill Book Company. Used with the permission of McGraw-Hill Book Company.]

and group-oriented system 4. In it, a police manager is simultaneously a member of one group, say, the chief's command staff, and the leader of another group, say, the Operations Bureau. The pattern of interaction is as a member of one group and as the leader of another, with the emphasis upon open, honest communications in an atmosphere of mutual confidence and trust. In a loose sense the traditional organization's managers perform a linkpin function, although it is man to man and is based on superior-subordinate interaction. However, in Likert's terms the linkpin function relies more on influence than on authority and connects groups rather than individuals.

BENNIS: ORGANIZATIONAL DEVELOPMENT

An organizational humanist, Warren Bennis's (1925–) criticisms of bureaucracy have been noted. Much of his work has been in the area of organizational development, which is:

> the name given to the emerging applied behavioral science discipline that seeks to improve organizations through planned, systematic, long-range efforts focused on the organization's culture and its human and social processes.[78]

Organizational development has two separate, but entwined, stems: the laboratory training stem and survey research feedback stem.[79] The laboratory approach involves unstructured experiences by a group from the same organization, the successor to stranger-to-stranger T-groups whose popularity had waned by the late 1950s. Laboratory training grew out of the work of Lewin and his Research Center for Group Dynamics.[80] The survey research feedback stem makes attitude surveys within an organization and feeds it back to organizational members in workshop sessions to create awareness and to promote positive change.[81] The survey research stem also grew out of Lewin's Research Center for Group Dynamics from which the senior staff—which had included McGregor—moved to the University of Michigan following Lewin's death in 1947. There they joined with the university's Survey Research Center to form the Institute of Social Research, where some of Likert's work was done.

In a sense, organizational development began as a result of people rejecting stranger-to-stranger T-groups.[82] The laboratory stem began working with groups from the same organization, and the survey research feedback stem began using measurements. Fairly quickly, the focus spread from groups in the same organization to entire organizations. To illustrate the earlier point that many of the behavioral system theorists are tied to organizational development, note that McGregor employed such an approach with Union Carbide in 1957 and Argyris used it with the U.S. Department of State in 1967.

Organizational development as we know it today is an early 1960s movement. In his classic *Changing Organizations* (1966) Bennis describes it as having the following objectives:

1. Improvement in the interpersonal competence of managers.
2. A change in values so that human factors and feelings come to be considered legitimate.
3. Increased understanding between and within groups to reduce tensions.
4. Development of more effective team management, meaning an increased capacity for groups to work together.
5. Development of better methods of resolving conflict, meaning less use of authority and suppression of it and more open and rational methods.
6. Development of open, organic management systems characterized by trust, mutual confidence, wide sharing of responsibility, and the resolution of conflict by bargaining or problem solving.[83]

Chapter 15, "Organizational Change," draws upon the literature of organizational development. To produce the types of climates Argyris, McGregor, Likert, and Bennis favor is hard work, and, despite good intentions by the organization at the outset, there is always the prospect of failure:

> The director of public safety in a major city wanted to implement a management by objectives (MBO) system. After discussions with the consultant who later directed the effort, it was agreed that this would take a long-term intervention. This effort focused on MBO as a rational management tool that had to be accompanied by behavioral shifts to be successful. The approach involved a survey research feedback component, training in MBO, and technical assistance in implementing it. After one year, the work had produced a good deal of paperwork, no small amount of confusion, and more than a little anger.
>
> The intervention failed because (1) the organization had not been prepared properly for change; (2) the project was seen as the director's "baby" and there was never widespread support for it; (3) many managers were threatened, denouncing it as "fad" or as an

attempt by top management to find a way to evaluate them unfavorably; (4) not all managers were trained due to cost and scheduling difficulties; (5) success in part depended upon people in the organization taking responsibility for training lower-level managers and supervisors, a feat they did not accomplish; (6) the consultant's reservations about the likelihood of success given the specifics of the situation were never given sufficient weight by him or by others at the times they were voiced; (7) the timelines for the project were too ambitious; and (8) the resources dedicated to change were not sufficient.

Organizations as Open Systems

Systems theory concepts have been discussed since the 1920s, but they came into general use only as recently as 1960. A system is a grouping of separate but interrelated components working together toward the achievement of some common objective. General systems theory (GST), on which the biologist Ludwig von Bertalanffy and the sociologist Talcott Parsons have written, is a broad conceptual framework for explaining relationships in the "real world" without any consideration of the specifics of a given situation.

Organizations may be characterized as closed or open systems. In actuality, there are no entirely closed or open organizations; these are only terms used to describe the extent to which an organization approximates one or the other.

The closed system view of an organization assumes complete rationality, optimizing performances, predictability, internal efficiency, and certainty.[84] Since all behavior is believed to be functional and all outcomes predictable and certain, the closed organization can ignore changes in the larger environment, such as political, technological, and economic.[85] Thus, the closed system organization sees little need for interaction with its environment. The police chief who denies that he needs an automated management information system (MIS) prohibits subordinates from talking with politicians, prefers the "tried and true" over recent innovations, and refuses to justify budget requests carefully in a tight economic environment is reflecting a closed system view. Traditional organizational theory and the closed system fall into the same stream of thinking and are compatible.

The police department as an open system is depicted in Figure 3-7. Open systems are described by Katz and Kahn as having the following characteristics:

1. Open systems seek and continuously import sources of energy, including money, recruits, and information as inputs.
2. Once imported, the energy is transformed by the subsystems comprising the throughput function. For example, recruits are trained.
3. Although some energy is used by the subsystems in the throughput function, such as the efforts associated with training recruits, open systems export the bulk of the energy transformed into the environment as products, services, such as the trained recruits who are now assigned to patrol and respond to calls, and other forms.
4. There is a cyclical relationship between the inputs, the throughput, and the outputs as the services exported into the environment furnish the source of energy to repeat the cycle. Outputs both satisfy needs and create new demands for outputs.
5. All forms of organization move toward disorganization or death; this entropic process is a universal law of nature. To survive, open systems reverse the process by acquiring negative entropy. The cyclical character of open systems

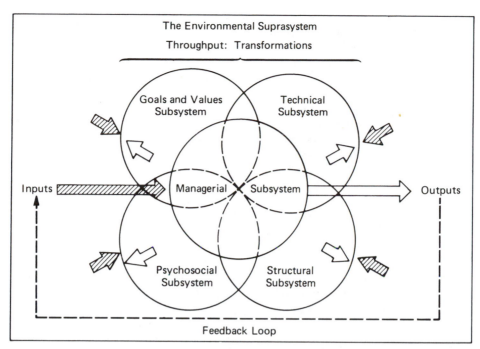

FIGURE 3-7. The Police Department as an open system. [From *Contingency Views of Organization and Management* by Fremont E. Kast and James E. Rosenzweig. © 1973, Science Research Associates, Inc. Reprinted by permission of the publisher with modifications.]

allows them to develop negative entropy by having energy flow continuously through them. Additionally, because open systems can import more energy than is expended, they have a storage capacity that allows them to survive brief interruptions of inputs. This may occur as one budget year ends and it is a short while until the city council enacts the new budget. Typically, the police department will have sufficient gasoline and other supplies to remain operational.

6. Open systems receive informational feedback as inputs from the larger environment in which they operate. As suggested by Figure 3-7, an open system has multiple points at which inputs occur. These inputs take place both through formal and informal exchanges. Police departments have a formally structured feedback loop to make them more responsive to control, and through it flows such things as technical evaluations of their programs and directions from the city council and the city manager. Open systems cannot absorb all informational and other inputs; excesses of inputs would overwhelm them. Therefore, open systems have a selective mechanism called "coding," which filters out some potential inputs and attunes them to important signals from the environment. A simple illustration of this principle is that, from among the dozens of daily telephone callers asking to talk to the chief of police, only a few actually get to do so. Switchboard operators, secretaries, and aides are taught to refer most callers to the appropriate department, handle the calls themselves, or connect them with someone empowered to deal with such matters. Yet the telephone calls of the city manager and certain other people will invariably find their way through these filters.

7. The continuous cycle of inputs, transformations, outputs, and feedback pro-

duces a steady state in an open system. A steady state is not a motionless or true equilibrium but a dynamic and continuous adjusting to external forces and of internal processes to ensure the survival of the system.

8. Over time open systems develop specialized subsystems, as shown in Figure 3-7, to facilitate the importation and processing of energy and to enhance its survival.

9. As specialization proceeds, its fragmenting effect is countered by processes that bring the system together for unified functioning, the purpose of the managerial subsystem depicted in Figure 3-7.

10. Open systems can reach the same final state even though they started from different sets of initial conditions and proceeded down different paths; this is the principle of equifinality.[86]

The subsystems identified in Figure 3-7 have been discussed in various ways; more specifically these overlapping subsystems have the following functions:

1. The managerial subsystem plays a central role in establishing goals, planning, organizing, coordinating, and controlling activities and in relating the police department to its environment.

2. Organizational goals and values represent an important subsystem; while the police department takes many of its values from the broader environment, such as the content of statutory law and appellate court decisions, it also influences society. An example illustrates the interplay between the police department's subsystems and the larger environment. Conditioned by the conservative nature of the organization in which they operate, which is reflected in the police department's goals and values subsystem, the top leadership of the managerial subsystem—in relating the police department to its environment—may take positions against abortions and the legalization of marijuana and for gun control and mandatory sentences.

3. The technical subsystem refers to the means required for the performance of tasks, including the knowledge, equipment, processes, and facilities used to transform inputs into outputs.

4. Individual behaviors, motivations, status and role hierarchies, group dynamics, and influence systems are all elements of the psychosocial subsystem.

5. The structural subsystem is concerned with the ways in which tasks are divided and how they are coordinated. In a formal sense, structure can be set forth by organizational charts, job descriptions, policies, and rules and regulations. Structure is therefore also concerned with patterns of authority, communication, and work flow. Too, the structural subsystem provides for a formalization of relationships between the technical and the psychosocial systems. However, many interactions that occur between the technical and psychosocial subsystems bypass the formal, occurring informally.[87]

Knowledge of open systems theory is important to the manager because it provides a view of the police department that is more consistent with reality; the police department is not a closed system but, rather, an open one having many dynamic interactions with the larger society in which it is embedded. Figure 3-8 demonstrates one aspect of these dynamic interactions, the relationship between the police department and external bodies in the fiscal management process.

Stressing the interrelatedness of the various subsystems and the interrelatedness of the police department with the larger world, open systems theory has the potential

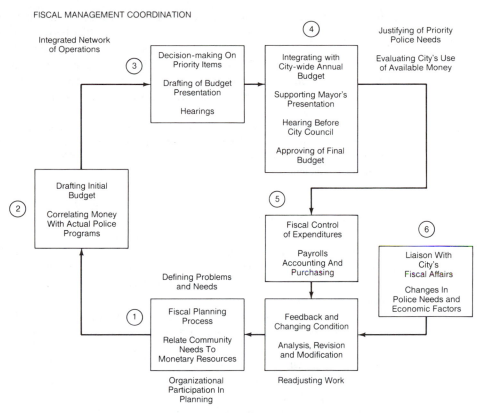

FISCAL MANAGEMENT COORDINATION

FIGURE 3-8. External relationships in the Houston Police Department's fiscal management process. [Source: Kent John Cabotar, *Measuring the Costs of Police Services* (Washington, D.C.: U.S. Department of Justice, National Institute of Justice, 1982), p. 114.]

to foster increased cooperation. Too, the emphasis of open systems theory upon achieving objectives serves to reinforce the need for purposeful behavior and may lead to greater effectiveness in achieving goals.

Critique of Open Systems Theory

Mayo's human relations school has been challenged on a number of grounds:

1. It rests on questionable research methods, a point raised earlier.[88]
2. The viewpoint that conflict between management and the worker can be overcome by the ''harmony'' of human relations attributes too much potency to human relations and ignores the potential that properly handled conflict has for being a source of creativity and innovation.
3. The single-mindedness with which advocates insisted on the importance of human relations was evangelistic.
4. Entirely too much emphasis was placed upon the informal side of organization to the neglect of the formal.
5. The attention focused on the individual and the group was at the expense of consideration of the organization as a whole.[89]

Human relations is also criticized as having a pro-management bias from several different perspectives. First, it saw unions as promoting conflict between management and labor, a condition antithetical to the values of human relations. Second, by focusing on workers, the Hawthorne studies provided management with more sophisticated means of manipulating employees. Finally, the end of human relations is indistinguishable from that of scientific management; both wanted a more efficient organization:

> Scientific management assumed the most efficient organization would also be the most satisfying one, since it would maximize both productivity and the workers' pay . . . the Human Relations approach was that the most personally satisfying organization would be the most efficient.[90]

Although the Hawthorne studies never showed a clear-cut relationship between satisfaction and job performance,[91] the human relations position that satisfied people are more productive has become a widely held and cherished belief. It is a logically appealing and commonsense position whose endless repetition has accorded it the status of "fact." However popular this "fact," the unqualified assertion that satisfied people are more productive is at odds with the research findings; there is no consistent relationship between job satisfaction and productivity.[92]

This does not mean that police managers should be unconcerned about any possible consequences of job satisfaction and dissatisfaction. Quite to the contrary, there are profoundly important organizational and humane reasons why they should be very concerned. On the positive side, job satisfaction generally leads to lower turnover, less absenteeism, fewer cases of tardiness, and fewer grievances and was the best overall predictor of the length of life in an impressive long-term study.[93] Conversely, job dissatisfaction has been found to be related to various mental and physical illnesses.[94] As a final note, some work on job satisfaction and productivity reverses the usual causal relationship, suggesting that satisfaction is an outgrowth of production.[95]

Maslow used a portion of his *Motivation and Personality* to attack the scientific method, claiming that its rigors limited the conclusions one could reach.[96] In turn, the scientific method has found it difficult to state the concepts of the need hierarchy in ways that they can be measured and the theory tested. Bennis reported that he was baffled to discover that little had been done to test the need hierarchy.[97] Despite the lack of research and the fact that the few existing studies do not support Maslow, there remains an almost metaphysical attraction to the need hierarchy,[98] a condition made even more perplexing by noting that Maslow's work on motivation came from a clinical study of neurotic people.[99]

In contrast to the lack of research on the need hierarchy, there has been considerable research on Herzberg's motivation-hygiene theory; after reviewing this evidence Gibson and Teasley conclude:

> It would be fair to summarize these efforts as mixed as regards the validation of the Herzberg concepts. The range of findings run from general support . . . to a vigorous condemnation of Herzberg's methodology.[100]

Behavioral systems theories have also been found wanting on a variety of grounds:

1. Insufficient attention has been paid to the organization as a whole, and too much emphasis has been placed upon the individual and groups.

2. Some theories, such as Argyris's immaturity-maturity theory, McGregor's theory X and theory Y, and Likert's systems 1, 2, 3, and 4, depend as much on setting the bureaucratic model up as a "straw man" to be knocked down as easily as they do their own virtues.

3. However attractive the arguments for organizational humanism, the data supporting them are not powerful and are sometimes suspect. For example, in commenting on McGregor's theory X and theory Y, Maslow notes that:

> a good deal of evidence upon which he bases his conclusions comes from my research and my papers on motivations, self-actualization, etc. But I of all people would know just how shaky this foundation is as a final foundation. My work on motivations came from the clinic, from a study of neurotic people . . . I am quite willing to concede this . . . because I'm a little worried about this stuff which I consider tentative being swallowed whole by all sorts of enthusiastic people.[101]

Concerns have also been expressed regarding what actually is being measured. For example, Johannesson claims that studies of job satisfaction and organizational climate are tapping the same dimension;[102] critics of Johannesson term his conclusion "premature and judgmental,"[103] while others argue that job satisfaction is the direct result of organizational climate.[104] Moreover, some data suggest conclusions that differ from certain of the logical positions taken by behavioral systems theorists. Argyris's argument that the narrow span of control makes people passive and dependent is a case in point. From a study of 156 public personnel agencies, Blau concluded that a narrow span of control provided opportunities for more mutuality in problem solving.[105] Although not stated directly, this also suggests the possibility that wide spans of control may produce less collaboration, since the manager has less time to share with each subordinate, and a more directive relationship.[106]

4. In one way or another, humanistic theories depend upon open and honest communications among organizational members in an environment of trust and mutual respect. A compellingly attractive theme, it gives insufficient weight to the consequences that can and do flow when authenticity meets power. Along these lines, Samuel Goldwyn is reputed to have said to his staff one day, "I want you all to tell me what's wrong with our operation even if it means losing your job."[107] The authenticity-power dilemma is not insurmountable; but it is a tall mountain whose scaling depends in large measure upon personally secure and nondefensive people dedicated to improving the organization and how it is experienced by its inhabitants.

5. In large measure the impetus to humanize organizations has been from the academic community; its belief that employees want more rewards than money from doing the work itself does not take into account the fact that some workers have a utilitarian involvement with the job. It simply provides the money necessary to live, and they save their energies and obtain their rewards from their families and other nonjob-related sources. Too, workers may not see attempts to broaden their jobs in the same light as theorists.[108]

Six American automobile workers spent four weeks in a Swedish Saab plant working to assemble engines as a team rather than on an assembly-line basis. Five of the six American workers reacted negatively to this experience. One of them expressed his dissatisfaction in the following way: "If I've got to bust my ass to be meaningful, forget it; I'd rather be monotonous."[109] While neither controlling nor entirely persuasive, findings such as these at least provide another framework for thinking about theories of organization.

Despite the fact that open systems theory has enjoyed some popularity since 1960, its use has not penetrated into police departments to any discernible degree. Disarmingly straightforward as a concept, its application requires the investment of resources beyond the reach of most police departments, particularly when considered in relationship to needs perceived as more directly relevant to their mission.

Bridging Theories

As noted earlier in this chapter, bridging theories are those that display a certain degree of empathy for both the traditional and open systems perspectives. Trying to place a range of theories under the traditional or open systems streams of thinking is not unlike the experience of trying to fit a square peg in a round hole. This difficulty is created by the simple reality that the work of some theorists produces thinking that does not focus solely or even largely on a single dimension. Additionally vexing is the fact that over time the importance that theorists and others attach to their work may change. Perhaps equally perplexing to those newly introduced to organizational theory is the array of classification schemes for presenting work in this area—which also may change over time. For example, at one time organic models of organization were differentiated from general systems models, although in 1967 Buckley noted that the modern concepts of systems are now taking over the duty of the overworked and perhaps retiring concept of the organic organization.[110] All of this is by way of noting that ultimately classification becomes a matter of judgment.

For present purposes, it is sufficient to understand that the designation "bridging theories" is intended to encompass a range of theories that can be conceived of as falling into the middle ground between traditional and open systems theory.

Under the broad heading of bridging theories, two subheadings of theories will be considered: general bridging theories and contingency theories. Note that, as the various theories are covered, mention is made of other ways in which these theories have been categorized.

General Bridging Theories

Within this section, the work of Chester Barnard (1886–1961), James March (1928–   ), and Herbert Simon (1916–) is treated. Barnard's thinking has also been identified by others as part of the human relations, social systems, and open systems schools; March and Simon's efforts are sometimes categorized as being part of a decision theory school.

Chester Barnard's principal career was as an executive with American Telephone & Telegraph, although he had other work experiences as well. During World War II, he was president of United Service Organizations, and from 1952–1953 he was the Rockefeller Foundation's president. In 1938, he wrote *The Functions of the Executive,* which reflected his experiences and thinking. Among his major contributions are the following ideas:

1. Emphasis is on the importance of decision-making processes and a person's limited power of choice, as opposed to the traditionalists' rational man.
2. An organization is a "system of consciously coordinated activities or forces

of two or more persons,'' and it is important to examine the external forces to which adjustments must be made.

3. Individuals can overcome the limits on individual performance through cooperative group action.

4. The existence of such a cooperative system depends on both its effectiveness in meeting the goal and its efficiency.

5. Efficiency, in turn, depends on organizational equilibrium, which is the balance between the inducements offered by the organization and the contributions offered by the individual.

6. The role of the informal organization insofar as it aids communication, cohesiveness, and individual feelings of self-respect.

7. Authority rests upon a persons' acceptance of the given orders; orders that are neither clearly acceptable nor clearly unacceptable lie within a person's zone of indifference.

8. Complex organizations are themselves composed of small units.

9. The traditional view of organizations is rejected as having boundaries and comprising a definite number of members. Included in this concept of organizations were investors, suppliers, customers, and others whose actions contributed to the productivity of the firm.

10. Executives operated as interconnecting centers in a communication system that sought to secure the coordination essential to cooperative effort. Executive work is the specialized work of maintaining the organization and its operation. The executive is analogous to the brain and the nervous system in relation to the rest of the body.[111]

These ideas of Barnard reveal an appreciation for both traditional and open systems theories. On the one hand, Barnard was concerned with formal structure, goals, effectiveness, and efficiency; on the other hand, he viewed organizations as cooperative systems, having an informal side and many relationships with the larger world. Effectively then, his thinking bridges the traditional and open systems streams of thinking.

Simon's *Administrative Behavior* has been mentioned with respect to its ''proverbs'' attack on the principles of organization, but it also made other noteworthy contributions. Simon believed that the ''anatomy of an organization'' was how the decision-making function was distributed; indeed, the central theme of *Administrative Behavior* is that organizations are decision-making entities.[112] Simon was, therefore, simultaneously interested in both structure and behavior. In *Organizations* (1958), March and Simon built on some of the ideas reflected in the earlier *Administrative Behavior*. *Organizations* presented March and Simon's ''administrative man'' who was a modification of the rational economic actor behaving in his own self-interest postulated by traditional organizational theory. Administrative man reflects the tension between the traditional theory's normative values of rationality, effectiveness, and efficiency and the open system's views of human behavior and the complexity of organizations. The administrative man:

1. Lacks complete knowledge of the alternatives available to him in making decisions.

2. Does not know the consequences of each possible alternative.

3. Uses a simple decision-making model that reflects the main features of decision situations, but not the complexity of them.

4. Makes decisions characterized as "satisficing," which are short of optimizing but satisfy and suffice in that they are "good enough to get by."[113]

Contingency Theory

In the late 1950s and early 1960s, a series of studies was carried out in England and in this country that were to lead ultimately to the development of what is presently referred to as situational or contingency theory. This approach holds—with respect to organizing, managing, leading, motivating, and other variables—that there is no one best way to go about it. Contingency theory does not, however, also assume that all approaches to a situation are equally appropriate. It is a bridging theory in that it favors neither traditional nor open systems theory; rather, it is the specifics of a situation that suggest which approach should be used.

An early study important to the development of contingency theory was reported on by Burns and Stalker in 1961; as a result of their analysis of the operations of some English industries, they decided that:

> we desire to avoid the suggestion that either system is superior under all circumstances to the other. In particular nothing in our experiences justifies the assumption that mechanistic systems should be superseded by the organic under conditions of stability. The beginning of administrative wisdom is the awareness that there is no one optimum type of management system.[114]

In 1965, another English researcher, Joan Woodward, confirmed and extended the work of Burns and Stalker by her finding that a traditional management system was appropriate for a mass-production technology, whereas the organic, flexible, adaptive system was better suited for handling less highly repetitive tasks.[115]

In this country, the 1966 publication of Harvey Sherman's *It All Depends* was an early major statement with a contingency theme on organizations; Sherman, an executive with the Port of New York Authority, believed in a "pragmatic perspective":

> There can be no ideal design or arrangement that will fit all times, all situations, all objectives, and all values . . . these forces are in constant flux . . . it is well to reassess the organization periodically. The very design of the organization structure is a significant force in the total situation and changes in it can alter the total situation.[116]

Forces that Sherman felt were particularly important included:

1. The enterprise's objectives and purposes, stated and implied.
2. The nature of the work to be done.
3. Technology, technological change, and the level of technological skills available to the organization.
4. The technological and formal interrelationships within the enterprise.
5. The psychology, values, and attitudes that prevail within the enterprise, particularly those of top management.
6. The interpersonal and sociological relationships within the enterprise.
7. Outside forces, such as changes in the economy, in technology, in laws, in labor relations, in the political situation and in broad sociological and cultural patterns.[117]

In the recent past, there have been a number of examples of a contingency approach short of an entire theory of organization. In 1964, Vroom developed a contingency model of motivation;[118] Fiedler's 1967 situational leadership approach is a contingency statement,[119] as is Katzell's theory Z.[120] This last concept is basically a midpoint between McGregor's theory X and theory Y; that is, theory Z holds that, depending on the specifics of each case, it may be appropriate to employ either theory X or theory Y.

Altogether, the broad and more specific approaches to organizations and behavior regardless of whether they were designated pragmatic, situational, or some other term received so much attention that in 1970 Lorsch and Lawrence noted:

> During the past few years there has been evident a new trend. . . . Rather than searching for the panacea of the one best way . . . under all conditions . . . investigators have more and more tended to examine the functioning of organizations in relation to the needs of their particular members and the external pressures facing them. . . . This approach seems to be leading to a "contingency" theory of organization.[121]

Prior to leaving contingency theory, it is appropriate to note that Burns and Stalker and Lorsch and Lawrence are also referred to in other literature as environmentalists, whereas Woodward is sometimes designated as technologist. Environmentalists are theorists who state basically that various types of environments face and interact with organizations. These environments reflect various degrees of complexity and uncertainty that impact upon the organization and its operation. In contrast the theorists such as Woodward maintain that technology—in the sense that methods used to get the work done—has a significant impact on how an organization is structured.

Critique of Bridging Theories

Bridging theories, in a sense, simultaneously confirm and disconfirm both traditional and open systems theories. In so doing, they place traditional and open systems theories into a perspective of being useful given appropriate qualifications. Barnard's and March and Simon's statements provide helpful orientations that are, however, somewhat limited by the absence of understandable guidelines as to their applications. Contingency theories of organizations rest presently on relatively limited research, often involving small samples of specific types of organizations. This, added to the fact that some of the important research has been done abroad in a similar but different culture, does not provide powerful data from which to generalize. Nonetheless, contingency theories of organizations provide an alternative and promising way in which to think about organizations as monolithic types—either closed or open.

Synthesis and Prognosis

Table 3-4 summarizes the three major streams of thought: (1) traditional theories, (2) bridging theories, and (3) open systems. Note that Table 3-4 also illustrates the interrelationships among the theories. For example, McGregor's theory Y and Likert's system 4 are consistent with each other. There is not, however, an absolute correlation among all theories found under the same major heading; whereas Argyris's state of maturity is compatible with both theory Y and system 4, it only falls within the

TABLE 3-4   The Interrelationships of the Three Major Streams of Theories

Theorists	Traditional theories	Bridging theories	Open systems theories
Taylor	Scientific management		
Weber	Bureaucratic model		
Fayol, Mooney and Reiley, Gulick, and Urwick	Administrative theory		
Mayo			Hawthorne studies and human relations
Maslow	Bottom three levels of need hierarchy		Top two levels of need hierarchy
Herzberg	Hygiene factors		Motivators
Lewin			Group dynamics
Homans			Internal-external systems
Argyris	Immaturity		Maturity
McGregor	Theory X		Theory Y
Likert	System 1	System 2 System 3	System 4
Bennis			Organizational development
Bertalanffy, Parsons, and Katz and Kahn			Systems Theory
Barnard		Cooperative system	
Simon and March		Administrative man	
Burns and Stalker, Woodward, Sherman and Lawrence and Lorsch		Organizational contingency theory	
Vroom		Expectancy theory	
Fiedler		Situational leadership	
Katzell		Theory Z	

same stream of thought as the Hawthorne studies. Thus, the use of Table 3-4 depends in some measure on knowledge gained in the preceding pages. Too, throughout this chapter, reference has been made at various points to material covered that was not a theory of organization. To repeat, the purpose of including it was to connect systems of thought as they were developed. Therefore, Table 3-4 includes macro theories of organization, along with some microlevel statements. Altogether, Table 3-4 does provide a comprehensive and easily understood overview of the theories covered and illustrates their interconnectedness.

For the vast majority of all organizations in the world, including the police, the bureaucratic model is going to remain overwhelmingly the dominant type of structure. This does not mean that police administrators should ignore or fail to try to reduce dysfunctional aspects of bureaucracy, but rather that reform efforts will generally take the form of improvements in how the bureaucratic model operates and is experienced by both employees and clients as opposed to abandoning it altogether. As discussed more fully in the next chapter, the police have experimented with structures that are alternatives to the bureaucratic model; from the late 1960s through the middle 1970s there was extensive experimentation nationally with team policing. As depicted in Figure 3-9, the Palo Alto Police Department shifted from a bureaucratic model to a team management/team policing concept that was closely aligned with the opens system stream of organizational theory. Approximately one year later the Palo Alto Police Department abandoned the team management/team policing model and returned to a traditional organizational form in which it has since remained. In 1986, one manager in the Palo Alto Police Department, who was there when all of the changes were made, stated that the abandonment of the new model was necessitated because planning for the open systems orientation went too fast and officers were not prepared for the new conditions.[122] Uniformed officers went from having to do only the initial investigation of a crime to also doing the follow-up investigation, which many officers were not sufficiently experienced to do. Additionally, the shifts in the responsibilities of many officers disrupted the patterns of communication and cooperation with other agencies, which further contributed to the decline in investigative effectiveness.

Attempts to modify bureaucracy, such as team policing, may succeed temporarily in large police departments, if only because such efforts produce a Hawthorne effect. However, in large-scale organizations over time, the latent power of bureaucracy will assert itself—because it remains a superior form of organization for which there presently is no viable long-term alternative—and efforts such as team policing will largely fall away. We have a view, which may be incorrect and is based largely on impressionistic data, that the long-term implementation of true alternative models to the bureaucratic model may be possible only in smaller police departments of something in the order of less than one hundred officers. This smaller scale facilitates interpersonal and group processes, such as communication, which can help maintain and institutionalize alternatives to the bureaucratic model. This is not a call to abandon efforts or experimentation with alternative organizational structures in policing; it is a call for realism and reason. The human systems approach is flawed by its small-group orientation in what is largely a large-scale organizational world. The data supporting the humanists, who make up a good part of the behavioral system theorists, are suspect on the basis of the often deductive posturing of this approach. What is left is that police managers must accept the bureaucratic form as a fact and embrace elements of the open system perspective largely on faith. Bridging theories, particularly contingency, represent a potentially rich source of satisfying the organizational imperatives of efficiency and effectiveness and of accommodating the needs of sworn officers and civilian employees.

Summary

External control of police departments requires that they be responsible to the societal demands placed upon them. This requirement carries with it the expectation that police departments will be efficiency oriented, but not internally democratic. This results in a basic tension between the existing bureaucratically structured department and some number of officers who want greater input into the organization and some increased control over work conditions and environment. While it is relatively easy to grasp the fundamentals of this issue, obtaining a solution to it has proven difficult and requires knowledge of organizational theory.

Organizational theory can be summarized as consisting of three major streams of thought: traditional organizational theory, open systems theory, and bridging theories. Traditional theory is comprised of three stems: scientific management, the bureau-

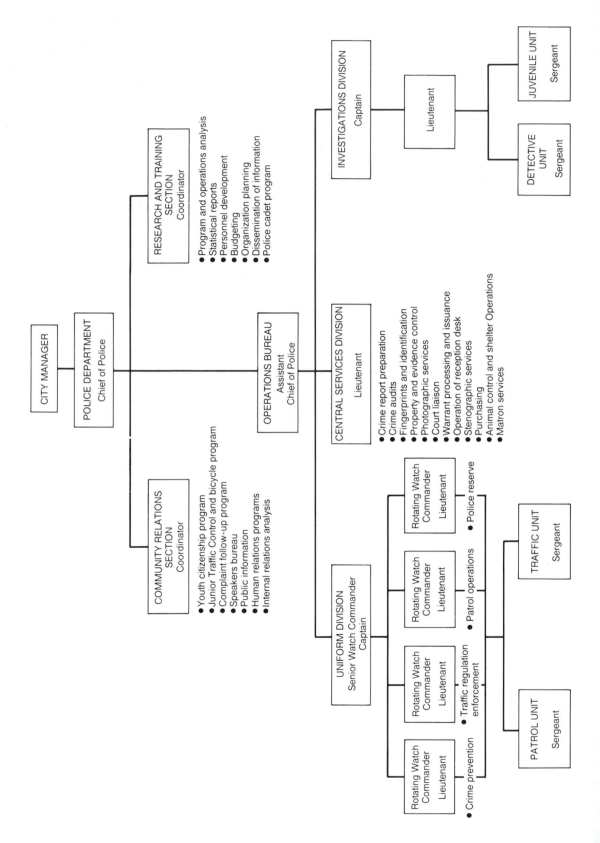

CITY MANAGER

POLICE DEPARTMENT
Chief of Police

COMMUNITY RELATIONS SECTION
Coordinator
- Youth citizenship program
- Junior Traffic Control and bicycle program
- Complaint follow-up program
- Speakers bureau
- Public information
- Human relations programs
- Internal relations analysis

RESEARCH AND TRAINING SECTION
Coordinator
- Program and operations analysis
- Statistical reports
- Personnel development
- Budgeting
- Organization planning
- Dissemination of information
- Police cadet program

OPERATIONS BUREAU
Assistant Chief of Police

CENTRAL SERVICES DIVISION
Lieutenant
- Crime report preparation
- Crime audits
- Fingerprints and identification
- Property and evidence control
- Photographic services
- Court liaison
- Warrant processing and issuance
- Operation of reception desk
- Stenographic services
- Purchasing
- Animal control and shelter Operations
- Matron services

INVESTIGATIONS DIVISION
Captain

Lieutenant

DETECTIVE UNIT
Sergeant

JUVENILE UNIT
Sergeant

UNIFORM DIVISION
Senior Watch Commander
Captain

Rotating Watch Commander
Lieutenant

Rotating Watch Commander
Lieutenant

Rotating Watch Commander
Lieutenant

Rotating Watch Commander
Lieutenant

- Crime prevention
- Traffic regulation enforcement
- Patrol operations
- Police reserve

PATROL UNIT
Sergeant

TRAFFIC UNIT
Sergeant

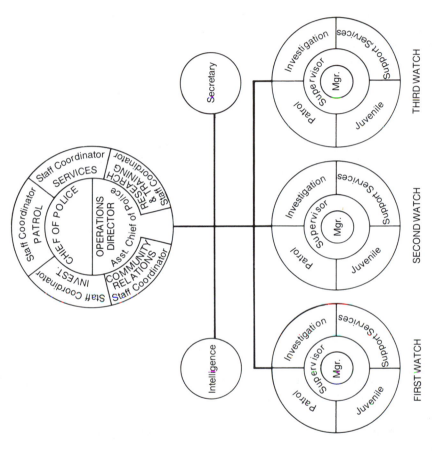

FIGURE 3-9. The shift in the Palo Alto, California, Police Department's organizational structure from the bureaucratic model (above) to a team concept (below) more closely aligned with the open system approach. [Source: Leo E. Peart, "Management By Objectives," *The Police Chief,* 38:4 (April 1971), p.55.]

cratic model, and administrative or management theory. Open systems theory also consists of three divisions: human relations, behavioral systems, and open systems theory. Bridging theories in some fashion represent the difficulty associated with putting a round peg in a square hole; bridging theories do not fall into either the traditional or the open systems streams of thought, but they do show a certain affinity for both perspectives; in this sense bridging theories can be conceived of usefully as occupying the middle ground between traditional and open systems theories. The two components to bridging theories are general bridging theories and contingency theories.

Virtually all police departments rest on traditional organizational theory. Although lengthy critiques have been made of traditional theory, the data upon which these critiques rest are not persuasive or powerful. Indeed, critiques have been made of all three major streams or organizational theory. For the foreseeable or near-term future—say, over at least the next three decades—significant movement away from the bureaucratic model by the police is unlikely. The police are hardly differentiated from most other organizations by this observation. The present reality is that bureaucratic organizations have achieved the very potency that Weber feared. The thorny but imminently necessary task facing police executives, perhaps their pre-eminent task, is to take the best features of the bureaucratic model and temper its debilitating effects with appropriate doses of other theoretical perspectives.

Discussion Questions

1. Why is knowledge of organizational theory important to police administrators and managers?
2. What is scientific management and what are three grounds on which it was attacked?
3. What are the seven characteristics of Weber's bureaucratic model?
4. Often overlooked in Weber's work on bureaucracy are two reservations that he expressed. What are they?
5. The most familiar and enduring acronym of administration was coined by Gulick. What is it and what does it mean?
6. Bennis makes certain criticism of bureaucracy, whereas Perrow raises certain defenses. Respectively, what are they and how are they similar or dissimilar?
7. What are the major stems or divisions of traditional and open systems organization theories?
8. Elton Mayo is regarded as the father of the human relations school. With which other body of theory did human relations collide and what were the consequences?
9. How can Maslow's need hierarchy, Herzberg's motivation-hygiene theory, McGregor's theory X and theory Y, Argyris's immaturity-maturity statement, and Likert's systems perspective be interrelated conceptually?
10. What are the characteristics of an open system, and how can they be illustrated as being present in a police department?
11. What are bridging theories?
12. Under the heading of contingency theory, one finds both technological and environmental perspectives. What do these terms mean?

13. What is the future of the police organizational structure over the foreseeable, near-term future?

Notes

1. Amitai Etzioni, *Modern Organizations* (Englewood Cliffs, N.J.: Prentice-Hall, 1964), p. 1.
2. Ibid., p. 1, with some additions.
3. Ibid., p. 1.
4. Talcott Parsons, *Structure and Process in Modern Societies* (Glencoe, Ill.: Free Press, 1960), p. 17.
5. Edgar H. Schein, *Organizational Psychology* (Englewood Cliffs, N.J.: Prentice-Hall, 1965), p. 9.
6. Peter W. Blau and W. Richard Scott, *Formal Organizations* (Scranton, Pa.: Chandler, 1962), p. 43, with some changes.
7. The treatment of the central issues of the four types of formal organizations is taken from ibid., pp. 43 and 55, with some changes.
8. Daniel A. Wren, *The Evolution of Management Thought* (New York: Ronald Press, 1972), p. 112.
9. Ibid., p. 114.
10. Ibid., pp. 114–115.
11. See the testimony of F. W. Taylor before the Special Committee of the House of Representatives Hearings to Investigate Taylor and Other Systems of Shop Management, January 25, 1912, p. 1387.
12. Wren, *The Evolution of Management Thought*, p. 115.
13. Frederick W. Taylor, *Principles of Scientific Management* (New York: Harper & Row, 1911), pp. 44–47.
14. See Frederick W. Taylor, *Shop Management* (New York: Harper and Brothers, 1911), for a discussion of this concept.
15. Ibid., p. 126.
16. Wren, *The Evolution of Management Thought*, p. 132. Not only did Bethlehem Steel abandon the system, but it also fired Taylor.
17. Ibid., p. 131.
18. L. P. Alford, *Henry Lawrence Gantt* (Easton-Hive Management Series: No. 6, 1972; facsimile reprint of a 1934 edition by Harper and Brothers), pp. 207 and 209.
19. Sudhir Kakar, *Frederick Taylor: A Study in Personality and Innovation* (Cambridge, Mass.: M.I.T. Press, 1973), p. 2.
20. Fremont E. Kast and James E. Rosenzweig, *Contingency Views of Organization and Management* (Chicago: Science Research Associates, 1973), p. 7.
21. Michel Crozier, *The Bureaucratic Phenomenon* (Chicago: University of Chicago Press, 1964), p. 3.
22. Max Weber, *The Theory of Social and Economic Organization*, trans. A. M. Henderson and Talcott Parsons (New York: Free Press, 1947), p. 337.
23. Ibid., p. 337.
24. Ibid., pp. 330–332, with limited restatement for clarity.
25. Ibid., p. 328.
26. On this point, see Nicos P. Mouzelis, *Organization and Bureaucracy* (Chicago; Aldine, 1967), pp. 20–21 and footnote 29 of that work.
27. H. H. Gerth and C. Wright Mills, *From Max Weber: Essays in Sociology* (New York: Oxford University Press, 1946), p. 50.
28. Wren, *The Evolution of Management Thought*, p. 230.

29. Henri Fayol, *General and Industrial Management,* trans. Constance Storrs (London: Sir Isaac Pitman, 1949), p. vi.

30. Ibid., pp. 19–41.

31. Ibid., p. 34.

32. The 1939 edition was co-authored, but the 1947 edition appeared under Mooney's name.

33. Luther Gulick, "Notes on the Theory of Organization," in *Papers on the Science of Administration,* eds. Luther Gulick and L. Urwick (New York: August M. Kelley, a 1969 reprint of the 1937 edition), p. 13.

34. L. Urwick, "Organization as a Technical Problem," in *Papers on the Science of Administration,* p. 52.

35. Taylor, *Shop Management,* p. 184.

36. Warren Bennis, "Organizational Developments and the Fate of Bureaucracy," *Industrial Management Review,* 7:2 (Spring 1966), pp. 41–55.

37. Herbert A. Simon, *Administrative Behavior* (New York: Free Press, 1945), p. 20. For additional criticism of the principles approach, see Dwight Waldo, *The Administrative State* (New York: Ronald Press, 1948).

38. J. Hage, "An Axiomatic Theory of Organizations," *Administrative Science Quarterly,* 10 (1965–1966), p. 305, Table 4.

39. Charles Perrow, *Complex Organizations* (Glenview, Ill.: Scott, Foresman, 1972), pp. 6–7.

40. Charles T. Goodsell, *The Case for Bureaucracy,* 2d. ed. (Chatham, N.J.: Chatham House Publishers, 1985), p. 11.

41. Ibid., pp. 11–12.

42. Alvin W. Gouldner, "Metaphysical Pathos and the Theory of Bureaucracy," *American Political Science Review,* 49 (June 1955), p. 501 as quoted by Goodsell at p. 12.

43. Goodsell, *The Case for Bureaucracy,* pp. 12–13.

44. Ibid., p. 29.

45. As early as 1924 researchers from the National Academy of Sciences had experiments under way; for present purposes, the work at the Hawthorne plant is described following the arrival of Mayo.

46. The definitive report of this research is F. J. Roethlisberger and William J. Dickson's *Management and the Worker* (Cambridge, Mass.: Harvard University Press, 1939). Roethlisberger came from Harvard with Mayo while Dickson was a company administrator.

47. The designation of this study as the bank wiring study is also found in the literature; banks were telephone switchboards.

48. There were actually two relay assembly test room studies, one following the other. The second one involved a change in the wage incentive and also confirmed the importance of the social group.

49. Roethlisberger and Dickson, *Management and the Worker,* pp. 58–59 and 180–183.

50. Bertram M. Gross, *The Managing of Organizations,* vol. I (New York: Free Press, 1964), p. 163.

51. Roethlisberger and Dickson, *Management and the Worker,* p. 522.

52. On this point, see ibid., pp. 179–186 and 448–458.

53. During the last two weeks of the switchboard wiring room study, there was a new supervisor, "Group Chief 2," who acted much more formally than did "Group Chief 1"; "GC-2" was regarded as a "company man." See ibid., pp. 452–453.

54. Ibid., pp. 21 and 397.

55. Etzioni, *Modern Organizations,* pp. 34–37.

56. Whitman Knapp, chairman, Commission to Investigate Allegations of Police Corruption and the City's Anti-Corruption Procedures, *Commission Report* (New York, 1972), pp. 4 and 65; also see Herman Goldstein, *Police Corruption* (Washington, D.C.: the Police Foundation, 1975), pp.

57. A. H. Maslow, "A Theory of Human Motivation," *Psychological Review,* 50 (July 1943), pp. 370–396.

58. These five elements are identified in A. H. Maslow, *Motivation and Personality* (New York: Harper and Brothers, 1954), pp. 80–92. Maslow later added a sixth category, "metamotivation," but it has never received substantial interest. See "A Theory of Metamotivation," *Humanitas,* 4 (1969), pp. 301–343.

59. Ibid., p. 91.

60. Robert M. Chiaramonte, "The Blue Max Award," *The Police Chief,* 11:4 (April 1973), pp. 24–25.

61. Wren, *The Evolution of Management Thought,* p. 324; Lewin lived in this country for the fifteen years preceding his death in 1947.

62. Ibid., p. 325.

63. Ibid., p. 325.

64. This case is reported in Paul Hersey and Kenneth H. Blanchard, *Management of Organizational Behavior,* 3d ed. (Englewood Cliffs, N.J.: Prentice-Hall, 1977), p. 139, with credit to "The Truth Hurts," *The Wall Street Journal,* no date. One of the key critics of T-groups has been George Odiorne.

65. George C. Homans, *The Human Group* (New York: Harcourt Brace, 1950), pp. 81–130.

66. Chris Argyris, *Personality and Organization: The Conflict Between System and the Individual* (New York: Harper and Brothers, 1957), pp. 58–66.

67. Ibid., pp. 76–122.

68. Chris Argyris, *Integrating the Individual and the Organization* (New York: John Wiley, 1964), p. 3.

69. For extended treatment of this subject, see ibid., pp. 146–191.

70. Ibid., p. 147.

71. Douglas McGregor, *The Human Side of Enterprise* (New York: McGraw-Hill, 1960), p. 6. Also see Louis A. Allen, "M for Management: Theory Y Updated," *Personnel Journal,* 52:12 (December 1973), pp. 1061–1067.

72. Ibid., p. 7.

73. Ibid., pp. 33–57.

74. The information on quality circles is drawn from W. Troy McClain "Focus on 'Quality Circles:' In Quest of Improved Police Productivity," *The Police Chief,* 52:9 (September 1985), pp. 50–54 and Joyce L. Roll, and David L. Roll, "The Potential for Application of Quality Circles in the American Public Sector," *Public Productivity Review,* vol. 7 (June 1983), pp. 122–142.

75. Rensis Likert, *The Human Organization* (New York: McGraw-Hill, 1967), p. 109.

76. Charles R. Swanson and Susette Talarico, "Politics and Law Enforcement: Implications of Police Perspectives," a paper presented at the 1979 meeting of the Academy of Criminal Justice Sciences, Table VI of the appendix.

77. Likert, *The Human Organization,* pp. 50–51.

78. Wendell L. French and Cecil H. Bell, Jr., *Organizational Development* (Englewood Cliffs, N.J.: Prentice-Hall, 1973). p. xiv.

79. Ibid., p. 21.

80. Ibid., pp. 21–25.

81. Ibid., pp. 25–26.

82. Ibid., p. 24.

83. Warren G. Bennis, *Changing Organizations* (New York: McGraw-Hill, 1966), p. 118.

84. Stephen P. Robbins, *The Administrative Process* (Englewood Cliffs, N.J.: Prentice-Hall, 1976), p. 259.

85. Ibid., p. 259.

86. Daniel Katz and Robert Kahn, *The Social Psychology of Organization,* 2d ed. (New York: John Wiley, 1978), pp. 23–30, with some change.

87. Kast and Rosenzweig, *Contingency Views of Organization and Management,* pp. 13–15, with changes and additions.

88. The Hawthorne studies have continued to excite the imagination. See, for instance,

H. M. Parsons, "What Caused the Hawthorne Effect?" *Administration and Society,* 10 (November 1978), pp. 259–283; Henry Lansberger, *Hawthorne Revisited* (Ithaca, N.Y.: Cornell University Press, 1958).

89. These points are drawn, with change, from William H. Knowles, "Human Relations in Industry: Research and Concepts," *California Management Review,* 2:2 (Fall 1958), pp. 87–105.

90. Etzioni, *Modern Organizations,* p. 39.

91. Edward E. Lawler, *Motivation in Work Organizations* (Monterey, Calif.: Brooks/Cole, 1973), p. 62.

92. Edwin A. Locke, "The Nature and Causes of Job Satisfaction," in *Handbook of Industrial and Organizational Psychology,* ed. Marvin D. Dunnette (Chicago: Rand McNally, 1976), p. 1332.

93. In this regard, see A. H. Brayfield and W. H. Crockett, "Employee Attitudes and Employee Performance," *Psychological Bulletin,* 52 (September 1955), pp. 394–424; V. H. Vroom *Motivation and Work* (New York: John Wiley, 1964); John P. Wanous, "A Causal-Correlation Analysis of the Job Satisfaction and Performance Relationship," *Journal of Applied Psychology,* 59 (April 1974), pp. 139–144; Niger Nicholson, Toby Wall, and Joe Lischerson, "The Predictability of Absence and Propensity to Leave from Employees' Job Satisfaction and Attitudes Toward Influence in Decision Making," *Human Relations,* 30 (June 1977), pp. 499–514; Phillip H. Mirvis and Edward E. Lawler, III, "Measuring the Financial Impact of Employee Attitudes," *Journal of Applied Psychology,* 62 (February 1977), pp. 1–8; Charles L. Hulin, "Effects of Changes in Job Satisfaction Levels on Employee Turnover," *Journal of Applied Psychology,* 52 (April 1968) pp. 122–126; A. H. Marrow, D. G. Bowers, and S. E. Seashore, *Management by Participation* (New York: Harper & Row, 1967); L. W. Porter and R. M. Steers, "Organizational Work and Personal Factors Related to Employee Turnover and Absenteeism," *Psychological Bulletin,* 80 (August 1973), pp. 151–176; Frederich Herzberg et al., *Job Attitudes: Review of Research and Opinion* (Pittsburgh, Pa.: Psychological Service of Pittsburgh, 1957); E. Palmore, "Predicting Longevity: A Follow-up Controlling for Age," *The Gerontologist,* 9 (1969), pp. 247–250.

94. See A. W. Kornhauser, *Mental Health of the Industrial Worker: A Detroit Study* (New York: John Wiley, 1965); R. J. Burke, "Occupational and Life Strains, Satisfaction, and Mental Health," *Journal of Business Administration,* 1 (1969–1970), pp. 35–41.

95. For example, Lyman Porter and Edward Lawler, *Managerial Attitude and Performance* (Homewood, Ill.: Dorsey Press, 1967); John E. Sheridan and John W. Slocum, Jr., "The Direction of the Causal Relationship Between Job Satisfaction and Work Performance." *Organizational Behavior and Human Performance,* 14 (October 1975), pp. 159–172.

96. Frank K. Gibson and Clyde E. Teasely, "The Humanistic Model of Organizational Motivation: A Review of Research Support," *Public Administration Review,* 33:1 (January–February 1973), p. 91. Several of the points made in the treatment of Maslow is drawn from this excellent analysis.

97. Bennis, *Changing Organizations,* p. 196.

98. Walter Nord, "Beyond the Teaching Machine: The Neglected Area of Operant Conditioning in the Theory and Practice of Management," *Organizational Behavior and Human Performance,* 4 (November 1969), pp. 375–401; also see Lyman Porter, "Job Attitudes in Management," *Journal of Applied Psychology,* 46 (December 1962), pp. 375–384, Douglas Hall and Khalil Nougaim, "An Examination of Maslow's Need Hierarchy in an Organizational Setting," *Organizational Behavior and Human Performance,* 3 (February 1968), pp. 12–35.

99. Maslow, *Motivation and Personality,* pp. 79–80.

100. Gibson and Teasley, "The Humanistic Model," p. 92.

101. Abraham Maslow, *Eupsychian Management: A Journal* (Homewood, Ill.: Dorsey Press, 1965), pp. 55–56.

102. R. E. Johannesson, "Some Problems in the Measurement of Organizational Climate," *Organizational Behavior and Human Performance,* 10 (August 1973), pp. 118–144.

103. W. R. Lafollette and H. P. Sims, Jr., "Is Satisfaction Redundant with Organizational Climate?" *Organizational Behavior and Human Performance,* 13 (April 1975), p. 276.

104. J. M. Ivancevich and H. L. Lyon, *Organizational Climate, Job Satisfaction, Role Clarity and Selected Emotional Reaction Variables in a Hospital Milieu* (Lexington: University of Kentucky Press, 1972).

105. Peter Blau, "The Hierarchy of Authority in Organizations," *American Journal of Sociology, 73* (January 1968), p. 457.

106. Perrow, *Complex Organizations,* p. 38.

107. Bennis, *Changing Organizations,* p. 77.

108. Jobs can be manipulated in three different ways: (1) jobs can be broadened by incorporating different tasks from the same skill level, referred to as "job enlargement"; (2) jobs can be made larger by giving some of the supervisor's tasks to the subordinate, called "job enrichment"; and (3) job enlargement and job enrichment may be employed simultaneously, also called "job enrichment."

109. "Doubting Sweden's Way," *Time,* March 10, 1975, p. 44.

110. Walter Buckley, *Sociology and Modern Systems Theory* (Englewood Cliffs, N.J.: Prentice-Hall, 1967), p. 43.

111. This concise summary of Bernard's contributions is drawn from Dessler, *Organization and Management,* pp. 44–45.

112. Simon, *Administrative Behavior,* p. 220.

113. James G. March and Herbert A. Simon, *Organizations* (New York: John Wiley, 1958), pp. 136–171.

114. Tom Burns and G. M. Stalker, *The Management of Innovation* (London: Tavistock, 1961), p. 125.

115. Joan Woodward, *Industrial Organization: Theory and Practice* (London: Oxford University Press, 1965).

116. Harvey Sherman, *It All Depends* (University: University of Alabama Press, 1966), p. 57.

117. Ibid., pp. 56–57.

118. Vroom, *Work and Motivation.*

119. Fred E. Fiedler, *A Theory of Leadership Effectiveness* (New York: McGraw-Hill, 1967).

120. Various names have been associated with theory Z. Writing in 1962, Harold J. Leavitt called for the use of "differentiating" approaches to structure and management, based on traditional and "newer" concepts, but did not use the term theory Z; see "Management According to Task: Organizational Differentiation," *Management International,* 2 (1962), pp. 13–22. On September 4, 1961, Raymond A. Katzell gave the presidential address to the Division of Industrial Psychology, American Psychological Association and, after referring to McGregor's theory X and theory Y, called for the use of theory alpha and omega, which combined the best features of McGregor's opposites; see *American Psychologist,* 17 (February 1962), pp. 102–108. Later, Lyndall F. Urwick specifically discussed what Leavitt generally, and Katzell more specifically, had addressed; see "Theory Z," *S. A. M. Advanced Management Journal,* 35:1 (January 1970), pp. 14–21.

121. Jay W. Lorsch and Paul R. Lawrence, ed., *Studies in Organization Design* (Homewood, Ill.: Irwin and Dorsey Press, 1970), p. 1.

122. Conversation of January 16, 1986, between Lt. J. Bonander, Palo Alto Police Department, and C. R. Swanson.

We trained hard . . . but it seemed that every time we were beginning to form up into teams we would be reorganized . . . I was to learn later in life that we tend to meet any new situation by reorganizing and a wonderful method it can be for creating the illusion of progress while providing confusion, inefficiency and demoralization.

PETRONIUS, 210 B.C.

Concepts of Police Organizational Design

Introduction

In the previous chapter the major theoretical concepts associated with organizations and the ways in which they function were covered. In this chapter, further attention is given to how these theories actually work in police organizations and additional related concepts are presented. Attention is also focused on line and staff relationships in police departments, why they evolved as they have, some of the reasons for the dissension that results from them, and some methods by which this dissension can be eliminated or at least minimized.

Organizing: An Overview

Police administrators modify or design the structure of their organization in order to fulfill the mission which has been assigned to the police. An organizational chart reflects the formal structure of task and authority relationships which has been determined to be most suited to accomplishing the police mission. The process of determining this formal structure of task and authority relationships is termed organizing. The major concerns in organizing are: 1) identifying what jobs need to be done, such as conducting the initial investigation, performing the latent or followup investigation, and providing for the custody of physical evidence seized at the scene of a crime; 2) determining how to group the jobs, such as those responsible for patrol, investigation, and the operation of the property room; 3) forming grades of authority, such as officer, detective, corporal, sergeant, lieutenant and captain; and 4) equalizing responsibility and authority, illustrated by the example that if a sergeant has the responsibility to supervise seven detectives, that sergeant must have sufficient authority to properly discharge that responsibility or he or she cannot be held accountable for any results.[1]

Specialization in Police Agencies

Central to this process of organizing is determining the nature and extent of specialization. Some 2,300 years ago, Plato observed that "each thing becomes . . . easier when one man, exempt from other tasks, does one thing."[2] Specialization or the division of labor is also one of the basic features of traditional organizational theory.[3] As discussed more fully later in this chapter, specialization produces different groups of functional responsibilities and the jobs allocated to meet those different responsibilities are staffed or filled with people who are believed to be especially qualified to perform those jobs. Thus, specialization is crucial to effectiveness and efficiency in large organizations. Yet, specialization makes the organizational environment more complex by complicating communication, by increasing the number of units from which cooperation must be obtained, and by creating conflict due to conflicting interests and loyalties. Too, specialization creates greater need for coordination and therefore additional hierarchy and can lead to the creation of narrow jobs which confine the incumbents and stiffle their willingness or capacity to work energetically in support of the police department's goals. Police departments are not insensitive to the problems of specialization and attempt through various schemes to avoid the alienation of employees. Personnel can be rotated to different jobs, they can be given additional responsibilities which challenge them, they can be involved in organizational problem solving such as through the use of quality circles, and the police department can try different forms of organizational structures. Thus, while specialization is an essential feature of large scale organizations, any benefits derived from it have their actual or potential costs.

One of the first police executives to systematically explore the relationship between specialization and the organizational structure was O. W. Wilson.[4] He noted that most small departments do not need to be concerned with widely developed specialization because in them the patrol officer is a jack-of-all-trades. Conversely, in large departments particular tasks (such as traffic enforcement and criminal investigation) are assigned to special units and/or individuals within the organization. There are a number of advantages to specialization in large departments:[5]

Placement of Responsibility. The responsibility for the performance of a given task can be placed on specific units or individuals. For instance, a traffic division is responsible for the investigation of all traffic accidents and a patrol division is responsible for all requests for general police assistance.

Development of Expertise. A narrow field of interest or attention can be the subject of specialized training; illustratively, a homicide detective could be sent to a forensic pathology class to further develop his or her investigative expertise. Further, the repetition of a task can develop a high degree of skill and ability. One example of such expertise in a large police agency is the Special Weapons and Tactics (SWAT) team that trains regularly to respond to critical incidents such as takeovers by terrorists or hostage situations.

Promotion of Group Esprit de Corps. Any group of specially trained individuals sharing similar job tasks, and to some degree dependent on each other for success, tend to form a highly cohesive unit with high morale.

Increased Efficiency and Effectiveness. Specialized units show a higher degree of proficiency in job task responsibility. For instance, a white collar fraud unit will ordinarily be more successful in investigating a complex computer fraud than a general detective division.

Specialization appears to be a sure path to operational effectiveness. It allows each employee to acquire expertise in one particular area so as to maximize his or her contribution to the overall department. However, as noted earlier, specialization has also been associated with increased friction and conflict within police departments. As units such as traffic, detective, and SWAT teams develop, an increase in job factionalism and competition also develops. The end result may be a decrease in a

FIGURE 4-1 Specialized patrol unit discusses geographical features of an area before saturation procedure in an effort to apprehend a rapist. [Courtesy of Maricopa County Sheriff's Office, Phoenix, Arizona.]

department's overall job performance as individuals within each group show loyalty primarily or only to their own unit. This traditional problem may be observed in the relationship between patrol officers and detectives. Patrol officers are sometimes reluctant to give information to detectives because they feel detectives will take credit for their work. Specialization also increases the number of administrative and command relationships, complicating the overall organizational structure. Additionally, each unit requires a competent leader. In some instances this competent leader must also be a qualified specialist. A thorny problem here is when the specialist does not qualify for the rank usually needed to head a major unit. An example of such a problem is observed in the staffing of an air patrol unit wherein the commanding officer may be a lieutenant or sergeant because that individual is the highest-ranking officer with a pilot's license. In this case, the level of expertise (high) does not coincide with the level of rank (lower) which may cause difficulties when trying to deal with other commanding officers of units who hold the rank of captain or major.

Finally, specialization may hamper the development of a well-rounded police program. As specialization increases, the resources available for general uniformed patrol invariably decrease, often causing a lopsided structure wherein the need for general police services are second to the staffing of specialized programs and units.[6]

Hierarchy: Spans of Control and Grades of Authority

A police administrator's potential to personally and successfully direct the efforts of others is greater than one person and less than infinity. At the same time, the principle of hierarchy requires that each lower level of an organization be supervised by a higher level. The span of control recognizes both the limitations on potential and the importance of the principle of hierarchy. The span of control is the number of subordinates a police administrator can personally direct effectively. Depending on the nature of the activities performed by subordinates, the skills of the subordinates, their educational level, their experience, and other variables, some police administrators can effectively direct a relatively large number of officers, whereas others are fully employed supervising only a few. As a rule of thumb, seven is generally regarded as the upper limit one person can effectively supervise. Decisions regarding span of control directly influence the number of levels in the organization hierarchy and, hence, its complexity. Recently, the term *span of management* instead of *span of control* has been used to describe the number of personnel a supervisor can personally manage effectively. The term *span of management* is broader than *span of control* and also encompasses factors relating to an individual's capacity to directly oversee the activities of others, such as a police manager's ability, experience, and level of energy.[7]

The principle of hierarchy requirement that each lower level of organization be supervised by a higher level results not only in the use of multiple spans of control, but also different grades of authority which increase at each successively higher level of the organization. This authority flows downward in the organization as a formal grant of power from the chief of police to those selected for leadership positions. These different grades of authority produce the chain of command. Although there are many similarities from one department to another, the American police service does not have a uniform terminology for grades of authority and job titles.[9] In recent years some police departments have moved away from using traditional military style ranks and have adopted, instead, alternative titles as summarized in Table 4-1.

TABLE 4-1   Traditional Police Ranks versus Alternative Titles

Traditional ranks	Alternative titles
Chief of Police	Director
Deputy Chief	Assistant Director
Colonel	Division Director
Major	Inspector
Captain	Commander
Lieutenant	Manager
Sergeant	Supervisor
Detective	Investigator
Corporal	Senior Officer/Master Patrol Officer
Officer	Public Safety Officer/Agent

However, in many departments there remains a distinction between rank and title.[8] In these, rank denotes one's place in terms of grade of authority or the rank hierarchy, while title indicates an assignment. Where this distinction is made, a person holding the title of "Division Director," for example, may be a captain, major, or colonel in terms of the rank hierarchy.

Organizational Structure and Design

Tansik and Elliott suggest that when we consider the formal structure (or pattern of relationships) of an organization, we typically focus on two areas:

1. The formal relationship and duties of personnel in the organization, which include the organizational chart and job descriptions;
2. The set of formal rules, policies, or procedures, and controls that serve to guide the behavior of organizational members within the framework of the formal relationships and duties.[10]

Organizational design focuses on two spatial levels of differentiation—vertical and horizontal, depicted in Figure 4-2. Vertical differentiation is based on levels of authority, or positions holding formal power within the organization; Table 4-2 reflects one range of vertical differentiation found in police agencies. Persons with vertical authority have the power to assign work and to exercise control to ensure job performance.[11] In Figure 4-2 the deputy chief has a span of control of three, all of whom are captains, and all to whom he or she can give assignments and control.

Horizontal differentiation, on the other hand, is usually based on activity. However, in some cases, horizontal differentiation is based on specific projects or even geographical distribution. For instance, many state police departments are responsible for large geographical areas. Their organizational structure often reflects horizontal differentiation based on location rather than function. Some of the more common ways in which activities of personnel are grouped within an organization (on a horizontal dimension) are as follows:

Grouping by Style of Service.   A police department usually has a patrol bureau and a detective bureau. The grouping of uniformed patrol officers on the one hand and of plainclothes investigators on the other illustrates how the former are grouped

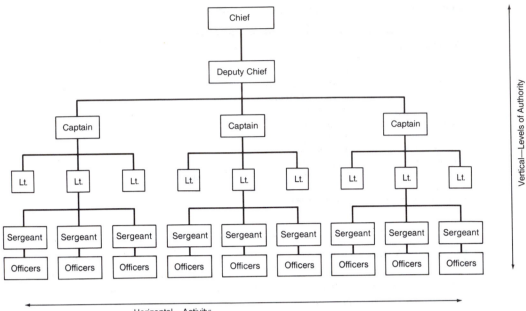

FIGURE 4-2. Organizational chart showing vertical and horizontal levels of differentiation. In some departments, especially large ones, a number of other ranks may be present within the chart.

because of the nature of their services (conspicuous, preventive patrol, and preliminary investigations), and how the latter are grouped also because of this same principle (follow-up investigations). This form of grouping also takes advantage of specialization of knowledge and skill and permits the pinpointing of responsibility for results.

Grouping by Geography. Where activities are widespread over any given area, it may be beneficial to provide local command. Instances of this type of operation are large city precincts or district-type operations as well as state police posts that are located throughout a state. An example of this appears in Figure 4-3B, later in this chapter. Even in the headquarters building, activities that are related usually share the same floor. Instances of this arrangement are records, communications, and crime analysis in close proximity to each other. This permits supervisors to become familiar with operating problems of related units and to coordinate the various efforts by more direct and immediate control.

Grouping by Time. This grouping occurs when the need to perform a certain function or service goes beyond the normal work period of a single eight-hour shift. Other shifts are needed to continue the effort. The division of the patrol force into three platoons each of which is responsible for patrolling the city during an eight-hour period, is an example of this differentiation process. This form of grouping tends to create problems of coordination and unity of direction because top administrators work normal day hours whereas many of their officers perform their functions on the evening and midnight shifts. The need to delegate authority becomes critical under these circumstances.

Grouping by Process. This involves the placing of all personnel who use a given type of equipment in one function. Examples of this include stenographic pools, crime laboratory personnel placed in a section to handle certain types of scientific equipment, and automotive maintenance units. This type of grouping lends itself to expertise involving a single process and makes the most efficient use of costly equipment.[12,13]

Top-Down Versus Bottom-Up Approaches

The level of complexity within a police organization is largely determined by the amount of horizontal and vertical differentiation that exists.[14] Size is often, but not necessarily related to complexity. Some organizations, even relatively small police departments, can be highly differentiated and quite complex in organizational design.

According to Hodge and Anthony, the differentiation process can occur in two basic ways in police agencies.[15] First, the "bottom-up" or synthesis approach focuses on combining tasks into larger and larger sets of tasks. For instance, a police officer's tasks may primarily involve routine patrol, but would dramatically increase in complexity when the officer is assigned preliminary investigative duties. Tasks become more complex and therefore require additional and varied levels of supervision and accountability. The "bottom-up" approach is shown in Figure 4-3A. Second, the "top-down" or analysis approach looks at the overall work of the organization at the top and splits this into increasingly more specialized tasks as one moves from the top to the bottom of the organization. The "top-down" approach considers the overall police mission—to protect and to serve the public. At the top level of a police agency this can be defined into various administrative tasks such as budgeting, political maneuvering, and leadership, whereas at the street level, such a mission is carried out through activities such as patrol and arrest. This type of approach is shown in Figure 4-3B.

Both approaches are commonly found in police organizations. The "top-down" analysis is often used in growing organizations since it is easy to visualize the set of tasks to be accomplished and then to break these sets down into specific tasks and subtasks. The "bottom-up" approach is often used during periods of retrenchment where organizational growth has declined, because combining tasks such as those found in patrol and detective bureaus can consolidate jobs or even units.

Flat Versus Tall Structure

Some organizations have narrow spans of management with tall structures and many levels, whereas others reduce the number of levels by widening the span of management at each level. Many narrower spans of control make a police department "taller." Show in Figure 4-4A, the California Highway Patrol (CHP) appears to have five levels. These levels are commissioner, deputy commissioner, assistant commissioner, field division chief, and area office commander. From a more functional perspective, each area office also has a chain of command consisting of four layers—captain, lieutenant, sergeant, and officer. Thus, when the rank layers in the area offices are considered, the CHP is a tall organization with a number of different levels of authority. Seven to nine levels of rank is fairly typical of large police organizations. Figure 4-4B displays each CHP area office by geographical grouping as described earlier in this chapter.

The complexity of a police department is increased by the proliferation of levels because they can negatively affect communication up and down the chain of command.

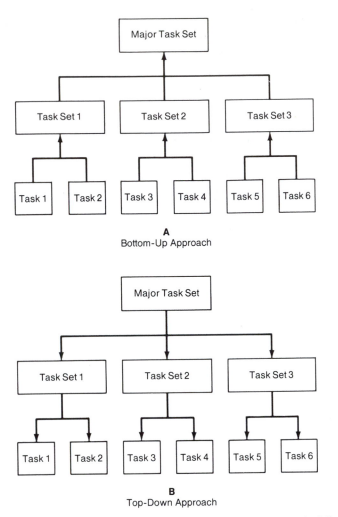

A
Bottom-Up Approach

B
Top-Down Approach

FIGURE 4-3. The bottom-up and top-down approaches to building structure around differentia-tion. [Source: B. J. Hodge and W. P. Anthony, *Organizational Theory: An Environmental Approach* Boston, Mass: Allyn & Bacon, 1979, p. 250.]

For example, during urban riots police departments found that an initially small incident grew rapidly beyond the ability of a small group of officers to control it. The process to get approval from senior police officials to send additional officers took so long that by the time the officers arrived at the scene, the once small incident had grown into an uncontrollable riot. Thus, most departments shifted the authority to deploy large numbers of police officers downward. In some cases this went all the way to the individual police officer at the scene. This example illustrates several important principles:

1. Narrow spans of control make police departments taller;
2. Taller organizations are complex and may react slowly during crisis situations as effective communication is hampered by the number of different levels present within the chain of command; and
3. Successful tall departments must develop policies and procedures that overcome problems created by increased complexity.

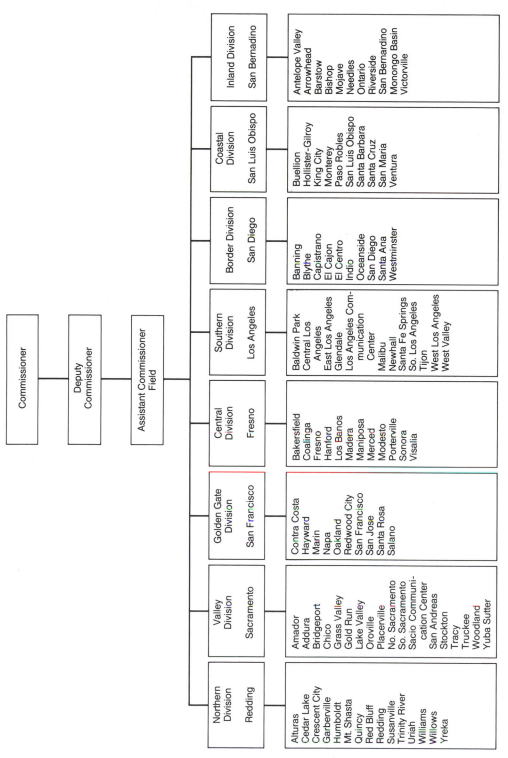

FIGURE 4-4A. Organizational chart for the California Highway Patrol (Field) with modification, showing five levels of control. [Courtesy California Highway Patrol, Sacramento, California, 1986.]

CHP GEOGRAPHICAL ORGANIZATION

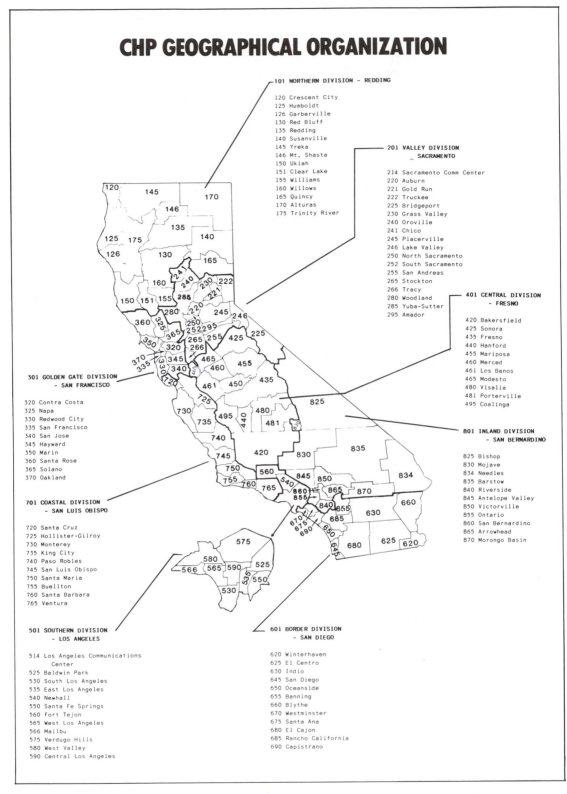

101 NORTHERN DIVISION - REDDING

120 Crescent City
125 Humboldt
126 Garberville
130 Red Bluff
135 Redding
140 Susanville
145 Yreka
146 Mt. Shasta
150 Ukiah
151 Clear Lake
155 Williams
160 Willows
165 Quincy
170 Alturas
175 Trinity River

201 VALLEY DIVISION
    _ SACRAMENTO

214 Sacramento Comm Center
220 Auburn
221 Gold Run
222 Truckee
225 Bridgeport
230 Grass Valley
240 Oroville
241 Chico
245 Placerville
246 Lake Valley
250 North Sacramento
252 South Sacramento
255 San Andreas
265 Stockton
266 Tracy
280 Woodland
285 Yuba-Sutter
295 Amador

401 CENTRAL DIVISION
    - FRESNO

420 Bakersfield
425 Sonora
435 Fresno
440 Hanford
455 Mariposa
460 Merced
461 Los Banos
465 Modesto
480 Visalia
481 Porterville
495 Coalinga

801 INLAND DIVISION
    - SAN BERNARDINO

825 Bishop
830 Mojave
834 Needles
835 Barstow
840 Riverside
845 Antelope Valley
850 Victorville
855 Ontario
860 San Bernardino
865 Arrowhead
870 Morongo Basin

301 GOLDEN GATE DIVISION
    - SAN FRANCISCO

320 Contra Costa
325 Napa
330 Redwood City
335 San Francisco
340 San Jose
345 Hayward
350 Marin
360 Santa Rosa
365 Solano
370 Oakland

701 COASTAL DIVISION
    - SAN LUIS OBISPO

720 Santa Cruz
725 Hollister-Gilroy
730 Monterey
735 King City
740 Paso Robles
745 San Luis Obispo
750 Santa Maria
755 Buellton
760 Santa Barbara
765 Ventura

501 SOUTHERN DIVISION
    - LOS ANGELES

514 Los Angeles Communications
    Center
525 Baldwin Park
530 South Los Angeles
535 East Los Angeles
540 Newhall
550 Santa Fe Springs
560 Fort Tejon
565 West Los Angeles
566 Mailbu
575 Verdugo Hills
580 West Valley
590 Central Los Angeles

601 BORDER DIVISION
    - SAN DIEGO

620 Winterhaven
625 El Centro
630 Indio
645 San Diego
650 Oceanside
655 Banning
660 Blythe
670 Westminster
675 Santa Ana
680 El Cajon
685 Rancho California
690 Capistrano

FIGURE 4-4B. Geographical organization of area offices for the California Highway Patrol. [Courtesy California Highway Patrol, Sacramento, California.]

110

Many police agencies, such as the Dallas Police Department, have redesigned their organizations to reflect larger spans of control or management and hence flatter organizational structures. Figure 4-5 represents only three major organizational levels—chief, bureau, and division. However, while this structure is flatter than the CHP, traditional grades of authority, such as sergeant and other ranks, also continue to exist in the Dallas Police Department. With higher educational standards for entry-level police officers and efforts toward professionalism, police organizational structures may reflect additional changes of this nature. Ultimately, however, the capacity to flatten out police organizational structures depends to no small degree on reducing the number of traditional ranks, a movement sure to be met with resistance because it means less opportunity for upward mobility.

McFarland points out that flat structures associated with wider spans of control offer numerous advantages over the more traditional tall structures. First, they shorten lines of communication between the bottom and top levels. Communication in both directions is more likely to be faster and more timely. Second, the route of communication is more simple, direct, and clear than it is in tall organizations. Third, distortion

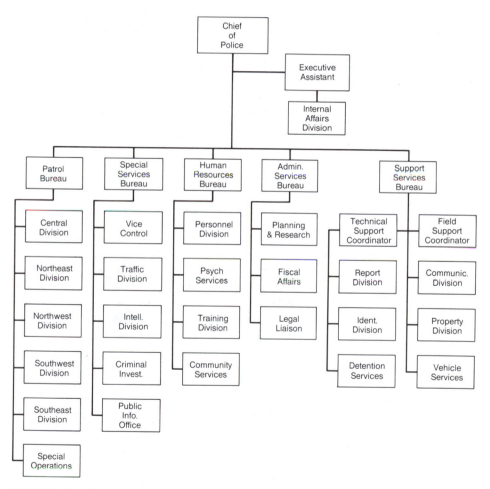

FIGURE 4-5. Flat organizational structure. [Courtesy Dallas Police Department, Dallas, Texas—1985.]

in communication is minimized by a reduced number of people being involved. Finally, and probably most importantly, flat structures are generally associated with employees with higher morale and job satisfaction as compared to employees in tall structured organizations.[16]

Flat structures do, however, place demanding pressures on supervisors, require high-caliber managers, and work best in organizations in which employees are held strictly accountable for measurable and objective results. Considering the role of the police and the continuing problems associated with evaluating police services, such a structure may cause inordinate stress on personnel. Top executives can attempt to direct the development of police agencies in such a way as to maintain structural balance. Some amount of hierarchy is needed for coordination, but the extremely tall police organization is neither needed nor particularly functional. In balance, presently no major city has successfully flattened out both the numbers of organizational layers or units and the traditional rank structure to any significant and continuing degree. Thus, any substantial flattening of a police organization is likely to be an experimentation in organizational design rather than becoming an institutionalized reform.

Types of Organizational Design

Four basic structural types of design may be found within organizations such as police. They are line, line and staff, functional, and matrix. These types exist separately or in combination.

Line Structure

The line structure is the oldest, simplest, and clearest form of organizational design. As illustrated in Figure 4-6, authority flows from the top to the bottom of the organization in a clear and unbroken line, creating a set of superior-subordinate relations in a hierarchy commonly called the chain of command. A primary emphasis is placed upon accountability by close adherence to the chain of command.

The term "line" originated with the military and was used to refer to those units which were to be used to engage the enemy in combat. Line also refers to those elements of a police organization which perform the work which the agency was created to handle. Stated somewhat differently, line units contribute directly to the accomplishment of the police mission. Thus, the primary line elements of a police department are uniformed patrol, investigation, and traffic. Within police agencies the line function may also be referred to as "Operations," "Field Services," or by some similiar designation.

The pure line police organization does not have any supporting elements which are internal or part of it such as personnel, media relations, training, or fiscal management. Instead, the line police organization totally uses its resources to provide services directly to the public. Typically found only in small towns, the line is the most common type of police organization due to the sheer frequency of small jurisdictions. However, most police officers work in larger departments which retain the basic line elements, but to which are added various types of support units. These larger police departments are often referred to as the line and staff form of organization.

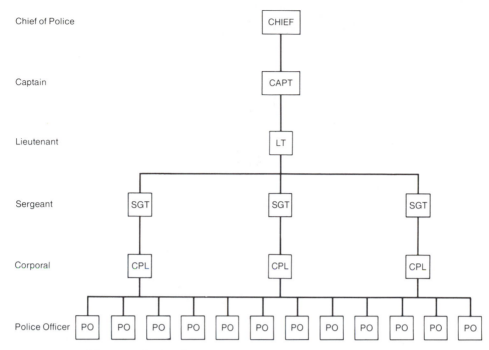

FIGURE 4-6. Line organizational structure in a small police department. [Courtesy of the Tigard Police Department, Tigard, Oregon.]

Line and Staff Structure

As more demands for services are placed on police departments, there is a need to add internal support functions so that the line functions can continue to provide direct services to the public. The addition of support functions to the line elements produces a distinct organizational form: the line and staff structure. The addition of a staff component to the line structure offers a number of advantages because such units are helpful in:

1. providing expert advice to line units in special knowledge areas as demonstrated by the opinions of legal advisors;
2. relieving line managers from performing tasks which they least prefer to do or are least qualified to do such as training and scientific analysis of physical evidence;
3. achieving department-wide conformity in activities that affect the entire organization such as disciplinary procedures; and
4. reducing or eliminating special problems such as corruption because of the greater expertise they bring to bear on the issue and the greater amount of time they have to devote to the problem.[17]

Staff is also referred to as "support" or "administrative" and all three terms are generally used to denote any non-line function. Staff functions will sometimes be further broken down into two types: auxiliary or support and staff services. Under this arrangement, auxiliary or support units, such as communications and crime labora-

TABLE 4-2 Line, Auxiliary, and Staff Functions

Line	Staff	
	Auxiliary	Staff
—Uniformed Patrol	—Crime Laboratory	—Personnel
—Investigations	—Detention and Jail	—Training
—Vice and Narcotics	—Records	—Planning and Research
—Traffic Enforcement	—Identification	—Fiscal/Budgeting
—Juvenile Service	—Communications	—Legal Services
—Crime Prevention	—Property Maintenance	—Media Relations
	—Transportation and Vehicle Maintenance	

tory services, are charged with the responsibility of giving immediate assistance to the operations of line elements. In contrast, staff units, such as personnel and training, provide services which are of less immediate assistance and are supportive of the entire police department. Table 4-2 identifies typical line, auxiliary, and staff functions. Depending on factors such as the history of the police department and the Chief's preferences, there is some variation as to how functions are categorized. Less frequently, legislative enactments may establish the organizational structure, which is another source of variation in how functions are categorized.

Figure 4-7 shows a line and staff structure. In it the Patrol and Detective Bureaus are line functions and the Support Services Division represents staff functions, but without any of the additional breakdown shown in Table 4-2. Note in Figure 4-7 that two types of staff report directly to the Chief of Police: 1) the generalist, illustrated by the Administrative Assistant and 2) the specialist, illustrated by Personnel and Internal Affairs Inspection. Because Fiscal Affairs reports directly to the Administrative Assistant, it is possible that the Administrative Assistant is actually a specialist in that area, but without more information than is shown that is by no means clear.

Functional Structure

The functional structure is one means by which the line authority structure of an organization can be modified. Hodge and Johnson state that functional structure ''is a line and staff structure that has been modified by the delegation of management authority to personnel outside their normal spans of control.''[18] Figure 4-9 shows a police department wherein the Intelligence Unit is responsible to three different captains whose main responsibility is for other organizational units.

The obvious advantage of this type of structure is in the maximum use of specialized units. Successful police work requires the coordination of various subunits or specialized resources to attain a desired objective. All too often, a coordinated effort organization-wide is prevented by competing goals, energies, and loyalties to internal subunits. A classic example can be found between patrol and investigative bureaus:

> Examples of police subunits organized on the basis of purpose of function are investigative bureaus, homicide, robbery, burglary or vice control squads, traffic enforcement details, etc. Each of these units is responsible for some function or purpose of the police mission, e.g., detection, apprehension and prosecution of robbery suspects, prevention of traffic

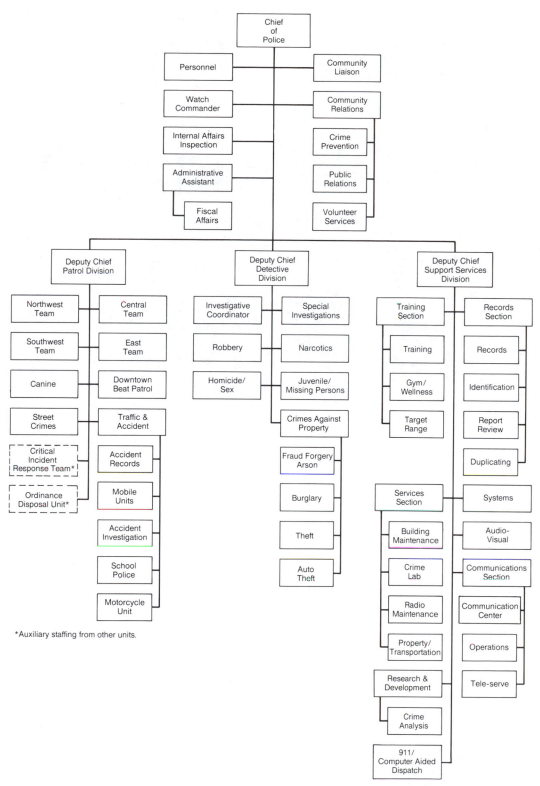

FIGURE 4-7. Line and staff structure in a police department. [Courtesy of the St. Paul, Minnesota, Police Department.]

*Auxiliary staffing from other units.

FIGURE 4-8. Units of the San Francisco's First Auxiliary Police Regiment pass in review in 1942. Although times have changed, many police agencies continue to support line officers with highly trained civilians acting in the capacity of auxiliary police officers. [Courtesy of the San Francisco Archives.]

accidents and apprehension of violators, suppression of vice activity, etc. Organization by purpose facilitates the accomplishment of certain assigned objectives by bringing trained specialists and specialized resources together under a single manager who can be held accountable for attainment of a desired state of affairs. The unit can be judged by what it accomplishes, not by its methodology. This type of organization is effective for gaining energies and loyalties of assigned officers because their purpose is clearly understood.

Difficulties arise when purposes overlap or conflict. A patrol unit and a specialized investigative unit may be jointly charged responsibility for the same task. For example, a local patrol precinct and a specialized robbery squad may share responsibility for reduction of the robbery rate in a certain high-crime area. Each of the units reports to a separate commander, both of whom are at least informally evaluated by how effectively robberies in that area are reduced. Each of the commanders may have his own ideas how this might be accomplished and each wishes to receive credit for improving the crime situation. This type of core-responsibility for the same results negates the advantage of specialization by purpose. It may result in the two units working at cross-purposes, refusing to share critical leads, and duplicating efforts. In this case, competition becomes dysfunctional and cooperation and communications between the patrol and investigative units are impaired.[19]

Some of these problems can be eliminated by police organizations using functional design. By forcing specific units to be responsible to a variety of other unit commanders,

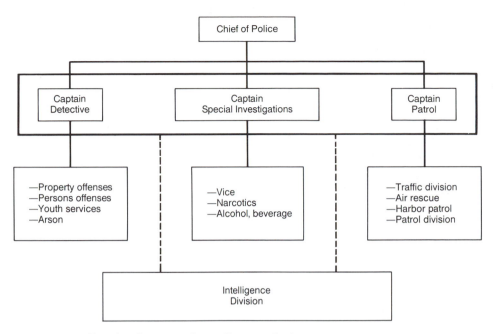

FIGURE 4-9. Functional structure in a police organization.

critical information is assured to reach other line officers. Sharing is promoted while competing loyalties are diminished.

The major disadvantage of the functional design is that it increases organizational complexity. In Figure 4-9, members of the Intelligence Division receive instructions from several superiors. This can result in conflicting directions and thus extensive functionalized structures are seldom found in police agencies. Law enforcement executives should explore the use of the functional design, but be ever cautious to the potential confusion that could result if the process is not properly monitored and controlled.

Matrix Structure

One interesting form of organizational design is variously referred to as "matrix" or "grid" structure. In some cases, the style has been inclusively part of "project" or "product" management. The essence of matrix structure is in the assignment of members of functional areas (e.g., patrol, detective, and support services) to specific projects (e.g., task forces and crime specific programs). The most typical situation in which the matrix approach is used is where a community has had a series of sensationalized crimes and the local police department announces it has formed a "task force" to apprehend the violator. One notable example of this occurred in 1981 in Atlanta, Georgia, where a "task force" comprised of over three hundred federal, state, and local law enforcement officers searched for the murderer of young males in that city. As a result of that combined effort, Wayne Williams was arrested and convicted. The advantage of this type of organizational design is in the formation of specific groups of individuals, combining varied talents and levels of expertise in order to fulfill a designated mission or goal. Quite often, the matrix structure is

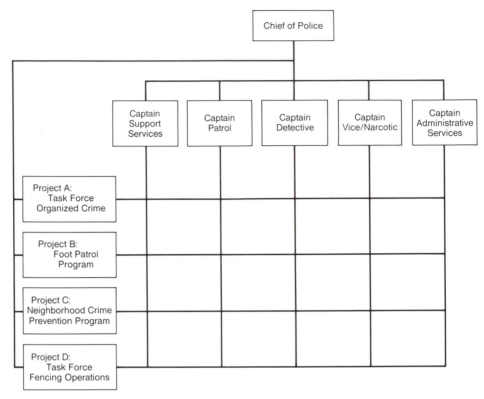

FIGURE 4-10. Matrix structure in a police organization.

used for relatively short periods of time when specific programs are conducted. After the assignment is completed, individuals return to their respective units.

Figure 4-10 displays the matrix design applied to a police organization. This chart reflects the basic line and staff elements found in most police agencies. However, four specific projects have been initiated which requires utilization of personnel from five different units. This then requires each project to organize along the lines suggested by Figure 4-11.

Although the matrix structure greatly increases organizational complexity, it has been successful only in the short term delivery of police services.[20]

Organizational Structure and Team Policing

Team policing is one of the most dynamic experiments that has altered the organizational design of police departments in both the United States and Great Britain. Table 4-3 contrasts key features of traditional and team policing. Team policing is an innovation most closely associated with open systems theory and it has enabled police personnel from various divisions to participate as full partners in the development of better ways to produce a superior police service delivery system.

Generally, team policing involves combining the officers responsible for line operations into a team with a leader. Each officer involved in the team has an opportunity to perform the patrol, traffic, and detective functions, and, where appropriate, the

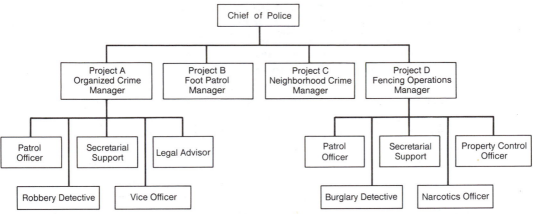

FIGURE 4-11. The detailed organization of projects.

TABLE 4-3 Comparison of Traditional and Neighborhood Team Policing

Traditional	Neighborhood team policing
1. Smallest patrol unit (precinct or division) has 100–250 officers.	1. Team has 20–30 officers.
2. Supervision is quasi-military.	2. Supervision is professional, with consultation, setting of objectives, an in-service training program, encouraging suggestions, permitting the exercise of responsibility within necessary limits.
3. Shift responsibility includes eight-hour tours, with only unit commanders—captains or inspectors—responsible for around-the-clock operations.	3. Team commander is responsible for all aspects of police service on an around-the-clock basis.
4. Assignment is on the basis of the first available car to a call for police service—with priority for emergency calls.	4. Team provides all police service for its neighborhood. Team members are sent out of the neighborhood only in emergencies. Nonteam members take calls in the neighborhood only in emergencies.
5. Officers are rotated to new divisions or assignments.	5. Officers are given extended assignments to a neighborhood.
6. Special police units (tactical, detective, etc.) operate in local neighborhoods without informing local patrol officials.	6. Special police units inform themselves of team goals and, whenever possible, consult in advance with the local team commander.
7. Community relations is seen as ''image building'' (special units for community relations plus speaking engagement for officials).	7. Community relations is seen as an essential patrol function, planned by the team commander and the team, and consists of good police service, friendly on street contacts, and attendance at meetings of various community groups.
8. Reactive policing (responding to calls) or aggressive policing (stop and frisk and street interrogations) are prevalent.	8. Decentralized planning (crime analysis, use of plainclothes or special tactics, investigations, preventive programs, referral programs, service activities).
9. Planning is centralized (innovation through orders from the chief or other important officials).	9. Planning is decentralized (innovation by team commanders, subject to review by their superiors).

From Peter Block and David Specht, *Neighborhood Team Policing* (Washington, D.C.: U.S. Government Printing Office, 1973), p. 2.

specialized functions of narcotics and vice, and juvenile control. Community relations is not considered as a specialization, since this function is considered the responsibility of every police officer. Each team is assigned a permanent sector or geographic area and is totally responsible for that area. Authority for internal team assignments, scheduling, and complete police service is given to the team leaders. The team is held strictly accountable for police service in its assigned area.[21]

A number of police departments have experimented with team policing, and the results have been mixed. In New York City; Dayton, Ohio; and Holyoke, Massachusetts; the programs were failures.[22] In New York City, officers continued to police in conventional ways, and low officer morale undermined the programs, as did similar problems in Dayton.[23] On the other hand, San Diego has reported success in redefining the role of officers and in improving work load management, and data from Rochester, New York, reveal improvements in crime control and investigative effectiveness. Furthermore, police from Albany, New York, and Los Angeles indicate that team policing was a qualified success in those cities in improving community attitudes about the police.[24] A repeated theme in analyses of the failure of some attempts at team policing has been the opposition of middle managers, because team policing reduces specialization and the numbers of levels in an organization, negating the importance of middle managers.

Although team policing has lost much of the luster it had during the mid-1970s, some of its failures may be more the consequence of poorly conducted organizational change than of the concept itself. There is also some limited research evidence that suggests that the implementation of team policing in large cities, but not necessarily smaller ones, may produce short-run benefits that ''wash out'' over time as the latent power of bureaucracy asserts itself;[25] Michels's ''iron law of oligarchy'' states that modern large-scale organizations tend toward centralization, even if this runs contrary to the ideals and intentions of both the leaders and the led.[26] Large police departments require a certain amount of specialization to handle diverse tasks efficiently, such as examining various types of physical evidence, and the amount of hierarchy required to coordinate the various specialized parts produces a tendency toward centralization.

Line and Staff Relationships in Police Agencies

The rapid growth in size of many police agencies has been accompanied by a corresponding rapid growth in specialization and a need for the expansion of staff services to provide support for operating units. This expansion and division of responsibility, which occurs in all police departments except those which are a pure line form of organization, is sometimes fraught with difficulty and dissension. If left uncorrected, these conditions will have a serious negative effect on both the quality and quantity of service a police agency is able to deliver to its citizens. The following represent some of the major causes of conflict between line and staff:

The Line Point of View

Some of the basic causes of organizational difficulties, as line operations view them, is that staff personnel attempt to assume authority over line elements instead of supporting and advising them.[27] Line commanders feel that the chief looks to them for accountability of the operation; therefore, staff personnel should not try to control their operation because they are not ultimately responsible for handling line problems. Another commonly heard complaint is that staff personnel sometimes fail to give sound advice because their ideas are not fully thought out, not tested, or "too academic." This attitude is easy for line commanders to develop because of the belief that staff personnel are not responsible for the ultimate results of their product and therefore propose new ideas too quickly.

Communications problems sometimes emerge between the staff specialist and line commanders. Staff personnel on occasion fail to explain new plans or procedures and do not give line commanders sufficient time to propose changes. For example, a major staff project was installed in a patrol operation after only a very brief period of time had passed from its announcement until the starting date. Some attempts were made to prepare the personnel for the project by the use of general orders and memos, but this was left to line supervisors to do, and they did not have enough information to fully explain the new program. This resulted in confusion. Individual officers were unsure of what they were to do, so they did little. It took several weeks to recognize the problem and several more weeks to explain, train, and guide the personnel to operate under the new plan. After a three-month delay, the plan began to show results. However, the crime picture for this period was the worst in four years. The chief placed the blame at his precinct commanders' doors. They, in turn, blamed staff for poor preparation and lack of coordination.

Line commanders frequently claim that staff personnel take credit for successful operations and point the finger of blame at the line commander when programs fail. In one department a new report-writing program was installed under staff auspices. This program was designed to improve the statistical data that the staff group would use in preparing the various departmental reports and also to help the patrol commander to evaluate patrol personnel. During the first year of the program several flaws showed up that prompted staff to write a report which stated that the patrol supervisors were not checking the reports carefully, and as a result erroneous information was appearing that made evaluation impossible. A retraining program was instituted and the defects were ironed out. The personnel assigned to do the training then wrote a report taking full credit for the improvement. The commander of the patrol division took a rather dim view of this self-congratulatory report since he along with some of his subordinates worked very closely with the training section in formulating the retraining program.

Operational commanders sometimes express the concern that staff personnel do not see the "big picture" because they have only limited objectives which reflect their own nonoperational specialties. For example, the personnel unit of one police department developed a test for the rank of lieutenant. Most of the sergeants who took the examination did poorly. Many became frustrated and angry because they had built up fine work records and believed that the examination procedure failed to accurately measure their potential ability for the rank of lieutenant. The members of the personnel unit who developed the examination procedure were not sympathetic and suggested that the department just did not have the caliber of personnel who could pass a valid examination. The line commanders claimed that the personnel unit did not know enough about the department's needs, and if they would put more effort into helping instead of "figuring out reasons why we're no good, then we'd be better off."

The Staff Viewpoint

Staff personnel contend that line commanders do not know how to use staff. Instead of utilizing their analytical skills, staff personnel feel that line commanders simply want to use them as writers. As an example, in one medium-sized department, the robbery case load was increasing at an alarming rate. When staff was approached to work on the problem, the detective chief told them how he saw the problem, asked them to prepare an order for his signature setting out the changes as he saw them, and refused any staff personnel the opportunity to contact the operating field units to determine what the problems were as they saw them.

Many staff personnel also feel that line officers are shortsighted and resist new ideas. As an example, a department had recently expanded and numerous personnel were promoted, but some of the personnel promoted to administrative and executive positions could not function effectively because they had not been properly trained to assume their new roles and responsibilities. The results were inefficiency and personal conflict. The planning and research officer had much earlier wanted to install a training program for career development for the ranks of lieutenant and above so there would be a trained group to choose from when needed. The planning and research officer blamed the line commanders for being shortsighted and not cooperating earlier to develop career development programs.

Solutions

The problems of line and staff relationships can be corrected. What is needed is: (1) a thorough indoctrination and training program and (2) clear definitions as to the task of each.

The line is principally responsible for successful operations of the department and therefore they must be responsible for operational decisions affecting them. Staff, on the other hand, exists to assist the line in reaching objectives by providing advice and information when requested to do so. This does not, however, prohibit staff from volunteering advice it believes is needed.

The use of staff assistance is usually at the option of line commanders but they must recognize that the chief can decide to use staff services to review any operation and that this decision is binding. As an example, a planning and research officer may be ordered by the chief to determine if patrol officers are being properly utilized. The patrol commander is responsible for making effective use of advice received under such circumstances. If the patrol commander disagrees with staff findings, then an opportunity for reply and review by a higher authority should be available.

Staff exists to help line elements accomplish the objectives of the department. To do this effectively, staff must know what line elements are doing. Illustratively, the personnel officer who does not know what tasks police officers must perform cannot effectively prepare selection standards for the hiring of personnel. Both staff and line must exert effort to ensure that staff stays in contact with what is going on in line units.

Line personnel are concerned primarily with day-to-day operating objectives within the framework of departmental goals. Staff can perform a valuable task for them by thinking ahead toward future problems and operations before they arise. The possibility of a plane crash is a subject that staff, in cooperation with line commanders, can anticipate. Thus, time-consuming planning and the development of orders and procedures can be accomplished by staff well before they are needed.

Line commanders should know what the various staff functions are and what they can contribute to the improvement of the line units. In some departments this can be done at meetings by allowing the staff heads to explain what they can do for the line commanders. At the same time line commanders can make known their expectations about staff support. Such discussions lead to closer coordination and to improved personal relationships that are essential for effectiveness. Staff's ideas will be more readily accepted if they demonstrate an understanding of line operations.

Staff activity deals primarily with change. However, people tend to resist change and ideas that threaten the status quo. Change by itself indicates the possibility that the old way is no longer acceptable. Staff should anticipate and dispel resistance to change by the following:

1. Determining to what extent the change proposed will affect the personal relationships of the people involved. Is the change a major one that will affect the social patterns established in the formal and informal organizations? Can the change be broken down into a series of smaller moves that will have less negative impact than a single large change?

2. Involving those most affected by the change in the early planning stages. When major changes are involved that will modify the relationships between line commanders and the people who work for them, opposition from commanders can be minimized if they participate from the early planning stages. While it may not be possible for everyone to actually participate, the use of representative groups of employees is often effective in helping to facilitate change.

3. Communicating throughout the entire planning stage. The personnel who will be affected by the change will accept it better if: (a) they believe it will benefit them personally—that it will make their work easier, faster, or safer. The change should be tied in as closely as possible with the individual's personal goals and interests—job, family, future; (b) the personnel have an opportunity to offer suggestions, ideas, and comments concerning the change as it affects them—provided these suggestions are sincerely wanted and are given serious consideration; and (c) they are kept informed of the results of the change.

In order to achieve their organizational objectives, a line commander should know how to use staff assistance. The specialized skills of staff people can be used to help achieve these goals more efficiently and economically. By involving staff in the problems of the line, staff personnel can become more effective by learning the line commanders' way of thinking. Line commanders must be able to identify their problems precisely before seeking assistance. They must not vaguely define a problem and then expect the staff unit to do all the work. It is also important for staff to keep other staff informed of decisions that will affect them. As an example, a department was given permission to hire and train 250 new officers, which was double the normal recruit class. The training unit was not advised of this until a week before the class was to start. Subsequently, many problems developed which could have been avoided.

Summary

This chapter elaborated on certain content from Chapter 3 and introduced related concepts. The major concerns in organizing are: 1) dividing the jobs, 2) grouping the jobs, 3) forming grades of authority, and 4) equalizing authority and responsibility. Specialization has both advantages and disadvantages. The advantages include placement of responsibility, development of expertise, promotion of esprit de corps, and increased efficiency and effectiveness. Among the disadvantages of specialization are increased friction and conflict, decreased job performance, complication of the command structure, difficulty in finding sufficient qualified leaders, and hampering the development of a well-rounded police program. Organizational design focuses on two spatial levels of differentiation: vertical, based on levels of authority, and horizontal, based on activity. Some of the ways in which horizontal differentiation occurs is through grouping by: style of service, geography, time, and process. According to Hodge and Anthony, the differentiation process can occur in two basic ways: 1) the bottom-up or synthesis approach and 2) the top-down or analysis approach. Police departments can be considered tall or flat. Tall organizational structures have many different layers which make them more complex and which can impair effective communication. Flat organizations have fewer layers, which is often the result of broadening the span of control, and tend not to suffer from as many communication problems as do the taller departments. Extremely tall organizations are neither needed nor particularly functional, although some amount of hierarchy is needed to coordinate the various parts of a large complex organization. However desireable theoretically, no major city has made significant and continuing inroads into reducing both the layers of organization and the height of the traditional rank structure.

There are four basic types of structural design which may be found in police agencies: (1) line, (2) line and staff, (3) functional, and (4) matrix. These types can exist separately or in combination. Statistically the line form of organization appears most frequently, but most police officers work in a line and staff structure. Team policing is an innovation in the way in which police services are delivered which is closely tied to open systems theory. Many police departments have experimented with team policing and the results have been mixed. One source of opposition to team policing has come from middle managers because team policing tends to flatten out the organization, negating the importance of middle managers. One of the continuing problems in all but the very smallest police departments is the tension between line commanders and staff specialists. Although the basic causes of these organizational difficulties are varied, there are strategies which can be employed as solutions to them.

Discussion Questions

1. What are some of the advantages and disadvantages of specialization?
2. Explain the concepts of vertical and horizontal differentiation as applied to organizational design.
3. What are the common ways of grouping activities?
4. What is meant by ''tall'' and ''flat'' organizational structures?
5. Identify and explain four basic types of structural design found in police agencies.

6. How do traditional and team policing differ?

7. What are the essential differences between line and staff in police departments?

8. What are some of the major sources of tension in line-staff relationships?

Notes

1. S. P. Robbins, *The Administration Process* (Englewood Cliffs, N.J.: Prentice Hall, 1976), pp. 17–18. This discussion of "Organizing an Overview" was adapted from this source.

2. *The Republic of Plato* trans. by A. Bloom (New York: Basic Books, 1968), p. 47.

3. For example, see Luther Gulick and L. Urwick, eds., *Papers on the Science of Administration* (New York: August M. Kelley, a 1969 reprint of the 1937 edition).

4. O. W. Wilson and R. C. McLaren, *Police Administration,* 3d ed. (New York: McGraw-Hill, 1972), p. 79.

5. Ibid., p. 81.

6. Ibid., p. 83.

7. N. C. Kassoff, *Organizational Concepts* (Washington, D.C.: International Association of Chiefs of Police, 1967), p. 22.

8. Wilson and McLaren, *Police Administration,* p. 56.

9. Ibid., p. 56.

10. D. A. Tansik and J. F. Elliot, *Managing Police Organizations* (Monterey, Calif.: Duxbury Press, 1981), p. 81.

11. Ibid., p. 81.

12. B. J. Hodges and W. P. Anthony, *Organizational Theory: An Environmental Approach* (Boston, Mass.: Allyn Bacon, 1979), p. 240.

13. Tansik and Elliot, *Managing Police Organizations,* p. 82.

14. Richard Hall, *Organizations: Structure and Process* (Englewood Cliffs, N.J.: Prentice-Hall, 1972), p. 143.

15. This section is a synopsis of the Nature and Process of Differentiation found in B. J. Hodge and W. P. Anthony, *Organizational Theory: An Environmental Approach* (Boston, Mass.: Allyn Bacon, 1979), p. 249.

16. Darlton E. McFarland, *Management: Foundations and Practices,* 5th ed. (New York: Macmillan, 1979), p. 316.

17. McFarland, *Management,* p. 309.

18. B. J. Hodges and H. J. Johnson, *Management and Organizational Behavior* (New York: John Wiley, 1970), p. 163.

19. Joseph J. Staft, "The Effects of Organizational Design on Communications Between Patrol and Investigation Functions," in U.S. Department of Justice, National Institute of Justice, Research Utilization Program, *Improving Police Management* (Washington, D.C.: University Research Corporation, 1982), p. 243.

20. Lawrence Sherman, Catherine Milton, and Thomas Kelly, *Team Policing: Seven Case Studies* (Washington, D.C.: The Police Foundation, 1973).

21. D. T. Shanahan, *Patrol Administration: Management by Objectives,* 2d ed. (Boston, Mass.: Allyn Bacon, 1985), p. 303.

22. William G. Gay, H. Talmadge Day, and Jane P. Woodward, *Neighborhood Team Policing: Phase I Report* (Washington, D.C.: U.S. Government Printing Office, 1977), p. 40.

23. Ibid., p. 40.

24. Ibid., p. 39, from Table 15.

25. Susette M. Talarico and Charles R. Swanson, "The Limits of Team Policing," *Police Studies,* 3:2 (Summer 1980), pp. 21–29.

26. See Robert Michels, *Political Parties* (New York: Dover, 1959).

27. Kassoff, *Organizational Concepts,* pp. 31–38.

Nothing quenches motivation as quickly as a slovenly boss. People expect and demand that managers enable them to do a good job. . . . People have . . . a right to expect a serious and competent superior.

PETER DRUCKER

Leadership

Introduction

An advertisement asserts that if an organization is having communication problems, it should turn to the telephone company for help, because "the system is the answer." In a similar fashion, for the past two decades police departments, like other organizations, have placed such a strong emphasis on the use of technology (e.g., computers) and on rational management systems (such as special budgeting and decision-making techniques) that leadership has received little attention. When first faced with the "budget crunch," many departments simply tried to use rational analytical tools to decide what programs to cancel or where the budget could be slashed. Faced with reduced resources on the one hand, and a public that needed and demanded quality police services on the other, chiefs of police tried to find ways to improve productivity. This tactic brought the chiefs full circle because leadership reemerged as an important topic. Although technology and rational management techniques unquestionably remain important, the role of leadership in making systems function at a high level has come to the front.

127

Leadership and Performance

The police leader is responsible for three equally important, but essentially different, broad responsibilities:

1. Fulfilling the mission of the police department;
2. Making work productive and subordinates achieving; and
3. Producing impacts.[1]

A number of factors impinge upon how well these responsibilities are met such as the chief's leadership style, community preferences, the resources available, and even how the chief was selected. Police leaders chosen by a competitive process or who are perceived by subordinates in the department as competent, are viewed consistently as having greater expertise and, consequently, have more influence and power.[2] There are, additionally, "habits of minds" that police leaders who meet their three key responsibilities effectively must practice:

1. They know where their time goes and manage it actively. They identify and eliminate things that need not be done at all; they delegate to others things that can be done as well or better by someone else. And they avoid wasting their own time and that of others.[3]
2. They focus on outward contribution. They gear their efforts to results rather than to work. They start out with the question, "What results are expected of me?" rather than with the work to be done, let alone with its techniques and tools.
3. They build on strengths—their own strengths, the strengths of their superiors, colleagues, and subordinates, and the strengths in the situation, that is, on what they can do. They do not build on weakness. They do not start out with the things they cannot do.
4. They concentrate on the few major areas where superior performance will produce outstanding results. They force themselves to set priorities and stay with their priority decision. They know that they have no choice but to do first things first—and second things not at all. The alternative is to get nothing done.
5. They make effective decisions. They know that this is, above all, a matter of system—of the right steps in the right sequence. They know that an effective decision is always a judgment based on "dissenting opinions" rather than on "consensus on the facts." And they know that to make many decisions fast means to make the wrong decisions. What is needed are few, but fundamental, decisions. What is needed is the right strategy rather than razzle-dazzle tactics.

If, as has been suggested, leadership is an intangible, the effects generated by its presence or absence and its character are not. Consider the following examples:

> Police officers, operating a dirty patrol vehicle, approached a motorist they had stopped for a traffic violation. Unkept in appearance, their conversation with the person was correct on the surface, but there was an underlying tone of arrogance.
> A sergeant, already thirty-five minutes late getting off duty, was enroute to the station when a burglary in progress call was given to another unit; he volunteered to help and subsequently was shot to death by two burglars.

The chief of police of a medium-sized city chronically complained to anyone who would listen that his commanders "aren't worth anything" and that he was "carrying the whole department on his back."

A visitor to a city approached an officer walking a beat and asked where the nearest car rental agency could be found; the officer replied "What the hell do I look like, an information booth?" and walked away. The next day she asked an officer standing on a street corner where the First National Bank Building was. The officer took the woman's arm, escorted her across the street and said, "Lady, you see that big building on the corner where we were just standing? Well, if it had fallen, we'd have both been killed by the First National Bank Building."

Based on limited new information, the commander of an investigations bureau reopened the case file on a convicted "no good" who had already served fourteen months for the offense in question. Subsequently, new evidence and a confession resulted in his release and the conviction of another person.

There are many different definitions of what leadership is, each reflecting certain perspectives. For example, leadership may be defined as the characteristics exhibited by an individual or as a function of a position within the police department's hierarchical structure, such as captain. However, a generally accepted definition is that *leadership is the process of influencing organizational members to use their energies willingly and appropriately to facilitate the achievement of the police department's goals.*

The Nature of Leadership, Authority, and Power

The definition of leadership given deserves some analysis. In Chapter 3, the basic rationale for the existence of organizations was given as being that they do those things that people are unwilling or unable to do alone. It therefore follows that police departments, as is true for other organizations, are goal directed. The behavior of its members should be purposeful and in consonance with the department's goals. By "using their energies appropriately," it is meant that morally and legally accepted means are employed in the discharge of duties. The terms *influencing* and *willingly* are related to the concepts of authority and power.

Although these are often treated synonymously, authority and power are allied, but separate, concepts. Authority is a grant made by the formal organization to a position, the incumbent of which wields it in fulfilling his or her responsibilities. The fact that a formal grant of authority has been made does not mean that the person receiving it also is automatically able to influence others to perform at all, let alone willingly as illustrated in the article "Police Balk at Issuing High Penalty Tickets."

Some power to induce performance is inherent in positions of authority. But to a significant degree that power, as suggested by Barnard, is a grant made by the led to the leader. The leader whose subordinates refuse to follow is not totally without power, for subordinates may be given verbal or written reprimands or suspensions, or be forced or expelled from the organization, or be fined, imprisoned, or executed, depending upon the specifics involved.[4] The use of this type of power must be considered carefully; failure to envoke it may contribute to a breakdown in discipline and organizational performance; the employment of it may contribute to morale problems, may

BOX 5-1.

Police Balk at Issuing High-Penalty Tickets

By CHARLES F. HESSER, *Special to The Journal-Constitution*

MIAMI—Remember the good old days when an erring motorist got a lecture and a warning instead of a scowl and a ticket from an attending officer?

Well, they're coming back to Florida—at least parts of it—if the Florida Fraternal Order of Police (FOP) and other assorted law enforcement agencies and individual officers have their way. Why? All because of another goof by the 1977 state legislature in "revising" Florida's nofault auto insurance law.

The legislature hiked fines for most traffic violations from $25 to $57.75—fines for drunken driving, however, went from $262 to $462—ostensibly to reduce insurance premiums for accident-free motorists and to aid victims of violent crime.

The FOP called the state's stiff new traffic fines "unrealistic." The FOP, with its 9,000 members, is urging all of Florida's 15,000 police officers to use more talking than ticketing, and passed a resolution calling for statewide support in repeal of the new law at next year's legislature.

"We urge all officers to use their lawful, discretionary authority whenever possible," said Robert Spiegel, FOP first vice president.

Circumstances that might warrant lectures and warnings, Spiegel said, would include driving "eight or nine" miles an hour above the speed limit, making an "improper left turn" or "narrowly running through a red light."

A policeman would have no leeway, he said, on cases such as reckless driving, drunken driving or excessive speed.

Spiegel explained that the FOP board of directors had acted because the new traffic ticket law, which went into effect July 1, does nothing to try to solve the problem of rising insurance rates and adds "unrealistic penalties to the citizen-consumer and visitors in the form of increased traffic fine surcharges."

The FOP said the new fine schedule is "unnecessarily punitive" and would create "confrontations" between officers and drivers in the form of high-speed chases and more verbal and physical assaults on police officers.

Hialeah Mayor Dale Bennett ordered his city's police department to stop using radar to reduce the number of $57.75 tickets issued for moving traffic violations. He instructed all Hialeah's officers to be "highly selective" when issuing citations.

Individual officers are fearful of talking for publication because of possible departmental discipline. In off-the-record talks, however, they're anything but the prototype of a heartless policeman silently peeling off a ticket while ignoring a motorist's apologies and pleas of poverty.

"There's no way I'm going to give a $57.75 ticket to someone making $125 a week," said a Dade County officer. "That's like taking food out of their mouths. If this law stays in effect, I won't write another traffic ticket for anything less than extreme reckless driving."

But Capt. John Hicks of the Florida Highway Patrol declared:

"This is a bad thing, with the FOP saying they're going to do more talking and less writing. Some habitual violators are going to take advantage of this.

"Then, when some officer does arrest him, he's going to get indignant. This kind of talk is bad for law enforcement."

Source: The *Atlanta Journal—Constitution,* July 24, 1977, p. 2-C.

divert energy from achieving goals, and may have other negative side effects, including calling into question the abilities of the leader involved:

A uniformed officer riding alone informed the radio dispatcher that he was stopping a possibly drunken motorist. His sergeant, who had only been promoted and assigned to the squad two weeks previously, heard the transmission and told the dispatcher that he would back up the officer. When the sergeant, a nine-year veteran of the force, but who had not served in any "street" assignment for the past six years, arrived, a Marine corporal was about to get into a taxi cab. When questioned by the sergeant, the officer who had stopped the Marine as a possible drunk driver related that the corporal had been drinking, but that it was a marginal case and after talking with him, the corporal agreed to park his car and had called the taxi cab from a nearby pay phone.

The sergeant talked to the Marine and concluded that he had drunk sufficiently to be charged with driving under the influence and directed the officer to arrest him. The officer declined and the sergeant, angrily said, "I think you don't want to arrest him because you're an ex-Marine . . . arrest him, that's a direct order." The officer refused again, the sergeant got into his car and left, and the Marine departed in the taxi cab.

Later when the sergeant filed charges for refusal to obey the direct order of a superior, the officer was suspended without pay for two days. The other squad members felt the sergeant was not "streetwise" and had acted in a petty manner. Over time, it became apparent to the sergeant's superiors that he had lost the respect and confidence of the squad and could not regain it. The sergeant was then transferred to a minor staff position where he had responsibility for several functions but actually supervised no one.

Leadership also arises, as demonstrated by the Hawthorne studies, out of the informal side of an organization. Members of a work group give one or more of their members power by virtue of their willingness to follow them. This power may be given on the basis suggested by Weber's charismatic leader; thus, officers may look more to a seasoned and colorful officer in their squad or one who has been decorated several times for heroism than to their sergeant, who represents Weber's rational-legal type of authority. During the late 1960s and 1970s, a variant of this situation was a problem more than occasionally in some departments as younger college-educated officers moved up in rank rapidly, passing less educated veteran officers. Dismissing them as "testtakers," the more experienced officers sometimes used the informal group to vie for leadership with the formally appointed leaders. If, however, the informal leaders support the police department's goals, they can be a significant additive and even help to compensate for mediocre formal leadership.

The Power Motivation of Police Managers

Power is an indispensable dimension of police departments. As we have seen, power is both a grant made from the led to the leader as well as an extension of the formal authority granted to a particular position such as sergeant. Power, however, is not always used for the same purpose; the term *power motivation* refers to the reasons, intentions, and objectives which underlie a police manager's use of power.[5]

Leadership requires that a person have an appreciation of the importance of influencing the outcome of events and the desire to play a key role in that process. This need for impact must be greater than either the need for personal achievement or the need to be liked by others. A police leader's desire for impact may take either of two forms; it may be oriented primarily toward (1) the achievement of personal gain and aggrandizement (a personalized power motivation), or (2) the need to influence others' behavior for the common good of the police department (a socialized power motivation). Additionally, police leaders have some desire to be accepted and liked, which is termed the *affiliation need*. Affiliation needs and aspirations are not power needs because they reflect a greater preoccupation with being accepted and liked than with having an impact upon events.

Table 5-1 summarizes the differences between managers who use personalized versus those who use social power. Hall and Hawker have developed an instrument for measuring personalized power, socialized power, and affilative needs. In Figure 5-1 the shaded portions of the personalized, socialized, and affiliative columns represents what Hall and Hawker regard, based on research by McClelland and Burnham, as the theoretically ideal profile for managerial success; note that the ideal profile contains a mix of power motivations and affiliative needs. Affiliative needs serve as a check on power motivations, helping to keep them in proper proportions. In the application of Figure 5-1, differences of more than 25 percentile points are required to denote a genuine preference for one approach in comparison to another. The dotted horizontal lines across the personalized, socialized, and affiliative columns reflect the scores of forty-three police managers from one medium-sized police agency and are intended as an illustration rather than as a generalization about police managers. Among the observations that can be made about the profile of those forty-three police managers as a group are (1) the preference for the use of personalized power as opposed to socialized power, and (2) a desire to be liked (affilative needs) which closely approximates their preference for personalized power. This suggests that as a group these police managers are somewhat ambiguous about how to use power. They want to be seen as strong and self-reliant, but also liked. Their scores also reflect the absence of a clearly unified approach to the use of power as well as the lack of a crystallized philosophy of management and are probably seen as somewhat inconsistent by their subordinates because of this.

TABLE 5-1

Police managers with personalized power tend to be:	Police managers with socialized power tend to be:
• Impulsive and erratic in their use of power	• Inhibited and self-controlled in their use of power
• Rude and overbearing	• Respectful of others' rights
• Exploitative of others	• Concerned with fairness
• Oriented toward strength	• Oriented toward justice
• Committed to the value of efficiency	• Committed to the value of working per se
• Proud	• Egalitarian
• Self-reliant; individualists	• Organization-minded; joiners
• Excited by the certitudes of power	• Ambivalent about power
• Competitive	• Collaborative
• Concerned with exceptionally high goals	• Concerned with realistic goals
• Defensive—protective of own sense of importance	• Non-defensive—willing to seek help
• Inspirational leaders	• Builders of systems and people
• Difficult to replace—leave a group of loyal subordinates dependent on their manager	• Replaceable by other managers—leave a system intact and self-sustaining
• Sources of direction, expertise and control	• Sources of strength for others

Personalized versus Social Power (From Jay Hall and James Hawker, ''Interpreting Your Scores from the Power Management Inventory,'' © Teleometrics International, The Woodlands, Texas, 1981). Special permission for reproduction is granted by the authors and the publisher, all rights reserved. The Power Management Inventory can be used with a variety of occupations.

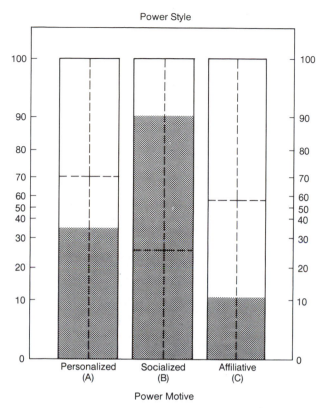

Power Style

FIGURE 5-1. The Mean Power Management Inventory Scores for forty-three police managers from one medium-sized department are indicated by the horizontal dotted lines and are contrasted from the ideal scores that are depicted by the shaded areas. The figure is from Jay Hall and James Hawker, ''Interpreting Your Scores from the Power Management Inventory,'' © Teleometrics International, The Woodlands, Texas, 1981, special permission for reproduction of the figure is granted by the authors and the publisher, all rights reserved. The data on the police managers are unpublished and in the files of C. R. Swanson.

The Leadership Skill Mix

As depicted in Figure 5-2 a police department can be divided into three levels and various mixes of three broad categories of skills associated with them.[6] The ranks indicated at each of the three levels of the organization identified in the figure are illustrative only and will vary depending upon departmental size and other factors. Additionally, in the discussion of these skills that follows, it should be noted that it is possible to include only a few of the many examples available.

Human Relations Skills

Human relations skills involve the capacity to interrelate positively with other people and are used at all levels of a police department. Examples include motivation, conflict resolution, and interpersonal communication skills. The single most important

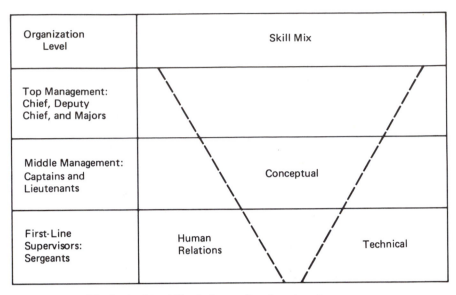

Organization Level	Skill Mix
Top Management: Chief, Deputy Chief, and Majors	
Middle Management: Captains and Lieutenants	Conceptual
First-Line Supervisors: Sergeants	Human Relations · · · · · Technical

FIGURE 5-2. The leadership skill mix in a police department.

human relations skill is communication; without it, nothing can be set in motion, and programs underway cannot be guided.

As one progresses up the rank hierarchy of a police department, typically one becomes responsible for more people but has fewer people reporting directly to him or her. The human relations skills of a police department's top managers remain important, however, as they are used to win political support for the agency's programs and to obtain the resources necessary to operate them. In particular, the chief's human relations skills are critical, as he is the key representative of the department to the larger environment. The way in which he "comes across" is to a certain degree the way in which some significant others—such as the city manager and members of city council—are going to come to regard the police department. The question of the fairness of that fact aside, the practical implication is that the chief must be aware and fulfill his symbolic leadership role.

Within the department, top management must communicate their goals and policies downward and be willing to receive feedback about them. As midlevel managers, lieutenants and captains play an important linking function, passing downward in implementable forms the communications they receive from top management and passing upward certain communications received from first-line supervisors. Because sergeants ordinarily supervise directly the greatest numbers of people, they use human relations with great frequency, often focusing on such issues as resolving interpersonal problems and working to gain or maintain the support of the informal group for departmental goals.

Conceptual Skills

Conceptual skills involve the ability to understand and also to interrelate various parcels of information, which often seem unrelated or the meaning or importance of which is uncertain. While this skill is utilized at all levels of the police department, the standards for handling the information become less certain and the level of abstraction necessary to handle the parcels becomes greater as one moves upward. Illustrative is the difference between a sergeant helping a detective to evaluate the legal significance of certain evidence and the chief sorting out and interrelating facts, opinions, and rumors about a productive but controversial police program supported and opposed by some combination of political figures, public interest groups, and the news media.

Technical Skills

Technical skills vary by level within a police department. Uniformed sergeants assigned to field duties must be able to help develop and maintain the skills of subordinates in such areas as the identification, collection, and preservation of physical evidence. As one progresses upward toward middle and top management, the range of technical skills narrows, and conceptual skills come to predominate. In that upward progression, the character of the technical skills also changes from being operations oriented to management oriented and gradually includes new elements, such as budgeting, planning, and the kind of decision making that increasingly requires the use of conceptual skills. To elaborate further, one may not be able to tell by the generic label whether a particular skill is, for example, technical or conceptual. A general understanding of the many aspects of financial management—such as is provided in Chapter 13—creates a conceptual skill, but the actual physical preparation of the budget is a technical skill required of middle-management or first-line supervisors, depending on the size and practices of a specific police department.

Theories of Leadership

Theories of leadership attempt to explain the factors associated with the emergence of leadership or the nature of leadership.[7] Included are (1) "great man" and genetic theories, (2) the traits approach, (3) behavioral explanations, and (4) situational theories.

"Great man" theories were advanced by Thomas Carlyle and Georg Wilhelm Friedrich Hegel.[8] Carlyle believed that leaders were unusually endowed individuals who made history. Reversing the direction of causality, Hegel argued that it was the events that produced the "great man." The "born leader" concept is associated with Francis Galton, who espoused that leaders were the product of genetics.[9]

It has also been maintained that leaders possess certain personality traits; for example, Field Marshal Montgomery believed that, although leaders were made, not born, they had certain characteristics such as an infectious optimism, confidence, intellect, and the ability to be a good judge of character.[10] Goode determined that the following traits were important for successful leadership:

1. The leader is somewhat more intelligent than the average of his followers. However, he is not so superior that he cannot be readily understood by those who work with him.
2. The leader is a well-rounded individual from the standpoint of interests and aptitudes. He tends toward interests, aptitudes and knowledge with respect to a wide variety of fields.
3. The leader has an unusual facility with language. He speaks and writes simply, persuasively and understandably.

4. The leader is mentally and emotionally mature. He has come of age mentally and emotionally as well as physically.

5. The leader has a powerful inner drive or motivation which impels him to strive for accomplishment.

6. The leader is fully aware of the importance of cooperative effort in getting things done, and therefore understands and practices very effectively the so-called social skills.

7. The leader relies on his administrative skills to a much greater extent than he does on any of the technical skills which may be associated directly with his work.[11]

Parenthetically, by administrative skills, Goode seems to mean what has been described previously as conceptual skills. Ralph Stogdill analyzed over two hundred studies in his 1948 and 1974 reviews of traits of leadership and following the second review described a leader as being:

> characterized by a strong drive for responsibility and task completion, vigor and persistence in pursuit of goals, venturesomeness and originality in problem solving, drive to exercise initiative in social situations, self-confidence, and a sense of personal identity, willingness to accept consequences of decision and action, readiness to absorb interpersonal stress, willingness to tolerate frustration and delay, ability to influence other persons' behavior, and capacity to structure social interaction systems to the purpose at hand.[12]

From an organizational standpoint, the traits approach has great appeal: find out who has these characteristics and promote them, and successful leadership will follow. However, C. A. Gibb has concluded that the numerous studies of traits do not reveal any consistent patterns,[13] and Walter Palmer's research does not provide support for the hypothesis that managerial effectiveness is a product of the personality characteristics of the individual.[14]

Other theories of leadership focus on the behavior of managers as they operate. Where trait theories attempt to explain leadership on the basis of what the leader is, behavioral theories try to do the same thing by concentrating on what the leader does.[15] This is referred to as style of leadership, meaning the continuing patterns of behavior as perceived and experienced by others that they utilize to characterize the leader. Various of these approaches are discussed in the section that follows. Although not exclusively, many of the styles reflect elements of scientific management's task-centered and human relations' people-centered orientations.

Situational leadership theories postulate that effective leadership is a product of the fit between the traits or skills required in a leader as determined by the situation in which he or she is to exercise leadership.[16] Illustrative are Frederick Fiedler's contingency model,[17] Robert House's path-goal theory,[18] Robert Tannenbaum and Warren Schmidt's authoritarian-democratic leadership continuum, and Paul Hersey and Kenneth Blanchard's situational leadership theory. The last two are covered in detail in the next section because of their interrelatedness with leadership styles.

Styles of Leadership

General interest in the topic of leadership and the various theories of it have generated both commentary and research on different schemes for classifying styles of leadership.

The purpose of this section is to provide a sense of some ways in which this subject has been treated and to discuss certain of the contributions in this area.

Lewin, Lippitt, and White: Authoritarian, Democratic, and Laissez-faire

Although these three styles of leadership had been identified in earlier works, the 1939 publication of Lewin, Lippitt, and White's classical study of boys' clubs has closely identified these approaches with them.[19]

The contrasting approaches of Lewin, Lippitt, and White's styles is detailed in Table 5-2. Briefly, they may be characterized as follows: (1) the authoritarian leader makes all decisions without consulting subordinates and closely controls work performance; (2) the democratic leader is group oriented and promotes the active participation of subordinates in planning and executing tasks; and (3) the laissez-faire leader takes a "hands-off" passive approach in dealing with subordinates.

White and Lippitt concluded that, although the quantity of work was somewhat greater under the autocratic leader, autocracy could generate hostility and aggression. The democratically controlled groups were about as efficient as the autocratically controlled ones, but the continuation of work in the former did not depend upon the presence of the leader. Under the laissez-faire leader, less work was produced, the

TABLE 5.2 The Authoritarian, Democratic, and Laissez-faire Leadership Styles

Authoritarian	Democratic	Laissez-faire
1. All determination of policy was by the leader.	1. All policies were a matter of group discussion and decision, encouraged and assisted by the leader.	1. Complete freedom for group or individual decision existed, with a minimum of leader participation.
2. Techniques and activity steps were dictated by the authority, one at a time, so that future steps were always uncertain to a large degree.	2. Activity perspective was gained during discussion period. General steps to group goal were sketched, and when technical advice was needed, the leader suggested two or more alternative procedures from which choice could be made.	2. Various materials were supplied by the leader, who made it clear that he or she would supply information when asked. Leader took no other part in work discussion.
3. The leader usually dictated the particular work task and work companion of each member.	3. The members were free to work with whomever they chose, and the division of tasks was left up to the group.	3. Nonparticipation of the leader was complete.
4. The dominator tended to be "personal" in his or her praise and criticism of the work of each member; remained aloof from active group participation except when demonstrating.	4. The leader was "objective" or "fact-minded" in his or her praise and criticism and tried to be a regular group member in spirit without doing too much of the work.	4. Spontaneous comments on member activities were infrequent unless questioned and no attempt to appraise or regulate the course of events.

From Figure 1, p. 32 in *Autocracy and Democracy* by Ralph K. White and Ronald Lippitt. Copyright © 1960 by Ralph K. White and Ronald Lippitt. Reprinted by permission of Harper & Row, Publishers, Inc.; an earlier version of this appears in Kurt Lewin, Ronald Lippitt, and Ralph K. White, "Patterns of Aggressive Behavior in Experimentally Created Social Climates," *The Journal of Social Psychology*, 10 (1939), p. 273.

work quality was poorer, and the work was less organized and less satisfying to members of the group.[20]

Tannenbaum and Schmidt: The Authoritarian-Democratic Leadership Continuum

In 1958, Tannenbaum and Schmidt published the leadership continuum depicted in Figure 5-3.[21] They believed that the successful leader could choose to be more or less directive depending on certain factors:

1. Forces in the manager, such as his or her value system, confidence in subordinates, leadership inclinations, and need for security in uncertain situations.
2. Forces in subordinates, including their needs for independence, readiness to assume greater responsibility, and interests, knowledge, and experience.
3. Forces in the organization, illustrated by prevailing views and practices, the ability of the group to work together effectively, the nature of the problem, and the pressures of time.[22]

Although their work is often simply presented as styles of leadership, by considering such variables and noting that these forces working together might suggest one leadership style instead of another, Tannenbaum and Schmidt's findings reflect a situational approach to leadership.

Downs: Leadership Styles in Bureaucratic Structures

In 1967, Anthony Downs described four types of leader behavior in bureaucratic structures: (1) climbers, (2) conservers, (3) zealots, and (4) advocates.[23]

Climbers are strongly motivated by power and prestige needs to invent new functions to be performed by their unit, particularly functions not performed elsewhere. If climbers can expand their functions only by moving into areas already controlled by others, they are likely to choose ones in which they expect low resistance. To protect their "turf," climbers tend to economize only when the resultant savings can be used to finance an expansion of their functions.[24]

The bias of conservers is toward maintaining things as they are. The longer a person is in the same job and the older one becomes, the lower one assesses his chances for advancement, and the stronger one becomes attached to job security, all of which are associated with the tendency to become a conserver. Climbers may become conservers when they assess their probability for advancement and expansion to be low. Desiring to make their organizational lives comfortable, conservers dislike and resist change.[25]

The peculiarities of the behavior of zealots stems from two sources: (1) their narrow interest and (2) the missionary-like energy that they focus almost solely on their special interest. As a consequence, zealots do not attend to all their duties and often antagonize other administrators by their lack of impartiality and their willingness to trample over all obstacles to further their special interest. Zealots rarely succeed

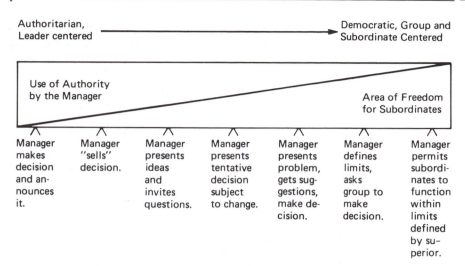

FIGURE 5-3. The authoritarian-democratic continuum.[Reprinted by permission of the *Harvard Business Review*. Exhibit from "How to Choose a Leadership Pattern" by Robert Tannenbaum and Warren H. Schmidt (May–June 1973). Copyright © 1973 by the president and fellows of Harvard College; All rights reserved.]

to high-level positions because of their narrowness and are, consequently, also poor administrators. An exception is when their interest comes into favor and they are catapulted into high office.[26]

Unlike zealots, advocates promote everything under their jurisdiction. To those outside their units, they appear highly partisan, but within their units they are impartial and fair, developing well-rounded programs. Loyal to their organizations, advocates favor innovation. They are also simultaneously more radical and more conservative than climbers. They are more radical in that they are willing to promote programs and views that may antagonize their superiors, if doing so will help their organization. They are more conservative because they are willing to oppose changes from which they might benefit but would not be in the best overall interest of their organization.[27]

Traditional versus Nontraditional Leaders

Traditional versus nontraditional leaders is a simple dichotomy, studies of which have revealed various attributes. As the two studies that follow suggest, however, they are distinguished by the traditionalist's preference for views associated with traditional organizational theory, whereas the nontraditionalists incorporate more thinking from open systems organizational theory.

COHEN: LEADERSHIP STYLES IN THE NEW YORK CITY POLICE DEPARTMENT

Bernard Cohen studied all commanding officers of the New York City Police Department holding the rank of captain or above, a total of 556 managers.[28] Of this number, 535 were white and the balance minorities, including 1 woman. The analysis of data revealed two separate sets of leaders: tradition oriented and reform oriented.

Tradition-oriented commanders had little education beyond high school, they tended to score low on civil service examinations and tests of executive ability, and their career advancement stemmed primarily from their seniority. Tradition-oriented commanders appeared to identify with the rank and file at the expense of top management, and this downward orientation was associated with a general refusal to accept management goals. As with Downs's conservers, they did not strive to get ahead and were satisfied with the organizational status quo. This leadership style is associated with the use of subjectivity and power, the use of street slang, and the expression of superiority over the "college boys" due to the tradition-oriented leader's "wider practical knowledge."

In contrast, Cohen's reform-oriented commanders were "college boys," having attended college or having earned a college degree. Unlike the tradition-oriented commanders who received higher performance evaluations from their superiors, the reform-oriented commanders as a group got poor evaluations, suggesting a certain degree of independence in expressing their views. Younger, and less senior, this group of leaders experienced career advancement in large measure because of their test scores. Reform-oriented commanders valued education and service to the community, favored severe punishment for brutality, corruption, and civil rights violations, and were less authoritarian than the traditionalists. New organizational goals were supported by the reform commanders, who also aspired to become part of upper levels of management. Altogether, reform-oriented leaders possess some of the qualities of Downs's advocates.

PURSLEY: A NATIONAL STUDY
OF POLICE EXECUTIVE LEADERSHIP

In a national study of a sample of police executive leadership, Robert Pursley looked at fifty-eight traditional and seventy-four nontraditional chiefs of police.[29] The nontraditionalist chiefs formed a relatively young, highly mobile, and well-educated group whose career development seems strikingly similar to that of young professional city managers; that is, when a good opportunity for advancement existed elsewhere, a move was made. The traditionalists displayed a very significant need to structure and control the work environment and the work-related activities of their subordinates. Their leadership style reflected a tendency toward centralization, a minimum of delegation, and little authority or power to initiate activities at subordinate levels. As opposed to the more authoritarian stance of the traditionalists, the nontraditionalists revealed a greater receptiveness to delegation and a willingness to accept the input of subordinates, traits associated with a more participatory, democratic approach to leadership.

The following "Interview with a Reform Chief" focuses on the late Victor Cizanckas who died of natural causes in 1981 while chief of police in Stamford, Connecticut. A progressive leader who embodied many of the qualities described by both Cohen and Pursley, Cizanckas reveals in the interview a wide range of issues involved in genuine reform.

Van Maanen: Station House Sergeants and Street Sergeants

In a study of a thousand officer police department, Van Maanen identified two contrasting types of police sergeants: "station house" and "street."[30] Station house sergeants

BOX 5-3.

Interview with a Reform Chief

Victor I. Cizanckas has been chief of the Stamford, Connecticut, Police Department since May 1977, when he was plucked from the Menlo Park, California, police in an apparent effort to reform the Stamford force.

The 43-year-old lawman began his enforcement career in Menlo Park in 1962 after an eight-year stint with the Marine Corps. He quickly worked his way up through the ranks, becoming chief of the California department in June 1968.

Cizanckas has long been involved in working for change in the criminal justice system. He has served on the California Council on Criminal Justice, the LEAA Manpower Development Committee, and the Advisory Committee of Project STAR (Standards, Training and Requirements).

In addition to his police duties in Stamford, Cizanckas works as a consultant with several public and private research-oriented organizations, including the Police Foundation, LEAA, and ABT Associates.

The holder of an A.A. in police science from the College of San Mateo and a B.S. in sociology from the College of Notre Dame, Cizanckas lectured throughout the United States and has held teaching positions in three colleges while pursuing his policing career.

A keen observer of the police scene, the chief is the author of almost two dozen articles, dealing with topics ranging from law enforcement management to vandalism.

This interview was conducted for Law Enforcement News by Harry O'Reilly and Dorothy H. Bracey.

Len: Could you describe some of the circumstances that greeted you on your arrival in Stamford in 1977?

Cizanckas: There was a challenge here, and there was a national search for a police chief in which I decided to participate and "won." I took the position on May 5, 1977. I was talking to the co-author of my book, Don Hanna, recently, describing what's been going on here for three years, and his comment was that I've had a negative learning experience. I think he's right.

Len: You were brought here with, if I under-stand it correctly, a mandate from the mayor to clean up the city of Stamford. How does a new police chief go about doing something like that?

Cizanckas: I would suggest to somebody else to do it cautiously; I did not, and it's taken its toll, I think, in many ways on the organization, on the people who work for me and people who have worked for me. Stamford is a unique city; there are just a lot of wonderful people here who are very proud of their city and its history. At the same time, Stamford is—and I use the term advisedly—totally corrupt. Wherever you look, you'll find corruption. It's a very sad set of circumstances. You have what could be one of the best cities in America giving way to an "old boy" system and a matrix, if you will, of, well, not "the Mafia" running the city, but there's Mafia here. It's a system where people serve themselves rather than the community; that's their primary objective. So you have a matrix of relationships that include Mafia, politicians, city workers, and contractors, and the list goes on and on. They've done very well by themselves, to the detriment of the community. I don't know what the total is, but it's millions.

Len: Your mandate definitely did encompass the whole city, though, not just the police department?

Cizanckas: It did encompass the whole city, and I approached it from that point of view. Simultaneously, we had a police department that was, well, political. Promotions, transfers, special assignments were called by a local contractor; that stopped. Tickets were fixed, cases were fixed; that stopped. When you start doing that, you start to take a toll. I collected 500 special police badges and took them away from people. That did not make a lot of friends. A number of department heads are no longer with the city. There's one under indictment being tried right now. They've been fired, indicted, exposed—it goes on and on.

Len: Were the investigations that led to the indictments of other city officials generated through your department?

Cizanckas: Yes.

Len: So that would mean, then, that you had

within your department a number of investigators who were trustworthy enough to perform these investigations in their own town and who had to be, of necessity, reform-minded themselves?

Cizanckas: A lot of people were waiting. In any system, no matter how corrupt, there are a lot of decent people, and they're sort of victims themselves. If the mayor or the administrator or police chief says "we're going to do it," they'll watch him for a while, and if they believe he means it and is not part of the system, they'll come through. In the Stamford Police Department itself we're talking about 90 percent honest cops—unfortunately part of an old system, so their reality is the Stamford police reality. They really don't know what's out there. They don't have a measuring stick; they can't set themselves up and say, "Well, we ought to be like this." They want to believe that they're good cops, and that they work for a good police department. When you expose it, there's a terrible price. It hurts them; it just blows them apart. Their pride is hurt, their pride in their job, in what they're dedicated to. It's hard.

Len: How many sworn personnel do you have?

Cizanckas: 243.

Len: Did you bring any of your own people with you when you came here?

Cizanckas: No.

Len: Would you do that again?

Cizanckas: Yes, I would not bring any. Let me explain. I've talked this over with a lot of my friends who are police administrators, and one of the things that has really crippled reform chiefs is they bring in staff, and they talk to each other and no one else. The real task is to find honest cops—they're part of the system, they know the players, and if they become committed you can do it. But if you isolate yourself from the rank and file, it's a disaster. They'll stall every kind of program you can think of, so that it's not institutionalized and it's not the product of the people who work there. Whatever we've done here is the product of the people who work here, and that's the difference. I believe in that.

Len: What was your initial approach to the press when you first took over the job?

Cizanckas: I decided, after consulting with a lot of my friends, that I would maintain a very high profile, I've had a very high profile here.

It's not my preference. I don't need press, and I don't need to read what I do.

Len: I gather from all of this that you emphatically denied the allegations that you came in riding on a white horse to save a department that didn't need saving.

Cizanckas: I came here with a mandate from the mayor—actually a mandate from the population—to clean up what was very bad. It's not over, by a long shot. It continues.

If at the time I had to write a book on Stamford, it would be treated as fiction. It's not real. They tried everything they can to wipe me out, to get me out of here. My own staff has betrayed me, blowing part of my undercover operations to try and embarrass me politically. They've undermined every effort I've put forward, but I've still got honest cops, and they're now in staff.

Len: To be able to function in a climate of negativity like this you've got a nucleus of good, solid police officers who are supportive and honest and helpful, who are with you. How about in terms of the public? What kind of support are you getting from them?

Cizanckas: Absolute. They want good government, most people do, and I have citizen groups, corporation groups, church groups, and I meet with all of them and I keep them advised. But it's a town job.

On that blown undercover operation, I brought somebody in with me and put him as an undercover operator. We opened up a variety store and he took numbers and sports betting. I ran it for 21 months without anyone knowing it. Somebody from my staff betrayed me, and after I was betrayed I had somebody else undercover. I guess if you want to know if I'm winning or losing, the best way is to quote somebody from the other side, talking about the blown undercover, and this was in June. "By blowing this," he's saying, "what he's proving so far is, you know who's winning? There's three rounds so far, and you know how many rounds the chief's got? He's got two rounds already." I had the third when the son of a bitch said that. It's real, but it's unreal.

Len: You have said that the goal of a reform chief is not to lock people up. Could you elaborate on that?

Cizanckas: Too many reform efforts are simply "let's make a few arrests, let's make some press releases, and tell everybody we've got the city cleaned up." That doesn't work. What you're talking about is social change, and it's way beyond arresting a few people. If you want to get into the academic side of it, you're doing organizational development which is changing the mores not only of a police agency but in this case of an entire city. The recurring theme, and something everybody said in this city when I first arrived, but which you have a hard time hearing now is, "one hand washes the other." Over and over again, I just made a lot of speeches about that and said that those people who say it better think about what they're saying, particularly if one hand happened to be very dirty. When you start changing a whole way of life, where if you have a position of power you can get a friend's ticket fixed—that is pervasive corruption, even though people think, well, that comes with their power position, there's no money exchanged but there's a favor. No money may change hands, but you pay a larger price than money. Everything disintegrates; there's no confidence in government, there's no confidence in the people who work for the government, so therefore the kinds of efforts that are necessary to serve the public properly—from every department, not only the police—are substandard.

Len: A number of the reform chiefs of the last decade have also been known as hit-and-run chiefs. Their tenures of office have been relatively short in the departments that they cleaned up. . . .

Cizanckas: You people say that, but you have to take a look at all the chiefs. The tenure of a police chief is relatively short; I think it's about two-and-a-half years now. I've been here three. And most of your reform chiefs usually are there beyond three years. I think there's also a life expectancy of a change agent. After a while, you reach the point of diminishing returns. The effort is the same, but the returns are less. Finally, you have hurt so many people and their extended families that you're no longer effective.

Len: So far as the individual is concerned, there is a sort of built-in half life?

Cizanckas: Yes, but who knows when it is? Someday I'll have to make that decision myself.

Len: Have you felt any explicit or implied threats to your own personal safety?

Cizanckas: A very explicit yes. It's very explicit on the tape I quoted from earlier that they were going to throw me out of office, run me out of town. I have been the subject of character assassination—I mean written character assassination, in letters. Everything I'm accused of I told my internal affairs unit to investigate.

My wife gets letters from people who run cemeteries saying, "we'll be happy to take care of your husband." I think that's an implied threat. The head of my internal affairs unit is Italian-American and his mother is old Italian from New York, Little Italy, and she's recovering from her third heart attack in a hospital. They called her to tell her, in Italian, that if her son makes another move he pays the price. That's very explicit. It put her back in intensive care.

It doesn't stop. They attack ministers who are in favor of social reform. . . .

Len: So what you're dealing with is a deeply-rooted clique that involves intermarriage, interrelationships on a business level. . . .

Cizanckas: Business, family social, and it's very very deep.

Len: And this is almost a kind of Borgia family that's in a power position, calling a lot of shots and wreaking a lot of financial havoc over the town?

Cizanckas: That's right. But let me say something. It goes way beyond financial havoc. It affects the quality of life. Deals are made in zoning, deals are made for buildings; everything starts to disintegrate. Deals are made in the Traffic Department. It just goes on and on, and it takes a terrible toll that's way beyond money.

Len: If you have a power nucleus like this, a controlling negative force up here somewhere, and you have the support of the general public, how does someone in your position or in a comparable position localize the small pockets of good people to combat this larger group of power people?

Cizanckas: There's one way, and that's to keep a very high profile. I don't keep anything from the press; I tell them everything, and it drives them crazy. It drives people crazy. I also meet with citizen groups, I meet with corporate executives. I've done three churches on a Sunday and a synagogue on Saturday, to tell them what I'm doing and ask for their support. The bottom line is that people want good government, they will support somebody that's trying to give it to them, and it will work. But it takes a terrible toll, psychologically, intellectually, and emotionally. The question is, how long can you last before you burn out.

Len: It's a human instinct to want to be loved and to be liked and accepted by people, and you can't do that.

Cizanckas: You can't do that; you give it up. When I formed my internal affairs unit. . . .

Len: There was no prior internal affairs division?

Cizanckas: Oh no. When I put them together I sat them down and I said to them, "When everybody in this town loves me, when the department is behind me more than 50 percent and everything is going OK, you open a case on me, because I've sold out." I am not going to be loved, I am not going to make friends, and that's a part of it.

Len: You've been able to do some recruiting since you've been here. What were your goals in this?

Cizanckas: The goals have been well-educated, intelligent, decent people, but there's a problem. You have to understand institutions, and let me leave this police department and talk about other police departments. I have seen white, middle-class, liberal, college-educated people with a sociology background enter a police department, and they've never spoken the vernacular, they've never been in the military, they watch their language. Within four weeks they're calling their nightstick a "nigger knocker." That's the nature of organizations. If the organization is bad, it takes a very strong personality not to want to belong to that and co-opt one's own values.

Len: That kind of individualism is often looked on as a negative thing, such as with Frank Serpico in New York. You're seen as being so atypical that no one accepts you.

Cizanckas: Absolutely. You're ostracized; you're a freak. They're talking about throwing the internal affairs officers out of the police officers association. The internal affairs officers are good cops who believe in what they're doing. And while they have had some officers found guilty of various things, they've cleared over 70 police officers. The name of the game in this town was that if a police officer made an arrest, the only way to beat the arrest was to

make an accusation against the police officer, then he'd fold the case and everybody is happy. What I told attorneys who came to my office when I first arrived was "I'll take your complaint and I'll investigate it, and as soon as your client's case is adjudicated we'll bring the other charge to the commissioner."

Len: You've made a number of changes in the training area relevant to the whole matter of corruption. Could you describe some of these?

Cizanckas: That's part of the gimmick. We teach such "weird" courses as ethics, interpersonal relationships, conflict resolution, professional responsibility, and the list goes on—weird topics for cops.

Len: Do you have your own training establishment?

Cizanckas: When I first came here we had a lot of turnover, and the state police academy could only handle so many, so we designed our own academy, which was certified. It was very different from the state police academy. In fact, our academy has not been replicated by the state, so we're now using the state academy; they pay all costs. They've included things like Project STAR. It's a greatly expanded curriculumn.

Len: Is recruit training done there?

Cizanckas: We do our own, and then we send them there.

Len: You said you had a turnover. Was there a mass exodus from the department?

Cizanckas: Yes, with the announcement of my coming a number of people left, and after my arrival a number of people left.

Len: Naturally, you're going to have to replace these people, or have had to replace them, so can it be assumed then that you have a lot of malleable young people in the lower echelons of your department?

Cizanckas: The problem is I can't reach them; the old guard reaches them first. It's a reality and I admit it, and it's a problem.

Len: On top of that, you can't recruit from all over, most of them are local people, so in many instances they're part of the old regime.

Cizanckas: It's a difficult proposition, as I said earlier. You can take the model recruit, but if you put him in an institution that has a value system that is not positive, not proper, that is corruptive, then that's what he becomes part of. I think one of the saddest case histories we have is the city of Denver in 1961, I think it was. Those police officers who went to prison as burglars did not become police officers to become burglars. Most of them are more purely motivated. They may want a civil service job and security, but they also want to serve. I think that's the greatest example of an institution doing somebody in from peer pressure.

When you talk about change, then you're changing a system, and it's more than making a couple arrests or firing a couple of people. It's a long hard process, but as we talked about earlier, there is a half life for people who do it, because the bottom line is if you're doing it properly there are a lot of people who are very upset with you.

Len: You're one of a few people in the country who have been a police chief executive on both coasts. Have you noted any significant differences?

Cizanckas: There is a major difference. The West Coast police are very professional—in how they write reports, how they handle things. Their educational level is higher. They really know their business. They're also plastic. That's the best way to describe them. I prefer it to what I found here. But on the other side of this, if you take an East Coast cop, and if you're hurt, if you're young, you're old, you're in trouble, they'll take care of you. You can rely on them coming to your house after hours to make sure you're OK. I've seen it. If a husband has a heart attack—I've seen it in many cases—the officer gets off duty, goes to the hospital to comfort the wife. You won't find that in a Western cop. An East Coast cop will drive her home, and when she's home by herself and her husband's in the hospital, they check the house. There's a great dichotomy. I've traveled across the country and I find that to be absolutely true. One of the best experiences I've had was in the city of San Antonio. I do weird things when I go to police chiefs' conferences— I don't go to the conference; I ride around in police cars in every city. I was with a Mexican-American patrol officer and I went out with him. He technically knew his business, I think, but personally. . . . He's not a Western cop, in San Antonio; I'm talking about the West Coast, where we have all the models. Everybody knew this cop by name, they flagged him down to tell him what's going on: "Yesterday there was a hit-and-run," for example, "and so-and-so did it."

There's a middle ground, but how do we accomplish that? I don't know. The morale is highest here when there's a snowstorm. There's no police work going on in the traditional sense. Everybody comes in their old clothes, nobody calls in sick. They're taking doctors and nurses to hospitals, they're taking people who need dialysis treatment to hospitals to be treated, they're taking groceries up to people who are snowed in, taking care of stranded motorists, and they all feel great. My feeling is that the mass media is in large part responsible for the poor police service we get in this country, because they portray a law enforcer Matt Dillon and they don't portray the humanist part of this job.

Len: But you constantly come across things like "don't give us all that social work stuff; we joined this job to fight crime."

Cizanckas: Absolutely. But when it's very clear what they're supposed to be doing on a given day, the level of job satisfaction is highest.

There's a great dichotomy between the police service officer and the law enforcement officer, and the reality is, as studies show, 80 percent of your time is spent on service calls. But we train for the 20 percent, we emphasize the 20 percent, and we reward for the 20 percent.

The other side of it is that when we have that type of service activity going on, it's one of the few times that a police officer can really judge the success of that he's doing. The rest of it is so ambiguous, it floats around. You know, "Well, I caught a burglar, and what's going to happen to him? He's going to get probation and he'll be back on the street." There's a frustration level that's so high. We even tell them in the academy, "Don't personalize it. If you make your arrest don't worry about it." And the officer say "Yes, I understand all of that. Burglars get probation, but not my burglars." It's a very frustrating job. And let me go beyond the media. Policing is one of the most esoteric professions in the nation. Very few people understand that. The citizen doesn't know what a cop does, because of the media, and they think that by his mere presence on the street he prevents crime. Well he does not. They think that having a cop on every block is going to make the community safe; it's not. And very few police officers really understand what their role in society is. I'll say this also: there are too many police administrators who do not understand what the role of the police officer is. If you have an administrator who makes an assumption about that role, it's not defined in any textbook you have. It's a tough job, and then when you come in from outside like I did, and you start to break the code— you say "we are not perfect, we have some problems"—even though I say 90 percent of my organization is humane, compassionate, they take care of you, if I say one cop is rotten, every other positive thing I say is forgotten and the only thing that's quoted is "he said this guy was a bad guy." And so all defense mechanisms go up and there's a closure of the ranks, and they say "this guy's not a cop, he's not on our side, he's not for us," when the reality is I am very much for them. I like cops. Let me expand on that. I think in too many cases police "reformers," who know what's good for the community, etc., they don't like cops. When you get underneath, they just don't like cops. I like cops; I think they're great, West and East Coast. They're out there doing something, a very demanding job that's little understood by the people they serve. But being a police officer is one of the most exciting professions, and one of the most demanding, both intellectually and physically.

Len: What do you see in your crystal ball for the future of Stamford, in relation to the conditions that existed when you first came here and the current situation?

Cizanckas: In the long run, I think the kind of things that we've done—reorganization, training, a new records room computerization—are really the foundation of any lasting reform, and I think they're finished. But they don't receive much press. The basic things are finished. I think that internally people know what kind of expectations they can have for themselves. So we've reached the point of institutionalizing these things; I don't think it will go back.

Len: And these things are not dependent upon one individual?

Cizanckas: If you do that, then you have not accomplished your mission or responsibility. A lot of people are afraid that things will go back if something happens to me or if I leave. My social scientist "hat" says no, but that's a guess. I hope not.

Source: Harry O'Reilly and Dorothy H. Bracey, "An Interview with Victor Cizanckas, Police Chief of Stamford, Connecticut," Law Enforcement News, March 24, 1980, pp. 8–10.

---

had been out of the "bag" (uniform) prior to their promotion to sergeant and preferred to work inside in an office environment once they won their stripes; this preference is clearly indicated by the nickname of "Edwards, the Olympic torch who never goes out" given to one such sergeant. Station house sergeants immersed themselves in the management culture of the police department, keeping busy with paperwork, planning, record keeping, press relations, and fine points of law. Their strong orientation to conformity also gave rise to nicknames as suggested by the use of "by the book Brubaker" to refer to one station house sergeant.

In contrast, street sergeants were serving in the field when they received their promotions. Consequently, they had a distaste for office procedures and a strong action orientation as suggested by such nicknames as "Shooter McGee" and "Walker the Stalker." Moreover, their concern was not with conformity, but with "not letting the assholes take over the city."

In addition to the distinct differences already noted, station house and street sergeants were thought of differently by those whom they supervised: station house sergeants "stood behind their officers" whereas street sergeants "stood beside their officers." Each of these two different styles of working as a sergeant also has its drawbacks and strengths. Station house sergeants might not be readily available to officers working in the field, but could always be located when a signature was needed and were able to secure more favors for their subordinates than street sergeants were. Although immediately available in the field when needed, street sergeants occasionally interfered with the autonomy of their subordinates by responding to a call for service assigned to a subordinate and handling it or otherwise, at least in the eyes of the subordinate officer, "interfering."

A consideration of Van Maanen's work leads to some generalizations about the future careers of station house versus street sergeants. The station house sergeant is learning routines, procedures, and skills that will improve future promotional opportunities. Their promotional opportunities are further enhanced by contacts with senior police commanders who can give them important assignments and who can, if favorably impressed, influence future promotions. In contrast, street sergeants may gain some favorable publicity and awards for their exploits, but they are also more likely to have citizen complaints filed against them, more likely to be investigated by internal affairs, and more likely to be sued. Consequently, very aggressive street sergeants are regarded by their superiors as "good cops," but difficult people to supervise. In short, the action-oriented street sergeant who does not "mellow out" may not go beyond a middle manager's position in a line unit such as patrol or investigation.

Price: Male and Female Police Leaders

The infusion of women into policing is basically a post-1972 movement triggered by the enactment of federal legislation covered from different perspectives in Chapters 2, 7, and 10. Although there were women in policing prior to that time, their numbers were insignificant, and they were invariably assigned to special functions, such as work with juveniles and vice. Moreover, prior to 1972 opportunities for the same general assignments as men and for promotion to leadership roles were virtually nonexistent.

Because of the only recent entry of women into policing, there has not been sufficient time for large numbers of them to advance to leadership positions and, consequently, there have been few studies of female leaders. In a study comparing twenty-six women holding the rank of sergeant or above with their male counterparts, Barbra Price found that women were superior at a statistically significant level on selected personality traits associated with leadership.[31] Specifically, Price found that women were more emotionally independent; more verbally and intellectually aggressive; more flexible and willing to part from routine and convention; had scores suggesting a more positive self-image, confidence, and social adequacy. Contrary to popular views, this sample of females was much lower on a measure of submissiveness than male leaders. Their scores also suggested a liberal perspective, and they were more creative and had less inclination toward authoritarian outlooks than did the male police leaders with whom they were compared.

Blake and Mouton: The Managerial Grid

Developed by Robert Blake and Jane Mouton, the Managerial Grid® has received a great deal of attention since its appearance in 1962 in the *Journal of the American Society of Training Directors*.[32] The Grid is part of the survey research feedback stem of organizational development and draws upon earlier work done at Ohio State University and the University of Michigan.[33]

Depicted in Figure 5-4, the Grid has two dimensions: (1) concern for production and (2) concern for people. Each axis or dimension is numbered from 1, meaning

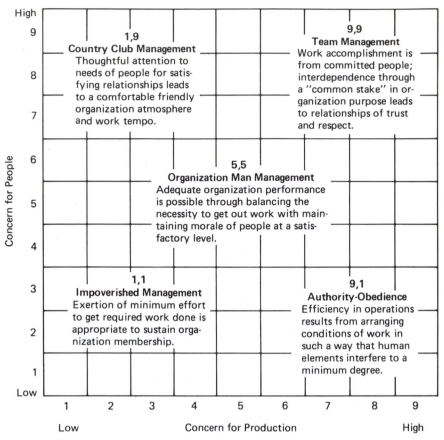

FIGURE 5-4. The managerial grid. [from *The New Managerial Grid* by Robert Blake and Jane Srygley Mouton. Houston: Gulf Publishing Company, Copyright © 1978, p. 11. Reproduced by permission.]

low concern, to 9, indicating high concern. The way in which a person combines these two dimensions establishes a leadership style in terms of one of the five principal styles identified on the Grid. The numbers associated with each of the styles reflect the level of concern for each of the two dimensions to the Grid. For example, 9,1 indicates maximum concern for production or the needs of the organization and a minimum orientation toward the needs of people in the organization.

Some of the leadership styles identified previously can be related readily to the Grid. Authoritarian leaders are represented by the 9,1 style; laissez-faire leaders by the 1,1; and democratic leaders by the 5,5. Additionally, the 9,1 and 9,9 styles are consistent, respectively, with the streams of thought summarized in Chapter 3 under the headings of "Traditional Organizational Theory" and "Open Systems Theory."

The leadership style of an individual can be identified by using a questionnaire based on the work of Blake and Mouton. Table 5-3 summarizes the leadership styles identified by 143 police supervisors and managers completing the Grid questionnaire; the police leaders involved came from four different states and represented a state investigative agency, a county police department, and three municipal departments.[34] "Primary style" indicates the style that the police leaders reported as preferring;

TABLE 5-3 Police Leadership Styles on the Managerial Grid

Backup styles	Primary styles					
	9,9	**5,5**	**9,1**	**1,9**	**1,1**	**Totals**
9,9		1	12	3	2	18
5,5	19		7	2	1	29
9,1	12	10		3	21	46
1,9	8	0	9		3	20
1,1	6	1	20	3		30
Totals	45	12	48	11	27	143

From Charles Swanson and Leonard Territo, "Police Leadership and Interpersonal Communication Styles," in *Police and Police Work*, ed. Jack R. Greene, (Beverly Hills, Calif.: Sage, 1982); with unpublished 1985 data from the files of C. R. Swanson added.

"backup style" reflects the style the police leaders would use if they were not able to continue using their primary.[35] According to the Grid, one moves from the "best" to the "worst" styles as one moves from a 9,9 through 5,5, 9,1 and 1,9 to the 1,1; the most desirable combination of a primary and backup style is the 9,9 with a 5,5 backup.

A difficulty in using the Grid questionnaire is that the data produced are no more accurate than the perceptions of self of the person completing the instrument. When working in an organizational development context, one way in which to overcome this is to have each manager complete the instrument and then to have each of his or her subordinates fill one out on how they experience the manager.

Hersey and Blanchard: Situational Leadership Theory

Hersey and Blanchard's situational leadership model was influenced greatly by William Reddin's 3-D management style theory.[36] While many situational variables are important to leadership—such as the demands of time, the leader, the led, the superiors, the organization, and job demands—Hersey and Blanchard emphasize what they regard as the key variables, the behavior of the leader in relationship to the followers.[37] Although the examples of situational leadership suggest a hierarchical relationship, situational leadership theory should have application when trying to influence the behavior of a subordinate, a boss, a friend, or a relative.[38]

Maturity is defined in situational leadership as the capacity to set high, but attainable, goals, the willingness to take the responsibility, and the education and/or experience of the individual or the group.[39] Age may be a factor, but it is not related directly to maturity as used in situational leadership theory.[40] An individual or group is not mature or immature in a total sense, but only in relationship to the specific task to be performed.[41] This task-relevant maturity involves two factors: (1) job maturity, the ability and the technical knowledge to do the task and (2) psychological maturity, feelings of self-confidence and self-respect about one's self as an individual.[42]

Figure 5-5 depicts the situation leadership model; the various levels of follower maturity are defined as:

- *M1:* The followers are neither willing nor able to take responsibility for task accomplishment.

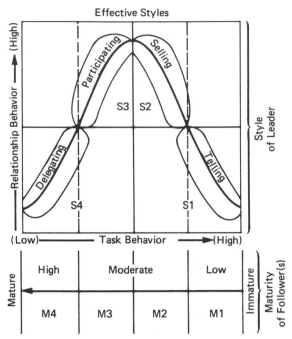

Effective Styles

FIGURE 5-5. The situational leadership model. [From Paul Hersey and Kenneth H. Blanchard, *Management of Organizational Behavior: Utilizing Human Resources*, 3rd ed., © 1977, p. 170. Reprinted by permission of Prentice-Hall, Inc., Englewood Cliffs, N.J.]

- *M2:* The followers are willing but not able to take responsibility for task accomplishment.
- *M3:* The followers are able but not willing to take responsibility for task accomplishment.
- *M4:* The followers are willing and able to take responsibility for task accomplishment.[43]

Task behavior is essentially the extent to which a leader engages in one-way communication with subordinates; relationship behavior is the extent to which a leader engages in two-way communication by providing socioemotional support, "psychological strokes," and facilitating behaviors.[44] The definition of the four basic styles associated with these two variables operates like the managerial grid and are described in the following terms:

- *S1:* High-task—low-relationship leader behavior is referred to as "telling," because this style is characterized by one-way communication in which the leader defines the roles of followers and tells them what, how, when, and where to do various tasks.
- *S2:* High-task—high-relationship behavior is referred to as "selling," because with this style most of the direction is still provided by the leader. He or she also attempts through two-way communication and socioemotional support to get the follower(s) psychologically to buy into decisions that have to be made.
- *S3:* High-relationship—low-task behavior is called "participating," because

with this style the leader and follower(s) now share in decision making through two-way communication and much facilitating behavior from the leader since the follower(s) have the ability and knowledge to do the task.

- *S4:* Low-relationship—low-task behavior is labeled "delegating," because the style involves letting follower(s) "run their own show" through delegation and general supervision since the follower(s) are high in both task and psychological maturity.

The bell-shaped curve in the style-of-leader portion of Figure 5-5 means that, as the maturity level of leader's followers develops from immaturity to maturity, the appropriate style of leadership moves in a corresponding way.[45]

To illustrate, the police leader who has a subordinate whose maturity is in the M2 range would be most effective employing an S2 style of leadership. The probability of success of each style for the four maturity levels depends on how far the style is from the high-probability style along the bell-shaped curve; Hersey and Blanchard describe these probabilities as for:

- M1:   S1 and S2 2nd, S3 third, S4 low probability
- M2:   S2 High S1 and S3 secondary, S4 low probability
- M3:   S3 High S2 and S4 secondary, S1 low probability
- M4:   S4 High S3 2nd S2 3rd, S1 low probability[46]

While it is easier said than done, the effective use of Hersey and Blanchard's model depends upon the police leader developing or having a diagnostic ability and the flexibility to adapt their leadership style to a given situation.[47]

The Leader and Conflict

Conflict is a condition in which at least two parties have a mutual difference of position, often involving scarce resources, where there is a behavior or threat of behavior through the exercise of power to control the situation or gain at the expense of the other party.[48] Competition differs from conflict in that, in the former, each party is bound to abide by the same rules.[49]

Conflict is a pervasive and perhaps inevitable part of human existence; it is not inherently "bad" or "good," and its consequences in the main depend upon how it is managed.[50] Viewed negatively, conflict is an energy-consuming and destructive phenomenon that divides individuals and groups within the police department, creates tension between representatives of the police department and other agencies, and results in acrimonious and combative exchanges. Viewed positively, conflict can:

1. Stimulate interest.
2. Prevent individual, group, and organizational stagnation.
3. Be a source of creativity and change as alternative ways of viewing things are aired.
4. Give individuals, groups, and organizations a distinctive identity by demarcating them from others.
5. Create group and organizational solidarity; and

6. Be an enjoyable experience of testing and assessing one's active use of his or her full capabilities.[51]

Although not unique to them, an unfortunate characteristic of many police departments is the view that conflict is destructive so that its positive aspects and potential benefits are overlooked and lost. To tap the useful dimensions of conflict, the police leader must be able to, as outlined in Table 5-4, distinguish between the presence of too much and too little conflict. Additionally, where conflict exists, there is a need to differentiate between pathologically and productively oriented situations. Pathological symptoms in conflict include:

1. Unreliable and impoverished communication between the conflicting parties.
2. The view that the solution of the conflict will result from the imposition of one view or position over the other.
3. A downward spiral of suspicion and hostility that leads to oversensitivity to differences and the minimization of similarities.[52]

Unresponded to, such symptoms are the prelude to hostile infighting, hardening of positions, and protracted opposition. In contrast, productively oriented conflict:

TABLE 5-4 Symptoms of Too Much and Too Little Conflict

Area of concern	General issue	Symptoms of too much conflict	Symptoms of too little conflict
Attitudes	Awareness of similarities and differences	Blind to interdependence	Blind to conflicts of interest
	Sophistication about intergroup relations	Unaware of dynamics and costs of conflict	Unaware of dynamics and costs of collusion
	Feelings and perceptions of own and other group	Elaborated stereotypes favorable to own and unfavorable to other group	Lack of consciousness of own group and differences from other group
Behavior	Behavior within groups	High cohesion and conformity; high mobilization	Fragmentization; mobilization
	Conflict management style of groups	Overcompetitive style	Overcooperative style
	Behavior between groups	Aggressive, exploitative behavior; preemptive attack	Avoidance of conflict; appeasement
Structure	Nature of larger system	Separate or underdefined common larger system	Shared larger system that discourages conflict
	Regulatory context for interaction	Few rules to limit escalation	Many rules that stifle differences
	Relevant structural mechanisms	No inhibiting third parties available	No third parties to press differences
	Definition of groups and their goals	Impermeably bounded groups obsessed with own interests	Unbounded groups aware of own interests

From L. Dave Brown, ''Managing Conflict Among Groups,'' in *Organizational Psychology,* 3d ed., ed. David Kolb, Irwin M. Rubin, and James M. McIntyre (Englewood Cliffs, N.J.: Prentice-Hall, © 1979), p. 383. Reprinted by permission of Prentice-Hall, Inc.

1. is characterized by open and honest communication, which reduces the likelihood of misperceptions and misunderstandings, allows each party to benefit from the knowledge possessed by the other, and promotes a mutual and accurate definition of the issues;

2. encourages the recognition of the legitimacy of the other's interests and of the need to search for a solution that is responsive to the needs of each party; and

3. fosters mutual respect and sensitivity to similarities and common interests, stimulating a convergence of positions.[53]

The way in which police leaders will handle conflict is to some extent bound up in their leadership style. Various methods for resolving conflict are summarized in Table 5-5. The use of denial or withdrawal corresponds to the 1,1 style from the managerial grid; suppression or smoothing over with the 1,9; power or dominance with the 9,1; compromise or negotiation with the 5,5; and collaboration with the 9,9. Each of the various methods identified may be appropriate or inappropriate at various times, and to return to an earlier point, good diagnostic ability and flexibility are again central attributes.

Leadership and Organizational Control

Because police leaders are responsible for the performance of their departments, they must be concerned with organizational control and organizational controls. Organizational control is synonymous with organizational direction and is normative, dealing with the future. In contrast, organizational controls consist of measurements of, information about, and analysis of what was and is.[54] Stated more simply, controls pertain to the means, control pertains to an end.[55]

Of necessity, the issues of organizational control and controls permeate police departments. Despite the definitions given, practical distinctions between them require some thought. For example, planning, budget preparation, and the written directive system of a police department—consisting of policies, procedures, and rules and regulations—are all control devices in that they all deal with preferred future states, positions, and behaviors. However, when an officer violates a rule and disciplinary measures are invoked, the system of controls is in operation. During the execution of a budget, a midyear review occurs in which performance over the first six months is summarized and analyzed and plans made for the remaining six months. Thus, this midyear review incorporates features of the system of organizational controls and control. Similarly, quarterly evaluations of police programs incorporate features of the system of controls and control, whereas the final program evaluation report is in the main part of the system of controls. Despite such variations, it is apparent that informed control is a function of the system of controls.

To give the police leader control, controls must satisfy the following specifications:

1. They must be specific and economical.
2. They must be meaningful, relating to significant events.
3. They must use the appropriate indicators.
4. They must be timely.
5. Their limitations must be understood.

TABLE 5-5 Methods for Resolving Conflict

Method	Results	Appropriate	Inappropriate	Skills required
Denial or withdrawal	Person tries to solve problem by denying its existence; results in win-lose	When issue is relatively unimportant; when issue is raised at inopportune time	When issue is important; when it will not disappear, but will build to greater complexity	Judgment of what is needed in the situation
Suppression or smoothing over	Differences are played down; results in win-lose	Same as above; also when preservation of relationship is more important than issue	When evasion of issue will disrupt relationship; when others are ready and willing to deal with issue	Empathy
Power or dominance	Authority, position, majority rule, or a persuasive minority settle the conflict; results in win-lose	When authority is granted by one's position; also when group has agreed on method of decision making	When those without power have no means to express their needs and ideas, especially if this lack of opportunity has the potential of future disruption	Decision making; running effective meetings
Compromise or negotiation	Each party gives up something in order to meet midway; results in some loss of each side's position	When both sides have enough leeway to give; when resources are limited; when win-lose stance undesirable	When original position is inflated or unrealistic; when solution must be watered down to be acceptable; when commitment by both parties is doubtful	Attentive listening and paraphrasing; problem solving
Collaboration	Individual abilities and expertise are recognized; each person's position is clear, but emphasis is on group solution; results in win-win	When time is available to complete process; when parties are committed to and trained in use of process	When time is limited; when parties lack training in or commitment to collaborative efforts	Attentive listening and paraphrasing; problem solving

From Lois Borland Hart, *Moving UP: Women and Leadership* (New York: Amacon, © 1980), p. 84. Reprinted with permission of Amacom, a division of the American Management Association. All rights reserved.

6. They must be as simple as possible.

7. They must be directed to those who can take the necessary action.[56]

Perhaps paradoxically, the tighter he or she attempts to control unilaterally, the less control a police leader actually has. A simple illustration of this point is taking a handful of sand and squeezing it forcefully; a great deal trickles out and is lost. Alternatively, the same amount of sand cupped loosely in the hand remains in place. By involving others, by sharing power, the police leader secures the greatest amount of control because individual commitment—the best and most effective type of control—is secured.

Summary

All police managers must be sensitive to their three main responsibilities: (1) contributing to the fulfillment of the department's mission, (2) ensuring that the effort of subordinates is productive and that they are achieving, and (3) producing impacts on their areas of responsibility. Meeting these key responsibilities effectively requires that the police managers, practice certain "habits of mind," such as employing their time wisely, building on the strengths that they and their subordinates have, and concentrating on the results to be achieved rather than on the units of work to be accomplished.

Whereas leadership can be seen as the qualities displayed by an individual or as the function of a position, such as major, within a police department, a generally accepted definition is that leadership is the process of influencing the members of an organization to employ appropriately and willingly their energies in activities that are helpful to the achievement of the police department's goals. "Influencing" and "willingly" are related to the concepts of authority and power. In the main, authority is a grant made from above by the formal organization, whereas power is a grant made from below, being confirmed on the leader by the led. However, one should not infer that those who have authority do not also have some power, for the bestowing of authority is accompanied inherently by at least some power.

Leaders at various levels of a police department have different blends of skills that they predominately employ. Human relations, conceptual, and technical are the three major types of skills that are employed in this skill mix. As one advances up the rank hierarchy of a police department, which can be organized under three groupings—first-line supervisors, middle managers, and top managers—the relative emphasis and importance of the three skills shift.

Leadership theories essentially try to establish what variables are related to the emergence of leadership or the nature of leadership itself. Illustrative are (1) great man and genetic theories associated variously with Carlyle, Hegel, and Galton; (2) the traits approach, which has historically enjoyed great appeal; (3) behavioral explanations, which center on what a leader does; and (4) situational statements, which maintain that effective leadership is the result of a good fit between the capabilities of a leader and the demands of a given condition.

The abundance of interest in the subject of leadership has produced alternative ways of classifying leadership styles. Schemes treated in this chapter include (1) authoritarian, democratic, and laissez-faire leaders; (2) the authoritarian-democratic continuum; (3) leader styles in bureaucratic structures; (4) traditional versus nontraditional police leaders; (5) station house versus street sergeants; (6) male versus female leaders in policing; (7) managerial grid styles; and (8) situational leadership.

A significant element of organizational life with which the police manager must deal is conflict, defined as a situation in which at least two parties have a mutual difference of position and in which one party employs or threatens behavior through the exercise of power to obtain control of the situation at the expense of the other party. Although the presence of conflict is often viewed as being undesirable, the absence of it is certainly unhealthy. Fundamental to any understanding of conflict is that the way in which it is handled is more a determinant of the ''goodness'' or ''badness'' of conflict rather than of any inherent characteristic of conflict itself. Leader styles may have certain pronounced preferences or tendencies for the way in which conflict is addressed; for example, the 9,1 style can be related to the use of power or dominance as a method of resolving conflict.

Organizational control and organizational controls are the devices by which the police manager shapes the course and events for the department. Organizational control and organizational direction can be equated usefully, and they are normative, futuristic statements. Measurements of, information about, and analysis of the past and present states are termed organizational controls. Organizational control and controls are differentiated further in that the former is a preferred state to be achieved whereas the latter are the means of achieving that preferred state.

Discussion Questions

1. What is a generally accepted definition of leadership?

2. What are the definitions of authority and power, and how are they related?

3. What distinctions can be made between personalized and social power?

4. Within the skill mix, which skill is most essential to top management? Why?

5. The traits approach to leadership has enjoyed great popularity. What is it and what evidence is there to support it?

6. What differences are there among authoritarian, democratic, and laissez-faire leaders?

7. What issues or forces did Victor Cizanckas discuss that are relevant to reform?

8. Is the research on police leaders by Cohen and Pursley related? If so, how?

9. What evidence is there to support the proposition that women can be effective leaders in policing?

10. What are the two key dimensions and five principal styles of the managerial grid?

11. What is conflict and is it good or bad for organizations?

12. Are there any differences between organizational control and controls? If so, what?

13. What specific skills are associated with each of the different methods of resolving conflict?

Notes

1. Peter F. Drucker, *People and Performance: The Best of Peter Drucker on Management* (New York: Harper's College Press, 1977), p. 28.

2. Patrick A. Knight and Howard M. Weiss, "Effects of Selection Agent and Leader Origin on Leader Influence and Group Member Perceptions," *Organizational Behavior and Human Performance,* 26 (August 1980), pp. 17–21. Also, see Thomas Henderson, "The Relative Effects of Community Complexity and of Sheriffs Upon the Professionalism of Sheriff Departments," *American Journal of Political Science,* 19 (February 1975), p. 126.

3. Peter F. Drucker, *The Effective Executive* (New York: Harper & Row, 1966), p. 23 and pp. 36–39. Points 2–5 were taken from this source at p. 24. Also see Eugene Raudsepp, "Why Managers Don't Delegate," *Journal of Applied Management,* 4:5 (September–October 1979), pp. 25–27.

4. The flip side of the coin is the question, "Under what conditions do organizational members voluntarily elect to leave, stay and protest, or simply stay?" An important book addressing these issues is Albert O. Hirschman, *Exit, Voice, and Loyalty* (Cambridge, Mass.: Harvard University Press, 1970).

5. The description of power motivation styles is drawn, with restatement into a police context, from Jay Hall and James Hawker, "Interpreting Your Scores from the Power Management Inventory" (The Woodlands, Tex.: Teleometrics International, 1981).

6. Variants of this model appear in the literature; see, for example, Ronald G. Lynch, *The Police Manager,* 2d ed. (Boston: Holbrook Press, 1978), Figure 1–2, p. 11; Calvin J. Swank, "Police Management in the United States: A Candid Assessment," *Journal of Police Science and Administration,* 4 (1976), pp. 90–93; Robert Katz, "Skills of an Effective Administrator," *Harvard Business Review,* 33:1 (January–February 1955), pp. 33–42.

7. Ralph M. Stogdill, *Handbook of Leadership: A Survey of Theory and Research* (New York: Free Press, 1974), p. 17.

8. Thomas Carlyle, *Heroes, Hero-Worship and the Heroic in History* (New York: A. L. Burt, 1902).

9. Francis Galton, *Hereditary Genius: An Inquiry into Its Laws and Consequences* (New York: D. Appleton, revised with an American preface, 1887).

10. Field Marshal Montgomery, *The Path to Leadership* (New York: Putnam, 1961), pp. 10–19. To some extent, Montgomery also holds with Carlyle in that the former asserted that the leader must be able to dominate and master the surrounding events.

11. Cecil E. Goode, "Significant Research on Leadership," *Personnel,* 25:5 (March 1951), p. 349.

12. Stogdill, *Handbook of Leadership,* p. 81, and "Personal Factors Associated with Leadership: A Survey of the Literature," *Journal of Psychology,* 25–26 (January 1948), pp. 35–71.

13. C. A. Gibb, "Leadership," in *Handbook of Sound Psychology,* vol. 2, ed. Gardner Lindzey (Reading, Mass.: Addison-Wesley, 1954).

14. Walter J. Palmer, "Managerial Effectiveness as a Function of Personality Traits of the Manager," *Personnel Psychology,* 27 (Summer 1974), pp. 283–295.

15. Gary Dessler, *Organization and Management: A Contingency Approach* (Englewood Cliffs, N.J.: Prentice-Hall, 1976), p. 158.

16. Stogdill, "Personal Factors Associated with Leadership," pp. 35–71; Dessler, *Organization and Management,* p. 169.

17. F. E. Fiedler, *A Theory of Leadership Effectiveness* (New York: McGraw-Hill, 1967). Fiedler has worked on a contingency approach to leadership since the early 1950s.

18. Robert J. House, "A Path-Goal Theory of Leader Effectiveness," *Administrative Science Quarterly,* 16 (September 1971), pp. 321–338.

19. See K. Lewin, R. Lippitt, and R. White, "Patterns of Aggressive Behavior in Experimentally Created Social Climates," *The Journal of Social Psychology,* 10 (May 1939), pp. 271–299; R. Lippitt and R. K. White, "The Social Climate of Children's Groups," in *Child Behavior and Development,* eds. R. G. Baker, K. S. Kounin, and H. F. Wright (New York: McGraw-Hill, 1943), pp. 485–508; Ralph White and Ronald Lippitt, "Leader Behavior and Member Reaction in Three Social Climates," in *Group Dynamics: Research and Theory,* 2d ed., eds. Dorwin Cartwright and Alvin Zander (New York: Harper & Row

1960), pp. 552–553; Ronald Lippitt, ''An Experimental Study of the Effect of Democratic and Authoritarian Group Atmospheres,'' *University of Iowa Studies in Childwelfare,* 16 (January 1940), pp. 43–195.

20. White and Lippitt, ''Leader Behavior and Member Reaction in Three Social Climates,'' pp. 539–545 and 552–553.

21. Robert Tannenbaum and Warren H. Schmidt, ''How to Choose a Leadership Pattern,'' *The Harvard Business Review,* 36:2 (March–April 1958), pp. 95–101.

22. Ibid., pp. 98–101.

23. Anthony Downs, *Inside Bureaucracy* (Boston: Little, Brown, 1967).

24. Ibid., pp. 92–96.

25. Ibid., pp. 96–101.

26. Ibid., pp. 109–110.

27. Ibid., pp. 107–109.

28. Bernard Cohen, ''Leadership Styles of Commanders in the New York City Police Department,'' *Journal of Police Science and Administration,* 8:2 (June 1980), pp. 125–138. References to Downs's types of leaders has been added.

29. Robert D. Pursley, ''Leadership and Community Identification Attitudes Among Two Categories of Police Chiefs: An Exploratory Inquiry,'' *Journal of Police Science and Administration,* 2:4 (December 1974), pp. 414–422.

30. John Van Maanen, ''Making Rank: Becoming an American Police Sergeant,'' *Urban Life,* 13:2–3 (October 1984), pp. 155–176. The distinction between station and street sergeants is drawn from Van Maanen's work with some restatement and extension of views. The speculation about future career patterns is the work of the present authors.

31. Barbra R. Price, ''A Study of Leadership Strength of Female Police Executives,'' *Journal of Police Science and Administration,* 2:2 (June 1974), pp. 219–226.

32. Robert R. Blake and Jane Srygley Mouton, ''The Developing Revolution in Management Practices,'' *Journal of the American Society of Training Directors,* 16:7 (1962), pp. 29–52.

33. The Ohio State studies date from the mid-1940s and identified the dimensions of consideration and structure; the University of Michigan studies date from the late 1940s and identified employee- and production- centered supervisors.

34. These data were gathered from police leaders attending training programs led by Ronald Lynch, Institute of Government, University of North Carolina, and/or Charles Swanson and Leonard Territo. Because of the way in which the data were obtained, they should be considered as illustrative rather than representative.

35. How long a leader will persist in a given style depends upon the strength of preference for the primary over the backup, which is measurable. In this regard, see Jack L. Kuykendall, ''Police Leadership: An Analysis of Executive Styles,'' *Criminal Justice Review,* 2:2 (Spring 1977), pp. 89–100.

36. Paul Hersey and Kenneth H. Blanchard, *Management of Organizational Behavior: Utilizing Human Resources,* 3d ed. (Englewood Cliffs, N.J.: Prentice-Hall, 1977), p. 105. Also, see William J. Reddin, *Managerial Effectiveness* (New York: McGraw-Hill, 1970).

37. Hersey and Blanchard, *Management of Organizational Behavior,* pp. 160–161.

38. Ibid., p. 161.

39. Ibid., p. 161.

40. Ibid., p. 163.

41. Ibid., p. 161.

42. Ibid., p. 163.

43. Ibid., p. 162.

44. Ibid., p. 168.

45. Ibid., p. 165.

46. Ibid., p. 168.

47. Ibid., p. 159.

48. Albert E. Roark and Linda Wilkinson, ''Approaches to Conflict Management,'' *Group and Organizational Studies,* 4 (December 1979), p. 441.
49. Ibid., p. 441.
50. Ibid., p. 440; on this point, also see Kenneth Thomas, ''Conflict and Conflict Management,'' in *Handbook of Industrial and Organizational Psychology,* ed. Marvin D. Dunnette (Chicago: Rand McNally, 1976), p. 889.
51. See Lewis A. Coser, *The Functions of Social Conflict* (Glenco, Ill.: Free Press, 1956); G. Simmel, *Conflict* (New York: Free Press, 1955); M. Deutsch, ''Toward an Understanding of Conflict,'' *International Journal of Group Tensions.* 1:1 (January–March 1971), p. 48.
52. Morton Deutsch, *The Resolution of Conflict* (New Haven, Conn.: Yale University Press, 1973), p. 353.
53. Ibid., p. 363.
54. Peter F. Drucker, *Management: Tasks, Responsibilities, Practices* (New York: Harper & Row, 1973), p. 494.
55. Ibid., p. 494.
56. Ibid., pp. 496–505.

The difference between the right word and the almost right word is the difference between lightning and lightning bug.

MARK TWAIN

Interpersonal and Organizational Communication

Introduction

Effective communication is essential in all organizations in which people deal with one another. It is very difficult to imagine any kind of activity that does not depend on communication in one form or another. Today's police managers are aware that the efficiency of their personnel depends to a great extent on how well the efforts of individual members can be coordinated. Since coordination does not just happen, managers must realize that communication is necessary, if their subordinates are to obtain the understanding and cooperation required to achieve organizational and individual goals.

A major role of today's manager is that of communicator. Managers at all levels of the police organization spend an overwhelming amount of their time in the process and problems of communication.

Research in recent years has indicated that communication is the number one problem in management, and lack of communication is the employees' primary complaint about their immediate supervisors.[1] The information contained in this chapter is intended to provide police managers with an overview of both interpersonal and organizational communications and provide specific information that will facilitate and enhance their communication skills.

The Communication Process

An explanation of communication begins with a basic problem—it cannot be examined as an isolated event. Communication is a process, and so it must be understood as the totality of several interdependent and dynamic elements. In the aggregate, communications may be defined as the process by which senders and receivers interact in given social contexts. Another understanding of this definition is that the process of communication requires that we examine the several elements that make up the process: encoding, transmission, medium, reception, decoding, and feedback.[2] Figure 6-1 illustrates this process graphically.

Encoding. Experience cannot be transmitted as experience. In conveying an experience to another person, we do not relive that experience with that person.

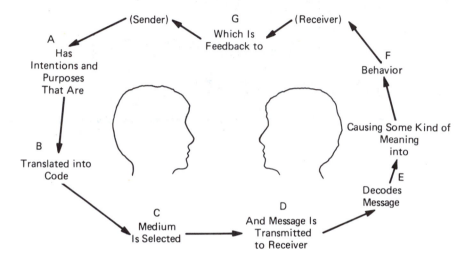

A. The sender has certain intentions, objectives, or purposes.

B. The sender translated these intentions into some code (language, nonverbal gesture, etc.), which becomes the message.

C. The sender then selects a medium (written or spoken words, music, art, etc.).

D. The sender uses the medium to transmit the message to the receiver.

E. The receiver "picks up" the message (listens, reads, watches, etc.) and decodes its meaning.

F. This meaning causes the receiver to behave in some manner.

G. This behavior gives the sender indications, or feedback, as to whether or not the receiver understood the meaning of the message.

FIGURE 6-1. The communication process. [From R. C. Huseman, "The Communication Process," in *Interpersonal Communication: A Guide for Staff Development* (Athens: Institute of Government, University of Georgia, August 1974), p. 22.]

Even in the most scrupulous reproduction of an experience, every element cannot be duplicated. At the very least, the time period is altered, and intervening experiences have altered us as individuals.

To convey an experience or idea to someone, we translate, or encode that experience into symbols. We use words or other verbal behaviors and gestures, or other nonverbal behaviors to convey the experience or idea. These symbols are our code; they stand for certain experiences; they are not experiences themselves.

Transmission.   Encoding involves only the decision to use a symbol for some concept. The element of transmission involves the translation of the encoded symbols into some behavior that another person can observe. The actual articulation (moving our lips, tongue, etc.) of the symbol into verbal or nonverbal observable behavior is transmission.

Medium.   Communication must be conveyed through some channel or medium. Media for communication may be our sight, hearing, taste, touch, or smell. Some other channels for media are television, telephone, paper and pencil, and radio. The importance of the choice of the medium should not be minimized. All of us are aware of the difference between a message that our superior delivers personally and the one that is sent through a secretary or by a memo. The medium, like the chosen symbol, has an effect on the meaning that the listener eventually attaches to the message in the process of decoding.

Reception.   For the receiver, the reception of the message is analogous to the sender's transmission. The stimuli, the verbal and nonverbal symbols, reach the senses of the receiver and are conveyed to the brain for interpretation.

Decoding.   The process of interpretation occurs when the individual who has received the stimuli develops some meaning for the verbal and nonverbal symbols and decodes the stimuli. For the receiver, then, decoding is analogous to the process of encoding for the sender. These symbols are translated into some concept or experience of the receiver. Whether the receiver is familiar with the symbols used, or whether interference, such as any physical noise or physiological problem, occurs, determines how closely the message that the receiver has decoded approximates the message that the sender has encoded. The success of the communication process depends on the extent to which the receiver's decoded concept is similar to the concept of the sender. It is for this reason that we hear the phrase, "meaning is in people." Truly, the external verbal and nonverbal symbols that we usually call the message are in fact only stimuli. The actual message is the decoded or interpreted concept of the receiver. This decoded concept is the receiver's meaning for the external stimuli.

Feedback.   When the receiver decodes the symbols transmitted, he or she usually provides some response or feedback to the sender. Feedback is a self-correcting mechanism. In our homes, thermostats, self-correcting mechanisms within the heating or cooling unit, will correct the temperature. In communication, responses to the symbols that we have sent act as regulators. If someone appears puzzled, we repeat the message or we encode the concept differently and transmit some different symbols to express the same concept. Feedback that we receive acts as a guide or steering device. Feedback promotes accuracy of communication. Feedback lets us know whether the receiver has interpreted our symbols as we intended. Feedback is, then, a crucial element in guaranteeing that the meaning that the sender intended to convey was in fact conveyed to the receiver.

Communication Barriers

Barriers to communication, or communication breakdowns, can occur at any place in the system. They may be the result of improper techniques on the part of either the sender or the receiver.

Sender-Caused Barriers. The sender hinders communications when

1. The sender is not clear about what is to be accomplished with the message.
2. The sender assumes incorrectly that the receiver has the knowledge necessary to understand the message and its intent and does not adapt the message to the intended receiver.
3. The sender uses a communication medium not suited for the message; for example, some messages are better transmitted face to face, others in writing or by illustrations.
4. The sender does not develop a mechanism for receiving feedback to determine if the message was understood correctly.
5. The sender does not interpret feedback correctly or fails to clarify the message on the basis of feedback from the receiver.
6. The sender uses language that causes the receiver to stop listening, reading, or receiving.
7. The sender analyzes the audience improperly.
8. The sender's background experiences and attitudes are different from those of the receiver, and the sender does not take this into account.

Receiver-Caused Barriers. The receiver hinders communication when

1. The receiver is a poor listener, observer, or reader and therefore misinterprets the meaning of the message.
2. The receiver jumps to conclusions.
3. The receiver hears or sees only certain parts of the message.
4. The receiver tends to reject messages that contradict beliefs and assumptions.
5. The receiver has other concerns such as emotional barriers, for example, being mentally preoccupied.

Other Barriers. Some other barriers to communication are

1. Noise, temperature, and other physical distractions.
2. Distance or inability to see or hear the message being sent.
3. Sender-receiver relationship, power structure, roles, and personality differences.

Information Flow and Directionality

Organizational systems of communication are usually created by setting up formal systems of responsibility and explicit delegations of duties, such as implicit statements of the nature, content, and direction of communication that are necessary for the performance of the group. Consequently, formal communication is required by the organization and follows the accepted pattern of hierarchical structure. Delegated authority and responsibility determine the path that communication should take, whether upward or downward. Messages that travel through the formal channels of any organization may follow routine patterns; they may be expected at a given time, or presented in a standard form, and receive a regularized degree of consideration.[3]

Most police managers prefer a formal system regardless of how cumbersome it may be because they can control it and because it tends to create a record for future reference. However, motivational factors of the individual and organizations affect the flow of communication. Employees typically communicate with those who help them to achieve their aims and avoid communicating with those who do not assist, or may retard, their accomplishing those goals; they direct their communications toward those who make them feel more secure and gratify their needs and away from those who threaten them or make them feel anxious or generally provide unrewarding experiences; and employees communicate in a manner that allows them to increase their status, belong to a more prestigious group, attain more power to influence decisions, or expand their control. The moving transaction identified as organizational communication can occur at several levels and can result in understanding, agreement, good feeling, and appropriate behavior; the converse may also be true.[4]

Downward Communication

Classical management theories place primary emphasis on control, chain of command, and downward flow of information. Downward communication is used by management for sending orders, directives, goals, policies, procedures, memorandums, and so forth to employees at lower levels of the organization. Five types of such communication within an organization can be identified.[5]

1. Job instruction-communication relating to the performance of a certain task.
2. Job rational-communication relating a certain task to organizational tasks.
3. Procedures and practices-communication about organization policies, procedures, rules, and regulations.
4. Feedback-communication appraisal of how an individual performs the assigned task.
5. Indoctrination-communication designed to motivate the employees.[6]

Other reasons for communicating downward implicit in this listing are opportunities for management to spell out objectives, change attitudes and mold opinions, prevent misunderstandings from lack of information, and prepare employees for change.[7] A study conducted by Opinion Research Corporation some years ago revealed surprisingly that large amounts of information generated at the top of an organization did not filter down to the working levels. Studies of the flow of communications within complex organizations repeatedly demonstrate that each level of management can act as an obstacle or barrier to downward communication.[8] In perhaps the best controlled experimental research in downward communication, Dahle[9] proved the efficacy of using oral and written media together. His findings indicate the following order of effectiveness (from most effective to least effective):

1. Oral and written communication combined.
2. Oral communication only.

3. Written communication only.
4. The use of the bulletin board.
5. The organizational grapevine.

The research conducted thus far seems to indicate that most downward channels in organizations are only minimally effective. Findings indicate further that attempts at disseminating information downward in an organization should not depend exclusively on a single medium or channel.

Upward Communication

Even though police administrators may appreciate the need for effective upward communication, they may not translate this need into action.[10] It becomes apparent at once that to swim upstream is a much harder task than to float downstream. But currents of resistance, inherent in the temperament and habits of supervisors and employees in the complexity and structure of modern police agencies, are persistent and strong. Let us examine some of these deterrents to upward communication.

BARRIERS INVOLVING POLICE ORGANIZATIONS

The physical distance between superior and subordinate impede upward communication in several ways. Communication becomes difficult and infrequent when superiors are isolated so as to be seldom seen or spoken to. In large police organizations, executives may be located in headquarters or operating centers that are not easily reached by subordinates. In other police agencies, executive offices may be placed remotely or executives may hold themselves needlessly inaccessible.

The complexity of the organization may also cause prolonged delays of upward communication. For example, let us assume that there is a problem at the patrol officer level that must be settled eventually by the chief executive or some other high-ranking officer. A patrol officer tells the sergeant about the problem, and they discuss it and try to settle it. It may take several hours or even a couple of days before all the available facts are compiled. The sergeant in turn brings the problem to the lieutenant, who feels compelled to reexamine all the facts of the problem and perhaps pursue it even further before forwarding it on to the next highest authority. Since each succeeding superior may be concerned that the problem could somehow reflect negatively on his or her ability, delays result that could mean that the problem is not brought to the attention of the chief executive for several weeks. In addition, as the information moves up the organizational ladder, there is a tendency for it to be diluted or distorted, since each supervisor consciously or unconsciously selects and edits information being passed up. The more levels of supervision the information passes through, the more it is filtered and the less accurate it becomes.

BARRIERS INVOLVING SUPERIORS

The attitude of superiors and their behavior in listening plays a vital role in encouraging or discouraging communication upward. If, in listening to a subordinate, a supervisor seems anxious to end the interview, impatient with the subordinate, or annoyed or distressed by the subject being discussed, a major barrier to future communication may be created.

There is always the danger that a supervisor may assume the posture that "no news is good news," when in fact a lack of complaints or criticism may be a symptom that upward communication is operating at a dangerously low level.

Supervisors may also assume, often incorrectly, that they know what subordinates think or feel and also believe that listening to complaints from subordinates, especially complaints about departmental policies or even specific supervisors, is an indication of disloyalty. This attitude tends to discourage employees with justifiable complaints from approaching their superiors.

One of the strongest deterrents to upward communication is a failure of management to take action on undesirable conditions previously brought to their attention. The result is that subordinates lose faith both in the sincerity of management and in the value of communication.

Some executives feel that they are too involved in daily problems and responsibilities to provide adequate time for listening fully to their subordinates ideas, reports, and criticisms. Nevertheless, many time-consuming problems could be minimized or eliminated if superiors would take time to listen to their employees, for in listening they can discover solutions to present problems or anticipate causes for future ones. The subordinate who has free access to a superior can get answers to many budding problems and thus eliminate the heavier demands that will result when the problems have become much more complex, emotion laden, and possibly even out of control.

Barriers Involving Subordinates

Communication may flow more freely downward than upward because a superior is free to call in a subordinate and talk about a problem at will. The subordinate does not have the same freedom to intrude upon the superior's time and is also discouraged from circumventing the chain of command and going over a superior's head or from asking for an appeal from decisions made by superiors. Thus, neither the system available nor the rewards offered to the subordinate for upward communication equal those for messages downward.

Management, on the other hand, can speed the flow of information by the use of written policies, procedures, general orders, meetings, and so forth. There are rarely comparable organizational vehicles available for the upward flow of communications. Further, tradition, authority, and prestige are behind communications downward.

In communicating upward, a subordinate must provide explanations for the desired communication and, in the final analysis, must obtain acceptance from someone with greater status who is also likely to be more fluent and persuasive than the subordinate. The superior probably has worked in a similar position at one time and knows the attitudes, language, and problems at that level. On the other hand, the subordinate who is communicating with a superior rarely understands the responsibilities or difficulties faced by the superior.

Finally, unless superiors are particularly receptive, subordinates generally prefer to withhold or temper bad news, unfavorable opinions, and reports of mistakes or failures. If a manager is defensive about listening to bad news, those who like and respect the manager will withhold information or minimize omissions and errors from friendly motives; others may withhold information from fear, dislike, or indifference.

Horizontal Communication

When an organization's formal communication channels are not open, the informal horizontal channels are almost sure to thrive as a substitute.[11] If there is a disadvantage in horizontal communication, it is that it is much easier and more natural to achieve than is vertical communication and, therefore, often replaces vertical channels rather than supplements them. Actually, the horizontal channels that replace weak or nonexistent vertical channels are usually of an informal nature. There are, of course, formal horizontal channels that are procedurally necessary and should be built into the system. Formal horizontal channels must be set up between various bureaus and divisions for the purposes of planning, interwork task coordination, and general system maintenance functions, such as problem solving, information sharing, and conflict resolution.

We can begin by acknowledging that horizontal communication is essential if the subsystems within a police organization are to function in an effective and coordinated manner. Communication horizontally among peers may also tend to furnish the emotional and social bond that builds *esprit de corps* or a feeling of teamwork. Psychologically, people seem to need this type of communication, and police managers would do well to provide for this need and thus allow peers to solve some of their own work problems together.

Suppose, for example, that patrol sergeant A is having great difficulty communicating certain mutually beneficial information to detective sergeant B because the police department requires strict adherence to the chain of command in transmitting information. As indicated in Figure 6-2A, sergeant A would have to go up through the various hierarchical complexities of the patrol division and back down through the detective division to communicate with sergeant B. The time being wasted and the level-to-level message distortion occurring in the classically managed organization was recognized by Fayol in 1916.[12] Fayol proposed the creation of a horizontal bridge (see Figure 6-2B) that would allow more direct communications between individuals within an organization. The major limiting factor to the use of Fayol's bridge is a loss of network control and the subsequent weakening of authority and random scattering of messages throughout the system. Such random communication channels can lead to diagonal lines of communication, such as direct communication between sergeant A in the patrol division and captain C in the detective division. Diagonal lines of communication are not in and of themselves bad; however, they are very difficult to control from the management point of view.[13]

Despite the need for formal horizontal communication in an organization, there may be tendency among peers not to formally communicate task-related information horizontally. For instance, rivalry for recognition and promotion may cause competing subordinates to be reluctant to share information. Subordinates may also find it difficult

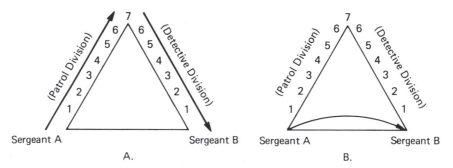

FIGURE 6-2. Horizontal lines of communication: A. Message path from sergeant A to sergeant B following the usual structured channels. B. Message path from sergeant A to sergeant B following Fayol's bridge. [From R. K. Allen, *Organizational Management Through Communication* (New York: Harper & Row, 1977), pp. 78–79. Reprinted by permission of Harper & Row, Publishers, Inc.]

to communicate with highly specialized people at the same level as themselves in other divisions.

In the main, then, formal horizontal communication channels are vital as a supplement to the vertical channels in an organization. Conversely, the informal horizontal channels, while needed socially, can be detrimental to the vertical channels. Informal horizontal channels may not only be carrying false or distorted information but sometimes tend to replace the vertical channels.[14]

The Grapevine

The best-known system for transmitting informal communication is the grapevine, so called because it meanders back and forth like a grapevine across organizational lines. The grapevine's most effective characteristics are that it is fast, it can be highly selective and discriminating, it operates mostly at the place of work, and it supplements and relates to the formal communication. These characteristics may be divided into desirable or undesirable attributes.

The grapevine can be considered desirable because it gives management insight into employees' attitudes, provides a safety valve for employees' emotions, and helps to spread useful information. Dysfunctional traits include its tendencies to spread rumors and untruths, its lack of responsibility to any group or person, and its uncontrollability. Attributes of the grapevine, its speed and influence, may work either to the good or to the detriment of the organization. The actual operation of the grapevine can be visualized in four ways (see Figure 6-3).[15]

1. The single strand chain: A tells B, who tells C, who tells D, and so on.
2. The gossip chain: A seeks and tells everyone else, thus being the organizational "Paul Revere."
3. The probability chain: A communicates randomly to D, F, G, and J, in

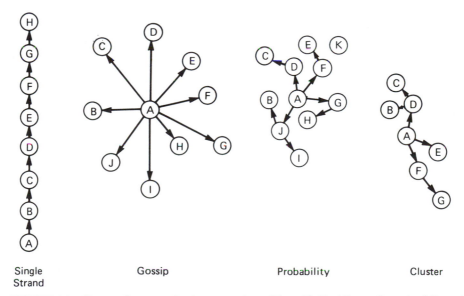

Single   Gossip   Probability   Cluster
Strand

FIGURE 6-3. Types of communication grapevines. [From H. H. Albers, *Organized Executive Action: Decision Making and Leadership* (New York: John Wiley, 1961), p. 343.]

accord with the laws of probability; then D, F, G, and J tell others in the same manner.

4. The cluster chain: A tells three selected others; perhaps one of them tells two others; and one of these tells one other person.

The grapevine is a permanent factor to be reckoned with in the daily activities of management, and no competent manager would try to abolish it. Rather, the astute manager should analyze it and consciously try to influence it.[16]

Interpersonal Styles of Communication: The Johari Window

A cross-cultural study involving respondents from the United States, Japan, and Great Britain revealed that approximately 74 percent of the managers cited communication breakdown as the single greatest barrier to organizational excellence.[17] A fact of organizational life is that, when management is effective and relationships among organizational members are sound, problems of communication breakdown tend not to be heard.[18] It is only when relationships among organizational members are fraught with unarticulated tensions that complaints about communication breakdown begin to be heard.[19] Two important points are implicit in this discussion:

1. The quality of relationships in an organization may dictate to a large extent the level of communication effectiveness achieved.
2. The quality of relationships, in turn, is a direct product of the interpersonal practices of an organization's membership.[20]

The single most important aspect of interpersonal practices is the way in which parties to a relationship communicate with each other. In 1955, Joseph Luft and Harry Ingham developed a communication model for use in their group dynamics training programs; this model has come to be known as the Johari Window, its designation as such arising from the use of portions of the first names of its developers.[21] Subsequently, Jay Hall and Martha Williams modified it to treat the Johari Window as an information flow and processing model. Through the use of a questionnaire developed by Hall and Williams, interpersonal styles of communication are identifiable.[22]

The Johari Window model is depicted in Figure 6-4 and has two key dimensions: exposure and feedback.[23] Exposure means the open and candid expression of the police manager's feelings, factual knowledge, guesses, and the like in a conscious attempt to share; together, these expressions are referred to as information. Untrue, frivolous, and kindred statements do not constitute exposure because they contribute nothing to promoting mutual understanding. Central to the use of exposure by the police manager is the desire to build trust and a willingness to accept a certain amount of risk. The feedback process entails the police leader's active solicitation of information that he or she feels others may have that he or she does not.

Figure 6-4 consists of four quadrants or regions, defined as follows:

1. Region I, termed the arena, is the area of the total space available in which information is shared equally and understood by the police manager and

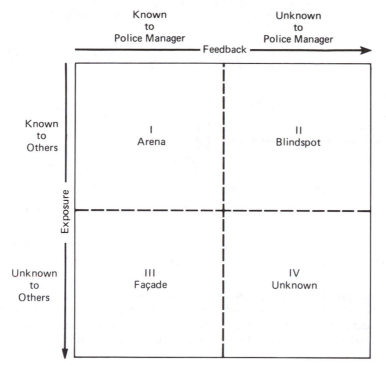

FIGURE 6-4. The Johari window. [From Jay Hall and Martha S. Williams, "How to Interpret Your Scores on the Personal Relations Survey," © Teleometrics International, The Woodlands, Texas, 1967, with minor modification. Special permission for reproduction is granted by the authors Jay Hall, PhD, and Martha S. Williams, PhD, and publisher, Teleometrics International. All rights reserved.]

others. This facet of the interpersonal relationship is thought to be the part that controls interpersonal productivity. The underlying assumption is that productivity and interpersonal effectiveness are related directly to the amount of mutually held information in a relationship. Therefore, the larger region I becomes, the more effective, rewarding, and productive becomes the relationship as well.

2. Region II, the blindspot, is that portion of the total space available that holds information known by others but unknown to the police manager. This area represents a handicap to the manager because one can scarcely understand the decisions, behavior, and feelings of others if one lacks the information on which they are based. However, others have a certain advantage to the extent that they have information unknown to the manager.

3. Region III, designated the façade, may also be considered an inhibitor of interpersonal effectiveness and productivity, due to an imbalance of information that favors the police manager. This is so because the police manager possesses information that is not known by others. The manager may withhold information that is perceived as potentially prejudicial to the relationship, out of fear, desire for power, or other related reasons. Essentially the façade serves as a protective front, but at the expense of keeping the arena from growing larger. Realistically, every relationship has a façade; the practical question is, How much is actually needed?

4. Region IV, the unknown, is the portion of the total space available that is

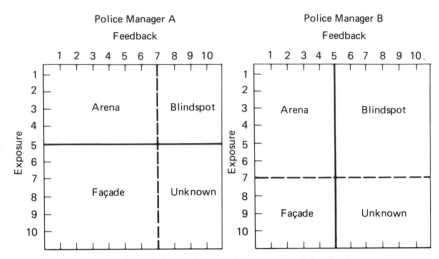

FIGURE 6-5. Illustration of the exchange of exposure and feedback.

unknown to both the police manager and others. This area is thought to contain psychodynamic data, unknown potentials, learned idiosyncracies, and the data base of creativity. However, as interpersonal effectiveness increases and the arena becomes larger, the unknown region shrinks.

As suggested, while the regions shown in Figure 6-4 are of equal size, when they are measured through the use of the Hall–Williams questionnaire, the ''Personnel Relations Survey,'' the regions vary in size. To illustrate, assume as shown in Figure 6-5 that there are two police managers. Manager B actively solicits information from manager A and as a result receives five ''parcels'' of information. Manager A is giving exposure, and manager B is receiving feedback, as depicted by the solid lines. Subsequently, the roles are reversed, and manager A receives seven ''parcels'' of information from manager B, as shown by the dashed lines. On the basis of this hypothetical exchange of feedback and exposure between managers A and B, the size of the quadrants or regions in their respective Johari Windows is established.

Basic Interpersonal Styles of Communication

Figure 6-6 shows the four basic interpersonal communication styles, which may be described in the following terms:

Type A. This interpersonal style reflects a minimal use of both exposure and feedback processes; it is, in effect, a fairly impersonal approach to interpersonal relationships. The unknown region dominates under this style, and unrealized potential, untapped creativity, and personal psychodynamics prevail as the salient influences. Such a style would seem to indicate withdrawal and an aversion to risk taking on the part of its user; interpersonal anxiety and safety seeking are likely to be prime sources of personal motivation. Police managers who characteristically use this style appear to be rigid, aloof, and uncommunicative. This style may often be found in bureaucratic organizations of some type where it is possible, and perhaps profitable, to avoid personal disclosure or involvement. Persons using this style are likely to be reacted to with more than average hostility, since other parties to the relationship

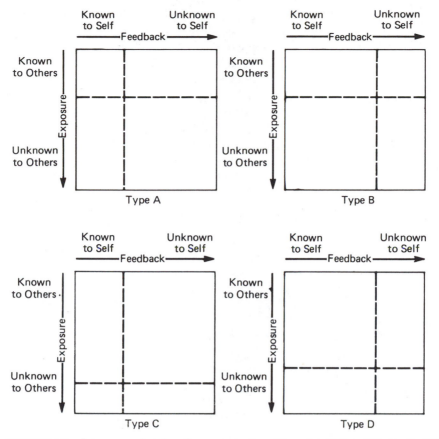

FIGURE 6-6. Interpersonal styles of communication. [From Jay Hall and Martha S. Williams, "How to Interpret Your Scores on the Personal Relations Survey," © Teleometrics International, The Woodlands, Texas, 1967. Special permission for reproduction is granted by the authors Jay Hall, PhD, and Martha S. Williams, PhD, and publisher, Teleometrics International. All rights reserved.]

will tend to interpret the lack of exposure and feedback solicitation pretty much in terms of their own needs and how this interpersonal lack affects need fulfillment.

Type B. Under this approach, there is also an aversion to exposure, but it is coupled with a *desire* for relationships not found in type A. Thus, feedback is the only process left in promoting relationships, and it is much overused. An aversion to the use of exposure may typically be interpreted as a sign of basic mistrust of others, and it is therefore not surprising that the façade is the dominant feature of relationships resulting from underused exposure coupled with overused feedback. The style appears to be a probing quasi-supportive, interpersonal ploy, and, once the façade becomes apparent, it is likely to result in a reciprocal withdrawal of trust by other parties. This may promote feelings of disgust, anxiety, and hostility on the part of others; such feelings may lead to the user being treated as a rather superficial person without real substance.

Type C. This interpersonal style is based on an overuse of exposure to the neglect of feedback. It may well reflect ego striving and/or distrust of others' opinions.

Individuals who use this style may feel quite confident of the validity of their own opinions and are likely to value authority. The fact is that they are often unaware of the impact they have on others. Others are likely to feel disenfranchised by individuals who use this style; they often feel that such people have little use for their contributions or concern for their feelings. As a result, this style often triggers feelings of hostility, insecurity, and resentment on the part of others. Frequently, others will learn to behave in such a way as to perpetrate the user's blindspot by withholding important information or by giving only selected feedback; as such, this is a reflection of the defensiveness that this style can cause others to experience.

Type D. Exposure and feedback processes are used to a great and balanced extent in this style; candor and openness coupled with a sensitivity to others' needs to participate are the salient features of the style. The arena becomes the dominant feature of the relationship, and productivity may be expected to increase as well. In initial stages, this style may promote some defensiveness on the part of others unused to honest and trusting relationships; but perseverance will tend to promote a norm of reciprocal candor over time such that trust and creative potential can be realized.[24]

Although not one of the basic styles, there is a fifth commonly appearing style, which we designate as type E. The type E style falls between types C and D, using both more exposure and feedback that type C but less than type D. In type E, there is slightly greater reliance on the use of exposure as opposed to feedback (see Table 6-1).

Police Managers and Interpersonal Styles of Communication

The mean Johari Window scores for 325 police managers are plotted in Figure 6-7. Note that the Johari Window yields the style associated with communicating with three different groups—(1) subordinates, (2) colleagues, and (3) superiors—and that there is some variance among the scores. This variance is even more striking when

TABLE 6-1 Mean Johari Window Interpersonal Communication Styles for Various Groups of Police Managers

Group	Number in group	Communication with		
		Subordinates	Colleagues	Superiors
1	27	E	E	E
2	26	E	C	B
3	21	A	C	C
4	38	B	C	E
5	41	E	C	E
6	40	E	E	E
7	24	E	C	E
8	30	D	D	D
9	19	C	D	C

These data were gathered by Ronald Lynch, Institute of Government, University of North Carolina, and/or Charles Swanson during 1975–1985. They include groups of managers from the southeastern United States, New Jersey, and Oregon. Managers from municipal and county police departments and sheriffs' offices are represented.

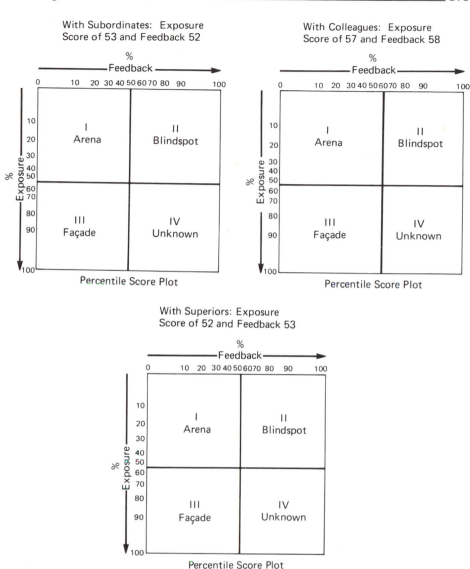

FIGURE 6-7. Mean Johari Window scores for 325 police managers. [The data depicted in these graphs are taken from Jay Hall, "Interpersonal Style and the Communication Dilemma: Utility of the Johari Window Awareness Model for Genotypic Diagnosis," *Human Relations,* 28 (1975), Table 3, p. 730. The graphs on which these data are displayed are taken from Jay Hall and Martha S. Williams, "How to Interpret Your Scores on the Personal Relations Survey," © Teleometrics International, The Woodlands, Texas, 1967. Special permission for reproduction is granted by the authors Jay Hall, PhD, and Martha S. Williams, PhD, and publisher, Teleometrics International. All rights reserved.]

examining the styles for eight different groups of police managers summarized in Table 6-1. Given such variance, it is difficult to make a unifying statement, but in general, type E is the most commonly occurring pattern among police managers.

As might be expected, there are correlations between grid management styles and Johari Window styles. These relationships are depicted in Table 6-2. To some

TABLE 6-2 Relationship of Grid Management and Johari Window Styles

Grid style	Johari window style
9,9 Team management	Type D
5,5 Organization management	Type E
9,1 Authority-obedience	Type C
1,9 County club management	Type B
1,1 Impoverished management	Type A

Data supporting these correlations may be found in Jay Hall, "Interpersonal Style and the Communication Dilemma: Managerial Implications of the Johari Awareness Model," *Human Relations,* 27 (April 1974), p. 391.

extent these associations raise a "chicken and egg question" as to whether the choice of grid styles produces the Johari style or whether the reverse is true.

Oral or Written Communication

Suiting the Medium to the Recipient

Although there is potentially a great variety of media available for issuing orders, the individual issuing the orders is generally forced to choose from among a few existing ones that have nothing more than tradition in their favor. When certain media have become established, all subsequent material is made to fit them. If, for example, an organization has a personnel policy manual, it may become the pattern to announce through a routine revision of the manual even those changes that may be of immediate and crucial interest to the employees. A change in the design of an application form would not elicit widespread interest, but a new system for computing vacation allowances is bound to interest everyone. Such differences in interest value are important factors in the proper selection of the media, but the medium must be available to choose from.

Written Communication

There tends to be considerable confidence in the written word within complex organizations. It establishes a permanent record, but a transmittal of information in this way does not necessarily assure that the message will be unambiguous to the receiver. Sometimes, in spite of the writer's efforts, information is not conveyed clearly to the recipient. This may result, in part, because the writer lacks the writing skills necessary to convey the message clearly and unambiguously. For example, the following information was taken from letters received by a county department and illustrates the difficulty some people have in communicating via the written form.

> I am forwarding my marriage certificate and six children. I have seven but one died which was baptized on a half sheet of paper.

> Mrs. Jones had not had any clothes for a year and has been visited regularly by the clergy.

Please find for certain if my husband is dead. The man I am living with can't eat or do anything until he knows.

I am very much annoyed to find you have branded my son illiterate. This is a dirty lie as I was married a week before he was born.

In answer to your letter, I have given birth to a boy weighing ten pounds. I hope this is satisfactory.

I am forwarding my marriage certificate and three children, one of which is a mistake as you can see.

Unless I get my husband's money pretty soon, I will be forced to lead an immortal life.

You have changed my little boy to a little girl. Will this make any difference?

I have no children as yet as my husband is a truck driver and works day and night.

I want money as quick as I can get it. I have been in bed with the doctor for two weeks and he doesn't do me any good. If things don't improve, I will have to send for another doctor.

In other instances, the writer may be communicating at too high a level for the recipient. The news article on the following page illustrates this point.

There is some evidence to suggest that police administrators are beginning to rely increasingly upon written communication as their dominant medium for transmitting information. This trend is occurring in part because of the realization that good records provide the greatest protection against the growing numbers of legal actions being taken against police departments by citizens, activists, interest groups, police unions, and so forth. Thus, even in those cases where initial contact with someone is made via oral communication, a follow-up memo or letter is frequently filed to verify the facts of the communication.

Oral Communication

There are some distinct advantages in oral communication to both the sender and the receiver.

The recipient of an oral order is able to probe for exactness wherever the meaning is not entirely clear, provided that the individual is not too unfamiliar with the subject matter. The recipient of the information may ask for a clarifying or confirming statement in writing, or a sketch or chart, or a demonstration of a manual operation. In this situation, both individuals are able to state their case so long as the elements of give and take are preserved.

The person issuing an order, on the other hand, has an opportunity for immediate feedback and can see whether the order has produced understanding or confusion. The person issuing the order can probably discern the recipient's attitude and determine whether it is one of acceptance or rejection, but the attitude of the person issuing the order will also be apparent to the recipient. It appears that an oral medium is highly suitable when it is believed that an instruction will be temporary. For example, a police sergeant instructing an officer to direct traffic at an intersection because of street construction will likely not put that instruction in writing if the problem is one of short duration. However, if the construction will be of long duration, a written order may be forthcoming, specifying that an officer will be assigned to direct traffic at this particular location until further notice. Further, the written order may also specify additional details such as the times the officer is expected to be at the location.

BOX 6-1.

What Is Your Fog Index

By GAYLE WHITE, *Constitution Staff Writer*

Shortly after he took office, former President Jimmy Carter sent out an executive order telling government executives to write their regulations in "plain English."

To understand Carter's memorandum, however, one would need at least the equivalent of a master's degree, Dr. Warren Blumenfeld says.

Blumenfeld is a professor of industrial psychology at Georgia State University. The readability index rating of Carter's memo was about 19, Blumenfeld said, which means that only a person with 19 or more years of formal education could be expected to understand it.

Blumenfeld and his students have studied various documents and works of literature, from Dr. Seuss' *The Cat in the Hat* to the federal food stamp eligibility act, to determine how easily they can be understood. Some of the studies have been presented before such professional groups as the American Psychological Association.

The field of readability was popularized by Rudolph Flesch in the 1940s, and modified by Robert Gunning into a rating called the "Fog Index," which Blumenfeld uses.

As Jefferson D. Bates explains in his book, "Writing with Precision," the first step in computing the "Fog Index" of a document is to choose a 100-word sample. Figure the average sentence length of the sample, then count the words with three or more syllables. Add the average number of words per sentence to the number of "difficult" words per hundred. Multiply the sum by 0.4. The product, or Fog Index rating, should be roughly equivalent to the grade level required to comprehend the document.

Determining readability is important, Blumenfeld said. "To the extent that you can get a reasonable match between the level of the document and the level of the target market, you've got a better chance of effective communication."

Or, in simpler terms—if you write on a level the people you want to reach can understand, they're more likely to do what you want them to.

A failure in communicating can be likened to the performance of a catcher and a pitcher in a baseball game, Blumenfeld said. "If a pitcher throws the ball at the catcher and the catcher doesn't catch it, it's the catcher's fault. If the pitcher throws the ball over the catcher's head and the catcher doesn't get it, it's the pitcher's fault."

If a writer states a concept clearly and effectively, at a level his audience can understand, and the reader fails to comprehend it, it's the reader's fault. But if the writer puts a concept into obtuse language and the reader fails to understand it, the lack of communication is probably the writer's fault.

In studying government documents, Blumenfeld and his associates also considered training manuals for people who must enforce them, and educational material to inform the public about them.

OSHA. Since the Occupational Safety and Health Act passed in 1970, businesses have struggled to conform to a program many failed to understand.

Blumenfeld assumed that the primary targets of OSHA materials were personnel directors and OSHA inspectors.

By considering the educational requirements of the two jobs and statistics gleaned from a professional personnel directors' association, Blumenfeld estimated the education level of OSHA inspectors at 16 years and the educational level of personnel directors at 16.31.

When he turned to Occupational Safety and Health Act itself, however, Blumenfeld found that it registered 30.79 on the readability scale. An executive order explaining it registered 23.66; the OSHA reporting regulations, 23.27; the OSHA inspector's manual, 20.47; and OSHA poster, 18.31.

Only OSHA directives, which registered 16.17, could be expected to be understood by the personnel managers and OSHA inspectors who must enforce the entire Occupational Safety and Health Act.

"The inappropriate reading level of OSHA materials for the intended readership . . . ," Blumenfeld wrote in a report of his study, "in turn will probably lead to continued decreases in morale, attitudes, credibility, and implementation. Possibly worst of all, it generates apparent 'busy work.' "

Internal Revenue Service Forms 1040 and 1040A. "We looked at the IRS instructions and plotted the long form and short form over the years," Blumenfeld said. "The short form (1040A) stays roughly at 12 years. It vacillates a little bit, but it's roughly high school equivalent or a little less. The long form (1040) contin-think it was about 15, which is college junior (level). You can be an accountant at 16." Specifically, 1976 instructions for the 1040 form were 14.16; 1040A instructions were estimated to require 12.45 years of education.

"You can have a cynical view," Blumenfeld said. "It's certainly cheaper for the government to process the short forms than it is to process the long forms. They can set the game up so that you'll say 'to heck with it all' and take the short form. That's a good deal for the government."

Catalogs of Georgia Tech and Georgia State. Blumenfeld began this study when a student asked him to interpret a paragraph of the catalog. Blumenfeld didn't understand it any better than the student.

The results of his study showed that to comprehend the full Georgia State catalog, one would need about 16 years of education—or a college degree. The Georgia Tech catalog scored even higher, 17.9, or a master's degree. "You would have had to have matriculated to understand the catalog," said Esther Blumenfeld, who has worked with her husband on several projects.

The 1976 Democratic and Republican Platforms. Two separate census Blumenfeld studied placed the educational level of the general U.S. population at just below high school graduate level, or somewhere between 11 and 12. The 1976 Republican platform checked out at 15.75; the Democratic platform at 17.41. "One would have to question whether or not they wanted them to be read," said Blumenfeld.

All documents aren't inappropriate for their audiences, however. The state driver's manual, for instance, checked out at 11.08, or high school junior level—appropriate for a state that awards driver's licenses at age 16.

The Good News translation of New Testament, undertaken specifically to make the Bible more readable, should be understood by eighth and ninth graders, compared to the Revised Standard version at 13.24 and the King James version at 14.99. Sales of the Good News version confirm its popular appeal. Time magazine called it "the greatest success story ever told."

Some other works and their scores: Dr. Seuss' *The Cat in the Hat*, 4.25; Erich Segal's *Love Story*, 7.64; the rules for "Monopoly," 11.41; *Playboy* magazine, 11.46; *Time* magazine, 10.62; the DeKalb County rabies control law, 19.23; the eligibility section of the food stamp act, 26.41; the Atlanta *Constitution*, 13.40.

Source: The Atlanta Constitution, October 10, 1978, pp. 1B and 6B.

Therefore, the method to be employed will sometimes be dictated by the duration of the problem.

Combining Oral and Written Media

Certain advantages are inherent in both oral and written orders and can be exploited according to each individual's situation. There are promising opportunities for using both oral and written form, where one or the other may have been used alone on previous occasions. For example, many police administrators have started using closed-circuit television combined with written communication to transmit information to their officers that may be especially sensitive or controversial. One police chief, upon creating an internal affairs unit, used his closed-circuit television to discuss the reasons that the unit was created and used that opportunity to answer a series of prepared questions that had been forwarded to him by officers who were concerned about the role and scope of this new unit. This televised presentation was given simultaneously with the newly developed procedure that detailed the organizational structure, the scope, and the responsibilities of this new unit.[25]

Organizational Communication

Organizational communication is viewed as the process of acquiring and organizing data about the internal workings of the organization as well as about the effects of its actions upon the external environment and the impact of the external environment upon the organization. The ability of the organization to scan the external and internal environment accurately to assess the variety of uncertainty involved reflects the degree of organizational intelligence. It is this intelligence that then becomes an input to the organizational decision making aimed at defining goals that are compatible with the external environmental conditions, at designing the organizational structure, and in assessing the functions requisite for the accomplishment of these goals. Operationally, the task of organizational communication is performed by employing a tool of information technology, both electronic and human. These two facets of information technology are inseparable and ought to be considered as two sides of the same coin.[26] (See Figure 6-8.) The news article "5 Police Workers to Testify at Hearing on '911' Calls' " illustrates the interrelationship of electronic and human communica-

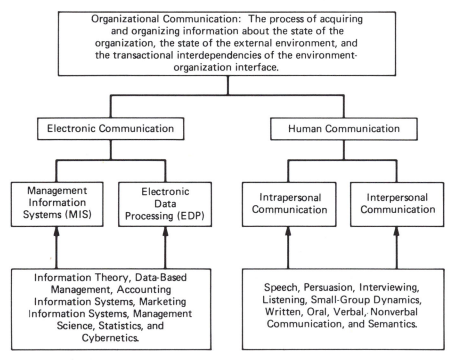

FIGURE 6-8. Organizational communication: A unified framework. [From A. G. Kefalas, "Organizational Communication: A Systems Viewpoint," in *Readings in Interpersonal and Organizational Communications*, eds. R. C. Huseman, C. M. Logue, and D. L. Freshly (Boston: Holbrook, 1977), p. 41.]

BOX 6-2.

5 Police Workers to Testify at Hearing on '911' Calls

By STEVE MARANTZ, *Globe Staff*

A Boston Police Department attorney said Friday that five department employees will be permitted to testify before the City Council's public safety committee tomorrow concerning the 911 emergency telephone system, but will not have to answer questions about the system's breakdown during a report of a South Boston rape in July.

The five employees, including two civilian dispatchers, two officers who arrested the rape suspect, and the head of the operations center, Lt. Paul Conway, are prevented from discussing the matter under a protective order obtained in Suffolk Superior Court, said Michael D. Powers.

Councilor-at-Large Albert L. O'Neil, chairman of the committee, has subpoenaed the employees in order to compel testimony concerning the South Boston rape, Powers said.

However, O'Neil said Friday that the employees will not be questioned specifically on the rape case, but on the general operation of the 911 system.

"We just want to know what steps they have taken to correct the system," said O'Neil.

The protective order was obtained in August because police personnel are not allowed to discuss a continuing rape investigation, Powers said.

James Sharkus, 29, is charged with aggravated rape, assault with intent to commit murder, robbery and assault and battery with a dangerous weapon in the South Boston case.

A witness has said that his two 911 calls to report the matter failed to get a response. The witness said he eventually hailed a passing police cruiser.

Commissioner Francis M. Roache has said the breakdown was due to a shortage of street patrol personnel. But other police officials have said the call for help was never put out to cruisers and that the breakdown occurred in the operations center.

A 911 study commission appointed by Mayor Flynn after the South Boston case reported last week that the 911 system was burdened by out-of-date technology, understaffing, and public misuse. The commission recommended it be improved with enhanced technology, more staffing, and a program to educate the public on its use.

Source: The Boston Sunday Globe, December 1, 1985, p. 34.

tions and the potential for tragic outcomes if both are not functioning properly and fully interrelated.

Summary

There is considerable evidence to support the premise that, for administrators to be truly effective, they must understand the dynamics involved in both interpersonal and organizational communications. It is not surprising when we learn that administrators who are successful are also effective communicators and have created communicative mechanisms within their organizations that avoid many of the pitfalls discussed throughout this chapter.

To understand the process of communication, we have examined several elements of the process. As a result, we now know that the communication process follows some fairly consistent patterns.

For example, the sender has certain intentions, objectives, or purposes, and translates these into some code (language, nonverbal gestures, etc.) that becomes the message. The sender then selects the medium (written or spoken words, music, art, etc.) and uses the medium to transmit the message to the receiver. The receiver in turn "picks up" the message (listens, reads, watches, etc.) and decodes its meaning. This meaning causes the receiver to behave in some manner, which gives the sender indications, or feedback, as to whether or not the receiver understood the meaning of the message.

Further, we have learned that barriers to communication or communication break-downs can occur at any place in the system and may result from either the sender or receiver. Since an information flow is multidirectional, (downward, upward, and horizontal), the police administrator must take every precaution possible to assure that barriers are not created in any direction that can disrupt the smooth flow of information throughout the organization.

The use of the Johari Window in this chapter has provided readers with an opportunity to examine and evaluate their own interpersonal styles of communication and to assess other styles as well. It is hoped that the insight gained provides the reader with an opportunity to make those adjustments deemed necessary to enhance their interpersonal communication style.

As we have learned, the police administrator may choose from among a number of ways to communicate. However, there tends to be considerable confidence in the use of written word in complex organizations. This is so, in part, because it establishes a permanent record that can be referred to readily. On the other hand, not all communications can or should be in writing. As we have seen, there are some distinct advantages in oral communication to both the sender and receiver.

Further, there will be those instances in which a police administrator may wish to combine both written and oral communications.

In the final analysis, there can be little argument with the conclusion that effective communication is essential in all organizations. A breakdown in the process of law enforcement not only results in less efficient organization but, as pointed out, may also result in the injury or death of some innocent person.

Discussion Questions

1. Discuss the elements that make up the communication process.
2. Discuss sender-caused barriers, receiver-caused barriers, and other barriers in communications.
3. Discuss the five types of organizational communication that have been identified.
4. Discuss in rank order, the most effective to the least effective, the means of downward communication according to Dahle.
5. The physical distance between superior and subordinate may impede upward communication. Why is this so?
6. What are the major desirable and undesirable traits of the organizational grapevine?
7. Discuss the four basic interpersonal styles of communication.
8. What are the advantages in oral communication to both the sender and receiver?
9. What are the advantages in combining both oral and written orders?
10. Why is effective communications in law enforcement so important?

Notes

1. *Interpersonal Communication: A Guide for Staff Development* (Athens: Institute of Government, University of Georgia, August 1974). p. 15.

2. Much of the discussion in this chapter on the communication process was developed by R. C. Huseman and incorporated into the publication *Interpersonal Communication: A Guide for Staff Development,* pp. 21–27.

3. P. V. Lewis, *Organizational Communication: The Essence of Effective Management* (Columbus, Ohio: Grid, 1975), p. 36.

4. Ibid., pp. 36–37.

5. Ibid., pp. 37–38.

6. D. Katz and R. L. Kahn, *The Social Psychology of Organizations* (New York: John Wiley, 1966), p. 239. As cited in Lewis, *Organizational Communication;* p. 38.

7. Lewis, *Organizational Communication,* p. 38.

8. R. L. Smith, G. M. Richetto, and J. P. Zima, "Organizational Behavior: An Approach to Human Communication," in *Readings in Interpersonal and Organizational Communication,* 3d ed., eds. R. C. Huseman, C. M. Logue, and D. L. Freshley (Boston: Holbrook Press, 1977), p. 11.

9. T. L. Dahle, "An Objective and Comparative Study of Five Methods of Transmitting Information to Business and Industrial Employees," Ph.D. dissertation, Purdue University, Lafayette, Indiana, 1954. As cited in Smith et al., "Organizational Behavior," p. 12.

10. Much of the discussion in this chapter on upward communication has been taken from E. Planty and W. Machaver, "Upward Communications: A Project in Executive Development," *Personnel,* 28 (January 1952), pp. 304–319.

11. Much of the discussion in this chapter on horizontal communication has been taken from R. K. Allen, *Organizational Management Through Communication* (New York: Harper & Row, 1977), pp. 77–79.

12. H. Fayol, *General and Industrial Administration* (New York: Pitman, 1949), p. 34. As cited in Allen, *Organizational Management Through Communication,* p. 78.

13. Allen, *Organizational Management Through Communication,* p. 78.

14. Ibid., pp. 78–79.

15. K. Davis, "Management Communication and The Grapevine," *Harvard Business Review,* (September–October, 1953), pp. 43–49. As cited by Lewis, *Organizational Communication;* p. 41.

16. Lewis, *Organizational Communication;* pp. 41–42.

17. J. Hall, "Interpersonal Style and the Communication Dilemma: Managerial Implications of the Johari Awareness Model," *Human Relations,* 27:4(April 1974), p. 381. For a critical review of communication literature, see Lyman W. Porter and Karlene H. Roberts, *Communication in Organizations* (Irvine: University of California Press, 1972).

18. Hall, "Interpersonal Style," p. 382.

19. Ibid., p. 382.

20. Ibid., p. 382.

21. As Joseph Luft describes this, "It is fairly well known now that Johari does not refer to the southern end of the Malay Peninsula. That's Johore. Johari is pronounced as if it were Joe and Harry, which is where the term comes from . . . Dr. Ingham and I developed the model during a summer laboratory session in 1955 and the model was published in the Proceedings of the Western Training Laboratory in Group Development for that year by the UCLA Extension Office." See Joseph Luft, *Of Human Interaction* (Palo Alto, Calif.: Mayfield, 1969) p. 6.

22. This questionnaire is termed the "Personnel Relations Survey" and is available from Teleometrics International, P.O. Box 314, The Woodlands, Texas 77380.

23. The description of the Johari Window is drawn, largely, with permission and minor modifications, from "How to Interpret Your Scores on the Personnel Relations Survey," © Teleometrics International, The Woodlands, Texas 77380.

24. The descriptions are taken by permission from ''How to Interpret Your Scores on the Personnel Relations Survey,'' pp. 4–5, with minor modification.

25. L. Territo and R. L. Smith, ''The Internal Affairs Unit: The Policeman's Friend or Foe,'' *Police Chief,* 43:7(July 1976), pp. 66–69.

26. A. G. Kefalas, ''Organizational Communications: A Systems Viewpoint,'' in *Readings in Interpersonal and Organizational Communication,* p. 42.

There's only one corner of the world you can be certain of improving and that's your own self.

ALDOUS HUXLEY

Human Resource Management

Introduction

Most authorities who examine the major issues involved in law enforcement come regularly to the same inescapable conclusion: namely, that the ability of a police department to provide high-quality service to its citizens and to solve its major operating problems will be significantly affected by the quality of its personnel and the ways in which they are managed.

As police departments have attempted to address external problems, such as rising crime rates, and internal problems, such as effectiveness of their operating units, they have undertaken many studies, entertained numerous theories, launched various experiments, and invested heavily in new equipment. In most of these efforts, however, it has been apparent that eventual success depends on the critically important element of human resources. Sound personnel practices, therefore, may well be the single most vital consideration in the quest for effective law enforcement.[1]

Since the late 1960s, the subject of human resource management has gained considerable prominence and visibility within the law enforcement community. A number of social, political, and economic factors have given impetus to the movement, including (1) the civil disorders and rapidly increasing crime rate during the 1960s, which resulted in the creation of two prestigious national commissions and numerous recommendations for improving the police service;[2] expansion of the labor movement within law enforcement, resulting in the revision of personnel policies relating to working conditions, training, discipline, and promotions; (3) the Equal Employment Opportunity Act of 1972, which induced many police departments to change personnel policies that discriminated against minorities and women in both employment and career development; and (4) a greater willingness on the part of courts and juries to award large cash settlements to citizens injured by police officers because of some act deemed negligent. Acts of negligence often involve the injury or death of innocent bystanders because of careless use of firearms or police vehicles and are frequently linked to inadequate selection procedures, training, or supervision.[3,4] These factors make it likely that considerable effort and time will be directed to all areas of human resource management.

Functions of the Police Personnel Unit

A sound personnel management program needs an adequately staffed and financed personnel unit reporting to the police chief. This unit must be specialized and have authority and responsibility to carry out its mission.[5] However, because of such factors as departmental philosophy, historical precedent, the chief executive's preference, intradepartmental power politics, and legislative requirements, broad statements about the functions of a police personnel unit are somewhat difficult to make.[6] However, a personnel unit is generally responsible for the following:

1. Preparing policy statements and standard operating procedures relating to all areas of the administration of human resources, subject to the approval of the chief executive of the agency.
2. Advising the chief executive of the department and other line officials on personnel matters.
3. Developing a performance evaluation system.
4. Creating an integrated management information system, which includes all necessary personnel data such as that pertaining to performance evaluation.
5. Maintaining an energetic and results-producing program to recruit qualified applicants.
6. Administering a carefully conceived process of selection; that is, administering a valid system for distinguishing those who are to be employed from those who may not be employed.
7. Establishing criteria for promotion to the various ranks, along with a method for determining the relative qualifications of officers eligible for such appointments.
8. Conducting a multifaceted staff development program for personnel of all ranks from entry through executive level.
9. Developing and administering position classification and assignment analysis to assure equal pay for equal work as well as to form the basis for staff assignment and evaluation.
10. Developing a plan of adequate compensation, distributed fairly among rank assignments according to difficulty and responsibility of assignments and

including provisions for differentials based on special assignments, shifts, or outstanding performance.

11. Representing the agency during negotiations with police employee groups and at other meetings with representatives of organized employees, such as at meetings pertaining to grievances and related matters.

12. Conducting exit interviews with resigning officers to identify, and subsequently correct, unsatisfactory working conditions.

13. Providing advice to managers and supervisors at all levels concerning human resource problems, with special attention to leadership and disciplinary problems, and administering reviews of disciplinary actions and appeals.

14. Conducting an ongoing personnel research program.

15. Representing the police department to the central personnel office or civil service commission.[7]

Inadequate Staffing Patterns

Few police agencies have viable, adequately staffed, and sufficiently supported personnel units that can maximize the agency's human resources. The most likely reasons for this problem are:

1. The failure of police management to determine its human resource objective. What does management really want its personnel arm—or, for that matter, its total personnel strength—to accomplish? Without clear-cut program objectives, it is difficult even for the best personnel administrator to adapt to the police function.

2. The inability or unwillingness of the police administrator to delegate clearcut authority to accomplish the human resource goals. The absence of clearcut lines of authority and responsibility is allowed to exist between field supervisors and the personnel staff. In some jurisdictions, civil service laws deny to the police chief, as well as to other line managers, sufficient authority over personnel matters. Without this authority, the personnel director is less than fully effective.

3. The inadequacy of total resources available to the police agency, leading to emphasis on field strength at the expense of personnel administration and frequently other management functions. While it is politically attractive to the chief to get as many officers into the field as possible, these officers may be underutilized unless there is adequate management direction.

4. The intransigence of some police officials and unions against changes in personnel practices and policies.[8]

Moreover, it is not uncommon to find departmental policy implicitly stating that the human resource is less important than are objects of capital expenditure. For example, in a number of cities, there are placards on the dashboards of police vehicles with a statement to the effect, ''This car cost the taxpayers of _____ $9,500—treat it with respect or you will be subject to disciplinary measures.'' Certainly no one would argue that a police officer having a vehicular accident is an unimportant event; accidents result in fewer cars being available for patrol service, thereby reducing coverage, and injuries may occur and liabilities may be created. But, in contrast, consider the sergeant with ten subordinates, each of whom earns $18,000 per year. Let us assume that the chief executive of that department sends the supervisor a memorandum at the beginning of each fiscal year stating, "You are responsible for the management of $180,000 of this organization's resources. Please ensure that the efforts of your subordinates are directed toward achievement of previously agreed-upon objectives." Would not this action, coupled with periodic monitoring, the implementation of any necessary corrective action, and comparison of year's and end results with anticipated outputs, be more beneficial to the public?

Police Personnel Selection

Although there are no hard and fast rules about the precise steps to be followed in the selection process, there is agreement that phases should proceed from the least expensive to the most expensive (see Figure 7-1).

The Initial Application

A prospective applicant will ordinarily make a preliminary visit to the police department, civil service commission, or central personnel office to obtain employment information. The results of such a visit should be several. The individual should come away with sufficient knowledge to make an informed decision concerning a career in policing. This will be gained through literature prepared especially for that purpose and by access to someone who can respond to questions accurately and in detail. If an individual clearly does not meet the minimum standards for employment, he or she should be so advised, along with possible remedial action, if any, that could be taken to qualify for consideration. Often overlooked by even seasoned personnel officers is the harm that can be done by treating an obviously unqualified prospective employee brusquely. Such action does little to mediate the person's disappointment and may cause the story of the treatment to be circulated among the individual's friends, reinforcing old stereotypes of the police and, in effect, dissuading other people from making application.

Among local units of government, most individuals will be required to visit the central personnel office, which serves all departments of city government, and submit an application. Alternately, it is not uncommon to find a civil service commission, consisting of a board of three to five prominent citizens, existing independently of the central personnel office. In such situations, the board would typically direct a professional staff that would perform most of the actual work. Historically;[9]

> The independent Civil Service Commission has often been limited to control over examinations for entry, promotions, and to the judicial function of hearing appeals from disciplinary actions.[10]

Where central personnel offices and civil service commissions exist concurrently in the same jurisdiction, the authority for matters not historically within the purview of the commission are retained by the central personnel office which constitutes no smaller number of functions or amounts of power. In some jurisdictions the central personnel office has virtually disappeared, supplanted by the civil service commission.

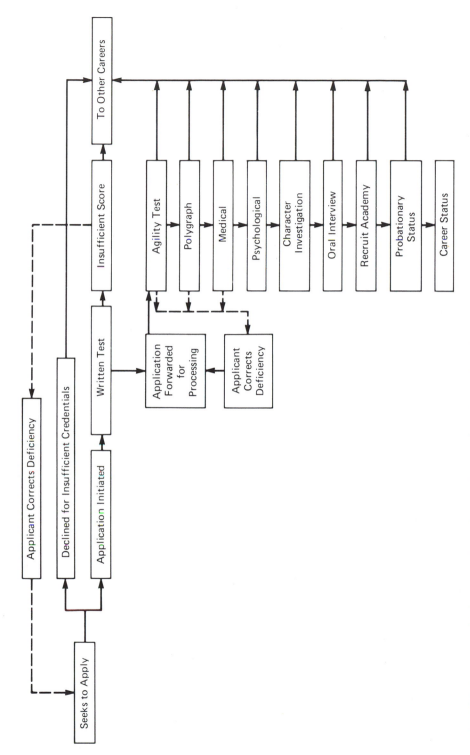

FIGURE 7-1. A model for processing police applicants. [From L. Territo, C. R. Swanson, Jr., and N. C. Chamelin, The Police Personnel Selection Process (Indianapolis, Ind.: © Bobbs-Merrill, 1977), p. 10]

Regardless of which arrangement prevails, the person seeking to make an application will have to demonstrate the meeting of certain criteria before the application is accepted; among these are citizenship, attainment of minimum age, and related factors. The candidate's application form is one of the most important sources of information about a candidate for a law enforcement agency. The data included in this form will provide much of the focus for the personnel investigator's line of inquiry, as it includes specifics related to the following: personal data; marital status and former marital status, including divorces, annulments, or widowhood; educational background; military service; foreign military services; foreign travel; veteran disability claims; employment record; financial history; criminal and juvenile record; motor vehicle operator record; family background; references; and willingness to undergo a polygraph examination.[11]

Where satisfactory proof of any of the basic criterion cannot be established, the application would be declined for insufficiency. An individual may later seek to reinstitute an application by correction of deficiencies or by obtaining and presenting additional documents.[12]

The Written Test

In 1972, Congress amended Title VII of the Civil Rights Act of 1964 and the Equal Employment Opportunity Commission (EEOC) was charged with the responsibility of administering its provisions. Title VII made it illegal to impermissably discriminate against any person on the basis of race, sex, color, religion, or national origin in employment decisions. An example of a permissible discrimination is refusing to hire a man to model women's lingerie; in this fact situation hiring only women would constitute a bona fide occupational requirement (BFOQ). "Employment decisions" is defined broadly and includes hiring, demotion, transfer, layoff, promotion, and firing decisions. Any procedure or requirement which is used in making these decisions comes under the scrutiny of EEOC. Thus, application forms, interviews, oral boards, written tests, probationary ratings, assessment centers, performance evaluations, education, background investigations, physical agility tests, and other logically related matters are all subject to EEOC review for a determination as to whether there has been an unlawful act of discrimination.

Initially EEOC focused on entry level requirements and testing because in many organizations there had been little genuine progress in hiring minorities. In more recent years, EEOC has directed greater attention to promotions and other personnel decisions as greater numbers of minorities had been hired and were effected by such decisions. A key concern of EEOC is whether selection devices, such as written entrance tests, are job related and predictive of future job performance.

The method by which a test can be shown to be associated with subsequent performance on the job is through a process of validation, the starting point for which is a job analysis. A job analysis reveals what the important tasks are for a position such as police officer as well as what specific knowledge and skills are needed to perform the job well.[13] Validation is a complex undertaking whose thorough treatment is not possible herein. However, some general statements are both proper and needed here. When the question is asked "Is this test valid?" what is really being asked is whether it is appropriate (valid) to make a decision about a person's ability to perform a particular job based on that person's score on a particular test.

TABLE 7-1 Hypothetical Group of Candidates for Employment as Police Officers

	White	Black	Totals
took test	400	100	500
passed	120	10	130
failed	280	90	370
passing rate	30%[a]	10%[b]	26%

[a] 120 (white passed) ÷ 400 (total white candidates) = 30% white selection rate

[b] 10 (black passed) ÷ 100 (total black candidates) = 10% black selection rate

Adverse Impact Calculation:

10% (black selection rate) ÷ 30% (white selection rate) = 33.3% or less than 80% (4/5ths)

A test that discriminates against a group of prospective or current employees and cannot be shown to be valid is impermissible discrimination under EEOC guidelines. However, if a police department or other employer can show that different test scores are associated with different levels of performance on the job, then even if the test discriminates against some identifiable group, including minorities, the courts are likely to find that it is a permissible discrimination, unless some other test would adequately meet the employer's needs and produce less of a discriminatory impact.[14]

Under EEOC guidelines, discrimination in testing occurs when there is a substantially different rate of selection in hiring, promotion, or other employment decision that works to the disadvantage of members of a race, sex, or ethnic group. This different rate of selection is termed "adverse impact" and is impermissible unless the test or other practice has been validated. As a rule of thumb, adverse impact occurs when the selection rate for any sex, race, or ethnic group is less than 4/5ths (80 percent) of the selection rate for the group with the highest selection rate.[15] Table 7-1 illustrates how the so-called "4/5ths rule" is applied; in that hypothetical case adverse impact is demonstrated and will be judged to be impermissible if the test has not been properly validated.

The 4/5ths rule does not allow up to 20 percent discrimination; it is not a legal definition, but a means of keeping attention focused on the issue. Regardless of the amount of difference in selection rates, other unlawful discrimination may exist and may be demonstrated through appropriate means. To use an extreme example, assume that the president of the local minority employee's association is very militant and vocal about his opposition to the current chief of police's policies. Further assume that the president's son applies for a job with the police department. All other applicants taking the written test mark their answers in ink, but the son is required to use a pencil. Later, the son is told that he failed the test because he left half of the answer sheet blank. An examination of that sheet reveals that half of his answers were erased and that the majority of the erasures involved correct responses. In this situation, an impermissible discrimination would be shown even if there was no adverse impact on minorities overall.

As reported in the accompanying article on a New York City sergeants' promotional examination, even when there has been careful effort made to validate a test, there may still be considerable controversy and the potential for litigation.

BOX 7-1.

'Unbiased' NYPD Exam Stirs Race Debate

By JENNIFER BROWDY

Suppose you are a police executive faced with the following scenario:

Your stated goal is to eliminate discrimination against minorities from your department. Your city has just spent a large sum of money to develop a police promotional test that is as culturally unbiased and job-related as possible, and you have gotten representatives from all factions within your department to agree that the test is indeed fair.

You administer the test, and receive surprising results: of those who passed, a shockingly disproportionate number are white.

Your minority officers raise a hue and cry, demanding that a quota system be implemented to increase their numbers in the supervisory ranks of the department. Your non-minority officers press just as firmly for promotions based on a strict merit system.

What would you do?

If you were New York City Police Commissioner Benjamin Ward, you would square your jaw and insist that the sacred precept of the merit system cannot be set aside for racial considerations.

The situation described above arose last month in New York when a sergeant's promotional exam was given to 11,593 police officers, many of whom had been originally hired under quota systems imposed by Federal courts. Of those who took the exam, 9,120 were white, 1,420 were black, 1,003 were Hispanic, 44 were Asian and 6 were American Indian.

The results showed that of the 1,037 officers who passed the test, 968 were white, 23 were black, 44 were Hispanic and 2 were Asian Americans. Translated into percentages, 10.6 percent of the whites who took the test passed, compared to 1.6 percent of the blacks and 4.4 percent of the Hispanics.

Obviously something is amiss in this situation, but just what it is no one involved has been able to explain.

"I don't know why so few blacks passed," said Officer Marvin Blue, president of the NYPD Guardian's Association, a black officers' group. Blue refrained from calling the test discriminatory, but said he wanted either a new test administered or a quota system used to insure more minority promotions.

Blaming the results on the cultural bias of the test is the easiest answer. But New York City, long the victim of racial discrimination lawsuits, spent $500,000 to develop a test that would be as fair and job-related as possible. A panel of attorneys and representatives from all police minority groups, as well as the Sergeant's Benevolent Association and the police administration, approved the test before it was administered.

"The process was legal, the test fair, but the results disparate," Commissioner Ward said. "That has not been explained yet."

Frederick Frank, vice president of Assessment Designs Inc., the Orlando, Fla., firm that developed the test, admitted that the development of standardized tests "is not a perfect science. But steps can be taken to make it as effective and fair and job-related as possible," he said. "And those steps were taken."

Sgt. Joseph Toal, president of the NYPD Sergeants Benevolent Association, said he believed the test was "fair, job-related and nondiscriminatory." The minority groups were "incorrect in calling for a quota," he said. "Everyone sat down and agreed the test was fair before it was given," he said. "We need sergeants very badly, and we want to see the people who passed be promoted. Anything else just ruins the system."

If all parties are in agreement that the test itself is unbiased, then the question becomes a bit more complicated. Why do minorities have such a bad track record on standardized tests?

The issue applies to more than just police Civil Service exams. A recent report published by Howard University's Institute for the Study of Educational Policy said black candidates for teaching positions are failing standardized tests in disproportionately larger numbers than whites. As a result, the report said, minority graduates in education are switching their career plans as word spreads of the mounting number of failures on the standardized tests.

The implications of this for policing are unsettling. How can a department improve minority representation if minorities either fail the Civil Service tests or opt to look for jobs in other occupational fields? Must the police administrator lower standards or implement a quota system in order to insure that minorities are properly represented?

"There is no happy solution," said Commissioner Ward of this problem. But, he said, he would not consider the idea of a quota system, because it would have a "devastating effect on the sense of fundamental fairness" among white men. If minorities continued to do poorly on the exams, he said, it might cause them to feel "they are in a second-class position" in the department, but his advice to those who felt this way was simple and direct: "Study long and study hard. That's what I did."

Newark Police Director Hubert Williams, another black police executive, said he "strongly supported" Commissioner Ward's policy.

Williams said that if he were faced with a similar situation, he would first make sure the test was "job-related and culturally neutral," and that it was "fairly administered, with proper notice given."

If all those requirements had been satisfied, he said, he would make his promotions from the top of the list on the basis of merit, not race.

The consequences of a racial quota system would be "quite severe" for a police department, Williams said. "Every police officer should feel they have an equal chance to compete. But as a police administrator, I think it would be extremely difficult to have quotas."

Law enforcement has a history of standing firmly behind the merit system for promotions and hiring. As far back as 1938, the International Association of Chiefs of Police passed a resolution supporting "the merit principle in recruitment, promotion and continuity in service of all police agencies."

In 1976 the IACP added a resolution recommending "that all criminal justice agency administrators implement the necessary recruitment policies, procedures and practices that will bring about a greater participation of qualified minority members in criminal justice agencies."

The pivotal word is "qualified." How does

a police agency find qualified minority candidates, and how does the agency rate their qualifications?

Both Ward and Williams said they felt more emphasis should be placed on the preparatory courses given at the Police Academy before promotional exams.

At the NYPD, Ward has promised to expand the prep classes and tailor them more closely to the needs of minority applicants. He is also planning to administer promotion tests every other year, rather than every four years as is currently the practice in New York, which may speed up the process of integrating minorities into the supervisory ranks.

There are other ways to improve the search for qualified minority police officers. Both Raoul Correa, a spokesman for the Houston Police Department, and John Green, a spokesman for the National Black Police Association, suggested that interviews should be added to the promotion procedure.

"I have yet to see an examination that can measure intangibles like personal presence and the ability to communicate with a variety of types of people," Green said. "I believe you can measure these types of qualities better through an oral interview."

Correa also said that one way to improve the showing of minorities in police promotional exams is to increase the department's attractiveness to minority recruits. One way to do this, he said, is to show them by example that minorities can succeed in police administration. In other words, nothing breeds success like success.

In the past in Houston, he said, many minority people who might have wanted to become police officers had been discouraged from seeking the position by the high failure rate of minorities on the police Civil Service exams. This was ultimately a factor in the low number of minorities in supervisory positions in the department, he said, because the pool of minority recruits taking the promotional exams was so small.

Correa said this situation has changed dramatically since 1982, when Police Chief Lee P. Brown, who is black, assumed command of the Houston Police Department.

"The hiring of black applicants has increased tremendously under Chief Brown," Correa said, attributing this in part to the immeasureable effect of Brown's status as a positive role model for minority youth.

"Chief Brown has demonstrated to minorities that the department is going places," Correa said. "There are a lot of qualified minority youth looking up to him now. He's kind of like an idol for them, and they're trying harder."

It may be that the process of integrating the upper echelons of policing is going to take a little longer than most minorities would like. In the meantime, police administrators are unlikely to wax enthusiastic about including racial

quotas in their promotional procedures. As Lieut. Armando Fontoura, president of the Police Management Association, put it: "Managers are people managers, and if people are promoted from the middle of the list over people from the top of the list, you are going to have problems."

Or, to paraphrase an old maxim, police officers are neither black nor white—they're blue.

Source: Law Enforcement News, September 24, 1984 pp 1, 8.

"Reverse Discrimination"

Under EEOC guidelines all discrimination is prohibited and there is no recognized "reverse discrimination" theory. Yet, when the courts mandate preferential hiring and promotional opportunities for minorities to correct for past employment practices, problems arise. Majority individuals, who are typically white males, label the preferential treatment as "reverse discrimination" and at odds with the merit principle. Moreover, as reflected in the article "Officers Charged in Variety of Crimes: Relaxed Recruiting Cited in Miami Police Scandals," relaxing standards to achieve important social goals may at least occasionally create problems in the operation of the police department.

BOX 7-2.

Officers Charged in Variety of Crimes: Relaxed Recruiting Cited in Miami Police Scandals

MIAMI (AP)—The arrest of Miami police officers last week on murder and drug-trafficking charges is the latest scandal to hit what law enforcement officials call the department's "Mariel generation," officers hired at a time when standards were relaxed.

The officers were accepted during the effort to strengthen the force after the 1980 "freedom flotilla" boatlift brought 125,000 Cuban refugees from Mariel, Cuba, including more than 5,000 criminals from the island's prisons.

In all, a dozen current and former Miami officers recruited to fight the ensuing crime wave in South Florida have been arrested, suspended or fired this year for crimes ranging from drug possession to first-degree murder.

And more officers are under investigation for a series of "home invasions," in which armed men seeking drugs or cash enter homes

and terrorize the occupants, said Lew Wilson, assistant chief of the Southern Region for the Florida Department of Law Enforcement.

Police officials say that rapid expansion of the force, coupled with pressure to increase minority hiring in the early 1980s, led the department to relax its standards, letting in candidates who might otherwise have been rejected.

"After the boatlift, we had to put people on the streets," department spokesman Reginald Roundtree said. He estimated that the department's 1,065 officers include at least 400, of various ethnic backgrounds, who were hired in the first years after the boatlift.

But Roundtree emphasized that most of the Mariel generation are "very good, competent police officers."

"There is nothing wrong with minority hiring," said Sgt. James Cox, president of the

Police Benevolent Assn. "But you have to hire the best, even if you have to go recruit at colleges."

Roundtree said the department has stopped hiring while it reviews its recruiting standards. A review committee set up in October is expected to deliver its report at the beginning of the new year.

Cox, a 27-year veteran, said increased temptation also is to blame for the scandals in the nation's No. 1 entry point for smuggled drugs.

He recalled that when he was on the vice squad 10 years ago, "street policemen never saw kilos of cocaine and people carrying hundreds of thousands of dollars. The biggest thing we ever had was a boatload of marijuana."

Last week's arrests and charges were the most serious to hit the department this year.

Three officers were arrested Friday and charged with the first-degree murder of three suspected drug dealers on July 28. The victims' bodies were found floating in the Miami River.

The officers charged with murder and two other officers, including one who recently resigned, also were charged with trafficking in cocaine. The ex-officer was still at large Saturday.

In an unrelated case Thursday, two officers were arrested and charged with trafficking in cocaine seized by the police.

Two other Miami officers were arrested earlier this month on cocaine charges. Two more were relieved of duty in connection with the investigation of the Oct. 9 theft of $150,000 from a police safe.

An officer and a retired officer were arrested in August and accused of selling weapons to undercover agents.

Source: The Los Angeles Times, December 29, 1985, Part 1, p. 19.

One of the regrettable side effects of trying to overcome years of blatant discrimination is the occasional tension between majority officers, who except for the need to meet a court mandate would have been promoted, and those who receive the preferential treatment. Despite the clear necessity to correct for long-standing discrimination in the work place, the use of such practices is difficult for the average officer to support. They feel that the "rules of the game" have been unfairly changed, that such preferential treatment needlessly endangers the public when the less able are hired or selected to lead. Even when a clearly superior minority officer, who would be promotable under any system, is selected ahead of them, their sense of anger may lead them to denigrate the minority officer's very real and substantial capabilities. Criticism of some methods, such as quotas, associated with correcting long-standing abuses in hiring and promoting are being heard from different quarters, including the U.S. Commission on Civil Rights. Minority leaders are apprehensive that in the emerging environment recent gains may be lost and discriminatory intentions can be masked as a "reform of the excesses of the application of EEOC guidelines by the courts."

BOX 7-3.

Curing Employment Bias Without More Bias

[*The following statement was issued January 17, 1984 by the U.S. Commission on Civil Rights concerning the Detroit Police Department's racial quotas for promotions.*]

The U.S. Commission on Civil Rights commends the city of Detroit for its desire to eradicate racial discrimination in its police department's employment practices and to increase the number of blacks in its police force. However, the commission deplores the city's use of a racial quota in its promotion of sergeants to lieutenants as one of the methods for achieving its laudable objectives.

The courts examining the validity of the

promotion quota concluded that the Detroit Police Department (DPD) engaged in pervasive discrimination against blacks from at least 1943 to the 1970's in all phases of its operations, including the hiring and promotion of employees, job assignments, and the treatment of black citizens. In July 1974, the city voluntarily adopted an affirmative action plan. One of the elements of the plan alters the method whereby sergeants are promoted to lieutenants. Prior to 1974, candidates for promotion who scored a minimum of 70 on a written test were ranked on a single list. Each candidate was accorded a numerical rating based upon a number of factors, including their score on the written examination, length of service, performance or service ratings determined by supervisors, degree of college education or credits, veterans' points, and an oral interview. Promotions were given to the highest ranking candidates on the list in numerical order until all available positions were filled.

The affirmative action plan does not change the basic criteria for determining which sergeants receive promotions to lieutenant. The plan, however, requires that two separate lists be compiled—one for black sergeants and the other for white sergeants. Rank on both lists is determined by use of the same numerical rating system in effect prior to 1974. Promotions are made alternately from each list so that one black officer is promoted for each white officer until 50 percent of the lieutenant corps is black, an event not expected to occur until 1990. Pursuant to the plan, a number of black sergeants have been promoted instead of white sergeants who would have ranked ahead of them if a single list had been used. The U.S. Supreme Court decided last week not to hear the case (*Bratton vs. City of Detroit*).

In the commission's view, enforcement of nondiscrimination law in employment must provide that all of an employer's discriminatory practices cease and that any identifiable individual who has been the direct victim of discrimination be returned to the place he or she would have had in the workforce in the absence of the employer's discrimination. Thus, each identifiable victim of the employer's discriminatory employment practices should be made whole, including the provision of back pay and restoration to his or her rightful place in the employer's workforce at the next available opening. Such

relief should also, when appropriate, accord a seniority status to the victim of discrimination higher than that of an innocent employee who would have been junior to the victim of discrimination in the absence of their employer's discrimination (here the innocent third party properly must share the burden of his or her employer's discrimination against identifiable victims in order to afford an adequate remedy to those victims). These kinds of relief, of course, must be available in cases involving a whole class of actual victims of discrimination, as well as cases involving only one such victim.

In addition, the use of affirmative action techniques, as tools to enhance equal opportunity for all citizens rather than as devices to penalize some on account of their nonpreferred racial, gender, or other status, should also be required of employers found to have discriminated, and encouraged for all employers who wish to improve the quality of their workforce. These techniques include: 1) additional recruiting efforts, aimed at increasing the number of qualified minority (or female) applicants from which the employer undertakes nondiscriminatory, race-and-gender-neutral hiring; 2) training, educational, and counseling programs for applicants and employees, targeted to attract minority (or female) participants and to enhance their opportunities to be hired or promoted on the basis of merit (rather than race or gender), but open to all on an equal basis.

"Simple justice" is not served, however, by perferring nonvictims of an employer's discrimination over innocent third parties solely on account of their race in any affirmative action plan. Such racial preferences merely constitute another form of unjustified discrimination, create a new class of victims, and, when used in public employment, offend the constitutional principle of equal protection of the law for all citizens. The DPD's promotion quota benefits nonvictims as well as victims of past illegal discrimination in promotions in derogation of the rights of innocent third parties, solely because of their race. Accordingly, it is a device that should be eschewed, not countenanced.

The commission believes that the use of racially preferential employment techniques, such as quotas, is not properly viewed as a situation pitting the interests of blacks against the interests of whites. Rather, each specific preferential plan favors members of the preferred group—of whatever race or gender—at the expense of the nonpreferred group, which inevitably includes persons of diverse ethnic, religious, or racial groups and sometimes includes females. Members of these groups have often been subjected to past discrimination.

The commission also rejects an "operational needs" justification for racial quotas, as Detroit advanced in favor of its needs to increase black police officers at all ranks, in order to achieve more effective law enforcement and reduce discriminatory treatment against black citizens, and that the promotion quota was a necessary means of meeting those objectives. This justification amounts to little more than a claim that only black police officers can effectively provide law enforcement services to black citizens or supervise lower-ranking black police officers. Such a claim has no place in a free, pluralistic society made up of many diverse ethnic and racial groups striving to achieve fully the goal of becoming one nation. If accepted, it would justify a claim that members of a racial or ethnic group can be properly served or treated only by fellow members of that group, e.g., only black teachers can teach black children— or that only white teachers can teach white children. This claim would, in the words of Chief Justice Earl Warren, "turn the clock back" (*Brown vs. Board of Education*, 1954) to the "separate but equal" days of the past, when public entities dispensed benefits, entitlements, and penalties of all kinds on the basis of a person's skin color. Such a claim, in short, would ultimately divide the nation rather than unite it.

Among the alternatives to racially preferential employment policies that a police department can use to meet its needs for more effective, and nondiscriminatory, law enforcement are: 1) vigorous enforcement of policies of nondiscriminatory treatment of all citizens by its members, including the disciplining or dismissal of offending officers, and 2) provision of training and counseling programs for its officers to instruct and counsel them in the requirements of nondiscriminatory law enforcement.

Nearly 25 years ago, Arthur L. Johnson, executive secretary of the Detroit Branch of the National Association for the Advancement of Colored People, testified about the poor relations between black citizens and the DPD before this commission's predecessor. He said, in part, "At absolutely no point in their experience do Negroes in Detroit see the law enforcement agency as being truly color-blind. . . ."

Unfortunately, the DPD's use of racial quotas demonstrates that it is still not truly color-blind, at least with respect to its employment practices.

Because the issues in the Detroit case are of such importance, the commission is disappointed that the Supreme Court has declined to hear the case. The issue of racial quotas in promotions, as well as in hiring, will undoubtedly be presented for Supreme Court review in the future. The commission hopes the Court will resolve the issue by reaffirming the principle of nondiscrimination and forbidding preferential treatment based on race, color, gender, national origin, or religion in favor of nonvictims of discrimination at the expense of innocent individuals.

Source: Law Enforcement News, February 13, 1984 pp 4, 12.

Physical Agility Testing

Prior to the enactment of Title VII in 1972, the principal physical requirement used in police officer selection was based on standards of height and weight. As is well known today, these standards adversely affected the employment of women and some ethnic groups with small body size, and are no longer used in selection.[16]

In developing physical standards for employment, some police departments sought quick solutions to their testing needs by using commercially available physical agility tests that "appeared" to be valid and nondiscriminatory. The greatest problem with such a solution is that unless these tests are based on a comprehensive job analysis of the jurisdiction in which they are used, they are as meaningless as the old height and weight requirements. Many other departments simply gave up physical ability testing altogether, fearing the costs associated with legal challenges to their tests. These departments have failed to recognize that increased costs in medical insurance, disability payments, damaged equipment, early retirement, and lost work time far exceed the potential savings of avoiding a legal challenge to physical ability testing.

Alternative Approaches

Booth and Hornick have developed a convenient and relatively easy method for evaluating the physical requirements of police officers in any size jurisdiction. Furthermore, based upon comprehensive job analyses, they have devised a content-valid, inexpensive, discriminating (but not discriminatory) physical agility test that was designed for this jurisdiction.

In their investigation of the physical requirements for a police officer's job in any jurisdiction, Booth and Hornick began with a review of some of the problems that may be attributable to a lack of physical fitness. For example, an examination of sick leave, injury claims, accidents, and similar data helped to target problem areas of particular significance in certain jurisdictions.

Where possible, they observed police officers performing their regular duties, as well as in their training activities. The most critical aspect of the investigation, however, was in providing the opportunity for police officers (and their supervisor) to relate to the researchers their perceptions of the physical requirements of the job. Although one-on-one interviews were valuable for this purpose, Booth and Hornick developed a brief questionnaire that permits all the officers this opportunity, regardless of department size.

The physical agility job analysis questionnaire they used is based upon previous research that examined general physical agility tests, research on the police officer's

FIGURE 7-2. Colorado police officers take part in physical agility tests that measure upper-body, leg, and grip strength; balance; and reaction time. [Photo courtesy of R. L. Albers, Aurora, Colorado, Training Bureau.]

job, and related domains. The questionnaire asked officers to rate the frequency and importance of a number of activities that are common to their jobs. All these activities represent normal police actions.

Moreover, the questionnaire was designed to measure five general areas of physical ability that have been identified as critical to the police officer's job in the injury investigations, job observations, and interviews. These five general areas are: (1) upper body strength, (2) leg strength, (3) grip strength, (4) balance/coordination, and (5) quick reactions. Frequency is rated on a six-point scale ranging from 1—"never performed" to 6—"performed more frequently than once per week." The importance of the various activities is rated on a five-point scale ranging from 1—"not important" to 5—"critically important." Questions related to additional areas of physical ability, as well as specific activities, are always part of the questionnaire.

Typical Questionnaire Results

Table 7-2 presents the results of a questionnaire that was administered to forty-two uniformed officers in a major Colorado city. Eighteen activities are listed in the order of their combined frequency and importance ratings. The five general areas of physical ability represented by these activities can be seen at the far right-hand side of the table.

Perhaps the most notable result in this table is the fact that the utilization of quick reactions is the most frequently performed and most critical physical activity of police officers. This result has been confirmed in every city in which Booth and Hornick conducted job analyses of the police officer's position. Despite the obviously critical nature of quick reaction time for police officers, however, it is rarely measured in initial selection. Since quick reactions are useful for everything from driving a police vehicle to physical confrontations with suspects, it is expected that preemployment screening on reaction time will result in fewer on-the-job accidents and injuries. This hypothesis is currently being examined in a statistical test validation program Booth and Hornick are conducting with several regional police departments.

For the most part, questionnaire results have confirmed their interview data and observations of police officers performing their regular duties. For example, running a short distance was reported as a relatively frequent activity, and was considered very important. Running long distances, however, was seldom done, and was considered less important. Many physical agility tests currently in use require long-distance runs, crawling, and the use of brute strength maneuvers such as forcing a door open. Yet, as the job analysis results of Booth and Hornick have demonstrated, these activities are among the least frequently performed and least critical of the many physical activities that police officers undertake.

Physical Agility Test

The results of analyses such as these have led to the development of a content-valid physical agility test comprised of five basic elements. The first element is a measure of reaction speed and peripheral vision using a device designed specifically for this purpose. The applicant sits in front of a large console consisting of twelve lights evenly spaced in a 120° curve around the individual. The applicant's reaction time is measured as the amount of time elapsed between the onset of one of these lights and the point at which the candidate reaches out to touch the light. Once a light is

TABLE 7-2 Summary of Physical Ability Survey From One City*

Combined ranking	Dimensions	Average frequency rating[1]	Average importance rating[2]	Combined average rating	Upper body strength	Leg strength	Grip strength	Balance	Reaction time
1	Utilize quick reactions	4.57	4.79	9.36					X
2	Utilize grip strength	4.38	4.64	9.02			X		
3	Utilize balance	4.33	4.58	8.91				X	
4	Run a short distance	3.98	4.38	8.36		X			
5	Wrestle—with help	3.45	4.69	8.14	X	X	X	X	
6	Wrestle—alone	3.19	4.83	8.02	X	X	X	X	
7	Leap over low obstructions	3.66	4.13	7.79		X		X	
8	Climb onto roofs	3.52	4.26	7.78	X	X	X	X	
9	Climb through windows	3.36	4.02	7.38	X	X	X	X	
10	Carry heavy objects	3.33	3.86	7.19	X	X	X		
11	Climb privacy fences	3.07	4.00	7.07	X	X	X	X	
12	Drag people—with help	2.76	4.10	6.86	X	X	X	X	
13	Drag people—alone	2.64	4.21	6.85	X	X	X	X	
14	Climb industrial fences	2.90	3.86	6.76	X	X	X	X	
15	Run a long distance	2.69	3.95	6.64		X			
16	Crawl	2.79	3.69	6.48		X			
17	Push disabled vehicle	3.36	3.02	6.38	X	X			
18	Force doors open	2.41	3.74	6.15	X	X			

* N = 42

[1] Frequency Rating

	Description
1	Never
2	Less frequently than once a month
3	Approximately once a month
4	More than once a month, but less frequently than weekly
5	Approximately once a week
6	More frequently than once a week

[2] Importance Rating

1 Not Important	2 Of Little Importance	3 Of Moderate Importance	4 Very Important	5 Critically Important

FIGURE 7-3. Measurement device for testing reaction, speed, and peripheral vision. [Photo courtesy Multidimensional Research, Aurora, Colorado.]

touched, it goes out and another light flashes on. This process continues for a random series of sixty lights. Measures from the digital readout provide information on peripheral vision and handedness, as well as overall reaction time. The other four events measure grip strength, coordination, and balance through a series of job-related activities such as climbing over a chain-link fence or through a standard-sized window opening.

Administration of this test in several cities has demonstrated that it has little adverse impact. Women, for example, perform as well as men on most of the elements of the test, particularly reaction time. Furthermore, although most physical ability tests favor the taller and heavier candidates, the test shows only minimal effects because of body size. This substantially reduces the test's adverse impact on certain protected classes. Nevertheless, the test has successfully screened out candidates who were overweight, uncoordinated, or in overall mediocre physical condition.

Although this test is content-valid, the researchers' goal was to guarantee its statistical validity and cost effectiveness. They intended to prove that the better a person performs on the test, the better that person's performance on the physical aspects of the job will be and the less likely that person will be to lose work days due to accidents and injuries on the job.

The Polygraph Test in Preemployment Screening

A source of constant amazement for many polygraphists is the willingness of law enforcement agencies to utilize the polygraph in criminal cases but an unwillingness to use it in the pre-employment screening process. The use of the polygraph in the preemployment screening process is a sound practice from practical, professional, and economic standpoints.

The term *polygraph,* when used in present-day terminology, refers most precisely to the multiple-pen subsystem that records the instrumental responses on a roll of paper. Contemporary polygraph equipment measures, simultaneously, three physiological responses: breathing patterns, blood pressure, and pulse and skin resistance to external current.

The polygraph examination should never be used as a substitute for a comprehensive character investigation; instead, it should be used as a management tool to supplement the overall screening process. Law enforcement agencies using the polygraph in the preemployment screening process have indicated that there have been many practical benefits derived from its use.

First, law enforcement agencies found that, when it was widely publicized that they were going to begin to use the polygraph to examine applicants, there were fewer numbers of undesirable applicants applying for positions with their agencies. This was supported by the decreasing percentage of applicants who were being eliminated at the conclusion of their background investigations.

Second, although it was difficult to prove empirically, there were some indications that the polygraph reduced the rate of turnover. This was accomplished by determining whether an applicant was seriously interested in pursuing a law enforcement career or was merely trying to find temporary employment. It is unreasonable to expect any young person to make a career commitment at the time of employment, but clear-cut cases of using the agency as a "temporary meal ticket" should be dealt with accordingly.

Third, by publicly announcing that it uses the polygraph to screen all law enforcement applicants, the law enforcement agency is letting its community know that it is determined to hire only those persons whose character and morals are above reproach.

Fourth, it is psychologically beneficial to veterans of the law enforcement agency to know that young rookie officers riding with them have been screened regarding their honesty, character, morals.[17]

These are but a few of the advantages gained by using the polygraph in the screening process.

Several years ago, Richard O. Arther, director of the National Center of Lie Detection, conducted a survey to determine what results other polygraph operators were having around the country with the use of polygraph in the preemployment screening process. The following are brief summaries of cases in which significant derogatory information was uncovered by law enforcement polygraphists while conducting examinations of law enforcement applicants.

> An applicant applying for a position with the Lower Merion, Pennsylvania, Police Department came to that agency highly recommended by a police lieutenant and his employer at a home for blind retarded children. During the polygraph examination the applicant admitted to at least fifty instances of sexually abusing the children.
> A police officer with an apparently good reputation applied for a position with the Iowa Bureau of Criminal Investigation. The police officer admitted to the polygraphist conducting the pre-employment examination that on several occasions he had stolen money from prisoners. He also admitted to other significant thefts.
> An applicant applying for a position with the Wichita, Kansas, Police Department admitted to the polygraphist that he had been involved in many burglaries. Their detective division was able to clear eight of their unsolved burglaries as a result of this applicant's confession.

A police officer employed by one California police department applied for a position with the Salinas, California, Police Department. He appeared to be a model police officer. His physical appearance was excellent, he was thoroughly familiar with the state codes, and his previous experience made him a potentially ideal candidate. During the pretest polygraph interview he made no admission of any wrongdoing. Only after he was confronted with the polygraph results indicating that he was being untruthful did he admit having committed over twelve burglaries while on duty and having used his police car to haul away the stolen property. He also admitted to planting stolen narcotics on innocent suspects in order to make arrests and on several occasions had sexual intercourse in his police car with girls as young as sixteen years of age.

An applicant applying for a position with the San Diego, California, Sheriff's Department admitted to that agency's chief polygraphist that on weekends he would go from bar to bar pretending to be drunk. He would then seek out people to pick fights with since he could only have an erection and orgasm while inflicting pain on others. He also admitted that he got rid of his frustrations by savagely beating "niggers, Chicanos, and long-haired pukes who cause all the trouble." The applicant was over six feet tall and weighed 250 pounds, thus adding impressive physical support to his deviant inclinations.[18]

An applicant applying for a deputy's position with the Leon County Sheriff's Department in Tallahassee, Florida, admitted to that department's polygraph operator that she was a member of a subversive political party and that she, along with other members of the party, were attempting to infiltrate the agencies of social control to cause whatever internal disruption they could to reduce the agencies' effectiveness and create moral problems. This applicant made the admission only after three test charts indicated deception on a question relating to the applicant's memberships in any subversive organizations. The applicant was a college graduate, extremely bright, articulate, and personable, had a good personal appearance, and appeared to be an outstanding applicant.

The rather interesting thing about these examples is the willingness of the applicants to make such damaging statements. Many polygraph operators have verified that this is a very common phenomenon, even in the pretest interview.

Psychological Stress Evaluator (PSE)

The psychological stress evaluator (PSE) is another type of detection instrument that is being used with greater frequency by law enforcement officers, during both preemployment screening and in criminal investigations. The psychological stress evaluator was developed by two retired Army intelligence officers and has been on the commercial market since 1970. This instrument capitalizes on the principle of involuntary physiological changes that are related to psychological stress. It is designed to display graphically certain stress-related components of the human voice's two modulations—the audible and inaudible.[19]

According to the developers of the PSE, there are inaudible frequency modulations in speech that are superimposed on those audible modulations of the voice that are heard. They further represent that internal stresses that are reflected in those audible variations of the voice are not totally controlled by the brain or thought processes and that those variations can be detected and recorded by their PSE device.

Two significant advantages are claimed for the PSE over other types of "lie detector" devices. First is its simplicity, in that it has relatively few moving parts and it is comparatively easy to learn to operate. Second, the PSE does not have to be used at the time of the interview or interrogation. A tape recorder is used to make a permanent record of the interview and the tape is later fed into the PSE and the voice reactions recorded on a chart. Users of this device frequently make tape recordings for clients over the telephone, run the tape on the PSE, and report the test to the client.

There is considerable debate at this time between the proponents of the polygraph and the proponents of the psychological stress evaluator. Each side claims that its instrument is better device for the detection of deception. It is highly recommended that law enforcement administrators scrutinize the merits and limitations of each instrument before making a decision regarding the suitability of one instrument over the other.[20]

When to Administer the Examination

There are no hard and fast rules regarding the exact point at which a polygraph or PSE instrument should be employed in the pre-employment screening process. However, there tends to be agreement that it should be used quite early in the screening process. Many law enforcement agencies using such instruments in their pre-employment screening process do so immediately after the applicant has passed all the written examinations and the FBI fingerprint record check has been returned to the agency from Washington, D.C. Investigators responsible for conducting character investigations are at a distinct advantage if they know as much about the applicant's background as possible before conducting their investigations. The polygraph or PSE examination may just possibly give them some important additional information that might not otherwise have been available when they started their investigation.

Any investigator who has had to conduct large numbers of character investigations will be the first to admit that occasionally an undesirable applicant slips through the administrative screen. The use of the polygraph or PSE will not eliminate this problem completely, but it will minimize the chance of such an applicant being employed.

Most reputable polygraph and PSE operators recommend very strongly that no one be disqualified solely on the basis of unexplained reactions. However, if a situation arises in which the instrument shows deception in a particular area, yet the applicant denies deception, this should raise the investigator's index of suspicion and extra scrutiny should be given to the area under consideration.[21]

Psychological Screening of Police Applicants

Since the Kerner's Commission recommendation in 1967 that all police officers be psychologically evaluated, psychological screening of applicants has become a routine component of the hiring process in many police agencies. Although the psychological evaluation process is widely used, it has not always been well understood or used to maximum effectiveness. Therefore, it is necessary to clarify some of the basic issues involved in effectively incorporating the "psychological" into the law enforcement administrative process.[22]

Stress, "Liability-Prone," and Negligent Admission/Retention

Research shows that excessive stress can lead to aggressive and unconventional behavior, as well as mental and physical dysfunctions on the job.[23] Police work is a well-known, high-stress occupation. Stress can be a significant factor in causing serious and expensive problems, but the stress tolerance level of officers or applicants can be a significant factor in preventing problems. (The topic of police stress is discussed in much greater detail in Chapter 8, ''Stress and Police Personnel.'') People have different ways of coping with stress. Some individuals are emotionally ''liability-prone.'' These individuals have an increased propensity to develop serious behavioral, psychological, and physical problems. They may become a serious threat to themselves, their fellow officers, the welfare of the community, and the agency budget.

Apart from the obvious moral obligation that law enforcement agencies have to ensure that their officers do not abuse their powers, inappropriate police behavior is expensive. The cost of investigating and processing personnel complaints is high. Disciplinary actions often include suspension, which reduces manpower. In addition, lawsuits and civil claims are costly in both dollars and manpower and are devastating to agency morale. The courts have identified ''negligent admission'' and ''negligent retention'' of officers as agency liabilities. (These issues are discussed in greater detail in Chapter 10, ''Legal Aspects of Police Administration.'') Most agencies can trace a major portion of their unfavorable incidents to a relatively small number of officers. It is in the area of identifying applicants whose behavior will be costly to the agency that psychological screening efforts can be most effective.

Strategies—''Select in'' or ''Screen out''

Too often, police administrators are led to believe in a ''select in'' strategy, which suggests that psychological evaluations can aid in selecting the best candidate for police work. This is not quite true. Psychological input can be helpful in deciding which individuals within an agency or department are suitable for specific assignments, such as Special Weapons and Tactics (SWAT), hostage negotiation, or bomb squads, but the most effective use of psychological evaluation is to ''screen out'' or identify those applicants who may not be emotionally suitable or may be a high risk for law enforcement.

The former strategy—''select in''—implies a precision and level of accuracy that psychologists do not possess and psychological procedures do not produce. In addition, this strategy ignores the possibility that future events, such as personal problems, could severely impact applicants initially judged to be acceptable and cause them to become high-risk employees at a later time.

Unsuitable applicants do not always appear to be inappropriate. Applicant pools approximate the normal curve—some individuals will appear to be excellent candidates, some will be obviously unacceptable, and the great majority will be somewhere in the middle. Applicants in this middle range who, in the judgment of a psychologist, demonstrate risk of engaging in liability-resulting behavior should be screened out. This decision is not always clear, but in admitting individuals to law enforcement, judgmental decisions should be made with caution.

Other mechanisms should exist in the screening process to minimize possible decision errors. Included should be an appeal or review process conducted at a higher administrative level.

How to Select and Best Use a Psychological Consultant

It would be ideal for law enforcement agencies to have a full-time mental health professional as part of the staff. In this case, the professional should be involved in an orientation period long enough to provide familiarity with police management, police officers' tasks, and criteria for successful job performance. Since the majority of police agencies do not have or cannot afford full-time mental health professionals, outside consultants are used for a variety of psychological services, including the psychological screening of applicants. Outside consultants may be psychologists, psychiatrists, management consultants, and, on occasion, physicians. Most often, a licensed professional or certified consultant is required.

An important consideration in choosing a professional for a department is the person's ability to relate to the police organization and to become knowledgeable in police consultation. Police agencies are approached by professionals from all areas and backgrounds who wish to become associated with an agency or propose a project on a fee-for-service or contract basis. In rural areas and small towns, police organizations sometimes develop working arrangements with university professors. In some cases, research academicians look upon police officers as subjects for data gathering and fail to understand totally the needs of police officers and administrators.

Academic persons working in applied areas or professionals who have done research in areas of police psychology are sometimes better prepared to begin consultation in law enforcement. It is, however, important that such professionals also possess training in the area of identifying clinical or personality issues that could impair police officers' performance. Consultants who are not familiar with the job should approach the consultation task initially as a student, and police agencies should insist on exposing them to relevant areas of police work.

The director or chief of police will often be the primary contact for the consultant. The psychological screening information is usually transmitted directly to him or her or to another previously designated representative. In most cases, the decision to hire is made by the chief of police after background results, medical results, psychological results, and, in some cases, polygraph results are available. Some agencies prefer either a "yes or no" response as to whether an applicant is suitable for police work. This response may be verbal, followed by a written report. Some police administrators prefer to meet with the consultant to discuss each applicant. However, in most cases, a detailed written report including the background as reviewed by the consultant, the results of any psychological tests administered, interview data, and a summary and recommendation is submitted to the department.

The consultant should function as part of a team that includes all those involved in processing applicants. It is strongly desirable for the consultant to meet with all persons in the system, including the training officers who will eventually complete the screening process by either recommending recruits for permanent status, probation, or termination. The consultant should know the training officer's perspective and be aware of any past psychological problems of the recruits. The training officer should know on what basis the psychologist will recommend marginal applicants be accepted with the hope they will develop as suitable officers during probation.

Consultants should be willing to explain and defend screening decisions should it become necessary. When an applicant appeals a disqualification, the consultant should be available to appear before a civil service board or in court, if necessary.

In many cases, a psychologist or other professional will be hired solely to provide preemployment psychological screening. After the agency develops confidence in him or her, the consultant may be called upon to perform psychological "fitness for duty" evaluations on officers who have demonstrated patterns of excessive-force complaints or highly unusual or "liability-prone" behavior. Also, officers applying for special assignments, such as bomb squad technicians or hostage negotiators, may be evaluated to ensure that the persons chosen are the best suited for the job. In these cases, the officer's personnel file and work history provide valuable information regarding past performance. Information on the number and nature of complaints against the officer, sick time taken, and performance under stress provides valuable input for the psychological consultant.

In all cases, it is important to remember that the decision as to who will be selected for employment and which officers will receive specialized assignments remains in the hands of the administration. The psychologist or consultant only provides specialized information and judgments that will be taken into consideration along with other important factors. In some instances, police administrators may choose officers who have not been recommended by the psychologist. Often, in these instances, the psychological consultant can identify areas of needed development and can suggest to the administration ways of supporting individual development.

SCREENING COMPONENTS

Police administrators and managers are often concerned with the validity of psychological tests. Psychological instruments and procedures were developed through scientific and statistical investigation, but the relevance of any single statistical score to a well-integrated psychological judgment is often overemphasized. Good decisions require information. The three best sources of information in evaluating law enforcement applicants are:

1. Psychological tests;
2. Background information; and
3. An in-depth or "Clinical" interview by a psychologist knowledgeable in law enforcement.

All information developed in the preemployment stages could reasonably be used by a clinical psychologist. Typically, most psychologists choose the Minnesota Multiphasic Personality Inventory (MMPI), the Sixteen Personality Factor Questionnaire (16PF), or the California Psychological Inventory (CPI). Extensive information exists on these instruments and their use in law enforcement screening,[24] however, psychologists may vary in the psychological tests they use depending on their training and experience.

Some psychological tests, such as the MMPI and the 16PF, can be computer scored, but a psychologist must review and interpret the results on an individual basis. Because most computer interpretations of the MMPI are based on the assumption that the test applicant is a mental patient or an outpatient in psychotherapy, negative or pathological information is likely to be emphasized. The MMPI can be extremely useful in screening, but it must be interpreted by a professional who is knowledgeable in both the test's subtleties and law enforcement.

The Psychologist as an Expert Judge

In the psychological screening approach, the psychologist plays a critical role in integrating psychological test results, background information, and interview data in order to arrive at a judgment of unsuitability. This is a "clinical" or expert judgment, not a statistical or scientific outcome. Studies have been done relating various kinds of biographical or psychological test score information to criterion variables, such as disciplinary actions, number of arrests made, commendations, sick time taken, on-the-job automobile accidents, and so on. These studies are helpful in suggesting which tests and criteria may be of potential benefit, but to rely totally on test scores and correlations would be inappropriate. It is the psychologist who is familiar with law enforcement who renders a clinical judgment that brings expertise and credibility to the screening process.

The psychological consultant, who is properly trained and working as support for management, can maximize the success and professionalism of the screening and selection process.

Psychologists cannot predict the future. However, assuming they know the intricacies of a police officer's job, they can develop relevant information regarding an individual's emotional functioning in a law enforcement position and render a judgment about an individual's suitability. Psychological screening minimizes the admission of inappropriate applicants and is consistent with the safeguards and precautions that the law and common sense dictate.

BOX 7-4.

Psychological Testing of Cops Proves Its Worth

By JOANNE HOOKER

Seven months after Susan Place, 17, and Georgia Jessup, 16, left their homes in Oakland Park for a day at the beach, their butchered, beheaded bodies were found in a shallow grave on Hutchinson Island.

The girls disappeared on September 27, 1972. One year to the day later, Martin County deputy sheriff Gerard Schaefer was convicted of the first-degree murders and linked to the murders or disappearance of two dozen other women.

Branded by newspapers as "the Bluebeard of the Beach," Schaefer, then 25, received two concurrent life sentences. At the time of the trial, Florida had no death penalty.

During pre-trial psychiatric examinations, the husky 6-footer told psychiatrists that all "indecent women should be destroyed for the good of society" and that he had killed cows and horses with a machete and later had sexual intercourse with the corpses.

Schaefer's bizarre psychosis did not prevent his being hired as a policeman—first at the 26-member Wilton Manors Department and then, after being fired for not having "an ounce of common sense," as a Martin County sheriff's deputy.

In 1974, less than a year after Schaefer's conviction, Florida's Police Standards Commission decided a statewide psychological testing program was needed to keep the "misfits" out of law enforcement.

"There were a number of sad situations in law enforcement at that time," said Joel Pate, chief of Florida's Department of Law Enforcement training bureau.

"But it was the deputy sheriff (Schaefer) who really created the push to weed out the bad apples. This man had been through other police agencies—he was a transient officer, and we knew our screening mechanism was allowing these people to get into enforcement ranks."

Backed by an initial $10,000 from the state university system, and a later grant of $143,000 from the U.S. Law Enforcement Assistance Administration, a team of psychologists from the University of South, Florida in Tampa, headed by Dr. Charles D. Spielberger, began researching what would become a six-year project.

The psychologists' goal was to design a battery of tests that would predict a recruit's success or failure as a police officer and warn an employer of a candidate's aberrant tendencies.

The problem was as complex as the police profession itself and the people who are drawn to it.

"Police officers have to be emotionally stable because we entrust an enormous amount of power to these people. They have to be compassionate and sensitive and at the same time deal with crimes of violence," said project coordinator Harry Spaulding.

"One bad apple has so much effect on the system. Even just one officer—so we're looking for people who are not fit for the job."

During the project's first year, the psychologists reached a dismal and discouraging conclusion. ". . . prevailing practices (of police selection) seemed to be based largely on unevaluated procedures that had evolved primarily on a trial-and-error basis." Spielberger told a national workshop on selection of law enforcement officers.

This trial-and-error method of hiring police officers has become very expensive—in the human terms of public trust and in money.

Allen Shoaff, chairman of law enforcement training at the Southeastern Institute of Criminal Justice in Miami, estimates that it costs taxpayers about $12,000 to put a recruit through the 22-week, 840-hour program.

Shoaff believes another level of screening is needed in law enforcement. "Agencies will not be hiring people who turn out to be unsuccessful or unproductive," he said. "If recruits can't pass the psychological tests right at the beginning they won't even get in (the academy)."

Or consider the cost of the man-hours and legal fees involved in investigating the lawsuits and complaints against police departments.

There are 91 lawsuits pending against Dade's 2,200-member Public Safety Department, including a $3 million suit by Nathaniel LaFleur, a sixth grade teacher who claims he was beaten by five police officers who mistakenly raided his home for drugs last February.

So far this year, Metro has received 577 complaints, 130 of those concerning the use of excessive force.

The City of Miami Police Department, with 650 members, received 291 complaints from January through October—40 of which were accusations of excessive physical force.

"Only 30 complaints overall were substantiated," said a Miami spokesman.

"But," countered a long-time investigator with the department, "it takes a lot of time to investigate everything. It's time we could use taking care of the public's needs."

In 1976, the psychologists began testing some 900 recruits in 11 Florida communities. The psychological battery, which takes about six hours, is given on the first or second day of academy classes. Only one recruit refused to take the voluntary tests.

During this validation period, the test results have not been used as a hiring tool, nor have they been shown to any law enforcement agency.

Although the recruits don't have to answer questions about their sex lives or how they feel about their parents, they are tested in three areas—ability/aptitude, interest and personality—and they are asked to fill out a biographical data sheet.

Out of these three areas, recruits are rated on: general suitability, work quality, relations with others and honesty and openness.

"We were looking to predict a recruit's success or non-success in police work and we were looking to weed out the clearly unsuitable people," said project coordinator Spaulding.

"There isn't a test existing which will weed out those officers with a propensity for brutality. But the tests will show instability. It will red flag those tendencies. If Schaeffer had taken the test he would have gotten an aberrant profile."

So far, test results have proven about 85 per cent accurate in predicting a recruit's success or failure in the law enforcement field.

Officers who were doing their jobs satisfactorily after a one-year probationary period or who were considered rehirable by their departments were defined as successful.

Unsuccessful officers were those recruits who failed the police academy or were not considered rehirable after they resigned or were fired.

In a group of 145 male Caucasian recruits, the test accurately predicted 84 per cent of the success and 71 per cent of the failures. In a group of 41 women recruits, the test accurately predicted 100 per cent of the successes and 78 per cent of the failures.

Certain profiles emerged. Successful Caucasian males were more likely to have participated in high school sports, moved fewer times as a child, needed less job encouragement and had higher values for achievement and contribution to society.

Successful women were less likely to be single than unsuccessful women.

As it is now in Dade, if a recruit passes a civil service exam, he is placed on an eligibility list. After a background check by the department's personnel selection unit, the recruit is interviewed by a three-member board composed of Metro staff psychologist Parke Fitzhugh, another police officer and someone from the personnel department.

If the recruit passes the interview board, he or she is given a physical and is scheduled for the next academy class.

Fitzhugh believes psychological testing is needed "to screen out those people who want to find a job with a uniform and authority."

He continued, "now when we look at a problem officer, we have to figure out if he brought the problem in with him or if police work caused the problem. If we spent some money on professional testing in the beginning, we might save money in the long run on lawsuits and investigations."

By December 1980, the intricate validation and cross-validation of test results will be completed.

By the spring of 1981, pending legislative approval, state officials foresee pre-employment psychological testing as mandatory for all recruits entering Florida's 428 police agencies.

With that, Florida, will join an elite cadre of only eight other states which require psychological testing of police officers. Those states are: Arkansas, Indiana, Minnesota, North Carolina, Oklahoma, Rhode Island, Tennessee and Vermont.

Minnesota began mandatory psychological testing in August 1976. "Psychological testing is an evaluation to determine if the applicant is free from any emotional or mental conditions which might adversely affect his performance of duties," said Mark Shields, head of that state's Peace Officers Standards and Training Board.

"And it gives the hiring authority a picture of this personality. It's up to them to use it as another tool in the evaluation of a candidate."

Throughout the research and validating process, the psychologists very carefully kept in mind one future pitfall—litigation. "We tried to make the test litigation proof," said Spaulding. "We asked ourselves, 'Is the test job related? Does it have to do with picking successful police officers?'"

Whether all this testing and training produces a better police officer is still open to question.

"We would like to assume a college-educated officer may be better able to handle some situations than non-college-educated officers," said Shields.

"In domestic disputes, a college-educated officer may prevent escalation of the situation to violence, but when you get into a riot situation and all hell is breaking loose, you can't tell one from another."

Source: The Miami News, December 26, 1979, pp. 5A.

The Character Investigation

With the exception of observing the probationary officer's actual performance under varied field conditions, the single most important element of the selective process is the character investigation. The basic course of action in the character investigation is to review and verify all responses made by the applicant as to his or her education, military service, prior employment history, and related matters, as well as to check the references listed and develop other references.

An editor once stated that the three basic rules for great journalists were "check your facts, check your facts, and check your facts." These "three basic rules" also apply to conducting the character investigation; making assumptions or failing to independently verify "facts" will result in an increase in negligent hirings. This creates, as is discussed in Chapter 10, "Legal Aspects of Police Administration," a liability problem because people who should not have been employed are hired. A case history illustrates this point:

On his initial employment form an applicant to a large city police department reported that he had served a tour of duty in the Coast Guard. Among the documents he showed the department's personnel investigators were the original copy of an honorable discharge as well as a DD 214 (Armed Forces of the United States Report of Transfer or Discharge). The investigators believed the discharge and DD 214 to be authentic. Still, they obtained an authorization for release of military records and medical information from the candidate. This release was then sent to the appropriate military records center. Meanwhile, the candidate's character investigation went on with respect to other factors. The candidate reported on his application form that following his discharge from the Coast Guard, he and his wife had spent 5 months traveling the country on money they had saved, thus there was no employment history during that time. When the military record information arrived, it was learned that he had, in fact, been honorably discharged, but in less than 30 days had reenlisted and 2 months into that tour of duty, he got drunk, badly beat up his wife, and assaulted military authorities who were sent to his quarters on base to handle the domestic disturbance. Subsequently, he was dishonorably discharged from the service. When questioned about it, he readily admitted to these facts and added that he was betting that either the department wouldn't check or that the record of the second enlistment wouldn't yet be in his permanent central personnel file if the department did check.

It is incidents such as these that have made many agencies realize that character investigations are very specialized and very demanding, and that a failure to properly conduct them will eventually produce results ranging from very serious to catastrophic.

Education

General agreement exists among law enforcement administrators as well as a broad segment of our nation's social and political leaders that the once-satisfactory entry standard of a high school education is no longer an acceptable minimum level. This position has been supported by three national commissions: the Wickersham Commission, 1931; the President's Commission on Law Enforcement and the Administration of Justice, 1967; and the National Advisory Commission on Criminal Justice Standards and Goals, 1973. The National Advisory Commission study recommended that:

> Every police agency should, no later than 1982, require as a condition of initial employment the completion of at least 4 years of education (120 semester hours or a baccalaureate degree) at an accredited college or university.[25]

It is apparent that neither has this higher education standard been met nor is there reason to believe that it will be met any time in the immediate future. This can be explained in part by considering that, in jurisdictions in which civil service commissions establish entrance requirements, the chief executive is limited in being able to change educational standards.[26] However, even with the absence of such a requirement, many police agencies report that they are attracting an ever-increasing number of applicants who have either completed some college work or are college graduates.[27]

It has been argued by some that police work, especially at the local level, does not require a formal education beyond high school because such tasks as directing traffic, writing parking tickets, conducting permit inspections, and performing clerical tasks do not require higher education. In addition, it has been suggested that a highly intelligent and well-educated person would soon become bored with these mundane and repetitive tasks and either resign or remain and become either an ineffective member of the force or a malcontent. However, in more progressive police agencies, such routine tasks have been turned over to civilian personnel or paraprofessionals and other governmental agencies. Thus, police officers are left with their more essential tasks, which include social control in a period of increasing social turmoil, preservation of our constitutional guarantees, and exercise of the broadest range of discretion—sometimes involving life and death decisions—of any government service. The need for police officers who are intelligent, articulate, mature, and knowledgable about social and political conditions is apparent.[28]

A number of agencies employing personnel who have college backgrounds have made some favorable reports about their performance as compared with those officers who did not have such a background. For example, one West Coast police department initiated a preemployment requirement of a four-year college degree.[29] The chief of that department reported that:

> Having employed four-year college graduates for over three years, we have found our crime rate down and yet we spend less for personnel. We have more applicants for patrolman jobs than we can use even though we have not advertised for applicants in over three years. We find we have an unusually low turnover in personnel and morale is high. We have few disciplinary problems because the men are more mature and do not feel they have to prove themselves. We have fewer citizen complaints because the men are not as threatened by abusive language and thus do not overreact. I foresee some of these men going on to other disciplines in public service and new professional public servants taking their place. The public through these men, will receive a better understanding of police problems, and better service will result.

A study of the New York City police revealed that:

> As a group, the men with at least one year of college education who remained on the force were found to be very good performers. They advanced through civil service promotion, but not disproportionately through the detective route of advancement, and they had fewer civilian complaints than average. The men who obtained college degrees, either before or after appointment to the force, exhibited even better on-the-job performance. They advanced through preferential assignments and civil service promotions, they had low incidence of all types of misconduct except harassment, on which they were average, they had low sick time and none had their firearms removed for cause.[30]

These findings were similar to the results of a Chicago Police Department study, which revealed that the highest-rated group of tenured officers were those with significantly higher education.[31] Other researchers have found that college-educated police officers are not only significantly less authoritarian than are noncollege-educated police officers but also less authoritarian than college graduates in other fields.[32]

Although much of the literature on this subject of higher education tends to extol the benefits to be gained by police departments that hire college graduates, some observers have taken a more cautious approach.[33,34,35,36] There is much evidence to suggest that the transition of going from an agency with none or few personnel with college backgrounds to one with many has created some difficulties for both the older, less educated personnel and the newer, better educated personnel. Several complaints heard consistently from the older, less educated personnel: namely, the new employees have unrealistic expectations and believe that they should be given preferential treatment in assignments and promotions because of their higher than average formal education, and they have an elitist attitude and believe that they are ''better'' than those who are less formally educated.

In one study, the college-educated officers of a department expressed a number of difficulties they had encountered. These were[37] (1) rejection by noncollege-educated peers; (2) command officers failure to encourage continuing education; (3) no reward system that encouraged education; (4) not being placed in specialized positions where their training and education could be most useful; (5) a slow promotional system; (6) no pay differential for their educational achievements; (7) little emphasis on a college education as long as the traditionalists were running the police organization; and (8) the absence of a mandatory retirement at an early age to make available openings in the higher ranks.

Thus, before making any dramatic changes in their entry and promotional standards, administrators should try to answer the following questions in relation to the needs of their agencies and communities.

- Will the increased educational level of police officers result in both a quantifiable and qualitative improvement in the delivery of social and crime control services?
- Will the college-educated officer have difficulty in identifying easily with or understanding the problems of lower- and working-class persons with whom much of police contact exists?
- Does education have a relatively uniform impact upon individuals, or is there some variance by discipline, that generally makes certain college majors more or less suitable for police work? (There tends to be a general lack of agreement, even among the proponents of higher education for police officers, about which academic skills are best suited to prepare individuals for a career in law enforcement.)
- Are many values attributed to education merely correlates of it, being provided instead by other functions of the psychological makeup and drives of individuals who pursue a college education: that is, are college graduates more highly motivated to achieve professional success because they went to college, or did they go to college because they were highly motivated to achieve professional success and simply viewed the college degree as a vehicle through which this end could be achieved.
- Are there differences in the attitude and job performance of those who bring a college degree to the organization when compared with in-service officers who obtained a degree over an extended period of time.
- If education reduces authoritarianism, does it do so to the extent that the amount remaining decreases effective performance field duties?[38]
- Should a law enforcement agency that is highly traditional, bureaucratized, and authoritarian in its leadership philosophy try to recruit college-educated personnel?
- What types of problems may occur if college-educated personnel are recruited into police departments where the majority of the personnel from the supervisory ranks upward are noncollege educated?
- Since supervisory, managerial, and planning roles tend to be more complex than those undertaken at the line level, would a mandatory higher education requirement be more realistic if it were directed toward individuals filling these positions rather than those at the entry and line levels?

Minorities and Women

Minority Recruitment

''Effectiveness'' is the traditional argument for increased minority recruitment. Police officers cannot be effective in a hostile environment—if they are unfamiliar with the culture of the community; if they feel alien to their environment; or if they are frightened, belligerent, hostile, or awkward. Citizens will not cooperate with them, will not report crimes, and will not aid in their investigations.[39] One solution sometimes employed by administrators is to assign police officers of the same ethnic background as the residents—Chicanos policing Chicanos, blacks policing blacks. There is evidence that racial or ethnic similarity can indeed improve community relations and reduce tensions. Dozens of cities, including Detroit, Baltimore, Washington, (D.C.) and New Orleans, have improved community relations by staffing troubled areas with police of the same racial or ethnic character as the neighborhood population.

One of the difficulties that even well-intentioned police administrators encounter is attempting to implement such a policy is the lack of sufficient numbers of personnel to fill such assignments. And minority recruitment, although not nearly as difficult as some contend, is still no simple matter. After decades of exclusion, suspicion, and discrimination, a passive "open door" policy is not sufficient. Peer group pressure—strong among young blacks—is one negative factor. Fear of failure, nonacceptance, or even outright discrimination is another. Furthermore, new job opportunities for minorities in other fields often appear more attractive than those offered in the police department.

Despite these obstacles, minority recruitment can be made more effective. For example,

> The department itself must initiate strong minority recruitment efforts. Recruitment relegated to a central city agency is not likely to be successful. Civil service boards have numerous other responsibilities, and few have the time or skills necessary to attract the type of candidate police departments require. Therefore, the department itself must assume the major responsibility for minority recruitment. This approach has proved highly effective in Detroit, Baltimore, Washington, D.C., New York City, and a number of other cities. The department must demonstrate a commitment to internal equal opportunity. It must be remembered that applicants are being asked to commit themselves to a new career. They need to know that the department recruiting them is also dedicated to helping them advance. Many departments—such as those in Boston, New Orleans, Dayton, New York, Miami, and St. Louis—have demonstrated such commitment by appointing qualified minority individuals, both from within and outside the department, to high positions. Most of these departments are also taking the potentially more important step of examining their promotional systems and removing as many of the discriminatory components as possible.
>
> The most effective recruiters of minority police applicants are successful minority officers. Such officers should be asked to direct or assist in the development of a minority recruitment program and be given the on-duty time and whatever support that might be required. Appearances at high schools, community group meetings, veterans' centers, and other gathering places for minority group individuals of suitable age have been especially helpful. In addition, these recruiting officers should encourage other beat officers to be alert for potentially qualified applicants. The patrol car itself can be an excellent recruiting tool if the officers are willing to expend the effort and are encouraged to do so. Some cities, such as St. Louis, provide up to five days of paid vacation to any officer who successfully recruits a new police officer. The response has been good.
>
> As promising individuals are identified they should be pursued by the department. Targeting individuals as prospective officers can be accomplished in much the same manner as the department "targets" an individual criminal. Potential applicants can be assigned to individual police officers, who will be expected to visit the applicants' homes and maintain regular contact with them, help the applicants prepare for their examinations, maintain

FIGURE 7-4. Patrol officer Douglas Wilson, San Antonio, Texas Police Department and a few of his friends. [Photo courtesy San Antonio Police Department.]

their determination through the long waiting period, and get through their training and probationary periods. This technique has been used successfully in private industry and by the Massachusetts State Police.

One other matter requires comment. It is frequently said that minority recruitment has been unsuccessful because of police departments that refuse to lower their standards to recruit minorities. One of the difficulties of discussing standards for police personnel is that the issue is seen in terms of "raising" or "lowering" requirements. Such code words as these really do not address the issue. Higher or lower standards are not at stake; rather, it is the standards that are relevant to the functions for which they are designed.

Employment of Women

Not too many years ago, it was common for police administrators to dismiss the notion that women could adequately perform functions normally falling within the exclusive domain of male officers—such as patrol work, nonfamily-related crime investigations, riding a motorcycle, and so forth. Legislative, administrative, and judicial action have long since resolved the question of whether or not women should be permitted to perform these functions, and women have put to rest the questions about their ability to handle these tasks. There is ample empirical evidence to support the proposition that carefully selected and carefully trained females can be as effective as police officers as carefully selected and carefully trained males. Not all women are suited for police work, nor are all men. This, however, is not meant to suggest that women have been universally and enthusiastically accepted by their male counterparts, but their employment opportunities and career advancement have improved immeasurably during the past decade.

The first women to be assigned to operating units that have traditionally been comprised exclusively of men usually experience the most serious difficulty. These women face certain psychological pressures that will not be encountered by men or by the women who will follow them months or even years later. For example, the first female police officers must perform their duties in an atmosphere of disbelief on the part of their supervisors and peers in their ability to deal physically and emotionally with the rigors of street work, particularly patrol functions. It must be remembered that peer acceptance is one of the greatest pressures operating within the police organizations.[40] The desire to be identified as a ''good officer'' is a strong motivating force, and a failure to achieve that goal in one's own eyes as well as in the eyes of one's peers can have a devastating and demoralizing effect.

For the rookie female officer, attaining the approval of her peers can be an even more frustrating task than it is for her male counterpart. As is true for her male counterpart, she must overcome her doubts about her own ability to perform her duties effectively, but unlike her male counterparts, she must also overcome the prejudice stemming from societal influences depicting the female as the ''weaker sex'' in every respect.[41] Also, unlike her male counterpart, she will very likely receive little support from her family, friends, and perhaps even her husband or other close male companions. Thus, additional pressures are imposed upon women choosing careers in law enforcement that are not imposed upon men, and these pressures may exist to an even greater degree with females of certain minority groups.

BOX 7-5.

Latin Policewomen

BILL GIEBRE, *Cox News Service*

MIAMI—When Elizabeth Martin told her family she was going to become a Miami police officer, her mother was stunned. She told Martin the family had sent her to a private school "to make you a lady."

When Andrea Landis informed her family of her plans to become a Miami police officer, her mother tried, unsuccessfully, to change her mind.

Elizabeth Alvarez didn't receive any direct family pressure to keep her from joining the Metro Public Safety Department. The pressure was cultural. Alvarez said the traditional His-panic upbringing discourages women from becoming police officers.

The three women are part of a small group in the two departments who have broken with their Latin backgrounds to enter police work. To Latins, the police force is a man's world.

Police recruiters for the city and the county—both of which are in the throes of heavy recruitment efforts—say the most difficult group to attract as job applicants are Latin females.

Of 122 females in the Public Safety Department, only 12 are Latin. In the Miami Police

Department, the ratio is even smaller: Only four of 51 female officers are Latin. Of the nine females now in training, one is Latin.

With the city under a federal mandate to promote Latins, blacks and women, the city's female Latin officers appear to have good chances of moving up. Landis, for example, is No. 11 on the promotion list, and is likely to move up before the list expires.

"In the Hispanic culture, (police work) is not considered appropriate for women—it's not a feminine occupation," says Manny Mendoza, an associate professor of political science and sociology at Miami-Dade Community College.

Police work is considered a "macho job" for males, says Mendoza, who is of Cuban descent. Mendoza is a member of the city of Miami's Affirmative Action Advisory Board.

Females are supposed to be "mothers and homemakers" and if they go to work they are supposed to go into the professions, such as law and medicine, Mendoza adds.

Carlos Arauz, assistant director of the Miami Human Resources Department, adds this: "In a majority of countries in Latin America, police officers are not seen as community servants, but as oppressors. . . . The image of police officers is not something a Latin woman associates with."

In the Latin family, the "woman always had the housewife role," says Randy Eques, Human Resources coordinator for the Public Safety Department.

Latin families "do not perceive (females) being police officers," says Miami police Maj. Robert Alba. "They place daughters on pedestals, think of them as mothers and housekeepers. Women are to bear children, not be police and firemen. And what the community perceives you as is the way you feel."

"There is a basic misconception among Latins that being a police officer is anti-feminine," says Martin, 29.

That was another argument her Cuban mother used six years ago to try to dissuade her from joining the force, she said.

"Latin females are raised to be feminine, and not to do anything without asking the man," says Martin. "The husband makes the decisions. Latin females stay at home, raise kids and get office jobs, if they work."

Martin tried the traditional route first. She got married right out of high school. But that ended in divorce and she went to work as a stewardess.

But when she lost her stewardess job because of a Pan Am cutback, she applied, with some encouragement from a Miami police officer, to the city's police department. She was single at the time.

She says that she probably would have had a difficult time joining the department had she been married to a Latin male. "Latin men couldn't handle women being police officers," Martin says.

"Latin women think you go out there and are kicking and fighting all the time." But of course that's not so. "You're not out there every day battling. More often than not, you are out there doing social work.

"There are times when I have had to fight," she says. But she adds that males tend to be less hostile toward female police officers.

"Latin women aren't into fighting," she says. "I don't want to get hurt. I try to use my head. Sweet talk is the best way to get them into my back seat.

"Usually I say, 'Come here and sit in my car and tell me all about it.'" With such a large Latin population, Martin says Latin females are valuable as translators and in certain sensitive assignments. One time, she adds, a male officer called her at home and asked if she would tell a Latin woman that her daughter had been killed in an accident.

For Martin, there is one male in her life who likes what she does: her 9-year-old son, who "thinks it's neat to have me as a police officer."

Andrea Landis, a Peruvian who came to the United States 13 years ago, didn't want a desk job. Six years ago, she decided against becoming a stewardess and became a Miami police officer because "it's different and challenging."

Her mother "had a fit. She thought it was dangerous." Her father was not alive when she applied for the job. Had he been, Landis says, he "would have killed me."

Latin families instill in females that they should "get married and raise a family," Landis says.

During the past six years, Landis has spent most of her time on patrol work, on the 3 P.M. to 1 A.M. shift.

Speaking Spanish helped Landis on one

occasion. She does not look typically Hispanic and was in the company of several Latin suspects who didn't know she could speak their language.

The two men were talking to each other in Spanish, and one told the other he was armed, Landis recalls. "I didn't wait to see what they were going to do," Landis says. She got the drop on them.

Landis' husband of two years, Vince Landis, is a Miami police sergeant who has no problem with his wife being a policewoman.

"She is a grown person and knows what the job entails," says Landis, who is of Irish and Italian decent. "I have no hangups about it. Women have their place in this world—whatever the calling is. I am encouraging her to go as high as she can."

Landis soon will return to work after a leave to have a baby, Tiffany Leigh, 2 months old.

"I'll let (Tiffany) make her own decisions" about her future, says her father. "If she wants to be a cop, that's OK; whatever the Lord wants her to be."

Source: The Tampa Tribune, November 29, 1980, p. 2-B.

Administrators can take a number of steps to facilitate the entry of females into their operating units. First, the introduction of policewomen, for example, in patrol activities, should be discussed in advance with male patrol officers to emphasize that female officers will be given neither preferential treatment nor preferential assignments. Second, field training officers and supervisors of rookie female officers must be individuals who will fairly and accurately assess performance without consideration of sex. Third, the chief administrator should issue a general order outlining the administrative expectations of women being assigned to previously all-male operating units.

For example, one chief of police issued a written order with nineteen guidelines to set the stage for the mass infusion of women into the patrol force. Some of these guidelines were women should be given the same assignments, privileges, and considerations as men; no special scout cars or special assignments should be created for women; women should be given the full range of assignments, including assignments to scout cars, footbeats, station duty, and traffic duty; women should be given consideration for certification to patrol alone when they have obtained the necessary experience.[42] This written order affirmed the chief's full support of the use of women in patrol work and probably reduced the potential for treating female patrol officers differently from their male counterparts.[43]

BOX 7-6.

How Good Are Women Cops?

By Tom Seligson

Kathy Burke has been a New York City cop for more than 15 years. For much of that time, the short, curly-haired detective worked undercover narcotics, buying drugs from pushers she would later arrest. She put more than 1000 dealers behind bars while risking exposure, rape and violent death. Now 41 and an investigator in the city's Major Case Squad, Burke obviously has paid her dues. Yet recently, while serving a subpoena, she encountered a clerk who could not believe she was a police officer.

"You mean that little girl's a detective?" said the clerk to Burke's partner.

"Yes, this little girl's a detective," Burke replied patiently. She is accustomed to such a reaction. For female cops, it's part of the job.

It has been 12 years now since women began joining our police forces in significant numbers. The discriminatory hiring practices that deterred many women—and restricted those hired to largely clerical functions—were prohibited in 1972 by the Equal Opportunity Act. For the first time, women were allowed on patrol and to perform all the other duties previously reserved for men. As a result, the number of female officers is now 19,668, or almost 5 percent of total officers (up from 1.5 percent in 1972). New York, for example, has 2109 female officers: Chicago has 740; and Los Angeles has 506. Moreover, women continue to swell the ranks. By the end of the decade, they may constitute 20 percent of our police force.

Many of the initial objections to women cops—that they were too weak physically and couldn't handle the stress—have been widely dispelled. Countless studies have proved female officers equal in competence to their male colleagues. "Female police officers are essential," says Tom Sardino, the chief of police in Syracuse, N.Y., and president of the International Association of Chiefs of Police. "I have talked to hundreds of law-enforcement executives throughout the world. I have not heard any of them register any kind of complaint regarding their ability." Clearly, women cops are up to the job.

But at what cost? Has it been hard for women, functioning in this hitherto all-male arena? What has been the impact on their personal lives, their families, their relationships in the community?

To find out how women officers are faring, I traveled around the country, talking to cops—both female and male—in big cities and small towns. I learned not only that the job has affected women but also that women, in turn, have had a decided impact on the job. Indeed, they are contributing to a whole new style of law enforcement emerging in America.

Why would a woman *want* to become a cop? Women become police officers for basically the same reasons as men: the excitement of the job, the opportunity for public service and the satisfaction of knowing that, out on the street, you're your own boss. Kathy Burke wanted to be a cop from the age of 13. "I had seen friends hurt from drugs," she recalls. "I wanted to rid the city of drugs."

Chris Lee and Marlene Willhoite, who are partners in San Francisco, left jobs in accounting and nursing to join the force. "I thought it would be a tremendous learning experience," says Chris, 32. "Both the physical training and the use of firearms." Marlene, 32, explains that she was bored working in a hospital. "I thought police work would be more exciting, and I was right."

Another appeal, of course, is the money. Louise Vasquez, a 49-year-old Miami homicide detective, got married right out of high school and had four kids. When her youngest child was 5, she and her husband divorced, and she was left with no means of support. Attracted by the secure income police work offered, she took the test for officer—and was hired. Now a highly decorated 18-year veteran, Vasquez has remarried, and her salary of more than $35,000 a year contributes to the raising of eight children.

Not that female cops don't earn their money. As demanding, dangerous and often thankless as police work is generally, for women the job has proven doubly taxing. First of all, they've had to deal with a public unaccustomed to the sight of a woman in uniform.

Mary Wamsley, 34, is a sergeant in Lakewood, Colo., a suburb of Denver. She started in 1974, the first year Lakewood allowed women on patrol. "The public was shocked," she recalls. "I remember getting a burglary-in-progress call one night and going up to the house, gun drawn. The man who called opened the door, saw me and slammed it. He called back to say, 'There's a girl outside with a gun who's part of the gang.' And this is even though I had my uniform on. They couldn't convince him I was a police officer. I had to wait in my car until a male officer showed up."

The surprise of the public was nothing compared with the initial reception female officers encountered from their male colleagues. "A lot of the men resented me," says Wamsley. "When I'd arrive as a backup, they'd act as if I wasn't there." Even worse than their cold shoulder was their protectiveness. "When I'd respond to something as minor as a barking dog or a stolen bicycle, I'd get a backup," Wamsley recalls.

Lucille Burrascano, 41, recently promoted to detective, was one of the first women to go on patrol in New York City. She too encountered inappropriate chivalry from the men.

"During training, I rode as the third person with two men. We're on a robbery run, the siren's blaring, and we pull up right in front of the door. We're supposed to come out with our guns drawn but, instead, one of the cops jumps out and opens the door for me. I said, 'What are you doing? This is not a date.' "

Other officers were downright hostile to Burrascano. "Before I went on patrol," she says, "one cop said to me, 'I would quit this job before I'd work with a woman.' "

The discrimination against Kathy Burke went so far as to actually jeopardize her life. While pursuing a drug dealer, she went into a building to make an arrest. Her commander held the backup unit, leaving her to fend for herself. "Let her be a cop," he said.

It is typical of Kathy Burke that she took the challenge in stride. "I knew I had to prove myself," she says. It wasn't until she followed her partner out a second-story window that Burke found herself accepted. "We were serving a warrant," she recalls, "and my partner went out onto what he thought was a ledge. Instead, he fell 10 feet to the ground. Instinctively, I followed him out. Fortunately, neither of us was hurt. After that, the men realized that anyone stupid enough to follow her partner out a window could be relied on."

John Gaspar, also a former partner of Burke's, feels confident that Kathy will fight with all her strength. "Pound for pound, she's like a terrier," he says.

Many women speak of having to "prove themselves." Often the judge is not the men, but themselves. "I was scared to death when I first went on patrol," says Mary Wamsley. "All I did was answer dispatch calls, looking straight ahead." Wamsley attributes the fear to her conditioning as a woman. "I was a daddy's girl," she says, "and it was hard for me to adopt the aggressive style of a cop. I would go home at night and cry. And the first time someone hit me, I went to the hospital. Not because I was hurt but because I was so shook."

Wamsley admits to having overcompensated for her passivity by becoming overly aggressive. "I got into a lot of fights," she says. "I was deliberately trying to be a man." It's an indication of how Wamsley has mellowed in her 11 years as a cop that, on the night I accompanied her on tour, she wore expensive French perfume.

It's easy to understand how they could be tempted to act like men, but the women who have succeeded as cops have come to learn that it's pointless to compete. "I had to arrest a guy for bank robbery who was 6 feet 7," says Kathy Burke, who stands 5 feet 2. "My partner was able to tackle him. No way was I gonna even try."

Ironically, this perceived weakness of women officers has, in effect, turned into an asset. Lucille Burrascano remembers arresting two men in a stolen car. "These guys were monsters," she says. "So big that I could not close the handcuffs. I asked one of them later on, 'How come you didn't put up a fight? I'm half your size.' He said, 'I knew I was under arrest and that, if I fought you, you would shoot me.' "

Another advantage female officers have is that they *are* still a novelty. "It's much easier for me, working plainclothes, to get into an apartment," says Kathy Burke. "No one suspects a woman is a cop. Cops are known as 'the man.' And if I ever have to draw my gun, it makes *much* more of an impact. A gun in the hands of a 5-foot-2 woman looks bigger than when held by a man. It looks like a cannon."

Burrascano discovered that she and her partner had their greatest success in breaking up family arguments. "Whoever was fighting, and sometimes it was two entire families, would stop when they saw us," she says. "Not only were we a novelty, but we were considered nonthreatening. Consequently, it was easier for us to defuse the situation."

This ability, whether it involves families or armed robbers, is acknowledged by male officers. Bob Davis, a member of the San Francisco vice squad, has trained or worked with close to 50 women. Davis maintains that he has not had *one* incompetent female partner. "I worked for nine months with one woman, and I had complete confidence in her. She had tremendous instinct: She spotted things I didn't see. And, of course, she was very good at defusing potentially explosive situations, which to me is the key to good police work. No smart cop wants to fight with crooks."

It appears that this calming, nonconfrontational approach is fundamentally altering our method of policing. "When I first came on the job," says Louise Vasquez, "I always heard that you had to be a macho tough guy to be a police officer. You got to be able to beat somebody up. I've seen men get into more fights, cause more injuries, kill more people and produce more complaints because of their need to prove their manliness. With women, it's just the opposite. They don't have to prove anything. And it's not because we're unable to be aggressive. Anybody can hit somebody on the head with a nightstick. Or shoot him. A gun is certainly gonna make me as tough as any man. But the women are less likely to use it. They're gonna find another way."

"I think the women are finally influencing the men into becoming less aggressive," observes Vasquez. "It's become a policy in our department that you try to get help. If you encounter a guy with a gun, you call for assistance. If two people do the job, it's less likely that someone's gonna get hurt."

To prove her point, Vasquez confides that, during her entire career, she has rarely pulled her gun, and she has fired it only once. Her preferred method of dealing with murder suspects talk. "The toughest guy in the world can be talked to," she explains. "They're used to dealing with other tough guys, so if you come on nice, it works."

Whatever approach they use, female officers generally find that it's not hardened criminals who pose their biggest problem. Ironically, they have more difficulty with other women. "To this day, I find that women don't like to be arrested by other women," says Mary Wamsley. "They either call me a lesbian, a dyke or a whole string of profanities."

Understandably, the loudest critics of policewomen always have been policemen's wives. They fear that female officers will not adequately protect their husbands and, perhaps even worse, that the long hours together will lead to an affair. Bob Davis' wife hated it when he worked with women. She was particularly jealous of Adele, his partner. "It was my own fault," concedes Davis. "I talked about her all the time."

Lucille Burrascano thinks cops' wives have a perfect right to be jealous. "When you spend eight hours a day with a partner, delivering babies, protecting one another in shoot-outs, going from one high-tension job to another, you can't help but be close. Also, quite frankly, policing is a highly emotional job. You have

moments of intense excitement. But to assume that two partners are going to have an affair is wrong. It depends on how good each of their marriages is. I'm single, and I rode for a while with a single man. He was great. But we never dated."

Kathy Burke had to sever a partnership because the man's wife felt threatened. But she herself has never experienced jealousy from her husband, maybe because he too is a cop. "He has always been supportive," she says.

Mary Wamsley has been married five years—her husband is a chief deputy district attorney—but when she was single, she found, as do many female cops, that her profession was a definite turnoff for most men. "I found in dating that a lot of men are intimidated by knowing I carry a gun," says Wamsley. "Also, that if we were out together and a fight broke out, I was more able to handle it than he was. My husband, however, doesn't give a rip."

But her husband *does* worry about her. "We have a code," says Wamsley. "I never go to work before he tells me to be careful. We've talked about the hazards of this job, and God knows he's seen me get injured (she has been stabbed and had her knee torn apart in the line of duty). But he knows I wouldn't be happy doing anything else."

Louise Vasquez says it's essential to separate family life from the job. Though encountering acts of violence almost daily, she does not allow herself to dwell on what she sees or relate any of it to her own family. Nevertheless, the mother of eight concedes that being a cop definitely influences the way she acts at home. "I think I've become a much more demanding mother. As a cop, you come across so many parents who don't care about their kids. It's caused me to be more concerned and more aware of what my own kids were doing."

However, none of her children has ever accused her of *acting* like a cop. And she's obviously set a good example: Her daughter-in-law, Patricia, recently left her job in public relations to join the Miami Police Department, and her daughter Becky also is considering quitting the post office to join the force.

What will happen to Patricia and Becky as a result of putting on a uniform, strapping on a gun and joining all the other mothers and sisters on patrol? Without question, the job will change them as women. "I've become much more outspoken," says Marlene Willhoite. "Now, if I have something on my mind, I'll talk about it, whereas before I kept it to myself." And Mary Wamsley says: "I've become much more cynical than my friends who aren't cops. I've seen a side of human nature that I wish I didn't know. But it's done good things for me too. It's made me more self-confident. I was a starry-eyed debutante when I started. Now I'd like to think I'm a pretty good cop."

Mary Wamsley is not unique. Women like her all across the country are proving themselves as police officers. Of course, they still face hurdles. Kathy Burke still encounters "dinosaurs" who think she belongs at home and who condescendingly call her "honey," "sister" or "dear." Marlene Willhoite and Chris Lee have to endure wisecracks—"Hey, you're like Cagney and Lacey!"—at least once a night.

Although Capt. Penny E. Harrington was just named police chief in Portland, Ore., so far only 6 percent of all women cops hold a rank higher than police officer. And Bob Davis predicts the real male resistance will develop when more women become supervisors, telling the men what to do. Lucille Burrascano goes so far as to say, "Women have two to three generations to go before they are truly accepted in a so-called 'man's job.' "

But women officers already have left their mark. They have shown that it is possible to be gentle and compassionate and still be a good cop. They have helped to humanize our police departments. They are a welcome addition to the ranks of America's finest.

Parade, March 31, 1985, pp. 4–7.

FIGURE 7-5. Officer instructing cadet on the proper way to complete a report form. [Photo Courtesy of the Sacramento, Calif. Police Department.]

Court-Mandated Recruiting and Employment

During the past decade there has been a growing number of cases in which federal judges have ordered police departments to utilize a quota system in their employment of minorities and women. Efforts by police administrators to resist such orders have for the most part met with little success. Such court-mandated recruiting and employment orders have generally been made after it has been demonstrated that a particular police department's hiring practices are intentionally or even unintentionally discriminatory.

BOX 7-7.

U.S. Judge Gives Preliminary OK to Minority and Female Hiring Plan for the San Francisco Police Department

A federal judge gave preliminary approval January 26 to a landmark discrimination case settlement requiring that minorities receive 50% and women 20% of all the city police officer appointments for the next 10 years.

The out-of-court settlement was signed and submitted to chief U.S. Dist. Judge Robert F. Peckham, climaxing a six-year struggle over a controversial lawsuit charging the city police department with employment discrimination.

At present, the 1,670-member police force includes about 200 minority persons and 60 women. City officials expect to enroll more than 600 recruits in the next two years.

The agreement established hiring quotas described by attorneys as among the highest ever set in a police employment discrimination case. Among other things, it also requires that:

—The city expand its existing police force by 340 positions within two years, at a cost to the city estimated at $14 million.

—The city award about $400,000 in back pay to minorities and women who can prove they were victims of discrimination in the past. Also, the city must set aside $500,000 to recruit and train new officers.

—The city virtually abolish seniority credit for police promotions, in order to speed the advancement of minorities and women, and that ultimately police promotions reflect the racial and gender proportions of the officers seeking the promotions.

—The city pay up to $385,000 in attorneys' fees to Public Advocates, the San Francisco law firm that represented a coalition of minorities and women who brought the discrimination suit against the city six years ago.

The hiring quotas established in the settlement were officially called "goals," but attorneys expressed full confidence that should the city, as a party to the settlement not reach those goals, the court action would quickly result.

"Those goals are very court-enforceable," said Lois Salisbury, an attorney for Public Advocates. "And this city, which is about 50% minority now, should have no difficulty finding qualified applicants."

In the settlement, the city does not directly concede discrimination against minorities and women. But it does promise to refrain from discrimination in the future. The quota system the settlement imposes would exist at least until 45% of the force is made up of racial minorities. No such goal is set for women. Women minorities would count as credit towards both the 50% minority and 20% female quotas set for future hiring.

The settlement was signed in the form of a proposed consent decree by Attorneys for Officers for Justice, a group of black police officers, and the rest of the coalition of minority and women's groups that brought the suit—along with lawyers for the city of San Francisco, the San Francisco Police Officers Assn. (a white officers' organization), and the U.S. Department of Justice.

The agreement had been approved earlier

this week by a 7 to 3 vote of the San Francisco Board of Supervisors.

The pact was approved with apparent reluctance by the supervisors, one of whom, Quentin Kopp, warned: "We're going to have a federal judge directing a substantial part of the operations of the police department."

Judge Peckham, receiving the proposed consent decree Thursday, noted that it formed a "substantial basis" for settlement of the long-standing suit. It was expected that the judge would give final approval soon.

The agreement was reached after six years of legal and political maneuvering, both in and out of court.

The organizations that brought the suit charged city officials manipulated police policies and physical and mental exams to effectively prevent racial minorities and women from being hired and promoted.

San Francisco homicide inspector Earl Sanders, a black officer, was the only witness ever called to testify in court proceedings.

He told the court that in 1964, when he took the police academy physical exam, city physicians found a "heart murmur" and "high blood pressure"—although his own doctor had said he was in excellent health.

Sanders said he heard a city physician say, "We already have 10 of them"—an apparent reference to 10 other black applicants.

Source: "Equal Opportunity Forum," *Affirmative Action Monthly,* February 1979, pp. 22.

Employment of Homosexuals

One of the more controversial police hiring practices during the past decade has been the active recruitment of homosexuals by the San Francisco Police Department. There is no evidence that other police departments will follow this practice, but one of the more interesting trends is the decision by some police administrators simply not to make an issue of sexual preference on the background investigations they conduct on applicants. For example, some police departments no longer question applicants about their sexual preference either on their applications or when administering the polygraph examination. There is no definite explanation to this change of attitude, but it is quite likely linked to an overall change in society's social and sexual mores as well as the concern by police administrators that if they do not voluntarily take the lead the federal courts may be called upon to intercede on the behalf of homosexuals as the courts have already done in the case of minorities and women.

BOX 7-8.

San Francisco Recruits Homosexual Police Officers

By SUSAN COHEN

San Francisco—one clue to John Abney's survival as a San Francisco sheriff's deputy is this piece of philosophy: "You have to learn to laugh at the fag jokes."

Abney is one of more than a dozen openly homosexual deputies in the sheriff's department, which guards the city's jails. He also is one of more than 350 homosexuals who've applied to join the San Francisco Police Department, which patrols the city's streets.

At a time when it still is routine in most jurisdictions to fire police officers for homosexuality, San Francisco has become the first city in the country to actively recruit gay cops.

"Every police force in the United States has had a policy of barring gays from the force.

But in five years there won't be a major urban area without gay officers," predicts Les Morgan, who at one time headed gay recruitment for the sheriff's and police departments.

For the last six months, Morgan, a social scientist who is homosexual, has been a volunteer for the police, meeting with gays and cooperating with the city's civil service system, which has been testing and screening applicants. The department, however, no longer is seeking applicants.

The campaign to hire gays was embraced by Police Chief Charles Gain, but Morgan admits it was greeted with less than total enthusiasm by the rank and file of San Francisco's finest.

"I'm told originally there was sort of a siege mentality, like the Russians were invading the U.S.," is the way Morgan describes it. "But when they saw we're not going to have a bunch of drag queens coming in here, the tension eased off."

The tension has not eased off enough, however, for a single San Francisco police officer to dare to acknowledge being gay, even though the chief and the head of the Police Officers Association state that there are homosexuals on the force.

"To have them come out of the closet and have them subjected to pressures, there's no point," argues police association president Bob Barry. "It will only raise a lot of moral questions in other officers' minds."

But Morgan disagrees. He hopes that with a big enough influx of gay recruits, no one rookie will be singled out for pressures, and attitudes will change among police as they have in the sheriff's department.

"Gays pay a lot of taxes in this city and they shouldn't be discriminated against in hiring," he says. "It's important that the community be adequately represented for the same reasons there should be blacks, women, Asians, and Chicanos."

The acceptance of homosexuals in the sheriff's department happened as gradually as their general acceptance as a sizable and politically influential part of San Francisco.

In 1961, when Undersheriff Charles Smith entered the department, he remembers there was a fellow rookie with an unfortunately high voice. Unfortunate because, Smith says, it led to the deputy being "terminated from the department on suspicion of being gay, even though he was married."

In 1972, Rich Hongisto was elected sheriff with the strong support of the gay community and a pledge to liberalize the department. It gave one new deputy the courage to allow a local gay newspaper to take a picture of him in uniform and write about his homosexuality.

The reaction among other deputies was mostly grumbling about the public nature of the disclosure, Smith recalls. But at the Alameda County Sheriff's Academy where the officer was sent for training, worse was in store.

"He was singled out," Smith says. "They tried to wash him out with a phony charge that he had cheated, and it took an investigation to show he had not."

It was in that atmosphere that Morgan was hired by Hongisto in 1974 as a civilian administrator and liaison to the gay community. One thing Morgan discovered was that even though homosexuals often were assaulted by gangs of roving punks in San Francisco, they were afraid to report it to the police.

One answer, he thought, was more gays in law enforcement.

The recruits who responded to Morgan's Outreach drive did not all identify themselves as being homosexual during the hiring process or even later, in the department. Someone posted a list of the new recruits with those suspected of being gay marked in red. The list was torn down.

There were jokes and jibes, but gradually most of the deputies found they were more comfortable telling others they were gay than concealing their personal lives.

"I was really petrified. I didn't know what was going to happen at all," says Sgt. Connie O'Connor of her decision to tell the sheriff that she was a lesbian. "I had just never really talked about my personal life too much, although I'm sure people suspected."

But, sitting on a review board screening applicants for the department, O'Connor heard some recruits state that they were gay.

"It was a little embarrassing. Here I was judging them and I'm closeted and they're open," she says.

Her decision not to conceal her sexual preference had no ill effects for O'Connor, 32, who today is in charge of one of the city's women's jails. But she believes lesbians in law enforcement have an easier time than homosexual men, because women officers "usually get called dikes even if they're not."

It took Sgt. Zapata a year of soul searching before he took aside some friends at a departmental Christmas party and said, "Hey, did you know I'm gay?"

"Some said, 'no,' " some said 'thought so,' but generally they all said it didn't make any difference," Zapata says. "I did it mostly to ease the pressures on me because I can't feel I'm being deceitful."

If to the public the image of homosexuals as effeminate and police as the ultimate in machismo are incongruous, they are not to Zapata. He thinks both stereotypes are incorrect.

Not only is there a wide range of behavior within the gay community, he says, but also "the macho image should be changed in any law enforcement agency anyway."

"It's not real. How can you fairly deal with people when you're spending all your time proving how tough you are?"

But Zapata believes deputies must be able

to convince suspects and the community that they are capable of handling tough situations and that "affected people or flamboyant people" wouldn't fare well as deputies.

Abney, 30, dark-haired and deep-voice, has a no-nonsense way about him and says that he is probably more conservative than his non-gay fellow deputies. He wants to join the police not only to do patrol work, but also to breach another barrier for homosexuals.

Abney says that the deputies who entered the sheriff's department as a result of the gay recruitment—90 per cent of whom remain— have blended into the agency. He, for instance, takes a female date to departmental get-togethers, explaining: "Why make some guy explain to his wife why two guys are there together."

"If somebody wants a cop, they don't care if it's a gay cop or a straight cop. It doesn't make any difference when you're on the job who you go to bed with at night."

Source: The Tribune (Chicago), May 7, 1979, p. 11.

Performance Evaluation

The process of performance evaluation is one that is too often disliked and misunderstood by both the individuals doing the evaluation and those being evaluated. This occurs many times because the purposes of the performance evaluation are simply not understood and the police department provides no clearly defined, unambiguous policy or procedure.

Purpose of Evaluation

Employee Performance. Appraisals serve as an aid in motivating employees to maintain an acceptable level of performance. In this sense, performance refers to more than just measurable units of work. Law enforcement is too complex an undertaking to base appraisals solely on how a person fulfills assigned tasks. In addition to an evaluation of how an officer performs physically, the appraisal must also address itself to aspects that are difficult to quantify, such as attitudes and traits, but are of utmost importance to the successful accomplishment of mission.[44]

Career Development. Personnel evaluations, if administered properly, pinpoint strengths that can be developed and weaknesses that should be corrected, thereby furnishing administrators with a developmental and remedial device of considerable worth. Those employees who consistently maintain a level of performance above the standards set by the department can, based upon their evaluations, be assigned to more responsible duties. Conversely, officers who are unable to meet reasonable standards can be given the guidance, supervision, and training necessary to save a career before it flounders.

Supervisory Interests. Systematic evaluations encourage supervisors to take a personal interest in the officers under their command. Within this context, appraisals can have a humanizing effect on supervision by holding commanders responsible for the performance of subordinates. Ideally, the program will foster mutual understanding, *esprit de corps,* solidarity, and group cohesiveness.

Salary Decisions. With the current managerial emphasis on rewards won on merit, personnel evaluations serve as a basis, often the only one, for pay increases. Officers with satisfactory appraisals will probably receive raises on time, whereas increases for those who fall below standards may be temporarily withheld. In industry, superior employees often receive early pay raises, an idea that may be of some value in police work, where it has not been used to any extent.

Selection Practices. When entry-level procedures are valid, most individuals selected for employment will make positive contributions to the department. If, however, many rookie officers in an agency are unable to perform adequately, something may be seriously wrong with the selection process. Personnel appraisal allows administrators to maintain a continuing check on entrance standards to determine if they are relevant or in need of modification. Furthermore, promotional examinations can be validated if supervisory and command evaluations are accurate.

Performance evaluations are sometimes used by employees as a legal defense to countermand allegations of misconduct by their departments. The following newspaper articles indicates how one police officer used her previous performance appraisals to enhance her chances of being rehired by the New York City Police Department after she was dismissed.

BOX 7-9.

New York Must Rehire Officer Who Posed Nude

NEW YORK (AP)—A police officer removed from her job for posing nude in a magazine was ordered reinstated with back pay by an appeals court Tuesday.

The officer, Cibella Borges, 27, was fired in 1983 for posing nude in a magazine called Pub nine months before she became a police officer. By a 3–1 vote, the state's appellate division, said the Police Department lacked the jurisdiction to fire the woman for behavior that occurred before her appointment.

During her time as an officer, her professional performance was judged "above standard" or "well above standard" by her supervisor.

"I will be back," Ms. Borges said in an interview on WNBC-TV.

She said she had been out of work since she was fired because prospective employers believed that she would be returning to the police force. She was vacationing in California and said she would return to New York today.

"The agonizing is over for Cibella," said Joseph O. Giaimo, Ms. Borges' attorney, in a telephone interview from the Bahamas. "We're flying high knowing she's going to be a policewoman again."

When told by a reporter that the court had ruled in favor of Ms. Borges, Mayor Edward I. Koch commented, "That's why we have courts. She's made her case. She's entitled to the relief the courts give her."

Koch said a decision on whether to appeal would be up to the city's corporation counsel, Frederick A.O. Schwarz.

Ms. Borges had accused the Police Department of applying a double standard for the behavior of ranking officials and lower level officers. Koch forgave Police Commissioner Benjamin Ward after he admitted having after-

hours encounters with a woman in his office on Rikers Island when he was the corrections commissioner.

Officer Joseph McConville, a Police Department spokesman, said the department refused to comment on the ruling because "we haven't had the opportunity to look at it yet."

Source: St Louis Post-Dispatch Wednesday, April 10, 1985 pp 2A, B1.

An Evaluation Policy

Naturally, it must be a first management priority to install an evaluation system that has a good chance of delivering. If a defective system is put into operation, nothing can be done to make it work. Once top management has drafted the right instrument, reasonable steps can be taken to see that it is utilized correctly. A policy declaration should be enacted that clearly informs personnel of all aspects of the plan. Ideally, the policy should address itself to a discussion of the topics that follow.

Coverage. Everyone on a police department beneath the chief executive should be evaluated formally by a superior. In the case of the highest level of management, the chief serves as the evaluator. One of the major reasons for appraising upper-echelon administrators is to motivate cooperation with the acceptance of the plan on the part of supervisory and line personnel. Nothing could be more subversive to the program than to institute a selective system of appraisal that eliminates certain individuals or classes of positions.

Preparation. Formal classroom instruction must be scheduled periodically for evaluators, especially line sergeants, who probably have the most challenging and rewarding job. At least four hours of yearly training is appropriate, with more when possible. The evaluation instrument should be accompanied by a written directive that explains, in detail, the elements of the process, including a step-by-step description of each factor on the form.

In addition to supervisory preparation, employees (i.e., patrol officers and civilian workers) must be prepared formally, although it should be more in the nature of an orientation than a classroom training session. Each prospective employee should be furnished with the policy pronouncement, a sample form, and a copy of the supervisory instructions regarding its use. An appropriate medium for the orientation is roll call training, reinforced by a training bulletin.

Frequency. The frequency with which employees should be evaluated varies. In recruit school, there may be value in appraising rookies formally on a weekly or, at the very least, monthly basis. Probationers, be they patrol officers or supervisors, should be evaluated quarterly. Yearly evaluations are appropriate for permanent employees. In special cases, these time frames may be narrowed in the interest of the department. For example, when a major deficiency has been noted on an officer's evaluation sheet, a special evaluation should be made prior to the next scheduled appraisal deadline.

Responsibility for Evaluation. Personnel evaluation is one responsibility that cannot be delegated except in the most extraordinary instances. Some scholars have taken the opposite tack, asserting that appraisals must be taken out of the chain of command because the close working relationship between a supervisor and his or her subordinates may stand in the way of a rater's objectivity. Another consideration is that the bond of camaraderie can be shattered by formal assessments. This may be so, but there is no suitable option available in police operations, so the responsibility for evaluations will continue to rest in the hand of supervisors directly in the chain of command of those to be appraised.

Use of Results. There is a wide divergence of opinion on just how the results of an appraisal should be used. Evaluations can form a basis for (1) the development of an employee's full potential, (2) making salary decisions, (3) determining training needs, (4) invoking discipline, and (5) determining promotability. On this last point, there has been widespread criticism that most appraisal systems do not predict, with any degree of accuracy, the ability of officers to succeed at the next level or rank. An officer's evaluations may show how good an officer he or she is, but do not adequately gauge potential as a sergeant. To end this problem, the International Association of Chiefs of Police has recommended that regular performance evaluations should be completed to assess an officer's in-grade progress, while a special form, called the promotional potential rating, should be completed after a candidate passes a promotional examination. Although the idea appears sound, it may be too late to wait until an individual passes a promotional exam to implement it.

Forms Control. A command decision must be made regarding the items to be included on evaluation forms, the number of different types of forms needed, and their distribution. The first point will be taken care of when the system is installed. However, there is always the temptation to design one form for everyone on the agency and to personalize it by changing the color and the name at the top to fit individual needs cosmetically. Of course, this practice is faulty, for there are differing qualities needed to fulfill the varied positions in a department. This is not to say that every level of rank on an agency should have a unique evaluation form. Certainly not. But those sworn positions that differ dramatically from all others deserve a special report form.

It appears that major police departments should draft unique forms for (1) officers attending recruit school, (2) probationary employees, (3) permanent nonsupervisory personnel, and (4) supervisors and middle managers. The appropriate evaluation form for top managers is a letter or memorandum from the chief of police. The purpose of the probationary report is different from the rest and as such should have a strong negative orientation because the major concern is to identify those persons who are incapable of effective performance.

There should be at least four copies of each report form so that both the evaluator and his or her subordinate can receive a copy, one can be filed in the appropriate division, and the last can be transmitted to the subject officer's personnel folder. Regardless of the system used, there should be ample space for a comment, in the form of a brief essay, by the rater. It is wise to implement an appellate process that equates roughly to grievance machinery, although no allowance need be made for extradepartmental appeals.

Focus on Results, Not on Personal Traits.   When objectives are not set and results not defined, means tend to become more important than ends, style replaces substance, and a preoccupation with procedure replaces the willingness to focus on performance as the basis of evaluation. Emphasis should be placed on job performance, not on personal characteristics.

Focus on Strengths, Not on Weaknesses.   A 10 percent improvement in what an officer does best will provide a far bigger yield than will a 10 percent improvement in what an employee does worst. More important, it is far easier to achieve. It is best to build into the evaluation process an emphasis on what employees do right, not on what they do wrong.

Salary Administration

Salary administration is one of the most critical components in the personnel administration function. The ability of a police agency to compete with business and industry in attracting the most highly qualified personnel will be directly affected by the wages and other benefits offered. Thus, one finds that considerable administrative time and effort are expended in developing and updating pay plans and salary schedules to assure that the police agency is in a sound competitive position in the labor market.[45]

When a pay plan is being developed, it must be remembered that it must accomplish several objectives, namely (1) to pay salaries that are equitable in relation to the complexity and responsibility of the work performed and to maintain internal equity in the relation of pay and employees; (2) to maintain a competitive position in the employment market and thereby attract and retain competent employees; (3) to provide data needed in budgeting, payroll administration, and other phases of financial and personnel management; (4) to stimulate personnel management and reward high-level performance; and (5) to provide an orderly program of salary policy and control.

Closely related to the development of the pay plan is the need for accurate information on existing employee benefits and trends regarding new benefits. Employee benefits include all payments in cash or in kind in excess of the base rate for time worked. For purposes of impact analysis, employee benefits can be classified into four basic categories: (1) income supplement (tax break) benefits, including issuance of uniforms, clothing allowance, paid medical and life insurance; (2) income supplement (trade-offs) benefits, including overtime pay, stand-by pay, and shift pay differentials; (3) good life benefits, including paid vacations, holidays, and recreational facilities; and (4) protection benefits, including sick leave and other paid leave, retirement pensions, and workmen's compensation.

Recent trends show considerable interest in a shorter workweek, early retirements, more paid holidays, longer vacations, payment for unused sick leave, and broader paid medical coverage for dental and eye care. Collective bargaining and rising expectations of employees are likely to increase the demands for new and improved fringe benefits. Every effort should be made to use employee benefits as a tool for attracting and retaining the best employees. Cost information on employee benefits is needed, not only to plan and implement a total compensation program but also to permit thorough explanations to employees and the public. Some police departments have prepared an information sheet for their employees that outlines the various fringe benefits enjoyed by their employees. Along with the dollar value of these benefits, this type of information is useful because it assists both the interested applicant and the employee in assessing more accurately actual earnings resulting from employment with the agency.

Salary Schedule

There is no standard salary structure that can be applied universally in police departments simply because of the structural diversity and variations in classifications that exist among them. There are, however, some standards that experience suggests should be applied in designing the police salary schedule. For example, there must be enough ranges to permit salary differentiation among all the subclasses in the classification plan and room enough in the total span of salaries to provide for significant differences in salary between successive ranks. There is a generally accepted rule of thumb that such classes within a class should be at least 5 percent apart. Thus, if a law enforcement agency chooses to have various grades of patrol officers, a 5 percent differentiation should exist in addition to longevity considerations. Differentials between subclasses of positions at successive organizational levels should be at least 10 percent and preferably 15 percent less.[46]

The salary schedule should be an integrated schedule. This means that successive rates should appear in successive ranges at different locations. For example, a portion of an integrated schedule with uniform 5 percent increments (rounded to the nearest $5.00) would look like this:

Grade	Minimum		Monthly rates intermediate		Maximum
7	$1,000	$1,050	$1,105	$1,160	$1,220
8	1,050	1,105	1,160	1,220	1,280
9	1,105	1,160	1,220	1,280	1,345

The regularity in such a schedule permits uniform percentage increases in grade upon promotion. There should be as much room as possible in the ranges for recognition of manner of performance and the increased effectiveness expected through length of service in position, that is, growth in the job.[47]

Assessment Centers

All organizations, whether public or private, share common personnel problems. The most significant of these involve the identification of talent, the development of human resources within the organization, and compliance with various legal requirements with regard to the selection and promotion of personnel. Many organizations have learned the hard way that effective performance at one level does not necessarily predict effective performance at a higher level.[48]

The task of selecting people for entry-level or promotional positions in law enforcement has produced various techniques over the years, few of which have been strong in their predictive aspects. The traditional methods of selection in police agencies are easy to attack for their inadequacies, but it is another matter to develop an economical, ethically sound selection system that can produce better results. One attempt at finding a more reliable way in which to predict future performance is through an assessment center.[49]

What Is an Assessment Center?

An assessment center is a method, not a place; it is a multiple assessment strategy. It involves multiple evaluation techniques, including various forms of job-related simulations, and may include interviews and psychological tests. Common job simulations include in-basket exercises, management tasks, group discussions, simulations of interviews with subordinates, fact-finding exercises, oral presentation exercises, and written communications exercises.[50]

The essentials of the assessment center method are described best in the definition presented in the standards and ethical statement endorsed by the Third International Congress on the Assessment Center Method held in Quebec, Canada, several years ago. The following is excerpted from this statement.[51]

To be considered as an assessment center, the following minimal requirements must be met:

1. Multiple assessment techniques must be used. At least one of these techniques must be a simulation. A simulation is an exercise or technique designed to elicit behaviors related to dimensions of performance on the job by requiring the participant to respond behaviorally to situational stimuli. Examples of simulations include group exercises, in-basket exercises and fact-finding exercises.

2. Multiple assessors must be used. These assessors must receive training prior to participating in a center.

3. Judgments resulting in an outcome (i.e., recommendation for promotion, specific training or development) must be based on pooling information from assessors and techniques.

4. An overall evaluation of behavior must be made by the assessors at a separate time from observation of behavior.

5. Simulation exercises are used. These exercises are developed to tap a variety of predetermined behaviors and have been pretested prior to use to insure that the techniques provide reliable objective and relevant behavioral information for the organization in question.

6. The dimensions, attributes, characteristics or qualities evaluated by the assessment center are determined by an analysis of relevant job behaviors.

7. The techniques used in the assessment center are designed to provide information which is used in evaluating the dimensions, attributes or qualities previously determined.

In summary, an assessment center consists of a standardized evaluation of behavior based on multiple inputs. Multiple trained observers and techniques are used. Judgments about behavior are made, in part, from specially developed assessment simulations.

These judgments are pooled by the assessors at an evaluation meeting during which all relevant assessment data are reported and discussed, and the assessors agree on the evaluation of the dimensions and any overall evaluation that is made.

What Is Not an Assessment Center

In an attempt to prevent misuse of the term *assessment center,* the Third International Congress on the Assessment Center Method identified activities that do not constitute the process:

1. Panel interviews or a series of sequential interviews as the sole technique.
2. Reliance on a specific technique (regardless of whether or not this is simulation) as the sole basis of evaluation.
3. Using only a test battery comprised of a number of pencil/paper measures, regardless of whether the judgments are made by a statistical or judgmental pooling of scores.
4. Single assessor or assessment.
5. The use of several simulations with more than one assessor when there is no pooling of data, i.e., each assessor prepares a report on performance in an exercise, and the individual reports (unintegrated) are used as the final product of the center.
6. A physical location labeled as an "assessment center" which does not conform to the requirements above.[52]

Historical Development of Assessment Centers

The first modern-day experiments with assessment centers were conducted by the Germans in World War I. Their objective was to select persons suited for intelligence assignments that required certain unique characteristics.[53] Simulation exercises were reactivated in World War II by German and British military psychologists to aid in the selection of military officers. In the United States, the Office of Strategic Services (OSS) used similar procedures for selecting intelligence agents. Candidates taking part in the OSS testing program participated in a wide range of paper-and-pencil tests, interviews, and simulations over a period of several days. The simulations were intended to reflect aspects of field intelligence work under wartime conditions, and some were, therefore, designed to be highly stressful.[54]

In the private sector, assessment centers have been employed since 1956, when they were introduced by the American Telephone & Telegraph Company. To date, over 100,000 people have been assessed by Bell companies alone. The use of such centers has grown particularly over the past six to eight years, and it is estimated that there are presently over three hundred assessment centers in operation in private business, including those of Standard Oil of Ohio, International Business Machines, General Electric, and Sears, Roebuck.[55] More recently, as their value has become clear, assessment centers have been modified for use in the public sector by such organizations as the Internal Revenue Service, the Social Security Administration, and the U.S. Army. Adapted to a wide variety of settings and organizations, these centers in both public and private agencies have been employed for the assessment of first-line supervisors as well as middle- and upper-level management positions and for identification of career development and training needs.[56]

Development of Simulation Exercises

The vast majority of simulation exercises created for the assessment centers are generally based upon the interviews of individuals who have served effectively in the position under consideration. For example, when the New York City Police Department created its assessment center, it was designed to assess the potential of high-level commanders for effectiveness in police management. Consultants who worked with the New York City Police Department to develop their assessment center interviewed a number of police captains to determine their job activities and their relation to the rest of the police organization. Based upon their study of the captain's role in the New York City Police Department, the consultants established a list of dimensions for evaluating an individual's potential for effectiveness as a police manager.[57] Then the consultants prepared a set of simulation exercises, background interviews, and paper-and-pencil tests to tap the identified dimensions of police management effectiveness. The simulations included[58]

1. *In-basket exercise.* Candidates assume the role of a newly appointed precinct commander and work through a packet of memos, letters, and other administrative materials such as would be found in a police commander's in basket.
2. *Television special exercise.* A group of four to six candidates with specially assigned roles engages in a leaderless group discussion to develop a television documentary about police work.
3. *Mrs. Hall's accident exercise.* Each candidate conducts an interview to learn as much as he can about the fictional case of Mrs. Hall who had an accident.
4. *Management cases exercise.* A group of six candidates participates in a leaderless group discussion to try to resolve five major problems relevant to the New York City Police Department.

FIGURE 7-6. A candidate is filmed during an Assessment Center simulated press conference. [Courtesy of the Fairfax County (Virginia) Police Department.]

The exercises employed should realistically simulate those encountered by the individuals in the positions for which they are applying.

Advantages of the Assessment Center

The assessment center technique offers a number of advantages over written tests and other management identification techniques. A number of important managerial abilities, such as planning and organizing, establishing priorities, leadership, relevant analytical skill, sensitivity to the needs of subordinates, management control, stress tolerance, and communications effectiveness, are very difficult to measure adequately with the use of written tests alone. Also, because of the job relevance and the procedures involved, assessment center results are generally readily accepted by individuals who object to traditional testing procedures. Some of the more significant advantages to the assessment center method are[59]

1. The exercises used are simulations of on-the-job behaviors.
2. A large amount of information is generated by each participant in a relatively short time.
3. A variety of methods is used.
4. The exercises are constant for all participants.
5. There is a consensus of judgment among the assessors for each participant.
6. The observers typically have no personal involvement with the participants.
7. The observers are well trained in evaluation procedures.
8. The observers are able to devote full attention to the task of assessing.
9. Information obtained can be used effectively to develop personnel. Individuals are provided with specific behaviorally referenced indicators of strengths and weaknesses, and developmental programs can be planned to strengthen weaknesses so that an individual may be promotable in the future.
10. Assessors involved receive valuable training in behavioral observation techniques, and this training carries over to their regular job performance.

Assessors

The role of the assessor is not to make promotion decisions. The assessors are to analyze behavior, make judgments about behavior, organize the information in a report, and make the report available to the individual making the promotion decision.[60]

As typically found in business organizations, assessors are managers who are one and sometimes preferably two levels higher than the position for which people are applying. This is based upon the assumption that prior experience in the job facilitates judgment of the candidate's aptitude for the position and is far enough away from the candidate to be assessed to ensure greater objectivity than their immediate supervisors might exercise. Also not to be overlooked is the credibility of the assessment center concept when upper-level officers are involved.[61] Depending on the number of candidates to be assessed and the time allotted for assessment, anywhere from three to six assessors may be needed.

Since the assessors may not be thoroughly familiar with the mechanics of operating the center and the instruments, a prime concern is training each assessor in the skills of being a keen observer of human behavior. A natural starting point in training is for prospective assessors to participate in the exercise themselves so they may experience the behavior they will be observing. Training in interviewing, observation of specific behavior, and precise analysis are also very important. Such training will very likely have to be provided by a professional who has extensive experience in this area of management. However, a large number of assessors may be trained at one time and the expense spread over considerable time as the assessors are used over the years whenever assessment centers are convened.[62,63]

Cost and Validity

In principle, assessment center methodology has merit, although the practical question of its cost makes it appear less attractive. Comparisons of "per candidate" costs in industry are not very instructive because, for example, companies treat assessors' costs differently. Two general observations are that assessment centers for police usually cost more than conventional testing procedures, and, beyond the conventional wisdom that "one gets what one pays for," it is difficult to show the cost benefits.[64] Yet there are two things to keep in mind concerning the cost of assessment centers. First, the center generates valuable information on which promotion decisions will be made.[65] Second, and just as important, the real costs in promotion decisions (and entry selection decisions, too) are not the direct cost of the instruments and the salaries of the personnel participating in the process but, rather, the costs to the organization of decision to promote individuals and elevate individuals to positions in which they do not perform well. These hidden and indirect costs can be staggering over a prolonged period of time. Put very simply, good police supervisors make fewer mistakes. Money spent to select effective supervisors on those who have the capacity to become effective supervisors pays off in superior organization performance.[66]

Civil service agencies know of assessment center validity research, and they usually find that the procedure is objective, especially when written examinations are included as part of the center.[67]

In analysis of over a dozen studies concerning the validity of assessment centers, Byham concludes

> This research and most other research indicate that assessment centers are better at predicting ratings of management potential and actual advancement than performance at first level. This is probably covered by the increasing importance of the management components of jobs as individuals rise in an organization. It is the management component that is most commonly and accurately measured in an assessment center.[68]

Employing Civilians in Police Work

Civilians are being employed by police departments in rapidly growing numbers in an increasing variety of activities. Moreover, the trend toward greater and more varied use of civilians is likely to continue. It appears that there are four major motivating factors leading to this greater use of civilian personnel: (1) the need to control costs yet improve service to citizens, (2) expert opinion supporting the need to use civilians for low-skilled "routine" tasks, (3) federal and state encouragement of the use of civilians, and (4) specific programs aimed at increasing the use of civilians.[69]

Cost pressures can be traced back to the urban population boom after World War II. Although the rapidly growing cities needed more services, particularly in law enforcement, a growth in police personnel was often deterred by tight city budgets and job competition from the private sector. In many departments, nonsworn personnel began to replace sworn officers in specialized jobs, and the trend has continued at a steady pace ever since.[70] The use of civilians has also been encouraged by leaders in law enforcement as well as from national commissions studying the practices of American law enforcement agencies. The most recent commission report recommended that

> Every police agency should assign civilian personnel to positions that do not require the exercise of police authority or the application of the special knowledge, skills, and aptitudes of the professional police officer.[71]

Several years ago, the Urban Institute conducted a survey of thirteen police departments in an effort to determine what types of functions were being performed by civilians and what types of overall benefits and problems have resulted from the process. Table 7-3 identifies the tasks being performed by civilians within these thirteen agencies. The findings of this study are as follows.[72]

1. Officers are relieved of such routine tasks as fingerprinting, dispatching cars, and handling prisoners.
2. Costs are reduced.
3. More uniformed personnel are available for more active law enforcement duties.
4. Service to the community is improved.

These findings are corroborated by the fact that almost half the thirteen departments have used civilians in communications, identification, or detention work for three to twelve years—and even longer in another fourth of those departments. Further, all thirteen cities intend to continue employing civilians. Police managers held very positive views toward civilians. They felt that the civilians were well qualified, exercised initiative, and helped to improve civilian-officer relations in general.

Most problems described by police managers were related to management issues, particularly civilians' low pay, lack of knowledge of police work, and inadequate training. The managers also expressed some concern about civilian tardiness, lack of dedication, excessive use of sick leave, and personality conflicts.

Officers in charge of civilians also expressed a very high opinion of the job performance of civilians. The thirty-three officers polled said that 75 percent of the tasks performed were very well done, 22 percent were fairly well done, and 3 percent were not so well done.

Seventy-two percent of those officers reported further that the civilians' work was very beneficial to the department, and 28 percent felt that their work was of some benefit; none reported very little or no benefit. Eighty-five percent felt more civilians should be hired. They thought civilians were most helpful by relieving officers for more critical duties; by assisting officers in various ways, including writing reports, fingerprinting, and handling prisoners; by providing information for action by the officers, and in communicating with the public.

One third of the officers in charge said that civilians had not caused problems for officers; but of those who acknowledged problems, 71 percent were attributed to

TABLE 7-3 Tasks Performed by Civilians

Identification	Detention
Fingerprint Technician:	Receives inmates and others awaiting trial
Takes fingerprints	Transports inmates
Lifts latent prints	Searches, fingerprints, and photographs inmates
Classifies, searches, verifies prints	Responsibility for well-being of inmates:
Communicates with other agencies	Allowing telephone calls
Operates microfilm reader	Health
Performs clerical function of above actions	Property safekeeping
Photography Technician:	Feeding
Takes photographs	Rehabilitation
Gathers physical evidence at crime scene	Educational programs
Performs field identification of disaster victims	Recreational programs
Makes plaster and rubber casts	Screens visitors
Processes film	Security check of facilities
Prepares slides	Provides court security
Prepares pictorial evidence	Enforces discipline from inmates
Takes motion pictures	Processes release
Operates video equipment	Operates computer
Operates drying, enlarging, and copying equipment	Checks Identification Department
Mixes chemicals	Analyzes Intoxometer
Stores and safeguards developing equipment	Serves as witness in court
Minor camera repair	Investigates in facility:
Instructs officers in use of equipment	Accidents
Other:	Deaths
Operates mobile crime investigations	Contraband evidence
Uses Intoxometer for breath tests	Irregular incidences
Receives, catalogs, and preserves property	Preserves evidence
Prepares property for disposition	Plans, coordinates, supervises work assignments of inmates
Operates teletype	Trains and instructs other correctional officers
Packages and mails evidence	Prepares records and reports
Gathers physical evidence of persons	Recommends new and revised policies and procedures
Prepares courtroom evidence	**Communications**
Testifies in court	Receives and/or transmits information
Develops and maintains training program	Gives general information to citizens
	Maintains location of all police units
	Determines if situation requires police action
	Notifies other emergency units
	Operates switchboard
	Monitors interdepartmental radio
	Performs clerical functions of above actions
	Trains new communications personnel

From A. J. Schwartz, A. M. Vaughn, J. D. Waller, and J. S. Wholey, *Employing Civilians for Police Work,* Washington, D.C.: U.S. Government Printing Office, July 1975), pp. 1–5.

deficiencies in management practices, 19 percent to personality conflicts, and 10 percent to a lack of dedication on the part of the civilians.

Officers suggested that civilians might be more helpful if departmental management practices were improved by providing additional training, permitting them greater responsibility and reducing their workload.

Cost Consideration

In transferring jobs from officers to civilians, a common goal is to reduce costs. Nineteen percent of the police managers interviewed listed cost saving as an objective, and 58 percent identified it as a realized benefit. Similar views were expressed by officers in charge of civilians and by the civilians themselves. Based on cost data and estimates provided by departments, there have been significant savings. But these savings often are offset partially by less obvious costs.

There are large local variations. For the thirteen cities as a whole, the average civilian salaries ranged from 22 to 25 percent less than that of patrol officers. But within the cities, civilian salaries ranged from 10 to 34 percent less than patrol officer salaries. Savings in overhead costs—generally meaning fringe benefits—also seem to be substantial in some cities but negligible or nonexistent in others.

Although variations in employee benefits and in budgeting and accounting procedures make detailed comparisons difficult, police managers have provided estimates of overhead costs for officers and civilians. In general, differences have diminished during the last ten years as cities, and particularly the larger departments, have begun providing similar benefits for police and civilian employees. Even so, overhead costs were estimated at 15 percent of salary for civilians and at 25 percent for officers—a difference of about 10 percent of salary. Thus the total savings—considering salaries plus benefits—from hiring civilians would be 29 percent rather than 23 percent when only salaries are considered.

Making generalizations about the costs of training patrol officers and civilians is also difficult. Size of classes, number of instructors and hours of instruction, and duration of training vary greatly. Nevertheless, average initial training and equipment costs have been estimated.

Training costs for patrol officers include recruit salaries, instruction, materials, and employee benefits but exclude on-the-job training after the formal training period. Total costs range from $3,000 to $10,000 with additional special training occasionally following recruit training. A reasonable average in thirteen cities is $6,500. In addition, new officers are commonly provided with uniforms, weapons, and peripheral gear such as belts and flashlights. The average cost of such equipment ranged from $265 to $705 and averaged $500.

Civilian training costs far less. While police recruit classes last twelve to twenty-three weeks, civilians generally receive largely on-the-job training, with close supervision for one month or less. Except for some specialized areas, formal training averages about one week and costs—including overhead—an estimated $289.

Thus, the average start-up cost for a patrol officer, including formal training, fringe benefits, and equipment, is $7,000. For an average civilian, it is $289—a savings of $6,711 or 96 percent.

Complaints of any kind from officers about civilians were few and minor as compared with the reported benefits. These evident savings are, however, partially offset by less evident costs. Police managers have generally ignored or de-emphasized these hidden costs. It has been the officers in charge and their civilian employees who have stressed the intangibles. While none considered the problems serious enough to outweigh the benefits, the problems do have cost ramifications.

When basic needs—such as competitive salaries, adequate supervision, and training—are not met, long-term costs results. These include

1. lack of job knowledge (a major problem identified by managers, officers, and civilians);
2. officer anxieties about the reliability of civilians and the degree to which officers can depend on them in emergencies;
3. higher civilian attrition rates (causing start-up costs to be repeated more often in jobs filled by civilians than in those filled by sworn officers);
4. costs of job supervision;
5. abuse of sick leave, tardiness, or other costs attributable to undesirable practices; and
6. officer concern that the use of civilians threatens job security, particularly when they fill jobs traditionally available to officers for light duty in case of physical disability.

In weighing the cost advantages of using civilians, these negative factors should be considered. Although the actual dollar cost of these intangibles is difficult to assess, individual departments should be able to estimate such costs based on past experience with civilian personnel and refine this estimate after gaining more experience.

Alternative Career Tracks

The financial rewards and professional status in most police departments are directed toward those individuals who become managers. The individual who has served as a patrol officer for twenty years and has retired, regardless of accomplishments, is frequently considered by peers to have been ''not very successful.'' However, by the very pyramiding nature of the existing organization structures of most police departments, 85 to 90 percent of all police officers will never rise above the rank of patrol officer, and it is not in the best interest of any organization to have a reward system that raises the expectation of so many to an unrealistic level.

One can find among the ranks of any police department many individuals who have neither the interest nor the aptitude to become managers, yet these same individuals feel compelled to pursue managerial positions because it provides the only major organizational alternative to achieving some degree of professional stature and monetary reward.

It is apparent that some new organizational models must be considered that can provide realistic and cost-effective alternatives. Among the alternatives is a dual career track system such as the one presented in Figure 7-7, which allows police officers to follow either the nonmanagerial professional police officer track or the professional police management track.

Such a system would greatly reduce the difficulties associated with the single track system because it would provide a realistic and viable alternative. Within the framework of such a model, the individual could remain within the patrol ranks in a nonmanagerial capacity yet still enjoy some of the professional and monetary rewards offered by the organization.

Table 7-4 outlines some of the recommended training and education components that can be built into the system to assure the systematic development of the individual along with quality control. Thus all police officers know precisely what they must do to move up either the professional police officer track or the professional police management track. This particular model may not be appropriate in its present form

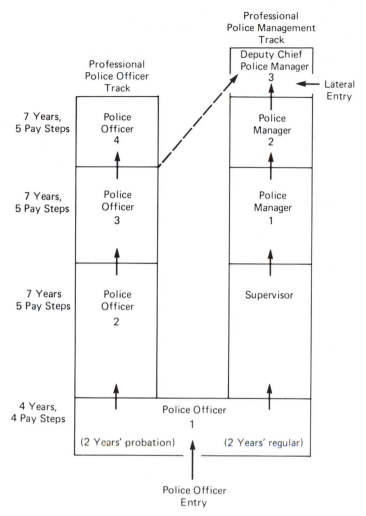

FIGURE 7-7. Professional career tracks. [Adapted from P. M. Whisenand. Police Career Development (Washington, D.C.: U.S. Government Printing Office, September 1973), p. 8.]

to meet the needs of some police departments, but it does provide a conceptual basis from which alternative models can be considered.

Retirement Counseling

Many police officers seem to experience considerable difficulty when they retire.[73] Consider the example that Joseph Wambaugh, in his book *The New Centurions*, relates: "It's your friend Andy Kilvinsky, Gus: your wife said that she was called tonight by a lawyer up in Oregon. Kilvinsky left you a few thousand dollars. He's dead, Gus. He shot himself."[74] This all too often is the result of retirement from police service. The stress of change becomes too much for the individual to cope with, and the path of least resistance is followed. There is stress connected with retirement. One study revealed that retirement is ranked tenth of forty-three items in difficulty of adjustment.[75]

TABLE 7-4 Professional Career Tracks: Training and Education

Training step	Training requirement	Police officer	Police management
5	Bachelor's degree and proven ability. These are minimum qualifications. Exempt positions can be filled from one or more of the ladders or laterally		Deputy chief, police manager 3
4	Bachelor's degree and 3,160 training points and seven years as a police officer 3 to be eligible for the three-day in-service selection and training program. Once passed, then a two-week in-service training program is provided. Annually, each person must earn 80 training points.	Police officer 4	Police manager 2
3	Ninety semester college hours, including 2,150 training points and seven years as a police officer 2 to be eligible for the three-day in-service selection and training program. Once passed, then a two-week in-service training program is provided. Annually, each person must earn 80 training points.	Police officer 3	Police manager 1
2	Sixty semester college hours, including 1,140 or better training points to be eligible for the three-day in-service selection and training program. Once passed, then a two-week in-service training program is provided. Annually, each person must earn 80 points 1 point = 1 training hour; 15 points = 1 semester hour.	Police officer 2	Supervisor
1	Six-month basic academy and twenty-four college semester hours.	Police officer 1	
Entry	High school diploma and the passing of other job-related tests.	Police officer entry	

Adapted from P. M. Whisenand, *Police Career Development*, Washington, D.C.: U.S. Government Printing Office, September 1973), p. 15.

One police psychologist identified this problem by describing police officers as people who face stress as a group. ''Similar to the military, police work is a way of life and retirement may present special problems. While many officers talk about putting in their twenty few make plans for that magic day.''[76]

A unique problem associated with police officer retirements relates to the relatively young age at which police officers are eligible to retire. Many police pension plans provide for retirement after twenty to twenty-five years of service. Therefore, many police officers are between forty-three and forty-eight years of age when they retire. This, for most American males, is the prime of their working lives. Very few people look forward to the prospect of starting a second career, and police officers are no exception. Very few can actually retire completely, in part because their pensions are inadequate to meet their financial obligations. Also, many are not psychologically prepared to sit around idly for the rest of their lives. Thus, many do continue working at some second career after retirement. Interestingly, even police departments that have comprehensive career development training programs never consider the need for retirement planning as a part of that program.

Program Development

The Kansas City, Missouri, police department recently developed a twenty-hour preretirement planning lecture series for law enforcement personnel with twenty-three or more years of service and civilian personnel with twenty or more years of service.[77]

Offered on an off-duty status over eight successive Tuesdays, each two- and one-half hour evening lecture addressed a specific topic of importance to a potential retiree. Department representatives and outside personnel with expertise in the various areas of retirement planning were invited to lecture on preretirement options and alternatives. A retirement planning resource handbook was provided for each participant to supplement verbal presentations.

Since the transition from employment to retirement can have a major impact on family life, spouses of department members were encouraged to participate in the program. Scheduling the lecture series in the evening hours made it more convenient for working spouses to attend.

Vocational psychologists believe that it is vital for the officer's spouse to be involved in the preretirement plan.[78] This is especially true for police officers who retire at a young age. Both partners must be made to realize the importance for the officer to develop long-term plans rather than to begin planning for retirement a few months ahead of time. It is also important to prepare the spouse for some of the changes that will occur when the officer is no longer an officer.

To make certain that department members were aware of the newly developed preretirement lecture series, a department memorandum not only acknowledged the new employee benefit program but also assured those individuals who were targeted for the first presentation that they were not being singled out for retirement but rather part of the initial group of department employees who would be invited to participate in the program.

Based on the experiences of other organizations that had developed preretirement programs, the promoters of the Kansas City program realized that getting a good turnout was essential in the implementation of an initial program. Because of many people's negative image of retirement, preretirement programs, in their early stages, often are not particularly popular or well attended. To combat this negative image and promote greater participation, preretirement orientation meetings were held to acquaint department personnel with the new program on a volunteer basis. The one-hour orientation meetings were scheduled on department time on all three shifts. The employee's commander/supervisor determined the best time for employee attendance based on division/unit workload. The orientation program included: a 16mm nineteen-minute color documentary entitled "A Week Full of Saturday," developed by Benefits Media, Inc., Rutherford, New Jersey. Rated excellent by numerous authorities in the retirement field, the documentary was used as a motivational opener to encourage personnel to participate in the lecture series. The documentary discusses such topics as financial planning, second careers, housing considerations, and retirement attitudes.

A twenty-minute verbal presentation on the importance of preretirement planning was offered. Included in the presentation were demographic statistics on aging, the fears/myths of retirement, and the eight topic areas to be covered in the lecture series. This was followed by a twenty-minute discussion period for question and answers.

Following the distribution of the department memorandum and the scheduling of orientation meetings, an article announcing the lecture series was included in the "Police News" (the department in-house publication), and a personal invitation from the chief of police was mailed to individual homes encouraging all eligible members and their spouses to participate in the program.

As a result of program publicity, twenty-eight department members (civilian and sworn law enforcement) and twenty-six spouses registered to attend the preretirement lecture series.

FIGURE 7-8. Major Arthur Barnett, commander of the Administrative Analysis Division and president of the Department's Credit Union, discusses the topic of investment planning at a session of the preretirement planning lecture series. [Photo Courtesy of the Kansas City (Missouri) Police Department.]

Program Content

Each evening of the lecture series was dedicated to a specific retirement topic. The eight-evening program included the following topics:

Assessment of Concerns.   A specialist in gerontology from Lincoln University, who had served as an observer to the White House Commission on Aging, discussed transitional barriers facing potential retirees and positive steps that can be taken to ensure a successful retirement. A panel comprised of past retired department members then shared with participants their personal experiences ''prior to'' and ''after'' their retirement from the department.

Pension System/Social Security.   A department administrator from the KCPD retirement program served as a lecturer on pension system policies and benefits. Following his presentation, a branch manager of the Social Security Administration explained how contributions are calculated, the procedure in requesting ''a statement of earnings,'' built-in ''cost of living'' adjustments, and the ''financial soundness'' of the Social Security system.

Physical/Mental Health.   A licensed counseling psychologist stressed to the participants that ''mental health'' was just as important an issue in preretirement planning as second careers, legal affairs, or financial planning. One's emotional and mental health have an impact on one's family, friends, and retirement alternatives. A professor from the Division of Geriatrics, School of Medicine, University of Missouri at Kansas City, then discussed the importance of nutrition, exercise, and aging versus sexuality. He stressed that how one exercises, eats, and thinks impacts his or her health and longevity.

Second Careers.   As indicated in the 170-page report, ''Aging in the Eighties,'' published by the National Council on Aging, 79 percent of the survey respondents stated they would engage in some type of postretirement paid work. In addressing this topic, the associate director for career development, at Rockhurst College discussed self-career analysis, transferrable job skills, and reentering the job market. A representative of the KCPD personnel division then discussed résumé writing, job interviewing, and the roles of employment agencies and executive consulting firms in second-career placement.

Consumer/Housing Considerations.   A family economics and management specialist from the University of Missouri explained how to get the most out of one's retirement dollar in a time of inflation and rising cost of living. Following her presentation, a local area realtor discussed residential vs. apartment, condominium, and mobile home living. Cost factors in buying and selling property, renting, and relocating to other parts of the country were also discussed.

Legal Affairs.   Because of the technical decisions facing potential retirees regarding legal considerations, a trust officer from a local bank was invited to address the topic of legal affairs. His in-depth presentation on wills, personal and living trusts, estate planning, probate, power of attorney, and tax shelters alerted participants to the need for legal planning in order to guarantee their independence, security, and financial peace of mind.

Insurance Options. A representative of the KCPD retirement system discussed the department's "carry-over" plans for health and life insurance. Even though retirees presently pay for their own individual/family health care coverage, the department provides retiring members with an opportunity to participate in a "group rate" plan. A chartered life underwriter then discussed life insurance, cash refunds, and variable annuities.

INVESTMENT PLANNING

The final evening of the lecture series was devoted to developing a money management plan to provide financial security in retirement. A financial advisor from a local investment firm and the president of the KCPD credit union discussed stocks, bonds, money market certificates, the Keough Act, and Individual Retirement Accounts.

Evaluation

In order to evaluate the success of the lecture series, a questionnaire was developed to measure the participants' knowledge of retirement issues. Administered prior to and at the conclusion of the program, an overall 20 percent increase in knowledge was realized. In addition to the questionnaire, the participants were requested to evaluate the content, materials, and lecture series presentations. Over 95 percent of the participants rated the lecture series as "very helpful" and would encourage other department members to participate in future sessions. Participants' comments ranged from "an excellent program," "extremely helpful," "long overdue," to "guest lecturers provided timely, in-depth presentations of tremendous personal benefit."

The preretirement lecture series demonstrated to the participants that the department had a deep and abiding interest in their welfare beyond their active service. Based on the participants' enthusiastic response, the program will be offered on a regular basis in the future.

Summary

There can be little argument that human resource management is one of the most important areas in police administration today because the quality of the service that a police department can deliver to its citizens can never exceed the quality of its personnel.

In this chapter we have examined some of the major components of police human resource management, drawn upon the latest state-of-the-art information from a wide variety of disciplines, and suggested ways in which police administrators can improve the overall effectiveness of their agencies within the confines of the resources available to them.

We began by discussing the functions of the police personnel unit and outlined the basic responsibilities of the unit. Some of these responsibilities included preparing policy statements and standard operating procedures in all areas of human resource administration; creating integrated management information systems; developing recruitment programs; developing selection, promotion, and career development programs; developing position classifications and pay plans; representing the agency during negotiations with police employee groups; conducting exit interviews; providing advice to management on human resource problems; and representing the police department to the central personnel office or civil service commission.

We then proceeded to discuss the process employed in selecting police officers—certainly one of the most important components of human resource management. Although there are no hard and fast rules about the precise steps to follow in the selection process, there is general agreement that the phases should proceed from the least expensive to the most expensive; namely, acceptance of the initial application; administration of the written test; physical agility test; polygraph; medical; psychological screening; and character investigation.

The issue of identifying the best level or most appropriate type of formal education for police officers is a rather thorny issue with considerable diversity of opinion among both practitioners and criminal justice educators. However, it does seem abundantly clear that police officers entering law enforcement during the decade of the 1980s will be far better educated than were their older counterparts. There will likely be benefits that accrue to the agencies they join, but there will also be some difficulties, especially in law enforcement agencies that are tradition bound and conservative in their organizational structure and dominant management styles.

On the subject of the recruitment of minorities and women, we concluded that the successful recruitment of minorities will be enhanced if the police department initiates a strong minority recruitment program, shows a commitment to internal equal opportunity, uses carefully selected minority officers in the recruiting process, and actively pursues promising individuals. Although police departments generally have not had great difficulty in recruiting good female applicants, administrators should be sensitive to some of the extra problems that females face upon entering law enforcement. This is especially true when a police department has had either no women or very few women employed as uniformed patrol officers. A failure to address some of the problems discussed in this chapter could result in a disproportionately high turnover rate of female officers.

As one of the more controversial components of human resource management, performance evaluation is often disliked and misunderstood by both the individuals doing the evaluation and those being evaluated. This occurs many times because their purposes are simply not understood by many of the people involved. The major purposes of performance evaluation are to aid employees in maintaining acceptable levels of behavior; to assist in career development; to encourage supervision to take a personal interest in officers under their command; to make salary decisions; and to evaluate the selection procedure.

Salary administration is one of the most critical components in the personnel administration junction. The ability of a police agency to compete with business and industry in attracting the most highly qualified personnel will be directly affected by the wages and other benefits offered. When a pay plan is being developed, it must accomplish the following: be equitable in relation to the work performed; maintain a competitive position in the employment market; provide data needed in budgeting; reward high-level performance; and provide an orderly program of salary policy and contract.

The task of selecting people for entry-level or promotional positions in law enforcement has produced various techniques over the years, none of which is strong in its predictive aspect. One attempt at finding a more reliable way to predict future performance is through an assessment center. An assessment center is a method, not a place; it is a multiple assessment strategy that involves multiple techniques, including various forms of job-related simulations, and may include interviews and psychological tests. Some of the more significant advantages to the assessment center method are use of simulations of on-the-job behaviors; a large amount of information is generated by each participant in a relatively short time; a variety of methods is used; the exercises are consistent for all participants; there is a consensus of judgment among the assessors for each participant; the observers are well trained in evaluation procedures; the observers are able to devote full attention to the task of assessing; information obtained can be used to develop personnel effectively; and assessors involved receive valuable training in behavioral observation techniques, which carries over to their regular job performance.

On the topic of civilians in police work, the literature indicates that civilians are being employed by police departments in rapidly growing numbers and in an increasing variety of activities, and it seems that this trend is likely to continue. There are four generally accepted reasons for this: namely, the need to control costs yet improve service to citizens; use of civilians for low-skilled and specialized tasks, thus freeing police officers to assume police functions; encouragement by the federal and state governments; and development of specific programs aimed at increasing the use of civilians. In our discussion of alternative career tracks, we examined some of the shortcomings of the traditional organizations, one of which is raising the expectations of its officers to an unrealistic level. It is apparent that most police organizations in this country give a disproportionate amount of the financial awards and status to those individuals who become managers. Thus the system has built into it features that make the managerial positions far more attractive than the nonmanagerial positions. But some 85 to 90 percent of able police officers will never rise above the rank of patrol officer. Alternatives for financial reward and status must be created. The model suggested in this chapter presents one alternative.

Finally, we discussed an often-neglected area of personnel administration: retirement counseling. There tends to be general agreement that many police officers experience considerable difficulty when they retire. Part of this is explained by the relatively young age at which they retire and the need to pursue a second career, often with little preparation, because they cannot realistically meet their financial obligations on their pensions. In addition, one police psychologist has noted that, as with the military, police work is a way of life and police officers frequently encounter difficulty when separated from those facets of police work that fill so many of their psychological needs. Because of these problems, it has been recommended that police departments institute preretirement counseling programs to start the employee thinking about retirement plans and adjustments and to create a setting in which questions, criticisms, and desires on the part of the worker can be voiced freely.

Discussion Questions

1. Since the late 1960s, the subject of human resource management has gained considerable prominence and visibility within the law enforcement community.

What are some of the major social, political, and economic factors that have given impetus to the movement?

2. What is the major purpose of the written examination?

3. Law enforcement agencies using the polygraph in the preemployment screening process have indicated that there have been many practical benefits derived from its use. What are these benefits?

4. What are the three best sources of information in evaluating law enforcement applicants?

5. What psychological tests are typically used to screen police applicants?

6. In one study, college-educated police officers expressed a number of difficulties that they had encountered. What were these difficulties?

7. Why is the recruitment of minority members into police departments no simple matter?

8. Why are the pressures imposed on females entering law enforcement frequently greater than those of their male counterparts?

9. What are the major purposes of performance evaluations?

10. When a pay plan is being developed, it must be remembered that it must accomplish several objectives. What are they?

11. In summary, of what does an assessment center consist?

12. What were the major topics discussed in the retirement counseling program of the Kansas City, Missouri, Police Department?

Notes

1. O. G. Stahl and R. A. Staufenberger, eds., *Police Personnel Administration* (Washington, D.C.: Police Foundation, 1974), p. III.

2. For a detailed analysis of these findings and recommendations, see The President's Commission on Law Enforcement and the Administration of Justice, *Task Force Report on the Police* (Washington, D.C.: U.S. Government Printing Office, 1967); *Report of The National Advisory Commission on Civil Disorder* (New York: The New York Times, 1968).

3. W. W. Schmidt, "Recent Developments in Police Civil Liability," *Journal of Police Science and Administration*, 4:3 (June 1976), pp. 197–202.

4. D. M. Walters, "Civil Liability for Improper Police Training," *Police Chief*, 38:11 (November 1971), pp. 28–36.

5. W. D. Heisel and P. V. Murphy, "Organization for Police Personnel Management," in *Police Personnel Administration* eds. O. G. Stahl and R. A. Staufenberger (Washington, D.C.: Police Foundation, 1974), p. 1.

6. L. Territo, C. R. Swanson, Jr., and N. C. Chamelin, *The Police Personnel Selection Process* (Indianapolis, Ind.: Bobbs-Merrill, 1977), p. 3.

7. Heisel and Murphy, "Organization for Police Personnel Management," pp. 8–11.

8. Ibid., pp. 1–2.

9. Territo, Swanson, and Chamelin, *The Police Personnel Selection Process*, p. 10.

10. Heisel and Murphy, "Organization for Police Personnel Management," p. 5.

11. Territo, Swanson, and Chamelin, *The Police Personnel Selection Process*, pp. 12, 13.

12. Ibid., p. 12.

13. Equal Employment Opportunity Commission, "Adoption of Questions and Answers to Clarify And Provide A Common Interpretation of The Uniform Guidelines on Employee Selection Procedures," *Federal Register*, March 2, 1979, p. 12007.

14. Ibid., p. 12003.
15. Ibid., p. 11998.
16. Walter S. Booth and Chris W. Horwick, ''Physical Ability Testing for Police Officers in the 80s,'' *The Police Chief* (January 1984). This discussion was taken with permission from this source pp. 39–41.
17. L. Territo, ''The Use of the Polygraph in the Pre-employment Screening Process,'' *Police Chief,* 47:7 (July 1974), pp. 51–53.
18. R. O. Arthur, ''How Many Robbers, Burglars, and Sex Criminals Is Your Department Hiring This Year?'' *Journal of Polygraph Studies,* 6:6(1971), p. 3.
19. Territo, Swanson, and Chamelin, *The Police Personnel Selection Process,* pp. 113, 114.
20. *The Use of Polygraphs and Similar Devices by Federal Agencies—Thirteenth Report of the Committee on Government Operations with Dissenting Views* (Washington, D.C.: U.S. Government Printing Office, 1976), pp. 5, 6.
21. Territo, Swanson, and Chamelin, *The Police Personnel Selection Process,* pp. 114, 115.
22. Susan Saxe and Joseph Fabricatore, ''Use of Psychological Consultants in Screening Police Applicants,'' *FBI Law Enforcement Bulletin* (August 1982). This discussion was adapted from this source, pp. 8–11.
23. W. D. Haynes, *Stress-Related Disorders in Policemen* (San Francisco: R & E Research Associates, 1978); R. H. Rahe and E. K. E. Gunderson, *Life Stress and Illness* (Springfield, Ill.: Charles C Thomas, 1974); M. Reiser, ''Stress, Distress and Adaptation in Police Work,'' *The Police Chief* (January 1976).
24. J. Gottesman, *The Utility of the MMPI in Assessing the Personality Patterns of Urban Police Applicants* (Hoboken, N.J.: Stevens Institute of Technology, 1975); S. J. Saxe and M. Reiser, ''A Comparison of Three Police Applicant Groups Using the MMPI,'' *Journal of Police Science and Administration,* vol. 4, No. 4 (1976); J. Fabricatore, F. Azan, and H. Snibbe, ''Predicting Performance of Police Officers Using the 16 Personality Factor Questionnaire,'' *American Journal of Community Psychiatry,* 6; 1, 1978; R. H. Blum, *Police Selection* (Springfield, Ill.: Charles C Thomas, 1964).
25. National Advisory Commission on Criminal Justice Standards and Goals: *Report on the Police* (Washington, D.C.: U.S. Government Printing Office, 1973), p. 369.
26. *The National Manpower Survey of the Criminal Justice System:* Volume Two. *Law Enforcement* (Washington, D.C.: U.S. Government Printing Office, November 1972), p. 20.
27. Ibid., p. 20.
28. National Advisory Commission, *Report on the Police,* p. 370.
29. D. P. Geary, ''College Educated Cops—Three Years Later,'' *Police Chief,* 37:8 (August 1970), p. 62.
30. B. Cohen and J. M. Chaiken, *Police Background Characteristics: Summary Report* (Washington, D.C.: U.S. Government Printing Office, November 1972), p. 20.
31. E. M. Baehr, J. E. Furcon, and E. C. Froemel, *Psychological Assessment of Patrolman Qualifications in Relation to Field Performance* (Washington, D.C.: U.S. Government Printing Office, November 1968), p. 212.
32. A. B. Smith, B. Locke, and W. F. Walker, ''Authoritarianism in Police College Students and Non-Police College Students,'' *Journal of Criminal Law, Criminology, and Police Science,* 59:3 (1968), pp. 440–443.
33. D. L. Carter, ''Issues and Trends in Higher Education for Police Officers,'' in *Issues and Trends in Criminal Justice Education* ed. G. D. Copus. Criminal justice monograph, (Huntsville, Tex.: Sam Houston State University, 8:5, 1978), pp. 9–19.
34. S. Gross, ''Higher Education and Police: Is There a Need for a Closer Look?'' *Journal of Police Science and Administration,* 1:4 (December 1973), pp. 477–483.
35. J. D. Jamison, ''Issues and Trends in Criminal Justice Education: The Philosophy of Curriculum Development,'' in *Issues and Trends in Criminal Justice Education,* pp. 2–8.

36. C. R. Swanson, Jr., "An Uneasy Look at College Education and the Police Organization," *Journal of Criminal Justice,* 5(1977), pp. 311–320.

37. R. C. Tojanowicz and T. G. Nicholson, "A Comparison of Behavioral Styles of College Graduate Police Officers vs. Non-College Going Police Officers," *Police Chief,* 43:8 (August 1976), p. 58.

38. Swanson. "An Uneasy Look at College Education and the Police Organization," p. 319.

39. For a comprehensive treatment of this topic, see R. Wasserman, M. P. Gardner, and A. S. Cohen, *Improving Police/Community Relations* (Washington, D.C.: U.S. Government Printing Office, June 1973). Much of the information in this chapter dealing with minority recruitment was taken from this source.

40. B. Washington. "Stress Reduction Techniques for the Female Officer," in *Job Stress and The Police Officer,* eds. W. H. Kroes and J. J. Hurreil (Washington, D.C.: U.S. Government Printing Office, December 1975), p. 36.

41. Ibid., p. 36.

42. Washington, D.C. Police Department, Circular 57, "Utilization of Policewomen on Patrol," April 17, 1972.

43. P. Block, D. Anderson, and P. Gervais, *Policewoman on Patrol: Major Findings.* First Report. Vol. 1 (Washington, D.C.: Police Foundation. February 1973), pp. 55–56.

44. W. Bopp and P. M. Whisenand, *Police Personnel Administration.* 2d ed. (Boston: Allyn & Bacon, 1980). Much of the discussion on performance evaluation was taken from this source.

45. J. N. Matzer, Jr., *Personnel Administration: A Guide for Small Local Governments* (Washington, D.C.: Civil Service Commission). Much of the information in this chapter dealing with salary administration was taken from this source.

46. C. F. Lutz and J. P. Morgan, "Jobs and Rank," in *Police Personnel Administration,* p. 39.

47. Ibid., p. 39, 40.

48. R. J. Filer, "Assessment Centers in Police Selection," in *Proceedings of the National Working Conference on the Selection of Law Enforcement Officers,* eds. C. D. Spielberger and H. C. Spaulding (Tampa, Fla.: University of South Florida, March 1977), p. 103.

49. R. Reinke, *Selection Through Assessment Centers: A Tool for Police Departments* (Washington, D.C.: Police Foundation, 1977), p. 1.

50. Filer, "Assessment Centers in Police Selection," pp. 103, 104.

51. Ibid., pp. 105, 106.

52. Third International Congress on the Assessment Center Method, *Standards and Ethical Considerations for Assessment Center Operators.* Quebec, Canada, May 1975, p. 3.

53. D. P. Slevin, "The Assessment Center: Breakthrough in Management Appraisal and Development," *Personnel Journal,* 57 (April 1972), p. 256.

54. M. D. Dunnette and S. J. Motowidlo, *Police Selection and Career Assessment* (Washington, D.C.: U.S. Government Printing Office, 1976), p. 56.

55. D. A. Kent, C. R. Wall, and R. L. Bailey, "A New Approach to Police Personnel Selection," *Police Chief,* 44:6 (June 1974), p. 73.

56. Ibid., p. 73.

57. Dunnette and Motowidlo, *Police Selection and Career Assessment,* pp. 56, 57.

58. Ibid., p. 56.

59. Filer, "Assessment Centers in Police Selection," pp. 105, 106.

60. W. J. Kearney and D. D. Martin, "The Assessment Center: A Tool for Promotion Decisions," *Police Chief,* 42:1 (January 1975), p. 32.

61. Ibid., p. 32.

62. Ibid., p. 32.

63. The following are some police departments that have utilized assessment centers: Chattanooga (Tenn.) Police Department, intermediate commander; Ft. Worth (Tex.) Police Department, patrol officers; Kansas City (Mo.) Police Department, sergeant and captain; Minneapo-

lis (Minn.) Police Department, detective; New York City Police Department, high-level commanders; Portland (Ore.) Police Department, intermediate commander; Rochester (N.Y.) Police Department, investigator; Savannah (Ga.) Police Department, chief of police; Washington (D.C.) Police Department, patrol officer and detective.

64. Reinke, *Selection Through Assessment Centers,* p. 4.
65. Kearney and Martin, "The Assessment Center," p. 33.
66. Ibid., p. 33.
67. Reinke, *Selection Through Assessment Centers,* p. 5.
68. W. C. Byham, "The Assessment Center as an Aid in Management Development," *Training and Development Journal,* 25:12 (December 1971), p. 15.
69. A. U. Schwartz, A. M. Vaughn, J. D. Waller, and J. S. Wholey, *Employing Civilians for Police Work.* (Washington, D.C.: U.S. Government Printing Office, July 1975), p. 1.
70. Ibid., p. 1.
71. National Advisory Commission, *Report on the Police,* p. 258.
72. Schwartz et al., *Employing Civilians for Police Work,* pp. 8–10.
73. K. E. Johnson, "Retirement Counseling," *FBI Law Enforcement Bulletin,* 47:6 (June 1978), pp. 28–31. Much of the discussion on retirement counseling was taken from this source.
74. J. Wambaugh, *The New Centurions* (Boston: Little, Brown, 1970), p. 297.
75. B. S. Dohrenwend and B. Dohrenwend, *Stressful Life Events, Their Nature and Effects* (New York: John Wiley, 1974), p. 50.
76. H. E. Russell and A. Beyel, *Understanding Human Behavior for Effective Police Work.* (New York: Basic Books, 1976), p. 292.
77. N. A. Caron and R. T. Kelly, "The Kansas City Police Department Pre-Retirement Lecture Series," *Police Chief,* 50:1 (January 1983), pp. 47–49.
78. E. H. Moore and G. Strub, *The Nature of Retirement* (New York: Macmillan, 1959), p. 198.

If, under stress, a man goes all to pieces, he will probably be told to pull himself together. It would be more effective to help him identify the pieces and to understand why they have come apart.

R. RUDDOCK

Stress and Police Personnel

Introduction

Historically, U.S. business and industry have been slow to identify and provide for the needs of workers. Largely because of the labor union movement, the U.S. worker has achieved a variety of benefits, ranging from increased wages to comprehensive medical care and retirement programs. The inclusion of mental health compensation as a significant management issue has evolved through a combination of union pressures and simple economics. A healthy, well-adjusted worker means increased efficiency and higher production for the corporation. As a consequence, job-related stress "has moved from the nether world of 'emotional problems' and 'personality conflicts' to the corporate balance sheet. . . . Stress is now seen as not only troublesome but expensive."[1]

Government and public service sectors generally lag behind industry and business in employee benefit innovations, and the mental health issue is no exception. However, the private sector's recent concern with the wide-ranging effects of job-related stress on workers is beginning to be shared by criminal justice authorities—or at least by those in law enforcement. More and more literature on stress factors in policing is becoming available to the law enforcement executive for use in developing programs designed to reduce stress among police personnel.[2]

What Is Stress?

Despite the volumes of research published on stress, the phenomenon remains poorly defined. Hans Selye, the researcher and theorist who pioneered the physiological investigation of stress, defines stress in the broadest possible terms as *anything that places an adjustive demand on the organism*. Identified as "the body's nonspecific response to any demand placed on it," stress may be either positive (*eustress*) or negative (*distress*).[3] According to this distinction, many stressful events do not threaten people but provide them with pleasurable challenges. The excitement of the gambler, the thrill of the athlete engaged in a highly competitive sport, the deliberate risk taking of the daredevil stunt man—these are examples of stress without *distress*. For many people, this kind of stress provides the spice of life.

Basowitz and his associates define stress as those stimuli that are likely to produce disturbances in most people. The authors postulate a continuum of stimuli that differ in meaning and in their anxiety-producing consequences:

> At one end are such stimuli or cues, often highly symbolic, which have meaning only to single or limited numbers of persons and which to the observer may appear as innocuous or trivial. At the other end are such stimuli, here called stress, which by their explicit threat to vital functioning and their intensity are likely to overload the capacity of most organisms' coping mechanisms.[4]

The authors also distinguish between pathological, neurotic, or harmful anxiety and the normal, adaptive, or healthy form of anxiety. In the first instance, anxiety is defined as a conscious and painful state of apprehension unrelated to an external threat. This kind of anxiety may render an individual incapable of distinguishing danger from safety or relevant information and cues from irrelevant ones. Ultimately, one's psychological and physiological functioning can become so reduced that death occurs. As the authors state, anxiety in this severe form is generally derived from "internal psychological problems and therefore is chronically present, leading to more serious, long-lasting somatic and psychological changes."[5] In the second instance, anxiety is defined as a state of increased alertness that permits maximum psychological and physiological performance. A state of fear, according to this formulation, is a simple form of anxiety characterized by the life-threatening or harmful nature of the stimuli. Unlike the more severe, harmful forms, simple forms of anxiety are temporal and beneficial to the individual. Of course, distinctions among the various levels of anxiety are difficult to make. For example, a person may react to a minimally threatening stimulus as though his or her life were in imminent danger. The fear response may have been appropriate and the overreaction inappropriate (perhaps indicative of psychological disturbance). Anxiety, then, can be defined as the individual's ability to cope with, or respond to, threatening situations.

Biological Stress and the General Adaptation Syndrome

Selye has formulated what he calls the general adaptation syndrome (GAS) to describe on the biological level how stress can incapacitate an individual. The GAS encompasses three stages of physiological reaction to a wide variety of *stressors*—environmental agents or activities powerful enough in their impact to elicit a reaction from the body: These three stages are (1) alarm, (2) resistance, and (3) exhaustion.

The alarm stage, sometimes referred to as an *emergency reaction,* is exemplified on the animal level by the so-called "fight or flight" syndrome. When an animal encounters a threatening situation, its body signals a defense alert. The animal's cerebral cortex flashes an alarm to the hypothalamus, a small structure in the midbrain that connects the brain with body functions. A powerful hormone called ACTH is released into the bloodstream by the hypothalamus and is carried by the bloodstream to the adrenal gland, a part of the endocrine, or ductless gland, system. There ACTH triggers the release of adrenin, which produces a galvanizing or energizing effect on the body functions. The heart pounds, the pulse races, breathing quickens, the muscles tense, and digestion is retarded or inhibited. The adjustive function of this reaction pattern is readily apparent, namely, preparing the organism biologically to fight or to run away. When the threat is removed or diminished, the physiological functions involved in this alarm, or emergency reaction, subside, and the organism regains its internal equilibrium.

If the stress continues, however, the organism reaches the resistance stage of the GAS. During this stage, bodily resources are mobilized to deal with the specific stressors, and adaptation is optimal. Although the stressful stimulus may persist, the symptoms that characterized the alarm stage disappear. In short, the individual seems to have handled the stress successfully.

Under conditions of prolonged stress, the body reaches a point where it is no longer capable of maintaining resistance. This condition characterizes the exhaustion stage. Hormonal defenses break down, and many emotional reactions that appeared during the alarm stage may reappear, often in intensified form. Further exposure to stress leads to exhaustion and eventually to death. Even before this extreme stage has been reached, however, excessive hormonal secretions may result in severe physiological pathology of the type that Selye calls "diseases of adaptation," for example, ulcers, high blood pressure, and coronary susceptibility.[6]

Psychological Stress

While life-threatening situations have understandably received considerable attention from researchers and theorists, there are many other circumstances in which the stress involved threatens something that the individual deems valuable: self-esteem, authority, and security, for example. The human being's highly developed brain, accumulated knowledge, and ability to perceive and communicate through the medium of symbols lead him or her to find unpleasant or pleasant connotations in an incredible number of situations and events. Human beings react not only to tangible, physical stresses but also to symbolic or imagined threats or pleasures.[7] The effects of the stimulus can vary widely, depending on a person's culture, personal and family background, experiences, and mood and circumstances at the time. The objective nature of an event is not nearly as significant as what the event means to a particular individual at any given time. People are able to influence the nature of stress through their ability to control and anticipate events in the environment. As anticipation can simplify stress, the lack of it does so even more. The unanticipated event often has the greatest impact on an individual and leaves the most persistent aftereffects.[8]

Reactions to Stress

Most people adjust their behavior to daily stress according to their adaptive range. At the high end of the range, when a person encounters an extremely demanding situation, his or her first reaction is usually anxiety, a varying mixture of alertness, anticipation, curiosity, and fear. At the low end of the range, when confronted with a stressful situation, an individual experiences a condition of overload. The ability to improvise deteriorates, and behavior is likely to regress to simpler, more primitive responses. Regardless of personality type, people under high stress show less ability to tolerate ambiguity and to sort out the trivial from the important. Some authorities report that people become apathetic and inactive when stress is either minimal or absent. As stress increases slightly, the person becomes attentive and more active. When stress increases further, the individual becomes either interested and curious or wary and cautious. Greater stress then results in emotional states of unpleasant anxiety or pleasant expectation. When stress becomes extreme, anxiety may increase until it threatens to overwhelm the individual. At this point, panic, accompanied by paralysis, flight, or attack, may occur. Under high levels of emotion, an individual becomes less discriminating and tends to make either disorganized or stereotyped responses, to lose perceptual judgment, and to idealize and overgeneralize.[9] As one police psychologist puts it, "People under stress make mistakes." In policing where job-related stress is involved, the kind of mistakes that are likely to occur can result in potentially irreparable, even fatal, consequences.[10]

Stress in Law Enforcement

Police work is highly stressful—it is one of the few occupations in which an employee is asked continually to face physical dangers and to put his or her life on the line at any time. The police officer is exposed to violence, cruelty, and aggression and is often required to make extremely critical decisions in high-pressure situations.

Stress has many ramifications and can produce many varied psychophysiological disturbances that, if sufficiently intense and chronic, can lead to demonstrable organic diseases of varying severity. It may also lead to physiological disorders and emotional instability, which can manifest themselves in alcoholism, a broken marriage, and, in the extreme, suicide. Three fourths of the heart attacks suffered by police officers are job-related stress, studies have shown. As a result, courts have ruled that a police officer who suffers a heart attack while off duty is entitled to workmen's compensation.[11] Thus, even a superficial review of the human, organizational, and legal impacts of stress-related health problems should sensitize every administrator toward the prevention, treatment, and solution of these problems.

Job Stress in Police Officers

In law enforcement, stressors have been identified in various ways.[12] Researchers such as Kroes,[13,14] Eisenberg,[15] Reiser,[16,17,18,19] and Roberts[20] have all conducted extensive studies into law enforcement occupational stress, and although they do not group these stressors in identical categories, they tend to follow similar patterns. Most of the law enforcement stressors can be grouped into four broad categories:

(1) organizational practices and characteristics, (2) criminal justice system practices and characteristics, (3) public practices and characteristics, and (4) police work itself.

One group of researchers interviewed one hundred Cincinnati patrol officers about the elements of their job that they felt were stressful. Foremost on their list of items were the courts (scheduling appearances and leniency), the administration (undesirable assignments and lack of backing in ambiguous situations), faulty equipment, and community apathy. Other items listed but not with so great a frequency were changing shifts, relations with supervisors, nonpolice work, other police officers, boredom, and pay.[21]

A survey of twenty police chiefs in the southeastern United States confirmed these findings. These chiefs, when asked about situations they felt were stressful for line personnel, listed lack of administrative support, role conflicts, public pressure and scrutiny, peer group pressures, courts, and imposed role changes.[22]

While working with the San Jose Police Department, one researcher was able to identify numerous sources of psychological stress that were basically reflections of his personal observations and feelings while performing the functions of a patrol officer for approximately two years. Some of these sources of psychological stress were poor supervision; absence or lack of career development opportunities; inadequate reward reinforcement; offensive administrative policies; excessive paperwork; poor equipment; law enforcement agency jurisdiction; isolationism; unfavorable court decisions; ineffectiveness of corrections to rehabilitate or warehouse criminals; misunder-

FIGURE 8-1. Mobile, Alabama, police officers called upon to control demonstrators protesting a work release program. [Photo courtesy of the *FBI Law Enforcement Bulletin.*]

stood judicial procedures; inefficient courtroom management; distorted press accounts of police incidents; unfavorable attitude by the public; derogatory remarks by neighbors and others; adverse local government decisions; ineffectiveness of referral agencies; role conflict; adverse work scheduling; fear of serious injury, disability, and death; exposure to people suffering and in agony, both physically and mentally; and consequences of actions, their appropriateness, and possible adverse conditions.[23]

It is interesting to note that an examination of the findings from a variety of police organizations tends to identify many of the same sources of psychological stress and similar reactions to it by police officers. This is true regardless of the geographical location or the organizational differences. The existence of these similarities is quite important, for it increases the possibility of creating programmatic solutions that have a high degree of applicability for a variety of law enforcement agencies that may on the surface seem to be dissimilar.

Stress Indicators

The Psychological Services Unit of the Dallas, Texas, Police Department has set forth in Table 8-1 its assessment of job-related stresses, the immediate response to stress, and the long-term response to stress. The unit has also developed a useful and practical guide to assist police supervisors in detecting the fifteen most prevalent warning signs of stress (see Table 8-2).

Alcoholism and Police Officers

Alcoholism in government and industry is not only widespread but also extremely costly—a fact established most convincingly by many independent researchers. Some 6.5 million employed workers in the United States today are alcoholics. Loss of productivity because of the disease of alcoholism has been computed at $10 billion.[24]

Although precise figures are not available to substantiate a high incidence of alcoholism among police, department officials have reported informally that as many as 25 percent of the officers in their respective departments have serious alcohol abuse problems.[25]

Alcohol problems among police officers manifest themselves in a number of ways. Some of these are a higher than normal absentee rate prior to and immediately following the officer's regular day off, complaints of insubordination by supervisors, complaints by citizens of misconduct in the form of verbal and physical abuse, intoxication during regular working hours, involvement in traffic accidents while under the influence of alcohol on and off duty, and reduced overall performance.

It has been suggested further that policing is especially conducive to alcoholism. Since police officers frequently work in an environment in which social drinking is commonplace, it is relatively easy for them to become social drinkers. The nature of police work and the environment in which it is performed provides the stress stimulus.[26]

Traditionally, police departments adhere to the "character flaw" theory of alcoholism. This philosophy calls for the denunciation and dismissal of an officer with an alcohol problem because recognizing him or her as a symptom of underlying problems reflects on the department. What is not considered is that alcoholism may result

TABLE 8-1. Short-term/Chronic Stress Reaction*

Job-related stressors	Immediate responses to stress			
	Personality	**Health**	**Job performance**	**Home life**
Administration	Temporary increases in:	Temporary increases in:	Job tension	"Spats with spouse"
Job conflict	Anxiety	Smoking rate	"Flying off the handle"	Periodic withdrawal
Second job	Tension	Headaches	Erratic work habit	Anger displaced to wife and children
Inactivity	Irritability	Heart rate	Temporary work decrement	Increased extra-marital activity
Shift work	Feeling "uptight"	Blood pressure		
Inadequate resources	Drinking rate	Cholesterol level		
Inequities in pay and job status				
Organizational territoriality	**Long-term responses to stress**			
Job overload	**Personality**	**Health**	**Job performance**	**Home life**
Responsibility for people	Psychosis	Chronic disease states:	Decreased productivity	Divorce
Courts	Chronic depression	Ulcers	Increased error rate	Poor relations with others
Negative public image	Alienation	High blood pressure	Job dissatisfaction	Social isolation
Conflict values	Alcoholism	Coronary heart disease	Accidents	Loss of friends
Racial situations	General malaise	Asthmatic attacks	Withdrawal	
Line of duty/crisis situations	Low self-esteem	Diabetes	Serious error in judgment	
Job ambiguity	Low self-actualization		Slower reaction time	
	Suicide			

* Adapted from W. H. Kroes, *Society's Victim—The policeman*, Psychological Services Unit, Dallas Police Department (Springfield, Ill.: Charles C. Thomas, 1976), p. 66.

TABLE 8-2.   Fifteen Most Prevalent Stress Warning Signs

Warning signs	Examples
1. Sudden changes in behavior. Usually directly opposite to usual behavior.	From cheerful and optimistic to gloomy and pessimistic
2. More gradual change in behavior but in a way that points to deterioration of the individual	Gradually becoming slow and lethargic, possibly with increasing depression and sullen behavior
3. Erratic work habits	Coming to work late, leaving early, abusing compensatory time
4. Increased sick time due to minor problems	Headaches, colds, stomach aches, etc.
5. Inability to maintain a train of thought	Rambling conversation, difficulty in sticking to a specific subject.
6. Excessive worrying	Worrying about one thing to the exclusion of any others
7. Grandiose behavior	Preoccupation with religion, politics, etc.
8. Excessive use of alcohol and/or drugs	Obvious hangover, disinterest in appearance, talk about drinking prowess
9. Fatigue	Lethargy, sleeping on job
10. Peer complaints	Others refuse to work with him or her
11. Excessive complaints (negative citizen contact)	Caustic and abusive in relating to citizens
12. Consistency in complaint pattern	Picks on specific groups of people (youths, blacks, etc.)
13. Sexual promiscuity	Going after everything all of the time—on or off duty
14. Excessive accidents and/or injuries	Not being attentive to driving, handling prisoners, etc.
15. Manipulation of fellow officers and citizens	Using others to achieve ends without caring for their welfare

Reproduced by permission of the Psychological Services Unit, Dallas Police Department.

from the extraordinary stress of the job and that eliminating the officer does not do away with the source of stress.[27]

Departmental Programs

There is no single "best way" for a department to assist its officers with a drinking problem, but some agencies have enjoyed a fair degree of success for their efforts. For example, the Denver Police Department is now utilizing its closed-circuit television system to teach officers who are problem drinkers and encourage them to join the in-house program. A major portion of the in-house program is designed to persuade the problem drinker, after he or she has digested a sufficient amount of the educational aspect, to enter the Mercy Hospital Care Unit and achieve the status of a recovering alcoholic.[28]

One researcher has concluded that it is the responsibility of the individual police agency and its administrators to recognize and accept the fact of alcoholism as a disease and to create a relaxed atmosphere and an in-house program for the dissemination of information relative to this problem. As indicated earlier, the objective of such a program is ultimately to persuade individual officers to enter a care unit for treatment. The combination of unsatisfactory performance, excessive costs, and the almost certain progressive deterioration of the individual officer to the point of unemployability, if the illness goes unchecked, creates a situation that conscientious chiefs of police should neither tolerate nor ignore.[29]

An essential point to remember is that, if drinking affects an officer's health, job, or family, immediate action is essential—the officer is probably an alcoholic.

Reports by the Denver Police Department indicate that the organization has benefited in specific ways since the implementation of their alcohol abuse program. Some of these specific benefits have been

1. Retention of the majority of the officers who had suffered from alcoholism.
2. Solution of a set of complex and difficult personnel problems.
3. Realistic and practical extension of the police agency's program into the entire city government structure.
4. Improved public and community attitudes by this degree of concern for the officer and the officer's family and by eliminating the dangerous and antisocial behavior of the officer in the community.
5. Full cooperation with rehabilitation efforts from the police associations and unions that may represent officers.
6. The preventive influence on moderate drinkers against the development of dangerous drinking habits may lead to alcoholism. In addition, an existing in-house program will motivate some officers to undertake remedial action on their own, outside the scope of the police agency program.[30]

Drug Use by Police Officers

Until recently, alcohol was almost exclusively the drug of choice among police officers. But the choice for some younger police officers is for illegal drugs. The news story on the following page illustrates this point.

In an effort to address this growing problem, the Legal Services Division of the International Association of Chiefs of Police has developed a model drug screening policy for police executives who are interested in establishing a method of testing for drug use in their departments. This model drug screening policy appears later in this chapter.

Suicide and Police Officers

Suicide as a problem for police officers can best be understood by examining the differences between younger and older officers. Suicide among young police officers is not particularly common, but when it does occur, it is frequently associated with divorce or other family problems. Among older police officers, suicide is more common and may be related to alcoholism, physical illness, or impending retirement.[31] Although hard data are not readily available, there is some speculation that suicides immediately after retirement may not be uncommon. Some researchers have suggested that police officers do not retire well. This fact is widely known within police departments, and it is not surprising to see newly retired officers becoming depressed and allowing their physical condition to deteriorate. As occurs with individuals in other occupations, police officers do not plan realistically for retirement. However, unlike workers in some other occupations, police officers are generally deeply involved with their work

BOX 8-1.

Drug Use by Cops Seen As Growing Problem

Top police executives say the use of illegal drugs by law enforcement officers is the biggest problem facing the law enforcement profession today, and they see a growing trend toward the frequent use of urinalysis to detect drug use among recruits and officers.

"We didn't have this problem in law enforcement years ago," said Neil Behan, the police chief of Baltimore County and president of the Police Executive Research Forum (PERF). "Our people, the young people were not using it to the degree that they are using it now," he said. "Society continues to change in regard to narcotic drugs and it's been on the increase these many years."

The people recruited 10 years ago, Behan said, were not likely to be drug users. However, he added, the young people that apply for police jobs now are very likely to have used them. "Ten years ago the number-one problem in law enforcement was corruption; now the number-one problem is the use of illegal drugs."

Chief Richard J. Koehler of the New York City Police Department sees the increased use of drug-detection tests on recruits as a mandate for police officials. "We have a responsibility under state law and the city's administrative code to maintain the fitness of the force. Illegal drug use requires someone to break the law and the use of drugs impairs somebody's ability to function."

According to Koehler, the NYPD's chief of personnel, the department has been giving urinalysis tests to recruits for the past several years. Koehler said that three urinalysis tests are given to recruits, one as an applicant just prior to testing, another while the recruit is still in the training academy and the last before the end of probation.

"We set a tone, particularly up front. We think of it as a socialization process. People are coming from society in general to be police officers with 30 to 35 percent of the population using narcotics, particularly marijuana. So we make it clear in the department that you don't use drugs. If you do, you'll get fired."

Koehler said that when the department tests a recruit's urine it is on the lookout for either illegal drug use or legal drugs illegally used.

The Chicago Police Department also gives urinalysis tests to recruits, as well as to selected in-service officers. According to Officer John Dineen, president of the Chicago Fraternal Order of Police Lodge 7, as an officer moves up in rank or applies for assignment in a special unit, he must submit to a urine test.

Over the past 20 months, 1,922 officers from different divisions have submitted to the drug tests. Of these, Police Superintendent Fred Rice announced that 81, or 4.2 percent, showed signs of illegal narcotics use.

These statistics include 58 security specialists—personal bodyguards—who were given the tests in June. Out of 58 officers tested, one failed when THC, the psychoactive ingredient in marijuana, was detected in his urine.

Chicago Police Department policy orders the reassignment to less sensitive positions of any officer who fails a drug test. Charges are then filed with the Police Board to have the officer dismissed from the force.

Although the tests are voluntary in the case of officers seeking a transfer, Dineen said, if an officer refuses to have a urine test the onus is him. "We've had classes for hostage negotiation training and when they were told they would have to voluntarily submit to an examination, about ten officers did not return to school the next day," he said.

It is no secret, Dineen said, that across the country people are "imbibing more and more" in the use of drugs and alcohol. "Whether it's marijuana, cocaine, heroin, barbiturates, amphetamines—there's more and more people getting involved and if you read the literature, if you're talking about the general population you're talking about 30 percent of the population becoming involved in some sort of chemical dependency."

Police agencies across the country have been implementing new means for assuring accuracy in marijuana testing, as well as ways of differentiating those applicants who have tried drugs in the past but who are not users from those who are still currently engaged in narcotic use.

At the Baltimore County Police Department, Chief Behan said, more information is being fed into computers to try to predict the success of a recruit in the future. One of the items entered is the applicant's prior drug history. "We wouldn't be hiring anyone who was any more than an experimenter," he said.

In New York, as in Chicago, termination is recommended for officers with a chemical dependency. If an officer is suspected of using illegal drugs, Koehler said, the supervisor makes an observation of the officer and then calls the department advocate's office to explain his suspicions. The supervisor then has the right to order that officer to take a drug test. If the officer refuses to take the test or the test proves positive, he is fired.

"Drug use is a crime," Koehler said. "In order to put the drugs in your body you must commit a crime. It's different from alcohol, which is protected under Federal law." Koehler said drug abuse and alcohol abuse differ in terms of the criminality of drug use and in the fact that drug use is not considered an illness under Federal law. For that reason, Koehler said, the department has no drug treatment program and no intention of starting one.

The 4.2 percent of the 1,922 Chicago officers who were found to be using drugs is a much lower proportion than the level found among the general population. Still, according to Dineen, there is a problem. "The biggest problem is that many corporations that will identify alcoholism as a sickness have now identified chemical dependency as a sickness and have programs to treat and retain those people in the work place," he said. "I know of no police department in this country that will retain an officer who has been identified as having a chemical dependency."

Behan said that within the Baltimore County ranks, any use of narcotics is unacceptable. "It's illegal and those who use it should be separated from this kind of work. Other professions should take the same attitude but they do not. They do not expel from their ranks those who they find to be users."

This is not the attitude in law enforcement, Behan continued. "It is a violation of the law and a police officer has no right to violate the law. The fact that they are users indicates their judgment could be impaired, their use of revolvers could be impaired and we don't want that to happen. In most cases we get rid of those people."

At present, the Chicago City Council is studying the possibility of ordering mandatory drug tests for some city employees. Dineen said that if the Council passes an ordinance to this effect, the FOP will take the city to court to protect the constitutional rights of officers. "That is not to say we are defending anyone who has violated the law, but we want to make sure the rights of all the officers are protected. We have the intention of bringing up this issue," he said, "at the negotiating table next month when we negotiate our contract."

In most departments, Behan said, on-the-job testing has not become a universal practice. "There is a trend toward that," he said. "If the abusing continues, you'll probably see an expansion of the idea of checking people. In this department, we give a urine test to every officer going into a narcotics squad. That's the way the trend is going, and you'll probably see more of that, not less."

Although none of the police officials questioned see a problem with substance abuse in their own departments, Behan said there is widespread concern within the law enforcement community. "We're concerned that drug abuse is out of control, especially cocaine, and we want to make sure that as we recruit and put people on special assignment that they are not drug users and do not become drug users after coming to us."

Both Koehler and Behan believe that proper training is the key to preventing a substance abuse problem within agencies. If an applicant has experimented with drugs in the past, Behan said, he would not be barred from joining the force, but if tests showed recent drug use or heavy drug use, that applicant would be deemed unacceptable.

At the NYPD, Koehler said, 3 percent of the applicants to the force are turned away because of narcotics use. Koehler said that while other departments using different approaches turn up positive results on 25 to 30 percent of the tests done on applicants, NYPD hopefuls are told that if there is any detection of drug use they will not be hired. "We tell them that when they take their written test," Koehler said. "From the very beginning of the investigative process all the way through the 18 months they're in the academy and on probation and in the field training program, we indicate that any sign of drug use is going to result in their termination. There has never been an exception where an officer has taken a test and we've gotten a hit. That person's fired."

Koehler believes that the socialization process at the very beginning has led to the 3 percent hits. "Our objective is not to catch people who have ever used marijuana. Our objective is to make sure that they don't use marijuana as police officers. When you look at 3 percent hits, the message is out."

Source: Law Enforcement News, September 23, 1985, pp. 1, 12.

 # MEMORANDUM

		TO	ACTION	INFO
DATE: August 27, 1986				
FROM: Legal Services Division				
SUBJECT: Attached Model Drug Screening Policy		Member Chiefs		X

The IACP model drug screening policy is intended to serve as a guide to the police executive who is interested in establishing a method for testing for drug use in a department. It is not meant to stand alone as a complete policy for a police agency. It may serve as a solid foundation for a final program design that must be shaped to the contour of the unique needs, legal requirements, case law and existing collective bargaining agreements of the implementing jurisdiction.

Drug testing is an emotional issue. It has raised concerns of possible violations of employees' privacy and other constitutional rights, concerns about the accuracy of these tests, and questions as to whether workers who are tested will be treated fairly.

The state of the law as it applies to mandatory drug screening for police employees, applicants, and sworn police officers is quite new and continues to emerge. Unfortunately, there exists no "bright line." The law is in the state of flux and will most likely remain that way for some time. In reviewing any drug screening policy, it is imperative to remember that the law enforcement community is dealing with a Fourth Amendment search according to the courts that have addressed this issue.

The Fourth Amendment, however, only prohibits unreasonable searches. According to the U.S. Supreme Court, a search is reasonable and, therefore constitutionally sound, if the need for the search outweighs its intrusion upon a person's personal rights. Since drug use among law enforcement personnel would clearly impact the public safety and public confidence in the integrity of law enforcement, it may be that the need for some sort of periodic drug testing of law enforcement officers outweighs any privacy rights that are implicated, especially where there exists a reason to believe an individual is ingesting drugs.

However, the due process clause guarantees that a person may not suffer punitive action as a result of inaccurate scientific procedures. Therefore, drug testing procedures must be carefully structured to ensure against false positive readings. Police administrators must ensure that the testing of the samples is conducted by a well-qualified laboratory that possesses quality control procedures. Furthermore, the "chain of custody" and security of the samples must be thoroughly documented to insure the integrity of the entire drug testing process.

As previously stated, there are several legal issues that must be taken into account by the police administration prior to implementing a drug testing program. They include the careful review of state statutes, city ordinances, civil service regulations, and case law. Any of these may restrict the administrator's ability

Memo
Page 2

to implement a drug testing program or may dictate the procedures to be used. Careful review of relevant employment and collective bargaining agreements must be undertaken to ensure the program complies with the agreement. In addition, administrators must be aware of the potential liability for negligent testing of employees such as not following the manufacturer's directions or for a breach of the chain of custody, or the improper disclosure of the findings of the list.

It has been argued that the Rehabilitation Act of 1973 precludes the use of urinalysis as the sole criteria to identify and discipline abusers. Further, the Act does protect former drug abusers, as a class, from discrimination in employment. However, it has never been held to protect current users that might be identified by such tests. At this stage, those individuals do not appear to meet the definition of "handicapped individual" set forth in the Act. This must be monitored carefully for decisions that do hold drug abusers fall within the definition of "handicapped individual."

The implementation process of a drug testing program is critical. Before beginning a testing program, a law enforcement agency must develop clear procedures, based upon a fully articulated written policy for dealing with the testing process and for dealing with employees that test positive. These procedures must be communicated clearly to all employees, enforced consistently, and applied fairly. They should be firmly based on the principles that drug abuse affects the health and safety of all law enforcement officers, employees, and the general public.

Below are some important guidelines for a law enforcement administrator to con-sider in designing a drug testing program:

- Demonstrate the need for drug testing in the agency. Articulate safety con-cerns and public expectations.

- Develop a specific substance abuse policy and program in consultation with all parts of the agency that may be affected. Union representatives, personnel managers, legal advisors and, most importantly, top mangement all must be involved.

- Notify employees of the policy. Tell them in advance the penalties that will be imposed for specified violations. If necessary, modify union agree-ments to reflect the agency's substance abuse program.

- Assure that all officers and employees have a clear understanding of the policy. The use of an informed concent form may be beneficial.

- Train all supervisors as to the policy and testing procedures. Supervisors should be trained as to what constitutes a "reason to believe" that an employee is using drugs. The observations of the supervisors must be objective and verifiable.

- Follow through. Do not let a substance abuse program become a "paper" policy.

- Test for substance abuse carefully. Follow the testing device manufacturer's instructions. Confirm all positive test results with another test. Make sure that persons who administer the tests and perform laboratory analyses are qualified to do so. Document the "chain of custody" and security of the samples.

- Notify employees of positive test results and provide them an opportunity to contest disciplinary actions taken on the basis of those results.

- Keep test results confidential. Do not release positive test results until their accuracy has been verified by a confirmatory test and, if possible, by corroborative evidence of substance abuse. Do not let anyone who does not need to know have the results.

It appears to be clear that reasonable drug testing procedures can be designed and used effectively within a law enforcement agency if carefully planned and imple-mented in compliance with statutory requirements, case law, and collective bar-gaining agreements. Because this is a controversial and rapidly changing area, judicial developments and legislative initiatives relating to drug testing must be continually monitored so that employee drug testing programs can be kept in compliance with new developments in the law.

until the actual moment of retirement. It is a shock to be estranged suddenly from a job that has occupied a major portion of one's life and has provided the source of so many social activities as well.[32]

These losses can have devastating effects upon retiring or retired police officers, but unfortunately most police departments, unlike many major industries, have not yet addressed themselves to this problem, which has no doubt led to an undetermined number of police suicides.

One study concluded that the data that are available indicate that male police officers are more likely to kill themselves than are men in other occupations.[33] For example, the suicide rate for members of the New York City Police Department from 1960 to 1967 was 21.7 per 100,000 per year. The rate from 1950 to 1965 was 22.7. This is higher than the suicide rate of 16.7 for all males in the United States during this period.[34]

In reported suicide rates for males in various occupations in the United States in 1950, police officers had the second highest rate of thirty-six occupations, at 47.6 per 100,000 per year. Only self-employed manufacturing managers and proprietors had a higher suicide rate. Clergymen had the lowest rate (10.6).[35]

Six possible clues have been outlined to help comprehend the high police suicide rates: (1) police work is a male-dominated profession, and males have demonstrated a higher successful suicide rate; (2) the use, availability, and familiarity with firearms by police in their work provide them with a lethal weapon that when used affords the user little chance of survival; (3) there are psychological repercussions of constantly being exposed to potential death; (4) long and irregular working hours do not promote strong friendships but do strain family ties; (5) there is constant exposure to public criticism and dislike for "cops"; and (6) judicial contradictions, irregularities, and inconsistent decisions tend to negate the value of police work.[36]

Some authorities believe that aggressive behavior stems not from internal drives but rather from societal frustration. In a sense they say that suicide and homicide are different manifestations of the same phenomenon. As acts of aggression, suicide and homicide cannot be differentiated with respect to the source of the frustration generating the aggression. Moreover, when the aggression legitimized by the aggressor is directed outward (other oriented) because of societal frustration, homicide results. Suicide or self-oriented aggression, a consequence of frustration, becomes a residual category or aggression for which outward expression against others is deemed illegitimate.[37]

In one study of suicides of twelve Detroit police officers who killed themselves between February 1968 and January 1976, Danto found that the group consisted of

> young men, married and for the most part, fathers, [who] came with backgrounds of unskilled employment prior to their police appointment, or military service, high school education or better, and some stable family life as measured by parents who were married and who had created families. The majority of the officers were white and had not been employed as police officers for many years. Many had received citations and commendations, as well as some reprimands. For some, service ratings were not good.
>
> The officers who committed suicide did so during the late hours of evening and early hours of morning. Most were either home or near loved ones or family when they died. They used firearms and fatally shot their heads and abdomens. Carbon monoxide was the second most common cause of death and many of the suicides, regardless of method, occurred in an automobile. Significant, perhaps, was that none of the officers was found in their uniforms at the time of their deaths.

Marital trouble appeared to be the most important precipitating stress. Many of the officers had received psychiatric consultation and treatment prior to their suicide; a few had asked for help directly.

The officers of the Detroit Police Department who committed suicide were different from the New York Police Department suicides. The Detroit group was younger, had less service time with the department, had a lower suicide rate within a police department, and less physical illness and police medical consultation histories, and fewer were single. In some respects they were similar: many had a history of alcohol abuse and dependency, had picked primarily firearms as their suicide method, and had suffered marital disharmony prior to their deaths.

Neither study proves that the police officer is any more prone to choose his profession because of its opportunities to express aggression than anyone else in society. The rising suicide and homicide rates for nonpolice persons should attest to that. Furthermore, since women have become more violent in terms of crime, homicide and suicide, we know that we are dealing with more general trend than a masculine assertion or aggression conflict. I do not feel that the police officer of today is more aggressive than most of the civilian population he serves.

By far and away the most upsetting problem for the suicidal police officer is his marriage. This marital discord is reflected both in the fact that the officer sometimes committed suicide following the murder of a significant person, but also killed himself in a location near to persons for whom he cared very deeply. To some extent, problems may be connected to his work because his hours are erratic, constantly subject to change, and the officer is subjected to danger which is beyond the reach of most civilian minds. Not only does his spouse have trouble accepting his working hours and risk of danger and injury, but she finds herself left out of his life as far as the police department is concerned. She is in competition with the department for her husband's interests and she finds that the military structure of the police department is such that her husband has become the property of the department. He is told how he will dress, where he will live (in terms of residency restrictions within the city), what hours he will work, what duty he will pull, and what danger he must face. He finds himself like a knot being pulled in a tug-of-war between the police department on one side and his wife and family on the other. For the officer who commits suicide it may be that he chooses death as a final exercise of control over his life, control that he feels others have removed from him. In this respect he may resemble the cancer patient who, when near death, commits suicide as his last expression of determination to decide his time and means of death, fearful that illness will rob him of that potency.

It would appear that the police officers in both police departments committed suicide in response to important personal problems.[38]

It has been suggested that the police suicide phenomenon should be viewed from a psychological basis that emphasizes both the unique and multideterminant aspects of an individual's behavior as well as the societal influences on that behavior. The human being is a frustrated and status-oriented social animal not isolated from peers. In many ways the American police officer is like a health professional. Officers frequently come in contact with the behaviorally different and socially ill citizens of our cities as part of their life's work. Likewise, when they are suffering unrelenting anguish, they often fear the loss of their jobs (perhaps realistically so because of parochial attitudes toward mental health held by their department) if they seek treatment. Yet the closest analogy, unfortunately, linking the police and health professionals is the reluctance of their respective colleagues to get them involved in treatment, in spite of their colleagues' awareness of their difficulties, because they may feel it is none of their business. A troubled police officer, like a health professional, is of no use to the public or to the profession if the officer does not seek treatment.[39]

Postshooting Trauma

For many years the FBI has compiled information concerning law enforcement officers who were killed in the line of duty. Until recently, however, there was little information regarding officers who killed in the line of duty either in their efforts to apprehend criminals or while defending themselves or others. The evidence is starting to mount that officers face very real and serious psychological and emotional side effects from these events. The following news story illustrates this point.

BOX 8-2.

If You Ever Have to Kill a Man, Never Look at His Face

MEMPHIS, Tenn. (UPI)—Eight years ago, patrolman John Thomas Cursey, 33, killed two holdup men during a liquor store robbery.

He shot one when the man turned on him with a gun, and the other when he ran. The second man did not die instantly.

"I heard him gasping for breath as he died," Cursey recalled. From this, he learned a lesson: "If you ever have to kill a man, never look at his face."

A few days after the killings, Cursey's buddies presented him with a fifth of whiskey. Over the label, they pasted a police photo of one of the dead bandits sprawled on the liquor store floor.

Six months later, Cursey was an alcoholic. He relived the killings night after night in his dreams. His wife left him and in 1976 the police department fired him because of his "uncontrollable" drinking. He couldn't hold a job.

Thursday, the city of Memphis' pension board awarded Cursey a lifetime disability pension of $5,500 a year—the first it has ever granted for psychological injuries.

Cursey, who reportedly collapsed in tears at the hearing, could not be reached for comment.

E. W. Chapman, Memphis' police director, said the board's decision was an indication that more and more people "have reached the realization that the psychological strain of being in police work is immense."

In an interview two years ago, Cursey re-called that the department had put 20 men on stakeout after a series of liquor store heists.

"The lieutenant called in eight of us and stood us up in front of him while he said, 'I want you to go out and kill those bastards. Don't come back until you've killed 'em.' "

It was February 3, 1970, when two men entered the liquor store where Cursey was watching from a back room. One, armed with a pistol, demanded cash. He struck the storekeeper over the head and Cursey burst in and leveled his shotgun at them.

"The guy with the pistol turned and started to aim at me. That was when I cut loose on him. I had to do it. It was either him, or me, or the manager." The man died instantly and the second robber was wounded.

"The other robber hesitated a moment and I begged him to give up. I said 'Please don't run or I'll have to kill you.' " He ran and I shot him just as he went out the door." He died 30 minutes later.

A psychologist, Dr. Lindley David Hutt, Jr., told the pension board Cursey was "what I would describe as a stable, hard working, family-oriented type of fellow with a good circle of friends," Hutt said. "His reaction to the incident was very severe anxiety and depressive neuroses, insomnia and a lack of concentration."

Source: The Times (Raleigh, N.C.), Feb. 17, 1978, p. 11-A. Reprinted by permission of U.P.I.

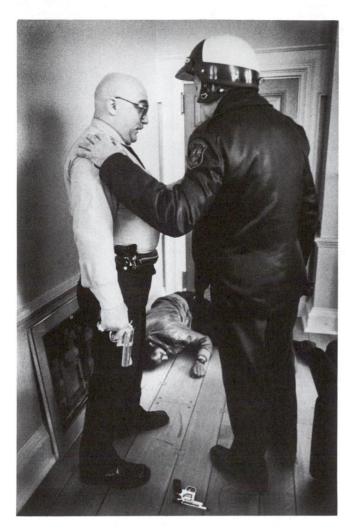

FIGURE 8-2. Pittsburgh police officer, left, is comforted by a fellow police officer after shooting a suspect after the man shot and wounded his wife. [Photo: courtesy John Kaplan, Pittsburgh Pa. Press.]

Responses from police officers who killed someone in the line of duty vary. In some cases, officers experience incredible guilt, feeling immobilized and perhaps even believe they have compromised their religious beliefs.[40] The other extreme is comprised of individuals who experience no guilt, as in the case of one officer who said to a police psychologist, "Doc, isn't it alright if I don't feel guilty? If I had another gun, I would have shot him six more times."

PATTERNS OF REACTION

The effects of a shooting are often varied among police officers, but interviews with officers who have experienced such incidents suggest that the following is a very common pattern.

Denial. The police officer does not believe the incident occurred and stands over the body in disbelief with shotgun or pistol in hand. The officer has not consolidated the entire event into his or her thinking system and there is momentary psychological shock. The activity leading up to the shooting has required the use of a reflexive behavior rather than a step-by-step thinking process. This disbelief or denial subsides

FIGURE 8-3. Wife of a Cincinnati police officer at her husband's funeral. The officer and his partner were killed by a robbery suspect. Friends of the slain officer also show the impact on them. [Photo courtesy of the Cincinnati (Ohio) Post.]

rather quickly as the police officer becomes aware of a dead body in front of him or her or a wounded subject needing help.

Gathering Facts. The police officer realizes that there is a need to present all of the facts relating to the sequence of events and the shooting must be justified. The officer is also beginning to prepare what will be an investigation by the homicide squad, internal affairs, and/or the administration. Police officers are trained to think in very factual terms when reporting such incidents. It is therefore suggested that it will probably not be wise for the police psychologist to speak to the police officer at that very moment. It would be best first to provide the officer with an opportunity to give the investigators all the factual information available at the moment.

Reporting Facts. The police officer presents the facts to the investigators hoping for support and vindication. If the officer receives this support, then the officer becomes less defensive. Up to this point the police officer is acting according to previous training. Fact gathering and reporting incidents are daily tasks for a police officer. The stages the officer enters next are beyond the scope of most training programs and are frequently psychologically threatening. It is at this point that the police officer is in need of stress management. The officer should be aware that he or she will be entering the following stages and should be assured that his or her responses are normal ones.

Physical Anxiety. The officer will experience a high amount of stress even if the officer is assured that the action taken was a correct one. The officer continues to respond to this experience in a fight/flight response. Having fought to save his or her own life by shooting another person, the officer begins to experience a response more akin to the flight response. The officer would like to get away from the situation and find some relief. The officer finds that he or she is unable to relax and wonders whether there is something physically wrong. This may manifest itself in the inability of the officer to sleep, and in frequent pacing, inability to sit still, and so forth. All police officers involved in a shooting incident should engage in some type of physical activity within twenty-four hours. Depending upon the officer's life-style, this could be a sedentary activity such as fishing, or active exercise, such as playing racquetball or baseball. This activity relieves the anxiety tension and continued state of preparedness in which the physical body of the police officer remains.

Peer Group Support. A rather significant phenomenon in the data accumulated is that police officers are often back at the police station wishing to speak to fellow officers within 48 hours of the incident. They are obviously seeking some peer reassurance. Some departments will give the police officer two or three days off with pay, yet the officer may insist on going back to the station and speaking with fellow officers. It is believed that this return to the station is necessary and healthy and reassures the officer that despite having taken someone's life, there are those who support the behavior.

Moral Questioning. After two or three days the police officer begins to think of the moral implications of the behavior. Within a few days the very strong value systems possessed by most police officers dramatically affect the officer's self-evaluation as a human being. It is at this point that a psychologist can be most helpful. Besides experiencing moral anxiety the officer may become concerned with his or her psychological state and wonder whether he or she is going to "lose it." The officer may be unable to speak to anybody about these problems and not know how to broach the subject. The situation gets rapidly out of hand and some police officers who have not had posttraumatic shooting counseling have expressed that they have died "a thousand deaths" since the shooting period. They continue to have nightmares about the incident and continue to expect some sort of high-level punishment of a religious nature. Their peers who deal with many of the same types of events are frequently unavailable. The macho image so important in the police culture does not often encourage the mutual sharing of emotionally wrenching experiences, and a police officer who has experienced a fatal shooting incident unfortunately will quite often not easily share those feelings. Officers also find they are not able to speak to their spouses or families. Even though the families may be supportive there is some suggestion that they do not form the same type of solid framework of peer group relationships as does the police culture, and the officer may believe that since they are not police officers they cannot understand his or her feelings. Thus the police officer quickly and unfortunately excludes important persons in his or her life, thus bringing about his or her own isolation and quite possibly ultimate immobilization.

Counseling. The most effective way to get a police officer into stress management counseling after such an incident is to establish a policy making such counseling mandatory. By making counseling mandatory, the decision-making responsibility is immediately taken from the police officer who is already suffering from extreme stress. Although there may be some momentary resistance toward such an order, it is up to the psychologist to bring relief to the police officer. The end result is usually the appreciation of the officer for having had such a counseling session.

The first counseling session is conducted with only the officer who is immediately assured of total confidentiality. No information is given to other people. Because the officer is being investigated by the department, the psychologist could easily be seen as another departmental inquiring force who is building a case against the officer if things have not been done according to department policy.

In many of these incidents an effort is made to have the police officer come back to the second session with his or her spouse. Again there is hesitation by the police officer who did not really want to involve the spouse. It is quite typical for a spouse to attempt to persuade the officer to transfer to a different kind of police work or even encourage the officer to get out of police work entirely. Now the officer not only has the stress of the incident, his or her own psychological stress and moral anxiety, but also the concern for his or her spouse and family. Thus the police officer is presented with incredible responsibility and decision making, a process for which the officer has probably not been trained.

The police officer and spouse are then given the option of attending future sessions. If it is believed that further support is needed, very strong encouragement is given to the officer and spouse to return. One study revealed that some 70 percent of all persons involved in such programs had returned for advice not only on police related matters but also for other personal problems. It is also significant that this group of police officers has been very active in referring other police officers to the psychologist.[41]

Stress and the Police Administrator

As any individual who has risen through the ranks of a police agency realizes, the types of problems and pressures encountered as an administrator are quite different from those encountered as a patrol officer. For either position, however, the end results of the stress can be equally menacing to the person performing the job.

The High Price of Success

One management expert has suggested that upward mobility in almost any type of bureaucracy tends to impose unique stresses upon individuals. These stresses occur in part because an individual often must sacrifice family relationships for career goals and because each promotion brings with it more responsibilities for the individual over wider-ranging areas and increased numbers of subordinates. In addition, young men and women who ascend the organizational ladder rapidly tend to generate considerable envy from their peers who believe that they have been passed over unfairly for promotion. Sometimes this envy manifests itself in negative interpersonal contacts between the superior and his or her less successful subordinates.[42]

Upward mobility regardless of age carries with it certain risks. The higher one rises in the organization, the harder the fall if one should err. The errors that occur in the higher levels of police organizations are likely to be bigger, more costly, and more painful personally than are those in the lower ranks. Because his or her errors are more obvious to a wider range of people, the individual becomes increasingly concerned about being viewed as incompetent. A person may also feel isolated as peers become subordinates and once-gratifying relationships with them become modified or perhaps even dissolved.

Moreover, at a certain point in the upward climb, usually close to the top, many executives experience a specific disappointment. Once having achieved a certain position, they discover that they still have the same frailties, inadequacies, and self-doubts except that now their younger and less experienced subordinates look to them for the answers to complex problems. Looking upward from the lower rungs of the hierarchy, subordinates often tend to view distant supervisors as omnipotent. They have a powerful impact on the organization and always seem to know what they are doing. When the younger person reaches these levels, he or she soon realizes that the giants were really human after all and that one does not acquire omnipotence merely from having achieved a certain position.[43]

Pressure from Above and Below

Subordinates do not always view their police superiors with respect, admiration, and awe. Kroes and others in their study of thirty administrators of the Cincinnati Police Department (twelve Captains and eighteen lieutenants) found that there was a tendency for patrol officers to blame their immediate supervisor for stressful conditions, when in some instances these superiors had little or no control over the factor inducing stress. Being blamed unfairly for their officers' problems can cause considerable anguish and frustration to superiors who are genuinely concerned about the welfare of their subordinates. This anguish is especially acute when the superior has a limited range of alternatives, authority, and resources available to correct those situations or factors that are stress inducing.[44]

Nevertheless, most police administrators do have some alternatives available that can be implemented within the framework of the organization's resources and budget. In addition to the creation of programs that assist police officers in coping with and reducing stress, considerable progress has been made in the selection and training of supervisory personnel who are better able to cope with the stress inherent in their responsibilities and who are also more sensitive to the needs of their subordinates.[45]

There is considerable evidence, from the available literature, that police administrators throughout the country experience similar types of personal, organizational, and community-initiated stress-inducing problems.

Midlife Crisis and the Middle-Aged Manager

Behavioral scientists have coined the phrase "midlife crisis" to describe some of physical and psychological changes some people may undergo between the ages of thirty-five and forty-five. For example, statistics provided by life extension examiners indicate that specific symptoms—such as extreme fatigue, indigestion, and chest pains—rise sharply among young executives just moving into top management.[46] One third of the symptoms found in the thirty to forty-year-old management groups can be traced to an organic cause, the examiners report.[47]

Although some explanations for this increase in symptoms are no doubt a product of the aging process itself, there are more pressing psychological forces. The British psychoanalyst Elliot Jaques contends that a peak in the death rate between thirty-five and forty is attributable to the shock that follows the realization that one is inevitably on a descending path.[48] This produces what for most men is a transitory period of depression. Depression increases a person's vulnerability to illness. There is much medical evidence that physical illness is likely to occur more frequently and more severely in people who feel depressed.

The middle-aged manager going through a midlife crisis may find himself running after his lost youth with vain cosmetic efforts, dressing in a manner comparable to men in their early twenties, buying sports cars, and seeking the companionship of much younger women. Carried to its extreme forms, the midlife crisis can be self-destructive to individuals and to the organization. Thus police organizations must take the middle-aged period seriously in their thinking, planning, and programming.

One of the needs for coping with midlife crisis is the opportunity to talk about it; therefore, a part of supervising and appraisal counseling should be devoted to some of the issues and concern of their conditions. Department educational programs should inform both managers and their spouses about this period of life and its unique pressures.

Stress and the Police Family

A law enforcement career is much more than a job or an occupation for the individual; it is a way of life for the officer, his spouse, and his family. A police officer's life becomes one of shared priorities between his family and the outside world in which he functions on an official basis. He brings the problems and frustrations encountered on the job home to the family. Conversely, he can vent the frustrations, tensions, and hostilities engendered by an unsatisfactory home life on the public.

Administrators are starting to recognize that the spouse and family are significant contributors to the success or failure in a law enforcement career. Marital and family strife, discord, and unresolved emotional problems affect a police officer's development, motivation, productivity, and effectiveness in ways that we are only beginning to appreciate and understand.

The excessive psychological pressures on officers to maintain self-control on the job drain their energies and can leave them totally depleted and unable to cope with problems at home. The wife and family who need and expect some time and attention in working out their own problems are confronted with a person who simply lacks the emotional resources to deal with one more stressful situation. Whether the problem is large and important or small and trivial is irrelevant to the emotionally depleted officer; the officer is unable to deal with it.[49]

Problems in Police Marriages

Marriages of law enforcement personnel are susceptible to certain kinds of stresses inherent in the nature of policing. Erratic work schedules, job pressures, and the

FIGURE 8-4. The Police Family. [Photo courtesy of the *FBI Law Enforcement Bulletin.*]

necessity for twenty-four-hour availability are a few factors that can drive a wedge between officers and their spouses. There is considerable evidence that police officers as an occupational group have one of the highest divorce rates in the country, and divorce seems to be especially prevalent among young police officers.

Some authorities point out that

> In large departments, it is easy to find numbers of patrol officers who are on their third marriage before age 30. There is no particular mystery with regard to the breakup of marriages existing prior to entry into police service. Many police officers are married within a few years after finishing high school and typically neither spouse had any realistic notion of what police service would mean in terms of its effect on family life. Police agencies that provide any orientation or counseling for spouses are increasing in number but they are still the exception rather than the rule.[50]

Earlier in this century, law enforcement personnel ranked thirtieth in divorce rates out of thirty-nine job categories.[51] Some occupations or professions ranked higher than police were physicians, lawyers, teachers, and salesmen. One explanation provided by Durner and others is that law enforcement officers during this earlier period constituted large numbers of Irish, Polish, and Italian Catholics. Thus it seems reasonable to assume that traditional condemnation of divorce by the Roman Catholic

Church kept the divorce rate from being a reliable indicator of the success or failure of law enforcement marriages.[52] Some authorities have suggested that divorce rates are merely the tangible expression of a far greater problem, dissatisfaction in marriage, whether or not it ends in divorce. Expressed dissatisfaction among married people is identified as a more accurate indicator of the number of people who are living in a state of marital discord and aggravation than is the actual divorce rate.

In the case of the police officer, an unhappy marriage becomes a social disability because of the officer's role as a controller of society. There is an urgent need to identify and overcome difficulties leading to marital dissatisfaction in police officers, for the plight of the officer's marriage affects everyone: the officer, his family, his offspring, and society as a whole. Generally, a long period of poor communication, confrontation, and frustration precedes the actual dissolution of a marriage.[53]

Job-Induced Problems

We spoke earlier of job-related pressures that are inherent in the law enforcement career. Unusual working hours, scattered weekends, excessive overtime, court appearances, and the constant presence of a gun in one's everyday life are enough to cause significant stresses and problems in a marital relationship. Most of these are obvious pressures to which most couples are able to adjust. There are stresses, however, that can have long-range and lasting effects on a relationship. Many of them create problems that have never been encountered, or even imagined by the couple until they are forced to cope with them following the marriage ceremony. In many instances, these stresses take their toll over an extended period of time, and neither party attends to the warning signals or is able to pinpoint the actual source of the difficulties.

Changing Work Schedules. Extensive disruption occurs in the family routine as a result of changing work schedules and may have an adverse effect on home life. Not enough time is spent with the children; weekends and holidays with the family are missed; the spouse dislikes and resents being home alone at night; and social events with friends and family are difficult to plan. Working overtime merely accentuates the problems of shift work and leaves even less time to spend with the family. The most important factor in all these missed opportunities is the lack of shared experience among husband and wife and children. The end result can be a loss of interest in one another and a resulting breakdown in communications.

Emotional Exhaustion. The inability to function effectively and deal successfully with people's problems confronts the police officer daily. This constant barrage of unsolvable problems, along with the various negative situations with which the officer constantly comes in contact, leads to frustration and psychological exhaustion. By the time the officer gets home, all his patience has been expended. Problems at home either seem insignificant or, at the other extreme, may serve to infuriate the officer. An outburst of displaced aggression may then be released upon the family. In any event, the family is the loser.

Negative Public Image. How other people behave toward us is a well-known determinant of social behavior. Most police believe that what they do is important, but they are also very conscious of what they believe the public opinion of them is. Perceived public animosity and disrespect impose the negative label of "cop" on the officer. Such a label has adverse effects not only on the officer but also on his close friends and family relations.

Overprotecting the Spouse and Family. One police psychologist points out that "because of the trauma and degradation they observe everyday, law enforcement officers tend to become overprotective of wives and families.[54] The job teaches and actively encourages an individual to become extremely observant and to develop suspiciousness as a part of his working personality. Often, without realizing it, the police officer carries over these characteristics, which are highly functional on the job, into his personal relationships to the degree that he becomes overly concerned about his spouse's and family's welfare. Wanting to know where his wife and children are, what they are doing, and who they are with at all times can impose irksome restrictions on the family. What the officer views as concern and love for his family can often be misinterpreted by his wife and children as a lack of trust and confidence on the part of an authoritarian husband and father who is not around most of the time.

Hardening of Emotions. To function adequately on the job, law enforcement officers often find it necessary to suppress their feelings. There is little room on the job for anger, disgust, tears, or sadness. Emotional suppression enables police officers to avoid deep personal involvement in the upsetting and occasionally traumatic incidents with which they have to deal on a daily basis. The "hardening" process helps police officers to perform unpleasant and distasteful but necessary tasks without any outward display of emotions. Unfortunately, it is impossible for the police officer to shed this stoic image with his uniform. Most officers bring this stoicism home to spouse and family who must try to relate to their impassiveness. Often, the spouse is unable to see, or even remember, the formerly cherished personal qualities of her partner, which he now hides because his career demands it.

Sexual Problems. Sexual problems between the officer and his spouse may be either a symptom or a cause of emotional conflict and estrangement—and often are both. Intimacy is an early casualty of the pressures that the officer experiences. Once the harmony between marital partners has been shattered, it becomes exceedingly difficult to restore. The consequence is a vicious circle in which frustration creates anxiety and self-doubt, which in turn results in further frustration. As one group of police psychologists points out,

> Sexual promiscuity can also be a problem when the parties, out of frustration, seek release outside of marriage. Some of the sexual problems emanate from factors relating to police work. For instance, the officer who works nights, whose wife works days, and both have different days off, encounter the basic problems of scheduling their sex life. In addition, if they also have children at home, the problem is exacerbated. Too frequently the couples do not put forth the effort to understand and tolerate these difficulties and to work out a compromise solution. Instead, they engage in open hostility toward each other and this creates feelings which in time can result in one or both partners seeking sexual partners elsewhere. This course of action, if discovered by the non-offending spouse, frequently results in the dissolution of the marriage.[55]

Infidelity on the part of the officer or spouse is a common source of domestic discord. Infidelity appears to be far more common among male officers than among their wives. In those cases, where the wife finds out about her husband's extramarital affairs, confronts him, and threatens to leave him, he usually undergoes severe depression and attitudinal and personality changes, which can result in serious problems for him both on and off the job.

Identity Problems.   Traditional roles of men and women in marriage have undergone rapid changes in the past several years. Many women, no longer content to live in a world circumscribed by child rearing and housework, are asserting their fundamental rights to seek a broader set of opportunities outside the home for personal growth and self-actualization. They set great store on their individuality—on their separate selves.

Marital problems may also result when the officer's wife believes that she has outgrown her husband and her social station as a police officer's wife. One case cited by a police psychologist concerned an officer's wife whose job involved circulating in highly sophisticated circles where her husband felt he did not belong: "This caused a serious strain in their relationship and they eventually sought counseling. If the officer's wife views his position as being one which does not have the degree of status or prestige she views as important to her own self-concept, then difficulties may emerge in the relationship."[56]

Problems with the Children.   Children of police officers may encounter negative reactions and rejections from both peers and schoolteachers because of their father's occupation. Juvenile problems also seem to become prevalent when the children of police families reach adolescence. Although many of these problems are between the children and their parents, serious delinquency is not uncommon and may involve school truancy, vandalism, alcohol and drug abuse, rebelliousness, and various other kinds of misconduct.

Psychologists interpret the delinquent actions of police officers' children as the rejection of the authority represented by their father's occupation. According to one group of police psychologists,

> Many times it is apparent that the officer is overprotecting his children and creating such an inhibiting home environment that they rebel. This phenomenon is far more common with adolescents who may feel trapped and stifled by their parent's protectiveness and act out in a manner that reinforces the parent's reason for overprotecting them.[57]

Once again, we see the familiar pattern of the vicious circle: the tighter the control, the more rebellious the juvenile becomes.

Marital Problems as an Administrative Concern

Until recently, law enforcement administrators have viewed marital problems among police personnel as a private matter involving only the officer and spouse. Fortunately, police executives are now beginning to view marital difficulties as an administrative problem. In acknowledgment of the magnitude and importance of marital problems and their far-reaching effects on job performance, some administrators have devised programs for solving, or at least reducing, marital problems within their organizations. As yet, however, these programs have not been implemented in the majority of departments. There is an urgent need to identify and overcome difficulties leading to marital discord and conflict among law enforcement personnel. The following are suggested programs for spouses of police officers that should help administrators reach this goal.

ORIENTATION PROGRAMS FOR SPOUSES

An orientation program for police spouses should make police wives more aware and understanding of the many activities of the police agency. It should provide a comprehensive view of operations within the department, levels of command, and the day-to-day duties performed by law enforcement officers. This program should also enable the spouse to ask top police administrators questions concerning the department's function, the officer's job role, and off-duty requirements such as attending political rallies, doing volunteer work, and giving presentations at luncheon meetings. There should also be an honest effort given to presenting a realistic view of the law enforcement field and of the problems encountered on the job.

INTERVIEW PROGRAMS WITH THE SPOUSES OF POLICE APPLICANTS

As part of the investigation of a police applicant, an interview could be conducted with his wife at home to help determine the compatibility of the couple and their life-style to a law enforcement career. This interview should be only one determinant in the selection of law enforcement personnel, because most pressures in law enforcement careers that result in marital problems are very difficult to foresee. From this interview, police administrators can gauge the willingness of the spouse to assume the burdens of a law enforcement marriage. Similarly, the spouse benefits by being able to ask questions about the job that her husband possibly cannot or will not answer.

RIDE-ALONG PROGRAMS

Law enforcement agencies should implement a ride-along program to provide spouses with firsthand observation and knowledge of the law enforcement officer's occupational role. This type of program also helps to familiarize the spouse with the police organization and its procedures.

PROGRAMS IN FIREARM USAGE AND SAFETY

Programs should be designed to introduce spouses to basic gun usage techniques and safety precautions since many people are frightened by the presence of firearms in their home. Instruction in the proper use and care of handguns should be given to reduce this stress situation for many couples. The spouse should be given opportunities to actually fire a weapon. Such programs provide the additional benefits of reducing the risk of a family member being injured accidentally.

An Exemplary Program

Dr. John Stratton, psychologist for the Sheriff's Department of Los Angeles County, has written about a program for spouses that was developed within this agency. Of the over four-hundred wives participating in the program, it was evaluated as follows:

FIGURE 8-5. Basic problems encountered in law enforcement marriages and solutions, as well as methods to improve communications, are among the subjects discussed by the department psychologist with spouses. [Photo courtesy of the Los Angeles County Sheriff's Department.]

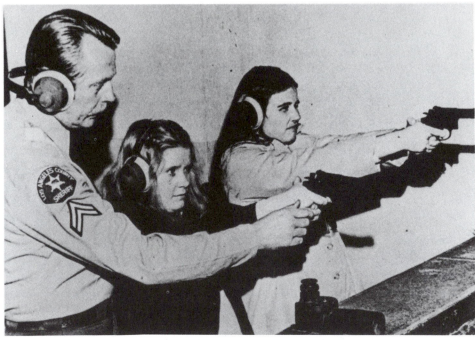

FIGURE 8-6. Spouses receiving instruction at the firing range. [Photo courtesy of the Los Angeles County Sheriff's Department.]

excellent, 62 percent; very good, 33 percent; good, 5 percent; fair, 0 percent; and poor, 0 percent.

Although the spouses viewed all segments of the program as valuable, they mentioned some aspects that they felt were especially beneficial, namely, that the department values the spouse as an important contributor, that their fears about firearms were allayed because they learned safety techniques and how to fire a gun, and that they were given the opportunity to experience patrol in realistic situations as opposed to what they generally saw on television and in the movies.

The following are some written responses from spouses who attended the program:

> It helped me realize that I was not the only one having problems. It rather relieved the tension that had been building up inside. It was nice to air out problems that others had in common with you.
> It lessened the fear that I have for this type of law enforcement work. The more you know about something, the less you will usually fear it.
> The friendships that developed among the spouses were really great. It helped make spouses more enthusiastic toward their husbands' work, which in turn makes it easier to understand problems that might be involved with their work. Also I know that I now don't feel ''apart'' or ''distant'' from my spouses's work experience.

There are obviously no simple solutions to the complex marital and family problems that afflict law enforcement personnel. The kinds of programs suggested are based on the premise that spouses who understands their mates' work, the nature of its responsibilities, and the types of personality and behavioral changes it may cause will be more supportive, patient, and understanding, thus increasing the possibility of a successful marriage.

Although these programs are extremely beneficial, they should be supplemented by marriage, family, and personal counseling services obtained from specialists employed by the agency or by referral to professionals in the community.

Employee Assistance Programs

In recent years an increasing number of police departments have developed Employee Assistance Programs (EAP) to assist police officers with many of the stresses associated with police work.[58] While offering programs to help employees to deal with personal or work-related problems clearly demonstrates management's concern for the health and welfare of the officers, part of the motivation is pragmatic in nature.

Enlightened police managers are aware that if employees are lost for reasonable and correctable reasons, the cost in experience lost and training new employees far outweighs the cost of prevention and health programs. Thus the concept of EAPs are a viable way of dealing with many of the problems experienced by police officers in their work.

EAP Criteria

An effective employee assistance program should provide twenty-four-hour availability for officers affected by traumatic incidents such as shootings, the death or wounding of an officer, exposure to mutilated victims, the death of a family member, or extended personal illness. Such programs typically deal with such stress-related factors as financial problems, alcohol or drug abuse, and retirement planning, and spouses' concerns are also encouraged. Some of these can be treated through counseling, seminars, workshops or other formalized programs. Group "therapy" with others who have experienced the same problems has proved extremely beneficial.

In establishing an EAP, several considerations must be addressed.

Confidentiality and Credibility. The credibility of those providing the assistance and the guarantee of confidentiality are essential for any program designed to provide assistance to employees. If the helper is believed to report negative information to the administration or is seen as one hired to get rid of problem employees, the program is doomed to failure.

Voluntary vs. Involuntary. People can be ordered to attend counseling, but they can't be forced to be involved in it or to be honest and open with the counselor. Although some people have benefited when forced to attend counseling sessions or alcoholism meetings, a program that people seek out on their own is generally more effective.

Status of Employee Assistance Program and Staff. The importance placed on the employee assistance program, the caliber of the staff, and the existence of independent ethical and professional standards are the key considerations in establishing an effective program.

Location and Accessibility of the Employee Assistance Program. These factors are crucial. For providing services to employees, a location away from headquarters generally seems the most beneficial. Some EAPs are set up in regular professional buildings, whereas others are set up in residential areas nearby. To be really functional in a law enforcement environment, an EAP must be accessible on a twenty-four-hour basis and allow direct access to the employee assistance personnel.

Division of Administrative vs. Treatment Preventive Services. EAPs are geared to provide assistance to employees with personal problems or job-related matters. Any problems related to job performance are an administrative area and should not be addressed by employee assistance program personnel. If the counselors' advice is ignored or doesn't change behavior, and the employee continues to perform poorly, administrative measures should be taken by supervisory and management personnel.

Additional Programs. Programs that contribute to employees' overall health, such as required yearly or biannual physical examinations, blood pressure screening and physical fitness programs that provide incentives for good physical health, benefit them both physically and emotionally. Providing information in the department's in-house newspaper or magazine on fitness and maintaining good emotional health can be very helpful.

Spouse orientation programs such as those discussed earlier are a very valuable component of any employee assistance program. All of the EAPs discussed call for a firm commitment from both the individual and the police department. And efforts toward increasing one's effectiveness in coping with stress are less successful in the absence of close cooperation between the individual officer and the department.

BOX 8-3.

Coping with Stress

For police and firemen who rushed to the scene of San Diego's disastrous air crash last September, the tragedy is not yet over. Months after a Pacific Southwest airliner collided with a small plane and plunged into a downtown neighborhood, claiming 144 lives, many of the emergency workers who confronted the human carnage were still trying to shake off the trauma. A few were paralyzed with anxiety whenever they tried to put on the uniform they wore on the day of the accident. Others suffered from hellish nightmares, insomnia, stomach ailments, migraines and partial amnesia about the terrible event. Says Alan Davidson, president of the Academy of San Diego Psychologists: "This has had an impact on the human psyche beyond what we can humanly know."

Davidson thinks that extensive dismemberment among the victims made the San Diego crash even more horrifying than most major accidents. Parts of bodies were strewn over lawns, houses and roads, and police said they could not walk down the street without stepping on human tissue. Emergency personnel were overwhelmed. They spent their first minutes in a semi-daze, trying to cover up the bloodiest scenes. Police who arrested people—for taking airplane parts or for not leaving the scene of a disaster—coped better. For such officers, say Psychologist Steven Padgitt, "there was some sense of purpose, some sense of being able to express the rage they were experiencing."

Twenty-five local psychologists provided free counseling to city workers and witnesses to the crash. About 100 sought treatment, most of them veteran police officers haunted by their inability to control the chaos and hysteria at the scene of the carnage. The first 16 policemen who came for help all used the word "macho" and talked of themselves as possible failures for seeking therapy. Most urged that the psychologist look at the video tapes and photographs of the site, partly to share their sickening feeling, partly to convince the therapist of their manliness. Says Davidson: "They didn't want it to appear that they'd been overcome by some small thing."

To unleash that suppressed rage, the psychologists prescribed jogging, target shooting or other sports. Explains Davidson: "We wanted the anger to come out in an appropriate, directed way rather than when they are arresting somebody." Standard behavioral modification techniques were used for sleeplessness and physical symptoms, and some psychologists tried hypnosis to deal with amnesia about the disaster. The most successful treatment, however, was simply empathy. Says Davidson: "They seemed to need to hear initially that they are normal, adjusted individuals who were put into a completely abnormal situation." Adds Gentry Harris, San Francisco psychiatrist who has worked extensively with disaster witnesses: "It's important to let the person know he's not some kind of screwball. He's still within the human family. We just need to make people recognize that they do have limitations."

Source: Time. January 8, 1979, p. 61.

Enhancement of Awareness and Self-esteem

There are a number of specific means that can be employed in reducing stress. On individual levels officers can decrease the impact of stress by increasing their understanding of the problems they are facing; that is, they should know the type of stressors they will likely encounter in their work and the physical and emotional effects these stressors may have on them. Self-understanding leads to increased knowledge of others, a deeper comprehension of one's own motivations, habits, idiosyncracies, and hangups and also diminishes the stress involved in interpersonal conflict. In addition, the self-assurance that comes with knowledge and understanding is a vital asset to the police officer. True self-confidence, not bravado, is required to react quickly, decisively, and effectively.

Psychologists use such terms as "ego strength" and "frustration tolerance" to refer to an individual's overall capacity for handling stressors of various kinds, especially those involving threats to self-esteem. Persons with high self-esteem are less prone to anxiety; when they experience frustration, they are more likely to deal realistically and directly with the source of their frustration than to divert their energies to substitute or alternative targets. Persons with low self-esteem, on the other hand, are less likely to deal constructively with frustration and stress.

> A person with low self-esteem not only has to attempt to solve the frustrating problem with which he is faced, but must also prevent any further loss of self-esteem. The latter task sometimes gets to be more important than the problem-oriented one, and the low [person] defends himself by hostility, withdrawal, excessive assertiveness in the use of power or insulting behavior. As the threat increases his anxiety, his thinking may become rigid and his solution of the problem at hand becomes less effective. On the other hand, the high self-esteem person is less diverted by a need to protect his self-esteem and can work more directly on the problem at hand. He approaches it with more confidence because his past experience has shown him that he can and does solve problems effectively. He can act directly on the problems and has little need to withdraw from them.
>
> Self-esteem is not a fixed quality in a person. No matter how secure a person is, there are going to be times when he feels blue, when he questions himself, when things happen that shake him up. A person's self-esteem may hover at lower levels on some days and higher on others. In fact, with extreme changes in life situations, a person's self-esteem can take remarkable nose dives or it may soar. New assignments, arrests, and case solutions can all have an influence on a police officer's esteem.[59]

Although one's self-esteem tends to increase from heightened understanding and mastery of specific job skills, it can also be improved by more direct methods of intervention. For example, one police stress control program makes use of training and rational self-assertion and also gives officers exposure to *cognitive restructuring:*

> The cognitive restructuring exercises are methods in which individuals are taught how their thinking process effects their emotional feelings and behavior. The negative or irrational self-statements which maintain the individual at a high level of anxiety are identified, and techniques to alter stress-inducing thoughts are initiated. . . . the aim of this instruction is to offer practical strategies for controlling disturbing self-talk without necessarily seeking professional assistance.[60]

A combination of assertiveness training and cognitive restructuring is also part of the program in "anxiety management training" that clinical psychologist Richard M. Suinn has developed for helping type A individuals (those who are especially prone to heart attacks) learn to cope more effectively with stressful situations.[61]

Physical Fitness: Exercise and Diet

Physical exercise can play an important part both in reducing stress and in increasing one's ability to cope with stressful situations. Although dedication and an unavoidable amount of discomfort are involved, especially in the early stages of a physical conditioning program, the results can be extremely rewarding to the individual. It is important that exercise become a part of a broader program aimed at improving overall physical fitness.

Although all types of physical exercise are beneficial, the greatest value is derived from aerobic exercises, those that involve the sustained exchange of oxygen. Aerobic exercises, in particular, benefit the cardiovascular system. Jogging, swimming, bicycling, tennis, and similar activities also improve muscle tone and physical strength.

Studies conducted by the Dallas Police Department, Los Angeles County Sheriff's Department, and the Aerobic Clinic of Dallas show the comparatively inferior condition of the average police officer. In the Dallas study, the participants in the experimental group who engaged in a consistent program of physical exercise demonstrated a 42 percent decrease in sick days. The control group showed a 5 percent increase in sick time.

After the physical training program, officers in the experimental groups averaged .91 commendations per man as compared with .67 commendations per man before the program. Complaints against officers for a six-month period before physical training were .24 per officer. After the program was completed, complaints dropped to .12 per officer. Overall job performance in the experimental group, as rated by the supervisors, increased by 15 percent.

Some of the areas showing improvement in the experimental group were job enthusiasm, self-control, job attitude, human relations skills, police image, and total performance. Of these, the two most affected by the training program were police image and self-control. One can conclude that the more physically fit an officer is and feels, the more self-assured and happy he is with himself.

Diet is another area that contributes significantly to physical well-being and is important in any stress management program. "Officers' diets, because of job demands and shift changes, are often nutritionally deficient. Eating the proper amount and type of food, aids health, reduces the effects of stress and enables the officer to perform effectively."[62]

Biofeedback and Relaxation Training

Because most people do not know how to relax, relaxation methods should be included in stress management programs. Techniques for relaxation are many and varied, ranging from such uncomplicated methods as listening to soothing instrumental music or practicing simple muscle relaxation to sophisticated approaches such as self-hypnosis, transcendental meditation, and biofeedback. Generally, some combination of these approaches is more successful and convenient than the use of a single method.

Deep muscle relaxation, as defined by Axelberd and Valle, is a procedure "whereby the person learns to identify tension in various muscles in his body and to reduce this tension by successively tensing and relaxing the affected muscle(s). The goal of this technique is to improve circulation and relieve the tension which could lead to more serious disorders."[63] The person is instructed just to tense his hands, biceps, face, shoulders, chest, stomach, legs, and feet and then to relax them and focus on the feeling that follows the muscle tensing. Breathing exercises are taught in conjunction with the deep muscle relaxation to increase the oxygen supply to the parts of the body involved in the exercise. Although not as vigorous as the aerobic exercises, deep muscle relaxation and breathing exercises are highly effective in the reduction of muscle tension, improving circulation, and diminishing the work that needs to be performed by the heart.[64]

These exercises may be augmented by the use of biofeedback, a technique that delivers both sociological and psychological benefits. Biofeedback training provides individuals with information about their bodies' function during ongoing physical conditions. Equipment is used to measure such variables as peripheral temperature, muscle tension, perspiration, and even brainwaves. Once a subject has been instructed in the use of biofeedback, he or she can learn to achieve some control over various physiological responses, particularly when the exercise in biofeedback is undertaken together with listening tapes that aid in deep relaxation.

Peer Counseling

Since there is evidence that many stress-related factors are linked directly to organizational policies and practices, police agencies should endeavor to reduce, modify, or eliminate those factors under their control. Some authorities suggest that the easiest way for administrators to identify those organizationally related job stressors is to use the consultant services of rank-and-file officers.

> The officer on the street has built up a wealth of experience and intimately knows the stressors which impinge upon him. By getting a group of experienced officers together to talk about stress problems, the most significant stressors can be identified. Once the major stressors are known, ideas need to be developed on how they may be eliminated. Since organizational change may be necessitated, the full cooperation of management is necessary in this process. It is also especially important to allow individual officers to participate in any decisions about eliminating a stressor which directly affects their job. Should it be found that a particular stressor is ''impossible'' to eliminate, rotation may be helpful. That is personnel could be rotated on and off assignments so that they are not trapped for long periods of time in an assignment which could cause a damaging degree of stress. In a practical sense these techniques involve training and stress awareness, insights into self and others, and specific skill training.[65]

In particular, the Boston Police Stress Program has made a pioneering effort in the use of peer counseling and has enjoyed considerable success in handling troubled officers with drinking, marital, family, and on-the-job problems.

Summary

Our objective throughout this chapter has been to present clear and straightforward discussions of major subjects in the area of stress that can be read with profit and interest by a person who does not necessarily possess a scientific background and training. We have tried to provide the reader with an orientation and introduction to the general topic of stress and some of its principal effects in terms of psychological, physiological, and social consequences and to acquaint the reader with some of the basic concepts and terminology relating to stress that are beginning to attain wider and wider currency among law enforcement personnel. It is quite apparent that some stress factors are unique to policing; others are comparable to the sorts of stress encountered in other occupations and professions. However, the latters' meaning and significance for the present account lie in how they interact with the unique stress factors in policing to create special problems in how to cope effectively with the total stress situation.

There is little doubt that some unmistakable trends are developing in the study and prevention of stress-related problems in police work. It appears that in the future we will witness a greater number of law enforcement administrators directing their professional efforts and organizational resources toward the creation of services that can deal effectively with job-related health and personal problems. The organizational changes that result will manifest themselves in a number of ways. We can expect to see an increasing number of law enforcement agencies implementing psychological and psychiatric assessment of police applicants. This will be done in part to screen out the emotionally unstable applicant.[66] Further, we will witness a dramatic increase in the number of law enforcement agencies that will make available to their personnel and their families in-house professional mental health specialists as well as referral services to community-based mental health specialists. We will also see a greater number of in-service training courses on this subject for both patrol officers and supervisors to assist them in recognizing and coping with job stress and the physical and psychological conditions associated with it.

This trend toward greater organizational sensitivity is indeed a welcome change and certainly long overdue. It is hoped that it will result in the reduction of alcohol and drug related problems, suicide, marital and other family problems, and premature retirements. In the final analysis, the police officer, his or her family, and the organization will be the beneficiaries.

Discussion Questions

1. What is the general adaptation syndrome?

2. How do most people react to stress?

3. Most law enforcement stressors can be grouped into four broad categories. What are these categories?

4. Alcohol-related problems among police officers manifest themselves in a number of ways. What are they?

5. What are some of the specific benefits reported by the Denver Police Department since it implemented its abuse program?

6. How do suicide patterns among younger and older police officers differ?

7. What are the typical phases officers go through in postshooting trauma?

8. It has been suggested that upward mobility in almost any type of bureaucracy tends to impose unique stresses upon individuals. Why is this so?

9. How do behavioral scientists define midlife crisis?

10. Marriages among law enforcement personnel are susceptible to certain kinds of stresses inherent in policing. What are some of them?

11. What are some of the specific means employed to cope with and reduce stress?

12. What should an effective employee assistance program provide to its personnel?

Notes

1. K. Slogobin, ''Stress,'' *New York Times Magazine,* November 20, 1977, pp. 48–55.
2. For a comprehensive treatment of literature on police stress, see L. Territo and H. J.

Vetter, (ed.), *Stress and Police Personnel,* (Boston: Allyn & Bacon, 1981). Much of the discussion in this chapter was drawn from this source.

3. H. Selye, *Stress Without Distress* (Philadelphia: Lippincott, 1974), p. 60.

4. H. Basowitz, H. Persky, S. J. Korchin, and R. R. Grinker, *Anxiety and Stress* (New York: McGraw-Hill, 1955), p. 7.

5. Ibid., p. 4.

6. Selye, *Stress Without Distress,* pp. 35–39.

7. J. C. Coleman, "Life Stress and Maladaptive Behavior," *The American Journal of Occupational Therapy,* (May–June 1973), 27:3 p. 170.

8. O. Tanner, *Stress* (New York: Time-Life Books, 1978).

9. For a comprehensive treatment of defensive behavior patterns, see J. M. Sawrey and C. A. Tilford. *Dynamics of Mental Health: The Psychology of Adjustment* (Boston: Allyn & Bacon, 1963), pp. 40–67.

10. J. G. Stratton, "Police Stress: An Overview," *Police Chief,* 45:4 (April 1978), p. 58.

11. "Compensation for Police Heart Attacks Allowed," *Crime Control Digest,* 9:10 (March 19, 1975), p. 3.

12. Stratton, "Police Stress," p. 58.

13. W. H. Kroes, B. L. Margolis, and J. Hurrell, "Job Stress in Policemen," *Journal of Police Science and Administration,* 2:2 (June 1974), pp. 145–155.

14. W. H. Kroes, *Society's Victim—The Policeman* (Springfield, Ill.: Charles C. Thomas, 1976).

15. T. Eisenberg, "Labor-Management Relations and Psychological Stress," *Police Chief,* 42:11 (November 1975), pp. 54–58.

16. M. Reiser, "Stress, Distress, and Adaptation in Police Work," *Police Chief,* 43:1 (January 1976), pp. 24–27.

17. M. Reiser, R. J. Sokol, and S. J. Saxe, "An Early Warning Mental Health Program for Police Sergeants," *Police Chief,* 39:6 (June 1972), pp. 38–39.

18. M. Reiser, "A Psychologist's View of the Badge," *Police Chief,* 37:9 (September 1970), pp. 24–27.

19. M. Reiser, "Some Organizational Stress on Policemen," *Journal of Police Science and Administration,* 2:2 (June 1974), pp. 156–165.

20. M. D. Roberts, "Job Stress in Law Enforcement: A Treatment and Prevention Program," in *Job Stress and the Police Officer: Identifying Stress Reduction Techniques,* eds. W. H. Kroes and J. Hurrell (Washington, D.C.: U.S. Department of Health, Education, and Welfare, 1975), pp. 226–233.

21. Kroes et al., "Job Stress in Policemen," pp. 145–155.

22. S. A. Somodevilla, C. F. Baker, W. R. Hill, and N. H. Thomas, *Stress Management in the Dallas Police Department* (Dallas: Psychological Services Unit, Dallas, Texas, Police Department, 1978), p. 6.

23. Eisenberg, "Labor Management Relations and Psychological Stress," pp. 54–58.

24. L. Dishlacoff, "The Drinking Cop," *Police Chief,* 43:1 (January 1976), p. 32.

25. Kroes and Hurrell, "Stress Awareness," in *Job Stress and the Police Officer,* p. 241.

26. Ibid., p. 241.

27. Ibid., p. 241.

28. Dishlacoff, "The Drinking Cop," p. 39.

29. Ibid., p. 39.

30. Ibid., p. 39.

31. J. A. Schwartz and C. B. Schwartz, "The Personal Problems of the Police Officer: A Plea for Action," in *Job Stress and the Police Officer,* p. 136.

32. Ibid., p. 136.

33. D. Lester, "Suicide in Police Officers," *Police Chief,* 45:4 (April 1970), p. 17.

34. P. Friedman, "Suicide Among Police," in *Essays in Self-destruction,* ed. E. Schneidman (New York: Science House, 1967).

35. S. Labovitz and R. Hagedorn, "An Analysis of Suicide Rates Among Occupational Categories," *Sociological Inquiry,* 41:1 (January 1971), pp. 67–72.
36. Z. Nelson and W. Smith, "The Law Enforcement Profession: An Incidence of Suicide," *Omega,* 1:4 (November 1970), pp. 293–299.
37. A. Henry and J. Short, *Suicide and Homicide,* (Glencoe, Ill.: Free Press, 1954), p. 15.
38. B. L. Danto, "Police Suicide," *Police Stress,* 1:1 (1978), pp. 32–36, 38, 40.
39. M. F. Heiman, "The Police Suicide," *Journal of Police Science and Administration,* 3:3 (September 1975), pp. 267–273.
40. Walter Lippert and Eugene R. Ferrara, "The Cost of Coming Out On Top: Emotional Responses to Surviving the Deadly Battle," *FBI Law Enforcement Bulletin* (December 1981), pp. 6–10. This discussion of Postshooting trauma was adapted from the source.
41. Ibid., pp. 6–10.
42. H. Levinson, "On Being a Middle-Aged Manager," *Harvard Business Review,* 47 (July–August 1969), pp. 55–57.
43. H. Levinson, *Executive Stress,* (New York: Harper & Row, 1970), pp. 95–97.
44. W. M. Kroes, J. J. Hurrell, Jr., and B. Margolis, "Job Stress in Police Administrators," *Journal of Police Science and Administration,* 2:4 (December 1974), pp. 381–387.
45. For a further discussion, see M. D. Dunnette and S. J. Motowidlo, *Police Selection and Career Assessment* (Washington, D.C.: Government Printing Office, 1978); J. F. Hooke and H. H. Kraus, "Personality Characteristics of Successful Police Sergeant Candidates," *Journal of Criminal Law, Criminology, and Police Science,* 62:1 (March 1971), pp. 104–106; J. Lefkowitz, "Evaluation of Supervisory and Training Programs for Police Sergeants," *Personnel Psychology,* 25:1 (January 1972), pp. 95–106; R. J. Levy, "Predicting Police Failure," *The Journal of Criminal Law, Criminology, and Police Science,* 58 (1967), pp. 265–276; R. Reinke, *Selection Through Assessment Centers: A Tool for Police Departments* (Washington, D.C.: Police Foundation, 1977).
46. Levinson, "On Being a Middle-Aged Manager." Much of the discussion of midlife crisis was taken from this source, pp. 51–60.
47. "Clinical Health Age 30–40," *Business Week,* March 3, 1956, p. 56.
48. E. Jaques, "Death and the Mid-life Crisis" *The International Journal of Psychoanalysis,* 46 (October 1965), p. 502.
49. For a further discussion, see J. G. Stratton, "Pressure in Law Enforcement Marriages," *Police Chief,* 42:11 (November 1975), pp. 44–47; B. Weber, "The Police Wife," *Police Chief,* 43:1 (January 1976), pp. 48, 49; C. Maslach and S. E. Jackson, "Burned-Out Cops and Their Families," *Psychology Today* (May 1979), pp. 59–62.
50. J. A. Schwartz and C. B. Schwartz, "The Personal Problems of the Police Officer" in *Job Stress and the Police Officer,* p. 134.
51. J. P. Lichtenberger, *Divorce: A Study in Social Causation* (New York: Columbia University Press, 1969), p. 96.
52. J. A. Durner, M. A. Kroeker, C. R. Miller, and W. R. Reynolds, "Divorce: Another Occupational Hazard," *Police Chief,* 42:11 (November 1975), p. 48.
53. Ibid., p. 50.
54. Stratton, "Pressure in Law Enforcement Marriages," p. 45.
55. Somodevilla et al., *Stress Management in the Dallas Police Department,* p. 12.
56. Ibid., pp. 13, 14.
57. Ibid., p. 13.
58. J. G. Stratton, "Employee Assistance Programs: A Profitable Approach for Employers and Organizations," *The Police Chief* (February 1985), pp. 31–33. This discussion of EAPs was adapted from this article.
59. International Association of Chiefs of Police, *Training Key #257* (Gaithersburg, Md: 1978), p. 3.
60. M. Axelberd and J. Valle, *Stress Control Program for Police Officers of the City of*

Miami Police Department. From Concept Paper #1, City of Miami, Florida, Police Department, November 14, 1978.

61. R. M. Suinn, "How to Break the Vicious Cycle of Stress," *Psychology Today,* 10 (December 1976), pp. 59, 60.

62. Stratton, "Police Stress," p. 76.

63. Axelberd and Valle, *Stress Control Program for Police Officers,* p. 10.

64. Ibid., p. 10.

65. Kroes and Hurrell, *Job Stress and the Police Officer,* p. 243.

66. For a comprehensive treatment of this topic, see L. Territo, C. R. Swanson, Jr., and N. C. Chamelin, *The Police Personnel Selection Process* (Indianapolis, Ind.: Bobbs-Merrill, 1977), Chapter 5, "Psychological and Psychiatric Assessment of Police Applicants."

"You, a lowly policeman is going to tell me how to run my department! . . . Get out!" and you had to go; he hated me. . . .

RANK-AND-FILE ORGANIZATION LEADER
JOHN CASSESE ON AN EARLY MEETING WITH
NEW YORK CITY POLICE
COMMISSIONER KENNEDY.

Labor Relations

Introduction

No single force in the past half-century has had as much impact on the administration of police agencies as collective bargaining by officers. Police unions represent a major force that must be reckoned with by police managers. In Chapter 1 brief mention was made of the evolution of this powerful phenomenon; this chapter begins with a more detailed exploration of these forces and then moves to cover the following important aspects of police collective bargaining: (1) the impact of unions, (2) the basis for collective bargaining, (3) police employee organizations, (4) establishing the bargaining relationship, (5) conducting negotiations, (6) grievances, (7) job actions, and (8) administrative reaction to job actions. This coverage provides a broad overview with supporting details, sufficient to understand the topic and also to create an appreciation for both its complexities and subtleties.

The Unionization of the Police

In Chapter 1 it was asserted that from 1959 through the 1970s, a number of events combined to foster public sector collective bargaining. The significant forces were identified as being (1) the needs of labor organizations, (2) the reduction of legal barriers, (3) police frustration with the perceived lack of support for their "war on crime," (4) personnel practices in police agencies, (5) salaries and benefits, (6) an increase in violence directed at the police, and (7) the success of other groups in making an impact through collective action.[1] Attention is now turned to a more thorough treatment of this topic.

THE NEEDS OF LABOR ORGANIZATIONS

The attention of labor organizations was devoted almost entirely to the private sector until the 1960s. However, as the opportunity to gain new members became increasingly constrained because of the extensive organization of industrial workers, unions cast about for new markets and statistics such as these impressed them:

> Public service is the most rapidly growing major sector of employment in the United States. In the last 30 years public employment has tripled, growing from 4.2 million to 13.1 million employees. Today nearly one out of five workers in the United States is on a government payroll.[2]

Thus, as with any organization that achieves its primary objective, labor groups redefined their sphere of interest to include public employees. Concurrently, there were stirrings among public employees to use collective action to improve their lot.

THE REDUCTION OF LEGAL BARRIERS

Although workers in the private sector had been given the right to bargain collectively under the federal National Labor Relations Act of 1935, it was another quarter of a century before the first state enacted even modest bargaining rights for public employees. Beginning with the granting of public sector collective bargaining rights in Wisconsin in 1959, many of the legal barriers that had been erected in the wake of the Boston police strike of 1919 began to tumble. Other states that also extended such rights to at least some classes of employees at an early date included California (1961) and Connecticut, Delaware, Massachusetts, Michigan, Oregon, Washington, and Wyoming, all in 1965. Many other states followed this lead, particularly during 1967–1974.[3] President John F. Kennedy granted limited collective bargaining rights to federal workers in 1962 by Executive Order 10988. The courts, too, were active in removing barriers; for example, in *Atkins* v. *City of Charlotte* (1969), the U.S. district court struck down a portion of a North Carolina statute prohibiting being or becoming a union member as an infringement on the First Amendment right to free association.[4] While *Atkins* involved firefighters, the federal courts reached similar conclusions involving Atlanta police officers in *Melton* v. *City of Atlanta* (1971)[5] and a Colorado deputy sheriff in *Lontine* v. *VanCleave* (1973).[6]

POLICE FRUSTRATION WITH SUPPORT FOR THE WAR ON CRIME

Historically, the police have felt isolated in their effort to control crime. This stems from two factors: perceived public hostility and the impact of the due process revolution.

The police perceive a great deal more public hostility than actually exists. Illustrative of this is a survey of one big-city department, which found that over 70 percent of the officers had an acute sense of citizen hostility or contempt.[7] In contrast, a survey conducted by the National Opinion Research Center revealed that 77 percent of the respondents felt that the police were doing a "very good" or "pretty good" job of protecting people in their neighborhoods, and a 1965 Gallup poll showed that 70 percent of the public had a great deal of respect for the police.[8] These data not withstanding, the police saw the public as hostile, and the most persuasive "evidence" of this emerged in the attempts to create civilian review boards, which carried several latent messages to police officers. First, it created anger with its implied allegation that the police could not, or would not, keep their own house in order. Second, it fostered the notion that politicians were ready to "throw the police to wolves" and thus were part of "them."

Particularly among street-level officers, the reaction of the police to the whirlwind of due process decisions, discussed in Chapter 1 under the heading of Scrutiny of the Police, was one of dismay at being "handcuffed" in attempts to control crime. It tended to alienate the police from the Supreme Court and to contribute toward a general feeling that social institutions that should support the police effort in combatting crime were, instead, at odds with it.

PERSONNEL PRACTICES

Past practices become precedent, precedent becomes tradition, and tradition, in turn, becomes the mighty anchor of many organizations. By the late 1960s, the tendency to question the appropriateness of certain traditions was pervasive. Police rank-and-file members were no exception. This tendency was heightened by the increased educational achievement of police officers. While management's general performance was often judged to be suspect, traditional personnel practices were the greatest concern, as these directly affected the individual officer.

Among the practices that were most distasteful to rank-and-file members were the requirement to attend, unpaid, a thirty-minute roll call immediately prior to the eight-hour tour of duty; uncompensated court attendance at hours or on days off duty; short-notice changes in shift assignments; having to return to the station from home for minor matters, such as signing reports, without pay or compensatory time for such periods; favoritism in work assignments and selection for attendance at prestigious police training schools; and arbitrary disciplinary procedures. Gradually, the gap between officers and management widened. Officers began turning to employee organizations to rectify collectively the shortcomings of their circumstance. Subsequently, the solidarity of police officers was to prove of great benefit to employee organizations.

In addition to providing material for ferment through illegal, ill-conceived, abrasive, or insensitive general personnel practices, police managers often unwittingly contributed to the resolve and success of police unions by their treatment of leaders of police employee associations. In Atlanta, the chief of police transferred the president of the Fraternal Order of Police fifty-one times in forty-five days for his activeness,[9] and in Boston, Dick MacEachern, founder and president of the then fledgling Police Patrolmen's Association, was transferred repeatedly from precinct to precinct and Mayor White subsequently refused to sign MacEachern's disability pension for the same reason.[10] Such actions provide free publicity, create a martyr (an essential for many social movements), put the leaders in contact with people they ordinarily would not meet, increase group cohesiveness, and provide compelling confirmation in the minds of rank-and-file members why they need and should join a union.

Salaries and Benefits

As did other government workers in the 1960s, police officers felt that their salaries, fringe benefits, and working conditions were not adequate. In 1961, mining production workers were averaging $111 a week in earnings, lithographers $114, tire and inner tube producers $127, and telephone line construction workers $133,[11] while the pay of police officers averaged far less. Even by 1965, the salary range for patrol officers in the larger cities, those with more than 100,000 in population, was only between $5,763 and $6,919.[12] The rank-and-file members believed increasingly that, if what was fairly theirs would not be given willingly, they would fight for it. In New York City, the Patrolmen's Benevolent Association (PBA) was believed to have been instrumental, from 1958 to 1969, in increasing entry-level salaries from $5,800 to $11,000 per year; obtaining longevity pay, shift differential pay, and improved retirement benefits; and increasing the death benefit from $400 to $16,500.[13] In 1968, the Boston PBA, in negotiating its first contract—which required mediation—obtained increased benefits for its members, such as an annual increase of $1,010, time and a half for all overtime including court appearances, and twelve paid holidays.[14]

Violence Directed at the Police

In 1964, there were 9.9 assaults per 100 officers; in 1969, this figure rose to 16.9. Prior to 1968, the killing of police officers by preplanned ambushes was unheard of; in that year, there were seven such incidents.[15] The escalating violence had considerable psychological impact on the police, who saw themselves as symbolic targets of activists attacking institutional authority. Rank-and-file members began pressing for body armor, special training, the placement of special weapons in all police cars, and sharply increased death benefits.

The Success of Other Groups

During the 1960s the police witnessed mass demonstrations on college campuses, which used many of the tactics associated with the civil rights movement. Among the campus demonstrations that were highly publicized were Berkeley (1964–1965), the University of Chicago (1965), Columbia University (1968), and San Francisco State College (1969). By 1970, campus demonstrations reached the point that, within ten days of President Richard Nixon's announcement to invade enemy sanctuaries in Cambodia, a total of 448 campuses were either shut down or otherwise affected by campus unrest.[16]

The analogy was not lost on the police: if concerted action could impact upon foreign policy, it could also be a potent force in winning benefits for the police. Moreover, the police began supplying their own success models. In 1966, Mayor Lindsay of New York City appointed an independent Civilian Review Board. In resistance, the PBA filed a petition to have the issue put to a citywide referendum and in the ensuing publicity campaign spent an estimated $250,000 to $1,000,000 to defeat the measure, not a small feat as both Senators Robert Kennedy and Jacob Javits had allied themselves with the mayor.[17]

The Impact of Unions

Despite the fact that police unionism as a viable force has had a history of less than thirty years, its impact has been considerable. Traditionally, public officials in general and law enforcement executives in particular have opposed the idea of police unions. A 1944 publication of the International Association of Chiefs of Police (IACP) concluded that police unions could accomplish nothing.[18] In a 1967 address to the State House at Annapolis, Maryland, Baltimore Police Commissioner Donald Pomerleau concluded that "a police union is not compatible with police responsibility."[19]

When such objections are distilled and analyzed, what often remains is the fear that police unions will result ultimately in reduced executive prerogatives. There can be little serious question that such fears have a reasonable and factual basis. As co-equal to management at the bargaining table, police unions represent a new power center that has in many instances effectively diminished management's unilateral and sometimes ill-considered exercise of control. In some matters administrators have simply made bad bargains, giving away prerogatives vital to the ability to manage properly. Far more difficult to assess are the consequences to the times that police executives have failed to act, or have acted differently, in anticipation of the union's stand.

Police unions have also impacted upon policy decisions in many ways. Civilian review boards were thwarted by police unions in New York City in 1966, in Boston in 1968, and in Baltimore in 1970, and in Detroit the union has had episodic battles with the Michigan Civil Rights Commission since that city's riots of 1967. The election of law and order candidates has long been a priority of police unions as illustrated by support for Sam Yorty in Los Angeles and Charles Stenug in Minneapolis.[20] In Portland, Oregon, the union is alleged to have been a potent force in producing the removal of key police officials by the mayor in 1981,[21] and during that same year the union in New York City, at least temporarily, halted a move toward one-officer cars,[22] while in Washington, D.C., Local 442 of the International Brotherhood of Police Officers was credited with the abolishment of three-member trial boards and revision of the department's internal disciplinary procedures.[23]

Police labor organizers often maintain that there is only one color that counts, the color of the uniform. Despite this low-pitched plea for solidarity among rank-and-file members, police employee associations and unions are believed by some observers to have contributed to racial tensions. Certainly, the thwarting of civilian review boards may be viewed by minorities as a hostile action; at least in some departments intradepartmental racial tensions may have worsened at times as the result of police associations or unions actions:

> Incidents that have served to widen the gulf between black and white policemen have occurred in cities throughout the country. The issues involved have varied: endorsement of George Wallace for United States President by the national president of the Fraternal Order of Police; support by police associations of white mayoralty candidates in contests with blacks; use of epithets by white policemen in referring to black members of the force; alleged discriminations against blacks in upgrading and promotions; and a brawl between white and black policemen at an annual . . . picnic.[24]

Such incidents created the feeling among blacks that white-dominated employee organizations were insensitive to issues affecting minorities. Consequently, blacks have tended to form their own organizations to address issues of importance to them.

It is incautious to make categorical statements about the impact of unionism on police professionalization, as it has had both positive and negative effects. Until the mid-1960s, police professionalization was conceived of as including all sworn officers.

BOX 9-1.

Tucker to Establish Police Review Boards

By CHRISTOPHER HEPP, *Inquirer Staff Writer*

Police Commissioner Kevin M. Tucker, in his first address to his department's commanders yesterday, said he intended to establish a number of internal reforms, including the creation of boards to review officers seeking promotions or transfers.

The plan was immediately attacked by officials of Lodge 5 of the Fraternal Order of Police, who said there was no need for the review boards.

"I was disappointed he did not run it by us before he went and told the commanders about it," Robert S. Hurst, FOP president, said yesterday. "I thought he knew more about labor relations. We feel, however, you don't run a department by committee. You run it by command."

Tucker, who was sworn in as commissioner Thursday, outlined his plans for the department in a brief address to several hundred police commanders at the Philadelphia Police Academy, 8501 State Rd. in the Northeast.

In addition to review boards to help him choose who to promote and who to transfer, Tucker told the commanders that he was putting together a management review of all current operations in the department, according to a department spokesman, Capt. John McLees.

He also ordered all commanders of uniformed units to be in uniform at all times while on duty, McLees said. Now, they are permitted to wear plain clothes.

Tucker's speech offered many of the command-level personnel their first in-person glimpse of Tucker, the former head of the Secret Service's Philadelphia office. Tucker is the first Philadelphia police commissioner selected from outside the department in 62 years.

After Tucker's 20-minute address, he asked the officers to form a receiving line so he could meet and shake hands with each individually, according to those in attendance.

"He was received well," said one captain.

According to officers who attended the address, Tucker said the promotion and transfer review boards would be made up of high-level police commanders. The panels would help Tucker in selecting those officers to be promoted and transferred.

The proposals appeared to be well-received among the commanders, according to several who were present. According to one, the review boards would be particularly helpful in Tucker's case, since as a departmental outsider Tucker has little or no personal knowledge of individuals seeking promotions or transfers.

"It seems to be a recognition that because he's from the outside, he does not know the people," said the same officer. "I think with the review boards, he's making up for what he lacks in organizational insight."

"I didn't notice anyone who was negative or critical," said one chief inspector. "I would be very surprised if he didn't have 100 percent backing among the commanders."

Source: The Philadelphia Inquirer, January 7, 1986, p. 5-B.

To the extent to which unionism drives a wedge between those at the lower reaches of the department and management, it negates police professionalization as conceived of for some number of years. Too, professionals traditionally have not participated in the labor movement. However, as many professional groups, such as the American Association for the Advancement of Science, the American Society of Civil Engineers, the American Nurses Association, and the American Association of University Professors (whose members have traditionally been considered professionals), come to act more like unions, there may be some redefinition of the relationship between a profession and unionism. The differences between labor and management have also served to foster a high degree of professionalization in the administration of police departments to deal with the existence and demands of unions.

Where the objectives of the union and the police administrator are the same, the union can be a powerful ally. Even when they are not the same, the union may line up behind a chief and provide support if the cost to the union is not too great. In such instances it may be simply a case of a display of police solidarity, the fact that the union likes a city manager or mayor even less than it likes its chief, the desire to improve the union's image by supporting something from which there is no apparent gain, or for some other reason. Too, when the union exercises its considerable political muscle, it can defeat important policy and program initiatives by the police chief, such as halting the use of one-officer cars as an alternative to two-officer units. It is here that the union confronts the police executive at a basic point: the control of the police department. One chief left a unionized department to take a similar position in another state which did not allow public sector collective bargaining. Over a period of time the city formerly employing him had given up control over many administrative matters as a substitute for demands made by the union for economic gains. As the chief himself put it: "I realized I had to get out because the union could do two things I couldn't; it could stop the department and it could start it." Although an extreme example, it does bring clearly into focus the issue of who controls the department for what purpose. Moreover, it squarely raises the issue of accountability: If police chiefs control increasingly less of their departments, to what extent can they be properly held accountable? Finally, presuming that a chief wants to administer for the common good, for the safety of the general public, but cannot do so, then for whose benefit is the department being operated?

The Basis for Collective Bargaining

Because each state is free to choose whether to provide for public sector collective bargaining and what that structure will be, there is considerable diversity with respect to the practices, policies, and legal provisions relating to bargaining by government employees.

Presently, more than 80 percent of the states have adopted one or another legislative framework permitting collective bargaining.[25]

Two long-time holdouts from extending collective bargaining rights to public employees, Ohio and Illinois, adopted such legislation effectively in 1984,[26] although bargaining rights in Illinois were not given to law enforcement officers until 1986. In general, the states without public bargaining laws are concentrated in the deep South; Florida is the only state in that region that is an exception. In some states, the collective bargaining law applies only to state or to local government employees, and coverage under the laws may differ with respect to the size of cities and counties and the occupational group such as police officers, teachers, and firefighters. In states that have comprehensive laws permitting the practice of collective bargaining by all government employees, the administration of the statute is often the responsibility of a state agency that functions as a labor commission and that may be designated as the Public Employees Relation Commission (PERC) or Public Employees Relation Board (PERB).

Just because there is no state statute permitting collective bargaining does not

Instructor from the Management Science Unit, Federal Bureau of Investigation Academy addressing police executives at a labor relations seminar sponsored by the Massachusetts Criminal Justice Training Council (Photo courtesy of the Federal Bureau of Investigation).

mean that it does not take place. In the absence of state legislation, bargaining may take place under terms of verbal or written agreements, executive orders, legislative resolutions, or local ordinances. These forces may also serve as a potent adjunct to state law in shaping the practice of bargaining. Where bargaining has gone on for some time despite the absence of some state provision for it, it does not mean that this will continue to be the case. In Virginia in 1974, for example, the attorney general ruled that, because there was no express statutory authority for it, units of government could not enter into collective bargaining agreements with their employees, thereby ending what had been a practice.

Employee Organizations

Knowledge of the various police employee organizations is essential to an administrator because these organizations tend to have their own philosophies and orientations. It is somewhat difficult to identify police employee organizations and those for whom they bargain accurately because one organization will succeed another and groups of police officers will choose to drop their affiliation with one union in favor of another.[27] Consequently, any such description is not unlike a photograph in that it depicts situations at a given time. In general, organizations that seek to organize police officers may be divided into three broad categories: subdivisions of industrial unions, independent government employee associations, and independent police-only associations.

Industrial Unions as the Parent Organization

The American Federation of State, County, and Municipal Employees (AFSCME) is the largest all-public-employee organization with an industrial union as parent. While police officers are bargained for separately, they belong to locals comprised of a variety of public employees. AFSCME's greatest police strength has traditionally been in Michigan, Connecticut, and Maryland. AFSCME is an American Federation of Labor–Congress of Industrial Organizations (AFL–CIO) affiliate.

Among federal workers, the American Federation of Government Employees (AFGE) is AFSCME's counterpart and is also an AFL–CIO affiliate. AFGE was founded in 1932, four years before AFSCME received its AFL–CIO charter. It has represented personnel from a number of federal agencies, including the Drug Enforcement Administration, the Border Patrol, protective officers with the General Services Administration, and deputy federal marshals. As is true for AFSCME, AFGE is an all-public-employee union.

The Service Employees International Union (SEIU) has been involved in organizing police officers two ways. The first was through a subordinate organization, the National Union of Police Officers (NUPO); the second has been to charter directly autonomous police locals. SEIU, unlike AFSCME and AFGE, is a mixed union admitting both private and public sector employees. NUPO was formerly designated the International Brotherhood of Police Officers but had to change its name because an organization by that name already existed. Knowledgeable observers characterize NUPO as virtually defunct, with by 1977 less than one third the members it had in 1969. SEIU strength historically has been primarily in Michigan, Louisiana, Missouri, South Carolina, and the Virgin Islands.

The International Brotherhood of Teamsters, Chauffeurs, Warehousemen, and Helpers of America (IBT or Teamsters) has had some interest in organizing the police for about two decades. The IBT either places police officers in mixed locals or in all-public-employee locals, such as Local 310 of the State of Minnesota, which includes state, county, and municipal employees. The Teamsters' greatest success in organizing police officers has historically been in rural, suburban, and western areas of the country, although it has had recent success in the Sunbelt states.

Independent Government Employee Associations

The National Association of Government Employees (NAGE) was founded in 1961 and organizes police officers through its surbordinate arm, the International Brotherhood of Police Officers (IBPO). IBPO was founded in 1964 in Rhode Island and became affiliated with NAGE in 1970. While IBPO's main strength is in New England, it also has locals in Texas, Utah, and California.

The Assembly of Government Employees (AGE) has almost no impact on police labor relations. Founded in 1952, AGE organizes on a governmentwide basis with most of its affiliates being at the state level, such as the 12,000-member Colorado State Employees Association. However, some number of police officers do belong, although they are believed to be only a very small percentage of the 700,000 members claimed by AGE.

Independent Police Associations

Independent police associations limit their membership to police personnel and may be national, statewide, or local. For twenty years following its founding in 1953, the International Conference of Police Associations (ICPA) was an association of associations with the purpose of exchanging information about police employee organizations. In 1973, however, ICPA decided to become a police union and to charter locals. By 1978, it represented about 182,000 officers in some 400 locals with heavy membership in New York, Illinois, New Jersey, and California.

At the ICPA's July 1978 convention in Toronto, Canada, the question of affiliation with the AFL-CIO split the member organizations evenly. Subsequently, at the ICPA's winter 1978 meeting in Phoenix, Ed Kiernan, Robert Gordon, and twenty-eight ICPA regional vice presidents resigned to form the International Union of Police Associations (IUPA). As president of the newly formed IUPA, Ed Kiernan submitted an application for a charter to the president of the AFL–CIO, George Meany. A review committee, composed of Jerry Wurf of AFSCME, Paul Hall of SEIU, and Howard McClennan of the International Association of Firefighters (IAFF), was appointed by Meany and in January of 1979 reported favorably on the matter. On February 20, 1979, the AFL–CIO Executive Board voted to extend a charter to the IUPA. In 1985 IUPA claimed 13,000 members nationwide.

The ICPA's loss of key executives and defection of member unions to the AFL–CIO left it weakened. Additionally, those associations that had elected not to follow Kiernan's lead were left with the ICPA's burden of $300,000 of outstanding debts; as the remaining local police associations began to resign from the ICPA to avoid being left "holding the bag," the ICPA became doomed as an organization.[28] Representatives of police associations from such places as New York, Detroit, St. Louis, and New Jersey subsequently formed the National Association of Police Officers (NAPO) with the intent that it should have a national, police-only, independent character, making it a successor to the ICPA in all significant respects.

The Fraternal Order of Police (FOP) has historically resisted labeling as a union. As a practical matter, however, where it represents police officers as a bargaining agent, it is a union. Founded in 1915, the FOP is not militant, largely because the lodge leadership positions tend to be dominated by low-ranking officers with long years of service. At least occasionally, this creates some dissatisfaction with younger, more militant officers who sometimes form rival organizations. In general, FOP membership is concentrated in the northeastern and southern states.

Some state police associations are independent, such as the Massachusetts Police Association and the Florida Police Benevolent Association; others, such as the Police Conference of New York, were formerly affiliates of the now nonexistent ICPA. Typically, state associations are not involved directly in negotiations. Instead, they provide services to their substate affiliates such as legal counseling, disseminating information, lobbying, and conducting wage and benefit surveys.

Because of the activeness of IUPA and IBT, the success of these groups in displacing independent police locals, and the advantages of affiliation of some type, we may expect the future to bring some erosion in the number of independent police locals.

Establishing the Bargaining Relationship

The Process

Assuming the existence of some legal provision for collective negotiations, the process of establishing a bargaining relationship is straightforward, although fraught with the opportunity for disputes. The mere fact that most members of a police department belong to a single organization does not mean that it automatically has the right to represent its members for the purposes of collective bargaining.[29] Those eligible to be represented may in fact select an organization to which they already belong for this purpose, or they may select another one. This choice must be made, however, in ways that conform to the legislation providing for collective bargaining if the employee organization hopes to gain certification by the PERC.

The union will begin an organizing drive, seeking to get a majority of the class or classes of employees it seeks to represent to sign authorization cards of which Figure 9-1 is typical. Once a majority, defined as 50 percent plus one of the employees eligible to be represented by the union, have signed cards, the union notifies the police department. If management believes that the union has obtained a majority legitimately and that it is appropriate for the class or classes of officers to be grouped together as proposed by the union, it will recognize the union as the bargaining agent of the officers it has sought to represent. Once recognized by the employer, the union will petition the PERC or other body responsible for administering the legislation for certification. In such cases, the PERC does not check the authorization cards, but only the appropriateness of the grouping of the officers. If the grouping is deemed appropriate by the PERC or similar administrative body, then the employee organization is certified as the bargaining representative.

If the employee organization is not recognized by management, it can petition PERC for an election; the petition must be accompanied by signed and dated representation cards from 30 percent of the group of employees the union seeks to represent.

INTERNATIONAL UNION OF POLICE ASSOCIATIONS

AUTHORIZATION FOR REPRESENTATION

Name _____ Telephone _____

Address _____

City _____ State _____ Zip Code _____

Name of Department _____

Job Title _____

I hereby authorize the International Union of Police Associations, affiliated with the AFL-CIO, to represent me as my Bargaining agent in matters of wages, hours and other conditions of employment.

Signature _____ Date _____

FIGURE 9-1. A typical authorization card.

BOX 9-2.

Unions Woo State and Local Cops

By R. Bruce Dold

Illinois state troopers and police in 17 local departments, including eight suburbs, filed notices Thursday that they will form collective bargaining units. The action came one day after a new state law guaranteeing the right to union negotiations went into effect.

Officials with several Illinois unions said efforts have begun to seek union recognition in dozens of other departments throughout the state, including the Cook County Sheriff's officers.

The law, which went into effect on Jan. 1, mandates collective bargaining rights in local departments with more than 35 members where unions file for recognition with the Illinois Labor Relations Board.

The law gives nonsupervisory police officers and firefighters basically the same collective bargaining rights that were provided to other Illinois public employees in 1984. The law doesn't affect Chicago police and firefighters because they are unionized, but it does provide for sharply increased pensions for widows of Chicago police officers.

The first bids for union recognition were filed Thursday morning by the American Federation of State, County and Municipal Employees [AFSCME] on behalf of Kane County Sheriff's police and three Downstate departments.

The Fraternal Order of Police filed later on behalf of Cicero, Calumet City, River Grove, Fox Lake, Lyons, Calumet Park, Flossmoor, Norridge, the McHenry County Sheriff's police,

the Illinois Department of State Police and four Downstate departments.

"We'll be filing for lots more," said Sally Kelsey, a spokesman for AFSCME. "These guys in a lot of cases have wanted to unionize for a long time." Police seeking union recognition must get the written consent of 30 percent of the members of a bargaining unit to file with the labor board.

The law grants bargaining units the right to seek arbitration for unresolved contract issues, but does not give them the right to strike. The decision of an arbiter could be rejected by a three-fifths vote of a governing body and sent back for further arbitration.

The law drew strong criticism from municipal and county government leaders, who contended that it will drive up the costs of local government. But its signing last month by Gov. James Thompson has left those officials largely resigned to working with union bargaining units.

Several unions are trying to organize the 1,700 to 2,000 Cook County Sheriff's police and deputies who could come under a new bargaining unit, according to a spokesman for Sheriff Richard Elrod.

A little more than half of the 35,000 police, firefighters and state troopers in Illinois are under union-negotiated contracts.

Source: The Chicago Tribune, January 3, 1986, p. 3.

A secret vote is then held at the direction of the PERC, with the ballot including the union or unions that are contesting the right to represent the officers along with the choice of no union. The union that receives a majority of the votes from among the officers who both are eligible to be represented by the employee organization and who actually cast ballots is then certified. Alternately, a majority of those casting ballots may vote for no union. In the event that no majority is achieved, a runoff election is necessary.

The Opportunity for Conflict

In establishing the bargaining relationship, there is ample opportunity for disputes to develop. Management may undertake a campaign to convince officers that they are better off without the union at the same time that the union is mounting its organizing drive. The employee organization may wish access to bulletin boards, meeting space, and mailing lists to publicize the advantages of unionizing to the officers, all of which management may not wish to provide. The decision as to what is an appropriate grouping of officers for the purposes of collective bargaining, technically referred to as *unit determination,* is profoundly significant and one about which management and the union may have sharp differences.

Questions such as the following may arise: Are lieutenants part of management and therefore not eligible for representation by the union for purposes of collective bargaining? Should civilian radio dispatchers be part of the same bargaining unit as uniformed officers? Should detectives be in a bargaining unit by themselves? These decisions are important because they may affect the operation of the police department, determine, to some degree, the dynamics of the employee organization, impact upon the scope of bargaining, affect the stability of the bargaining relationship, or even be decisive in the outcome of a representation election.[30]

Both the union and management are pragmatic when it comes to defining the appropriate bargaining unit. In general, both may prefer a broad unit, the union, because the numbers will give it strength while management resists the proliferation of bargaining units because each one that is recognized officially must be bargained with separately. Here, too, despite a similar orientation, disputes may arise. The union may know that it has the support of only one category of employees, for the purposes of illustration, detectives, and seeks to represent them as a single bargaining unit. Management may feel that particular union is too militant and, consequently, favors, as a part of a hidden agenda, the inclusion of detectives in a wider unit as a means of promoting the election of a more moderate union that is also seeking to represent employees.

What constitutes an appropriate unit may be defined by state law. For example, in Massachusetts the appropriate unit for the state police is all ranks up to and including sergeant; in Nebraska all ranks subordinate to the chief may be placed in one unit.[31] The most common method of unit determination, however, is for the PERC or similar administrative body to make decisions on a case-by-case basis, applying certain criteria stipulated in the legislation.[32] Among the criteria often identified are the desires of the employees, the "community of interests" shared by employees, the need to avoid creating too many bargaining units, the effects on efficiency of operations, and the history of labor relations in the police department.

Legislation establishing the right to bargain collectively enumerates certain unfair labor practices for management and employee organizations. Certain of these may come into play during the union's organizing period, particularly if management mounts a countering campaign:

> it is an unfair labor practice, sometimes referred to as an "improper practice" or "prohibited practice," for a public employer to:
>
> **(1)** interfere with, restrain or coerce public employees in the exercise of their enumerated rights;
>
> **(2)** dominate or interfere with the formation or administration of an employee organization;
>
> **(3)** discriminate in regard to hire or tenure of employment or any term or condition of employment to encourage or discourage membership in any employee organization;
>
> **(4)** discharge or otherwise discriminate against an employee because he had filed charges or given testimony under the act; and

(5) refuse to bargain in good faith with the duly designated bargaining agent.

Similarly . . . it is an unfair labor practice for an employee organization to:

(1) restrain or coerce employees in the exercise of their enumerated rights;
(2) cause or attempt to cause an employer to interfere with, restrain or coerce employees in the exercise of their enumerated rights;
(3) restrain or coerce employers in the selection of their representatives for the purposes of collective bargaining or the adjustment of grievances; and
(4) refuse to bargain in good faith.[33]

The interpretation of these provisions would be a function of the PERC; for example, a police union may claim that the employer is engaging in an unfair labor practice by having its managers conduct a surveillance of the union's meeting place during organizing rallies. After conducting a preliminary investigation, the PERC, if substantiating evidence were found to support the claim, would order a hearing. In this example, assuming the necessary presentation of evidence, the PERC would issue a cease-and-desist order requiring the police department not to engage in such activities, which clearly is an unfair labor practice by the employer.

Negotiations

Selection of the Management and Union Teams

Figure 9-2 depicts a typical configuration of the management and union bargaining teams. The union's chief negotiator will usually not be a member of the bargaining unit; rather he or she will be a specialist brought in to represent it. This ensures a certain level of expertise, wider experience, an appropriate degree of objectivity, and an autonomy that comes from knowing that, once the bargaining is over, he or she will not be working daily for the people sitting across the table. It is not automatic that the union president will be a member of the bargaining team, although customarily some union officer is, and often it is the president. Accompanying the union's chief negotiator and president will be two or three team members who have conducted in-depth research on matters relating to the bargaining issues and who will have various types of data, facts and documents—such as wage and benefit surveys, trends in the consumer price index, and copies of recent contracts for similarly-sized jurisdictions—with them. Although there will only be several union research team members at the table, they will have had assistance in gathering their information from others in the union. Unless the union's chief negotiator is an attorney, there will seldom be an attorney sitting at the table with the union's team.

The composition of management's negotiating team is also depicted in Figure 9-2; the chief negotiator may be the director of labor relations for the unit of government involved or a professional labor relations specialist. Some jurisdictions prefer the latter because, if there are acrimonious occurrences, once the bargaining is over the director of labor relations can step back into the picture and assume a relationship with the union that is unscarred by any incidents. The chief of police should not appear at the table personally, but a key member of the command staff who has his

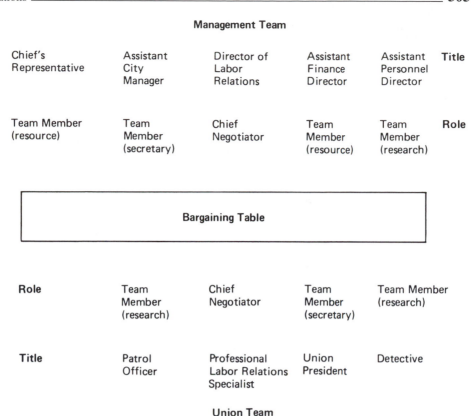

Management Team

Chief's Representative	Assistant City Manager	Director of Labor Relations	Assistant Finance Director	Assistant Personnel Director	**Title**
Team Member (resource)	Team Member (secretary)	Chief Negotiator	Team Member (resource)	Team Member (research)	**Role**

		Bargaining Table	

Role	Team Member (research)	Chief Negotiator	Team Member (secretary)	Team Member (research)
Title	Patrol Officer	Professional Labor Relations Specialist	Union President	Detective

Union Team

FIGURE 9-2. The management and union bargaining teams. [From Charles W. Maddox, *Collective Bargaining in Law Enforcement* (Springfield, Ill.: Charles C Thomas, 1975), p. 57, by permission and with modification.]

confidence should. The appearance of the chief at the table makes the task of leadership more difficult; to appear there on equal footing with the union's bargaining team on one day and then to step back atop the organizational hierarchy on the next requires greater adjustments by both the chief and the union members than the creation of any benefits associated with his presence are worth. Although not depicted in Figure 9-2, an assistant city attorney may also sit with the management team.

The issues, the way in which they are presented, and the flexibility that both sides have will impact strongly upon how the bargaining sessions will go. Perhaps equally important are the decisions made as to who will represent each side in what role at the table. It is not uncommon in evolving or newly established bargaining relationships to find that both parties put great effort into preparing for negotiations but make the selection of their representatives without the same thought. Zealots, those with "axes to grind," and firebrands are poor choices as are those with sarcastic, acrid, or abrasive personalities. The purpose of bargaining is to produce a bilateral written agreement to which both parties will bind themselves during its lifetime. This is not only a profoundly important task, but one that is sufficiently difficult— witness the collapse of the mayor of Toledo, Ohio, in 1979 following an all-night bargaining session with representatives of 3,500 striking city employees—without including people on either side who have an agenda other than negotiating in good faith or whose personalities create yet another obstacle. For these reasons, management must exercise careful consideration in deciding who will represent the police department at the table and, if necessary, influence the selection of the city's other representatives.

The Scope of Bargaining

The scope of bargaining refers to the decision as to what aspects of the employment relationship should, or should not, be subject to joint determination at the bargaining table.[34] Management prefers a narrow scope of negotiations since it means less shared power; the union's preference is for the widest possible scope. An analysis of police contracts reveals that only 9 percent had the "strongest" management rights clauses, suggesting that administrators have not been vigorous in preserving their managerial prerogatives by limiting the participation of labor organizations in the decision-making process.[35] The applicable state statute may categorize matters within the scope of bargaining as being either mandatory or nonnegotiable, with other matters not specifically identified considered permissible.

The level of specificity in the wording of the scope of bargaining provision varies from state to state. For example in Alaska, California, Connecticut, Kentucky, and Florida, the mandatory scope of bargaining provided for statutorily, essentially includes the "terms and conditions of employment, including wages and hours," whereas Nevada's statute covering local government employees enumerates over twenty specific factors within the mandatory scope of negotiations, such as the total number of days work required of an employee in a work year.

As a rule of thumb, the scope of bargaining typically makes policy decisions by management a reserved preserve. However, "since virtually every proposal submitted by either party at the bargaining table affects policy and employment conditions—the turf of management on the one hand and employees on the other—it is often a difficult task to identify which proposals fall into the reserved policy category."[36] When the courts have been called upon to decide the issue, they have recognized the impracticability of drawing a hard and fast line between "terms and conditions of employment," which are bargainable, and "policy determinations," which are ordinarily not.[37] In accommodating these two considerations, one often-cited case held that, while management is not required to negotiate a policy decision, it must negotiate with respect to the impact of the policy decision on the conditions of employment.[38] Thus, the policy decision to use civilians in office work positions to free the more costly time of sworn officers for field duties or to replace two officer cars with one officer car is not negotiable, but its impact is—and may meet stiff opposition from the employee organization as in Boston—although some civilianization has occurred without significant union opposition in such places as New York City, New Haven, Baltimore, Dayton, and Hartford.[39]

Preparing for Negotiations

Management can ill afford to simply wait until the employee organization prepares its demands and presents them; effective action requires considerable effort on management's part before it receives the union's proposal. Management's negotiating team must be selected, agreement with the union obtained on the site where the actual negotiations will take place, the bargaining schedule must be established in conjunction with the union, and various types of data and information gathered, tabulated, and analyzed. While final preparations for negotiating will begin several months prior to the first bargaining sessions, the preparation process is a continuous one; management should begin preparing for the next year's negotiations as soon as this year's are completed. The demands not obtained by the union in the past year may be brought up again in this year's bargaining sessions, and management should be prepared for this.

Various types of records should be kept and summaries made of such factors as the union membership; types and outcomes of grievances; the costs of settling grievances; the numbers, kinds, and consequences of any contract violations by the employee organization; the subject matters brought before the union-management committee during the life of the expiring contract and the disposition of them; and the themes reflected in the union's newsletter. Additionally, just as the employee organization's bargaining team is doing, the management team must be familiarizing itself with changes in the consumer price index and provisions of recent contracts in similarly situated jurisdictions and conducting its own wage and benefit survey or cooperating with the union on one.

From all these and other sources, it is essential that management do three things. First, it must develop fairly specific anticipations as to what the union will be seeking and the relative importance of each demand to the union. Second, it must develop its position with respect to the anticipated preliminary demands that it believes the union will present. Third, it must develop the objectives that it seeks to achieve during the forthcoming process of bilateral determination. If it is not already an institutionalized practice, arrangements should be made to have the union submit its demands in writing some agreed-upon number of days before the first scheduled round of negotiations. These demands may be submitted in either the form of a proposed contract or as a "shopping list," which simply lists the demands being made. The presentation of the demands in writing before the first bargaining session allows for a more productive use of the time allotted for the first negotiating session.

If management has done a good job, there will be relatively few surprises when the proposed contract is submitted. Surprises do not indicate that management's preparation was wasted; the knowledge gained through the process of anticipating the union's demands add to the negotiating team's depth of understanding and overall confidence, key ingredients of bargaining table success. It is difficult to know precisely when management's bargaining team is prepared, but a lack of preparation is detected easily and is capitalized upon by the employee organization.

The Negotiating Sessions

The publicity and attending atmosphere preceding the negotiating sessions focuses considerable attention on them and may be barometers of, or influence, the way in which they unfold. However, prebargaining publicity is also part of attempts to influence public opinion, to impress the public or rank-and-file members with the city's or union's resolve, and to create a façade behind which both sides may maneuver for advantage. Thus, one should not be too encouraged or discouraged about the content of such publicity; it should be considered and evaluated, but not relied on solely as an informational source.

The number of bargaining sessions may run from one to several dozen, lasting from thirty minutes to ten or more hours, although half-day sessions are more common, depending on how close or far apart the union and management are when they begin to meet face to face. Traditionally, any means of making verbatim transcripts, such as the use of a stenographer or tape recorder, have generally been excluded from the bargaining sessions, as it was believed that they tended to impede the progress of negotiations because people would begin speaking for the record.

In a related vein, the enactment of Florida's "sunshine law" opened up many previously closed governmental meetings to the general public, including bargaining sessions, and stirred up some controversy. Advocates of the legislation argued that it opened government up to the people and would make it both more responsive and responsible. With respect to its application to collective negotiations, critics of the law maintained that the real bargaining would be done secretly, that the scheduled public bargaining sessions would be merely a ritualistic acting out of what had been agreed upon privately, and that real negotiating would be difficult because both sides would tend to "play to the audience." This last point is underscored by one negotiator's wry observation that bargaining under the sunshine law was like "a Roman circus with kibitzers."[40]

At the first meeting, friendly conversation may be passed across the table or there may be merely strained greetings before the formal session begins. Much like the prenegotiations publicity, this may, or may not, be reflective of how the session will go. Friendly conversation may suggest that rapid and amicable bargaining will follow, but, instead, no mutually acceptable positions are reached because the friendly conversation has veiled only thinly the hostility or aggressiveness of one or both sides, which quickly comes to the fore. On the other hand, strained greetings may reflect the heavy responsibility that each party to the negotiations feels and quick progress may follow.

Representatives of the Florida Police Benevolent Association at the bargaining table with State of Florida officials during the negotiations for members of the State Law Enforcement Supervisors Unit. (Photo courtesy of the Florida Police Benevolent Association.)

In the initial session, the chief negotiator for each party will make an opening statement; management's representative will often go first, touching on general themes such as the need for patience and the obligation to bargain in good faith. The union's negotiator generally will follow this up by voicing support for such sentiments and will outline what the union seeks to achieve under the terms of the new contract. Ground rules for the bargaining may then be reviewed, modified as mutually agreed upon, or developed. The attention then shifts to the terms of the contract that the union is proposing and the contract is examined thoroughly in a "walkthrough" during which time management seeks to learn what the union means by particular wording. This is a time-consuming process but of great importance because both parties need to share a common understanding of what it is they are attempting to commit each other to or there will be frequent unresolved conflicts and many complex and expensive grievances filed during the lifetime of the contract. For purposes of illustration, the union may have proposed that "vehicles will be properly maintained to protect the health and safety of officers." Discussion of this proposal may reveal that their expectations are much more specific:

1. This is to apply to all vehicles, including marked, semimarked, and unmarked.
2. Each patrol vehicle, whether marked, semimarked, or unmarked, will be replaced at 60,000 miles.
3. All vehicles will be equipped with radial tires.
4. Plexiglass protectors will be installed between the front and rear seats.
5. Shotguns in locking mounts accessible from the front seat will be provided for in all marked and semimarked cars.
6. First-aid kits of a particular type will be placed in all vehicles.

Another illustration is reflected in Table 9-1; assuming that the union is seeking a two-year contract and wants a 20 percent raise during the lifetime of the contract, there are several ways that the cost of that raise might be spread. Management must find out what the union is bargaining for in very specific terms and then cost it out so that the administration knows the budgetary implications of its commitments and counterproposals beforehand.[41] The walkthrough may take several sessions to complete; during this time, little bargaining is being done, as management is basically attempting to obtain clarity about what the union's expectations are.

For bargaining purposes, the union will have categorized the clauses in the proposed contract as being (1) "expendable," meaning that under certain circumstances it will be withdrawn as a symbol of good faith; (2) a "trade-off," indicating that it will be dropped as total or partial payment for obtaining some other benefit; (3) "negotiable," meaning that the benefit needs to be obtained in one form or another; and (4) "nonnegotiable," meaning that the benefit is wanted exactly as proposed.[42] Management will study the information gained from the walkthrough for several days, and then both parties will return to the table. Management then responds to the union's proposal by indicating which clauses it: (1) "accepted," (2) "accepted with minor modification," (3) "rejected," and (4) to which it wishes to make its own proposals and counterproposals. Management cannot simply reject a clause out of hand; to do so would not constitute bargaining in good faith. Instead, it must give a reason for the rejection that is reasonable, such as an actual inability to pay.

Having been told formally of management's position on the contract proposed, the bargaining begins, concentrating on the items on which agreement can be reached

TABLE 9-1. Alternative Ways to Costing out a 20 percent Raise over a Two-Year Contract

1. 10% increase each year of contract	
Year 1 cost: 10% of $1,019,200	= $101,920
Year 2 cost: 10% of year 1	
wages, $1,121,120	= 112,112
plus continuation of year 1	= 101,920
	$315,952
2. 15% increase in year 1; 5% in year 2	
Year 1 cost: 15% of $1,019,200	= $152,880
Year 2 cost: 5% of year 1 payroll	
of $1,172,080	= 58,604
plus continuation of year 1	= 152,880
	$364,364
3. 20% in year 1; nothing in year 2	
Year 1 cost: 20% of $1,019,200	= $203,840
Year 2: no new increase but	
continuation of year 1 raise	= 203,840
	$407,680

Source: W. D. Heisel and Gordon S. Skinner, *Costing Union Demands* (Washington, D.C.: International Personnel Management Association, 1976), p. 13.

immediately or fairly rapidly. Such an approach helps to foster a spirit of mutualism that can be useful in dealing with the issues about which there are substantial differences. As bargaining enters the final stages, the issues that must be dealt with usually become fewer but also more difficult in terms of securing agreement about them.

At such points, "side trips" may threaten to make the sessions unproductive. These side trips may involve wild accusations, old recriminations, character assassinations, or discussion of a specific clause in philosophical or intellectual terms as a means of not dealing with the concrete realities that may be threatening and anxiety provoking for one or both parties. At these times a caucus or even a slightly longer space of time than ordinary until the next session may give enough time for tempers to calm or for more perspective to be gained.

Ultimately, unless a total impasse is reached, agreement will be obtained on the terms of a new contract. The union's membership will vote on the contract as a whole. If approved by the membership, the contract then goes before the necessary governmental officials and bodies, such as the legislative unit that appropriates the funds, for its approval.

Bargaining Impasse Resolution

Even parties bargaining in good faith may not be able to resolve their differences by themselves and require the invocation of some type of impasse resolution technique. The essence of all bargaining impasse resolution techniques is the insertion of a neutral third party who facilitates, suggests, or compels an agreement. Of present concern are the three major forms of impasse resolution: mediation, fact-finding, and arbitration. All, several, or only one of these techniques may be provided for in a particular jurisdiction. In Massachusetts and Iowa for example, all the techniques are provided for by state statute. In Tennessee, covered workers have access only to mediation and fact-finding, whereas issues involving Rhode Island state police officers go to arbitration if an agreement is not reached in thirty days.[43]

MEDIATION

"Mediation arises when a third party, called the mediator, comes in to help the adversaries with the negotiations."[44] This person may be a professional mediator, a local clergyman whom both parties respect and have confidence in, or some other party. The mediating will most often be done by one person, although three- and even five-member panels may be used.

In most states mediation may be requested by either labor or management, although in some states both parties must request it, and in others the PERC can intervene on its own initiative. The mediator may be appointed by the parties to the negotiations or by a governmental body. Meeting with labor and management either jointly and/ or separately,[45] the task of the mediator is to build agreement about the issue or issues involved by reopening communications between the two groups. An analysis of various experiences suggests that 50 to 70 percent of the issues going to mediation are resolved successfully.[46]

The mediator will remove himself or herself from a case when (1) an agreement is reached, (2) one of the parties to the negotiations requests his or her departure, (3) the agreed-upon time comes to use the next step in the impasse resolution procedure, or (4) the mediator feels that his or her acceptability or effectiveness is exhausted.[47] Since the mediator is without any means to compel an agreement, a chief advantage to the process is that it preserves the nature of collective bargaining by maintaining the decision-making power in the hands of the parties involved. Balancing this advantage, however, is the belief that the effectiveness of mediation depends upon a certain level of sophistication by those conducting the negotiations, and where this condition does not exist, the mediator may spend more time simply educating the two parties than in helping them resolve their differences.[48]

FACT-FINDING

The designation of this technique as fact-finding is something of a misnomer; one study found that about half the respondents were sure of the facts and another 28 percent were only in "slight doubt" with respect to them.[49] Much of the work in fact-finding is the interpretation of facts and determining what weight to attach to them.

Appointed in the same ways as are mediators, fact-finders also do not have the means to impose a settlement of the dispute. Fact-finders may sit alone or as part of a panel, which often consists of three people. If a panel is used, a common procedure is for management and labor each to appoint a representative and those two pick the third person who is designated as the neutral. If the two appointed members cannot agree on the third, then the PERC, the American Arbitration Association (AAA), or other body or official as provided for in the applicable state law will do so. In some states the representatives that management and labor placed on the panel have no part in the selection of the neutral, it being a decision of the PERC. Rarely does a panel consist of three neutrals due to the cost. If a single fact-finder is used, the parties may agree upon one: he may be appointed by a body such as the PERC; or a group such as the AAA supplies a list of names and labor, and then management and the union take turns striking off names from a list of seven until only one remains, that person being then appointed as the fact-finder.

The fact-finding hearing is quasi-judicial, although less strict rules of evidence are applied. Both labor and management may be represented by legal counsel, verbatim transcripts are commonly made, and each side generally presents its position through the use of a single spokesperson along with some exhibits. Following the closing arguments, the fact-finder will prepare the report containing his or her recommendations that must be submitted in a specified number of days, such as within thirty days of appointment or ten days following the close of the hearings. A finding of one study was that 89 percent of the disputes submitted to fact-finding are resolved,[50] although other research found that the fact-finder's recommendations were the basis for settlement of 60 to 70 percent of the issues.[51]

In the majority of instances, the fact-finder's recommendations will be made public at some point. However, the report should first be given to the two parties for their use for some specified period of time so that they might carry out further negotiations free of distractions. While there is some minor debate as to whether fact-finders should even make recommendations, the majority position is described aptly by the view that fact-finding without recommendations is "as useful as a martini without gin."[52]

ARBITRATION

In most respects—including the selection and appointment of arbitrators and as a process—arbitration parallels fact-finding; it differs chiefly in that the "end product of arbitration is a final and binding decision that sets the terms of the settlement and with which the parties are legally required to comply."[53] The arbitrator's jurisdiction may apply to all matters or may be limited, as in cases involving municipal employees in Maine, in that it is binding only with respect to noneconomic issues. Although the term "advisory arbitration" is occasionally encountered, it is a contradiction of terms because arbitration is compulsory and binding; "advisory arbitration" is, instead, another term that is used occasionally to describe the process of fact-finding.[54] Arbitration may be compulsory or voluntary:

> it is compulsory when mandated by law, regulation and/or Executive Order and is binding upon the parties even if one of them is unwilling to comply. On the other hand it is voluntary when the parties undertake of their own volition to use the procedure. Voluntarism could be the result of a statute which permits, rather than requires, the parties to submit disputed issues to binding arbitration on their own initiative. It could also arise from the parties' own initiative with respect to future contract impasses pursuant to a permanent negotiation procedure.[55]

Even when entered into voluntarily, however, arbitration is compulsory and binding upon the parties who have agreed to it.

Although some states now permit strikes under certain conditions, the more prevalent public policy choice has been no strikes, particularly with respect to providers of services viewed as critical, most notably correctional, police, fire, and hospital workers.[56] Simultaneously, the final step provided for in resolving most bargaining disputes has been some provision short of arbitration. The net result was that labor was denied the use of its ultimate tactic, the strike, and also had no neutral "final court of appeal" in which to resolve a bargaining impasse. The inherent unfairness of this situation became easier to deal with as public sector collective bargaining began gaining acceptance, and by 1985 the number of states providing arbitration for public employee bargaining disputes numbered 24.[57] Although compulsory arbitration tended initially to be provided for only those occupational groups viewed as providers of critical services, there has been some movement to broaden the coverage to include other or all types of employees.[58]

One form of bargaining impasse arbitration that began to emerge about 1973 is final offer selection (FOS); presently less than a dozen states provide for some form of it. In FOS, each party submits its last offer, and the arbitrator or arbitrators select, without modification, one of them as being final and binding. Although FOS may be done on an item-by-item basis, as for example in the case of police and firefighters in Massachusetts and Michigan, it is usually done on a package or whole-contract basis.[59] Ohio's 1984 public bargaining law gives all employees except public safety personnel the right to strike, with a ten-day mandatory advance notice. As an alternative to the use of a strike, public safety personnel in Ohio are given item-by-item final offer selection (FOS).

Although court cases have challenged the use of arbitration on the basis of its being an unlawful delegation of power, the courts have generally upheld its use.[60] Moreover, even in considering the ability to pay, several courts have held that the employer must make available the funds necessary to implement an agreement that has been reached by the parties.[61]

In one unusual situation, a contract was also found to take precedence over a city's charter:

> The Michigan Supreme Court backed up a line of Michigan Employees Relations Commission decisions, in *Detroit Police Officers Association v. City of Detroit and Michigan Employment Relations Commission* (1974), and held that a residency requirement cannot be imposed upon the police even if a voter referendum amended the city charter to establish such a requirement. The court explained that "residency is a mandatory subject of bargaining under PERA (the state bargaining law) and collective bargaining cannot be avoided through the enactment of a city ordinance."[62]

Grievances

Why Grievances Are Inevitable

There is a notion that, once the bargaining is completed and an agreement signed, the most difficult part of labor relations has been passed through and easy times are ahead. Such a notion is natural. Bargaining is high drama, with a great deal of attention focused upon it by the news media and the community. The production of an agreement acceptable to both the union and management is in fact a significant achievement. Beyond it, however, is the day-to-day administration of the contract during its lifetime. Since the contract outlines the duties and rights of each party in its dealings with the other, it is ironically not only the basis for accord, but also for conflict:

> It would, of course, be ideal for all concerned, including the public, if in the negotiation of the agreement both parties were able to draft a comprehensive document capable of foreseeing and forestalling all potential disputes which might arise during its life. Unfortunately, such crystal-ball vision is usually lacking, particularly when the parties are pressured to obtain agreement in a period of negotiation tensions and time deadlines. It is not

humanly possible in a new collective bargaining relationship to draft such a perfect document.

Therefore it is inevitable that questions will arise concerning the interpretation and application of the document drafted in the haste and pressure of contract negotiations. What is the meaning of a particular clause of the agreement? How does it apply, if at all, to a set of facts which occurred after the agreement was signed? These questions are not at all uncommon in any contractual relationship.[63]

The Definition of a Grievance

While in common usage a grievance is a complaint or expression of dissatisfaction by an employee with respect to some aspect of employment, what can be grieved formally is usually defined within the contract itself. Grievances may be limited to matters discussed specifically in the contract, primarily contract related, or anything pertaining to the job, as is seen in these clauses from three different agreements:

1. A grievance is defined as a complaint arising out of the interpretation, application or compliances with the provisions of this agreement.

2. For the purpose of this agreement the term "grievance" shall mean the difference or dispute between any policeman and the Borough, or a superior officer in the chain of command, with respect to the interpretation, application, claim or breach, or violation of any of the provisions of this agreement, or with respect to any equipment furnished by the Borough.

3. A grievance, for the purposes of this article, shall be defined as any controversy, complaint, misunderstanding or dispute arising between an employee or employees and the City, or between the Brotherhood and the City.

The Grievance Procedure

The grievance procedure is a formal process that has been the subject of bilateral negotiations and that is detailed in the contract. It involves the seeking of redress of the grievance through progressively higher levels of authority and most often culminates in binding arbitration,[64] as in cases in Beaumont, Texas, Pittsburgh, Pennsylvania, Sacramento, California, and Grand Rapids, Michigan, by a tripartite panel or a single neutral. A typical sequence of steps would include the following:

Grievances shall be presented in the following manner and every effort shall be made by the parties to secure prompt disposition of grievances:

Step 1.

The member shall first present his grievance to his immediate supervisor within five (5) days of the occurrence which gave rise to the grievance. Such contact shall be on an informal and oral basis, and the supervisor shall respond orally to the grievance within five (5) working days.

Step 2.

Any grievance which cannot be satisfactorily settled in Step 1 shall be reduced to writing by the member and shall next be taken up by his division commander. Said grievance shall be presented to the division commander within five (5) working days from receipt of the answer in Step 1. The division commander shall, within five (5) working days, render his decision on the grievance in writing.

Step 3.

Any grievance not satisfactorily settled in Step 2 shall be forwarded, in writing, within five (5) working days, to the Chief of Police, who shall render his written decision on the grievance within five (5) working days.

Step 4.

If the grievant is not satisfied with the response of the Chief of Police, he will forward his written grievance within five (5) working days to the City Manager, who will have ten (10) working days to reply, in writing.

Step 5.

If the grievance has not been settled to the satisfaction of the grievant in Step 4, the matter will be subject to arbitration. An arbiter will be selected, without undue delay, according to the rules of the American Arbitration Association. The arbiter will hold an arbitration hearing. When the hearing has ended, the arbiter will be asked to submit his award, in writing, within fifteen (15) days. His decision shall be final and binding on both parties.[65]

Because the union must share equally the cost of arbitration with management, the decision to take a grievance to the last step is customarily the prerogative of the union rather than the individual officer who is grieved.

Not only are the steps of the grievance procedure enumerated in the agreement, but also such matters as the manner of selecting the tripartite panel or the single neutral, along with their duties and powers. If the panel is used, management and the union each appoints one member and those two appoint the third; where the two cannot agree upon the neutral, the contract may provide for the referral of the choice of a chairperson to a designated agency[66] such as the American Arbitration Association, the Federal Mediation and Conciliation Service, or a state agency. Where a single arbitrator is used, a variety of techniques are employed in selection, ranging from agreement on the person by the union and management on a case-by-case basis, to the appointment of a permanent arbitrator during the lifetime of the contract, to having an outside agency submit a list of qualified arbitrators from which management and the union take turns eliminating names until only one remains or they agree to accept any of some number remaining, such as three.

The arbitration hearing is quasi-judicial with more relaxed rules of evidence than are found in either criminal or civil proceedings. Witnesses may, or may not, be sworn, although they generally are. Ordinarily, since the arbitrator is a creature of the parties to the proceeding, he or she will be guided by them on the decision of whether to swear witnesses but will require an oath where the parties cannot agree on the matter. The burden of proof is on the grieving party, except in discipline cases where it always is on the employer. The parties may be represented by legal counsel at the hearing, and the format will generally be obtaining agreement of what the issue is, the opening statements by each side (with the grieving party going first), examination and cross-examination of witnesses, and closing arguments in the reverse of the order in which the opening statements were made.

Arbitration Issues and Decision Making

There is great variety as to what ends up before an arbitrator, and one has only to review *Labor Arbitration in Government,* a monthly summary of awards and fact-finding recommendations to appreciate the diversity of issues. For example, the Boston Police Superior Officers Federation argued unsuccessfully that the transfer of primary authority for enforcing sick leave regulations from the commanding officers of districts to staff inspection was a violation of their contract[67] and in Auburn, New York, a member of Security and Law Enforcement Employees Council 82 under indictment maintained that the city had deprived him of the opportunity to obtain double pay for working holidays by keeping him on the payroll but not actually permitting him to work. The city negated the grievant's claim by pointing out that, because criminal proceedings were pending against the officer, it could do no more than maintain him on the payroll, but on a nonduty status, during that period.[68]

Despite the many different types of matters that can be and are grieved, the largest single category of cases, about 90 percent of the total, brought to an arbitration hearing are those involving discipline against the officer. While some arbitration decision making is not difficult because one side chooses to take a losing case to arbitration, because of its symbolic importance, the need to appear supportive of union members, or to be seen as strongly supporting one's managers, other decisions are complex as they seek to obtain equity in a maze of conflicting testimony, ambiguous contract language, changes from past practices, credibility of evidence, and valid and persuasive cases by both parties that emphasize the relative importance of different factors. Arbitrators often employ checklists in conducting the hearings to ensure that all relevant points are covered. In a discipline case, the list might include the following:

1. Was the rule that management sought to enforce, along with the possible consequences of noncompliance, properly promulgated, so that the grieving officer was aware of what was expected and that discipline would in all probability result from disobedience?
2. Did the police department make a fair and objective investigation into the alleged wrongdoing and all of its surrounding circumstances?
3. Does the penalty invoked meet the test of being even-handed?
4. Does the evidence support the employer's conclusion that a disciplinary offense was committed?
5. If the evidence does support the police department's conclusion, was the penalty imposed appropriate with respect to the notion of progressively more serious discipline and/or justified by the gravity of the offense?[69]

If an employee is found to have done what he or she was accused of, the arbitrator may then consider certain factors that might mitigate the severity of the penalty, including the officer's years of service to the department; the provocation, if any, that led to the alleged offense; the officer's previous disciplinary history, including the numbers, types, and recency of other violations; the consistency with which the applicable rule is enforced; and the penalties applied for similar offenses by other officers.[70]

Table 9-2 summarizes the actions ordered by arbitrators in police grievance cases; the percent column adds up to more than 100 percent because of multiple responses; e.g., an officer could be reinstated and given back pay or reinstated with a reprimand or suspension.

One study of police grievances that were arbitrated reveals that the officer involved in the grievance was assigned to uniformed patrol 84 percent of the time, another police officer was involved in the incident slightly more than half the time (56 percent of the cases), the grieving officer's supervisor supported him or her 14 percent of the time, and in exactly three-quarters of the cases the officer involved had a clear disciplinary record.[71] Given that police unions must be selective in terms of the

TABLE 9-2. Actions Ordered by Arbitrators in Police Grievance Cases

Action Ordered	Percent
Officer awarded back pay	39.1
Department to change practices, such as discipline	32.8
Reinstatement of officer	29.7
Officer suspended	21.9
Discharge of officer	10.9
Reprimand issued to officer	6.3

Source: Helen Lavan and Cameron Carley, "Analysis of Arbitrated Employee Grievance Cases in Police Departments," *Journal of Collective Negotiations in the Public Sector,* 14: 3 (1985), from Table 1, p. 250.

cases they take to arbitration, the results are not too surprising: the union won 77 percent of the grievances.

A key advantage to arbitration is the speed with which issues are heard and a decision made as compared with seeking resolution of the dispute in court. The deadline for issuance of the award may be established by statute, the parties, by some governmental authority, such as PERC, the arbitrator, if he or she is acting as an independent and is without other guidance, or the body appointing the arbitrator.[72] The American Arbitration Association requires arbitrators to render their decision in writing within thirty days of (1) the conclusion of the hearing, (2) the receipt of the hearing transcript, if one has been made, or (3) the receipt of posthearing briefs.[73] In general, except in such instances as fraud or bias by the arbitrator, the hearing officer's decision, where binding arbitration is provided for, will not be reviewed by the courts.

Job Actions

"Job action" is a label used to describe several different types of activities in which employees may engage to express their dissatisfaction with a particular person, event, or condition or to attempt to influence the outcome of some matter pending before decision makers. Job actions carry the signal "we are here, organized, and significant, and the legitimacy of our position must be recognized."

Through job actions, employees seek to create pressure that may cause the course of events to be shifted to a position more favorable or acceptable to them. Such pressure may come from a variety of quarters, including the city manager, elected officials, influential citizens, merchant associations, political party leaders, and neighborhood groups. Under such pressure, administrators may agree to something that they might not under more relaxed circumstances. When ill-advised agreements are made, they may be attributable at a general level to pressure but on a more specific plane to such factors as stress, miscalculations, the desire to appear responsive to some superior or constituency, or the mistaken belief that the implications of a hastily conceived and coerced agreement can be dealt with effectively later. Four types of job actions are recognizable: the vote of confidence, work slowdowns, work speedups, and work stoppages.

BOX 9-3.

Anatomy of a Grievance: Partners in Crime Busting Are Vindicated

Talented Murder Sleuths Were Harassed, Improperly Punished, D.C. Board Says

By JOHN WARD ANDERSON, *Washington Post Staff Writer*

It was a murder case that tested the ingenuity and resourcefulness of homicide investigators Tom Kilcullen and Bill Corboy. There was no body to prove that a murder actually had been committed in the District, and to compound matters the D.C. police department refused to pay for their trip to Harrisburg, Pa., to interview witnesses and gather evidence.

So they took a vacation day, jumped into Kilcullen's station wagon and drove to Harrisburg, where they spent hours with the FBI and local police piecing together a case against two men who abducted a young woman, drove her to the District, raped her in a hotel here, then shot her to death and dumped her body into the Potomac River.

No trace of Patsy Gaisior was ever found, but when the two men accused in her death came to trial in D.C. Superior Court—one in August 1983 and the other seven months later—prosecutors won convictions on the basis of Corboy and Kilcullen's investigation, much of it conducted on their own time.

It was the sort of dedication that had earned the homicide investigation partners a reputation among other detectives, prosecutors and even public defenders as "the perfect team."

Then it all came apart. Corboy and Kilcullen fell out of favor with their superiors and their partnership was disbanded. They were transferred to a different shift and their days off were changed. Corboy was eventually dropped from the homicide squad and sent back to a foot patrol in the 4th police district. Last year, while on duty, he was thrown from a motorcycle in an accident that left him partially disabled and his future in doubt.

"It was a tragic and stupid loss for the city," said a ranking prosecutor in the U.S. attorney's office. "He was born to be a homicide investigator."

Now, the city's Public Employees Relations Board has upheld a hearing examiner's ruling that Corboy and Kilcullen were unfairly harassed and improperly punished because of the anti-union animus of police officials. Those officials, including Deputy Chief Alfonso Gibson, head of the department's Criminal Investigations Division and one of the city's top police officials, subjected the pair to arbitrary threats, reprisals and discrimination, the examiner found.

The decision was hailed by Corboy's and Kilcullen's colleagues, one calling it a "monument" to their "fortitude, gumption and tenacity."

"They really did make a perfect pair. There was almost too much talent there to stay together," said another prosecutor, adding that the story of their partnership is about being "broken up and broken."

At 28, Corboy was the youngster, detailed part time to homicide, where he pored over old case jackets with a seemingly photographic memory for detail. His colleagues considered him one of the best new investigators the department had ever had, with innate investigative skills that earned him a nickname: The Future.

Kilcullen, now 42, was the savvy veteran, a teacher at the prestigious homicide school who had solved 88 percent of the 156 cases he had investigated in 12 years in the homicide branch—one of the best arrest rates in the department. He had a knack for recognizing and nurturing talent, colleagues say, and in Corboy he saw the makings of a great detective, someone who could carry on a tradition of excellence.

Once "The Future," Corboy is now called "The Yo-Yo," a reference to the changes in his fortune that started in the fall of 1983. It was then, after being on a "temporary detail" to the homicide branch for 2½ years, that Corboy started asking about being promoted from officer to detective, with the accompanying pay raise, and being assigned to the squad full time.

He asked the police union, the Fraternal Order of Police, to look into his status. Deputy Chief Gibson called Kilcullen on the carpet for giving his young partner "bad advice" about going to the union, according to the PERB.

Both men filed an unfair labor practice complaint in December 1983 with the PERB and were criticized by their superiors for being disloyal. The two were split up and Corboy was later transferred from the homicide squad.

The change in partners, the hearing examiner later found, "was intended to teach Officer Corboy and Detective Kilcullen a lesson . . . primarily as a punitive measurement."

After Corboy was transferred from the homicide squad, he was sent to the 4th District. Last October, as he was returning a stolen motorcycle to the police station, he rounded a corner and hit some gravel on the road, and the motorcycle spun out from under him.

Doctors put two three-inch pins in his left knee to bolt seven fractures together. Now he walks with a limp and is assigned to a desk. He has no police powers, no badge, no gun. Instead of investigating murders, he answers telephones.

"My authority has been suspended because of my condition," he explained recently. "If someone calls in with a tip, I log it in. I just answer the phones, or if there is substantial information, I can do some background investigation in the office."

Although the hearing examiner ordered that the police department "and all its agents and officials shall cease and desist from taking reprisals, retaliation and discriminatory actions against Officer Corboy and Detective Kilcullen," he did not order any corrective or punitive measures.

Chief of Police Maurice T. Turner Jr. said in an interview last week that the department would comply with Corboy's wishes to return to the homicide branch but that any move depends on his physical condition. Turner said Corboy would be promoted as soon as he "can pass a physical" and his leg does not prohibit him from performing police duties.

The labor dispute pitted Corboy and Kilcullen against the Metropolitan Police Department of the District of Columbia and codefendants Deputy Chief Gibson, Lt. John Harlow and Capt. Jimmy Wilson, who was then head of the homicide branch and is now inspector in charge of the department's Internal Affairs Division.

Papers filed with the PERB about the unfair labor practice complaint, are replete with contradictory statements made during 12 days of bitter testimony last year.

According to the hearing examiner's decision, which PERB upheld last month after an appeal by the police department, the examiner frequently chose to believe Corboy and Kilcullen's version of the facts and "did not credit" the testimony of the police department's witnesses.

A key element were notes taken by Corboy and Kilcullen after conversations they had with officials and others in the homicide branch.

On numerous occasions when witnesses for the police department said they could not recall details of conversations or contradicted Corboy and Kilcullen's version, the partners offered their notes to support their testimony.

The police department countered that the notes were "reworked statements" that had been "cleverly distorted" by Corboy and Kilcullen.

As a result of the allegations, Corboy and Kilcullen asked Assistant U.S. Attorney Steve Gordon to testify as a character witness in their behalf. When Deputy Chief Gibson learned of Gordon's plans to testify, he called U.S. Attorney Joseph diGenova and said it would "strain relations" and would not "serve to foster a unifying and amicable relationship" between their offices, according to memos on the call written by Gibson and diGenova.

The hearing examiner later found that, while the phone call "could be perceived as threatening," it did not prevent Gordon from testifying. "It is reasonable to conclude, however, that the telephone call was an effort to impede the proceedings in this case," the examiner wrote.

And, in every instance in which the notes were offered as evidence, the hearing examiner deemed them accurate. The examiner also pointed to numerous occasions when he could find no "credible" evidence to support the police department's version of events.

Gibson called the PERB ruling a "departmental matter" and said he did not want to discuss it. Inspector Wilson said he has "always honored the role of the union" and that changes in Corboy's and Kilcullen's assignments were "made with the intent to increase the effectiveness of the total [homicide] unit." Lt. Harlow is on leave and could not be reached for comment.

Police Chief Turner said that in his opinion, the hearing examiner did not question the "veracity" of police officials, but simply ruled that the officials were "retaliatory."

Turner said he has not yet decided if he will punish the three officials who the PERB said violated Corboy and Kilcullen's rights. "If it does come, it will probably be a reprimand. . . . It could be a written warning" placed in their personnel files.

Gary Hankins, labor committee chairman of the FOP, said last week, "There should be disciplinary action against the people found guilty of the violations, and there should be stern action.

"Police officers are especially sensitive to hypocrisy because we chose a profession that has as its goal the equal application of the law and the protection of the weak against the strong. To see these kinds of problems in our own ranks rankles a police officer and shakes his faith not only in the department but the very basis of our profession."

One legacy of the case has been a notice posted on police department bulletin boards throughout the city reaffirming the right of officers to use the FOP to settle grievances. The notice, which the PERB ordered posted for 60 days, states that "Improper efforts by any officials of the department to discourage such communications or to intimidate members are unlawful and will be punished."

In the homicide branch, where Kilcullen and other detectives still phone Corboy for advice on cases, most are looking forward to his return.

"If someone in my family was murdered, or I was murdered, I want Corboy to work it," a longtime veteran of the branch said. "If Corboy comes back and says I've exhausted all the means, I'm satisfied with that."

Meanwhile, Corboy divides his time between answering phones and going to a physical therapist to try to regain full use of his leg. Doctors, who had said he would never be a police officer again, now say it should be about two years before he's well enough to return to full duty.

Corboy is more optimistic. "When I go down to the therapist's office, I work just as hard there as anywhere else," he said. "I hope by the end of the year to be strong enough to run again and go up and down stairs."

Source: The Washington Post, August 8, 1985, pp. C1 and C7, reprint by permission.

The Vote of Confidence

The vote of confidence, which typically produces a finding of no-confidence when taken, has been used sparingly in law enforcement. It is the method by which rank-and-file members formally signal their displeasure with an administrator and his policies. While votes of confidence have no legal standing, they may have high impact because they are a public and often highly publicized statement. No-confidence votes have played roles in forcing the removal of Chief Robert Digrazia in Montgomery County, Maryland, and perhaps in the retirement of Chief Harold Bastrup in Anaheim, California.[74] Other chiefs receiving votes of no-confidence in the past include Harry Caldwell in Houston, John Rhoads in Prince Georges County, Maryland, and Carl Calkins in Long Beach, California.

While votes of no confidence may produce changes in the leadership of a police department, it is by no means certain that it will. Moreover, such votes may be interpreted as a sign that a chief is making much needed improvements. Following the 1978 vote on Houston's Chief Caldwell, Dale Harris of the Chamber of Commerce said that the vote was to be expected because management was being very aggressive and "exposing a lot of past corruption."[75] Houston City Councilman Louis Macey echoed this stance by observing that "you've got a chief now who is clamping down, making the police officers, at least in the public view, toe the line."[76]

Work Slowdowns

A work slowdown means that, although officers will continue to provide all the usual services, less initiative is used and work is done at a measured pace so that each unit of work takes longer to complete, causing productivity to drop. As productivity decreases, certain benefits are lost and work begins to accumulate. Pressures begin to mount as more and more people begin to perceive the loss of those benefits and experience the delivery of services on an untimely basis. These people then begin using whatever avenues are open to them to try to establish a normal state of affairs by, for example, calling the mayor, complaining to the chief of police, or writing to the members of the city council.

The California Highway Patrol has used a slowdown in the writing of traffic citations to create pressure by cutting revenue; in Phoenix, Arizona, officers slowed down investigations by following regulations meticulously;[77] and in Long Beach, California, members of the Police Officers Association (POA) implemented their notion of "professionalism" to protest a 5.4 percent raise, when they had asked for 10.8 percent; the POA's professionalism resulted in fewer arrests being made due to the "thorough investigation" of cases and the writings of lengthy reports on those investigations.[78] Slowdowns have also occurred in other cities, including Columbus, Georgia, Compton, California, and Louisville, Kentucky. In Louisville, thirty-six officers were suspended when, minutes after the contract in force expired, thirty-two police cars were disabled by flat tires and the radio system was deliberately jammed.[79]

Work Speedups

As the term suggests, the work speedup is an acceleration of activity resulting in a large increase in the productivity of one or more types of police services. The purpose is to create pressure through overproduction. To stimulate contract negotiations, New York City transit police ticketed three times the average number of subway riders for usually ignored violations such as smoking and littering in the hope that angered riders would demand the contract be finalized so that things would return to normal.[80] Other cities, such as Chicago, have had "ticket blizzards"—periods of abnormally high issuances of traffic citations. In Holyoke, Massachusetts, a city of 50,000 persons, police officers handed out 2,000 parking tickets, ten times the normal amount, in less than a week to protest stalled negotiations with the city; not to be outdone, Mayor Ernest Proulx ordered "meter maids" to ticket all illegally parked cars belonging to officers and barred officers on the night shift from using the parking lot behind City Hall.[81] Strict law enforcement tactics, resulting in increased productivity with its attending pressures, have also been used in Fairfax and Arlington counties, Virginia, to protest announced pay raise limitations or to protest pay raises offered.[82]

Work Stoppages

Work stoppages may involve the virtually total withholding of production in one or a limited number of areas of police service or may involve the ultimate job action, the strike, which represents a total withholding of the services of labor.

Examples of work stoppages, in the narrow context, include police officers in Cincinnati, Ohio, refusing to give traffic citations and officers in Phoenix, Arizona, declining to write parking tickets or issue traffic citations for minor violations and refusing off-duty jobs directing traffic around construction sites.[83] In San Diego, members of the POA campaigning for a 22.5 percent pay increase wore black arm bands during a moratorium on traffic citations that lasted ten days; during this period an average of 15 citations per day were issued as compared with the normal daily average of 880.[84]

Although only eleven states—Alaska, Hawaii, Idaho, Illinois, Minnesota, Montana, Ohio, Oregon, Pennsylvania, Vermont, and Wisconsin—have granted at one time or another the limited right to strike to some employees, nationally there are numerous illustrations of police officers striking, including New Orleans; San Francisco; Montebello, Monterey, and Vallejo, California; Pontiac, Michigan; Baltimore; Memphis; Lorain, Cleveland, Youngstown, Warren, and Steubenville, Ohio; Tucson; Detroit; Tuskegee, Alabama; Skokie, Illinois; Albuquerque; Biloxi, Mississippi; New Bern, North Carolina; and sheriffs' deputies in Santa Barbara and Salinas, California, and Jefferson County, Alabama.

Strikes may take a variety of forms such as "sick out" or "blue flu," as has happened in Honolulu; Gennesee County, Michigan; and San Jose, California. In Winthrop, Massachusetts, the entire day shift called in sick;[85] in Harvey, Illinois, twenty-one officers were separated from the service by the chief when they were absent from their jobs for ten days;[86] and in Joplin, Missouri, officers were afflicted with the "bluebonic plague." Strikes thinly veiled as resignations have occurred in Poplar Bluff, Missouri, where twenty-one officers resigned en masse;[87] in Ontario, Oregon, where thirteen officers quit their jobs; in Lafayette, Georgia, where the entire twenty-five-member police department resigned because town officials didn't grant them a 4 percent across-the-board pay increase;[88] and in Oklahoma City. In

New Orleans police officers while on strike in 1979.

Oklahoma City, a land area larger than Los Angeles, all but 16 of 597 officers quit, many throwing their badges on the desk of City Manager Howard McHahan, including one officer recuperating from wounds received while attempting to make an arrest, who was carried into the city manager's office on a stretcher.[89]

While strikes or other job actions are often for reasons that are on the face immediately identifiable as economic, such as a pay raise, others are less clearly so, as in 1979 when the Birmingham police struck when the city announced plans to change the carrier of the city's health insurance coverage from one company to another.[90] Birmingham's policy was to give preference for doing business with the city to companies located within the city, and when Blue Cross-Blue Shield made public its plans to move out of the city, another insurance carrier, whose coverage was not as attractive to the police, was selected. The strike by the police, joined by other city employees, however, forced the city to abandon such a shift for at least one year. A mixture of both economic and social factors may cause the rank and file to act also. In Newark, New Jersey, officers threatened a blue flu if attempts were made to make them abide by the city's residency requirement, a move seen by the police as working an economic hardship on them, along with having significant impact on their families.[91]

The Political Context of Job Actions

While job actions frequently center on economic factors, they may be initiated for reasons that exist almost purely in the political context of police work. Cincinnati officers struck in 1979 to protest the death of Melvin Henze, the fourth Cincinnati officer to die in the line of duty in ten months.[92] The officers flung the keys to their cruisers at a statue honoring the department's dead and walked off the job. The president of the Fraternal Order of Police, Elmer Dunway, told officers not to return to work until after a city council meeting at which police wives and others intended to press for improved weapons, body armor, and the institution of two-officer patrol units. Cincinnati police officers had also complained that lenient judges and parole boards were releasing criminals "to prey upon society" in a city where law enforcers are "grossly undermanned." Within weeks of the strike the Cincinnati City Council voted to give police officers .357 caliber magnum handguns with hollow-point expansion bullets, a move that pleased the officers and their families but drew criticism from black community leaders. Also, in 1979, hundreds of Prince Georges County, Maryland, police officers stayed home from work, without a strike vote, to voice their bitterness at circumstances surrounding the manslaughter conviction of Terrence Johnson for the slaying of two Prince Georges County police officers. The officers felt that the media had misrepresented them and that the county citizens had abandoned them by virtue of what the officers saw as a lenient verdict.[93]

Administrative Reaction to Job Actions

Anticipatory Strategies

There are no simple answers for what police administrators should do in the face of a job action. A short period of ignoring a work slowdown may see its natural dissipation, or it may become more widespread and escalate. Disciplinary action may effectively end a job action, or it may simply serve to aggravate the situation further, causing the job action to intensify and become more protracted. In choosing a course of action, one must read the environment, assess the situation, review alternatives, decide on a course of action, implement it, monitor the impact, and make adjustments as necessary. In short, it is a decision-making process, albeit a delicate one.

The best way in which to handle job actions is for both management and the union to take the position that they have mutual responsibilities to avoid them. This may, however, not be uniformly possible; a union leadership that is seen to be too cooperative with management may, for example, be discredited by rank-and-file members and a sickout may occur. Negotiations that do not meet expectations, however unrealistic, of militant union members may produce a walkout. In general, the following can be expected to reduce the possibility of a job action.[94]

1. The appropriate city officials, both appointed and elected, union leaders, and management must be trained in the tenets and practices of collective bargaining, particularly as they relate to mutual trust and the obligation to bargain in good faith.

2. Formal and informal communications networks should be used freely within city government, the police agency, and the union for the transmission of messages between them. The timely sharing of accurate information is essential to good labor relations in that it reduces the opportunity for misinformation or noninformation to create distance and build barriers.

3. On a periodic basis, key managers from the police department, along with the staff and its labor relations unit, should meet with union leaders and the representatives, including elected officials, of the city who are responsible for the implementation of its labor relations program. This serves to strengthen existing communications networks, it establishes the possibility to open new networks, and it is a continuing affirmation of the mutualism that is central to the process of collective bargaining.

4. Well before any job actions occur, management must develop and publicize the existence of a contingency plan that contemplates as many of the problems as reasonably can be foreseen with respect to each type of job action. For example, in planning for a strike, one must consider such things as how will the rights and property of nonstrikers be protected?[95] What security measures are to be invoked for government buildings and property? What are the minimum levels of personnel and supplies required? What special communications arrangements are necessary? Does the city's insurance extend to coverage of potential liabilities to employees and property? What legal options exist and who has authority to invoke them under what circumstances? What coordination arrangements are needed with other police departments and governmental agencies? What effect will various strike policies have upon labor relations after the strike? How will nonstriking officers and the public react to various strike policies? May a striking employee injured on the picket line be placed on sick leave? Do striking employees accrue leave and retirement credit for the time they were out?

5. In attempting to determine the possibility of various job actions, the philosophy, capabilities, strengths, weaknesses, and propensities of the union, its officers, negotiators, legal counsel, and its members must be assessed. That, along with an estimate of the financial resources of the union, will be useful in anticipating the actions in which it is likely to engage and toward which planning can be directed. Although the hallmark of good planning is that it

provides properly for future states of affairs, management is most likely to underestimate the union's capabilities, and the planning bias should, therefore, be toward an overstatement of what is possible.

During the Job Action

Using a strike as an illustration, police managers must appreciate its long-range implications. The striking officers are engaging, as is the employer, in a power struggle that has an economic impact on both parties. The union is not attempting to divest itself of its employer, and for both legal and practical reasons, the employer cannot unilaterally rid itself of its relationship with the union; at some point in the very near future, it is most likely that they will resume their former relationship.[96] Considering this, managers must be temperate in their private and public remarks regarding striking officers; emotionally laden statements and cynical characterizations regarding strikers may provide a degree of fleeting satisfaction, but at some cost to the rapidity with which antagonisms may be set aside and the organization restored to its normal functioning. The union leadership and the rank-and-file membership have the same obligation; in the face of either management or the union not fulfilling their obligation, it becomes even more important that the other side be restrained in their remarks, or the ensuing trail of recriminations and biting comments will lead only to a degeneration of goodwill and the production of hostility, both of which will have negative effects on future relations.

Managers should strive to maintain a fair and balanced posture on the subject of the strike, and their dominant focus should be on ending it. Additionally,

1. No reaction to a strike or other job action should be taken without first anticipating the consequences of a reaction from the union and the officers involved. For example, the decision to seek an injunction ordering the officers to terminate the action and return to work could result in the officers disobeying the order and forcing a confrontation with the court issuing the order. A public statement that all officers involved in the action will be fired places the chief in the difficult position after the conflict is terminated of either firing participating officers or, in the alternative, losing face with his employees.

2. All management responses to a strike should be directed toward terminating it only, and not toward an ulterior purpose, such as trying to ''bust'' the union. There have been job actions in which the employer's sole objective was to destroy the union, an objective that frequently results in aggravated hostility between the employer and the union, the chief and officers participating in the action and among the officers themselves. The long-range effect of this approach is to injure the morale of the police department, affecting the quality of police services and ultimately the level of service to the public.[97]

The degree of support that nonstriking employees, the media, the public, and elected and appointed officials will give management in the event of a strike is a product not only of the soundness of management's position but also of how effective management is in communicating. For a department whose work force is depleted by a walkout, personnel are a scarce resource and not to invest it in communications efforts is a natural temptation tinged heavily by the reality of other needs that must also be considered. To be borne in mind, however, is the perspective that the effective use of some personnel in communications efforts may shorten the strike.

It is essential during a strike that communications be rapid, accurate, consistent, and broadly based. Nonstriking employees may be kept informed by the use of the daily bulletin, briefings, or other devices. Letters may be sent to the homes of striking officers informing them of the applicable penalities for their actions, the status of negotiations, and management's present position with respect to these issues. Facsimile letters for this and other actions should already have been prepared as part of the development of the contingency plan.

Personal appearances by police managers before neighborhood groups, professional associations, civic clubs, and other similar bodies can be useful in maintaining calmness in the community, in providing one means of informing the public of special precautionary measures that they can take to protect themselves, and in galvanizing public opinion for management's position. Care must be taken to ensure that in this effort the needs of lower socioeconomic groups are not overlooked; they are not likely to be members of the Kiwanis or the local bar association, and special attention must be given as to how they too will be informed and their needs listened to.

In the Aftermath

At some point the strike will either collapse, as it did among New Orleans officers in 1979, or an agreement will be reached, or both sides will agree to return to the bargaining table upon the return of personnel to the job. Often, a tense atmosphere will prevail for some time. Nonstrikers will resent any threats made and any damage to their personal property. Those who walked out will view those who continued to work as not having helped to have maintained the solidarity necessary for effective job actions. Union members dissatisfied with what the strike did or didn't produce may engage in petty harassments of nonstrikers, display thinly veiled contempt for management, or surreptitiously cause damage to city property. Management's posture during the strike can in part reduce the tensions inherent in the poststrike adjustment period, but it cannot eliminate the need for responsible action by the union or overcome the intransigence of a subversely militant union.

As soon as an agreement ending the strike is reached, a joint statement with the union should be released announcing it and highlighting the key features of the settlement, and letters should be sent to the homes of all officers urging them to put aside the matter and to return to the business of public service with renewed commitment. All personnel in the department should take particular care not to discriminate between those who struck and those who did not.

Among the other items of business that must be handled after a strike relate to whether strikers are to be disciplined, although the union will typically insist upon amnesty for all striking officers as a precondition to returning to the job; what disciplinary measures are to be taken against those who destroyed private or public property during the course of the strike; what measures are to be taken against those who undertook various actions against officers who did not walk out; and the securing of a union commitment not to act in any way against nonstrikers and to actively discourage such actions by union members.

Some of what management does during and after a strike may be provided for by legislative enactment, which either requires or makes possible certain decisions. In Indiana, striking public employees cannot be paid for the days they missed during the walkout. In Texas, striking officers may be fined up to $2,000, cannot receive a pay increase for one year, and are placed on probation for two years, and the courts may fine the union $2,500 to $20,000 per day during the strike.

As a final note, there has been some experimentation with reconciliation meetings of parties to promote goodwill. Experience has demonstrated that, in most cases, the wounds are so fresh and the feelings so intense that it simply creates the opportunity for an incident; in one notable instance, a reconciliation party resulted in two hours of strictly staying in groups of strikers and nonstrikers and ultimately in a mass fight at the buffet table.[97]

Summary

From 1959 through the 1970s seven forces were at work contributing to the evolution of collective bargaining by public sector employees, including: 1) the needs of labor organizations; 2) the reduction of legal barriers; 3) police frustration with a perceived lack of support in the war on crime; 4) insensitive personnel practices; 5) inadequate salaries and fringe benefits; 6) a sharp upswing in violence directed at the police; and 7) the success of other groups in using collective action to attain their objectives.

Unions have successfully fought the hiring of lower-salaried civilians to replace police officers working inside at routine desk and clerical jobs. Although the officers would not have lost their jobs, they would have been returned to street duty, where they would have to endure the extremes of weather and other unpleasant conditions. Unions have also displayed political muscle in defeating the institution of civilian review boards, electing pro-police candidates to office, altering the disciplinary processes of their departments, halting the use of one-officer cars as an alternative to two-officer cars, and obtaining more powerful weapons for the police to use—even in the face of opposition by minorities, and other actions. All of these actions confront police executives at a basic point: the control of the police agency.

Over 80 percent of the states have adopted legal provisions permitting the practice of public sector collective bargaining. In states with comprehensive laws, there is usually an agency that functions as a labor commission and may be titled a Public Employees Relations Commission (PERC).

Police employee organizations that represent their members for bargaining purposes are called unions. These organizations vary as to their philosophy and orientation and may be any of the following: (1) subdivisions of industrial unions, (2) independent government employee associations, and (3) independent police-only associations.

Merely because a majority of officers belong to a police employee organization does not mean that the association bargains for the officers. An appropriate number of signed authorization cards must be obtained from the group of officers that the union seeks to represent, and the grouping of the officers—the unit—must be determined to be appropriate by the PERC. Under certain conditions, an election by secret ballot may be required and any of three outcomes may arise: (1) the union or a particular union from among several competing unions may gain a majority vote, (2) there may be a runoff election, or (3) the officers eligible for union membership may vote for no union.

During the time that a bargaining relationship is being established, there are frequent chances for conflict to occur. These may represent conflicts over access to bulletin boards, meeting space, or more substantial matters. Of particular concern to both management and the union is that each party observe the other's rights and not engage in unfair labor practices.

Considerable effort is expended before management and the union arrive at the bargaining table; the members of the respective bargaining teams must be selected with care; the issues to be presented must be identified and researched; a site must be selected; and common procedures must be agreed upon by both parties, among other matters.

Bargaining can be tough work, with progress difficult to come by. Even when there has been a general spirit of mutualism among the negotiating parties, a single hotly contested item can grind progress to a halt. In these situations, a cooling-off period may be sufficient to get negotiations back on track, or it may be necessary to resort to one of the major forms of resolving bargaining impasses.

The achievement of a written contract obtained through bilateral negotiations is a noteworthy accomplishment, one often heralded in the media. However, the hard work is not over. For a year or whatever period the contract covers, the parties to the agreement must daily live under the terms that they have mutually agreed will regulate their relationship. Despite the best of intentions and efforts and the existence of well-intended and reasonable people, it is inevitable that differences are going to occur as to what a particular clause means, allows, requires, or prohibits. When presented formally, these differences are called grievances and ultimately may be settled by arbitration.

When unionized officers are displeased with such things as the progress of negotiations or when they want to influence or protest a decision, they may engage in job actions such as (1) votes of confidence, (2) work slowdowns, (3) work speedups, and (4) work stoppages. Although strikes by police are almost always illegal, numerous examples of them exist. The administrative handling of job actions is an issue requiring sensitivity and good judgment. The best posture regarding job actions is one in which management and the union agree that they have a joint obligation to avoid them; however, management as a practical matter must plan for the worst scenario, and its bias should be to overestimate the negatives in the situation to be faced. In contrast, management's public pronouncements must be statesmanlike.

Discussion Questions

1. There are three broad categories of police unions. What are they?

2. What is unit determination and why is it important?

3. What parties in what roles sit at the bargaining table?

4. Of what significance is the scope of bargaining?

5. With respect to the scope of bargaining, what do the terms "mandatory," "non-negotiable," and "permissible" mean?

6. What is a "walkthrough"?

7. How are expendable, trade-off, negotiable, and non-negotiable union proposals distinguished?

8. What are the three major types of impasse resolution?

9. Are grievances inevitable in labor relations?

10. What are the major forms of job actions?

11. What can Chiefs of Police do to reduce the possibility of a job action by unionized officers?

Notes

1. These themes are identified and treated in detail in Hervey A. Juris and Peter Feuille, *Police Unionism* (Lexington, Mass.: Lexington Books, 1973).

2. C. M. Rehmus, "Labor Relations in the Public Sector," Third World Congress, International Industrial Relations Association, in *Labor Relations Law in the Public Sector,* eds. Russell A. Smith, Harry T. Edwards, and R. Theodore Clark, Jr. (Indianapolis, Ind.: Bobbs-Merrill, 1974), p. 7.

3. The Public Service Research Council, *Public Sector Bargaining and Strikes* (Vienna, Va.: Public Service Research Council, 1976), pp. 6–9.

4. 296 F. Supp. 1068, 1969.

5. 324 F. Supp. 315, N.D. Ga., 1971.

6. 483 F. 2d. 966, 10th Circuit, 1973.

7. President's Commission on Law Enforcement and Administration of Justice, *Task Force Report: The Police* (Washington, D.C.: U.S. Government Printing Office, 1967), p. 144.

8. Ibid., p. 145.

9. Charles A. Salerno, "Overview of Police Labor Relations," in *Collective Bargaining in the Public Sector,* eds., Richard M. Ayres and Thomas L. Wheeler (Gaithersburg, Md.: International Association of Chiefs of Police, 1977), p. 14.

10. Rory Judd Albert, *A Time for Reform: A Case Study of the Interaction Between the Commissioner of the Boston Police Department and the Boston Police Patrolmen's Association* (Cambridge, Mass.: M.I.T. Press, 1975), p. 47.

11. From various tables, U.S. Department of Labor, *Employment and Earnings,* 8:4 (October 1961).

12. Bureau of the Census, *Statistical Abstract of the United States, 1975* (Washington, D.C.: U.S. Government Printing Office, 1975), p. 162.

13. John H. Burpo, *The Police Labor Movement* (Springfield, Ill.: Charles C Thomas, 1971), p. 34.

14. Albert, *A Time for Reform,* p. 29. Several recent studies have reported that market forces other than unions explain better the rise in public employees' salaries than does union activity.

15. These data were extracted from the Federal Bureau of Investigation's *Uniform Crime Reports* (Washington, D.C.: U.S. Government Printing Office, 1965 and 1970).

16. William W. Scranton, chairman, *Report of the President's Commission on Campus Unrest* (Washington, D.C.: U.S. Government Printing Office, 1970), p. 18.

17. Sterling D. Spero and John M. Capozzola, *The Urban Community and Its Unionized Bureaucracies* (New York: Dunellen, 1973), p. 183.

18. International Association of Chiefs of Police, *Police Unions and Other Police Organizations* (Washington, D.C.: International Association of Chiefs of Police, 1944), pp. 28–30.

19. From the March 16, 1967 statement of Commissioner Donald Pomerleau on the unionization of the Baltimore Police Department at the State House, Annapolis, Maryland.

20. Juris and Feuille, *Police Unionism,* p. 155.

21. "Portland Shocks Zap Police Chief, Narc Squad," *Law Enforcement News,* 7:12 (June 22, 1981), pp. 1 and 12.

22. "NYC Police Union Slams Brakes on One-Man Patrol Car Proposal," Law Enforcement News, 7:19 (November 9, 1981), p. 1.

23. "DC Union Pact Dumps Trial Boards," *Law Enforcement News,* 7:12 (June 22, 1981), p. 1.

24. Jack Stieber, *Public Employee Unionism* (Washington, D.C.: Brookings Institution, 1973), p. 62.

25. David Lewin, "The Climate for Public Sector Labor Relations in the 1970's: A Changing of the Guard," the 1977 meeting of the American Society for Public Administration.

26. James K. McCollum and Roger S. Wolters, "Public Sector Bargaining Legislation in Illinois and Ohio, 1983," *Journal of Collective Negotiations in the Public Sector,* 14:2 (1985), pp. 161–172.

27. Portions of this section, revised and with additional information, are drawn from Charles R. Swanson, "A Typology of Police Collective Bargaining Employee Organizations," *Journal of Collective Negotiations in the Public Sector,* 6:4 (1977), pp. 341–346.

28. "Labor News," *Police Magazine,* 2:3 (May 1979), pp. 46–47.

29. William J. Bopp, *Police Personnel Administration* (Boston: Holbrook Press, 1974) p. 345.

30. See Richard S. Rubin et al., "Public Sector Unit Determination Administrative Procedures and Case Law," Midwest Center for Public Sector Labor Relations, Indiana University Department of Labor Contract J-9-P-6-0215, May 31, 1978.

31. Government Employee Relations Report, "State and Local Programs" (Washington, D.C.: The Bureau of National Affairs, 10–21–85), pp. 77, 89. (Hereafter GERR.)

32. In this regard, see Stephen L. Hayford, William A. Durkee, and Charles W. Hickman, "Bargaining Unit Determination Procedures in the Public Sector: A Comparative Evaluation," *Employee Relations Law Journal,* 5:1 (Summer 1979), p. 86.

33. These points are drawn from the private sector National Labor Relations Act, Section 7 amended, which has served as a model for the portion of many public sector laws pertaining to unfair labor practices. Also, see Russell A. Smith, Harry T. Edwards, and R. Theodore Clark, Jr., *Labor Relations Law in the Public Sector* (Indianapolis, Ind.: Bobbs-Merrill, 1974), p. 108.

34. Paul Prasow et al., *Scope of Bargaining in the Public Sector—Concepts and Problems* (Washington, D.C.: U.S. Department of Labor, 1972), p. 5. For a more extended treatment of the subject, see Walter Gershenfeld, J. Joseph Loewenberg, and Bernard Ingster, *Scope of Public-Sector Bargaining* (Lexington, Mass.: Lexington Books, 1977).

35. Steven A. Rynecki, Douglas A. Cairns, and Donald J. Cairns, *Police Collective Bargaining Agreements* (Washington, D.C.: National League of Cities and Police Executive Research Forum, 1978). For a dissenting view, see Steven C. Kahn, "The Scope of Collective Bargaining in the Public Sector: Quest for an Elusive Standard," *Employee Relations Law Journal,* 1 (Spring 1979), p. 562.

36. Kahn, "The Scope of Collective Bargaining in the Public Sector," p. 562.

37. Ibid., p. 565.

38. *West Irondequoit Teachers Ass'n* v. *Helsby,* 35 N.Y.2d 46, 87 LRRM 2618 (1974).

39. Hervey A. Juris and Peter Feuille, *Police Unionism* (Lexington, Mass.: Lexington Books, 1973), p. 133.

40. Donald Slesnick, "What Is the Effect of a Sunshine Law on Collective Bargaining: A Union View," *Journal of Law and Education,* 5 (October 1976), p. 489.

41. On costing out contracts, see Marvin Friedman, *The Use of Economic Data in Collective Bargaining* (Washington, D.C.: Government Printing Office, 1978).

42. Charles W. Maddox, *Collective Bargaining in Law Enforcement* (Springfield, Ill.: Charles C Thomas, 1975), p. 54.

43. There are also other types of statutory regulations affecting the police; illustratively, in Nevada, Ohio, and New Jersey the police cannot join or belong to a union with nonpolice members; on this and related points see GERR, pp. 3–139 for a state-by-state summary of collective bargaining laws.

44. Arnold Zack, *Understanding Fact-finding and Arbitration in the Public Sector* (Washington, D.C.: Government Printing Office, 1974), p. 1. A well-regarded work on this topic is William E. Simkin's *Mediation and the Dynamics of Collective Bargaining* (Washington, D.C.: Bureau of National Affairs, 1974).

45. Ibid., p. 1; most characteristically the mediator meets with labor and management separately.

46. Thomas P. Gilroy and Anthony V. Sinicropi, "Impasse Resolution in Public Employment," *Industrial and Labor Relations Review,* 25 (July 1971–1972), p. 499.

47. Zack, *Understanding Fact-finding and Arbitration,* p. 1.

48. Gilroy and Sinicropi, "Impasse Resolution," p. 499.

49. William R. Word, "Fact Finding in Public Employee Negotiations," in *Collective Bargaining: Non-profit Sector,* ed. Charles S. Bunker (Columbus, Ohio: Grid, 1973), p. 217.

50. James L. Stern, "The Wisconsin Public Employee Fact Finding Procedure," *Industrial and Labor Relations Review,* 20 (October 1966–1967), pp. 3–29.

51. Gilroy and Sinicropi, "Impasse Resolution," p. 501.

52. Robert G. Howlett, "Fact Finding: Its Values and Limitations—Comment," Arbitration and the Expanded Role of Neutrals, Proceedings of the twenty-third annual meeting of the National Academy of Arbitrators (Washington, D.C.: Bureau of National Affairs, 1970), p. 156.

53. Zack, *Understanding Fact-finding and Arbitration,* p. 1.

54. Ibid., p. 1.

55. Ibid., p. 1.

56. J. Joseph Loewenberg et al., *Compulsory Arbitration* (Lexington, Mass.: Lexington Books, 1976), p. 152.

57. In 1985 these states were Alaska, Connecticut, Delaware, Hawaii, Illinois, Indiana, Iowa, Maine, Michigan, Massachusetts, Minnesota, Montana, Nevada, New Hampshire, New Jersey, New York, Ohio, Oregon, Pennsylvania, Rhode Island, Texas, Vermont, Washington, and Wyoming. In some of these states arbitration is available to all public employees whereas in others only to special categories of workers, such as police officers, prison guards, workers in mental health facilities, and fire department employees. In three of these states—Delaware, Maine, and New Hampshire—the general rule is that wages, salaries, pensions, and insurance are not subject to arbitration, although even these three states show variation. New Hampshire does not permit arbitration on cost items, whereas Delaware allows arbitration on everything except wages and salary. See GERR, pp. 3–139.

58. Loewenberg et al., *Compulsory Arbitration,* p. 152.

59. Council of State Governments and the International Personnel Management Association, *Public Sector Labor Relations* (Lexington, Ky.: Council of State Governments, 1975), p. 38. In Iowa, the arbitrators may take the last offer of either party or the fact-finder's recommendation.

60. One exception is *City of Sioux Falls* v. *Sioux Falls Firefighters Local 813, 535* GERR B-4 (1973), a Fourth Judicial Circuit Court of South Dakota decision.

61. Council of State Governments, *Public Sector Labor Relations,* p. 31. The state courts were those of Rhode Island and Kentucky and involved teachers and firefighters, respectively.

62. Ibid., p. 28.

63. Arnold Zack, *Understanding Grievance Arbitration in the Public Sector* (Washington, D.C.: U.S. Government Printing Office, 1974), p. 1.

64. A 1978 study of police contracts found that 75 percent provided for binding arbitration of grievances at the last step; 4 percent advisory arbitration, the equivalent of fact finding; 10 percent determination by some management person; with the balance being miscellaneous such as a final determination by the civil service commission or binding arbitration entered into voluntarily. See Rynecki, Cairns, and Cairns, *Police Collective Bargaining Agreements,* p. 19.

65. Maddox, *Collective Bargaining in Law Enforcement,* p. 109.

66. Zack, *Understanding Grievance Arbitration in the Public Sector,* p. 4.

67. *Labor Arbitration in Government,* "Special Orders Create New Sickness Reporting Mechanism," 9:1 (January 1979), p. 3.

68. *Labor Arbitration in Government,* "Premium Holiday Pay While Not on Active Duty Status," 9:2 (February 1979), p. 8.

69. Maurice S. Trotta, *Arbitration of Labor-Management Disputes* (New York: Amacon, 1974), p. 234, with changes.

70. Ibid., p. 237, with changes.

71. See Helen Lavan and Cameron Carley, "Analysis of Arbitrated Employee Grievance Cases in Police Departments," *Journal of Collective Negotiations in the Public Sector,* 14:3 (1985), pp. 250–251.

72. Zack, *Understanding Grievance Arbitration in the Public Sector,* p. 32.

73. Ibid., p. 32.

74. David Marc Kleinman, "Zinging It to the Chief," *Police Magazine,* 2:3 (May 1979), p. 39.

75. Ibid., p. 44.

76. Ibid.

77. *Crime Control Digest,* 10:25 (July 21, 1976), pp. 3–4.

78. *Crime Control Digest,* 5:28 (July 16, 1971), p. 7.

79. *Crime Control Digest,* 10:30 (July 26, 1976), pp. 7–8.

80. *Crime Control Digest,* 6:43 (October 27, 1972), p. 10.

81. *The Atlanta Constitution and Journal,* April 3, 1977, p. B-19.

82. *Crime Control Digest,* 10:27 (July 5, 1976), p. 8.

83. *Crime Control Digest,* 10:25 (June 21, 1976), pp. 3–4.

84. *Crime Control Digest,* 4:11 (June 5, 1970), p. 13.

85. *Crime Control Digest,* 4:5 (March 11, 1970), p. 13.

86. *Crime Control Digest,* 3:20 (December 17, 1969), pp. 8–9.

87. *Crime Control Digest,* 4:5 (March 11, 1970), p. 13.

88. *The Atlanta Constitution,* May 16, 1979, p. C-1.

89. *Crime Control Digest,* 9:43 (October 27, 1975), p. 8.

90. *The Atlanta Journal,* May 4, 1979, pp. A-1, A-26.

91. *Crime Control Digest,* 6:6 (February 11, 1972), p. 4.

92. *The Washington Post,* May 9, 1979, p. A-7.

93. *The Washington Post,* April 3, 1979, pp. C-1, C-3.

94. On September 29, 1976, Richard M. Ayres presented a paper, "Police Strikes: Are We Treating the Symptom Rather Than the Problem," at the eighty-third International Association of Chiefs of Police Meeting, Miami Beach, Fla. Although it is not quoted here, some of his themes may be identifiable and his contribution in that regard is acknowledged.

95. This list of questions with some modification and additions is drawn from Charles C. Mulcahy, "Meeting the County Employees Strike," in *Collective Bargaining in the Public Sector,* eds. Richard M. Ayres and Thomas L. Wheelen, (Gaithersburg, Md.: International Association of Chiefs of Police, 1977), pp. 426–430. Also see Carmen D. Saso, *Coping with Public Employee Strikes* (Chicago: Public Personnel Association, 1970).

96. Harold W. Davey, *Contemporary Collective Bargaining* (Englewood Cliffs, N.J.: Prentice-Hall, 1972), p. 195.

97. John H. Burpo, *Labor Relations Guidelines for the Police Executive* (Chicago: Traffic Institute, Northwestern University, 1976), p. 14, with modifications and additions.

98. Lee T. Paterson and John Liebert, *Management Strike Handbook* (Chicago: International Personnel Management Association, 1974), p. 42.

Law is order, and good law is good order.

ARISTOTLE

Legal Aspects of Police Administration

Introduction*

One of the primary characteristics of our nation's law is its dynamic nature. Rules of law are promulgated in three basic ways: by legislation, by regulation, and by court decision. Statutes and ordinances are laws passed by legislative bodies, such as the United States Congress, state legislatures, county commissions, and city councils. These lawmaking bodies often produce legislation that establishes only a general outline of the intended solution to a particular problem. The legislation authorizes a particular governmental agency to fill in the details through rules and regulations. Such rules and regulations have the full force of the law.

When the solution to a legal dispute does not appear to be specifically provided by an existing statute, rule, or regulation, a judge may rely upon prior decisions of that or other courts which have previously resolved disputes involving similar issues. Case decisions can be reversed or modified by a higher-level court or by passage of

* This chapter represents a substantial rewrite by Donald D. Slesnick and Janet E. Ferris of the text, which was authored by Jack Call and Don Slesnick for the first edition. A concerted effort has been made to render this chapter as readable for the administrator as possible. In some instances, this has resulted in the exclusion of certain legal details from the text. However, the notes at the end of the chapter offer additional information for those who desire a more expanded discussion.

new legislation. Sometimes judges must develop their own tests or rules to fairly resolve an issue through creative interpretation of a statute or constitutional provision.

Clearly, the fluid nature of our lawmaking system renders it impossible to offer a definitive statement of the law that will remain true forever or perhaps even for very long. The task of stating rules of law is complicated further by the vast number of legislative bodies and courts in this country. Statutes and judge-made law may vary considerably from state to state and from one court to another. However, interpretations of the U.S. Constitution and federal law by the U.S. Supreme Court are binding on all other courts, be they state or federal, and, therefore, are given special attention in this chapter.

The reader should view the material that follows as instructive background rather than as an authoritative basis for action. Police administrators should always seek qualified legal counsel whenever they face a problem or a situation that appears to possess legal ramifications. A primary objective of this chapter is to make police administrators more capable of quickly determining when they face such a problem or situation.

Liability for Police Conduct

One of the most troubling legal problems facing police officers and police departments in recent years has been the expanded impact of civil and criminal liability for alleged police misconduct. It is commonplace to hear police spokespersons complain that law enforcement officers are widely hampered by the specter of being undeservedly sued for alleged improper performance of duty. Although one may argue that the magnitude of police misconduct litigation may be overstated, the amount of litigation appears to be increasing, and is apparently accompanied by a movement toward larger monetary damage awards.

Basic Types of Police Tort Actions

A tort may be defined as the infliction of injury upon one person by another person. Assault, battery, false imprisonment, false arrest, invasion of privacy, negligence, defamation, and malicious prosecution are examples of torts that are commonly brought against police officers.[1]

In our system of government, there are court systems at both federal and state levels of government. However, federal courts are intended to be courts of somewhat limited jurisdiction and generally do not hear cases involving private, as opposed to public, controversies unless a question of federal law is involved or the individuals involved in the lawsuit are residents of different states. Even then, the suit may usually be decided in a state court if both parties to the controversy agree to have the dispute settled there. As a result, historically most tort suits have been brought in state courts.

However, a recent trend in the area of police misconduct litigation is the increase in the number and proportion of these suits that are being brought in federal courts. There are two legal vehicles by which federal courts can acquire jurisdiction of these suits.

The first is what is often referred to as a ''1983'' lawsuit. This name derives from the fact that these suits are brought under the provisions of Section 1983 of Title 42 of the United States Code. This law passed by Congress in the aftermath of the Civil War and commonly referred to as the Civil Rights Act of 1871 was designed to secure the civil rights of the recently emancipated slaves. It prohibits depriving any person of life, liberty, or property without due process of law. When a police officer is alleged to have acted improperly, for example, in conducting an illegal search, that officer can be sued in federal court by alleging that he or she deprived the person searched of his or her constitutional right under the Fourth Amendment to be free from unreasonable searches and seizures, and did so while acting within the scope of employment as a police officer.

The second legal vehicle for acquiring federal jurisdiction is to allege what some commentators call a ''Bivens'' tort. The name derives from the lawsuit that established this method for acquiring federal jurisdiction, *Bivens* v. *Six Unknown Federal Narcotics Agents.*[2] Bivens-type suits are usually brought when the plaintiff wants to sue a federal employee.

The preceding discussion demonstrates that three basic types of tort actions may be brought against police for misconduct: traditional state law torts, Section 1983 torts, and Bivens torts. This classification is important in that the type of tort action brought will determine who can be sued, the kind of behavior that will result in liability, and which immunities might be available to the defendants.

Who Can Be Sued

At common law, police officers were held personally liable for damage caused by their own actions that exceeded the boundaries of permissible behavior. This rule applied even though the officer may have been ignorant of the boundary established by the law. Unjust as many of such results may often seem, the rule establishes one of the traditional risks of policing.

A more difficult question concerns whether the supervisors of the officer and/or the governmental unit by which he is employed can be sued for his misbehavior.

Generally, an effort to impose liability on a supervisor for the tortious conduct of his employee is based on the common law doctrine of respondent superior. That doctrine, also called vicarious liability, developed along with the growth of industrial society, and reflected a conscious effort to allocate risk to those who could afford to pay for the complained of damages.[3]

Although American courts have expanded the extent to which employers can be sued for the torts of their employees, they have traditionally been reluctant to extend the doctrine of vicarious liability to police supervisors and administrators.[4] There appear to be two primary reasons for this reluctance.

The first is that police department supervisors and administrators have limited discretion in hiring decisions.[5] The second reason is that police officers are public officials whose duties are established by the governmental authority that created their jobs rather than by their supervisors or police administrators.[6] Therefore, a police supervisor does not possess as much ability to control the behavior of his employees as does his counterpart in private industry.

The court decisions that have refused to extend vicarious liability to police supervisors or administrators do not go so far as to insulate them from liability for acts of their subordinates in all cases. If the supervisor authorized the misbehavior, was present at the time of the misbehavior and did nothing to stop it, or otherwise cooperated in the misconduct, he can be held partially liable for the officer's tortious behavior.[7] However, these situations are not classic examples of vicarious liability; rather they are instances in which it can be said that the supervisor's own conduct is, in part, a cause of the injury giving rise to the lawsuit.[8]

The courts' general reluctance to hold police supervisors and administrators vicariously liable for the misdeeds of their subordinates applies to each of the three basic types of tort actions identified earlier, although the law regarding Bivens torts is somewhat unsettled in this area.[9]

A second difficult question with respect to who may be sued for damages caused by police misconduct concerns the liability of the police department and the governmental unit of which the department is a part.[10] To answer this question, it is necessary to briefly consider the concept of sovereign immunity.

At common law in England, the government could not be sued because the government was the king, and, in effect, the king could do no wrong. Although this doctrine of sovereign immunity was initially adopted by the American judicial system, it has undergone extensive modification by court decisions and acts of legislative bodies.

The courts were the first to chip away at the doctrine as it related to tort actions in state courts. Most of the courts taking this action did so on the basis that the doctrine had been created initially because the times seemed to demand it, and thus the courts should abrogate the doctrine because modern times no longer justified it. Kenneth Culp Davis, a commentator on administrative law, reported that eighteen courts "had abolished chunks of sovereign immunity" by 1970, twenty-nine had done so by 1975, and thirty-three by 1978.[11]

Davis noted that the trend toward abrogation of sovereign immunity by judicial action was on the wane by 1976 and that the state legislatures had become the primary movers toward limiting or eliminating the doctrine. As a result of combined judicial and legislative action, by 1978 only two states still adhered fully to the traditional common law approach that government was totally immune from liability for torts occurring in the exercise of governmental functions.[12]

Law suits brought in federal courts against state and local officials are analyzed somewhat differently. The courts first examine the claim asserted by the plaintiff in the case, and will then determine whether the relief requested can be imposed against the defendants named in the action. For governmental officials and governmental entities named as defendants, the plaintiff's ability to succeed will depend upon which immunities are available to those defendants. These immunities will be applied to determine whether governmental defendants remain in the lawsuit and whether damages can be assessed against them.

In federal lawsuits against a state, or state officials sued in their official capacities, the courts have concluded that the Eleventh Amendment to the United States Constitution precludes awards of monetary relief.[13] The courts have arrived at this result by deciding that the essence of the Eleventh Amendment is its protection of state treasuries against damage awards in federal court. The U.S. Supreme Court recently extended this principle to bar the recovery of attorneys' fees against state officials sued in their official capacity under 42 U.S.C. 1983.

The Eleventh Amendment does not, however, preclude courts from ordering state officials to do certain things in the future,[14] even if such orders will require the expenditure of substantial sums from the state treasury.[15] The rationale behind such orders is that federal courts can require that the actions of state officials comport with the federal constitution. The U.S. Supreme Court decided in 1984 that the federal courts' authority to insist that state officials act in a manner consistent with the federal constitution does not allow those courts to consider allegations that a state official violated state law; such claims must be addressed in state courts.

Individuals pursuing damage claims under Section 1983 against local government officials, and state officials who are sued in their individual rather than official capacities will have to overcome the defense available to such parties of "qualified, good-faith immunity." Such official immunities are not creatures of Section 1983; they arose from traditional, common law protections that were historically accorded to government officials. Basically, the good faith immunity doctrine recognizes that public officials who exercise discretion in the performance of their duties should not be punished for actions undertaken in good faith. Imposing liability on public officials in such situations would inevitably deter their willingness to "execute . . . [their] office with the decisiveness and the judgment required by the public good."[16]

Over the years, the courts have struggled to develop a test for "good faith." In 1975, the U.S. Supreme Court articulated such a test that considered both the official's state of mind when he committed the act in question (the subjective element) and whether the act violated clearly established legal rights (the objective element).[17]

However, seven years later the Supreme Court decided that the subjective element of the text should be dropped, leaving only the standard of "objective reasonableness."[18] Now, a court must only determine whether the law at issue was "clearly established" at the time the challenged action occurred. Furthermore, if the plaintiff's allegations do not show a violation of clearly established law, a public official asserting good faith immunity will be entitled to dismissal of the lawsuit before it proceeds further.[19]

The immunities available to state and local officials are generally designed to protect individuals from liability arising out of the performance of official acts. With the Eleventh Amendment providing similar protection to the states, the question of the immunity of a local government was raised. Initially, the U.S. Supreme Court concluded that Congress had not intended to apply 42 U.S.C. 1983 to municipalities, thereby giving municipalities what is called "absolute," or unqualified immunity from suit.[20] Upon reexamination of this issue in the 1978 case *Monell* v. *Department of Social Services*,[21] the Court decided that Congress had intended for Section 1983 to apply to municipalities and other local government units. The Court further concluded that although certain other immunities were not available to a municipality in a Section 1983 lawsuit, the municipality could not be held liable solely because it employed an individual who was responsible for Section 1983 violations. The Court made it clear that local government entities will be liable under Section 1983 only when that government's policies or official procedures could be shown to be responsible for the violation of federally protected rights.

Unfortunately, the *Monell* decision did not fully articulate the limits of municipal liability under Section 1983. The result has been considerable litigation to establish when a deprivation of federally protected rights actually results from enforcement of a municipal policy or procedure, and at what point an official's actions can be fairly treated as establishing the offending policy.[22]

More recently, the Supreme Court has held that "single acts of police misconduct" do not, by themselves, show that a city policy was involved in the alleged tortious act.[23] A lower federal court has since acknowledged that it may be questionable whether an alleged policy of inadequate training or negligent hiring will suffice to impose liability on a municipality for the unconstitutional actions of its police officers.[24]

Scope of Liability

In general, state tort actions against police officers provide a greater scope of liability than do the Section 1983 and Biven suits. That is, in tort actions under state law, a greater range of behavior is actionable.

The types of torts under state law that commonly are brought against police officers may be categorized as intentional or negligence torts. An intentional tort is one in which the defendant knowingly commits a voluntary act designed to bring about certain physical consequences. For example, the tort of assault is the purposeful infliction upon another person of a fear of a harmful or offensive contact. If X points an unloaded pistol at Y, who does not know the pistol is unloaded, X has created in Y an apprehension that Y is about to experience a harmful contact from a bullet. X voluntarily lifts the pistol and points it at Y, fully expecting that it will cause Y to be apprehensive about being hit by a bullet. Thus, X is liable to Y for the intentional tort of assault.

The tort of negligence involves conduct that presents an unreasonable risk of harm to others which, in turn, is the proximate cause of an actual injury. Whereas in an intentional tort the consequences following an act must be substantially certain to follow, in the tort of negligence the consequences need only be foreseeable. When X drives his car through a stop sign, even though unintentional, and hits the side of Y's car, X's behavior presents an unreasonable risk of harm to others and is the proximate cause of the damage to Y's car. Although X would have been negligent for "running the stop sign" even if he had not hit another car, he would not have committed the tort of negligence in that he had caused no injury.

As noted earlier in this chapter, most lawsuits against police officers are based on the intentional torts of assault, battery, false imprisonment, and malicious prosecution.[25] Suits against police officers for intentional torts can be brought as state tort actions, Section 1983 suits, or Bivens suits. While suits against police officers for negligence torts can be brought as state tort actions, the issue is not so clear-cut with regard to Section 1983 and Bivens suits.

Generally damages assessed in civil litigation for negligence are ordinary (compensatory) damages that are paid by the employing governmental entity (or its liability insurance carrier), on behalf of the defendant officer. Therefore, as a general rule, the individual employee is not required to pay ordinary damages that result from a civil negligence suit. This is so because normally when a governmental employee is performing his duties within the scope of his employment, he is deemed to be the agent or representative of the employing agency, and therefore not personally liable for his acts. However, where punitive damages are assessed for conduct which is grossly negligent, wanton, or reckless, the individual who has been responsible for such acts is personally liable, and generally speaking these assessments are not absorbed by the employing governmental entity nor by liability insurance. Thus, a law enforcement employee who acts in a reckless, wanton, or grossly negligent manner will be subject to, and personally liable for, a punitive damage award.

Immunities

In this constantly changing area of the law, the U.S. Supreme Court has established a rule that police are entitled to "qualified" immunity for acts made in good faith and which can be characterized as "objectively reasonable." In *U.S.* v. *Leon*,[26] the Court focused on the objectively ascertainable question of whether a reasonably well-trained officer would have known that the act committed was illegal. Subsequently, the Court following that logic held that if police personnel are not "objectively reasonable" in seeking an arrest warrant, they can be sued personally for money damages despite the fact that a judge has approved the warrant. In fact, the Court stated that a judge's issuance of a warrant will not shield the officer from liability if a "well-trained officer in [his] position would have known that his affidavit failed to establish probable cause and that he should not have applied for the warrant."[27] Thus, while public officials exercising discretion (for example, judges and prosecutors) have absolute immunity for their unreasonable acts, the only person in the system left to sue for damages for a wrongdoing will be the police officer unless his or her acts can be attributed to the policy or procedural custom established by the employing governmental agency.

Trends in Tort Liability for Police Supervisors and Administrators

Although there has been a traditional reluctance to hold police supervisors or administrators liable for the misbehavior of their subordinate officers, some courts have been increasingly willing to extend liability to these officials where the plaintiff has alleged negligent employment, improper training, or improper supervision.[28]

Under the first of these, negligent employment, a police official may be held liable for his failure to conduct a thorough investigation of a prospective employee's suitability for police work where he or she hires an applicant with a demonstrated propensity "toward violence, untruthfulness, discrimination or other adverse characteristics."[29] Of course, under this theory, the injuries suffered by the plaintiff would have to have been the result of the negative trait that had been demonstrated by the individual prior to his employment as an officer. If the negative trait is not demonstrated until after employment, a party injured by the officer may be able to sue a police official successfully for negligently retaining the officer or otherwise failing to take appropriate remedial action. In some circumstances, the official may not be able to dismiss an officer who has demonstrated unfitness, but he still might be found liable if he negligently assigns the unfit officer to duties where the public is not protected adequately from the officer's particular unfitness. Finally, the official is potentially liable for negligently entrusting a revolver to an officer who has a history of alcohol or drug abuse or misuse of a weapon.

Suits alleging that police officials improperly trained a police officer have been particularly successful where firearms were involved in inflicting the injury. Courts have stressed that the "law imposes a duty of extraordinary care in the handling and use of firearms"[30] and that "public policy requires that police officers be trained in the use of firearms on moving and silhouette targets and instructed when and how to use them.''[31] Suits alleging lack of necessary training are also becoming increasingly successful in cases involving the use of physical force to overcome resistance, the administration of first aid, pursuit driving, and false arrest.[32]

Another emerging theory of recovery against police officials is an allegation of failure to properly supervise or direct subordinate officers. This type of suit is typically brought where officials have failed to take action to rectify a recurring problem exhibited in the conduct of police operations by subordinates.[33] An interesting recent development in this area concerns the situation in which the police department issues a written directive that establishes a policy more stringent than the law requires. In several cases involving such a situation, the courts have held that the written directive establishes a standard of conduct to which police officers must conform or face the possibility of civil liability for their actions.[34]

The last area to which courts have given recent increased attention concerns cases in which it is alleged that the police officer failed to provide needed medical care to people with whom the officer came in contact.[35] Although the incidents giving rise to such allegations can occur in a variety of situations, they seem to occur with greatest frequency when the plaintiff has been in custody or has been mistakenly thought to be intoxicated when he was actually suffering from a serious illness. There are four theories of recovery on which these cases are based: (1) failure to recognize and provide treatment for injury, (2) failure to provide treatment upon request, (3) failure to provide treatment upon recognition of an injury, and (4) negligent medical treatment. Suits in the first three categories may allege either negligent conduct or intentional behavior. Some courts have held that police officers do not have a duty to care for injured persons with whom they come in contact,[36] although such a holding is not likely to occur when the injured person is in their custody.

Administrative Discipline: Due Process for Police Officers

The Fifth and Fourteenth Amendments to the U.S. Constitution state that ''no person shall be . . . deprived of life, liberty, or property, without due process of law.''

Liberty and Property Rights of Police Officers

There are two general types of situations in the disciplinary process in which an employee of a law enforcement agency can claim the right to be protected by the guarantees of due process.[37] The first type involves those situations in which the disciplinary action taken by the government employer threatens liberty rights of the officer. The second type involves a threat to property rights.

Liberty rights have been defined loosely as those involving the protection and defense of one's good name, reputation, and position in the community. It has, at times, been extended further to include the right to preserve one's future career opportunities as well. Thus, where an officer's reputation, honor, or integrity are at stake because of government-imposed discipline, due process must be extended to the officer.[38]

It should be noted that the use of the "liberty rights" approach as a basis for requiring procedural due process has proven extremely difficult. The Supreme Court further restricted the use of this legal theory by holding that it can be utilized only when the employer is shown to have created and publicly disseminated a false and defamatory impression about the employee.[39]

The more substantial and meaningful type of due process guarantee is that pertaining to the protection of one's property. Although the general concept of property extends only to real estate and tangible possessions, the courts have developed the concept that a person's property also includes the many valuable intangible belongings acquired in the normal course of life such as the expectation of continued employment. However, not all employees are entitled to its protection.

The courts have consistently held that an employee acquires a protected interest in a job only when it can be established that there exists a justifiable expectation that employment will continue without interruption except for dismissal or other discipline based on just or proper cause. This expectation of continued employment is sometimes called "tenure" or "permanent status."

In 1972, the Supreme Court issued two landmark decisions on tenure.[40] In one of these cases, the plaintiff was a state university professor who had been hired under a one-year contract, and had been dismissed at the end of that year without notice or a hearing. The Court held that the professor was not entitled to notice or a hearing because under the circumstances the professor had no tenure since he had no justifiable expectation of continued employment after his contract expired. Therefore, he had no vested property interest protected by the Fourteenth Amendment. The other case also involved a state university professor employed on a one-year contract, but this professor had taught previously in the state college system for ten years. Under these circumstances, the Court held that the professor had acquired de facto tenure (a justifiable expectation of continued employment) and, therefore, possessed a vested property interest protected by the Fourteenth Amendment.

Since property rights attach to a job when tenure has been established, the question of how and when tenure is established becomes crucial. Public employment has generally used certain generic terms, such as "annual contract," "continuing contract," and "tenure" in the field of education or "probationary" and "permanent" in civil service systems to designate the job status of employees. However, court decisions indicate that it is the definition of these terms as established by the employer rather than the terms themselves that determines an employee's legal status. Thus, the key to the establishment of the rights of an employee is the specific wording of the ordinance, statute, rule, or regulation under which that person has been employed.[41]

Merely classifying job holders as "probationary" or "permanent" does not resolve the property rights question. Whether or not a property right to the job exists is not a question of constitutional dimension; rather, the answer lies in a careful analysis of the applicable state and local laws that might create legitimate mutual expectations of continued employment.[42]

Federal courts have been inclined to read employment laws liberally so as to grant property rights whenever possible. For example, the Fifth Circuit Court of Appeal found that a city employment regulation that allows termination "only for cause" created a constitutionally protected property interest.[43] A federal district court held that a Florida Statute (Section 112.532) known as the "Law Enforcement Officers' and Correctional Officers' Bill of Rights," created a property interest in employment because of its disciplinary notice provisions.[44] That approach is consistent with other jurisdictions in which state statutes have been interpreted to give property interests in a job to local government employees.[45]

Once a liberty or property right has been established, certain due process guarantees attach to protect the employee. The question becomes, "What process is due?"[46]

The question of due process for police officers falls into two categories: procedural and substantive. The former, as its name implies, refers to the legality of the procedures used to deprive police officers of status or wages, such as dismissal or suspension from their job. Substantive due process is a more difficult and elusive concept. We will simply define substantive due process as the requirement that the basis for government disciplinary action is reasonable, relevant, and justifiable.

Procedural Due Process

Kenneth Culp Davis has identified twelve main elements of a due process hearing:

> (1) timely and adequate notice, (2) a chance to make an oral statement or argument, (3) a chance to present witnesses and evidence, (4) confrontation of adverse witnesses, (5) cross-examination of adverse witnesses, (6) disclosure of all evidence relied upon, (7) a decision based on the record of evidence, (8) a right to retain an attorney, (9) a publicly-compensated attorney for an indigent, (10) a statement of findings of fact, (11) a statement of reasons or a reasoned opinion, (12) an impartial deciding officer.[47]

The courts have not examined all the trial elements in the context of the police disciplinary process. However, there are cases that have held that the police officer must be informed of the charges on which the action is based,[48] given the right to call witnesses,[49] confronted by the witnesses against him,[50] permitted to cross-examine the witnesses against him,[51] permitted to have counsel represent him,[52] have a decision rendered on the basis of the record developed at the hearing,[53] and have the decision made by an impartial hearing officer.[54]

A question that has proven particularly troublesome for the courts is whether or not due process requires that an evidentiary hearing be held prior to the disciplinary action being taken. In *Arnett* v. *Kennedy,* a badly divided Supreme Court held that a "hearing afforded by administrative appeal after the actual dismissal is a sufficient compliance with the requirements of the Due Process Clause."[55] In a concurring opinion, Justice Powell observed that the question of whether a hearing must be accorded prior to an employee's removal "depends on a balancing process in which the government's interest in expeditious removal of an unsatisfactory employee is weighed against the interest of the affected employee in continued public employment."[56] In *Mathews* v. *Eldridge,* the U.S. Supreme Court set forth the competing interests that must be weighed to determine what process is due: (1) the private interest that will be affected by the official action; (2) the risk of an erroneous deprivation of such interest through the procedures used, and the probable value, if any, of additional or substitute procedural safeguards; and (3) the government's interest, including the function involved and the fiscal and administrative burdens that the additional or substitute procedural requirement would entail.[57]

In 1985, the Court further clarified the issue of pretermination due process in *Cleveland Board of Education* v. *Loudermill.*[58] The Court found that public employees possessing property interests in their employment have a right to "notice and an opportunity to respond'' prior to termination. The Court cautioned that its decision was based on the employee also having an opportunity for a full post-termination hearing. Therefore, assuming that a public employee will be able to challenge the termination in a full-blown, evidentiary hearing after the fact, pretermination due process should include an initial check against mistaken decisions: essentially, a determination of whether there are reasonable grounds to believe that the charges against the employee are true and support the proposed action. The Court went on to describe an acceptable pretermination procedure as one that provides the employee with oral or written notice of the charges against him, an explanation of the employer's evidence, and an opportunity to present his side of the story. The Court reasoned that the governmental interest in the immediate termination of an unsatisfactory employee is outweighed by an employee's interest in retaining employment and the interest in avoiding the risk of an erroneous termination.[59]

Thus, it is clear that those public employees who can legitimately claim liberty or property right protections of due process for their job are guaranteed an evidentiary hearing. Such hearing should be conducted prior to disciplinary action being taken unless the prediscipline protections just mentioned are provided, in which case the full-blown hearing may be postponed until afterward.

For those administrators with a collective bargaining relationship with their employees, where minimal procedural safeguards are provided in contractual grievance-arbitration provisions, that avenue of relief may very well provide an acceptable substitute for constitutionally mandated procedural rights.[60]

Substantive Due Process

As mentioned earlier, due process requirements embrace substantive as well as procedural aspects. In the context of disciplinary action, substantive due process requires that the rules and regulations on which disciplinary action is predicated be clear, specific, and reasonably related to a valid public need.[61] In the police environment, these requirements present the greatest challenge to the commonly found departmental regulations against conduct unbecoming an officer or conduct that brings discredit upon the department.

The requirement that a rule or regulation be reasonably related to a valid public need means that a police department may not intrude into the private matters of its officers in which it has no legitimate interest. Therefore, there must be a connection ''between the prohibited conduct and the officer's fitness to perform the duties required by his position.''[62] In addition, the conduct must be of such a nature as to adversely affect the morale and efficiency of the department or have a tendency to destroy public respect for and confidence in the department.[63] Thus, it has been held that a rule prohibiting unbecoming conduct or discrediting behavior cannot be applied to the remarks of a police officer that were highly critical of several prominent local figures but were made to a private citizen in a private conversation in a patrol car, and were broadcast accidentally over the officer's patrol car radio.[64]

The requirements for clarity and specificity are necessary to ensure (1) that the innocent are not trapped without fair warning, (2) that those who enforce the regulations have their discretion limited by explicit standards, and (3) that where basic First Amendment rights are affected by a regulation, the regulation does not operate unreasonably to inhibit the exercise of those rights.[65]

The courts' applications of these requirements to unbecoming conduct and discrediting behavior rules have taken two courses. The first course, exemplified by *Bence* v. *Breier,* has been to declare such regulations unconstitutional because of their vagueness. In its consideration of a Milwaukee Police Department rule that prohibited "conduct unbecoming a member and detrimental to the service," the court found that the rule lacked

> inherent, objective content from which ascertainable standards defining the proscribed conduct could be fashioned. Like beauty, their content exists only in the eye of the beholder. The subjectivity implicit in the language of the rule permits police officials to enforce the rule with unfettered discretion, and it is precisely this potential for arbitrary enforcement which is abhorrent to the Due Process Clause.[66]

The second course taken by the courts has been to uphold the constitutionality of the regulation because, as applied to the officer in the case at hand, it should have been clear to him that his behavior was meant to be proscribed by the regulation. Under this approach, the court is saying that there may or may not be some circumstances in which the rule is too vague or overbroad, but the rule is constitutional in the present case. Thus, it should be clear to any police officer that fleeing from the scene of an accident[67] or making improper advances toward a young woman during the course of an official investigation[68] constitutes conduct unbecoming an officer or conduct that discredits the police department.

Many police departments also have a regulation prohibiting neglect or dereliction of duty. While on its face such a rule would seem to possess some of the same potential vagueness and overbreadth shortcomings characteristic of the unbecoming conduct rules, it has fared better in the courts since the usual disciplinary action taken under neglect-of-duty rules nearly always seems to be for conduct for which police officers could reasonably expect disciplinary action. The courts have upheld administrative sanctions against officers under neglect-of-duty rules for sleeping on the job,[69] failing to prepare for planned demonstrations,[70] falsification of police records,[71] failure to make scheduled court appearances,[72] failure to investigate a reported auto accident,[73] and directing a subordinate to discontinue enforcement of a city ordinance.[74] The courts have refused to uphold disciplinary action against a police chief who did not keep eight-to-four office hours,[75] and against an officer who missed a training session on riot control because of marital problems.[76]

Damages and Remedies

In determining an employee's entitlement to damages and relief, the issue of whether the employer's disciplinary action was justified is important. For example, when an employee's termination was justified, but procedural due process violations occurred, the employee can recover only nominal damages in the absence of proof of actual compensable injuries deriving from the due process violation. Upon proof of actual injury, an employee may recover compensatory damages, which would include damages for mental and emotional distress and damage to career or reputation.[77] However, injury caused by the lack of due process when the termination was justified will not be compensable in the form of back pay.[78]

Constitutional Rights of Police Officers

Free Speech

The First Amendment of the U.S. Constitution prohibits Congress from passing any law "abridging the freedom of speech." It has been held that the due process clause of the Fourteenth Amendment makes this prohibition applicable to the states, counties, and cities as well.[79]

Although freedom of speech is one of the most fundamental of all constitutional rights, the Supreme Court has indicated that "the State has interests as an employer in regulating the speech of its employees that differ significantly from those it possesses in connection with regulation of the speech of the citizenry in general."[80] Therefore, the state may place restrictions on the speech of its employees that it could not impose on the general citizenry. However, these restrictions must be reasonable.[81] Generally, disputes involving infringement of public employee speech will be resolved by balancing the interests of the state as an employer against the employee's constitutional rights.[82]

There are two basic situations in which a police regulation or other action may be found to be an unreasonable infringement upon the free speech interests of an officer. The first is when the action is overly broad. A Chicago Police Department rule prohibiting "any activity, conversation, deliberation, or discussion which is derogatory to the Department" was ruled overly broad because it prohibited all criticism of the department by policemen, even if the criticism occurred in private conversation.[83] The same fate befell a New Orleans Police Department regulation that prohibited statements by a police officer that "unjustly criticize or ridicule, or express hatred or contempt toward, or . . . which may be detrimental to, or cast suspicion on the reputation of, or otherwise defame, any person."[84]

A second situation in which a free speech limitation may be found unreasonable is in the way in which the governmental action is applied. The most common shortcoming of police departmental action in this area is a failure to demonstrate that the statements by the officer being disciplined adversely affected the operation of the department.[85] Thus, a Baltimore police regulation prohibiting public criticism of departmental action was held to have been applied unconstitutionally to a police officer who was president of the police union and who had stated in a television interview that the police commissioner was not leading the department effectively and that "the bottom is going to fall out of this city."[86]

A more recent basis for enforcing employees' First Amendment freedom of speech is that of public policy. The Eighth Circuit held that discharging an employee who violated the police department's chain of command by reporting misconduct to an official outside of the city violated the employee's First Amendment rights. The court reasoned that the city's interest in maintaining discipline through the chain-of-command policy was outweighed by the public's vital interest in the integrity of its law enforcers, and by the employee's right to speak out on such matters.[87] However, the same court upheld a department's refusal to promote a fire captain who, as union president, had issued a letter to the public in which he accused the chief of destroying the department.[88]

Other First Amendment Rights

A basic right of Americans in our democratic system of government is the right to engage in political activity. As with free speech, the government may impose reasonable restrictions upon the political behavior of its employees that it could not impose on the citizenry at large. It is argued that if the state could not impose some such restrictions, there would be a substantial danger that employees could be pressured by their superiors to support political candidates or causes that were contrary to their own beliefs under threat of loss of employment or other adverse action against them for failure to do so.[89]

At the federal level, various types of partisan political activity by federal employees are controlled by the Hatch Act. The constitutionality of that act has been upheld by the U.S. Supreme Court.[90] Many states have similar statutes, which are usually referred to as "little Hatch" acts, controlling political activity by state employees. The Oklahoma version of the Hatch act, which was upheld by the Supreme Court,[91] prohibited state employees from soliciting political contributions, joining a partisan political club, serving on the committee of a political party, being a candidate for any paid political office, or taking part in the management of a political party or campaign. However, some states, such as Florida, specifically prohibit local governments from limiting the off-duty political activity of their employees.

Whereas the Supreme Court decisions might appear to have put to rest all controversy over the extent to which the government can limit political activity by its employees, that has not been the case. In two more recent cases, lower courts have placed limits on the authority of the state in limiting the political activity of state employees.

In Pawtucket, Rhode Island, two firemen ran for mayor and city councilman, respectively, in a nonpartisan election, despite a city charter provision prohibiting all city employees from engaging in any political activity except voting and privately expressing their opinions. In granting the firemen's requests for an injunction against the enforcement of this provision, the court ruled that the Supreme Court precedents did not apply to the Pawtucket charter provision because the statutes upheld in the prior decisions had prohibited only partisan political activity.[92] In a very similar case in Boston, however, the court upheld the police departmental rule at issue there on the basis that whether the partisan-nonpartisan distinction was crucial was a matter for legislative or administrative determination.[93]

In a Michigan case, the court declared unconstitutional two city charter provisions that prohibited contributions to or solicitations for any political purpose by city employees because it was overly broad.[94] That court specifically rejected the partisan-nonpartisan distinction as crucial, focusing instead on the office involved and the relationship to that office of the employees whose political activity was at issue. For example, the court saw no danger to an important municipal interest in the activities of a city employee "who is raising funds to organize a petition drive seeking a rate change from the Public Service Commission."[95]

Thus, whereas the Supreme Court has tended to be supportive of governmental efforts to limit the political activities of government employees, it is clear that some lower courts intend to limit the Supreme Court decisions to the facts of those cases. Therefore, careful consideration should be given to the scope of political activity to be restricted by a police regulation, and trends in the local jurisdiction should be examined closely.

The cases just discussed dealt with political activity, as opposed to mere political affiliation. May a police officer be relieved of his or her duties because of his or her political affiliations on the basis that those affiliations impede his or her ability to carry out the policies of superiors with different political affiliations? The Supreme Court addressed this question in a case arising out of the Sheriff's Department in Cook County, Illinois.[96] The newly elected sheriff, a Democrat, had discharged the chief deputy of the Process Division and a bailiff of the Juvenile Court, both of whom were nonmerit system employees, because they were Republicans. The Court ruled that it was a violation of these employees' First Amendment rights to discharge them from nonpolicymaking positions because of their political party memberships.[97]

Nonpolitical associations are also protected by the First Amendment. However, it is common for police departments to prohibit officers from associating with known felons or other persons of bad reputation on the basis that "such associations may expose an officer to irresistible temptations to yield in his obligation to impartially enforce the law, and . . . may give the appearance that the community's police officers are not themselves honest and impartial enforcers of the law." Sometimes the prohibition is imposed by means of a specific ordinance or regulation, whereas in other instances the prohibition is enforced by considering it conduct unbecoming an officer. Of course, if the latter approach is used, the ordinance or regulation will have to overcome the legal obstacles discussed earlier, relating to unbecoming conduct or discrediting behavior rules.

As with rules touching upon other First Amendment rights, rules prohibiting associations with criminals and other undesirables must not be overly broad in their reach. Thus, a Detroit Police Department regulation that prohibited knowing and intentional associations with convicted criminals or persons charged with crimes except in the course of an officer's official duties was declared unconstitutional because it proscribed some associations that could have no bearing on an officer's integrity or the public's confidence in an officer. The Court cited as examples an association with a fellow church member who had been arrested on one occasion years ago, and the befriending of a recently convicted person who wanted to become a productive citizen.[98]

The other common difficulty with this kind of rule is that it is sometimes applied to situations in which the association has not been demonstrated to have had a detrimental effect on the performance of the officer's duties or on the discipline and efficiency of the department. Thus, one court has held that a police officer who was a nudist but was fully qualified in all other respects to be a police officer could not be fired simply because he was a practicing nudist.[99] On the other hand, another court upheld the firing of a police officer who had had sexual intercourse at a party with a woman he knew to be a nude model at a local "adult theater of known disrepute."[100] The court viewed this behavior as being of such a disreputable nature that it had a detrimental effect on the discipline and efficiency of the department.

The First Amendment's protection of free speech has been viewed as protecting means of expression other than verbal utterances.[101] That issue as it relates to an on-duty police officer's personal appearance has been addressed by the Supreme Court decision in *Kelley* v. *Johnson*,[102] which upheld the constitutionality of a regulation of the Suffolk County, New York, Police Department that established several grooming standards for its male officers. The Court in *Kelley* held that either a desire to make police officers readily recognizable to the public or a desire to maintain an esprit de corps was a sufficiently rational justification for the regulation.

Searches and Seizures

The Fourth Amendment to the U.S. Constitution protects "the right of the people to be secure in their persons, houses, papers, and effects, against unreasonable searches and seizures. . . ." This guarantee protects against actions by the states as well as by the federal government.[103] Generally, the cases interpreting the Fourth Amendment require that before a search or seizure can be effectuated, the police must have probable cause to believe that a crime has been committed and that evidence relevant to the crime will be found at the place to be searched. Because of the language in the Fourth Amendment about "persons, houses, papers, and effects," for years the case law analyzed what property was subject to the amendment's protection. However, in an extremely important case in 1967, the Supreme Court ruled that the amendment protected individuals' reasonable expectations of privacy and not just property interests.[104]

The Fourth Amendment usually applies to police officers when at home or off duty as it would to any other citizen. However, because of the nature of the employment, a police officer can be subjected to investigative procedures that would not be permitted when an ordinary citizen was involved. One such situation arises with respect to equipment and lockers provided by the department to its officers. In this situation the officer has no expectation of privacy that merits protection.[105] The rights of prison authorities to search their employees was at issue in a 1985 Iowa case. There the court refused to find a consent form signed as a condition of hire to constitute a blanket waiver of all Fourth Amendment rights.[106]

Another situation involves the ordering of officers to appear at a lineup. Requiring someone to appear in a lineup is a seizure of his or her person and, therefore, would ordinarily require probable cause. However, a federal appeals court upheld a police commissioner's order to sixty-two officers to appear in a lineup for the purpose of identifying officers who had allegedly beaten several civilians. The court held that in this situation "the governmental interest in the particular intrusion (should be weighed) against the offense to personal dignity and integrity." Because of the nature of the police officer's employment relationship, "he does not have the full privacy and liberty from police officials that he would otherwise enjoy."[107]

To enforce the protections guaranteed by the Fourth Amendment's search and seizure requirements, the courts have fashioned the so-called "exclusionary rule," which prohibits the use of evidence obtained in violation of the Fourth Amendment in criminal proceedings. No cases have held specifically that the exclusionary rule applies to disciplinary hearings. The cases dealing with the exclusionary rule's applicability to other kinds of administrative hearings are so inconsistent that it is impossible to predict how the courts would decide the issue when police disciplinary hearings are concerned.[108]

Right Against Self-Incrimination

On two occasions the Supreme Court has addressed questions concerning the Fifth Amendment rights of police officers who are the subjects of investigations. In *Garrity* v. *New Jersey*,[109] a police officer had been ordered by the attorney general to answer certain questions or be discharged. He testified and the information gained as a result of his answers was later used to convict him of criminal charges.

The Fifth Amendment protects an individual from being compelled "in any criminal case to be a witness against himself."[110] The Supreme Court held that the information obtained from the police officer could not be used at his criminal trial because the Fifth Amendment forbids the use of coercion of this sort to extract an incriminating statement from a suspect.

In *Gardner* v. *Broderick*,[111] a police officer had declined to answer questions put to him by a grand jury investigating police misconduct on the grounds that his answers might tend to incriminate him. As a result, the officer was dismissed from his job. The Supreme Court ruled that the officer could not be fired for his refusal to waive his constitutional right to remain silent. However, the Court made it clear that it would have been proper for the grand jury to have required the officer to answer or face discharge for his refusal so long as the officer had been informed that his answers could not be used against him in a criminal case and the questions were related specifically, directly, and narrowly to the performance of his official duties. The Court felt that this approach was necessary to protect the important state interest in ensuring that police officers were performing their duties faithfully.

As a result of these cases, it is proper to discharge a police officer who refuses to answer questions that are related specifically and directly to the performance of his duties, and who has been informed that any answers he does give cannot be used against him in a criminal proceeding.[112]

Historically, it was not uncommon for police departments to make use of polygraph examinations in the course of internal investigations. The legal question that has arisen most frequently is whether an officer may be required to submit to such a procedure under threat of discharge for refusal to do so. There is some diversity of legal authority on this question, but the majority of courts that have considered it have held that an officer can be required to take the examination.[113]

An Arizona court overturned a county merit system commission's finding that a polygraph examination could be ordered only as a last resort after all other investigative efforts had been exhausted, and held that

> a polygraph is always proper to verify statements made by law enforcement officers during the course of a departmental investigation as long as the officers are advised that the answers cannot be used against them in any criminal prosecution, that the questions will relate solely to the performance of official duties, and that refusal will result in dismissal.[114]

On the other hand, a more recent decision of the Florida Supreme Court held that the dismissal of a police officer for refusing to submit to a polygraph test constituted "an unjust and unlawful job deprivation." Further, the court recognized that granting to public employers a carte blanche authority to force employees to submit to unlimited questioning during a polygraph test would conflict with the employee's constitutional right of privacy, and would abrogate his or her protection against self-incrimination.[115]

Other Grounds for Disciplinary Action

Sexual Conduct

The cases in this area tend to fall into two general categories: cases involving adultery and cases involving homosexuality.

Most cases of the 1960s and 1970s were in general agreement that adultery, even though committed while the policeman was off duty and in private, created a proper basis for disciplinary action.[116] The courts held that such behavior brings adverse criticism upon the agency, and tends to undermine public confidence in the department. However, one case involving an Internal Revenue Service agent suggests that to uphold disciplinary action for adultery, the government would have to prove that the employing agency was actually discredited, and further stated that the discreditation will not be presumed from the proof of adulterous conduct.[117]

More recently, the Supreme Court justices appeared to be divided on the issue of extramarital sexual activity in public employment. In 1984, the Sixth Circuit held that a Michigan police officer could not be fired solely because he was living with a woman to whom he was not married (a felony under state law).[118] In 1985, the Supreme Court denied review of that decision over the strong objection of three justices who felt the case "presented an important issue of constitutional law regarding the contours of the right of privacy afforded individuals for sexual matters."[119]

The issue of homosexual activity as a basis for discharge was recently presented to the Supreme Court. Oklahoma had a law permitting discharge of schoolteachers for engaging in "public homosexual activity."[120] The lower court held the law to be facially overly broad and therefore unconstitutionally restrictive. The Supreme Court affirmed the decision.[121] Another federal court held that the discharge of a bisexual guidance counselor did not deprive the plaintiff of her First or Fourteenth amendment rights. The counselor's discussion of her sexual preferences with teachers and other personnel was not protected by the First Amendment. Her equal protection claim failed because she did not show that the heterosexual employees would have been treated differently for communicating their sexual preferences.[122] Additionally, a discharged homosexual Navy petty officer was not reinstated because of the court's determination that his discharge was not in violation of the constitutional right of privacy or equal protection.[123]

Residency Requirements

A number of local governments have established requirements that all or certain classes of their employees live within the geographical limits of the jurisdiction. These residency requirements have been justified by the governments imposing them as desirable because they increase employees' rapport with, and understanding of, the community. When police officers were concerned, it has been asserted that the presence of off-duty police has a deterrent effect on crime and results in chance encounters that might lead to additional sources of information.

Prior to 1976, challenges to the legality of residency requirements for public employees dotted the legal landscape. The challenges had persisted in spite of the U.S. Supreme Court's denial of an appeal from the decision of the Michigan Supreme Court that Detroit's residency requirement for police was not irrational.[124] In 1976, the Supreme Court in *McCarthy* v. *Philadelphia Civil Service Commission* ruled that Philadelphia's residency requirement for firemen did not violate the Constitution.[125]

Since the *McCarthy* decision, the legal attacks on the residency requirements have subsided. The cases now seem to be concerned with determining what constitutes residency. The most obvious means of attempting to avoid the residency requirement (by establishing a second residence within the city) appears doomed to failure unless the police officer can demonstrate that he or she spends at least a substantial part of his or her time at the in-city residence.[126] A strong argument has been made that, in areas where housing is unavailable or prohibitively expensive, a residency requirement is unreasonable.[127] In upholding the application of such requirements, courts have focused on the issues of equal enforcement and the specificity of the local residency standard.[128]

Religious Belief or Practice

In part, Title VII of the Civil Rights Act of 1964 prohibits religious discrimination in employment. The act defines religion as including "all aspects of religious . . . practice, as well as belief, unless an employer . . . is unable to reasonably accommodate to an employee's . . . religious . . . practice without undue hardship on the conduct of the employer's business."[129] Title VII requires reasonable accommodation of religious beliefs, not accommodation in exactly the way the employee would like. Title VII also does not require accommodation which spares the employee any cost whatsoever.[130] For example, an Albuquerque fireman who was a Seventh-Day Adventist refused to work the Friday night or Saturday day shifts because they fell on what he believed to be the Sabbath day. Although department policy would have permitted the fireman to avoid working these shifts by taking leave with pay, taking leave without pay, or trading shifts with other firemen, he refused to use these means and insisted that the department find other firemen to trade shifts with him or simply excuse him from the shifts affected by his religious beliefs. The department refused to do either. Under these circumstances, the court ruled that the department's accommodations to the fireman had been reasonable and that no further accommodations could be made without undue hardship to the department. Therefore, the fireman's discharge was upheld. However, as the court itself emphasized, decisions in cases in this area will depend on the particular facts and circumstances of each case. Recently, the courts have held that the termination of a Mormon police officer for practicing plural marriage (polygamy), in violation of state law, was not a violation of his right to freely exercise his religious beliefs.[131]

Moonlighting

Traditionally, the courts have supported the authority of police departments to place limits on the outside employment of their employees.[132] Police department restrictions on "moonlighting" range from a complete ban on outside employment to permission to engage in certain endeavors, such as investments, rental of property, teaching of law enforcement subjects, and employment designed to improve the police image. The rationale in support of moonlighting prohibitions is that "outside employment seriously interferes with keeping the [police and fire] departments fit and ready for action at all times."[133]

However, in a Louisiana case, firemen offered unrefuted evidence that moonlighting had been a common practice before the city banned moonlighting; during the previous sixteen years, no firemen had ever needed sick leave as a result of injuries suffered while moonlighting; there had never been a problem locating off-duty firemen to respond to an emergency; and moonlighting had never been shown to be a source of fatigue that was serious enough to impair a fireman's alertness on the job. Under these circumstances, the court ruled that there was not a sufficient basis for the prohibition on moonlighting and invalidated the ordinance.[134]

Misuse of Firearms

Because of the obvious dangers associated with the use of handguns and other firearms, it is not surprising that police departments customarily regulate the use of such weapons by their officers. The courts have held that such regulations need only be reasonable and that the burden rests with the disciplined police officer appellant to demonstrate that the regulation is arbitrary and unreasonable.[135] Moreover, the cases suggest that the courts are inclined to grant great latitude to police department administrators in determining when their firearm regulations have been violated.[136]

Police firearm regulations tend to address three basic issues: (1) requirements for the safeguarding of the weapon, (2) guidelines for carrying the weapon while off duty, and (3) limitations on when the weapon may be fired.

There is little case law dealing with regulations concerning the safeguarding of an officer's weapon. However, a New York court has held that an officer could not be disciplined for neglecting to safeguard his weapon when the evidence showed that the weapon had been stolen during a burglary of the officer's room while he was asleep.[137]

Regulations concerning the firing of a weapon are difficult to construct with precision.[138] Applying these regulations to actual situations is equally difficult. An important caution relates to an earlier discussion of the fact that some courts in damage suits have held police officers subject to a higher standard of care than the law itself would require, because the department's regulations established a higher standard. Although police departments should not necessarily refrain from establishing exacting requirements as to when their officers can fire their weapons, police administrators should be aware of the possible effect such action could have in civil damage actions.[139]

Alcohol and Drugs in the Work Environment

It is common for police departments to require that their officers not be under the influence of any intoxicating agent while on duty. Even in the absence of such specific regulation, disciplinary action has been upheld when they were taken against an officer who was suspected of being intoxicated while on duty by charging him with neglect of duty or violation of a state law.[140]

Regulations that prohibit being under the influence of an intoxicating or mind-altering substance have been upheld uniformly as reasonable because of the hazardous nature of a police officer's work, and the serious impact his or her behavior or misbehavior is sure to have upon the property and safety of others. The necessity to require a clear head and rational action, unbefuddled by alcohol or drugs, is clear.[141] A Louisiana court upheld a regulation that prohibited an officer from consuming alcoholic beverages on or off duty to the extent that it caused the officer's behavior to become obnoxious, disruptive, or disorderly.[142]

Effective enforcement of regulations against an officer's being under the influence of drugs or alcohol will occasion situations when a police supervisor or administrator will order an officer to submit to one or more tests to determine the presence of the prohibited substance in the subject's body.

It has been held that a fireman could be ordered to submit to a blood sampling when reasonable grounds existed for believing that he was intoxicated, and that it was permissible to discharge the fireman for his refusal to comply with the order.[143]

More recently the courts have also been asked to review police department policies that require officers to submit to urinalysis for the purpose of determining the presence of drugs or alcohol. The prevailing view appears to be that totally random, unscheduled urine testing is unacceptable, but that particular officers can be required to submit to urinalysis if there exists a "reasonable suspicion" that the officer has been using a prohibited substance.[144] The results of such compulsory tests are appropriate evidence for introduction in administrative discharge proceedings.[145] Decisions involving other governmental employees and similar kinds of personal intrusions (e.g., strip searches of prison guards) seem to support the view that random testing is unreasonable under the Fourth Amendment.[146] This is a rapidly developing area of law that needs to be carefully monitored.

Terms and Conditions of Employment

Wage and Hour Regulations

The Fair Labor Standards Act (FLSA) was initially enacted by Congress in 1938 to establish minimum wages, and to require overtime compensation in the private sector. In 1974, amendments to the act extended its coverage to state and local government employees, and established special work period provisions for police and fire. However, in 1976 the U.S. Supreme Court ruled that the extension of the act into the realm of traditional local and state government functions was unconstitutional.[147] Almost a decade later, the Supreme Court surprisingly reversed itself thus bringing all local police agencies under the coverage of the FLSA.[148] Shortly thereafter, Congress enacted the Fair Labor Standards Amendments of 1985 (effective April 15, 1986) which set forth special wage and hour provisions for government employees in an effort to reduce the monetary impact of the overtime requirements on state and local governments.

Generally, all rank-and-file law enforcement officers are covered under the FLSA. Exemptions include elected officials, their personal staffs, and those employees in "policymaking" positions. The law requires that overtime be paid to police personnel for all work in excess of 43 hours in a 7-day cycle or 171 hours in a 28-day period. Employers are allowed to establish or negotiate a work/pay period as they see fit within those boundaries. (The FLSA sets minimum standards that may be exceeded by offering greater benefits.) The appropriate wage for overtime hours is set at 1½ times the employee's regular rate of pay. This may be given in money or compensatory time. Public safety officers may accrue a maximum of 480 hours of "comp" time, which, if not utilized as leave, must be paid off upon separation from employment at the employee's final regular rate or at the average pay over the last three years, whichever is higher.

Of special interest to police agencies is that off-duty work and special details for a separate independent employer voluntarily undertaken by the employee are not utilized for calculating overtime payment obligations. Thus, specific hourly rates may still be negotiated for such work.

Since the new provisions discussed previously were only recently placed into effect, it is exceedingly difficult to offer definitive guidance to police administrators as to the precise application and interpretation of the 1985 amendments. Therefore, the readers should seek legal guidance to ensure that wage and hour regulations are appropriately implemented and enforced.

Age-Based Hiring and Retirement Policies

State and local governments have adopted a variety of personnel policies to ensure that police officers are in adequate mental and physical condition in order to perform the normal and the unexpected strenuous physical activities of the job satisfactorily and safely. Based upon the assumption that increasing age slows responses, saps strength, and increases the likelihood of sudden incapacitation because of breakdowns of the nervous and/or cardiovascular systems, many police departments and state law enforcement agencies have established mandatory hiring and retirement ages.

During the 1970s the courts allowed employers much latitude in enforcing retirement age requirements, finding such standards to be rationally related to a legitimate state interest in seeing that officers were physically prepared to protect the public's welfare.[149] In more recent decisions, however, the Supreme Court has significantly restricted the employer's ability to require that an employee be terminated upon reaching a certain age.

The Age Discrimination In Employment Act (ADEA) is a federal law that prohibits discrimination on the basis of age against employees who are between the ages of forty and seventy, unless age is shown to be a "bona fide occupational qualification (BFOQ) reasonably necessary to the normal operation of the particular business."[150] The Supreme Court has held that the BFOQ exemption is meant to be an extremely narrow exception to the general prohibition of age discrimination contained in the ADEA.[151] For an employer to successfully demonstrate that its age-based mandatory retirement rule is valid, it must first prove the existence of a job qualification reasonably necessary to the essence of its operation. Second, the employer must show that it has reasonable cause, based upon fact, for believing that substantially all persons in the prohibited age group would be unable to perform the job duties safely and efficiently, or that it is impractical or impossible to accurately test and predict the capabilities of individuals in the excluded group.[152]

In another 1985 decision, the Supreme Court stated that stereotypical assumptions about the effects of aging on employee performance were inadequate to demonstrate a BFOQ. Instead, the Court held that employers are required to make a "particularized, factual showing" with respect to each element of the BFOQ defense.[153]

The federal courts have considered an ADEA challenge to a New York State law setting a maximum age of twenty-nine for those applying for jobs as police officers. The court concluded that age twenty-nine was not a BFOQ, and ruled that the requirement was a violation of the law. The court noted that the employer has the same burden of proof to justify an age-based hiring standard as it does to justify an age-based retirement requirement.[154]

Summary and Conclusion

In recent years there has been a significant increase in the amount of litigation involving police agencies and their officers. A substantial portion of this litigation has stemmed from efforts by citizens to receive compensation for injuries allegedly caused by department policy and the actions of police department employees. Such suits are brought as state tort actions, Section 1983 claims, or Bivens-type suits. In state tort actions, the plaintiff alleges that his or her injury was caused by conduct that constitutes a tort under state law, such as assault, battery, false imprisonment, or false arrest. A Section 1983 claim is brought under a federal statute that permits relief from infringements of rights created by the Constitution or by federal law by persons acting under color of state law. A Bivens-type suit also provides relief from infringements of constitutional rights and serves primarily to fill some "holes" left by Section 1983.

All three types of suits have limitations on who can be sued. The police supervisor and administrator are generally not liable solely by virtue of their status as the employer of the officer whose conduct caused the injury, unless the supervisor or administrator specifically authorized or cooperated in the officer's conduct that led to the injury. However, in an increasing number of cases, supervisors and administrators have been found liable for the misbehavior of their subordinates when plaintiffs were able to demonstrate that the former were negligent in the employment, training, or retention of their subordinates.

The governmental body that employs the officer accused of culpable behavior was traditionally shielded from liability by the doctrine of sovereign immunity. In recent decades, the protection of sovereign immunity in state tort actions has been eroded substantially by legislative and judicial action, but it remains an important restriction on the amount of recovery that can be obtained against the government.

Plaintiffs seeking recovery for injuries caused by police conduct are also limited by the judicial extension of immunity to public employees. In suits based on federal law, an absolute immunity is extended to prosecutors, and to judicial and quasijudicial officials. A qualified immunity is extended to other officials while they are acting in a discretionary capacity, in good faith, and in a reasonable manner. However, a defendant is not acting in good faith if his or her conduct violates settled law. In state tort actions, absolute immunity is still usually extended to public officials in their exercise of discretionary functions.

Disciplinary actions against police officers raise issues concerning procedures that are required by the due process guarantees of the U.S. Constitution. Due process protections apply when property interests or liberty interests of a public employee may be affected by disciplinary action. Supreme Court cases suggest that in determining when property and liberty interests evoke due process guarantees, the Court will carefully examine whether the local government intended to create a protected interest in the public employee.

When due process is mandated, procedural protections are required by the Constitution in taking disciplinary action against a police officer. Court decisions have extended to the police officer rights to be given notice of the charges, to call witnesses, to be confronted by and cross-examine adverse witnesses, to have counsel, and to have a decision based on the record of a hearing conducted by an impartial party. The evidentiary hearing may be postponed until after the disciplinary action is taken when risk-reducing protections, such as written notice of and opportunity to rebut the reasons for the action, are afforded the employee.

Due process also requires that disciplinary rules be clear, specific, and reasonably related to a valid job requirement. Accordingly, a disciplinary rule must address conduct that has an impact upon an officer's fitness to perform his or her duties, adversely affects departmental morale or efficiency, or undermines public confidence in the department. The rule must be clear enough to give fair warning, to control the discretion of administrators, and to avoid a "chilling effect" on the exercise of constitutional rights by officers. Many departments prohibit conduct "unbecoming an officer" or "tending to bring discredit upon the department." The application of due process protections to rules of this nature has resulted in some rules being declared unconstitutional for vagueness. Other courts have upheld the constitutionality of such rules because in various disciplinary situations, it should have been clear to the officer that the rule was intended to prohibit his or her conduct.

Sometimes disciplinary rules attempt to prohibit conduct of police officers that is protected by the Constitution. Rules infringing upon the free speech of officers may be upheld if the legitimate interest of the governmental employer is found to be more important than the officer's free speech interest. However, such rules frequently run afoul of the Constitution because they are too broad, or because the department failed to demonstrate that the officer's speech produced an unjustifiable adverse effect on the department's ability to perform.

Rights regarding political participation are also protected by the First Amendment to the Constitution. However, the federal Hatch Act and similar state laws that prohibit nearly all partisan political activity by public employees, have been upheld by the Supreme Court. Nevertheless, courts have struck down prohibitions that extended to nonpartisan political activity or political activity, which seemed only remotely related to an important governmental interest. Dismissals of nonpolicymaking public employees for reason of political party affiliation have been held illegal.

In other areas affected by the First Amendment, courts have generally upheld rules prohibiting police officers from associating with criminals or other undesirables so long as the rule is not too broad, and it can be demonstrated that the association has a detrimental effect on the department's operation. With regard to freedom of expression, the Supreme Court has upheld the establishment of grooming standards for police officers.

Courts have held that the Fourth Amendment protection against unreasonable searches and seizures does not prevent a department from searching lockers and equipment issued to officers, or from ordering officers to appear in a lineup when there is a strong governmental interest at stake.

The constitutional right against self-incrimination does not prohibit a police department from ordering an officer to answer questions directly related to the performance of his or her duties. Although there is some disagreement among courts considering the question, most courts have also held that officers may be required to take polygraph examinations under the circumstances just described.

Other issues regarding disciplinary action against police officers include:

1. Adultery has generally been upheld as a proper basis for disciplinary action.
2. Homosexuality. The key seems to be whether the employee's homosexuality

impairs the efficiency of the agency, and only flagrant displays of homosexual conduct have generally been found to have such an effect.

3. Residency. A department can require its officers to live within the geographical limits of its jurisdiction.

4. Religious preference. A department must reasonably accommodate the religious practices of its officers without imposing an "undue hardship" upon itself or other employees.

5. Moonlighting may be prohibited.

6. Regulations relating to the use of weapons issued to officers will be upheld so long as they are reasonable.

7. Regulations prohibiting intoxication or impairment of an officer's ability to perform while on duty as a result of the influence of drugs or alcohol carry a strong presumption of validity. Police officers can probably be ordered to take blood, breathalyzer, or urinalysis when there is a reasonable suspicion of abuse or influence.

In administrative matters unrelated to the disciplinary process, the Supreme Court has held that police departments must comply with the minimum wage and overtime requirements of the Fair Labor Standards Act. Persons between the ages of forty and seventy may not be discriminated against in employment decisions unless age is a bona fide occupational qualification reasonably necessary to the operation of the department's business.[155]

Discussion Questions

1. What are the two vehicles by which federal courts can acquire jurisdiction of tort suits that have traditionally been brought in state courts?

2. What is sovereign immunity and how has it changed in this country?

3. How are intentional and negligent torts different?

4. Of what importance is the doctrine of "respondent superior" to police administrators?

5. What are procedural and substantive due process?

6. What are the twelve elements of a due process hearing?

7. In what three ways are rules of law promulgated?

8. Of what importance is the distinction between ordinary and punitive damages?

9. What are liberty rights and property rights?

10. To what extent may police administrators legally restrict the exercise of First Amendment rights by police officers?

Notes

1. False arrest is the arrest of a person without probable cause. Generally, this means making an arrest when an ordinarily prudent person would not have concluded that a crime had been committed or that the person arrested had committed the crime. False imprisonment is the intentional illegal detention of a person. The detention that can give rise to a false imprisonment claim is any confinement to a specified area and not

simply incarceration in a jail. Most false arrests result in false imprisonment as well, but there can be a false imprisonment after a valid arrest also, as when the police fail to release an arrested person after a proper bond has been posted, the police unreasonably delay the arraignment of an arrested person, or authorities fail to release a prisoner after they no longer have authority to hold him. "Brutality" is not a legal tort action as such. Rather, it must be alleged as a civil (as opposed to a criminal) assault and/or battery. Assault is some sort of menacing conduct that puts another person in reasonable fear that he or she is about to have a battery committed upon him or her. Battery is the infliction of harmful or offensive contact upon another person. Harmful or offensive contact is contact that would be considered harmful or offensive by a reasonable person of ordinary sensibilities. See Clarence E. Hagglund, "Liability of Police Officers and Their Employers," *Federation of Insurance Counsel Quarterly*, 26 (Summer 1976), p. 257, for a good discussion of assault and battery, false arrest, false imprisonment, and malicious prosecution as applied to police officers.

2. 403 U.S. 388 (1971). [Citations to case opinions give the volume number in which the opinion is located, followed by the name of the reporter system, the page number, the court if other than the Supreme Court, and the year in which the opinion was rendered.]

3. See William L. Prosser, *Handbook of the Law of Torts*, 4th ed. (St. Paul: West, 1971), p. 69 for a good discussion of the philosophical basis for and development of the doctrine of vicarious liability.

4. Wayne W. Schmidt, "Recent Developments in Police Civil Liability," *Journal of Police Science and Administration*, 4 (1976), p. 197, and the cases cited therein.

5. [T]he courts have very generally drawn a distinction between a sheriff and a chief of police, holding that the deputies of the former are selected and appointed by the sheriff and act purely as his representatives, but that police officers are generally not selected exclusively by the chief of police, and are themselves officers and do not act for the chief of police in the performance of their official duties," *Parish* v. *Meyers*, 225 P. 633 (Wash. 1924).

6. *Jordan* v. *Kelly*, 223 F. Supp. 731 (1963), p. 738.

7. Ibid., p. 739.

8. Schmidt, "Recent Developments in Police Civil Liability," p. 197.

9. Michael P. Lehman, "Bivens and Its Progeny: The Scope of a Constitutional Cause of Action for Torts Committed by Government Officials," *Hastings Constitutional Law Quarterly*, 4 (1977), pp. 531, 572–575.

10. Prosser, *Handbook of the Law of Torts*, pp. 977–978.

11. Kenneth Culp Davis, *Administrative Law of the Seventies* (Rochester, N.Y.: Lawyers Cooperative, 1976), p. 551 and p. 207, 1978 Supplement.

12. In most states in which abrogation of sovereign immunity has occurred, the abrogation has not been total. In some states, the abrogation is an unconditional waiver of sovereign immunity, but the waiver extends only to certain activities, to cases in which the employee had a particular state of mind, to liability not to exceed a designated monetary amount, or to only a particular level of government. In some states, the waiver of sovereign immunity is effective only if the governmental unit being sued is insured for the potential loss. Yet another approach taken by some states is not to allow government units to be sued but to require indemnification of public employees who have been sued successfully. (For an example, see *Florida Statutes*, Chapter 768.28.)

13. *Hans* v. *Louisiana*, 134 U.S. 1 (1890), *Edelman* v. *Jordan*, 415 U.S. 651 (1974), *Scheuer* v. *Rhodes*, 416 U.S. 232 (1974).

14. *Alabama* v. *Pugh*, 438 U.S. 781 (1978).

15. *Davis* v. *Scherer*, 104 S.Ct. 3012 (1984).

16. *Scheuer* v. *Rhodes*, 416 U.S. 232, 240 (1974).

17. *Wood* v. *Strickland*, 420 U.S. 308 (1975).

18. *Harlow* v. *Fitzgerald*, 457 U.S. 800 (1982).

19. *Mitchell* v. *Forsyth,* 105 S.Ct. 2806 (1985).

20. *Monroe* v. *Pape,* 365 U.S. 167 (1961).

21. 436 U.S. 658 (1978).

22. See, for example, *Rookard* v. *Health and Hospitals Corp.,* 710 F2d 41 (2d Cir 1983).

23. *Oklahoma City* v. *Tuttle,* 105 S.Ct.2427 (1985), but see: *Pembaur* v. *Cincinnati,* U.S.__, No. 84–1160 (1986).

24. *Fundiller* v. *City of Cooper City,* Case No. 84–5104, (11th Cir. 1985).

25. Hagglund, ''Liability of Police Officers and Their Employers,'' p. 257.

26. 468 U.S.____(1984)

27. *Malley* v. *Briggs,* No. 84–1586 (S. Ct. 1986).

28. Schmidt, ''Recent Developments in Police Civil Liability.''

29. Ibid., p. 198.

30. *Wimberly* v. *Patterson,* 183 A.2d 691 (1962), p. 699.

31. *Piatkowski* v. *State,* 251 N.Y.S. 2d 354, (1964), p. 359.

32. Schmidt, ''Recent Developments in Police Civil Liability,'' p. 199.

33. *Fords* v. *Breier,* 383 F. Supp. 505 (E. D. Wis. 1974).

34. *Lucas* v. *Riley,* Superior Court, Los Angeles County, Calif. (1975); *DeLong* v. *City of Denver,* 530 F. 2d 1308 (Colo. 1974); *Grudt* v. *City of Los Angeles,* 468 P. 2d 825 (Cal. 1970); *Dillenbeck* v. *City of Los Angeles,* 446 P. 2d 129 (Cal. 1968).

35. *AELE Law Enforcement Legal Defense Manual,* ''Failure to Provide Medical Treatment,'' Issue 77–6 (1977).

36. Ibid., and cases therein.

37. See, generally, Joan Bertin Lowy, ''Constitutional Limitations on the Dismissal of Public Employees,'' *Brooklyn Law Review,* 43 (Summer 1976), p. 1; Victor G. Rosenblum, ''Schoolchildren: Yes, Policemen: No—Some Thoughts About the Supreme Court's Priorities Concerning the Right to a Hearing in Suspension and Removal Cases,'' *Northwestern University Law Review,* 72 (1977), p. 146.

38. *Wisconsin* v. *Constantineau,* 400 U.S. 433 (1970); *Doe* v. *U.S. Department of Justice,* 753 F. 2d 1092 (D.C. Cir. 1985).

39. *Codd* v. *Velger,* 97 S.Ct. 882 (1977). See also, *Paul* v. *Davis,* 424 U.S. 693 (1976), which held that injury to reputation alone does not constitute a deprivation of liberty. Also see *Swilley* v. *Alexander,* 629 F. 2d 1018 (5th Cir. 1980) where the court held that a letter of reprimand containing untrue charges that was placed in an employee's personnel file infringed on his liberty interest.

40. *Board of Regents* v. *Roth,* 408 U.S. 546 (1972); *Perry* v. *Sindermann,* 408 U.S. 593 (1972).

41. *Arnett* v. *Kennedy,* 416 U.S. 134 (1974); *Bishop* v. *Wood,* 426 U.S. 341 (1976). See Robert L. Rabin, ''Job Security and Due Process: Monitoring Administrative Discretion Through a Reasons Requirement,'' *University of Chicago Law Review,* 44 (1976), pp. 60, 67, for a good discussion of these cases, also: *Bailey* v. *Kirk,* No. 82–1417 (10 Cir. 1985).

42. See Carl Goodman, ''Public Employment and the Supreme Court's 1975–76 Term,'' *Public Personnel Management,* 5 (September–October 1976), pp. 287–289.

43. *Thurston* v. *Dekle,* 531 F. 2d 1264 (5th Cir. 1976), vacated on other grounds 438 U.S. 901 (1978).

44. *Allison* v. *City of Live Oak,* 450 F. Supp 200 (M.D. Fla. 1978).

45. See, e. g., *Confederation of Police* v. *Chicago,* 547 F. 2d 375 (7th Cir. 1977).

46. *Parratt* v. *Taylor,* 451 U.S. 527 (1981).

47. Davis, *Administrative Law of the Seventies,* p. 242.

48. *Memphis Light, Gas & Water Division* v. *Craft,* 436 U.S. 1 (1978); also: *Okeson* v. *Tolley School Dist.,* 760 F. 2d 864 (8th Cir. 1985).

49. In re Dewar, 548 P. 2d 149 (Mont. 1976).

50. *Bush* v. *Beckman*, 131 N.Y.S. 2d 297 (1954); *Gibbs* v. *City of Manchester*, 61 A. 128 (N.H. 1905).
51. *Morrissey* v. *Brewer*, 408 U.S. 471, 489 (1972).
52. *Goldman* v. *Kelly*, 397 U.S. 254 (1970). See also *Buck* v. *N.Y. City Bd. of Ed.*, 553 F. 2d 315 (2nd Cir. 1977), *Cert den*, 438 U.S. 904 (1978).
53. *Morrissey* v. *Brewer*, Ibid.
54. *Marshall* v. *Jerrico, Inc.*, 446 U.S. 238 (1980) and *Hortonville J.S.D. No. 1* v. *Hortonville Ed. Assn.*, 426 U.S. 482 (1976); and *Holley* v. *Seminole County School Dist.*, 755 F.2d 1492 (11th Cir. 1985).
55. 416 U.S. 134 (1974), p. 157.
56. Ibid., pp. 167–168.
57. 424 U.S. 319, 335 (1975).
58. 105 S. Ct. 1487 (1985).
59. Ibid., at 1494.
60. *Gorham* v. *City of Kansas City*, 590 P. 2d 1051 (Kan. S. Ct. 1979) and *Winston* v. *U.S. Postal Service*, 585 F. 2d 198 (7th Cir. 1978).
61. *Bence* v. *Breier*, 501 F. 2d 1185 (7th Cir. 1974).
62. *Perea* v. *Fales*, 114 Cal. Rptr. 808 (1974), p. 810.
63. *Kramer* v. *City of Bethlehem*, 289 A. 2d 767 (1972).
64. *Rogenski* v. *Board of Fire and Police Commissioners of Moline*, 285 N.E. 2d 230 (1972). See also, *Major* v. *Hampton*, 413 F. Supp. 66 (1976), in which the court held that an IRS rule against activities tending to discredit the agency was overbroad as applied to a married employee who had maintained an apartment for illicit sexual liaisons during off-duty hours.
65. *Grayned* v. *City of Rockford*, 408 U.S. 104 (1972), pp. 108–109.
66. *Bence* v. *Breier*, p. 1190.
67. *Rinaldi* v. *Civil Service Commission*, 244 N.W. 2d 609 (Mich. 1976).
68. *Allen* v. *City of Greensboro, North Carolina*, 452 F. 2d 489 (4th Cir. 1971).
69. *Petraitis* v. *Board of Fire and Police Commissioners of City of Palos Hills*, 335 N.E. 2d 126 (Ill. 1975); *Haywood* v. *Municipal Court*, 271 N.E. 2d 591 (Mass. 1971); *Lewis* v. *Board of Trustees*, 212 N.Y.S. 2d 677 (1961). Compare *Stanton* v. *Board of Fire and Police Commissioners of Village of Bridgeview*, 345 N.E. 2d 822 (Ill. 1976).
70. *DeSalvatore* v. *City of Oneonta*, 369 N.Y.S. 2d 820 (1975).
71. *Marino* v. *Los Angeles*, 110 Cal. Rptr. 45 (1973).
72. *Guido* v. *City of Marion*, 280 N.E. 2d 81 (Ind. 1972).
73. *Carroll* v. *Goldstein*, 217 A. 2d 676 (R.I. 1976).
74. *Firemen's and Policemen's Civil Service Commission* v. *Shaw*, 306 S.W. 2d 160 (Tex. 1957).
75. *Martin* v. *City of St. Martinville*, 321 So. 2d 532 (La. 1975).
76. *Arnold* v. *City of Aurora*, 498 P. 2d 970 (Colo. 1973).
77. *Carey* v. *Piphus*, 435 U.S. 247 (1978).
78. *County of Monroe* v. *Dept. of Labor*, 690 F. 2d 1359 (11th Cir. 1982).
79. *Gitlow* v. *New York*, 268 U.S. 652 (1925).
80. *Pickering* v. *Board of Education*, 391 U.S. 563 (1968), p. 568.
81. *Keyishian* v. *Board of Regents*, 385 U.S. 589 (1967).
82. *Pickering* v. *Board of Education*.
83. *Muller* v. *Conlisk*, 429 F. 2d 901 (7th Cir. 1970).
84. *Flynn* v. *Giarusso*, 321 F. Supp. 1295 (E.D. La. 1971), p. 1299. The regulation was revised and later ruled constitutional in *Magri* v. *Giarusso*, 379 F. Supp. 353 (E.D. La. 1974). See also *Gasparinetti* v. *Kerr*, 568 F. 2d 311 (3rd Cir. 1977).
85. *In re Gioglio*, 248 A. 2d 570 (N.J. 1968); *Brukiewa* v. *Police Commissioner of Baltimore*, 263 A. 2d 210 (Md. 1970); *Kannisto* v. *City and County of San Francisco*, 541 F. 2d 841 (9th Cir. 1976). Compare *Magri* v. *Giarusso; Hosford* v. *California State Personnel Board*, 141 Cal. Rptr. 354 (1977); *Simpson* v. *Weeks*, 570 F. 2d 240 (8th Cir. 1978).

86. *Brukiewa* v. *Police Commissioner.*
87. *Brockell* v. *Norton,* 732 F. 2d 664 (8th Cir. 1984).
88. *Germann* v. *City of Kansas City, Mo.,* 776 F. 2d 761 (8th Cir. 1985).
89. *Broadrick* v. *Oklahoma,* 413 U.S. 601 (1973) and *Reeder* v. *Kansas City Bd. of Police Comm.,* 733 F. 2d 543 (8th Cir. 1984).
90. *United Public Workers* v. *Mitchell,* 330 U.S. 75 (1947); *U.S. Civil Service Commission* v. *National Association of Letter Carriers,* 413 U.S. 548 (1973).
91. *Broadrick* v. *Oklahoma.*
92. *Magill* v. *Lynch,* 400 F. Supp. 84 (R.I. 1975).
93. *Boston Police Patrolmen's Association, Inc.* v. *City of Boston,* 326 N.E. 2d 314 (Mass. 1975).
94. *Phillips* v. *City of Flint,* 225 N.W. 2d 780 (Mich. 1975). But compare *Paulos* v. *Breier,* 507 F. 2d 1383 (7th Cir. 1974).
95. Ibid., p. 784.
96. *Elrod* v. *Burns,* 427 U.S. 347 (1976). See also, *Ramey* v. *Harber,* 431 F. Supp. 657 (W.D. Va. 1977) and *Branti* v. *Finkel,* 445 U.S. 507 (1980).
97. *Connick* v. *Myers,* 461 U.S. 138 (1983); *Jones* v. *Dodson,* 727 F. 2d 1329 (4th Cir. 1984).
98. *Sponick* v. *City of Detroit Police Department,* 211 N.W. 2d 674 (Mich. 1973), p. 681, but see: *Wilson* v. *Taylor,* 733 F. 2d 1539 (11th Cir. 1984).
99. *Bruns* v. *Pomerleau,* 319 F. Supp. 58 (D. Md. 1970). See, also, *McMullen* v. *Carson,* 754 F. 2d 936 (11th Cir. 1985), where it was held that a Ku Klux Klansman could not be fired from his position as a records clerk in the sheriff's department simply because he was a Klansman. The Court did uphold the dismissal because his active KKK participation threatened to cripple the agency's ability to effectively perform its public duties.
100. *Civil Service Commission of Tucson* v. *Livingston,* 525 P. 2d 949 (Ariz. 1974).
101. See, for example, *Tinker* v. *Des Moines School District,* 393 U.S. 503 (1969).
102. 425 U.S. 238 (1976).
103. *Mapp* v. *Ohio,* 367 U.S. 643 (1961).
104. *Katz* v. *United States,* 389 U.S. 347 (1967).
105. See *People* v. *Tidwell,* 266 N.E. 2d 787 (Ill. 1971).
106. *McDonnell* v. *Hunter,* __F. Supp.__, 23 GERR 1078 (S.D. Iowa 1985).
107. *Biehunik* v. *Felicetta,* 441 F. 2d 228 (1971), p. 230.
108. Basil J. Mezines, Jacob A. Stein, and Jules Gruff, *Administrative Law* (New York: Matthew Bender, 1979), pp. 27–29, 29–30, and supplements thereto.
109. 385 U.S. 483 (1967).
110. The states are bound by this requirement as well. *Malloy* v. *Hogan,* 378 U.S. 1 (1964).
111. 392 U.S. 273 (1968).
112. *See: Gabrilowitz* v. *Newman,* 582 F. 2d 100 (1st Cir. 1978). Cases upholding the department's authority to order an officer to take a polygraph examination include *Eshelman* v. *Blubaum,* 560 P. 2d 1283 (Ariz. 1977); *Dolan* v. *Kelly,* 348 N.Y.S. 2d 478 (1973); *Richardson* v. *City of Pasadena,* 500 S.W. 2d 175 (Tex. 1973); *Seattle Police Officer's Guild* v. *City of Seattle,* 494 P. 2d 485 (Wash. 1972); *Roux* v. *New Orleans Police Department,* 223 So. 2d 905 (La. 1969); *Coursey* v. *Board of Fire and Police Commissioners,* 234 N.E. 2d 339 (Ill. 1967); *Frazee* v. *Civil Service Board of City of Oakland,* 338 P. 2d 943 (Cal. 1959); and *Hester* v. *Milledgeville,* Case No. 85–8010 (11th Cir. 1985). Cases denying the department's authority include *Molino* v. *Board of Public Safety of City of Torrington,* 225 A. 2d 805 (Conn. 1966), *Stape* v. *Civil Service Commission of City of Philadelphia,* 172 A. 2d 161 (Pa. 1961), and *Farmer* v. *City of Fort Lauderdale,* 427 So. 2d 187 (Fla. 1983), *Cert denied,* 104 S. Ct. 74 (1984).
113. *Eshelman* v. *Blubaum,* p. 1286.
114. *Farmer* v. *Ft. Lauderdale.*
115. *Faust* v. *Police Civil Service Commission,* 347 A. 2d 765 (Pa. 1975); *Steward* v. *Leary,*

293 N.Y.S. 2d 573 (1968); *Brewer* v. *City of Ashland,* 86 S.W. 2d 669 (Ky. 1935); *Fabio* v. *Civil Service Commission of Philadelphia,* 373 A. 2d 751 (Pa. 1977).

116. *Major* v. *Hampton,* 413 F. Supp. 66 (1976).
117. *City of North Muskegon* v. *Briggs,—F. 2d—*(6th Cir. 1984).
118. 53 U.S.L.W. 3909.
119. *National Gay Task Force* v. *Bd. of Ed. of Oklahoma City,* 729 F. 2d 1270 (10th Cir. 1984).
120. *Bd. of Ed.* v. *National Gay Task Force,* 53 U.S.L.W. 4408, No. 83–2030 (1985).
121. *Rowland* v. *Mad River Sch. Dist.,* 730 F. 2d 444 (6th Cir. 1984).
122. *Dronenburg* v. *Zech,* 741 F. 2d 1388 (D.C. Cir. 1984).
123. *Detroit Police Officers Association* v. *City of Detroit,* 190 N.W. 2d 97 (1971), appeal denied, 405 U.S. 950 (1972).
124. *McCarthy* v. *Philadelphia Civil Service Comm.,* 424 U.S. 645 (1976).
125. *Miller* v. *Police Board of City of Chicago,* 349 N.E. 2d 544 (Ill. 1976); *Williamson* v. *Village of Baskin,* 339 So. 2d 474 (La. 1976); *Nigro* v. *Board of Trustees of Alden,* 395 N.Y.S. 2d 544 (1977).
126. *State, County, and Municipal Employees Local 339* v. *City of Highland Park,* 108 N.W. 2d 898 (1961).
127. *Hameetman* v. *City of Chicago,* 776 F. 2d 636 (7th Cir. 1985).
128. 42 U.S.C. §200e(j).
129. *Pinsker* v. *Joint Dist. No. 28J,* 554 F. Supp. 1049 (D. Colo. 83).
130. *United States* v. *City of Albuquerque,* 12 EPD 11, 244 (10th Cir. 1976), See, also *Trans World Airlines* v. *Hardison,* 97 S.Ct. 2264 (1977).
131. *Potter* v. *Murray City,* 760 F. 2d 1065 (10th Cir. 1985).
132. *Cox* v. *McNamara,* 493 P. 2d 54 (Ore. 1972); *Brenckle* v. *Township of Shaler,* 281 A. 2d 920 (Pa. 1972); *Hopwood* v. *City of Paducah,* 424 S.W. 2d 134 (Ky. 1968); *Flood* v. *Kennedy,* 239 N.Y.S. 2d 665 (1963). See also *Trelfa* v. *Village of Centre Island,* 389 N.Y.S. 2d 22 (1976). Rules prohibiting law enforcement officers from holding interest in businesses that manufacture, sell, or distribute alcoholic beverages have also been upheld. *Bock* v. *Long,* 279 N.E. 2d 464 (Ill. 1972); *Johnson* v. *Trader,* 52 So. 2d 333 (Fla. 1951).
133. Richard N. Williams, "Legal Aspects of Discipline by Police Administrators," Traffic Institute Publication No. 2705 (Evanston, Ill.: Northwestern University, 1975), p. 4.
134. *City of Crowley Firemen* v. *City of Crowley,* 264 So. 2d 368 (La. 1972).
135. *Lally* v. *Department of Police,* 306 So. 2d 65 (La. 1974).
136. See, for example, *Peters* v. *Civil Service Commission of Tucson,* 559 P. 2d 698 (Ariz. 1977); *Abeyta* v. *Town of Taos,* 499 F. 2d 323 (10th Cir. 1974); *Baumbartner* v. *Leary,* 311 N.Y.S. 2d 468 (1970); *City of Vancouver* v. *Jarvis,* 455 P. 2d 591 (Wash. 1969). But compare *Thompson* v. *Lent,* 383 N.Y.S. 2d 929 (1976), and *Glover* v. *Murphy,* 343 N.Y.S. 2d 746 (1973).
137. *Glover* v. *Murphy.* Compare *Taylor* v. *Police Board of Chicago,* 378 N.E. 2d 1160 (Ill. 1978).
138. *Peters* v. *Civil Service Commission of Tucson* contains a portion of such a regulation that illustrates this point. See Lay Gerald Safer, "Deadly Weapons in the Hands of Police Officers, On Duty and Off Duty," *Journal of Urban Law,* 49 (1971), p. 565, for a good discussion of possible statutory approaches to the question of when police officers should be permitted to use deadly force.
139. *Chastain* v. *Civil Service Board of Orlando,* 327 So. 2d 230 (1976), p. 232.
140. *Reich* v. *Board of Fire and Police Commissioners,* 301 N.E. 2d 501 (Ill. 1973).
141. *Krolick* v. *Lowery,* 302 N.Y.S. 2d 109 (1969), p. 115, *Hester* v. *Milledgeville,* 598 F. Supp. 1456, 1457, n2 (M.D. Ga. 1984).
142. *McCracken* v. *Department of Police,* 337 So. 2d 595 (La. 1976).
143. *Krolick* v. *Lowery.*

144. *City of Palm Bay* v. *Bauman*, 475 So. 2d 1322 (Fla. 5th DCA 1985).

145. *Walters* v. *Secretary of Defense*, 725 F. 2d 107 (D.C. Cir. 1983).

146. *Security and Law Enforcement Employees, District Counsel 82* v. *Carly*, 737 F. 2d 187 (2d Cir. 1984): *Division 241 Amalgamated Transit Union* v. *Suscy*, 538 F. 2d 1264 (7th Cir. 1976) *cert. denied* 429 U.S. 1029 (1976); *McDonnell* v. *Hunter*, 612 F. Supp. 1122 (S.D. Iowa 1984), aff'd 746 F. 2d 785 (8th Cir. 1984).

147. *National League of Cities* v. *Usery*, 426 U.S. 833 (1976).

148. *Garcia* v. *San Antonio Transit*, 105 S. Ct. 1005 (1985).

149. *Massachusetts Board of Retirement* v. *Murgia*, 427 U.S. 307 (1976).

150. 29 U.S.C. 623(f).

151. *Western Airlines* v. *Criswell*, 105 S. Ct. 2743, 2751 (1985), and *Dothard* v. *Rawlinson*, 433 U.S. 321, 329 (1977).

152. *Usery* v. *Tamiami Trail Tours, Inc.*, 531 F. 2d 224 (5th Cir. 1976).

153. *Johnson* v. *Mayor and City Council of Baltimore*, 105 S. Ct. 2717, 2722 (1985).

154. *Hahn* v. *City of Buffalo*, 770 F. 2d 12 (2d Cir. 1985).

155. The co-authors of this chapter have extensive legal experience. Donald D. Slesnick II practices public sector labor and employment law in Miami, Florida. His clients include fifteen police personnel collective bargaining units. Prior to entering private practice a decade ago, he served as director of Personnel and Labor Relations of the Metro-Dade County Public Safety Department, director of Employee Relations and Legislative Affairs of the Dade County School Board, and general labor counsel of the Florida Police Benevolent Association. Slesnick is a past chairman of the Florida Bar Labor and Employment Relations Law Committee, and is currently the co-chairman of the American Bar Association's State and Local Government Collective Bargaining Committee. Janet E. Ferris currently serves as general counsel of the Florida Department of Law Enforcement, a post she has held since 1982. Previously, she was an assistant state attorney in Broward County, Florida, and an assistant attorney general of the State of Florida. After assisting the state legislature in the composition of the Racketeer Influenced and Corrupt Organizations ("RICO") Act, she was appointed as the first chief of the attorney general's civil RICO section. Ms. Ferris is a regular lecturer to various professional law enforcement and legal associations and at the Organized Crime Institute.

The great challenge of the eighties is not the training of workers but the retraining of managers.

JOHN NAISBITT

Information Systems and Applications

Introduction

In the last fifteen years, there has been a tremendous increase in computer automation in law enforcement. This technological trend has brought about dramatic changes in police personnel, roles, and services, and for the most part these changes have resulted in increased police efficiency and effectiveness.

Unlike years past, computers are no longer very expensive first-time investments requiring outside subsidies or matching federal grants for their purchase. Today's computers provide even the smallest departments with the capability of becoming automated at a cost they can afford. Further, the networking or "tying together" of small computers can surpass the memory capacity that was previously available in large and expensive mainframe computers.

The information society so accurately predicted by futurists of the 1960s is now an American reality in which "individual and organizational survival is dependent on the ability to access information."[1] Law enforcement agencies are vast information-processing organizations. All too often, managers and the general public think of police work in terms of physical security, patrol cars, weaponry, crime control, and traffic enforcement. In fact, most police work involves the collection, manipulation, structuring, collating, and dissemination of information, so much so, that an automated records and communication system is no longer viewed as a luxury but a necessity.

Planning for Computerization

The term *planning* is a loosely defined and poorly understood concept.[2] Stated simply, planning is a process that attempts to link information from the past with probable future events. The decision to purchase an automated records system requires careful and proper planning considerations. Many police chiefs have been faced with the dilemma of implementing such a system without having the necessary information and knowledge on which to base correct decisions.

Technological Expertise

Law enforcement administrators sometimes make the mistake of relying on information pertaining to computers that they or others in their department have gained on a hobby basis. Often some member of their agency recently purchased a home computer and now feels competent to automate the police records division. The pitfalls of this approach are obvious as the complexities and extensiveness of such a project may well be beyond the capabilities of such personnel. For the most part, police chiefs are general managers, and as such they should seek specialized advice. There are a number of sources from which this help can be obtained.

One source is the outside consultant. Most cities have a number of consulting firms that specialize in office automation. Although these consultants may have the technological knowledge to ascertain and evaluate a number of computer systems, they may not understand the needs of the police organization. Ideally, the consultant should have police experience, hopefully at a supervisory or management level, in addition to extensive technological knowledge. Realizing that this type of consultant may be hard to find, especially in nonmetropolitan areas, the police chief may have to rely on a number of specialty journals or seminars in order to obtain an objective evaluation of the current, state-of-the-art computer systems.

Another source of valuable information for the police chief may be in the local university or community college. Higher educational facilities often have a department of criminal justice or law enforcement with a faculty member specializing in the area of automation and technology. Such persons are able to provide the valuable and critically important technological expertise that is necessary during the computerization process.

Needs Assessments

One of the major problems observed in the planning process for computerized systems in law enforcement is the lack of a valid needs assessment. A needs assessment is basically a statement that gives the goals and objectives for the system to be purchased. What specific functions will the computer perform? This question appears to be basic; however, it is frequently overlooked in the planning process. Certain variables— such as the size of the department, the number of calls received in a year, the budget allocation for spending, and the like—provide valuable insights and limitations on the type and size of computer that would be necessary to perform the functions required within a police department. Many chiefs make the mistake of buying computers with capabilities that either far exceed or fail to match their needs. The result is having a greater deal of capability that is not used or having a system that is inadequate to perform the tasks for which it was purchased. Too, contrary to popular belief, the computer cannot do "everything." Automation is not a cure-all for problems within the department's information-processing system.

During the needs assessment stage, a consultant or outside source can also serve a very useful function. Many times, the outside reviewer can provide valuable points that otherwise would have been overlooked by the internal administrator or manager. The old proverb "not being able to see the forest because of the trees" often is true during the needs assessment stage. Obviously, the chief can become so involved in the department that he or she will fail to consider a number of important points.

Hardware and Software Compatibility

Computer hardware is a term used to describe the components of a computer system such as input/output devices, data storage devices, and the central processing unit (CPU).[3] Hardware is the actual physical mechanisms of a computer, whereas software is the directive programming and operational systems that provide instructions to the CPU and other hardware devices. Software (computer programs) is the common communication medium between the user and the computer.[4] During the planning process, it is critically important to match these two integral components—hardware and software—to provide smooth and efficient operation and subsequent goal achievement.

Compatibility refers to the capability of a computer hardware system to run a software package. A number of computer systems are limited to specific operating systems and computer languages. Thus, to achieve compatibility a careful planning process is required.

Applications

Literally thousands of software packages are available that provide singularly or in combination a number of functions directly related to law enforcement. Records management, data analysis, graphics, telecommunications, and word processing are application programs that currently exist in the software market. Most of these software packages require little customizing or adapting for police usage.

In addition to these general purpose programs, a number of software packages are specifically designed for use in law enforcement. One of the first attempts to maximize compatibility between computer hardware systems by means of a shared software package evolved through the cooperation of the Bureau of Justice Statistics, the U.S. Department of Justice, and the International Association of Chiefs of Police. The main program, called POSSE (Police Operations Systems Support-Elementary) is a relatively low-cost computer system that stores a variety of management reports. The main program interfaces with three other limited-use data-management systems:

—CASS (Crime Analysis System Support) is a generalized, automated crime analysis system that provides crime/suspect correlations, crime patterns, target profiles, forecasting, and resource allocation studies.[5]
—IMIS (Investigative Management Information System) is a criminal investigation moni-

FIGURE 11-1 In 1939, the San Francisco Police Department announced that it would use a "mechanical brain" to analyze crime. The cards were punched in the machine in the foreground, sorted in the machine on the left, and "analyzed" and printed by the last machine. Current computer and software technology advancements have gone far beyond this once state-of-the-art capability. [Courtesy of the San Francisco Archives.]

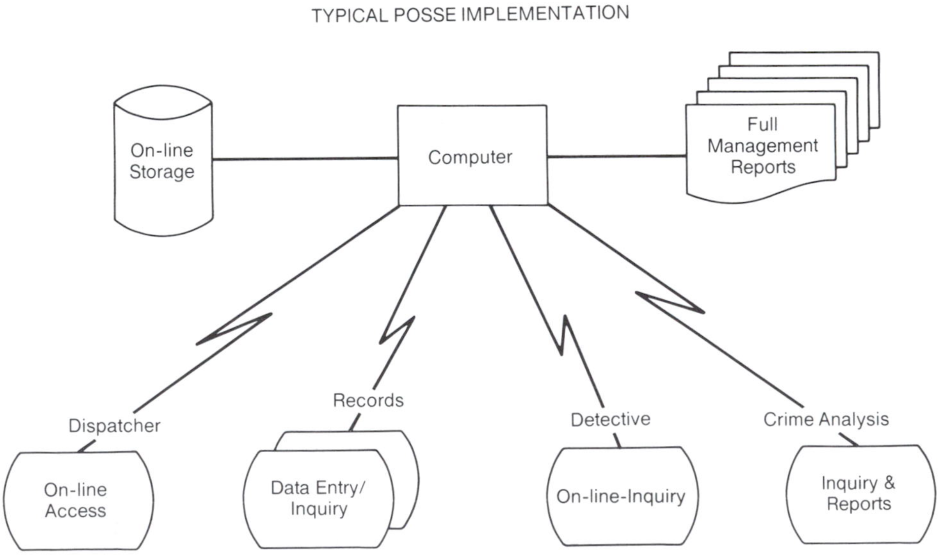

TYPICAL POSSE IMPLEMENTATION

On-line Storage — Computer — Full Management Reports

Dispatcher — On-line Access

Records — Data Entry/ Inquiry

Detective — On-line-Inquiry

Crime Analysis — Inquiry & Reports

FIGURE 11-2 Diagram of the typical POSSE computer system. [Courtesy Hadron System Products Group (Formerly Simeon Incorporated) Fairfax, Virginia.]

toring system that provides feedback on workload, performance, case status, and support budget requests.

—FMIS (Fleet Management Information System) is a fleet management system which assesses vehicle and equipment class performance, monitors fuel consumption, and provides support for budget requests.

The POSSE system represents just one of a number of software packages designed to service law enforcement agency needs. Most packages incorporate a series of subprograms that manipulate stored data into some type of meaningful report. A good example is the Uniform Crime Report (UCR) schedules that are routinely made by police agencies on a monthly basis. Stored data regarding the number of offenses is tabulated, and a report is generated that is then submitted in accordance with FBI guidelines. Most of the features available in specifically designed software packages fall into one of three broad-based categories: (1) Operations (Data Base Information), (2) Management and Administration (Data Base Management), and (3) Communication and Training (Data Base Sharing).

Operations

Law enforcement agencies are excellent examples of information-processing systems. The information may be as mundane as tracking a parking ticket through the system or as complex as an analysis of crime trends in an area.[6] Traditionally, most agencies have captured information on original police reports and stored it in vast warehouse rooms called "Records Division." Police records usually include information about persons, locations, vehicles, offenses, incidents, and so on that establishes a large, centralized data base. The problem with nonautomated systems is that specific information cannot be retrieved immediately nor can such information be statistically manipulated without many hours of hand tabulation. The man-hours expended in such efforts and the large volume of report forms to be analyzed necessitates computerization.

Automated Records Systems

An automated records system enables police agencies to maintain large data bases with an immediate search and retrieval capability. In this manner, law enforcement personnel have almost instantaneous access to individual criminal histories, outstanding warrants, traffic information, field contacts, investigations, and the like. Further, these systems usually provide data summaries and displays that allow police analysts to recognize patterns in reported incidents and to match suspects, vehicles, and weapons with criminal activities.

These systems can be either very simple (store, sort, and retrieve) or extremely complex with a variety of added features. Some of the more advanced systems incorporate:

- —Special Hazard Denotations: Small one- or two-word messages that are highlighted or flash in order to catch the operator's attention. A common hazard message is "Armed and Dangerous" when describing a particular suspect.
- —Address Verification Files: A subprogram that automatically searches the

---

WANTED/HAZARD

LEADS NAME DISPLAY

LEADS NUMBER: 46   UPDATE DATE: 2/11/88

NAME: BROWN, LEROY JAMES   FBI: 12345AB123
                                                       FDLE: 987654XXX
MONIKERS: BAD LEROY   HCSO: 999999210

SEX:	M	RACE:	W	DOB:	7/08/50	ANTI-SOCIAL-TRAITS
HGT:	6'5"	WGT:	240	SSNO:	123-45-6789	RESISTS ARREST
EYES:	BLU	HAIR:	BRN	PHONE:	555-1234	

                                            OPERATORS LICENSE   ST   YR
SCARS-MARKS-TATTOOS   ABCD—123456   AZ   88
JAGGED SCAR ON CHIN

                                            ASSOCIATED VEHICLES LIC PLT ST
LAST KNOWN ADDRESS   80 CHOP HARLEY MC   M-1234   AZ
100 N. PLAZA WAY   85 RED CADILLAC 2DR ABC-123 AZ

* * * * * * * * * * * * * *

FIGURE 11-3 The Law Enforcement Automated Data System—LEADS front name page. An excellent example of an automated records system. Note the special hazard denotation and moniker file. [Courtesy Robert W. Taylor and Associates, Tyler, Texas.]

address entered and confirms its location giving dispatch directions and names of residents.

- —Phonetic Files: A subprogram designed to list sound-alike names with different spellings. For instance, the last name "Martinez" may be queried under the phonetic spellings of "Martenes," "Martins," or "Martines." Obviously, such an automated file would be invaluable concerning names of different nationality pronounced the same way although spelled differently.

- —Monikers Files or AKA Files: This system can list an alias for a given individual or query an individual by the name entered. The nickname "Scarface" may be the only name heard by a victim or witness. By entering the moniker, the identities and criminal histories of all persons known as "Scarface" are obtained.

One of the more innovative and interesting projects that is directly related to improving automated records systems is "live reporting."[7] Police officers produce reports by telephoning a record specialist who directly enters the information into the computer. In this manner, the system produces professionally typed reports and serves as the primary source of management information that is accessible instantaneously from remote locations.

Additionally, with the advent of programmable, battery-powered, notebook-sized computers that weigh less than four pounds, with a full-sized keyboard, a built-in telephone modem, and preprogrammed word processing and communications, some police departments, such as those in St. Petersburg and Ocala, Florida, are pioneering the use of portable computers for writing formatted police reports in the field.[8]

These new techniques greatly enhance existing automated records systems by (1) reducing time spent by uniform police officers in preparing reports, thus increasing officer, and supervisor "street time"; (2) providing instant "on-line" management information and instant retrieval of reports from any remote location, such as the precinct or detective office; (3) reducing office space used to maintain "hard copies" in filing cabinets or vaults by "storing" reports in computer memory; (4) improving the quality, accuracy, and timeliness of crime analysis, management reports, and Uniform Crime Reports (UCR) by electronically processing, aggregating, distributing, and filing of these documents; and (5) improving the quality, legibility, and accuracy of police reports.[9]

Crime Analysis

The statistical analysis of data and the organization of information into manageable summaries provides law enforcement with meaningful tools in which to combat crime. The crime problem has continued to grow in terms of quantity, sophistication, and complexity, thereby forcing police officers and investigators to seek additional help in enforcement techniques. The purpose of crime analysis is to organize massive quantities of raw information, from data bases utilized in automated records systems, and to forecast specific future events from the statistical manipulation of this data. In theory, crime analysis provides a thorough and systematic analysis of data on which to make rational decisions regarding past, present, and future actions.[10]

Crime analysis is not limited solely to reported crime information. Attention has also been given to the statistical analysis of intelligence information. Kinney reports that criminal intelligence analysis can support investigators, decision makers, and policymakers in their attempt to prevent and control crime.[11]

FIGURE 11-4 Crime specific targeting in a residential neighborhood. [Courtesy of Maricopa County Sheriff's Office, Phoenix, Arizona.]

Some of the more common crime analysis techniques are:

- —Crime Specific Analysis: A tabular or graphic display of reported crimes within a given pattern of time and/or location. It is often used to detect robberies or burglaries that cluster in specific locations during various time periods.
- —Link Analysis: A graphic portrayal of associates between individuals or organizations, charted from available information to a given point in time. This is invaluable in putting many identities in proper relational perspective. It is most frequently used as an investigative and briefing aid.[12]
- —Telephone Toll Analysis: Computerized reports derived from court ordered long-distance telephone billings of suspects in illegal narcotics trafficking. Reports indicate number and frequency of calls that are displayed in numerical, chronological, and geographical order. Link Analysis can be used to show the relationship between billing numbers and the numbers called.[13]
- —Visual Investigative Analysis (VIA): Charting that depicts key events of criminal activity in chronological order. VIA is used to show the degree of involvement of subjects. This method is especially convincing in conspiracy cases and can also be used as a planning tool to focus the resources of an investigative effort.[14]
- —Case Analysis And Management System (CAMS): Computerized case management in which large amounts of data are compiled and indexed for easy retrieval of specific items. This system is used to clarify relationships and to calculate the probability of associations.[15]

Although not all of these techniques are fully automated, the basic procedures follow a flow-chart configuration that provides a sound basis for software design. Combining these techniques with a statistical packages (such as SPSS/X, ABSTAT, SAS or STATPRO) produces a strong capability for forecasting and prediction.

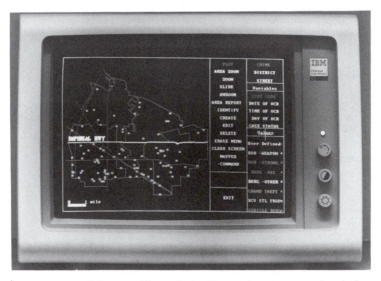

FIGURE 11-5 Crime specific analysis: Electronic street map pinpointing crime in a city overlayed in police beats. Note the clustering effect in certain areas as presented by LandTrak, a software package that displays data using graphic mapping and charting on an ordinary personal computer monitor. [Courtesy Criterion Inc., Dallas, Texas; photograph by Martin Trailer Photographics, San Diego, California.]

Some police departments, such as the Portland, Oregon, Police Bureau have placed renewed emphasis on crime analysis through field report formats. Each incident is coded for easy computer entry and captures detailed information about the victim as well as the suspect and modus operandi. Figure 11-6 displays this unique report coding style.

Investigations and Case Management

The RAND study of detectives identified a number of functions performed by investigators.[16] The study questioned whether many of these functions (such as preparing cases for prosecution, apprehending suspects, engaging in intensive investigations when there are no suspects, conducting pro-active investigations, and performing administrative tasks and paperwork related to these functions) should be performed at all by detectives.[17] The study concluded that these functions could be performed better (more effectively) and at a lower cost (more efficiently) by patrol officers and clerical personnel.[18] The present process of investigation was concluded to be so chaotic and complex that all of the functions could not be adequately performed by a single individual.

In direct response to this study and in an attempt to coordinate activity between investigators and prosecutors, a number of automated case management systems were designed. These systems assign cases to individual detectives and then monitor the progress of the investigation from case opening to final disposition. Although most such systems are internal to police agencies, some, like the Prosecutor's Management and Information System—PROMIS, attempt to coordinate activities between law enforcement and prosecution.[19] The computerization of the ''assembly-line'' production of case investigation and prosecution reduces fragmentation of responsibility and control. Further, the automation of such a process allows evaluation at various points or stages in the ''assembly-line'' by means of the application of a uniform set of criteria. In this manner, more important cases (based on the gravity of the crime and the suspect's prior record) can receive special attention while assuring an even-handed treatment of cases of less seriousness.[20]

Management and Administration

One of the most important benefits stemming from the use of computers in law enforcement is the monitoring and improvement of officer productivity, a task long associated with management and administration. The assumption is that managers, when given precise information regarding personnel resources and capabilities, should be better equipped to make correct decisions. These types of computerized systems that serve the needs of managers and administrators throughout an organization are termed ''decision support systems.''[21] Although a number of computer-based decision support systems are available to the law enforcement manager, the most critical involve productivity and personnel evaluations.

Productivity and Personnel Evaluation

Most automated records systems provide data sheets or summaries of officer activity over a given period of time. These usually include the number of arrests (felony and misdemeanor) made by each officer, the number of tickets written by each traffic

COPIES	CASE NUMBER	PORTLAND POLICE BUREAU INCIDENT REPORT	REFER CASE NUMBER	ACCOMPANYING REPORTS:	Crime Analysis Info.

COPIES (left column checkboxes):
- ☐ DET
- ☐ CAU
- ☐ Central
- ☐ East
- ☐ North
- ☐ TRF
- ☐ DA
- ☐ DVD
- ☐ ID
- ☐ Prop Rm
- ☐ Crime Prev.
- ☐ Intell
- ☐ Patrol Support
- ☐
- ☐
- ☐
- ☐
- ☐
- ☐
- ☐
- ☐
- ☐

PORTLAND POLICE BUREAU — INCIDENT REPORT

ACCOMPANYING REPORTS:
- ☐ INCIDENT   ☐ PROP. RCPT.
- ☐ SPECIAL
- ☐ CUSTODY   ☐ TRF. ACC.

CLASSIFICATION   CLR   DATE/TIME REPORTED   DATE/TIME OCCURRED

TYPE ACTIVITY   LOCATION OF OCCURRENCE   N
☐ Radio ☐ Phone
☐ S/I

ONE SENTENCE SUMMARY OF INCIDENT

PERSONS   V-Victim   C-Complainant   R/O-Registered Owner   W-Witness   P-Parent   F-Firm Name   Additional Persons in Narrative Y N

Code	NAME: LAST	FIRST	MIDDLE	CRN	Sex	Race	DOB

HOME ADDRESS   HOME PHONE

BUSINESS/SCHOOL ADDRESS   WORK HOURS   BUSINESS PHONE

| Code | NAME: LAST | FIRST | MIDDLE | CRN | Sex | Race | DOB |

HOME ADDRESS   HOME PHONE

BUSINESS/SCHOOL ADDRESS   WORK HOURS   BUSINESS PHONE

| Code | NAME: LAST | FIRST | MIDDLE | CRN | Sex | Race | DOB |

HOME ADDRESS   HOME PHONE

BUSINESS/SCHOOL ADDRESS   WORK HOURS   BUSINESS PHONE

SUSPECTS A&B   M-Missing   R-Runaway   D-Deceased   Additional Suspects Coded on Another Incident Y N

| Code | NAME | CRN | Sex | Race | DOB/AGE |

HT   WT   HAIR   EYES   ADDRESS   PHONE   In Custody Y N

OTHER DESCRIPTION (FACIAL HAIR, CLOTHING, ETC.)

| Code | NAME | CRN | Sex | Race | DOB/AGE |

HT   WT   HAIR   EYES   ADDRESS   PHONE   In Custody Y N

OTHER DESCRIPTION (FACIAL HAIR, CLOTHING, ETC.)

COMPUTER ENTRY

VEHICLE   S-Stolen   U-Unauthorized Use   R-Recovered   L-Locate   A-Abandoned   T-Towed   V-Victim's Veh.   SP-Suspect Veh.

☐ Person

| Code | LICENSE NUMBER | State | Year | Type | VIN | STLN/RECD VALUE |

OPR
☐ Vehicle

Year   MAKE   MODEL   STYLE   COLOR

OPR
☐ Crime

| Deliq. Payments | Keys in Vehicle | Theft Ins. | Permission Given | Body Damage | 7 5 3 1 | Transmission | CHARGE/CITE NO. |
| Y N | Y N | Y N | Y N | Y N | 8 6 4 2 | ☐ Standard ☐ Auto | |

TOWED BY/TOWED TO   ☐ Dept. Req. HOLD Y   REASON   UNIT & PERSON NOTIFIED
☐ Private Rq. N

OPR
☐ Prop

O.R.S. 162.375 SECTION 212 INITIATING A FALSE REPORT. (1) A PERSON COMMITS THE CRIME OF INITIATING A FALSE REPORT IF HE KNOWINGLY INITIATES A FALSE ALARM OR REPORT WHICH IS TRANSMITTED TO A FIRE DEPARTMENT, LAW ENFORCEMENT AGENCY OR OTHER ORGANIZATION THAT DEALS WITH EMERGENCIES INVOLVING DANGER TO LIFE OR PROPERTY (2) INITIATING A FALSE REPORT IS A CLASS C MISDEMEANOR.

OPR
☐ Book

☐ I UNDERSTAND THAT I AM LIABLE FOR ALL TOWING AND STORAGE COSTS INCURRED DURING THE RECOVERY OF THIS VEHICLE.

☐ I WILL TESTIFY AS A WITNESS AGAINST THE DEFENDANT WHEN HE/SHE IS CHARGED WITH A CRIME.

☐ RELEASED PROPERTY/VEHICLE TO

OPR

☐ THE NAMED CHILD (ADULT) IS PRESENTLY A RUNAWAY (MISSING) AND I REQUEST THAT HE/SHE BE TAKEN INTO CUSTODY FOR THEIR OWN PROTECTION.

SIGNATURE OF PERSON REPORTING THE INCIDENT

| Physical Force Used by Police? Y N | Identification Division notified? Y N | Follow-up required? Y N | Crime Prev. Info desired? Y N | Outside agency notified Y N | Which one: |

| REPORTING OFFICER(S) | BPST | Prec/Div | Rlf/Shft | Assn/Dist | Reviewed By | PAGE OF |

CASE NUMBER (vertical, right margin)

PPB-11-9/83

FIGURE 11-6 Criminal incident report with accompanying coding sheets designed for easy computer entry of suspect and witness information, vehicle descriptions, and modus operandi. [Courtesy Portland Police Bureau, Portland, Oregon.]

WORTHLESS DOCUMENT	TYPE OF DOCUMENT:				AMOUNT OF LOSS	

□1. Money Order □2. Credit Card □3. Personal □4. Payroll □5. Travelers □6. Other

REASON FOR REJECTION OF W. DOC:

□1. NSF □2. RTM □3. Sig. Irreg. □4. Acct. Closed □5. Utl □6. Forged □7. Stolen □8. Fict. Print □9. Raised □10. Post Dated □11. Pre Dated □12. Other

HOW DOCUMENT WAS WRITTEN:

□PEN WRITTEN □TYPEWRITTEN □HANDWRITTEN □PROTECTOGRAPHED □OTHER   Check Acct. No.

Any part of document written in presence of victim/witness Y N	WHAT PART?	TYPE PROPERTY OBTAINED

Name
Address: Date _____ No. _____

IDENTIFICATION USED BY SUSPECT:

Pay to order of: _____ Amount: _____

DOCUMENT ACCEPTED BY:

Bank
Branch:

DOCUMENT IN CUSTODY OF:

□ Property Rm   □ Crime Lab   □ Other
□ Fraud Office   □ Compl.

Print Name of Maker

PROPERTY	S-Stolen L-Lost D-Damaged F-Found K-Safekeeping R-Recovered E-Evidence								
Code	Qty	ITEM	BRAND	Model/Style	SERIAL NO.	COLOR	Engravings/Pecularities	SIZE	VALUE

PROPERTY RECEIPT NUMBER(S)	ADDITIONAL PROPERTY ON SPECIAL REPORT Y N	PROPERTY IN CUSTODY OF	SERIAL NO. CHECKED BY

NARRATIVE

FIGURE 11-6 *(Continued)*

INCIDENT REPORT CODING SHEET Blocks 1-8
(Alphabetical Order)

1. Type of Premises

Airport/Depot	24
Apparel-Clothes, Shoes, Fur	41
Apt/Duplex/Condo	11
Auditorium/Stadium/ Museum	23
Auto/Truck/Etc.	601
Bridge/Viaduct/Tunnel	63
Bowl/Skate/Pool HL/Arcade	32
Bus	602
Business Office-Unspf	492
Cabin	13
Camper/Trailer	603
Cemetery	73
Church	25
Club/Dorm/Rooming Hse.	12
Concession Stand	391
Construction Site	791
Const-Bldg. Elec. Plmb.	47
Convenience Store	39
Dept./Variety Store	40
Dev. Farm Land/Pasture	75
Dock/Pier/Wharf	53
Driveway	64
Factory/Warehouse	50
Farm Bldg-Barn, Shed, Etc.	52
Financial, Bank, Ins.	34
Freeway	61
Furniture/Appliance	43
Golf Course	70
Govt. Office/Service	21
Grocery	38
Hardware/Sporting Goods	44
Hotel/Motel	14
Light Rail/Train	605
Liquor Store	493
Logging Site	76
Jewelry/Camera	42
Marina	46
Medical/Dental/Hospital	36
Mobile Home	101
Mot. Vhcl./Sales	45
Mot. Vhcl Service Parts	451
Night Club/Tavern	33
Not Applicable	97
Nursing/Retirement Home	111
Other Buildings	59
Other	98
Other Road	62
Park/Campground/Beach	71
Parking Structure	641
Pharmacy/Drug Store	37
Private School/College	26
Public Safety Facility	20
Public School/College	22
Restaurant	30
Serv.-Gas, Grooming, Rental	35
Shopping Mall	604
Single Family Residence	10
Social Service Agency	494
Stereo Equip Store	491
Street/Alley/Sidewalk/ Bus Stop	60
Ship/Boat	792
Theater	31
Unknown	99
Unspecified Business	49
Unspf Resid Bldg/Garage	51
Utility Gas/Elec./Phone	351
Water/Shoreline	72
Woods/Forest/Mts.	77
Yards/Related Area	74

2A. Method/Point of Entry

Attempted Forced Door	011
Attempted Forced Door w/Deadbolt Lock	012
Attempted Window	013
Climbed over Dividr/Gate/ Countr/Fence/Etc.	024
Forced Door	031
Forced Window	032
Forced Dividr/Gate/Contr	034
Forced Hood/Trunk	035
Forced Roof	036
Forced Wall	037
Forced Door w/Deadbolt Lock	0311
Legal Entry	990
Manipulated lock on door	010
Not Applicable	97
Open Door	026
Open Window	027
Open Vent	028
Other	98
Unlocked Door	021
Unlocked Window	022
Unlocked Ventilator	023
Unlawful-Hood/Trunk	025

2B. Alarm Systems

Alarm System Activated	01
Alarm System-Not Activ/ Inop.	02
Alarm System-Not Activ/ Not On	03
Alarm System-Not Activ/ Unknown Reason	04
No Alarm System	05
Alarm Defeated	06

7. Unusual Actions

Apologizes	28
Approach Victim	12
Assume Disguise/Deformity	37
Bad Odor	36
Bomb/Arson-Covr Crime	154
Bomb/Arson-Device O/S	153
Bomb/Arson-Prior Threat	151
Bomb/Arson-Warning	152
Bunco/Con Game	58
Bunco/Fraud DOC	57
Carries Weapon	49
Change ID #	55
Claims Family Hostage	04
Claims Found Money	38
Claims Gunman O/S	02
Cleans Off Fingerprints	48
Defeat Alarm	26
Defecates	19
Disconnects Phone	52
Does Not Speak	29
Drunk/On Drugs	34
Eat/Drink at Scene	21
Engage Victim in Gambling	39
Escape Route Open	53
Excessive Charges	43
Hides on Premises	07
Holds Hostage	05
Homicide-Dismember	161
Homicide-Hide/Transport	163
Homicide Sex Act	162
Jumps from Auto	14
Limps	35
Leave Jewelry/Security	41
Leave Other Valuables	27
Mask/Disguise	01
Molests	45
Not Applicable	97
Nude/Partial Dress	46
Obtain Pymt in Advance	42
Other	98
Phony Quiz Game	44
Prey on Homosexuals	47
Profane Language	31
Pull Curtains	25
Questions Victim	13
Ransack, Messy	18
Ransack, Neat	17
Remove ID #	56
Request Admittance	33
Run from Behind	11
Sadistic Acts	09
Shoplifts	231
Smash/Grab	23
Smokes	51
Speaks with Accent	32
Steal Prop from Auto	221
Susp Call Prior to Crime	54
Threaten Victim Family	03
Tie/Gag Victim	06
Unknown	99
Use Match/Flashlight	24
Uses Notes	08
Vandalizes	22

3. Instrument/Force Used

Brick/Rock	05
Bunco-Con Game/Bank Ex	082
Bunco-Fraud Docmt	081
Bunco-Pigeon Dr/Jam Boy	083
Bunco-Unspecified	084
Celluloid Strip/Credit Card	15
Check Protector	22
Club/Bludgeon	04
Consumer Fraud	088
Explosive	06
Glass Cutter	075
Hands/Feet	16
Hand Gun	011
Home Repair Fraud	085
Key	13
Knife	021
Mace	12
Mail fraud	086
Match/Lighter	11
Medical Fraud	087
Not Applicable	97
Other	98
Pipe	073
Pipe/Bolt Cutter	072
Poison	17
Prying Tool/Screwdriver	071
Rifle	012
Saw	076
Shotgun	013
Simulated Gun	015
Siphon	077
Slide Hammer/Ignit Punch	21
Telephone	18
Threatening Note	03
Thrown Object	09
Unknown	99
Unspf Gun	014
Unspf Cutting Inst	022
Vehicle	19
Wire	14
Wrench/Pliers/V Grips	074

6. Location of Property when Stolen

Bike Rack	26
Cash Register/Box	18
Cooler/Freezer	17
Driveway/Carport	29
Fuel Tank	15
Garage	09
Hotel/Motel Room	25
In Cabinet	21
In Coin Machine	23
In Mail Box	28
In Purse/Bag	24
In Safe	22
Locker	27
Not Applicable	97
On/In Desk	14
On Person	19
On/Under Counter	11
Other	98
Park	05
Parking Lot	06
Porch	07
Residence	08
Shelves/Racks	12
Shopping Cart	13
Sidewalk	04
Storage Area	16
Street/Alley/Hwy	02
Unknown	99
Vehicle	01
Yard	03

4. Location of Victim at Time of Crime

Business Office	11
Church	18
Driveway/Carport	23
Garage	07
Hospital	14
Hotel/Motel Room	15
In Residence	06
Lobby/Hallway/Stairs	22
Not Applicable	97
Out of City/State/Cnty	24
Park	16
Parking Lot	05
Porch/Patio	21
Public Store	09
Restaurant	12
School/Grounds	17
Sidewalk	04
Street/Alley/Hwy	02
Tavern/Night Club	13
Unknown	99
Unspf Public/Other	98
Vacation	19
Vehicle	01
Work	08
Yard	03

5. Victims Activity at Time of Crime

Answer Door	09
Argument/Fight w/Suspect	03
Attending School	15
Conduct Prsnl Bus	04
Enter Building	13
Hitchhiking	11
Inside Residence	08
Leaving Building	14
Not Applicable	97
Observing Suspect	17
Other	98
Phone Conversation	07
Recreation Activity	21
Riding in Vehicle	05
Shopping	16
Sleeping	12
Socializing	19
Talking with Suspect	02
Unknown	99
Waiting for Ride	06
Walking	01
Working	18
Working in Yard	22

8. Type of Evidence

Blood	01
Bullets/Casings	02
Cigarette	20
Clothing	03
Credit Card	21
Documents	04
Drugs	05
Explosives/Fireworks	06
Fingerprints	07
Hair/Fibers	08
Money	09
Not Applicable	97
Other	98
Paint	10
Photos	11
Semen	12
Shoe Impression	13
Slugging Weapon	18
Tire Impression	14
Tool Impression/ Door Knob	15
Tools	22
Unknown	99
Vehicle	17
Weapons	16

1
2
3
4
5
6
7
8

FIGURE 11-6 *(Continued)*

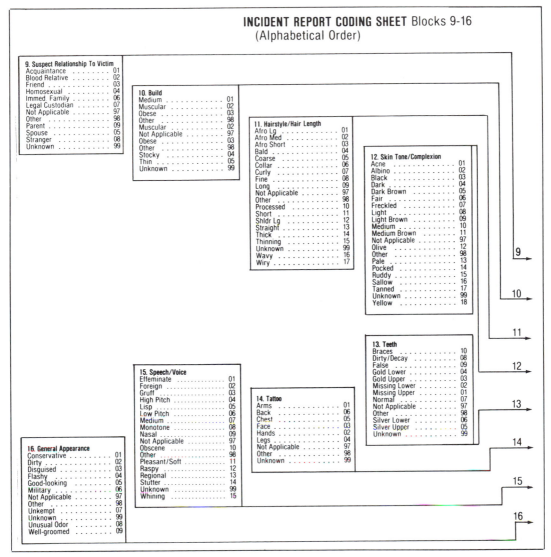

INCIDENT REPORT CODING SHEET Blocks 9-16
(Alphabetical Order)

9. Suspect Relationship To Victim

Acquaintance	01
Blood Relative	02
Friend	03
Homosexual	04
Immed. Family	06
Legal Custodian	07
Not Applicable	97
Other	98
Parent	09
Spouse	05
Stranger	08
Unknown	99

10. Build

Medium	01
Muscular	02
Obese	03
Other	98
Muscular	02
Not Applicable	97
Obese	03
Other	98
Stocky	04
Thin	05
Unknown	99

11. Hairstyle/Hair Length

Afro Lg	01
Afro Med	02
Afro Short	03
Bald	04
Coarse	05
Collar	06
Curly	07
Fine	08
Long	09
Not Applicable	97
Other	98
Processed	10
Short	11
Shldr Lg	12
Straight	13
Thick	14
Thinning	15
Unknown	99
Wavy	16
Wiry	17

12. Skin Tone/Complexion

Acne	01
Albino	02
Black	03
Dark	04
Dark Brown	05
Fair	06
Freckled	07
Light	08
Light Brown	09
Medium	10
Medium Brown	11
Not Applicable	97
Olive	12
Other	98
Pale	13
Pocked	14
Ruddy	15
Sallow	16
Tanned	17
Unknown	99
Yellow	18

13. Teeth

Braces	10
Dirty/Decay	08
False	09
Gold Lower	04
Gold Upper	03
Missing Lower	02
Missing Upper	01
Normal	07
Not Applicable	97
Other	98
Silver Lower	06
Silver Upper	05
Unknown	99

15. Speech/Voice

Effeminate	01
Foreign	02
Gruff	03
High Pitch	04
Lisp	05
Low Pitch	06
Medium	07
Monotone	08
Nasal	09
Not Applicable	97
Obscene	10
Other	98
Pleasant/Soft	11
Raspy	12
Regional	13
Stutter	14
Unknown	99
Whining	15

14. Tattoo

Arms	01
Back	06
Chest	05
Face	03
Hands	02
Legs	04
Not Applicable	97
Other	98
Unknown	99

16. General Appearance

Conservative	01
Dirty	02
Disguised	03
Flashy	04
Good-looking	05
Military	06
Not Applicable	97
Other	98
Unkempt	07
Unknown	99
Unusual Odor	08
Well-groomed	09

9
10
11
12
13
14
15
16

FIGURE 11-6 *(Continued)*

unit, and other related standard indicators. A common problem associated with such tabulations is that they lead to a wrong assumption: By increasing the amounts reported in each category of officer activity, there is a proportionate increase in the quality of police service. Unfortunately, the concepts of police productivity and quality of service are often misinterpreted.[22] As Hernandez has pointed out, "In order to effectively deal with the concept of police productivity, one must come to grips with identifying the mission, goals and objectives of the police agency."[23]

With this in mind, decisions and actions should be based on the appraisal of the best available data inseparably linked with overall agency needs and goals. By far the most exhaustive study assessing police productivity with computerized data-based systems is that conducted by Danziger and Kraemer.[24] Their study indicated that the productivity of professional workers and managers who undertake semistructured tasks and are dependent on a rich information environment is greatly enhanced by computer technology.[25] Further, they associate "enhanced productivity" with "case-oriented" objectives and performance measures—a critical point for evaluation.[26]

One of the more useful software packages in this area is CAPE—Computer Assisted Personnel Evaluation. The CAPE system includes a series of performance-evaluation manuals designed to assess the various job classifications in law enforcement such as officer, investigator sergeant, and lieutenant. Manuals, which were developed and tested in various law enforcement agencies, consist of a series of five-point behaviorally anchored rating scales that describe the specific duties of each separate job classification. There are more than four hundred separate scales grouped into fifteen different job categories from which a department may select for use in evaluating any job classification.[27] Although CAPE is specifically designed for promotion and selection appraisals, minor modifications would allow the program to assess productivity measures.

Fiscal Management and Analysis

Historically, the computer process entered the business world through the automation of payroll and billing. Payroll was an easy task for computers and high-speed printers. Then too, the rigid bookkeeping regulations required in accounting practices lend themselves well to the automation process.

In the public sector, and more specifically concerning law enforcement, a number of software packages are available to facilitate the budget process. Police agency budgets are part of an overall municipal or state budget which is enacted and controlled by that government. Many of the administration and record-keeping functions of a police budget are the responsibility of another department of that government. However, most police agencies do keep an ongoing accounting of expenditures and for this purpose a number of software packages perform in-house accounting tasks adequately.

"Spreadsheet" programs are especially well-suited for budget development. The

TABLE 11-1 **Flagstaff Budget Worksheet Fiscal Year 1986/87**

	Police				
Account	**Current year**	**Expended thru 12/31**	**Estimate 1/1–6/30**	**Total estimate this year**	**Estimate next year**
Salaries	2,063,803.00	1,016,897.71		1,016,897.71	
Overtime	226,025.00	101,341.64	125,659.00	227,000.00	250,000.00
Pension Contributions	76,319.00	38,473.63		38,473.62	
Social Security	161,878.00	77,290.01		77,290.01	
Industrial Accident Insurance	43,597.00	22,714.35		22,714.35	
Clothing Allowance	23,000.00	13,141.37	13,000.00	26,141.00	42,480.00
Group Insurance	43,770.36	24,384.27		24,387.27	
Shop Labor	700.00	4,017.75	400.00	4,417.00	1,000.00

Spreadsheet Budgeting using Lotus 1–2–3 (Courtesy Flagstaff, Arizona, Police Department.)

BOX 11-1.

Calif. Police Redesign Micro into Multiuser System

By EDWARD WARNER, *CW Staff*

SACRAMENTO, Calif.—The California State Police headquarters here has implemented a cost-conscious solution to its need for desktop computing power. Able to afford only one IBM Personal Computer XT, the agency configured that computer into a multiuser system supporting 14 terminals.

The terminals provide word processing and filing functions for the agency and will eventually be able to access a copy of the state police's criminal data base, when a 70M-byte hard disk storage unit is added to the system soon. In all, said Schnoer Sherman, the man who configured the system, it provides $25,000 worth of processing power, based on the cost of using personal computers instead of terminals.

The system cost the agency $18,000, including the host.

The key to the four-month-old system's multiuser capabilities is its QNX operating system, one which Sherman described as being outwardly like the Unix operating system, but inwardly different. QNX, from Quantum Software, Ltd., of Canada, cost the agency $650 and came equipped with built-in word processing, file management and communications software, said Sherman, the agency's DP coordinator and staff services analyst.

"This is the best single piece of software I've ever seen in my life," Sherman enthused.

The operating system's built-in communications software, in conjunction with the multiuser system's three modems, allows the system to communicate with terminals in use at the agency's command centers in Los Angeles, San Francisco, Fresno, Calif., and elsewhere in Sacramento.

When the 70M-byte hard disk is installed, Sherman added, the system will download the state police data base on wanted suspects from the state's Teale Data Center. The agency currently accesses that data base on-line, but experiences slowed data retrieval that in-house storage of a data base copy would solve, he said.

The agency's system has four Tab Products, Inc. 132/15 terminals and six Teleray Trend Data Corp. terminals hard-wired to 10 of 16 ports available on the XT. Sixteen ports on an XT? It is possible, Sherman explained, through the addition of two eight-port serial cards from Control Systems Corp. and a 16-port bracket on the back of the computer.

The state police bought the Teleray terminals, which had been leased by other California state agencies, by paying off the $160 "balloon" at the end of each terminal's lease period. Sherman said he replaced the Teleray terminals' black-and-white screens with amber screens to ease viewing during word processing, a function that he said occupies at least six people in his office at any one time.

Though the system is only four months old, Sherman said most of the office's paperwork is already being done on it, and several files in a personnel data base have been stored on the system.

Sherman said the biggest hang-up with a multiuser system based on an IBM Personal Computer XT is its storage demands. To remedy that hang-up, the Personal Computer XT's 10M-byte hard disk storage unit capacity will soon be augmented by a Tallgrass Technologies Corp. 70M-byte disk.

Sherman said two other state agencies have sent representatives to look at the state police multiuser system and that, were the QNX software used in conjunction with a group of Teleray terminals and an IBM Personal Computer host, state agencies could have a multiuser system for less than $15,000.

Courtesy of ComputerWorld Magazine, July 23, 1984.

spreadsheet is a powerful tool designed mainly for handling quantitative information in a two-dimensional table (rows and columns). Beyond basic statistical analysis and mathematical tabulation, some spreadsheet programs provide sophisticated financial modeling capabilities designed specifically to assist top executives in decision making.

General Management Functions and Microcomputers[28]

With the recent advent of low-cost microcomputers, many law enforcement agencies are discovering new ways of keeping records and expediting paperwork. From a clerical standpoint, the introduction of word-processing programs has totally revolutionized the secretarial role. Word processing greatly speeds report writing and editing when compared to traditional typewriting, dictation, or handwriting. Erasure is fast and easy and allows the user to compose and edit simultaneously, producing a faster, better written copy without several drafts.[29] Further, most word-processing programs can be customized to handle standardized departmental forms and reports.

Another important set of software programs useful for law enforcement falls in the general description of "data base management." This is a term used to describe the range of programs functioning as computerized file clerks in an electronic file cabinet.[30] Through the use of general purpose data-base management programs like Condor, DBASE III, or Info Star, law enforcement agencies can build their own applicational files. As Benton, Stoughton, and Silberstein explain:

> Personnel management is an obvious choice for a data-base program. Each employee would be included, along with such pertinent information as employment type (civilian, sworn peace officer, supervisory, line, probationary, permanent, etc.), salary, overtime, authorized absences. By maintaining such a data base, the department would be free to perform a variety of analyses at any time. For example, a supervisor could locate potential leave abuses or identify the need for increased staffing by looking at sick leave or overtime used by each unit or by individuals on a monthly or quarterly basis. Scheduling staff for training, tracking the end of probationary status, or remembering when to conduct personnel reviews are just some of the many management functions aided by a locally available data-base system.
>
> Inventory control of equipment, vehicles, stolen property and evidence could also benefit from a data-base file system. There are commercial packages specially designed for inventory records or the department can create its own.[31]

Jail and Prisoner Management

Although jail and prisoner management are not the responsibility for many local and state law enforcement agencies, it is often a major function for county sheriffs. An example of a common software package designed for this task is JAMS-II-Jail Administration Management System.[32] JAMS-II simplifies jail record keeping and offers administrators up-to-the-minute information on the inmate population. JAMS-II, as well as other jail and prisoner management software, performs the following functions:

- —Booking: Automatically generates a booking number and captures all the information necessary to complete the booking record. A detailed account of personal property and cash removed from the inmate is maintained and a paper copy of the booking record is generated.
- —Updating: Changes and records corrections quickly and efficiently. Updating functions include: inmate releases, cell moves, and changes in holds, warrants status, medical status, visiting and phone privileges, charge dispositions, scheduled court appearances, and sentence calculation/outdates.

- —Record Inquiry: Retrieves selected portions of an inmate record and displays them on an operator's terminal. Staff may display current information or historical records, and a paper copy may be printed.
- —Daily Log/Audit Trail: Collects and prints the shift log of activities. The log includes all bookings, releases, and tallies for the shift. Every system transaction is logged to an audit file which may be printed or stored for processing later. The audit file contains the operator ID number, date and time of usage, record accessed, and transaction.
- —Medical Accounting: Maintains medical information for each inmate. The medical module is protected from unauthorized use by a special security feature.
- —Classification/Pretrial Release: Supports inmate classification and pretrial release programs, and supplies information for indigence and bail/release recommendations.
- —Inmate Cash Accounting: Accounts for inmate cash, allowing the jail to keep track of cash on hand, commissary purchases, other cash expenditures, as well as cash deposits.
- —Billing: Produces billing reports and agency invoices which detail the particulars of inmate housing.

Communications and Manpower Allocation Design

In the last twenty-five years, computer automation has not been the only rapidly growing industry affecting law enforcement. Another major advancing technology during this same time period has been that of radio communications. The portable radio is as common now in police work as the "billy club" was a century ago. The advent of computer and communication technologies has provided the individual police officer with increased levels of safety and given police executives additional tools with which to manage the workforce.[33]

CAD System Overview

The development of computer-assisted or computer-aided dispatch (CAD) plans, which combine modern communication and automated record systems, has enabled police managers to improve the allocation or use of uniformed officers assigned to patrol duties.

A number of CAD system software packages are available in the law enforcement market. Most packages offer dispatch speed and flexibility well beyond any manual system. Uniformed officers are dispatched based on the type of incident and the location. When this information is entered, the CAD system responds with detailed information about that location, such as verification of address, best access route, dangers near the location (e.g., known dangerous felons and "biker" hangouts), immediate past police or emergency service history (within the last twenty-four hours), and any other information that previously was entered. Additionally, most systems maintain a dynamic status review for available personnel and suggest the closest available unit to the location. In systems incorporating automatic transponders within patrol vehicles, units are visually monitored and assigned in coordination with the computer suggestion. Enhanced CAD systems utilize mobile digital terminals (MDTs)

ASPRIN* Communication Plot

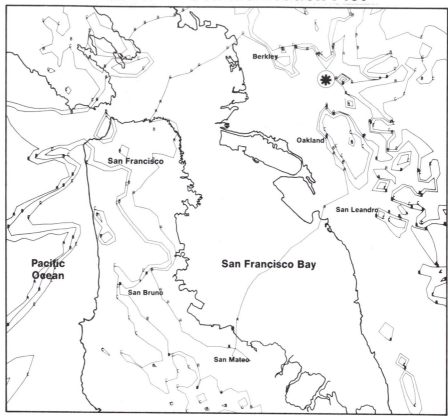

Talk-In 850 MHz Reliability A = 95%
B = 80%
C = 50%

FIGURE 11-7 Automated System Prediction for Radio Intregrated Networks (ASPRIN). This schematic represents the latest in computer-communication linkages applied to law enforcement applications. The chart measures communication reliability based on geographical setting in the San Francisco Bay area. In this manner, police communication devices can be strategically placed to increase radio and CAD reception reliability. [Courtesy of ElectroCom Automation, Inc., Arlington, Texas.]

placed within each patrol car. Dispatching can then be conducted electronically from the host computer to each MDT, eliminating most of the mundane and routine voice communication of the past.

Mobile digital terminal and CAD systems provide a number of important advantages for the individual police officer as well as the law enforcement agency:

- —Officers are free to query names and license plates directly through records and warrant files without interfering with radio communications or requesting the time of a dispatcher. Thus, CAD systems provide an interface or direct computer-to-computer linkage between local systems and county, state and/ or federal criminal justice information systems, such as the National Crime Information Center (NCIC);

- —Document control numbers and initial report formats can be directly entered into the automated records system, thereby eliminating certain clerical functions;
- —Exact addresses can be displayed with nearest cross streets, map coordinates, and in some cases even floor plans;
- —Coordination of all emergency agencies to include fire and ambulance services can be visually monitored by the officer and the dispatch center;
- —Response time is dramatically decreased as the complete dispatch process from call-in to arrival time is fully automated;
- —Automatic processing of incident information via a preformatted incident form is completed;
- —Geo-coding is utilized to identify responsible agencies; assign the nearest unit; capture reported, dispatched, arrival, and completion times; and verify address locations;
- —The status of patrol units and personnel is constantly maintained which enhances officer security and safety;
- —CAD systems enable the accumulation of large amounts of data over time which can be used in basic crime analysis and manpower allocation planning to assign personnel when and where crime is highest or calls for service are heaviest. This is the primary goal in manpower allocation design;
- —To have officers available when and where services are needed.

For the most part, CAD systems and manpower allocation design models have been parallel in development. The most intricate plans combine the immediate data

FIGURE 11-8 Computer-assisted dispatch (CAD) system utilizing mobile digital terminals (MDT's) in patrol vehicles. [Courtesy of Los Angeles Police Department.]

base from a CAD system with an ongoing allocation format. To understand this unique convergence of advancing computer and communication technology with allocation modeling, it is important to assess various developments.

Manpower Allocation Design—Early Developments

The analysis of police patrol allocation in the United States began with the work of August Vollmer in Berkeley, California, during the early 1900s. Vollmer established a list of police functions that still appears in the literature on municipal policing.[34] With little variation, that list of police functions consists of: crime prevention, crime repression, apprehension, criminal investigation, public service, maintenance of peace and security, regulation of noncriminal activities, traffic control, and provision of emergency services. According to Vollmer, these functions combined are the police mission. He was the first to associate these functions with a territorial unit of work or the "beat." Vollmer's contribution to patrol allocation can be viewed in two perspectives. First, he placed a priority emphasis on the study of beat construction by formulating a standard for allocation: patrol officers should be distributed by area in proportion to the amount of work to be done.[35] Second, Vollmer initiated the advancement of technological innovations in patrol assignments, especially in the use of communications.

In 1920, Fosdick expanded on Vollmer's earlier thoughts. Noting that patrol deployment must change and alter with new political, economic, employment, residential, and crime-occurring conditions, Fosdick proposed that the type and mode of patrol must adapt to new situations.[36] He was the first to recognize a relationship between a changing community environment and the need for a patrol strategy or allocation design.

Smith's *Police Systems in the United States* (1929), recognized still another important aspect of patrol deployment. Indicating that patrol had been traditionally "distributed on an equal, or nearly equal, basis throughout the twenty-four hours of the day," despite marked increases in workload and crime occurrences, Smith was the first to advance the use of crime analysis in allocation design.[37] For the first time, patrol distribution was related to activity and crime documentation by police records. This was an important step for allocation design, as managers recognized the need to deploy personnel in an effort to maximize patrol activity during those times of highest crime and workload occurrence.

THE HAZARD MODEL

In 1941, O. W. Wilson, then Chief of Police at Wichita, Kansas, established the "relative need" approach to police deployment. Emphasizing the redistribution of patrol forces based on a set of "proportionate need factors," Wilson called for the application of law enforcement to the locations, during the times and toward the particular criminal violations that represented the greatest demands on the police.[38]

Elaborating on his original work, Wilson formulated a deployment scheme that was based on allocation by hazard.[39] The formula was first initiated in the Los Angeles Police Department in 1953 and, with relatively minor changes, is still in use today. Each type of crime is given a weighted hazard score, and by prioritizing the incidence of crime, a total weighted sum for each region is calculated. The patrol force is then allocated accordingly.

Manpower Allocation Design: Post-1960 Developments

In the early 1960s, Phoenix, Arizona modified the hazard model somewhat for its own use. The Phoenix model includes considerations of any delay in responding to a call for police service, travel time to the location of the call, and the amount of time actually used in providing whatever police services are needed.[40] Currently, Phoenix is able to provide police, fire, and emergency medical service cars with mobile graphics on their MDTs. These graphics can display, for example, a diagram of a building, including the floor plan and the location of stairwells and other related features.

Crowther, in 1964, suggested a series of computer programs for the allocation of patrol personnel in St. Louis.[41] The St. Louis model allows for the patrol force to be distributed on the assumption that up to 15 percent of calls for police service may not be responded to immediately. Instead, calls are placed in line or queue and handled as patrol units come back in-service from other calls.

The Law Enforcement Manpower Resource Allocation System (LEMRAS) is very similar to the St. Louis model.[42] A key variation is the LEMRAS method for prioritizing calls. Calls for services are categorized by event codes. These codes are then assigned to one of three priority levels which designate the length of time the call will be held in queue. For example, a "cold" burglary may be placed in priority three, whereas a robbery in progress is assigned a priority one. Calls are then dispatched

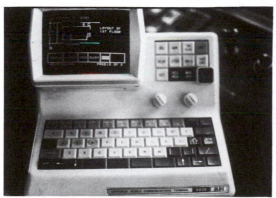

FIGURE 11-9 The Phoenix Graphics System is one of the most advanced MDT systems available to police, fire, and other emergency service agencies. Each vehicle is equipped with an MDT displaying both a written description and a visual diagram of the building queried. [Courtesy of the Phoenix Fire Department, Phoenix, Arizona.]

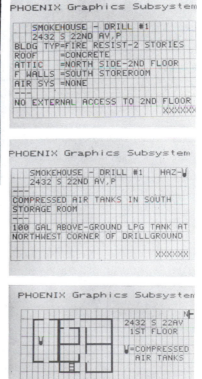

in order of decreasing priority. Thus, all priority one and two calls would be dispatched before any priority three call, thereby decreasing the delay for any high priority incident.

In 1969, Larson designed a simulation model which bases the allocation of the patrol force on factors such as expected time of travel to the location of a call in relationship to the geographical characteristics of the city, the number of patrol cars on duty, and the demands for service in specific rectangular sectors.[43] Larson's model, in contrast to LEMRAS, uses more than three priority levels for calls placed in line or queue.

Developed in 1975, the Patrol Car Allocation Method (PCAM) is based heavily on Larson's program.[44] PCAM does not attempt to equalize the calls for service workload across watches or shifts. Instead, its goal is to deploy officers so that dispatch delays and response times can be optimized.

The Shoup-Dosser or split force model was first proposed in 1964, although actual use of it was not made until later.[45] It is based on the assumption that police officers have a direct and quantifiable effect on the crime rate within each geographical area. The ideal situation for this model is to have enough officers at any given moment to match the demand for police service, while at the same time having enough of a preventive patrol force distributed to minimize criminal activity. Thus, the patrol force is split into response and preventive duties.

The hypercube queuing model was developed in 1977 by Larson.[46] It assists police managers in the design of individual patrol beats. The goal of the model is to provide maximum relevant information about the ability of patrol units to answer service calls in the various patrol beats. A key objective of this is equalization of the work load between patrol units.

Deployment Plans in General

The preceeding material covers the major evolutions in police patrol allocation/CAD models. Only those studies and models that are well known have been analyzed. There are numerous other designs, which, however, are rarely mentioned in the literature.[47]

One of the pronounced shortcomings of police patrol allocation designs, in general, lies in the area of evaluation. The evaluation of patrol deployment plans has not been well developed and has failed to make use of experimental design.[48] What is required to further the advancement of patrol deployment is a carefully designed experiment that measures the effect of innovations in police strategies and schemes. For example, very few of the noted patrol allocation designs have ever been implemented to measure what the police actually did.[49] Instead, they attempted to measure the effect of increased or decreased response times, elapsed times, police presence, work load, calls for service, and the like. Further, only recently have social scientists begun to review and critique patrol allocation plans.

Training

In the 1960s and even into the early 1970s, an enormous amount of excitement was generated over the potential of the computer as a tool to aid learning. It was confidently predicted that computer-assisted instruction (CAI) would soon be an integral part of classroom procedures.[50] William and Betty Archambeault have defined computer-assisted instruction as "the use of the computer to aid instruction which places the learner in a conversational or interactive mode with a computer that has a prepro-grammed study or instructional plan."[51]

The advent of the microcomputer has sparked even more fascination about the possibilities of CAI. These small, relatively inexpensive machines now make it possible for most school districts to at least experiment with CAI. Similar application of computer use has been tested in industry. Computer-based training (CBT) has emerged as an alternative delivery style for employee skill acquisition and improved retention of learned material.[52] The use of computers in both education and training has provided the basis for extensive research and development by many multinational corporations. Bell Laboratories' Richard Davis predicts that by 1990 about 10 percent of all industrial training will use computers in some form, and that this figure will increase to 50 percent by the year 2000.[53]

In the area of law enforcement training, computer-based education has recently developed as a viable and realistic entity. The application of PLATO (Programmed Logic for Automated Teaching Operations) in various courses at the Police Training Institute, University of Illinois, was the first to raise considerable interest in the field.[54] Today, three general recognized types of CAI programs are utilized in law enforcement training—tutorial, drill and practice, and simulation.

Tutorial CAI

In tutorial programs, instruction takes place solely between the student and the computer. Based on the traditional "Socratic" method of teaching, the computer presents a logical progression of facts, information, and questions.[55] This type of program mimics the lecture-style format in classroom instruction utilizing written versus oral communication. Feedback is provided to student answers and the program allows for review in a related field when incorrect responses are recorded.

Drill and Practice CAI

Drill and practice CAI software is designed to work in cooperation with an instructor to intensify and review previously taught material. After a period of instruction by the course teacher, the student is tested on the material by the drill and practice program. The computer presents a question that in turn is answered by the student. The computer checks the answer and returns appropriate feedback if correct. If the answer is incorrect, a group of review questions pertaining to the studied material is presented. The procedure continues in this manner until the correct responses have been recorded.

Simulation CAI

Simulation CAI program packages are much more advanced than the previously mentioned types of software. Like drill and practice, they are designed to be used in conjunction with an instructor. However, simulation CAI provides the opportunity not only to respond to given questions but also apply previously learned problem-solving skills to a specific "real-life" situation.[56] Simulation CAI utilizes audio and visual elements to present a realistic scenario for the student. In each presented "game" or situation, the student must make decisions and judgments based on a variety of behavioral instincts and/or intellectual skills. For instance, the Federal Law Enforcement Training Center (FLETC) at Glynco, Georgia, has designed a simulation courseware involving "shoot, don't shoot" exercises. A laser disc is employed to score accurate "shots" fired by students while encountering different environments. Shooting proficiency and decision-making skills are evaluated through "computer assisted target analysis" (CATA) programs.[57] Simulation CAI has an immense potential in law enforcement training from personnel selection and promotion (e.g., real-life situations and video scenes require an individual to apply agency policy) to top executive development and testing (e.g., individuals must play a "game" in which decision trees lead to effective outcomes during crisis events such as terrorist attacks, floods, earthquakes, and the like).[58] In general, simulation CAI courseware can be utilized in any area in which individuals must learn specific values and rationales from a behavioral science and apply them to a dynamic and ever-changing environment.

CAI Effectiveness

Most of the research attempting to evaluate the effectiveness at CAI on general police training has been very positive. Wilkenson has shown that adults prefer to learn, or actually learn better when the following conditions exist:[59]

- —Courses are presented in a single concept manner with heavy emphasis on the application of the concept to relevant real world problems.
- —New material is presented at a pace that permits mastery of one idea at a time with frequent summarization.
- —Projects are self-directed and the pace of study is controlled by the learner.
- —The study environment eliminates risk taking, such as asking questions in public.
- —The material is presented in a manner that promotes learning in the fastest and easiest way possible.

General CAI courseware appears to meet many of these conditions and as such has been found to reduce learning time and improve learning skills for students within law enforcement training arenas.[60]

The Impact of Automation on Law Enforcement

The socioeconomic impact of the computer revolution has received considerable attention by futuristic writers. Most noteworthy are the observations of Naisbitt, who asserts that power is directly related to "information control."[61] Those individuals who have information knowledge can create an economic value and reality. One can support Naisbitt's argument by observing the well-documented increase in white-collar and service jobs as manufacturing jobs have declined. Fundamental shifts in an industrial society will occur, but not necessarily along the lines that economists, planners, political scientists, and bureaucrats usually monitor. Toffler suggests that civilization has grossly fragmented or "de-massified" into a number of idiosyncratic

FIGURE 11-10   Simulation CAI: IRS agents-in-training utilize portable computers to assist in audit and fraud investigations. [Courtesy of Federal Law Enforcement Training Center, Glycno, Georgia.]

and socially diverse institutions that he calls the techno-sphere, the socio-sphere, the info-sphere, the bio-sphere, the power-sphere, and the psycho-sphere.[62] He argues that the more mass society fractures and the more economy becomes differentiated, then the more information must be exchanged to maintain integration in the system. This has brought about the revolution of the Third Wave or the dependence on technology and information sharing.[63] Toffler, as well as many others, has dedicated considerable time and effort in attempting to assess the impact of this change on society and world civilization in general.[64]

Paradoxically, there is little empirical research focusing on the impact of automation on the police, an institution that often reflects societal attitudes and perspectives.[65] Sykes has, however, pointed out that the reform movement toward professionalism during the last twenty years required the use of computerization of records and reports. He writes:

> Police professionalism primarily stressed efficiency and technical competence in crime control. Implicitly this assumed a centralized, systematic information-gathering process. Automation became a necessary complement in the effort to supervise, evaluate, and maintain more direct administrative control over line officers in terms of this professional role. Information gathering and processing so essential for efficient crime control, due to technical innovations in silicon chip technology, now assumes more significance than in the past.
>
> . . . If the ''professional'' focus in policing as a crime-control activity fosters the need for more efficient information gathering, coding, storing and processing for use by the criminal justice system automation of management information provides more complete

data on personnel and other resources to be used in decision-making by police managers. Information on workloads, scheduling, performance, budgeting, and program evaluation will substantially enhance the ability of police executives to know what is happening within their organizations and allegedly provides the data necessary to use resources in a more organizationally responsible manner. In plain terms, the automation of police agencies is almost an inevitable reform given the emphases of the professional movement with its complementary efforts to develop sophisticated police management.[66]

Police Role

The increased demand for information for criminal justice agencies and police management needs may alter the existing role of individual police officers. Bittner has provided a colorful and dramatic image of the ''soldier-bureaucrat,''[67] as an individual totally controlled by administrative tasks, unable to perform rudimentary duties, and make discretionary judgments. Sykes suggests an even darker scenario as the ''line officer, metaphorically speaking, could become an appendage of the machine.''[68]

In essence, has computerization and the subsequent need for information provided unnecessary shifts in the police role? If so, an interesting issue may arise. Who controls whom? Does the officer generate a report that becomes bits of information for processing or does the computer (regulated by management) demand that certain bits of information be processed?

The scenario as described by Bittner and Sykes is not unrealistic, especially when one evaluates the changing emphasis on recruit entrance requirements. Many police departments require a college degree or at least two years of higher education as a result of the professionalization movement. Today's agencies prefer that entering law enforcement candidates have a familiarity with computers and computer applications in criminal justice. Hence, the subtle shifting of education (for police recruits) from broad-based social and behavioral science programs to a more technically oriented background. This type of education is contradictory to the original rationale for recommending higher education among police officers. The 1967 President's Commission on Law Enforcement and Administration of Justice, after exhaustive review of the preceeding ten years (which were characterized by massive unrest, turbulence, and violence) recommended that police officers be schooled in basic human relations and social/behavioral sciences in an effort to reduce racial bias and social prejudices.[69] We need officers who can relate to people and not machines. Is the pendulum swinging back to narrow, technically oriented programs for police officers? If so, is this the type of officer that the community really wants?

Some proponents might argue ''yes'' as the automation explosion has developed a new type of crime and criminal. The uneducated, blundering ''con'' of the past has been replaced by a sophisticated, technically smart thief who utilizes the computer as an instrument of crime. The increasing cases of computer fraud, credit card manipulation, and automation theft have provided police with new arenas for investigation which they are ill prepared to handle. However, these are jobs for specialized investigators not line officers.

Today's police officers still require the ability to relate to various people under strained conditions in often hostile environments. Peacekeeping involves extralegal intervention into human situations that call for judgment and skill in relating to people.[70] For this challenge, police officers must understand their role in the community as aided by, and not controlled by, the technological marvels of automation.

BOX 11-2.

Micros: Most Powerful Crime Fighters Yet

By RONALD K. OLSEN, *Special to GCN*

The most powerful modern weapon available today in the war against crime is neither a laser nor a nuclear device, it is a microcomputer.

Many of today's criminals are intelligent, highly educated and very sophisticated. These criminals permeate the government scene. They could be anyone, from the local contractor who collects the garbage to the multi-national conglomerate furnishing weapons systems, or from the GS-7 clerk who handles the imprest fund to the top executive of the agency. They cost the taxpayer billions of dollars.

Here is where the big money is. Here is where the big crooks are. They must be rooted out and stopped. . . . They must be apprehended. . . . They must be prosecuted. . . . They must be stripped of their ill-gotten gains. . . . And, they must be incarcerated!

This is a very difficult job. These criminals are sly and nefarious individuals who are not obvious. They are cunning and subtle. The evidence of their crimes is buried under a mountain of paper or in the bowels of their computers.

Therefore, the people who are going to investigate these matters must also be intelligent, sophisticated, highly trained and able to use their own computers as tools for investigating these complex crimes.

They must know how to sift through these mountains of paper. They must know how to operate their own computers to probe the innermost recesses of the suspect's computer and glean the kernels of evidence in a legal manner, preserve them in a proper manner, and be able to present them to the jury in a manner acceptable by the court.

Microcomputer technology has evolved to the point where several highly portable units are now available for use in the field by investigators and auditors. At the same time, some very powerful software has been developed to allow investigators and auditors to analyze vast amounts of both quantitative and qualitative data, thereby making these individuals far more productive.

The President's Council on Integrity and Efficiency (PCIE) has endorsed the use of the microcomputer. Under this endorsement several thousand investigators and auditors have and will be using portable microcomputers to increase the efficiency and effectiveness of their work. The PCIE has established a computer committee to enhance the computer audit and investigative skills of the offices of inspectors general.

The committee, chaired by June Gibbs Brown, former inspector general, NASA, assembled a task force headed by Bill Colvin, deputy inspector general, NASA. The task force has identified the microcomputer hardware and software technical requirements; coordinated the procurement of microcomputer systems; identified needed and required training; designed the training (four courses) around the specific needs of federal investigators and auditors; and designed the classrooms and coordinated the installation of microcomputer hardware and software.

After that they initially taught each of the courses at the training sites, at which time the permanent instructors were taught; established a microcomputer users group to function as a technical resource group and to pursue other interests of the committee; and assigned responsibility for preparing microcomputer audit guidelines.

The training programs, modified to be more specifically aimed at the investigative community are available at the Federal Law Enforcement Training Center, Glynco, Ga. These programs, for investigators who may have no prior computer experience, are designed to teach the use of the microcomputer as an investigative tool. Specifically, this program teaches the use of a computer to investigate any type of activity in which much information or many records must be analyzed, synthesized, and summarized.

(For additional information on enrolling in the computer related courses, call or write the Computer/Economic Crime Branch, Federal Law Enforcement Training Center, Glynco, Ga. 31524; telephone 912–267–2342,

FTS 230–2342. Or the Office of State and Local Programs, 912–267–2345, FTS 230–2345. These courses are open to all federal law enforcement agencies as well as state and local police.)

The microcomputer can be used to quickly collect, display and analyze evidence in support of an investigation. It is small, portable and permits ready utilization on virtually any investigative site. The microcomputer can be used to arrange, summarize, and display evidence, and to prepare effective investigative reports.

In addition to being able to do analysis very quickly, the microcomputer allows the investigator many more options on what evidence can by sought and how to seek that evidence. Data can be downloaded from virtually any mainframe and manipulated within the microcomputer. The results show the investigator exactly who should be interviewed, and exactly what questions should be asked that witness.

The word processing capability of the microcomputer is so powerful and user-friendly that some of the agencies have made policy statements prohibiting the use of them for that purpose. So many of the inspector general personnel were using them as word processors that they were unavailable to be used by the investigators.

However, in the field, this outstanding capability is a distinct blessing. Often, the agency will type up a report immediately after obtaining the evidence or interview. The microcomputer can then communicate those reports to the home office where they can be printed and waiting to be reviewed by supervisory personnel the next day.

All financial investigators have had the experience of spending hours doing the calculation to support a net worth analysis of a suspect, only to have new evidence discovered that requires it to be done over. The microcomputer, with its ability to automatically recalculate a worksheet, has eliminated these hours of toil.

The investigator now has a tool that can quickly and easily convert the data to clearly understood graphs and charts. The use of the graphics capability of the microcomputer is threefold: it can present the data in a format that is easily recognized and understood; it can highlight and emphasize that portion of the data that is most important; the graphs and charts can also be used as outstanding analytical tools.

The computer use capability of the investigators has given Health and Human Services Inspector General Richard Kusserow's agents the weapons they need "to allow us to hit the crooked provider (of health care services) where it hurts most . . . in the pocketbook." He estimates that indictments backed by computer—derived evidence, could save $1 billion a year in false cost reports filed against Medicare, Social Security and Workers Compensation programs.

Department of Transportation investigators, working with state highway officials have been using the same techniques for some months, including use of the graphic display capability to persuade grand juries in highway-construction bid-rigging criminal indictments.

The Department of Labor Office of Inspector General has had its investigators and auditors using the microcomputers for some time. One of the first cases in which the microcomputer was used heavily, involved allegations of conspiracy, mail fraud, benefit plan bribery and aiding and abetting. It was tied to a major organized crime family and included potential kickbacks of at least $130,000 in connection with the pension and welfare funds of five different union locals.

The case involved an allegation that the defendant received what amounted to an interest free loan over a period of several years with the amount varying from month to month. One of the things DOL was asked to do was to determine the amount of money that would have been required to pay interest on the loan, at the prime rate, over the period of time that the defendant had the money, and to come up with the answer in 10 days.

The microcomputer automatically computed the interest with the time limit. However, new evidence revealed that incorrect information had been provided and it had to be done over. With new entries keyed in, the computer automatically recomputed the interest well within the time allotted.

Another DOL case with 8,000 checks was easily handled by the computer. The checks had only to be examined one time, then keyed into the computer for analysis. Another case needed an analysis of 5,000 telephone calls. The numbers were entered at random into the computer, which then automatically sorted and printed them in their numerical order, verifying an organized crime connection.

The Internal Revenue Service has so many diverse uses for the microcomputer that it expects to purchase between 12,000 and 17,000 units by May 1985. Some agents in the Boston district are currently armed with portable computers and have probably a score or more of instances where the agents have taken the portable out into the field and actually worked a case on it.

Agents in the New York office are setting up microcomputer workstations at home. They each have microcomputers with floppy disk drives and printers at their residences. Unless there are specific reasons for them to report to their offices, they work their cases at home, sending the data to the office over the telephone lines. Productivity has been increased to a significant extent.

The NASA Office of Inspector General has become very sophisticated in the use of the microcomputer. In its audit report, "Acquisition, Utilization, Accountability, and Cost of Spares—Space Shuttle Main Engine," issued on September 7, 1984, the office used graphs generated by the microcomputer to illustrate audit findings. It made for such a clarity of the message that there was an excellent acceptance of the findings.

In another NASA case, the automatic recalculating capability of the microcomputer was so necessary that Bill D. Colvin, the deputy inspector general said, "The case could not have been accomplished within the necessary timeframe without the microcomputer." He added that, "Even additional manpower could not have accomplished the job that was done by the microcomputer."

After the microcomputer had been used by investigators and auditors for about two years, the PCIE Computer Committee agreed the project was nearing an appropriate stage to be independently evaluated.

Therefore, they arranged to have Dr. Robert W. Lissitz, chairman and professor, Department of Measurement, Statistics and Evaluation, University of Maryland, to do a "Statistical Analysis of the Effects of Using a Microcomputer System for Field Audits and Investigations Conducted by the Offices of Inspectors General." That analysis has been completed and was published on August 15, 1984.

The analysis did both a case study and a survey of first line supervisors to determine the effects of using a microcomputer. The analysis showed the use of microcomputers will often save days of effort on the part of investigators and auditors. And in some cases the use of a microcomputer allows for activities that would not otherwise be possible. The analysis stated, "It is likely that in the near future microcomputers will become very common."

In fact, many of the people in the investigative community believe that all future investigations, other than small uncomplicated criminal activity, will have to be done with the aid of the computer. From now on, the investigator who cannot use the computer will receive the dull, routine assignments. All investigations that are the least bit complex or lengthy will have to be done with the aid of the microcomputer.

The future is now. Crimefight with the computer.

Source: Courtesy of *Government Computer News,* June 7, 1985.

Summary

The advent of computerized systems has drastically affected law enforcement organization, personnel, and services. The vast amount of data and information collected by police agencies demand an efficient system that offers immediate retrieval capabilities. Further, the issue of police accountability for actions and expenditures requires the tabulation of information into meaningful summaries and statistics in which managers can measure and justify operational decisions.

The implementation of a computerized system requires exhaustive planning, often involving technical areas beyond the scope of the law enforcement executive. Police administrators should rely on technological expertise in the development of accurate and precise needs assessments. These organizational evaluations should attempt to match perfectly the computer hardware and software system capable of meeting the department's goals and fiscal limitations. The most important consideration in adopting such a system is a thorough understanding of the computer applications available for law enforcement. These applications fall into three categories: (1) Operations (Data Base Information), (2) Management and Administration (Data Base Management), and (3) Communication and Training (Data Base Sharing).

For the operation of any police agency, an automated records system will increase management efficiency. Added statistical analysis of crime data will yield meaningful tools necessary to judge and evaluate officer productivity. General management functions for microcomputers include word processing, automated budgeting, personnel management, scheduling, inventory systems, and various data base filing systems.

We have seen great advances not only in computer technology but also in the radio communications industry. The combination of these two technologies has given law enforcement a substantial increase in efficiency. The development of computer-assisted dispatch (CAD) systems that provide immediate data for manpower allocation design has allowed patrol deployment to be based on sophisticated mathematical and game theories instead of mere intuition. Computers have also entered the training arena, opening new horizons in increased skill levels and improved effectiveness. Computer-assisted instruction (CAI) has been reviewed by three general program types—tutorial, drill and practice, and simulation.

Notwithstanding the dramatic effect that computer automation has had on law enforcement agencies and organizations, we still must be ever cognizant of the role of the individual line officer. Policing is a human task requiring exceptionally good judgment and skill in relating to people. Although technological advances have promised to increase the efficiency and effectiveness of the police, the true test for successful law enforcement will always rest on the sensitivity and professionalism of the individual officer.

Discussion Questions

1. Why is automation no longer viewed as a luxury but a necessity for most police agencies?

2. Discuss some of the most important considerations in planning for a computerized system.

3. Explain the terms "hardware," "software," and "compatibility."

4. What is an automated records system and how does it increase police efficiency? Explain some of the features found on an advanced records system.

5. What is CAPE?

6. What is a "spreadsheet" program?

7. What is a CAD system? Discuss some of the important advantages developed with a CAD system.

8. What is and who developed the "hazard model" of manpower allocation design?

9. Explain the three types of computer assisted instructions: tutorial, drill and practice, and simulation.

10. Discuss the negative as well as the positive impacts of automation on law enforcement.

Notes

1. W. G. Archambeault and G. J. Archambeault, *Computers in Criminal Justice Administration and Management* (Cincinnati, Ohio: Anderson, 1984), p. 4.
2. J. K. Hudzik and G. W. Cordner, *Planning in Criminal Justice Organizations and Systems* (New York: Macmillan Publishing, 1983), p. 33.
3. Archambeault and Archambeault, *Computers in Criminal Justice,* p. 16.
4. Ibid., p. 27.
5. G. Robertson and S. Chang, "Crime Analysis Support System," *The Police Chief* (August 1980), pp. 41–43.
6. R. E. Bensmiller, *Local Crime Information Computer* (Whitsett, Tex.: Bensmiller Computer Service, 1982), p. 1.
7. D. A. George and G. H. Kleinknecht, "Computer Assisted Report Entry—CARE," *FBI Law Enforcement Bulletin,* 54 (May 1985), pp. 3–7.
8. For more detailed information, refer to internal policies and directives from the City of St. Petersburg, Florida, Police Department and the City of Ocala, Florida, Police Department. Both agencies are experimenting in the use of "lap" computers for the generation of police reports.
9. George and Kleinknecht, "Computer Assisted," p. 3.
10. J. B. Howlett, "Analytical Investigative Techniques," *The Police Chief* (December 1980), p. 42.
11. J. A. Kinney, "Criminal Intelligence Analysis: A Powerful Weapon," *International Cargo Crime Prevention* (April 1984), p. 4.
12. D. M. Ross, "Criminal Intelligence Analysis," *Police Product News* (June 1983), p. 45.
13. Ibid., p. 45.
14. Ibid., p. 45.
15. Ibid., p. 49.
16. J. Chaiken, P. Greenwood, and J. Petersilia, "The Rand Study of Detectives," in C. Klockars, *Thinking About Police: Contemporary Readings* (New York: McGraw-Hill Publishing, 1983), pp. 167–184.
17. Ibid., p. 178.
18. Ibid., p. 179.
19. Institute for Law and Social Research, Inc. *Prosecutor's Management and Information System (PROMIS), New Orleans,* (Ann Arbor, Mich.: Inter-University Consortium for Political and Social Research, 1984).
20. Ibid., p. i.
21. Refer to Peter G. W. Keen and Michael S. Morton, *Decision Support Systems: An Organizational Perspective* (Reading, Mass.: Addison-Wesley Publishing, 1978) and S. L. Alter, *Decision-Support Systems: Current Practices and Continuing Challenges* (Reading, Mass.: Addison-Wesley Publishing, 1980).
22. Lucious Riccio, "Police Data as a Guide for Measuring Productivity," in Alvin Cohn (ed.), *The Future of Policing* (Beverly Hills, Calif.: Sage Publishing, 1978).
23. Ernie Hernandez, Jr., *Police Handbook for Applying the Systems Approach and Computer Technology* (El Toro, Calif.: Frontline Publications, 1982), p. 19.
24. James N. Danziger and K. L. Kraemer, "Computerized Data-Based Systems and Productivity Among Professional Workers: The Case of Detectives," *Public Administration Review,* 45 (January/February, 1985), pp. 196–209.
25. Ibid., p. 206.
26. Ibid., p. 206.
27. G. W. Smith and M. W. Lehtinen, "Better Personnel Evaluation—With Computers," *Law Enforcement News,* Vol. XI, No. 3 (February 11, 1985), p. 7.
28. Much of this section is condensed from an excellent article that applies open market

software to police applications by W. Benton, D. Stoughton, and J. Silberstein, "A Fast and Easy Way to Build a Software Library," *Law Enforcement News,* 11:3 (February 11, 1985), pp. 6–12.

29. Ibid., p. 6.
30. Ibid., p. 6.
31. Ibid., p. 7.
32. JAMS-II is a program developed by SEARCH under grants awarded by the Bureau of Justice Statistics. SEARCH, the National Consortium for Justice Information and Statistics, is a nonprofit corporation governed in the interest of the criminal justice community by appointees of the governors of the states. For over ten years SEARCH has been a pioneer in the exploration of information technology for law enforcement, courts, and corrections. Much of the information regarding JAMS-II is taken from the SEARCH Group, Inc. brochure on the software package.
33. P. K. Wormeli, "Hi-Tech: Changing the Nature of Policing," *Law Enforcement News,* Vol. XI, No. 3 (February 11, 1985), p. 1.
34. G. E. Misner and R. Hoffman, *Police Resource Allocation* (Berkeley, Calif.: University of California Press, 1967), p. 7.
35. August Vollmer, "The Police Beat" in *Police Patrol Readings,* ed. Samual G. Chapman (Springfield, Ill.: Charles C Thomas, 1964), p. 189.
36. Frank E. Walton, "Selective Distribution of Police Patrol" in *Police Patrol Readings,* ed. Samual G. Chapman (Springfield, Ill.: Charles C Thomas, 1964), p. 177.
37. Ibid., p. 177.
38. Ibid., p. 178.
39. O. W. Wilson, *Police Planning* (Springfield, Ill.: Charles C Thomas, 1958), p. 81.
40. Rand Corporation, "Methods for Allocating Police Patrol Resources," in *Issues in Police Patrol,* ed. Thomas J. Sweeney (Kansas City, Mo.: Kansas City Police Department, 1973), p. 244.
41. Robert F. Crowther, *The Use of a Computer System for Police Manpower Allocation in St. Louis, Missouri, Part I, Manpower Requirements for Calls Answering Services* (Terre Haute: Indiana University Press, 1965), pp. 1–2. Also see Thomas McEwan, *Allocation of Patrol Manpower Resources in the St. Louis Police Department* (St. Louis: Metropolitan Police Department, 1966), pp. 6–48.
42. Rand Corporation, "Methods for Allocating," p. 247.
43. See Richard C. Larson. *Urban Police Patrol Analysis* (Cambridge, Mass.: MIT Press, 1972).
44. Jan Chaiken and Peter Dormant, *Patrol Car Allocation Method: Users Manual* (Santa Monica, Calif.: The Rand Corporation, 1975).
45. Carl S. Shoup and Douglas Dosser, "Standards For Distributing A Free Governmental Service: Crime Prevention," *Public Finance* 19, 1964.
46. Richard C. Larson, *Hypercube Queuing Model: Users Manual,* (New York: Rand Corporation, 1977).
47. For a detailed explanation of less cited patrol allocation models refer to: Gregory L. Campbell, *A Spatially Distributed Queuing Model for Police Patrol Sector Design* (Cambridge, Mass.: MIT Press, 1972); Richard Mudge, *A Description of the New York City Police Department RMP Allocation Model* (New York: Rand Institute, 1974); Peter Kolesar, *A Simulation Model of Police Patrol Operations* (New York: Rand Institute, 1975); Wayne Bennett and John DuBois, *The Use of Probability Theory in the Assignment of Police Patrol Areas* (Washington, D.C.: U.S. Government Printing Office, 1970); Kenneth Chelst, *An Interactive Approach to Police Sector Design* (Cambridge, Mass.: MIT Press, 1974); Spencer B. Smith, *Superbeat: A System for the Effective Distribution of Police Patrol Units* (Chicago: Illinois Institute of Technology, 1973).
48. Wilson and Boland, "Effect of Police on Crime," p. 383.
49. Ibid., p. 383.

50. Refer to a number of the early works on computer-assisted instruction by D. Coulson, "Factors in Learning," *Journal of Educational Psychology,* 14 (1962), pp. 133–147; J. W. Loughary (ed.), *Man-Machine Systems in Education* (New York: Harper & Row Publishers, 1966); and J. C. Meridith, *The CAI Author and Instructor* (Englewood Cliff, N.J.: Educational Technology Publications, 1971).

51. Archambeault and Archambeault, *Computers in Criminal Justice,* p. 118.

52. P. H. Seldon and N. L. Schultz, "What the Research Says About CAI's Potential," *Training,* 14 (1982), pp. 61–65.

53. Ibid., p. 62.

54. Paul Palumbo, "Firearms Training: Computer-Assisted Target Analysis," *The Police Chief,* 50 (May 1983) pp. 67–69.

55. C. J. Flammang and R. O. Walker, "Training: A Rationale Supporting Computer Assisted Instruction," *The Police Chief,* 49 (August 1982), pp. 60–62.

56. Archambeault and Archambeault, *Computers in Criminal Justice,* p. 125.

57. Palumbo, "Firearms Training," p. 67.

58. Archambeault and Archambeault, *Computers in Criminal Justice,* p. 125.

59. Tom Wilkenson, "The Use of Computers in Police Training," *The Police Chief,* 51 (April 1984), p. 49.

60. R. O. Walker and C. J. Flammang, "Instructional Application of Computer-Based Education in Police Training," *Journal of Police Science and Administration,* 9 (Spring 1981), pp. 224–228.

61. John Naisbitt, *Megatrends: Ten New Directions Changing Our Lives* (New York: Warner Books, 1982).

62. Alvin Toffler, *The Third Wave* (New York: William Morrow, 1980).

63. Ibid.

64. Refer to the works of Alvin Toffler, *The Eco-Spasm Report* (New York: Bantam Books, 1975); A. Toffler, *Future Shock* (New York: Random House, 1970); E. Cornish, *The Study of the Future* (Washington D.C.: World Future Society, 1977); G. T. Molitor, "The Information Society: The Path to Post-Industrial Growth," *The Futurist* (April 1981) pp. 23–30; J. Naisbitt, *Megatrends* (New York: Warner Books, 1982). For references that relate directly to futuristics and the police, refer to William L. Tafoya, *Futuristics: New Tools for Criminal Justice Crime Prevention, Parts I, II, and III,* Unpublished manuscript (Quantico, Va: FBI Academy, Management Science Division, 1986).

65. For an excellent review of the impact of automation on police reform refer to G. W. Sykes, "The Functional Nature of Police Reform: The 'Myth' of Controlling the Police," *Justice Quarterly* (March 1985), pp. 53–65 and G. W. Sykes, "The Impact of Automation on Police Organization: The New Reformers?" A paper presented at the Annual Conference of the Academy of Criminal Justice Sciences, Las Vegas, Nevada (March 1985). Much of the discussion in this book regarding the impact of automation on police was derived from Sykes' work.

66. Sykes, "The Impact of Automation on Police Organization," pp.3–4.

67. Egon Bittner, *The Functions of the Police in Modern Society* (Washington, D.C.: U.S. Government Printing Office, 1971).

68. Sykes, "The Impact of Automation on Police Organization," p. 6.

69. President's Commission on Law Enforcement and Administration of Justice, *Task Force Report: The Police* (Washington, D.C.: U.S. Government Printing Office, 1966).

70. Sykes, "The Impact of Automation," p. 11.

Decision Making

Introduction

Decision making is a complex process that includes not only procedures for reaching a sound decision on the basis of pertinent knowledge, beliefs, and judgments but also procedures for obtaining the required knowledge, ideas, and preconditions. Moreover, in the case of important decisions, these procedures may involve many minor decisions taken at various stages in the decision-making process. For example, a chief's decision to automate the records division by purchasing a computer and software usually follows a series of decisions. First, the chief decides that the present manual system is not adequate. Second, a decision is made to evaluate the number of systems available on the open market. This decision probably accompanied the decision to address the city council for additional funding with which to purchase the necessary equipment. And finally, the chief resolves that records division personnel must be retrained to operate in an automated system. These minor decisions were only part of the overall process in arriving at a major decision. Thus, the decision to take a certain action, if sound, should be based on the judgment that this action probably will have more desirable results than any other action, and this judgment may be based on conclusions as to the probable consequences of alternative decisions.[1]

399

Decision making also involves the application of our knowledge, our experience, and our mental and moral skills and powers to determine what actions should be taken to deal with a variety of problem situations. Moreover, this decision-making process includes the application of logic for testing conclusions and the use of ethics for testing judgments.[2] For instance, an individual officer's decision to arrest a violent, drunk husband at a family disturbance will usually be based on the officer's past knowledge that if the current situation is left unattended, the probable result will be a criminal act involving assault, wife or child abuse, or even murder. Ethically, the officer is bound to deter crime and as such will take the necessary course of action to prevent the physical harm of any family member.

Decision making is a responsibility that all police officers come to accept routinely. These decisions may be as ordinary as deciding whether to write a motorist a traffic citation or as complex as a split-second decision whether to shoot at someone. The quality and types of decisions made by police managers in their policy formulation and by the street-level officer in invoking arrest action will be based, in part, upon the personality characteristics of the individual making the decision, the recruiting and career development practices of the police department, and, equally important, the type of community being served. For example, one merely has to read the works of Wilson[3] and Skolnick[4] to conclude that enforcement decisions that appear to be quite adequate for one community may be totally unacceptable for another; that recruitment practices that would be acceptable to one community would be objected to by another. Thus, there is no single model that police administration can follow to make the best decisions all the time. However, certain principles, when understood and applied carefully, can result in good decisions being made much of the time. Although sometimes not understood as such, planning is basically part of the decision-making process, and as such will be treated accordingly.

Planning

Police administrators sometimes do not appreciate the importance of planning because of their pattern of career development. It is ironic that the pattern of career development for typical police managers carries with it seeds that sometimes blossom into a negative view of planning. Having spent substantial portions of their careers in line divisions, such as patrol and investigative services, planning may be seen as "clerical" or "not real police work." Further, because many agencies have a "planning and research" unit, there is a natural tendency to believe that planning should occur only in that area by individuals assigned to that task. However, planning is an integral element of good management and good decision making.[5] Management needs to anticipate and shape events; it is weak if it merely responds to them.[6] The police manager whose time is consumed by dealing with crises is symptomatic of a department with no real planning or decision-making process. Police departments are sometimes said to be practicing "management by crisis"; in fact, it is "crisis by management."[7] That is, the lack of attention given by police managers to planning creates an environment in which crises are going to occur with regularity. This is so because management by crisis produces a present-centered orientation in which considerations of the future are minimal. In contrast, planning can be expected to:

1. Improve analysis of problems.
2. Provide better information for decision making.

3. Help to clarify goals, objectives, and priorities.
4. Result in more effective allocation of resources.
5. Improve inter- and intradepartmental cooperation and coordination.
6. Improve the performance of programs.
7. Give the police department a clear sense of direction.
8. Provide the opportunity for greater public support.
9. Increase the commitment of personnel.

In short, competent planning is a sure sign of good police administration and the first step in accurate decision making.[8]

Definitions of Planning

There are no simple definitions of planning. The word *planning* became common terminology in the vocabulary of criminal justice, with the introduction of the Omnibus Crime Control and Safe Streets Act of 1968. However, what appeared to be missing in that now-famous document was an examination of what planning actually involved, or what it meant in the operation of criminal justice organizations. Hudzik and Cordner have defined planning as, ''thinking about the future, thinking about what we want the future to be, and thinking about what we need to do now to achieve it.''[9] Stated more succinctly, planning involves linking present actions to future conditions. Planning is defined by Mottley as:

> A management function concerned with visualizing future situations, making estimates concerning them, identifying the issues, needs and potential danger points, analyzing and evaluating the alternative ways and means for reaching desired goals according to a certain schedule, estimating the necessary funds and resources to do the work, and initiating action in time to prepare what may be needed to cope with changing conditions and contingent events.[10]

There is also the assumption that planning is oriented toward action, which means that thinking is only a part of planning; the real purpose is determining what an organization should do, and then doing it. And finally, planning is associated with empirical rationalism: planners gather and analyze data and then reach an objective conclusion.

Planning Approaches

A variety of approaches is employed in the planning processes. Each is unique and can be understood as a *method* of operationalizing the word ''planning.'' There are basically five major approaches to planning: (1) Synoptic, (2) Incremental, (3) Transactive, (4) Advocacy, and (5) Radical.

Synoptic Planning

Synoptic planning or the rational-comprehensive approach is the dominant tradition in planning. It is also the point of departure for most other planning approaches, which, in general, are either modifications of synoptic planning or reactions against it. Figure 12-1 represents the typical synoptic model. It is based on "pure" or "objective" rationality and attempts to assure optimal achievement of desired goals from a given situation.[11] This model is especially appropriate for police agencies as it is based on a problem-oriented approach to planning. It relies heavily on the problem identification and analysis phase of the planning process and can assist police administrators to formulate goals and priorities in terms that are focused on specific problems and solutions that often confront law enforcement. For instance, police administrators are more apt to appreciate a planning model centered around problem-oriented goals and priorities (such as the reduction of burglaries in a given residential area) than around more abstract notions (such as the reduction of crime and delinquency).[12] Then, too, police departments are designed for response, and it is easier to mobilize individual officers and gain cooperation between police units if concrete goals and objectives are set in reaction to a given problem.

Synoptic planning consists of eleven progressive steps. Each step is designed to provide the police manager with a logical course of action:[13]

PREPARE FOR PLANNING

Hudzik and Cordner point out that the most important aspect of planning is that it takes place in advance of action.[14] Therefore, the task of planning should be a detailed work chart that specifies (1) what events and actions are necessary, (2) when they must take place, (3) who is to be involved in each action and for how long, and (4) how the various actions will interlock with one another.[15]

Police managers need to understand that when a course of action and its consequence seem "patently clear," a grand planning event may be unnecessary and inefficient. However, when consequences are not clear, or when undiscovered courses of

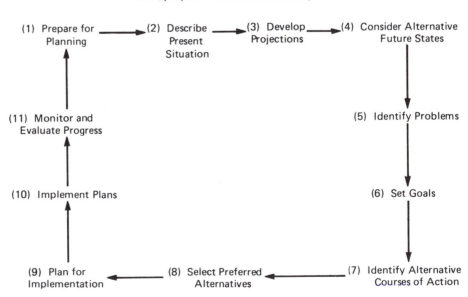

FIGURE 12-1. The synoptic or traditional planning model. [From Robert Cushman, *Criminal Justice Planning for Local Governments* (Washington, D.C.: U.S. Government Printing Office, 1980), p. 26, with minor modification.]

action may be better, the value of planning increases greatly.[16] This assumes that decision making is ongoing and that planning attempts to predict or at least partially control the future.[17] Police managers, then, must be prepared to address the vast array of possibilities that may arise from a given course of action. It is during this stage that the police chief organizes the planning effort with a central theme—what are we trying to accomplish and what type of information is required to understand the problem?

DESCRIBE THE PRESENT SITUATION

This step is often forgotten or overlooked by police administrators because of the desire to immediately eliminate the problem. Planning must have a means for evaluation, and without an accurate beginning data base there is no reference point on which to formulate success or failure. Weiss states that a primary purpose for planning is in evaluation, or comparing "what is" with "what should be."[18] To this end, police chiefs following this model must describe the current situation; describe crime and criminal justice system functions (What exactly do police, courts, and corrections do?); and analyze community characteristics associated with crime (Is the community conservative or liberal? Does any religious or political agenda affect the situation?).

DEVELOP PROJECTIONS AND CONSIDER ALTERNATIVE FUTURE STATES

Projections should be written with an attempt to link the current situation with the future, keeping in mind the desirable outcomes. One projection should at least dwell on the status quo. What will happen if the police do nothing? In some instances, it may be best to eliminate police presence. For example, a police chief may decide that the best course of action is to reduce police visibility. This tactic has been successful where a high probability for violence between a group of people and the police exists—such as rock concerts, outlaw biker parades, and demonstrations. It is important for the police executive to project the current situation into the future to determine possible, probable, and desirable future states while considering the social, legislative, and political trends existing in the community. What may work in one city may not work in another. For instance, a parade of gay activists marching in San Francisco may be somewhat of a common occurrence, whereas the same type of activity in another city may be received differently.

IDENTIFY AND ANALYZE PROBLEMS

The discovery of problems assumes that a system to monitor and evaluate the current arena is already in place. The final step in the synoptic model addresses this concern. However, closely related to the detection and identification of issues is the ability of the police manager to define the nature of the problem; that is, to be able to describe the magnitude, cause, duration, and expense of the issues at hand. This provides a clear conceptual picture of the present conditions confronting the chief in which to develop means for dealing with the problem. It is here that the chief develops a detailed understanding of the problem and ensuing issues. At this point, the planning process allows for estimations of the gap between the probable future and desired outcomes—or how serious and complex the problem really is. A complete understanding of the problem leads to the development of means to deal with the issues.

Set Goals

A goal is an achievable end state that can be measured and observed. Making choices about goals is one of the most important aspects of planning.[19] However, without the previous steps, goal setting has little meaning. It makes no sense to establish a goal that does not address a specific problem. Remembering that police departments are "problem-oriented," choices about goals and objectives should adhere to the synoptic model.

Hudzik and Cordner point out that several kinds of choices must be made concerning goals:

> Several kinds of choices must be made. First, choices must be made about preferred states or goals. An important and sometimes ignored aspect of this choice involves the choice of the criteria for measuring goal attainment. This is often hard, much harder than setting the goal itself. For example, the goal of a juvenile treatment program may be to reduce recidivism among those treated. Yet, in measuring goal attainment several questions arise. First, what constitutes recidivism? Technical or status violation? Arrest for criminal violation? Conviction on a criminal violation, and only for those crimes against which the juvenile program may have been directed? Also, over how long a period will recidivism be monitored? A year? Two years? Five years? Ten Years? It is not that those questions cannot be answered, but securing agreement on the appropriate criteria becomes a major difficulty.[20]

The following steps attempt to link set goals with desired outcomes through the establishment of specific means.

Identify Alternative Courses of Action

Alternatives are means by which goals and objectives can be attained. They may be policies, strategies, or specific actions aimed at eliminating a problem. Alternatives do not have to be substitutes for one another or perform the same function. For instance, improving officer-survival skills through training, modifying police vehicles, issuing bulletproof vests, utilizing a computer-assisted dispatch program, and increasing first-line supervision may all be alternatives in promoting officer safety.

It is important that the activities (the means) that a police department engages in actually do contribute to the achievement of goals (the ends). If the means are not connected to the ends, then a police agency could expend a great deal of resources in activities that keep personnel busy, but do not contribute to fulfilling key objectives or responsibilities.

Means-Ends Analysis. Depicted in Figure 12-2 is a means-ends analysis chart. This is one method of trying to ensure that the police department's programmatic efforts and expenditures do make an appropriate contribution toward arriving at the desired state. Means-ends analysis charting is also a very effective method in which alternatives can be identified in the planning process.

The following procedure is used to develop a means-ends analysis chart:

1. At the center of a page, state the objective you are trying to achieve. In the case of Figure 12-2, this is stated as "to reduce assaults on officers by 50 percent in fiscal year (FY) 1989 as compared to fiscal year 1988." Note that an objective differs from a goal in that an objective can be achieved within one year.

2. Identify the "whys" of trying to attain the objective. Place these statements above the objective on the work page. Figure 12-2 identifies four such "whys,"

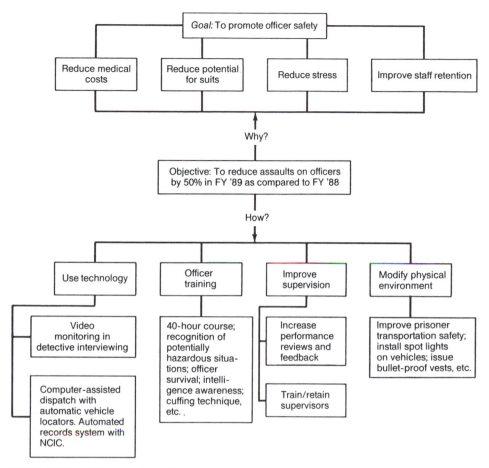

FIGURE 12-2. Means-ends analysis chart.

namely reduce medical costs, reduce potential for civil suits, reduce officer stress, and improve officer retention.

3. Identify and select the "hows" to obtain the objective. Referring again to Figure 12-2, four major "hows" or means are specified: use technology, increase officer training, improve supervision, and modify the physical environment.

The police manager should realize that the means-ends analysis chart does not select alternatives; that is discussed in the following step of the synoptic planning model. However, means-ends analysis is an excellent method of brainstorming that assists the police chief in identifying alternative courses of action designed to achieve specific goals and objectives.[21]

SELECT PREFERRED ALTERNATIVES

The selection process for deriving at a preferred course of action or alternative is often fraught with complexity. The issue has been researched for several decades by scholars in business management, public administration, systems science, and criminal justice in order to assist decision makers in this process. Three basic techniques to select alternatives are discussed here: (1) strategic analysis, (2) cost-effectiveness analysis, and (3) must-wants analysis.

1. *Strategic Analysis:* The first study addressing the selection of preferred courses of action originated at the U.S. Naval War College in 1936 and has been popular in police management circles.[22] Since that time, the model has been refined into a more systematic and objective treatment.[23] The process is shown as a diagram in Figure 12-3.

In order to visualize how the technique can be applied and selections made, it will be helpful to use an example currently confronting law enforcement managers, e.g., the issue of automating a records division with particular reference to the improvement of officer-generated reports by use of lap computers.

Given a set of possible alternatives or courses of action, the number of alternatives can be reduced in the following ways:

First, through making suitability studies of all alternatives. That is, each course of action is evaluated in accordance with general policies, rules, and laws. For example, in some jurisdictions it is illegal to maintain an automated records system that contains arrest and conviction data of juveniles in order to safeguard the juvenile's reputation. A manual records system is deemed more secure since access can be totally controlled.

Second, the retained and suitable alternatives are subjected to feasibility studies. These include the appraisal of the effects of a number of factors weighed separately and together. Continuing with the example, the feasibility of an automated records system would be judged on the basis of meeting: (1) The existing standards of operation (e.g., Will an automated records system do everything the manual system can do?); (2) the conditions of the operational environment (e.g., Is the police department

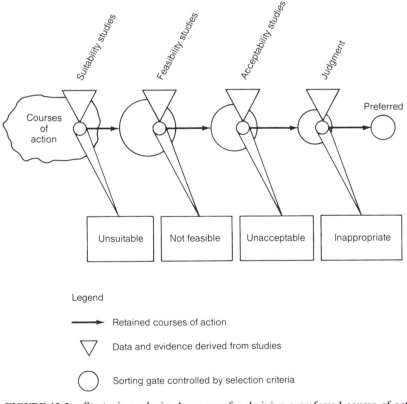

FIGURE 12-3. Strategic analysis: A process for deriving a preferred course of action [Source: C. M. Mottley, "Strategic Planning," *Management Highlights*, 56, September 1967.]

facility large enough to accommodate a computer? Is it air-conditioned? Does it have proper electrical outlets?); (3) the restrictions imposed by the state of the art (e.g., Is the desired software compatible with the existing computer system?); and (4) limitations on the resources available (e.g., Is the cost for an automated records system beyond police funding approval? Can the records division personnel be retrained and how much will that cost?).

Third, the retained courses of actions (those judged to be suitable and feasible) are then analyzed in acceptability studies. Four principal factors are combined and enter into this evaluation: (1) The cost of each alternative; (2) the performance received; (3) the effect of the alternative on the entire system; and (4) the time involved in implementation and setup. These factors are applied to each alternative to reveal critical limits and trade-offs. Finally, a judgment is rendered that selects the preferred course of action.

2. *Cost-Effectiveness Analysis:* This technique is sometimes called cost-benefit or cost-performance analysis. The purpose of this form of selection is that the alternative chosen should maximize the ratio of benefit to cost. The concept is based on economic rationalism: Calculations are made ''scientifically'' through the collection of data and the use of models in an attempt to maximize benefits and minimize costs. A model is a simplified representation of the real world that abstracts the cause-and-effect relationships that are essential to each course of action or alternative.[24] Using the example of automating a records division, each course of action would be analyzed in an attempt to compare the cost in dollars of each segment of the system (mainframe, software, lap computers) with the benefits (increased officer safety, more efficient crime analysis, and subsequent apprehension that diminishes property loss and injury). In the analysis of choice the role of the model (or models, for it may be inappropriate or absurd to attempt to incorporate all the aspects of a problem into a single formulation) is to estimate for each alternative (or course of action) the costs that would be incurred and the extent to which the objectives would be attained.[25] The model may be as complex as a set of mathematical equations to a purely verbal description of the situation, in which intuition alone is used to predict the outcomes of various alternatives. Figure 12-4 is the structure of cost-effectiveness analysis.

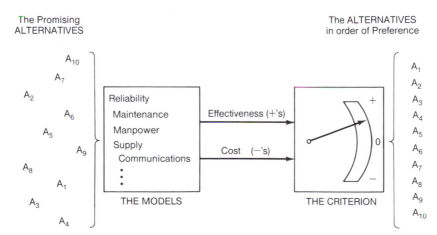

FIGURE 12-4. The structure of cost-effectiveness analysis [Source: E. S. Quade, ''Systems Analysis Techniques for Planning-Programming-Budgeting,'' in F. J. Lyden and E. G. Miller, *Planning, Programming, Budgeting: A Systems Approach to Management* (Chicago, Ill.: Markham, 1972), p 250.]

It is important to note that each alternative is weighed against a criterion: the rule or standard by which to rank the alternatives in order of desirability. This provides a means to analyze cost against effectiveness.[26] Unlike strategic analysis, alternatives are not dismissed from the process but ranked in order of preference.

3. *Must-Wants Analysis:* This method of selecting a preferred course of action combines the strengths of both strategic and cost-effectiveness analyses. Must-wants analysis is concerned with both the subjective weights of suitability, feasibility, and acceptability as well as the objective weights of costs versus benefits.

In this method of selection a ''must-wants chart'' is developed to assist the police administrator. Returning to the example of automating a records division and improving officer-generated reports by the use of laptop computers, Figure 12-5 provides a chart for evaluating three alternative brand-name laptop computers, namely the Ericsson Portable, the Heath ZP 150, and the Hewlett-Packard Portable PLUS. The must-wants chart is constructed in the following manner:

1. ''Musts'' are placed at the top of the page. These are conditions that are set by the police chief and that absolutely have to be met in order for an alternative (in this case a specific laptop computer) to continue to be a viable choice. Failure of any alternative to meet a ''must'' condition immediately eliminates it from further consideration. In Figure 12-5, note that Alternative B, the Heath ZP 150, did not conform to the ''must'' of having a minimum 128K RAM internal drive, and was eliminated.

2. ''Wants'' are conditions, performances, characteristics, or features that are desirable, but not absolutely necessary. They are listed below the ''musts'' and the corresponding data for each ''want'' are completed for each alternative which was not discarded at the previous step.

3. Weight (the column marked ''wt.'' in Figure 12-5) reflects the subjective importance of the ''want'' as determined by the police chief. Weight has a scale of 1 (lowest) to 10 (highest).

4. Score (the column marked ''sc.'' in Figure 12-5) is the evaluation of the actual existence of ''wants'' by the chief. A scale of 1 to 10 is also used in this column. The score is set by the administrator to reflect an assessment of the subjective or actual existence of the ''want.'' In this example, the want of ''excellent screen visibility with high resolution'' is a subjective evaluation, while ''IBM compatible'' can be objectively determined. In general, the scoring of wants should be based on a limited number of factors because too many could distort the choice of an option.

5. The weight and score for each ''want'' is multiplied (wt × sc in Figure 12-5) and summed. The sum of each wt × sc column is called the performance total for ''wants'' objectives.

6. The second part of the must-wants chart, shown in Figure 12-6, is called the ''possible adverse consequences worksheet.'' On this worksheet, statements concerning possible detriments or negative outcomes are listed for each alternative. The probability and seriousness of each comment is subjectively scored. The probability of an adverse consequence happening is scored on a scale from 1 (very unlikely) to 10 (certain to happen). Seriousness is scored on the same type of scale with 1 representing ''extremely unserious'' and 10 denoting ''very serious.'' The final scores are summed and used in the last choice, the selection step.

7. Some advocates of using must-wants chart recommend that the totals of the possible adverse consequences work sheet only be considered advisory while others recommend that the performance totals for each alternative be mathematically reduced

MUSTS		Alternative A: Ericsson Portable			Alternative B: Heath ZP 150	Alternative C: Hewlett-Packard PLUS		
Total purchase price not to exceed $3,000		$2,995			$1,995	$2,295		
Maintenance contract not to exceed $300/yr.		225			195	250		
Minimum 128K RAM		256K			32K	128K		
Minimum one disk drive		yes				yes		
Receivable within 30 days		yes			NO GO	yes		
Local area dealership within 20 miles of police department		yes				yes		

WANTS	wt		sc	wt × sc			sc	wt × sc
Minimum total price	7	$2,995	5	35		$2,295	8	56
Lowest maintenance contract per year	4	225	8	32		250	6	24
High Random Access Memory (RAM) cap.	8	512K	7	56		896K	8	64
Good power supply, constant	6	yes	8	48		yes	7	42
Built-in AC adapter	5	yes	9	45		no	6	30
Rechargeable battery pack	5	no	6	30		yes	8	40
Excellent keyboard functioning/response	9	very good	8	72		good	7	63
Good keyboard layout	4	very good	9	36		not standard	6	24
Large, well-defined keys	7	excellent	9	63		OK	7	49
Excellent screen visibility with high resolution	10	plasma type excellent	10	100		LCD type fair	7	70
Good graphics capability	2	good	8	16		good	8	16
Built-in printer	5	yes	8	40		no	2	10
Internal modem standard with price	5	option only	4	20		option only	4	20
IBM compatible	10	yes	10	100		with addition	4	40
Standard 5¼″ diskette drive	7	yes	8	56		no, 3½″ disk	4	28
Standard Random Operation Memory (ROM) chip	7	no	2	14		yes, 192K	8	56
Light weight	3	16.8 lbs.	7	21		10 lbs.	8	24
Durable and long-wearing outer cover	8	yes	6	48		yes	8	64
PERFORMANCE TOTAL, WANTS OBJECTIVES				832				720

FIGURE 12-5 Must-Wants Chart for Selecting a Laptop Computer. [Source: "Laptops to Go," *PC Magazine*, 24: 5 (December 10, 1985), pp. 124–141. The "results" in the illustration of must-wants analysis are hypothetical and should not be used as a basis of action.]

Alternative A: Ericsson Portable PC				Alternative C: Hewlett-Packard PLUS			
	Proba-bility	Serious-ness	P × S		Proba-bility	Serious-ness	P × S
No rechargeable battery pack, will require a moderately expensive option	10	3	30	Will require adding ThinkJet printer, ex-pensive option	10	6	60
Not a well-known brand of computer, may be hard to get parts	6	4	24	Will require HP interface for IBM compatibility	10	2	20
A bit heavy for officers to carry in and out of patrol cars	8	2	16	HP parts are more expen-sive than other brands	6	4	24
				Batteries only good for an 8 hour period of time, may not last an entire shift	2	4	8
			70				112

FIGURE 12-6   Possible Adverse Consequences Worksheet—Laptop Computers.

by the value of the possible adverse consequences score. If this latter approach is used, the alternative with the highest total points should be chosen. Referring to Figure 12-7, Alternative A would be selected with a total point score of 762.

Despite the "rational" and "objective" appearance of the must-wants analysis approach, there are a number of subjective scores, weights, and probabilities in the chart. The "bottom line" values in Figure 12-7 (762 and 608) were calculated on subjective measures. The real value in must-wants analysis is in the methodology. The chief must not become a captive of the device and follow the results mechanistically. He or she should use a must-wants chart to consider and weigh the intangibles that are not easily quantifiable between alternatives. The value of must-wants analysis is not in the end product, but rather in the sharpening of differences or similarities between alternatives or courses of action.

As with must-wants charts, the other two approaches (strategic and cost-effective-ness analyses) are methods of selecting a preferred alternative or choosing a desired course of action. In the final analysis, the judgment of the police chief plays a key and indisputable role, one that cannot be taken lightly or afford to be ill-informed about the alternative courses to be made.

	Ericsson Portable alternative A	Hewlett-Packard PLUS alternative C
MUSTS:	All Met	All Met
WANTS PERFORMANCE TOTAL:	832	720
POSSIBLE ADVERSE CONSEQUENCES		
TOTAL:	−70	−112
	762	608

FIGURE 12-7   The Final Step in Must-Wants Analysis—Selecting an Alternative. The alternative with the highest point value should be chosen.

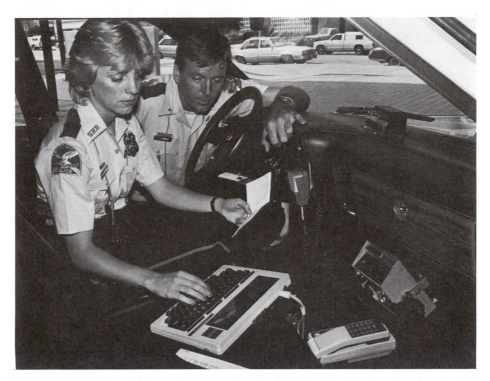

FIGURE 12-8 Officers using a lap computer via a cellular telephone hook-up in a marked police vehicle [Courtesy of St. Petersburg, Florida, Police Department and GTE Mobilnet, Inc.]

PLAN AND CARRY-OUT IMPLEMENTATION

Once a preferred course of action is selected, the next step in the synoptic planning model is to implement the chosen alternative. Implementation requires the chief to execute plans that fulfill the objectives or goals of the process. The classic work on implementation was conducted by Pressman and Wildavsky in Oakland, California.[27] In that study, the authors contend that the process of implementation alone can produce complexities in the future. An example of this phenomenon is observed in any organization undergoing change. The very process of change often causes anxieties within personnel, disputes over responsibilities, and restructuring of the organization. Organizational change is discussed in Chapter 15. But as an illustrative point, consider again the case of automating a police records division. Certainly, the automation process will cause most of the records clerks to reassess their value as workers. Some may think that the computer will eliminate their position whereas others will resist being retrained because they have little or no previous familiarity with computers. Then too, who will manage the new computerized center? What will happen if the software has minor ''bugs'' or faults? Who will fix the hardware if it breaks? Thus, a whole series of new issues and questions arise from the implementation of a computer into a police department.

In any event, the police administrator must be aware that implementation requires a great deal of tact and skill. It may be more important ''how'' an alternative is introduced to a police department than ''what'' it actually is.

MONITOR AND EVALUATE PROGRESS

The final step of the synoptic planning model is evaluation: Were the objectives achieved? Were the problems resolved? The answer to these questions should be obtained through a system that monitors the implementation process.

Evaluation requires comparing what actually happened with what was planned for—and this may not be a simple undertaking.[28] Feedback must be obtained concerning the results of the planning cycle, the efficiency of the implementation process, and the effectiveness of new procedures, projects, or programs. This is an important step of synoptic planning—trying to figure out what, if anything, happened as a result of implementing a selected alternative. It is for this reason that baseline data is so critical (Step 2—Describe the Present Situation). Hudzik and Cordner point out that evaluation completes the cycle of rational planning.[29] The issue of identifying problems must be considered again. Does the original problem still exist or was it solved? Is there a new problem?

SUMMATION OF THE SYNOPTIC PLANNING APPROACH

Considerable attention has been given to synoptic planning because it is the most widely used approach in police management. Most other approaches have been derived from the model just described. Synoptic planning basically comprises four activities: preparing to plan, making a choice between alternatives, implementation, and evaluation. The eleven-step approach is a refinement of this cyclical process.

The approaches to follow are other methods commonly used in business forecasting or social planning. Although these approaches are not used as extensively in police management as the synoptic approach, they too deserve some attention.

Incremental Planning

Incremental planning levels a series of criticisms at synoptic planning, including its tendency toward centralization, its failure to appreciate the cognitive limits of police executives (decision makers), and unrealistic claims of rationality. Incrementalism concludes that long-range and comprehensive planning are not only too difficult, but inherently bad. The problems are seen as too difficult when they are grouped together and easier to solve when they are taken one at a time and broken down into gradual adjustments over time. The incremental approach disfavors the exclusive use of planners who have no direct interest in the problems at hand and favor a sort of decentralized political bargaining that involves interested parties. The incrementalists feel that the real needs of people can best be met this way and the "tyranny of grand design" avoided.[30]

Transactive Planning

Transactive planning is not carried out with respect to an anonymous target community of "beneficiaries" but in face-to-face interaction with the people who are to be affected by the plan. Techniques include field surveys and interpersonal dialogue marked by a process of mutual learning. For example, in planning a crime-prevention program in a particular neighborhood, the police might go to certain randomly selected houses to talk to residents about unreported crime, their concerns and fears, and the rise in residential burglary rates. The residents receive crime-prevention techniques and a more secure feeling knowing that the police are concerned about their neighborhood. The police department also receives benefits; intelligence information is gathered about strange persons or cars in the area, a more aware citizenry is likely to detect and report crimes, and a more supportive public attitude concerning the police is developed.

Advocacy Planning

Advocacy planning grew up in the 1960s in the adversary procedures modeled by the legal profession. This approach is usually associated with defending the interests of the weak—the poor and politically impotent, for example—against the strong. Beneficial aspects of this approach include greater sensitivity to unintended and negative side effects of plans.

Radical Planning

Radical planning has an ambiguous tradition with two mainstreams that sometimes flow together. The first mainstream involves collective action to achieve concrete results in the immediate future. The second mainstream is critical of large-scale social processes and how they permeate the character of social and economic life at all levels, which, in turn, determine the structure and evolution of social problems.

Types of Plans

From an applications perspective, the planning process yields an end product—the plan. These can be categorized by use and are delineated into four groups:[31]

1. Administrative or management plans include formulation of the department's mission statement, goals, and policies; the structuring of functions, authority, and responsibilities; the allocation of resources; personnel management; and other concerns whose character is that they are prevalent throughout the entire agency. An administrative plan appears in the appendix to this chapter. Note that this plan is expressed as a general order. General orders are issued to cover standing or long-term situations. In contrast, special orders are issued to cover unique nonrecurring events, such as a visit by the President of the United States, which last for only a limited and specific period of time. Parenthetically, the announcement of promotions, transfers, and other such actions are made known in personnel orders.

2. Procedural plans, in line with many but certainly not all management plans, are ordinarily included as part of a police department's written directive system, a copy of which is assigned to every officer and is updated periodically. Procedural plans are the guidelines for the action to be taken under specific circumstances and detail such matters as how evidence is to be sent or trans-

ported to the crime laboratory, the conditions under which male officers may search arrested females and the limits thereto, and how to stop and approach traffic violators.

3. Operational plans are the work programs of the line units (such as patrol and detectives) as established by an analysis of the need for services.

4. Tactical plans involve planning for emergencies of a specific nature at known locations. Some tactical plans are developed in anticipation of such emergencies as the taking of hostages at a prison or a jailbreak and are subject to modification or being discarded altogether in peculiar and totally unanticipated circumstances. Other tactical plans are developed for specific situations as they arise, such as how to relate to a demonstration in the park or a march on city hall. Although well-operated police agencies invest considerable effort in developing tactical plans that may seldom or never be used, their very existence stimulates confidence among field officers and lessens the likelihood of injury to officers, the public, and violators.

Effective Plans

Regardless of how plans are classified, the bottom line is that organizations with a formal and continuous planning process outperform those without one. This discrepancy in performance increases as the larger environment becomes more turbulent and the pace and magnitude of change increase.[32] This is the type of environment that police administrators have faced in recent years and is illustrated by Proposition 12 in California, which severely limited police expansion; fuel shortages and the attending swift rise in fuel prices; the unionization of police officers and job actions, such as strikes and demonstrations; the escalation of litigation by the public and police department employees; and times of fiscal restraint producing cutbacks in the availability of resources.[33]

Considering these and other circumstances, police administrators must not only have a planning process and plans but also must be able to recognize characteristics of effective plans:

1. The plans must be sufficiently specific so that the behavior required is understood.

2. The benefits derived from the achievement of the goals associated with the plan must offset the efforts of developing and implementing the plan, and the level of achievement should not be so modest that it is easily reached.

3. Involvement in their formulation must be as widespread as is reasonably possible.

4. They should contain a degree of flexibility to allow for the unforeseen.

5. There must be coordination in the development and implementation of plans with other units of government whenever there appears even only a minimal need for such action.

6. They must be coordinated in their development and implementation within the police department to ensure consistency.

7. As may be appropriate, the means for comparing the results planned for versus the results actually produced must be specified prior to implementation. For tactical plans, this often takes the form of an analysis, referred to as the "after-action report."

Planning and Decision Making

As stated previously, planning is the first integral part of decision making. Planning is primarily concerned with coming to understand the present situation (problem) and widening the range of choices (alternative or courses of action) available to the police chief (decision-maker). Therefore, planning is aimed at providing information (a plan) whereas decision making is aimed at the use of this information to resolve problems or make choices.[34]

Decision Making

The literature dealing with decision making in the police management field is not very extensive, and most of it is devoted to methods of applying the decision-making process. Whereas in theory it should be easy to divide decision-making processes into discrete, conceptual paradigms, in reality, it is extremely difficult to separate one approach from another.

However, three models derived from decision-making theory appear to be basic in most of the literature. They are: 1) the rational model, 2) the incremental model, and 3) the heuristic model.

The Rational Model

The traditional theory of management assumes that people are motivated predominantly by "economic incentives" and will, therefore, work harder given the opportunity to make more money. The "economic actor" concept also prevails in early decision-making theory. In Chapter 3, the scientific management approach developed by Taylor was presented. Within this concept, the economic person is presumed to act in a rational manner when faced with a decision-making situation. The assumptions for this rational behavior are (1) that a person has complete knowledge of all alternatives available to him or her, (2) that a person has the ability to order preferences according to his or her own hierarchy of values, and (3) that a person has the ability to choose the best alternative for him or her. Money is usually used as a measure of value for the decision maker. It is considered only natural that a person will want to work harder if that person can maximize the return of money by so doing. But these assumptions are difficult for a person to achieve in real life. Just by looking at the first assumption—that a person has knowledge of all available alternatives and their consequences in any given decision situation—we can see how impossible it would be to fulfill these requirements in most circumstances.

There is some evidence to suggest that administrative rationality differs from the "economic actor" concept of rationality because it takes into account an additional spectrum of facts relative to emotions, politics, power group dynamics, personality, and mental health. In other words, the data of social science are facts just as much as the carbon content of steel, but they are difficult and, in many cases, impossible to quantify with a high degree of accuracy.[35]

Police administrators bring to administrative decision making their own personal value system that they inject into the substance of decision making while clothing their decision with a formal logic of the "good of the organization." They clothe

the decision with the official mantle of the department's logic and respectability while their eyes remain fixed on more personal goals. But this does not lead to chaos, because there is frequently a large element of commonality in personal value systems as related to organizational goals.[36] For example, the police executive who develops and directs a specialized unit to solve a series of murders will be accomplishing a law enforcement goal: to apprehend criminals. Although the executive's personal motives are to gain public success of his or her unit, the personal objectives are in line with the organizational goals. Thus, conflict does not arise, unless the personal values begin to compete with the department's mission.

In an earlier chapter the work of Gulick and Urwick was discussed as a description of administrative behavior focusing on the work of the chief executive. Part of their theory includes the act of making rational choices by following prescribed elements of work (PODSCORB). Their contribution set the stage for the rational model of decision-making by suggesting that executives follow orderly and rational steps before making decisions. Subsequently, Simon responded to these assumptions in his article "The Proverbs of Administration," in which he outlined several requirements for a scientifically based theory of administration.[37] Simon's article was then included in his *Administrative Behavior* (1947).[38]

Simon explains that rational choices are made on a "principle of efficiency." His model of rationality contends that there are three essential steps in decision making; (1) list *all* of the alternative strategies, (2) determine and calculate *all* of the consequences to each strategy, and (3) evaluate *all* of these consequences in a comparative fashion.[39] Whereas Simon is given credit for the development of this approach, its comprehensive expansion can be observed in the literature of several other theorists. Drucker's concept of the "Effective Executive," Iannone's "style" in *Supervision of Police Personnel,* and Sharkansky's decision-making model in *Public Administration* all exhibit an expansion of Simon's original work.[40] The rational model, now often referred to as the rational-comprehensive model, sets forth a series of formalized steps toward "effective" decision making. These steps can be generally observed and listed as follows:

1. Identify and define the problem
2. Ascertain *all* information regarding the problem
3. List *all* possible alternatives and means to solving the problem
4. Analyze the alternatives and assess the facts
5. Select the appropriate alternatives; find the answer

It is important to observe the elaboration on Simon's original method. The decision-making model assumes an ideal condition whereby the decision-maker is aware of *all* available information related to the problem and has an unlimited amount of time in which to explore and narrow down proposed alternatives by a "rational" and comparative process. Unfortunately, actual practice rarely allows for the ideal.

Highly criticized for being too idealistic and irrelevant to the administrative functions of a police organization, the rational decision-making model has been subjected to harsh criticisms. Many of these criticisms were noted as limitations by proponents of the method. For instance, Sharkansky provided a detailed discussion of "roadblocks" to the fulfillment of the rational-comprehensive model in practical administration.[41] He documented constraints in the collection of all available data and emphasized contingencies in the human ability to make decisions. Additionally,

Simon elaborated on the concept of a "rational man." Noting that man was "bounded" by a triangle of limitations, he stated:

> On one side, the individual is limited by those skills, habits, and reflexes which are no longer in the realm of the conscious . . . on a second side, the individual is limited by his values and those conceptions of purpose which influence him in making decisions . . . and on a third side, the individual is limited by the extent of his knowledge that is relevant to his job.[42]

It is apparent that Simon not only understood the decision-making process but also the "human" factors associated in the term of "rationality." A prerequisite to "effective" decision making is an acute awareness of the social, environmental, and organizational demands placed on the administrator. Simon accurately stresses that one's ability to make rational decisions is bounded by the limitation of his or her knowledge of the total organization.[43] From this critical observation, Simon formulates a modified rational-comprehensive idea entitled, "bounded rationality."[44] The emphasis, of course, is on man's inherent limitations to make decisions. Refer to Figure 12-9.

The Incremental Model

Another important approach concerning the modification of rational decision making is the "incremental" and "muddling through" theories explored by Lindblom.[45] Based on his study of governmental institutions in the United States, Lindblom states that the decision-making process is so fragmented and so complex, incorporating the interaction of various institutions, political entities, pressure groups, and individual biases, that rationality can have only a marginal effect. That is, for the police administrator there are a set of limiting political factors (such as the mayor's wish to be reelected), that prevents the decision-making process from being truly rational. For elected sheriffs, the political agendas may be so strong that purely rational decision making is inhibited.

Lindblom asserts that decision making is serial, that it is limited by time and resources as it gropes along a path where means and ends are not distinct, where goals and objectives are ambiguous, and where rationality serves no purpose. Contending that police managers and administrators "play things safe" and opt to move very slowly (incrementally) in decision making, Lindblom proposes that managers "muddle through" problems rather than analytically choosing decisions.[46] In Lindblom's view, decision making that occurs through a series of incremental steps provides

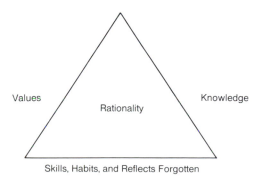

FIGURE 12-9. Simon's concept of bounded rationality.

the police administrator (and hence the public) with a number of safeguards against error:

> In the first place, past sequences of policy (decision) steps have given him knowledge about the probable consequence of further similar steps. Second, he need not attempt big jumps toward his goals that would require predictions beyond his or anyone else's knowledge, because he never expects his policy (decision) to be a final resolution of a problem. His decision is only one step. . . . Third, he is in effect able to test his previous predictions as he moves on to each further step. Lastly, he often can remedy a past error fairly quickly—more quickly than if policy (decision) proceeded through more distinct steps widely spaced in time.[47]

Lindblom's ideas have support, if not in theory, at least in practice, as many police managers find them to be "a description of reality."[48]

The Heuristic Model

In another opposing concept to rationality and logic, Gore identifies the crucial element of humanism in decision making. He presents a "heuristic model" appropriately referred to as "the gut level approach" when considering the police organization.[49] The seasoned patrol officer frequently refers to an unknown quality or phenomenon known as "moxie" or the ability to be "street-wise." This unknown dimension is captured in Gore's decision-making method for police administrators. In an antithesis to the rational model, Gore identifies a process by which a decision is the product of the maker's personality. Gore views the heuristic process "as a groping toward agreements seldom arrived at through logic . . . the very essence of those factors validating a decision are internal to the personality of the individual instead of external to it."[50] Whereas the rational method is concrete, formalized by structure and calculations, the heuristic concept is nebulous, characterized by "gut feelings reaching backward into the memory and forward into the future."[51]

For Gore, decision making is basically an emotional, nonrational, highly personalized, and subjective process. Therefore, the facts validating a decision are internal to the personality of the individual instead of external to it. The key word in this statement is "validating"; it is intended to convey a sense of personal psychological approval or acceptance. The optimum situation is to select that decision alternative that creates the least anxiety or disruption to the individual's basic needs, wants, and desires. In effect, every "objective" decision should be modified or adjusted to meet the emotional needs of the various members of the police department who will be affected by the decision. The passage from which this statement was taken provides additional insight into Gore's heuristic decision-making scheme:[52]

> Whereas the rational system of action evolves through the identification of causes and effects and the discovery of ways of implementing them, the heuristic process is a groping toward agreement seldom arrived at through logic. The very essence of the heuristic process is that factors validating a decision are internal to the personality of the individual instead of external to it. Whereas the rational system of action deals with the linkages between a collective and its objectives and between a collective and its environment, the heuristic process is orientated toward the relationship between that private core of values imbedded in the center of the personality and its public counterpart, ideology. The dynamics of personality are not those of logic but rather those of emotion.[53]

In other words, although logic and reason may be the basic intellectual tools needed to analyze a given problem or to structure a series of solutions to a given situation, logic and reason may not prove to be completely effective in establishing intraorganizational agreement in connection with any given decision.[54]

Applauded for its contribution to the decision-making process, Gore's approach is also highly criticized as being too simplistic and nonscientific. Souryal writes that "Gore's analysis is too unreliable . . . it could complicate an existing situation, promote spontaneity, discredit the role of training and delay the advent of professionalism" in police organizations.[55] This is an unfair assessment of the method. Gore views heuristic applications as adjuncts or alternatives to rational models. Further, some type of credibility must be assessed to that vague, unknown, and nonmeasurable entity we call "experience," "talent," or the "sixth sense." It was these elements that Simon had so much trouble with in calculating his "bound and limited" argument regarding the rational model. In any event, Gore's contributions remain as an opposite to decision making based solely on figures, formulas, and mathematical designs.

Alternative Decision-Making Models

A more recent attempt to outline various approaches to the decision-making process is Allison's account of the 1962 Cuban Missile Crisis.[56] He contends that the rational decision-making model, although most widely used, is seriously flawed. Allison presents two additional models (the organizational process model and the government politics model) to explain decision making during crisis events that police and other government agencies often face. The organizational process model is based on the premise that few major government decisions are exclusively the province of a single organization. In other words, police agencies are dependent on information and advice from other governmental units (like the mayor's office, the FBI, and the district attorney's office) to make major decisions that affect public policy. The government policies model purports that major government policies are rarely made by a single rational actor, such as the chief of police. Rather, policy and general decision making is the outcome of a process of bargaining among individuals and groups to support those interests. Implicit in both of the models is that the decision-maker requires direction from his or her internal staff as well as support from other governmental agencies in the making of important decisions. This is especially true during crisis situations.[57]

Other alternative models to decision making have evolved from the systems approach to management as described in Chapter 3. These techniques are vastly influenced by large, complex systems of variables. The application, collection, and analysis of data from decision making within the organization is called "operations research."[58] In response to a need for a management-science that addressed complex problems involving many variables, such as government planning, military spending, natural resource conservation, and national defense budgeting, operations research employs the use of mathematical inquiry, probability theory, and gaming theory to "calculate the probable consequences of alternative choices" in decision making.[59] As a result, techniques such as Program Evaluation and Review Technique (PERT) and Planning, Programming, and Budgeting Systems (PPBS) were developed for use in managerial planning, forecasting, and decision making.[60] By their very nature, these techniques must structure the system for analysis by quantifying system elements. This process of abstraction often simplifies the problem and takes it out of the real world. Hence, the solution of the problem may not be a good fit for the actual situation.

PERT is a managerial attempt to convert the disorganized resources of people, machines, and money into a useful and effective enterprise by which alternatives to problem solving can be assessed. This process is conducted by a cost-effective analysis or an estimation for each alternative of the costs that would be incurred and the extent to which the objectives would be attained, which is similar to those discussed in the synoptic planning model.

Another model, the decision tree, is illustrated in Figure 12-10. In this model, the probabilities for various outcomes are calculated for each branch of the tree. In the example used in Figure 12-10, the first branch of the trunk has three possible outcomes: 1) arrest at the scene by a patrol officer, 2) no arrest at the scene, and 3) arrest at the scene by a detective. Note in Figure 12-10 that the probabilities for those three events total 1.0, which is the mathematical value for certainty; all possible outcomes for that branch of the example are accounted for. The next higher branch of the example decision tree deals with the various types of evidence obtained from investigation and the final branches deal with the probability of arrest associated with the gathering of each type of evidence. Decision trees are very useful in analyzing situations and for reference when series of decisions that flow from one event are involved. For example, decision trees would be useful to the Commander of a Detective Bureau in formulating policy and guidelines on when to continue or inactivate an

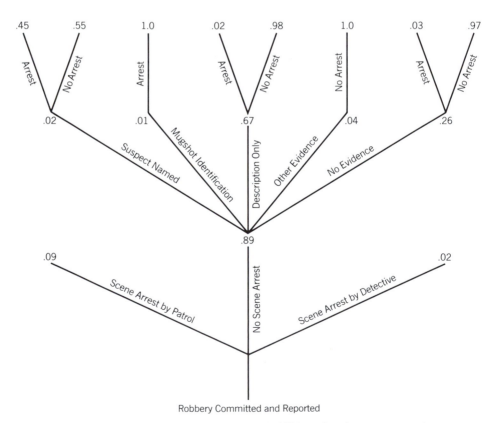

FIGURE 12-10 Decision tree of hypothetical probabilities of various outcomes in a robbery investigation.

investigation based on the types of evidence which were involved in order to make best use of investigative resources. In this regard, decision trees can be seen as a tool of operations research. If an administrator is facing a decision for which there is no actual data, a decision tree can still be useful in analyzing the situation and the "probabilities" can be the administrator's own subjective estimations based on past experience.

These approaches are highly sophisticated elaborations of the rational model utilizing quantitative techniques. The weakness of the methods are in their practicality to real-world situations in which time and resources are not directly structured to gather intelligence about every problem and possible alternative. Further, these models assume that human biases will not enter the decision-making process. The most critical aspect of the approaches appear to be in their overriding insistence that decision making is not a human activity but the product of some scientific, computerized, and unimpressionable robot that digests quantitative information.

Wildavsky has continually warned that the application of decision making to costs, benefits, resources, and budgets frequently results in the adoption of meaningless data and places unwarranted stimuli into the process.[61]

Types of Decisions

Regardless of the model employed, a number of types of decisions exists. Each type may represent a different method, or several types may be arrived at from the same technique. The more important aspect here is that decisions can be recognized and classified for study and review:

- A *decision by avoidance* is made by not making a decision about an idea that has been proposed; the idea is therefore disposed of and the police manager's inaction results in a continuation of things as they are. The key thing about this style is that not making a decision is effectively a decision against change and a decision for the status quo.

- *Individual, authority-based decisions* leave room for some real conferring, whereas authoritarian decisions do not. It is useful here to observe that decisions made on the basis of expert power are authoritative, but are not authoritarian.

- The *statistical average* of the individual decisions involves passing out forms, individually ranking alternatives without discussion, averaging the individual rankings to identify statistical average, and selecting the one ranked highest. This approach reduces the effect of extreme decisions. However, the lack of discussion reduces the amount of information commonly shared and understood.

- *Minority decisions* are those in which a vocal minority dominates discussions and ultimately the selection of the decision itself.

- *Majority rule decisions* are based on a majority vote. Although consistent with democratic practices, up to 49 percent of the people voting may feel no commitment to the course of action selected and this approach could badly split a police command staff into two roughly even and warring camps.

- *General consensus decisions* involve genuine discussion and sometimes spirited debate. General consensus decisions are based on collective agreement; they are not the same as majority rule or total agreement decisions in that the final decision forged is one which has the support of all those who participated in the process even though they might not favor every specific of the decision. A key advantage of this and the next type of decision is that by allowing

BOX 12-1.

A Case Study is Decision-Making: "Attention, MOVE. This is America"

In the early morning hours of May 13, 1985, the Philadelphia Police Department engaged the radical cult MOVE—a name that apparently meant nothing. Police Commissioner Gregore Sambor bellowed over a police bullhorn: "Attention, MOVE. This is America. You have to abide by the laws of the United States." What followed was one of the most devastating police battles in the history of law enforcement. After a day-long siege, Police Commissioner Sambor made the decision to drop two one-pound charges of Du Pont Tovex—a TNT-related blasting agent used in mining—atop MOVE's rooftop bunker. The bomb apparently sparked a fire, fueled by stored gasoline inside the house. The impending result reduced most of two tree-lined city blocks to smouldering rubble. Over $7 million in damages: 61 houses destroyed, 250 people homeless, and 11 MOVE members, including 5 children, killed during the episode.

What events led to the decision that ended in such a tragedy? Why would the police even consider a bomb as a viable alternative? How did the police commissioner arrive at this course of action? These questions and others provide an interesting basis in which to analyze police executive decision making.

First, consider the synoptic planning approach. Was there an accurate and detailed description of the problem? Apparently not, as police testified that they were unaware of the stored gasoline and the number of children in the house. Did police executives exhaust the number of possible alternatives? Possibly. Police tactics included the use of tear gas, water cannons, attempted SWAT assaults, and selective sniper fire. However, each attempt was futile against the MOVE fortified house.

From the rational decision-making model, one could assume that Police Commissioner Sambor might have considered retreat. All else had failed and back-up plans were deemed not feasible. For example, hostage negotiators were not utilized because of the violent past history of the group; and the intended plan to use a crane to knock down fortifications was aban-doned as city streets were too narrow. Certainly, police could have fallen back and attempted to arrest suspects at a later time, when the heat and emotion of urban confrontation was less.

Looking at the incremental model, what events precipitated the police strike? The incident was the second violent confrontation between Philadelphia police and MOVE. The first incident occurred in August, 1978, when police attempted to evict the leader and founder of the group MOVE, Vincent Leaphart (calling himself John Africa) from a house less than five miles away from the current situation. During that confrontation, one police officer was killed and twelve other police and firemen were injured. As a result, nine MOVE members including John Africa were convicted of murder and sentenced to prison. Within a week previous to the current incident, MOVE leaders had demanded the release of their jailed "brother" as the condition for ending their continued confrontation with police. When the city refused, MOVE threatened to blow up the entire residential block. With that risk, the Mayor (Wilson Goode), Police Commissioner Sambor, and other government officials justified the May 13th police strike. Moving in at dawn, police hoped to take the MOVE group by surprise. After some ten hours of siege, police used a helicopter to drop the bomb in hopes that the charge would blow a hole in the roof through which tear gas and water could be dispersed. However, the bomb sparked a fire. If the decision was made from a series of incremental steps, why wasn't the fire department standing by for a fire contingency? The fire department responded a full 40 minutes after the house was engulfed in flames. Why weren't ambulances called to nearby locations to reduce their response time? After all, previous contact with MOVE had resulted in violence. The decision had not been made rationally or incrementally.

In all probability the decision to use a bomb on the May 13th MOVE incident came heuristically—at the "gut level" of Police Commissioner Gregore Sambor, himself a 35-year police veteran. The decision was not without some rationality: the bomb was supposed to be nonincendiary and an air strike from above would not further endanger police officers on the ground. The decision to use explosive entry devices must have sounded good to police officers after some 90 minutes of a full-fledged fire fight with MOVE dissidents, wherein over 7,000 rounds of police ammunition was expended. As expressed by one officer, "We wanted action but we never expected this."

The purpose of this case study is not to criticize the Philadelphia Police; hindsight is always 20–20. The important element, here is for students and police executives to realize that decision making *always* involves planning for the unexpected. No one decision-making model guarantees success, and what works one time may not work the next.

Source: Marci McDonald, "Attention, MOVE. This Is America." *MacLeans* (May 27, 1985), pp. 28–29.

active participation, people develop a sense of "ownership" about the decision and are, therefore, much more likely to support it.

- *Total agreement decisions,* in which every individual agrees on every point, are statistically possible, but as a practical matter they occur only infrequently. On very key issues it might be important to obtain genuine total agreement, particularly because of the commitment it brings; however, attaining total agreement is extremely time consuming and costly, and therefore is used sparingly. Sound decision making requires that when a group is immediately in total agreement about a course of action, some time could be profitably spent examining the unspoken (and therefore unexplored) underlying rationale and assumptions which may have produced total agreement—but be totally wrong.[62]

To this point, we have mainly concentrated on individual decision making. However, police administrators rarely act alone. They are surrounded by deputy chiefs, bureau commanders, and division captains who provide input into the working structure of a police department. Their actions in the decision-making arena are critically important to the success or failure of a specific decision, and therefore require exploration.

Group Decision Making

Research on group problem solving reveals that this approach has both advantages and disadvantages over individual problem solving. If the potential for group problem solving can be exploited, and if its deficiencies can be avoided, it follows that group problem solving can attain a level of proficiency that is not ordinarily achieved. The requirement for achieving this level of group performance seems to hinge on developing a style of leadership that maximizes the group's assets and minimizes its liabilities. Since members possess the essential ingredients for the solution, the deficiencies that appear in group solutions reside in the processes by which group solutions are developed. These processes can determine whether the group functions effectively or ineffectively. With training, a leader can supply these functions and serve as the group's central nervous system, thus permitting the group to emerge as a highly efficient entity.[63]

FIGURE 12-11 The Anatomy of a Disaster. Incremental steps in Philadelphia's attempt to evict MOVE [Courtesy *Newsweek Magazine*, May 27, 1985.]

FIGURE 12-12 Philadelphia's Osage Avenue and environs after the decision to bomb MOVE headquarters. [Courtesy Tannenbaum/SYGMA.]

FIGURE 12-13 A common group decision making technique: The decision table. [Courtesy Tyler Police Department, Tyler, Texas.]

Group Assets

A number of advantages are found in group decision making. They are:

Greater Total Knowledge and Information.   There is more information in a group than in any of its members; thus, problems that require utilization of knowledge (both internal and external to the police agency) should give groups an advantage over individuals. If one member of the group (e.g., the police chief) knows much more than anyone else, the limited unique knowledge of lesser informed individuals could serve to fill in some gaps in knowledge.

Greater Number of Approaches to a Problem.   Most police executives tend to get into ruts in their thinking, especially when similar obstacles stand in the way of achieving a goal, and a solution must be found. Some chiefs are handicapped in that they tend to persist in their approach and thus fail to consider another approach that might solve the problem in a more efficient manner. Individuals in a group have the same failing, but the approach in which they are persisting may be different. For example, one police administrator may insist that the best way to cope with the increasing number of robberies of local convenience stores in a community is to place the businesses under surveillance by specially trained police officers who are equipped with sufficient firepower to either arrest or shoot the robbers if necessary. Another police administrator might insist that the best way to reduce the number of robberies is through the implementation of crime-prevention programs designed to employ procedures that would make the businesses in question either less attractive or less vulnerable to robberies (e.g., keep the amount of cash available down to a minimum, remove large signs from the front of the store windows that block the view of passing patrol cars and other motorists). It is sometimes difficult to determine which approach or approaches would be most effective in achieving the desired goal. But undue persistence or allegiance to one method tends to reduce a decision group's willingness to be innovative.

Participation in Problem Solving Increases Acceptance.   Many problems require solutions that depend upon the support of others to be effective. Insofar as group problem solving permits participation and influence, it follows that more individuals accept solutions when a group solves the problem than when one person solves it. When the chief solves a problem alone, then he or she still has the task of persuading others. It follows, therefore, that when groups solve such problems, a greater number of persons accept and feel responsible for making the solution work. A solution that is well accepted can be more effective than a better solution that lacks acceptance. For example, the decision to establish a crime prevention program in a ghetto neighborhood must have support from the level of chief to individual beat officer. Although other measures to reduce crime (like increasing the number of patrol officers or stricter enforcement of juvenile gang activity) might have a more substantial impact, it is important to remember that most of the program participants must support the effort.

Better Comprehension of the Decision.   Decisions made by an individual but that are to be carried out by others must be communicated from the decision maker to the decision executors. Thus, individual problem solving often requires an additional state—that of relaying the decision reached. Failures in this communication process detract from the merit of the decision and can even cause its failure or create a problem of greater magnitude than the initial problem that was solved. Many police organizational problems can be traced to inadequate communication of decisions made by superiors and transmitted to officers who have the task of implementing the decision. The chances for communication failures are reduced greatly when the individuals who must work together in executing a decision have participated in making it. They not only understand the solution because they saw it develop, but they are aware of the several other alternatives that were considered and the reasons they were discarded. The common assumption that decisions supplied by superiors are reached arbitrarily, therefore, disappears. A full knowledge of goals, obstacles, alternatives, and factual information tends to open new lines of communication, and this communication in turn is maximized when the total problem-solving process is shared.

This maxim is especially important concerning law enforcement because officers assigned to regular "beats" or "districts" often provide the administrator with additional information or new dimensions to the problem. Additionally, almost any new program aimed at reducing crime in a specific area (neighborhood crime prevention or neighborhood watches) must necessarily include the patrol officer for implementation and success.

Group Liabilities

Notwithstanding the benefits of group decision making, a number of liabilities are worth mentioning as a precautionary measure:

Social Pressure. Social pressure is a major force for increasing conformity. The desire to be a good member and to be accepted may become more important than whether or not the objective quality of a decision is the most sound. Problems requiring solutions based upon facts, independent of personal feelings and wishes, can suffer in group problem-solving situations.

It has been shown that minority opinions in leaderless groups have little influence on the solution reached, even when these opinions are the correct ones. Reaching agreement in a group often is confused with finding the right answer, and it is for this reason that the dimensions of a decision's acceptance and its objective quality must be distinguished.

Individual Domination. In most leaderless groups, a dominant individual emerges and captures a disproportionate amount of the influence in determining the final outcome. Such individuals can achieve this end through a greater degree of participation, persuasive ability, or stubborn persistence (wearing down the opposition). None of these factors is related to problem-solving ability, so that the best problem solver in the group may not have the influence to upgrade the quality of a solution (which the individual would have had if left to solve the problem alone). The mere fact of appointing a leader causes this person to dominate a discussion. Thus, regardless of the individual's problem-solving ability, a leader tends to exert a major influence on the outcome of a discussion. In police circles, the influence of the chief's opinion is undeniable. All too often, the chief dominates the group process so much that participation is squelched. The chief needs to be aware of his or her influence and make a cognitive effort to listen rather than dominate.

Conflicting Secondary Goals: Winning the Argument. When groups are confronted with a problem, the initial goal is to obtain a solution. However, the appearance of several alternatives causes individuals to have preferences, and, once these emerge, the desire to support a particular position is created. Converting those with neutral viewpoints and refuting those with opposing viewpoints now enters the problem-solving process. More and more, the goal becomes having one's own solution chosen rather than finding the best solution. This new goal is unrelated to the quality of the solution and, therefore, can result in lowering the quality of the decision.

Factors That Can Serve as Assets or Liabilities

Depending on the skill of the discussion leader, some elements of group decision making can be assets or liabilities:

Disagreement. Discussion may lead to disagreement and hard feelings among members or it may lead to a resolution of conflict and hence to an innovative solution. The first of these outcomes of disagreement is a liability, especially with regard to the acceptance of solutions; the second is an asset, particularly where innovation is desired. A chief can treat disagreement as undesirable and thereby reduce both the probability of hard feelings and innovation. The skillful police administrator creates a climate for disagreement without risking hard feelings because properly managed disagreement can be a source of creativity and innovation. The chief's perception of disagreement is a critical factor in utilizing disagreements. Other factors are the chief's permissiveness, willingness to delay reaching a solution, techniques for processing information and opinions, and techniques for separating idea elicitation from idea evaluation.

Conflicting versus Mutual Interests. Disagreement in discussions may take many forms. Often, participants disagree with one another with regard to the solution, but when the issues are explored, it is discovered the solutions are in conflict because they are designed to solve different problems. Before there can be agreement on a solution, there must be agreement as to the problem. Even before this, there should be agreement on the goal as well as on the various obstacles that prevent the goal from being reached. This is where the synoptic planning model can be an invaluable tool. Once distinctions are made among goals, obstacles, and solutions (which represent ways of overcoming obstacles), the opportunities for cooperative problem solving and reduced conflict are increased.

Often, there is also disagreement regarding whether the objective of a solution is to be of the highest quality or merely acceptable. Frequently a stated problem reveals a group of related, but separate problems, each requiring a separate solution so that a search for a single overall solution is impossible. Communications are often inadequate because the discussion is not synchronized, and each person is engaged in discussing a different aspect of the problem. Organizing the discussion to systematically explore these different aspects of the problem increases the quality of solutions. The leadership function of guiding such discussions is quite distinct from the function of evaluating or contributing ideas.

When the discussion leader helps separate different aspects of the problem-solving process and delays the inclination of the group to come to a quick but not well-thought-out solution, both the quality of the solution and acceptance of it improve. When the leader hinders or fails to facilitate the isolation of these processes, there is a risk of deterioration in the group process. The leader's skill thus determines whether a discussion drifts toward conflicting interests or whether mutual interests are located. Cooperative problem solving can only occur after the mutual interests have been established, and it is interesting how often they can be found when a discussion leader makes this a primary task.

Risk Taking. Groups are more willing than individuals to reach decisions that involve risk. Taking risks is a factor in the acceptance of change, but change may either represent a gain or a loss. The best protection against the latter outcome seems to be primarily a matter of the quality of a decision. In a group situation, this depends upon the leader's skill in utilizing the factors that represent group assets and avoiding those that make for liabilities.

Time Requirements. In general, more time is required for a group to reach a decision than for an individual to reach one. Insofar as some problems require quick decisions, individual decisions are favored. In other situations, acceptance and quality are requirements, but excessive time without sufficient returns also presents a loss. On the other hand, discussion can resolve conflicts, whereas reaching consensus has limited value. The practice of hastening a meeting can prevent full discussion, but failure to move a discussion forward can lead to boredom and fatigue, and group members may agree to anything merely to put an end to the meeting. The effective utilization of discussion time (a delicate balance between permissiveness and control on the part of the leader), therefore, is needed to make the time factor an asset rather than a liability. Unskilled leaders either tend to be too concerned with reaching a solution and, therefore, terminate a discussion before the group's agreement is obtained, or tend to be too concerned with getting "input," allowing discussion to digress and become repetitive.

Who Changes. In reaching consensus or agreement, some members of a group must change. In group situations who changes can be an asset or a liability. If persons with the most constructive views are induced to change, the end product suffers, whereas if persons with the least constructive points of view change, the end product is upgraded. A leader can upgrade the quality of a decision because the leadership position permits the individual to protect the person with the minority view and increase the individual's opportunity to influence the majority position. This protection is a constructive factor because a minority viewpoint influences only when facts favor it.

In many problem-solving discussions, the untrained leader plays a dominant role in influencing the outcome, and when this person is more resistant to changing personal views than are the other participants, the quality of the outcome tends to be lowered. This negative influence of leaders was demonstrated by experiments in which untrained leaders were asked to obtain a second solution to a problem after they had obtained their first one. It was found that the second solution tended to be superior to the first. Since the dominant individual had influenced the first solution and had won the point, it was not necessary for this person to dominate the subsequent discussion that led to the second solution. Acceptance of a solution also increases as the leader sees disagreement as producing ideas rather than as a source of difficulty or trouble. Leaders who see some of their participants as troublemakers obtain fewer innovative solutions and gain less acceptance of decisions made than do leaders who see disagreeing members as persons with ideas.

Brainstorming

Brainstorming is a special case or type of group decision making developed initially in advertising to help trigger creativity. The idea behind brainstorming is to bring a group together and to establish an environment in which individuals within the group can present any idea that seems to apply even remotely to the subject being considered with the understanding that criticism will be withheld unless it can somehow improve on the original idea.[64] The practitioners of brainstorming have been able to determine some specific procedures that improve the effectiveness of the brainstorming sessions. Karass points out that:

1. The sessions should last forty minutes to an hour, although brief ten- to fifteen-minute sessions may be effective if time is limited.
2. Generally, the problem to be discussed should not be revealed before the session.
3. The problem should be stated clearly and not too broadly.
4. A small conference table that allows people to communicate easily should be used.[65]

This approach can be useful in dealing with many public policy or administrative problems. When the major problem is one of discovering new ways of dealing with a situation, brainstorming may prove useful. One of the most difficult aspects of brainstorming, however, is creating a situation in which it can occur. Most of the "rules of the game" are based on an implicit level of trust between individuals that sometimes does not exist in a politically volatile organization. This kind of trust must be developed for the procedure to be successful; thus, people tend to become freer and better able to use the process as they have repeated experiences with it.[66]

Major Sources of Power in Group Decision Making

As a part of a group decision-making process, it is useful to understand the sources of power. Some people believe that power can only be bestowed by external sources, for example, being appointed as supervisor gives a person power.[67] Karass notes that most sources of power can be generated internally by the individual without explicit bestowal by others. Internally generated power, according to Karass, can arise from these sources:

1. Ability to provide reward. Rewards need not be financial but can be the ability to fulfill another's needs. Certainly, police work can have intrinsic rewards such as the satisfaction of arresting a particularly violent suspect, the saving of a person's life at an automobile accident, or delivering a baby in the back seat of a patrol car.

2. Commitment. Lack of commitment to a specific solution gives the individual more power compared to an individual who feels that he or she must have their own solution adopted.

3. Time. The person who can "wait it out" and who does not feel a sense of time urgency derives power vis-à-vis the person who is pressed for time.

4. Effort. Doing one's homework, or putting in sufficient effort to truly understand the nature of the decision being considered creates power as compared to those who did not put in such effort.

5. Uncertainty tolerance. Power is derived by those who can tolerate ambiguity or uncertainty for a longer period.

6. Ability to provide punishment. This can be done by withholding promotions, salary increases, and choice assignments.

7. Alternatives. The individual who can provide viable alternatives for the group to consider gains relative power.

8. Legitimacy. This may be the most powerful source of power since it is derived from such sources as the law and civil service regulations. In police circles, for example, rank carries legitimacy and is often documented in written regulations.

9. Bargaining skills. This skill can be learned and leads to power in negotiating situations. An example of this is a detective who attends a hostage negotiation seminar; his or her capacity is improved by developing interpersonal communications and bargaining skills and by learning to maintain emotional control in tense situations.

10. Information control. Control of information, through tactics such as selective transmission or distortion of the message, can transform the controller of information into the actual decision maker.[68]

Checklist and Rating Scales to Assess the Group Decision-Making Process

A checklist of questions for evaluating decision-making behavior, and a rating scale of decision-making behavior, both of which are given, have been developed by Patton and Griffin to assist either group leaders or participants in the group decision-making process in assessing and improving the process. The rating scale can be most helpful in identifying specific parts of the decision-making behavior that are weak. It is sometimes easier to improve one particular type of behavior at a time than it is to try "to do better" in a general way.[69]

Personality Characteristics of Decision Making

It has been suggested by Katz and Kahn that among the more important personality dimensions of policymakers that may affect their decision are (1) their orientation to power versus their ideological orientation, (2) their emotionality versus their objectivity, (3) their creativity versus their conventional common sense, and (4) their action orientation versus their contemplative qualities.[70]

BOX 12-2.

Checklist of Questions for Evaluating Decision-Making Behavior

This checklist can be used in the form provided; however, all of us as individuals observe the behavior of others through filters provided by our own unique experience or biases.

1. Is your group careful to identify mutual concerns, as they seek a solution to a group problem?

2. Does your group determine the degree of the members' concern about a problem before attempting to solve it?

3. If some members are greatly concerned and others concerned very little, are attempts made to identify concerns that are complementary, even if different?

4. If members differ in their degree of concern about a problem, are efforts made to identify superordinate goals to which all members can make a commitment?

5. In analyzing an identified problem, does your group carefully compare the existing conditions with the specific situation or conditions desired?

6. In considering the existing condition, does your group carefully identify impelling and constraining forces?

7. Is the desired condition clearly specified as a goal to be achieved by your group?

8. Does your group obtain sufficient relevant and valid information?

9. Does your group clearly identify various possible approaches?

10. Is sufficient creativity achieved in seeking to identify various possible approaches?

11. Are criteria for evaluating a proposal clearly identified by your group?

12. Are reasonable predictions made of the degree to which each proposal probably would achieve the desired goal (new condition)?

Source: B. R. Patton and K. Griffin, *Decision-Making Group Interaction* (New York: Harper & Row, 1978), p. 196.

Ideology versus Power Orientation

A police department dominated by a power-driven chief will find its policy decisions moving in the direction of survival and aggrandizement of the chief rather than toward the healthy development of the total department. The following actual case illustrates how this may occur.

A newly appointed police chief selected from outside his department made a decision to implement team policing in one section of the city. The experiment enjoyed some success,

BOX 12-3.

A Rating Scale of Decision-Making Behavior

Instructions: On each bipolar scale indicate the degree to which your group (as you see it) accomplishes each identified behavior. Use the following scale as a conceptual system for evaluation.

Poor	Fair	Average	Good	Excellent
1	2	3	4	5

Circle the appropriate evaluation code number for each item of behavior. For example, if you believe that the appropriate response to item 1 should be "fair" or "2," then you should circle that number, and so on.

	Poor	Fair	Average	Good	Excellent
1. Each member's degree of concern regarding a particular problem is identified by the group before they attempt to solve it.	1	2	3	4	5
2. If some members are less concerned than others, an effort is made to reach some understanding of each other's viewpoint.	1	2	3	4	5
3. In analyzing a particular problem, existing conditions are carefully compared with the specific condition desired.	1	2	3	4	5
4. Both impelling and constraining forces (reasons for making a change and reasons for not changing) are carefully identified in analyzing a problem.	1	2	3	4	5
5. When the group analyzes a problem they state exactly what they hope to achieve when it is solved.	1	2	3	4	5
6. Relevant, valid information is secured when needed	1	2	3	4	5
7. Imaginative approaches are encouraged by the group in seeking to identify all possible approaches to a problem.	1	2	3	4	5
8. Various different possible approaches to a problem are clearly identified before the group chooses one of them.	1	2	3	4	5
9. Guidelines are clearly identified by the group for evaluating various proposed solutions.	1	2	3	4	5
10. Reasonable predictions are made regarding the probable outcomes for each proposed approach.	1	2	3	4	5
11. Agreement by the group is achieved					

	Poor	Fair	Average	Good	Excellent
regarding the most desirable solution to an identified problem.	1	2	3	4	5
12. A detailed plan of action is developed once a problem solution has been chosen.	1	2	3	4	5
13. When resources are required that are not controlled by the group, the attitudes of persons controlling these resources are assessed.	1	2	3	4	5
14. Members of the group effectively employ the techniques of advocacy in mobilizing required resources that are controlled by persons outside of the group.	1	2	3	4	5

Source: B. R. Patton and K. Griffin, *Decision-Making Group Interaction* (New York: Harper & Row, 1978), p. 197.

and as a result the chief was beginning to gain national recognition via articles in police journals, guest speaker appearances at national conferences and so forth. There was considerable speculation within the ranks of his police department that the chief was using the police department as an experimental laboratory to test the team policing concept and also as a staging area of self-aggrandizement in the hopes of eventually moving to some larger police department.

The team policing project had been in operation for approximately six months when the chief made a decision to implement it throughout the entire city. The decision was made, in fact, because this would have been the first time team policing had been tried on such a large scale in the United States and would most certainly have thrust the police chief into the national spotlight.

The chief's entire command staff was opposed to the move because there were still some personnel and operational problems that had not been worked out in the experimental team policing area. In addition, there was considerable resistance to the concept among rank-and-file personnel. There was sufficient evidence to support all these concerns. A confrontation occurred between the police chief and his entire command staff. The command staff threatened to resign en masse if the chief tried to implement the plan. The city manager became embroiled in the confrontation and decided to support the command staff. The chief was fired, and with his dismissal the entire team policy project was abandoned.

In the final analysis, the chief's quest for self-aggrandizement and his own personal ambitions were perceived by his command staff and many rank-and-file officers as not being congruent with the organizational welfare or with their own personal welfare.

However, in some instances, the power interest of the police executive and organizational welfare coincide. The questions to be answered are: How pertinent are the contributions of the leader to the organization, and what is left for the department when the top leader has moved on?

A police department may have a remarkable chief executive whose brilliant rise in the agency has been accompanied by new organizational developments and substantial benefits to the organization, and when this does occur, such a person may be classified as having an ideological orientation. In reality, however, few organization leaders are ideological crusaders or power-driven survivalists or self-aggrandizers. Most decision makers represent combinations of these value orientations and often use practical compromises to achieve power.

Emotionality versus Objectivity

All individuals are to some extent susceptible to interjecting emotional components into the decision-making process. To a great extent, the degree to which either one's emotions or objectivity intervene will depend upon the characteristics of the decision makers and the variables involved in the situation calling for a decision. However, some decision makers seem to possess a higher degree of chronic emotional biases with accompanying momentary emotional impulses than do others. For example, time after time in World War II, Hitler made military decisions reflecting his need to project the image of Germans as supermen. His armies, though outflanked, were never to withdraw but were to fight to the death. The Germans suffered unnecessary losses on the Russian front, in Egypt, and finally on the Western front because decisions were made not only on the basis of objective military strategy and tactics but also on the basis of Hitler's unconscious need to avoid any display of weakness.

Some personality characteristics are capable of activating defense mechanisms in the decision-making process. These psychological characteristics can block or distort the analysis of the problem or the assessment of consequences. Experimentation has shown that defense mechanisms can change the perception of incoming information. Threatening and unpleasant facts are often denied, ignored, or distrusted. Police executives whose defensiveness results in their avoiding certain types of unpleasant information may be reinforced in their blindness by subordinates who keep such facts from them.

Creativity versus Common Sense

Some individuals are gifted in originality; they are able to see new relationships and to impose new structure upon old facts. Others may have a marked ability in making commonsense judgments requiring the evaluation of many relevant factors and the accurate prediction of likely outcomes. Although not logically antithetical, these two abilities do not often occur in the same person. Some individuals by virtue of their enthusiasm, originality, and creativity do not examine the flow of their ideas with searching criticism. Such an attitude would inhibit the creative process. On the other hand, the person seeking to make a balanced judgment and concerned with giving the appropriate weight to competing plausible notions is unlikely to produce a new solution. Occasionally, the two abilities are combined in a person who can move from a phase of creativity to a phase of criticism.

In general, the power to make policy is in the hands of people of good judgment rather than with creative police managers. The police chief with good judgment can single out subordinates to perform the innovative function. Creative police managers can supplement their talents by surrounding themselves with individuals of good sense, yet still have the problem of making the final judgment. It is understandable, then, that the most original minds in any organization are rarely found in top positions. The complexities of organizational life, with its many conflicting demands on the police chief, means that critical and judgmental abilities are the essential requirement at this level.

Action Orientation versus Contemplation

Another personality characteristic relevant to organizational functioning is the capacity for action, the ability to act upon judgments. Many people have excellent ideas; not nearly as many translate their ideas or even make their decisions into the required implementing actions. Many individuals make that translation in what is called the "action paragraph," acting only when the situation compels it or when they are otherwise forced to perform. As a result, the opportunity for action is sometimes lost entirely.

Impact of Personality Traits on Decision Making

In the final analysis, an understanding of personality characteristics is essential if one is to understand the decision-making process. An individual's intellect, reasoning powers, emotions, and biases enter into most decisions, and even when decisions appear to be based almost entirely upon hard data, the data that are selected for inclusion in the decision-making process are influenced to some degree by emotion and feeling.[71]

In fact, it is rarely possible to make decisions that are completely free from inherent discrimination of some kind. Biases may be introduced into the process in many ways, and, whether through ignorance or carelessness, many decision makers appear to overlook the bias of their methods. They tend to use the decision-making processes with which they are most comfortable or familiar without any real concern for their fairness. This practice may produce conflict in circumstances when the chief is called on to defend a decision from attack by advocates of a rejected course of action who contend that their disadvantaged position had resulted from biased or unfair decisions.[72]

Holland's study of decision making and personality concluded that:

> Intelligent persons can think their own thoughts. Moreover, a measure of critical introspection is imperative in a well-lived life. They must recognize outward signs of anxiety, depressions, peculiar habits and mechanisms and view these as symptoms of causes which lie in repressed drives or counter drives. Most highly civilized people are shocked when they recognize powerful negative emotions in themselves. Yet we all have hostilities and fears and we can learn to discharge these without damage. Administrators can admit punitive, egotistical drives for power and omnipotence and deal with these wisely, with a sense of amusement at themselves or even recognize irrational, perfectionistic compulsions as signs of their own overdeveloped conscience. They can get their centers of gravity back in their own hands and away from the primitive impulses and counteracting inhibitions.[73]

Qualities Common to Effective Decision Makers

When beginning to analyze the way in which successful police managers work, it becomes apparent that their success is not a matter of luck. Those who make effective decisions share certain common characteristics. An understanding of these characteristics provides an opportunity to position and analyze oneself in comparison with those who make effective decisions. An understanding of these characteristics helps, too, in analyzing areas in decision making.[74]

Marvin has summarized what he assesses to be the twelve most common characteristics of effective decision makers.[75] According to Marvin, decision makers are:

1. **Synoptic.** Effective decision makers focus on the big picture in a perspective permitting searching out, identification, and assessment of promising opportunities and potentials. They have a firm grasp on the available alternatives and are able to make the best choice from them.

2. **Dissatisfied.** They know that there is a better way and they take steps to find it. Decision makers are "boat rockers." The thing that prompts action, decision-making action, is an inherent belief that things could be better.

3. **Sensitive.** They maintain an acute sensitivity to situations before, during, and after decision making. They keep their thinking tuned to the times.

4. **Catalytic.** Those who make effective decisions assume a personal responsibility for seeing to it that decisions are made, and on time. They recognize that decision making may involve many people and that someone must take the initiative in seeing to it that the decision-making task is done the way it should be done.

5. **Opportunistic.** Good decision makers are those who are not afraid to make new moves. They do not do one thing too long. They move to new assignments that increase and broaden their responsibilities. They move around as opportunities arise.

6. **Skill directed.** Effective decision makers do not adopt the "try and see" attitude of those who accept challenges blindly. They do things they know they can do well and capitalize on their in-house resources.

7. **Innovative.** Creative input is critically important in decision making; the ideas in creative decision making are not all ideas of the decision makers themselves. They come from a variety of different sources.

8. **Forward thinking.** Effective decision makers are always searching for opportunities and do not wait for opportunities to come to them.

9. **Resourceful.** Effective decision makers utilize the counsel of those best informed and involve others on the basis of participation in proportion to their potential contributions.

10. **Evaluative.** Good decision makers know what they are doing. They know because they ask the right questions and they are not satisfied until they get the answers to the questions they ask.

11. **Expedient.** Good decision makers know the effective ways of getting things done, now. The effective way is not always the orderly way, the easy way, or the proper way according to the book.

12. **Courageous.** Effective decision making involves risk that is commensurate with responsibilities, awards, and results required. Good decision makers are those who willingly accept responsibilities for the things they do. Good decision makers weigh risks, responsibilities, rewards, and results to the best of their ability. Admittedly drawing upon intuition and prescience, they act. Those lacking this kind of courage rarely make effective decisions.

The profile of the effective decision maker developed by Marvin, and shown in Figure 12-14, provides decision makers with a model with which to compare them-

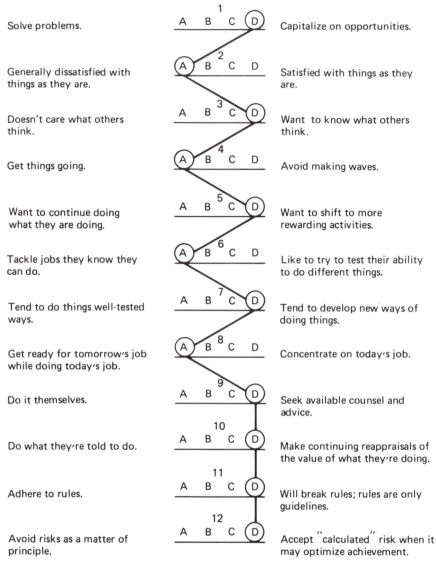

	1	
Solve problems.	A B C Ⓓ	Capitalize on opportunities.
Generally dissatisfied with things as they are.	Ⓐ B C D	Satisfied with things as they are.
Doesn't care what others think.	A B C Ⓓ	Want to know what others think.
Get things going.	Ⓐ B C D	Avoid making waves.
Want to continue doing what they are doing.	A B C Ⓓ	Want to shift to more rewarding activities.
Tackle jobs they know they can do.	Ⓐ B C D	Like to try to test their ability to do different things.
Tend to do things well-tested ways.	A B C Ⓓ	Tend to develop new ways of doing things.
Get ready for tomorrow's job while doing today's job.	Ⓐ B C D	Concentrate on today's job.
Do it themselves.	A B C Ⓓ	Seek available counsel and advice.
Do what they're told to do.	A B C Ⓓ	Make continuing reappraisals of the value of what they're doing.
Adhere to rules.	A B C Ⓓ	Will break rules; rules are only guidelines.
Avoid risks as a matter of principle.	A B C Ⓓ	Accept "calculated" risk when it may optimize achievement.

FIGURE 12-14 Decision-making profile for top performers. These twelve characteristics are not presented in any order of relative importance; however, when a decision maker consistently deviates from this model, the quality and even the quantity of his or her decisions will likely be diminished greatly. [From P. Marvin, *Developing Decisions for Action* (Homewood, Ill.: Dow Jones-Irwin, 1971), p. 47.]

selves. The twelve characteristics are not presented in any order of relative importance; the line through them reflects the path of the profile of good decision makers. The quality of the decisions by police managers will be affected by the extent to which they conform to or deviate from this path.[76]

Comparing one's own decision-making profile with that of effective decision makers provides a working tool for use in developing a more effective decision-making posture. Characteristics common to effective decision makers provide a useful frame of reference. The opportunities to improve one's posture lie in target areas in which one's personal profile departs from that of effective decision makers.[77] For example, Figure 12-15 provides an analytical composite of a hypothetical profile as compared with the top performer profile. Variance in each respective target area reveals where effort can productively be exerted to strengthen one's decision-making posture.[78]

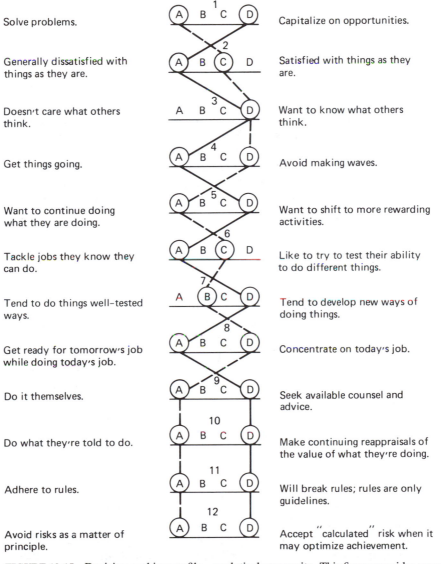

Solve problems.	Capitalize on opportunities.
Generally dissatisfied with things as they are.	Satisfied with things as they are.
Doesn't care what others think.	Want to know what others think.
Get things going.	Avoid making waves.
Want to continue doing what they are doing.	Want to shift to more rewarding activities.
Tackle jobs they know they can do.	Like to try to test their ability to do different things.
Tend to do things well-tested ways.	Tend to develop new ways of doing things.
Get ready for tomorrow's job while doing today's job.	Concentrate on today's job.
Do it themselves.	Seek available counsel and advice.
Do what they're told to do.	Make continuing reappraisals of the value of what they're doing.
Adhere to rules.	Will break rules; rules are only guidelines.
Avoid risks as a matter of principle.	Accept "calculated" risk when it may optimize achievement.

FIGURE 12-15 Decision-making profile—analytical composite. This figure provides an analytical composite of a hypothetical profile in comparison with the top performer profile. Variance in each respective target area reveals where one must place the emphasis in taking steps to strengthen one's decision-making posture. [From P. Marvin, *Developing Decisions for Action* (Homewood, Ill.: Dow Jones-Irwin. 1971), p. 49.]

Common Errors in Decision Making

Analysis of the decision-making process indicates that certain types of errors occur at a higher frequency than others. Nigro and Nigro[79] have indicated that these are: (1) cognitive nearsightedness, (2) the assumption that the future will repeat the past, (3) oversimplification, (4) overreliance on one's own experience, (5) preconceived notions, (6) unwillingness to experiment, and (7) reluctance to decide.[80]

Cognitive Nearsightedness

The human tendency is to make decisions that satisfy immediate needs and to brush aside doubts of their long-range wisdom. The hope is that the decision will prove a good one for the future also, but this actually is to count on being lucky. The odds for such good fortune to occur consistently across all decisions are poor.

Attempting to find a solution which is a "quick fix" may create infinitely greater difficulties in the future. An example of this phenomenon is observed in barricaded hostage situations, in which the chief wants to assault the location immediately with a SWAT team. In crisis situations such as this, time has always proven to be an ally of the police.[81] Unfortunately, the complicated environment in which police officials function, sometimes creates pressure to act on relatively narrow considerations of the moment. Also related to cognitive nearsightedness is the "narrow view" or the consideration of only one aspect of a problem while neglecting all other aspects of that problem.

Assumption That the Future Will Repeat Itself

In making decisions, police officials must try to forecast future conditions and events. Human behavior controls many events; in relatively stable periods of history, the assumption can safely be made that employees, client groups, and the public in general will behave much as they have in the past. The present period is, however, far from stable; many precedents have been shattered, and police officers along with other public employees can behave in sometimes surprising ways. Very rarely do dramatic changes occur without some warning signals. Early trends frequently can serve as valuable indicators of future behavior, but the police administrator must make the effort to be aware of these trends and develop strategies to cope with them.

Oversimplification

Another tendency is to deal with the symptom of a problem rather than with its true cause because the actual cause may be too difficult to understand. It is also easier for those participating in a decision-making process to understand a simpler solution: it is more readily explained to others and therefore more likely to be adopted. Although a less-involved solution may actually be the better one, the point is that the decision maker looking for an acceptable answer may take the first simple one, no matter how inferior it may be to other, somewhat more complicated, alternatives.

Overreliance on One's Own Experience

In general, law enforcement practitioners place great weight on their own previous experience and personal judgment. Although the experienced police executive should be able to make better decision than the completely inexperienced one, a person's own experience may still not be the best guide. Frequently, another police executive with just as much experience has a completely different solution and is just as certain that his or her solution to a problem is the most satisfactory one. In fact, past success in certain kinds of situations may be attributable to chance rather than to the particular action taken. Thus, there is frequently much to be gained by counseling with others whose own experience can add an important and uniquely different dimension to the decision-making process.

Preconceived Notions

In many cases, decisions allegedly based on facts actually reflect the preconceived ideas of the police executive. This appears to be dishonest, and it is dishonest if the facts are altered to justify the decision. However, in many cases, individuals are capable of seeing only those facts that support their biases. Administrative decisions might be better if they were based on social science findings, but such findings are often ignored if they contradict the ideas of the police chief.[82] In administrative policymaking, conclusions are often supported by a structure of logic that rests dangerously on a mixed foundation of facts and assumptions.[83] Decision makers may appear as if they are proceeding in an orderly way from consideration of the facts to conclusions derived logically from them, when, in fact, what sometimes occurs is that the conclusion comes first and then the facts are found to justify them.

Unwillingness to Experiment

The best way in which to determine the workability of a proposal is to test it first on a limited scale. However, pressure for immediate large-scale action often convinces the police chief that there is not time to proceed cautiously with pilot projects, no matter how sound the case for a slow approach. Sometimes police executives are reluctant to request funding and other needed support from the small-scale implementation of new programs for fear that such caution may raise doubts about the soundness of the programs. In all fairness to the cautious police administrator, sometimes this assessment has merit.

Reluctance to Decide

Even when in possession of adequate facts, some people will try to avoid making the decision. Barnard speaks of the natural reluctance of some people to decide:

> The making of a decision, as everyone knows from personal experience, is a burdensome task. Offsetting the exhilaration that may result from a correct and successful decision is the depression that comes from failure or error of decision in the frustration which ensues from uncertainty.[84]

The Future Police Decision Makers

Harland Cleveland, former U.S. Assistant Secretary of State, has developed a profile of what he believes will be required for future executives in both the public and private sectors to be effective decision makers. He states that:

> The new style public-private horizontal systems will be manned by a new breed of men and increasingly women. I call them the public executives, people who manage public responsibilities whether in public or private organizations. They will climb ladders of specialized achievement, into positions that require them to "get it all together." Their administrative style will have to be adjusted to an environment which is still described by drawing square and static diagrams on two dimensional charts; it will feel more like a continuous chemical reaction in a liquified solution. From this analysis of the executive "a jungle of close decisions, openly arrived at"—I have tried to derive a description of the kind of person who will climb into our aristocracy of specialized achievement to try his or her hand at general management. My estimate is that before the end of this decade we will need a million of them at any one time in the United States alone.[85]

Apart from the physical capacity to operate under the pressure of executive responsibility, Cleveland believes that the following predictions can be made with some assurance about executive style in complex systems:

1. The future executive will be more intellectual than the executive of the past and capable of plunging into the complex staff work in which the options are analyzed and the real decisions made. If the executive is not personally plowing through the analysis, then the executive is not making decisions but is merely presiding while others decide. The obligation to think will be the one executive function that cannot be delegated.

2. The future executive will be a low-key individual with a soft voice and a high boiling point. On this point much of the evidence is already in. Even in the administration of infantry divisions, fighter squadrons, and warships at sea, the people who are running things find less and less need for a loud voice or a parade ground manner. If they want to reach large numbers of people, they ask for an electronic amplifier. If they have orders to give subordinates, they are increasingly likely to call a meeting and act by consensus—or at least to formulate the command as a suggestion.

3. The executive of the future will show more talent for many-sided consensus than for two-sided debating and will develop a taste for ambiguity. Individuals who say that they cannot get on with their part of a job until the lines of authority and responsibility are clarified may simply not yet have learned that ambiguity is an important part of systems management, and, in fact, responsibilities may be intentionally blurred for the benefit of the organization. Individuals who understand and promote the principle of constructive ambiguity are likely to be executives for the world of tomorrow.

4. The future executive will have the optimism of the doer and the determination to organize the future in a different way. Gloom and reluctance are often the hallmarks of expertise; the sum of specialized advice is usually to proceed cautiously and to do nothing. Only the executive supply with a pinch of unwarranted optimism for the stew of calculated costs and carefully evaluated benefits.[86]

FIGURE 12-16 During future crisis situations, police executives will be forced to make decisions influencing a wide range of organizational, community, and political issues. [Courtesy of San Diego Police Department.]

Effective police executives of the future will reflect these same qualities. Additionally, police managers must be aware that their organizations are drastically influenced by a continuously changing relationship between the police department and the community. This relationship should be viewed as a source of knowledge about how to make appropriate changes.

Summary

Decision making is an integral part of the responsibilities of all administrators, yet it is clear that some individuals are more effective at it than others. We have attempted to examine the decision-making process in a way that would assist readers in evaluating and enhancing their own decision-making skills.

Planning was discussed as an integral first step in the decision-making process. Special attention was given to the synoptic planning model and three methods of selecting a preferred course of action: strategic analysis, cost-effectiveness analysis, and must-wants analysis. Other planning approaches mentioned were the incremental, transactive, advocacy, and radical techniques. Various types of plans were identified as well as the characteristics of effective plans.

The major strengths and weaknesses of major decision-making models were discussed, including rational decision making, incremental decision making, and heuristic decision making. Attention was also given to certain alternative decision making models and types of decisions.

In the discussion of group decision making, it was learned that this approach has some very distinct advantages and disadvantages. The advantages of group decision making include a greater knowledge and information from the group than from any of its members; a greater number of approaches to a problem likely to be considered;

an increase in the potential for acceptance by individual members; and a better understanding of the decision. The liabilities of group decision making include the desire
to be a good group member and to be accepted, which tends to silence disagreement
and favors consensus; the potential of individual domination from a person who
does not possess the greatest problem-solving ability; and conflicting secondary goals,
such as the desire to win an argument rather than to obtain the best possible solution.

The ways in which one's own personality characteristics can affect the types of
decisions one makes was examined. These characteristics include orientation to power
versus ideology, emotion versus objectivity, creativity versus conventional common
sense, and action versus contemplation. Effective decision makers share certain characteristics: they are synoptic, dissatisfied, sensitive, catalytic, opportunistic, skill directed,
innovative, forward thinking, resourceful, evaluative, expedient and courageous. There
are also certain decision-making errors that occur with a higher frequency than others:
cognitive nearsightedness, assumption that the future will repeat the past, oversimplification, overreliance on one's own experience, preconceived notions, unwillingness
to experiment, and reluctance to decide. The chapter concluded with a section on
the future police decision makers.

Discussion Questions

1. Discuss the synoptic planning approach. Describe three methods of selecting a
preferred course of action.
2. Compare and contrast five planning approaches.
3. What are the difference between administrative, procedural, operational, and tactical
plans?
4. Discuss Simon's concept of "bounded rationality."
5. Explain Lindblom's theory of incremental decision making.
6. How does Gore view the decision-making process?
7. According to Katz and Kahn, what are some of the more important personality
dimensions of policymakers that will affect their decisions?
8. Discuss the twelve most common characteristics of effective decision makers according to Marvin.
9. Analysis of the decision-making process indicates that certain types of errors occur
at a higher frequency than others. What are they?

Notes

1. G. S. Fulcher, *Common Sense Decision-Making* (Evanston, Ill.: Northwestern University
Press, 1965), p. 4.
2. Ibid., pp. 4–5.
3. J. Q. Wilson, *Varieties of Police Behavior* (Cambridge, Mass.: Harvard University Press,
1978). In this study, Wilson considers how the uniformed officers of eight communities
deal with such offenses as assault, theft, drunkenness, vice, traffic violators, and disorderly
conduct. He also analyzes the problems facing the police administrator both in deciding
what patrol officers ought to do and then in getting the officer to do it; how patrol officers
in various cities differ in performing their functions; and under what circumstances such
differences are based on explicit community decisions.

4. J. H. Skolnick, *Justice Without Trial* (New York: John Wiley, 1966). This book is based on the author's actual participation as a detective plus comparative community and case material. He discusses key issues such as the organization of the police in America; the effects of police bureaucracy on criminal justice, narcotics, and vice investigation; the informer payoff and its consequences; and the relation between the police and black citizens. His findings are analyzed in light of organizational and legal controls over the police and their effect on the decision-making processes with law enforcement.

5. Israel Stollman, "The Values of the City Planner," in *The Practice of Local Government Planning*, eds. Frank S. So et al. (Washington, D.C.: International City Management Association, 1979), p. 13.

6. Ibid., p. 13.

7. Robert C. Cushman, *Criminal Justice Planning for Local Governments* (Washington, D.C.: U.S. Government Printing Office, 1980), p. 8; five of the elements identified are provided by Cushman, and the others have been added.

8. Ibid., p. 8.

9. John Hudzik and Gary Cordner, *Planning in Criminal Justice Organizations and Systems* (New York: Macmillan, 1983), p. 1.

10. Charles M. Mottley, "Strategy in Planning." In J. F. Lyden and E. S. Miller, *Planning Programming Budgeting* (Chicago, Ill.: Markham, 1972), p. 127.

11. The term *pure* or *objective rationality* is taken from the alternative planning models identified by Tony Eddison, *Local Government: Management and Corporate Planning* (New York: Harper & Row, 1973), pp. 19–23.

12. Cushman, *Criminal Justice Planning for Local Governments*, p. 4.

13. The synoptic model is thoroughly discussed in R. C. Cushman, *Criminal Justice Planning for Local Governments*. Some of the following information relating to the model is paraphrased from that work.

14. Hudzik and Cordner, *Planning in Criminal Justice*, p. 10.

15. Ibid., p. 24.

16. Ibid., p. 10.

17. Ibid., p. 10.

18. Carol Weiss, *Evaluation Research: Methods of Assessing Program Effectiveness* (Englewood Cliffs, N.J.: Prentice-Hall, 1972), p. 7.

19. P. Davidoff and T. A. Reiner, "A Choice Theory of Planning," *Journal of American Institute of Planners* (May 1982), pp. 103–115.

20. Hudzik and Cordner, *Planning in Criminal Justice*, p. 14.

21. R. G. Lynch, *The Police Manager* (Boston, Mass.: Holbrook Press, 1975), p. 144.

22. U.S. Naval War College, *Sound Military Decisions* (Newport, R.I.: U.S. Naval War College, 1942).

23. The following discussion of strategic analysis is taken from Charles M. Mottley's "Strategic Planning," *Management Highlights*, Release 56, Office of Management Research, U.S. Department of the Interior (September 1967), pp. 103–119.

24. E. S. Quade, "System Analysis Techniques for Planning-Programming-Budgeting." In F. J. Lyden and E. G. Miller, *Planning, Programming, Budgeting: A Systems Approach to Management*, 2d ed. (Chicago, Ill.: Markham, 1972), p. 249.

25. Ibid., p. 249.

26. Ibid., p. 249.

27. J. L. Pressman and Aaron Wildavsky, *Implementation* (Berkeley, Calif.: University of California Press, 1973).

28. Hudzik and Cordner, *Planning in Criminal Justice*, p. 196.

29. Ibid., p. 196.

30. The last portion of this paragraph is taken, with some restatement, from Stollman, "The Values of the City Planner," pp. 14–15.

31. A number of sources identify plans according to their use; see O. W. Wilson, *Police Planning*, 2d ed. (Springfield, Ill.: Charles C. Thomas, 1962), pp. 4–7; Vernon L. Hoy,

"Research and Planning," in *Local Government Police Management,* ed. Bernard L. Garmire (Washington, D.C.: International City Management Association, 1977), pp. 374–375.

32. Stanley S. Thune and Robert J. House, "Where Long-Range Planning Pays Off," *Business Horizons,* 13 (August 1970), pp. 81–90.

33. For information on managing organizational decline and cutback, see Elizabeth K. Kellar, ed., *Managing with Less* (Washington, D.C.: International City Management Association, 1979); Jerome Miron, *Managing the Pressures of Inflation in Criminal Justice,* (Washington, D.C.: U.S. Government Printing Office, 1979).

34. Hudzik and Cordner, *Planning in Criminal Justice,* p. 195.

35. J. M. Pfiffner, "Administrative Rationality," *Public Administration Review,* 20:3 (Summer 1960), p. 126.

36. Ibid., p. 128.

37. Herbert A. Simon, "The Proverbs of Administration," *Public Administration Review,* Winter 1946, 6, pp. 53–67.

38. Herbert A. Simon, *Administrative Behavior* (New York: Macmillan Publishing, 1961 a reprint of 1947 edition), p. 39.

39. Ibid., p. 40.

40. For a complete discussion of the rational-comprehensive model, see Peter F. Drucker, *The Effective Executive* (New York: Harper & Row, Publishers, 1967). N. F. Iannone, *Supervision of Police Personnel* (Englewood Cliffs,: Prentice-Hall, N.J., 1970). Ira Sharkansky, *Public Administration* (Chicago: Markham, 1972).

41. See Sharkansky, *Public Administration* p. 44 and Sam S. Souryal, *Police Administration and Management* (St. Paul, Minn.: West Publishing, 1977), p. 315.

42. Simon, *Administrative Behavior,* p. 40.

43. Ibid., p. 40.

44. See Paul M. Whisenand and R. Fred Ferguson, *The Managing of Police Organizations,* 2d ed. (Englewood Cliffs, N.J.: Prentice-Hall, 1978), pp. 202–203, for a discussion of Simon's "bounded-rationality" concepts.

45. Charles F. Lindblom, *The Policy-making Process* (Englewood Cliffs, N.J.: Prentice-Hall, 1968).

46. Ibid., p. 209.

47. Charles F. Lindblom, "The Science of Muddling Through," *Public Administration Review* 19, Spring 1959, p. 86.

48. Jack Kuykendall and Peter Unsinger, *Community Police Administration* (Chicago: Nelson-Hall, 1975), p. 132.

49. William J. Gore, *Administrative Decision-Making: A Heuristic Model,* (New York: John Wiley, 1964).

50. Ibid., p. 12.

51. Souryal, *Police Administration and Management,* p. 318.

52. L. G. Gawthrop, *Bureaucratic Behavior in the Executive Branch* (New York: Free Press, 1969), pp. 98–99.

53. W. J. Gore, *Administrative Decision-Making: A Heuristic Model,* p. 12.

54. Gawthrop, *Bureaucratic Behavior,* p. 99.

55. Souryal, *Police Administration and Management,* p. 319.

56. Graham T. Allison, *Essence of Decision: Exploring the Cuban Missile Crisis* (Boston, Mass.: Little, Brown, 1971).

57. Some of this discussion was excerpted from an excellent review of Allison's book by Robert B. Denhardt, *Theories of Public Organization* (Monterey, Calif.: Brooks/Cole, 1984), pp. 81–85.

58. John Ott, "The Challenging Game of Operations Research," in Max S. Wortmann and Fred Luthans, eds. *Emerging Concepts of Management* (London: Macmillan, 1970), p. 287.

59. Ibid., p. 287.

60. Peter P. Schoderbeck, "PERT—Its Promises and Performances" in Max S. Wortman and Fred Luthans, *Emerging Concepts in Management,* p. 291 and E. S. Quade, "Systems Analysis Techniques for Planning-Programming-Budgeting," *Rand Report,* p. 3322 (Santa Monica, Calif.: Rand Corporation, 1966), p. 7.

61. Aaron Wildavsky, *Speaking Truth to Power: The Art and Craft of Police Analysis* (Boston, Mass.: Little, Brown, 1979), p. 84.

62. This information appears in the *Jail Management Seminar Notebook* located in the Jail Center at the National Institute of Corrections Library, Boulder, Colorado. No author or source is indicated. We continue to search for a citable source.

63. N. R. F. Maier, "Assets and Liabilities in Group Problem Solving: The Need for Integrated Function," *Psychology Review,* 74:4 (July 1967), pp. 239–248. Much of the information in this chapter dealing with the discussion of group decision making was obtained from this source.

64. Gortner, *Administration in the Public Sector,* (New York: John Wiley, 1977), p. 124.

65. C. S. Whiting, "Operational Techniques of Creative Thinking," *Advanced Management Journal,* 20:28 (October 1955), pp. 24–30.

66. Gortner, *Administration in the Public Sector,* p. 124.

67. W. H. Bricker, *Decision-Making Process* (San Jose, Calif.: Lansford, 1973), p. 8.

68. C. L. Karass, *The Negotiating Game* (Cleveland, Oh.: World, 1970).

69. B. R. Patton and K. Griffin, *Decision-Making Group Interaction* (New York: Harper & Row, 1978), pp. 196–198.

70. Much of the discussion on these four personality dimensions of decision makers that follows has been drawn extensively from D. Katz and R. L. Kahn, *The Social Psychology of Organizations* (New York: John Wiley, 1966), Chapter 10, "Policy Formulation and Decision-Making," pp. 290–294.

71. A. J. DuBrin, *Fundamentals of Organizational Behavior* (New York: Pergamon Press, 1974), p. 76.

72. A. Easton, *Decision-Making: A Short Course for Professionals,* Lesson I (New York: John Wiley, 1976), p. 35.

73. H. K. Holland, "Decision-Making and Personality," *Personnel Administration,* 31:3 (May-June 1968), pp. 28–29.

74. P. Marvin, *Developing Decisions for Action* (Homewood, Ill: Dow Jones-Irwin, Inc., 1971), pp. 36–37.

75. Ibid., p. 46.

76. Ibid., pp. 46–47.

77. Ibid., pp. 48–49.

78. Ibid., p. 49.

79. Much of the information in this chapter dealing with the discussion of common errors in decision making was obtained from F. A. Nigro and L. G. Nigro, *Modern Public Administration,* (New York: Harper and Row, 1977), pp. 226–232.

80. Katz and Kahn, *Social Psychology of Organization,* p. 285.

81. Robert W. Taylor, "Hostage and Crisis Negotiation Procedures: Assessing Police Liability," *TRIAL Magazine,* 19:4 (March 1983), pp. 64–71.

82. See for example A. Leighton, *Human Relations in a Changing World* (Princeton, N.J.: Princeton University Press, 1949), p. 152.

83. Ibid., p. 152.

84. C. Barnard, *The Functions of the Executive,* (Cambridge, Mass.: Harvard University Press, 1938), p. 189.

85. H. Cleveland, "The Decision Makers," *The Center Magazine,* (September-October 1973), p. 14.

86. Ibid., pp. 14–15.

An Administrative Plan

KENTUCKY STATE POLICE GENERAL ORDER	KENTUCKY STATE POLICE			
			3-1-85	AM-C-10
		Date of Issue	Effective Date	Identifier
SUBJECT		Reference		
INVENTORY OF KENTUCKY STATE POLICE PROPERTY				
Distribution		Recinds, Amends, or Special Instructions		

POLICY

Control and accountability of Kentucky State Police property is an important function that involves all personnel within the Department. The following guidelines address several areas concerning the control of that property.

PROCEDURE

A yearly inventory will be conducted at every Division, Branch, Post, Section and Unit level where property is assigned.

The Supply commander shall establish an inventory schedule and assign Supply personnel to conduct the inventory.

The Supply commander shall notify each commander of the area to be inventoried at least five (5) working days before the inventory will be conducted.

Supply personnel conducting the inventory shall take with them two (2) inventory printouts to be obtained from Data Processing no earlier than 30 days prior to the inventory.

The inventory will be conducted by Supply personnel and the Division, Branch, Post, Section or Unit commander, or his representative, of the area inventoried. Each item on the inventory printout will be visually checked and a mark made on the printouts in a manner indicating the property was accounted for. Once all property is checked, the inventory officer and Division, Branch, Post, Section or Unit commander, or his representative, shall reach an agreement on an accounting of all property. Should property be missing, a notation will be made on both inventory printouts indicating what items are missing. The commander affected shall then sign both inventory printouts. He will retain one (1) copy and the inventory officer will return one (1) copy to Supply to be retained as a permanent record. The inventory officer shall also sign and date both inventory printouts verifying that the inventory is accurate and correct.

Should property be discovered missing during the inventory, the affected commander shall initiate a memorandum through channels to his Division Director setting forth the circumstances surrounding the issue. The Division Director shall then review the report and make a determination on what action should be taken. Once a decision is made, the commander affected shall be notified in writing of that decision. A copy of the action shall also be forwarded to the Supply commander who must ensure action is taken in removing the property from the inventory system. The Supply copy of the correspondence must be attached to the inventory printout for the particular area involved to document the removal of property from the inventory system.

<u>Division, Branch, Post, Section And Unit Commanders Shall Cause A Yearly Inventory To Be Made Of Property Assigned To Individual Personnel Under Their Command.</u>

At least once yearly an inventory will be made of property assigned to individual personnel. Inventory printouts may be obtained through the Supply Section listing the property assigned. At the conclusion of the inventory both inventory printouts will be signed and dated, verifying inventory is accurate and correct, by the officer conducting the inventory. One (1) copy will be forwarded to Supply and one copy retained.

Should property be discovered missing, the commander shall require the individual concerned to address the circumstances surrounding the issue on a memorandum relative to the issue. The report will then be forwarded through channels to the Division Director for final action. A copy of the final action will be forwarded back through channels to the commander, the individual officer concerned and also the Supply commander who shall ensure the property is removed from the inventory system and the record retained as a permanent record.

<u>Lost Property</u>

Should property be lost by individual personnel between inventories, the circumstances will be addressed in the same manner as property discovered missing during an inventory as discussed above.

<u>Stolen Property</u>

When an item of agency property has been stolen, a memorandum outlining the details, along with a list of the stolen items, will be forwarded through channels to Supply. The Supply commander shall cause the property to be removed from the inventory system. The Supply Section shall then notify the appropriate Finance & Administration Section by memorandum listing the items deleted, along with other pertinent information. All correspondence will be retained in a Stolen Property File at Supply. Should the property be recovered, Supply shall be notified and will take appropriate action in re-entering the property into the inventory system.

<u>Changes In Division, Branch, Post, Section or Unit Commanders</u>

When a Division, Branch, Post, Section or Unit changes commanders, an immediate inventory shall be completed by the involved commanders. If a discrepancy is noted and cannot be resolved by the commanders, then either commander has the option to request an audit by Supply. Then, if the discrepancy is not resolved by the Supply commander, the Division Director, or if the Division Director is a concerned party, the Commissioner will resolve the issue.

Commanders assuming command of a particular area shall sign and date an inventory printout and forward to Supply to be retained. He shall also retain one (1) copy for his records.

Exchange Of Property Between Commanders

The exchange of property between commanders shall be documented by submitting a Property Inventory Change Card (KSP-300) to Supply. If property is exchanged and a KSP-300 is not submitted, responsibility shall be with the commander giving up the property. Both commanders involved shall sign the KSP-300.

Property Requiring A Property Number

All items of property purchased by this agency which meets the following criteria shall be marked with a Property Number for perpetual inventory:

1. Any non-expendable item which costs fifty dollars ($50.00) or more; and

2. Regardless of cost;
    Binoculars,
    Battery, electric and gasoline powered items;
    Pictures and wall hangings.

In certain instances, the Supply Section may purchase through Surplus Properties items costing less than $50.00. If such items are non-expendable and will be placed in use within the agency for an extended period of time, that property will be assigned a Property Number for inventory purposes.

Purchase Documents/Obtaining A Property Number

We must ensure that all property requiring a Property Number is entered into the inventory system.

When purchases are made through Supply and delivery made at Supply, a number will be affixed to the property and property will be entered into the inventory system before delivery is made to the person ordering. During this process a Property Number will be entered onto purchase documents before those documents are forwarded to Fiscal Affairs for payment. Appropriate inventory records will be delivered with the property by Supply.

When possible, all shipments in the Frankfort area should be made to the Supply Section. In certain instances, however, such as at the Forensic Laboratories Section, this may not be feasible. If delivery is made directly to another section, it will be that section commander's responsibility to ensure Supply is provided the necessary information to obtain Property Numbers and provide Supply with necessary information to enter property into the inventory system.

When a post or section outside the Frankfort area purchases property requiring a Property Number the following guidelines shall apply. Once property is received, a Local Purchase Order shall be initiated unless the item appears on a purchase document already received from Fiscal Affairs. You shall enter onto the L.P.O. or purchase document the date item was received. You should then call the Supply Section and provide them with the necessary information to obtain a property decal for the property. Once a Property Number is obtained, the number must be entered onto the L.P.O. or purchase document and then forwarded to Fiscal Affairs for payment.

Supply will forward to you a Property Number decal and two (2) Property Inventory Records. The property decal shall be affixed to the property immediately upon receipt. One (1) Inventory Record stamped "Section Copy" shall be retained at your level; the other marked "Supply Copy" shall be signed by the person responsible for the property and returned immediately to Supply.

Should Fiscal Affairs receive a L.P.O. or purchase document requiring a Property Number, and a number has not been entered, they will take appropriate action to obtain the necessary information.

Not least among the qualifications of an administrator is his ability as a tactician and gladiator in the budget process.

FREDERICK C. MOSHER

Financial Management

Introduction

The historical importance of financial mangement to this country's very existence is unmistakable; the issue of taxation without representation was part of the disagreement with England that led ultimately to the American Revolution. The present importance of financial management in government is readily established by examining the content of daily newspapers.[1] Stories may note the arrest and indictment of an official for embezzling public funds, the defeat or passage of a bond referendum to construct a jail, an auditor's report that describes the police department's accounting procedures for handling funds for informants and narcotics purchases as "woefully inadequate," the closing of a school or precinct station because funds were no longer available to operate it, or the efforts of local officials to obtain the state legislature's approval to levy new taxes or to increase the levels of existing ones.

In Chapter 12 the view that some police managers have of planning was discussed. Relatedly, some police administrators see budgeting and financial management in a similar vein. The mistaken view that financial management is "only detailed clerical work" and therefore unattractive and unimportant deserves some attention here.

First, financial management does involve some detailed effort. The product of that effort is attended by the possibility of uncomfortable or potentially severe consequences for misjudgment. For example, the dramatic rise in gasoline prices in 1979 and 1980, which far exceeded what was judged to be likely, resulted in some police agencies having to limit the numbers of miles patrolled daily, the purchasing of smaller cars, the cost of driver training programs to increase fuel economy, and the need to return to the legislative body for additional funds. In this last regard, the Maryland State Police had to request an additional $525,000 in one year, and Detroit's city-wide annual budget for gasoline was found to have been inadequate by some $2,000,000.[2]

A second factor related to viewing financial management as unattractive work is that it offers little of the excitement, attention, or perhaps even "glamor" that directing a noteworthy major investigation does. However, success in obtaining and shepherding resources increasingly involves the need for creativity and is a potentially rich source of job satisfaction. As to financial management not being "real police work," the validity of that statement diminishes as one advances up the hierarchy, incurring at each successive level a set of new responsibilities that renders operational prowess less relevant.

Politics and Financial Management

Gangs swarmed around two of Newark, New Jersey's police stations and smashed the windows out of forty-six cruisers, and the following weekend more than forty of that city's traffic signals were disabled. In both instances police officers reported having seen nothing.[3] Newark's chief said he thought some officers were "probably involved," and the president of Newark's Patrolmen's Benevolent Association told reporters he was "assuming" that police were responsible for the squad car episode. In San Jose, California, the Peace Officers Association took the city to arbitration when the pay schedule was changed from every two weeks to monthly.[4] In both cities, the issue was financial; in Newark, the mayor had announced plans to lay off 200 of the city's 1,160 officers, and in San Jose, a change in the structure of budget execution allegedly produced some lost earnings for union members.

Budgeting is inherently a political process. Anything done through government entails the expenditure of public funds.[5] If politics is regarded in part as a conflict over whose preferences shall prevail in the determination of policy, the outcome of this struggle is recorded in the budget.[6] Thus, the single most important political statement that any unit of government makes in a given year is its budget. Essentially the budget process confronts decision makers with the gambler's adage, "put your money where your mouth is."[7] Because often increasing demands are made on resources that are declining, stable, or outstripped by the claims made on them, the competition for appropriated funds is keen and often fierce as the police and other departments seek to make the best case they can for their own budget. Beset by competing demands from each department of government, assailed by informal "arm twisting," influenced by media reports of public opinion on various subjects, confronted by special-interest groups with different priorities, and in consideration of their own values and judgments, those who appropriate the funds are making a highly visible and often controversial political decision when they enact a budget. Because legislatures allow public officials, such as city managers and police chiefs, some discretion in how they execute a budget, they too are making political decisions whose impact—as seen in the cases of Newark and San Jose—may evoke strong reactions.

While its political orientation is inescapable, a budget is more than an indicator of who won and who lost, who was able to form effective coalitions and work out acceptable compromises and who was not able to perform this feat, and whose policies are in ascendancy and descendancy; it is also a key managerial tool.[8]

State and Local Financial Management

The States' Role in Local Finance

There are numerous examples of private sector organizations that have had severe financial problems, including Chrysler, Lockheed, and Penn Central. Historically, local governments have also not been without a certain degree of financial fraility. In the last 150 years, over 6,000 units of local government have defaulted on their financial obligations, although about two thirds of these came during the decade that followed the economic crash of 1929.[9] States simultaneously contribute to, and attempt to help, local government avoid financial difficulties. They contribute to the problem by mandating programs that require the expenditure of local funds. Examples of such mandated programs include the training of peace officers, proscribing levels of police service, and establishing special disability and retirement benefits for police.[10] Our national government also contributes in a similar fashion; for example, it is estimated that programs legislated by the federal and state government cost Iowa cities $50,000,000 to $60,000,000 annually.[11]

As the sovereign and superior governmental entity for the geographic areas they encompass, the states have constitutional responsibilities over local government.[12] Under the legal doctrine known as Dillion's rule,[13] no local government may organize, perform any function, tax citizens, or receive or spend money without the consent of the state. With an eye toward helping local government avoid financial woes, state laws, which vary, may control (1) the revenue structure of local governments and methods of tax collection; (2) budgeting, accounting, and financial reporting practices; (3) cash collection, deposit, and disbursement procedures; and (4) procedures for incurring debt, the types of debts that may be issued, and the level of debt that is allowable.

A general model of how states assist local government is depicted in Figure 13-1; such efforts require the state to commit significant resources, another sign of the importance attached to them. In New York, for example, the financial activities of the 9,100 units of local government are monitored and supervised by three state agencies, the most significant being the Department of Audit and Control, which employs 420 people and expends $7.5 million annually in this effort.[14]

Local Administration

In addition to whatever requirements are established by the federal and state governments, the practice of local financial management is also shaped by a number of other forces, including the city charter, ordinances, executive orders, regulations, and practices. Of considerable impact is the political structure of the unit of government. In city manager and strong mayor cities, these figures play dominant roles in their

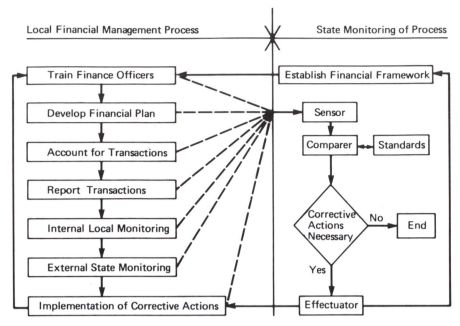

FIGURE 13-1. A general model of a state fiscal monitoring system. [From Paul Moore and Alan G. Billingsley, "Financial Monitoring of Local Governments," *State Government*, 52 (Autumn 1979), Exhibit 1, p. 157.]

respective systems in the development of what is termed an executive budget. In weak mayor systems, the city council is the dominant force in the development of what is termed a legislative budget. Under this arrangement, a city council budget committee has responsibility for preparing the budget. A budget staff frequently serves this committee by providing administrative support. The heads of the various departments, including the police, and their budget staffs deal directly with the council budget committee and its staff in formulating the budget. Under the declining commissioner plan, three to seven elected officials serve as both members of the local legislative branch of government and as heads of one or more departments of city government. One of the commissioners receives the title of mayor, but it is largely ceremonial, akin to a weak mayor system. Under the commissioner plan, the budget preparation process may follow any of several patterns: (1) the commission as a whole may be the dominant force, (2) the commission may have a budget officer attached directly to it, or (3) the preparation of the budget may be guided by a budget officer assigned to the commissioner of finance, but who serves at the pleasure of the commissioners as a whole to ensure responsiveness to them.

Definitions of a Budget

The word "budget" is derived from the old French *bougette*, meaning a small leather bag or wallet.[15] Initially, it referred to the leather bag in which the chancellor of the exchequer carried the documents to English Parliament stating the government's needs and resources.[16] Later, it came to mean the documents themselves. Currently, "budget" has been defined in many ways, including a plan stated in financial terms, an estimate of future expenditures, an asking price, a policy statement, the translation of financial resources into human purposes, and a contract between those who appropriate the funds and those who spend them.[17] To some extent, all these are true and help us to understand something about budgets, but they lack the feature of being comprehensive.

Even more "comprehensive" definitions of a budget reflect different notions. The definitions that follow represent, successively, the budget as a management tool, the budget as a process, and the budget as politics:

> The budget is a comprehensive plan, expressed in financial terms, by which a program is operated for a given period of time. It includes: (a) the services, activities, and projects comprising the program; (b) the resultant expenditure requirements; and (c) the resources usable for their support.[18] In Sunnyvale, California, each year a ten-year budget is adopted using the term Resource Allocation Plan (RAP), which reflects a strong planning orientation in the use of that city's fiscal resources.

> The budget is a unified series of steps taken to implement a government's policy objectives. It involves the development of a documented work program . . . the careful linkage of the program with a formal, comprehensive financial plan, and the carrying out of the entire scheme through an administrative arrangement.[19]

> The budget is a device for consolidating the various interests, objectives, desires and needs of our citizens.[20]

Budgets may also be defined as operating and capital. An operating budget is usually for one year and is for items that have a short life expectancy, are consumed in the normal course of operations, or are reincurred each year. Included in operating budgets are batteries, paper, duplicating and telephone expenses, as well as salaries and fringe benefits. There is a great deal of diversity in how different jurisdictions treat their capital budgets. "Capital Project" or "Capital Improvement Plan" (CIP) is often used to denote expenditures to buy land or to construct or for a major renovation of public facilities. Normally three to five years are needed to complete the development of, and paying for, a CIP. Depending on the guidelines that a jurisdiction uses, vehicles, furniture, and other equipment may or may not be included in the CIP. If not included in the CIP, such objects as police vehicles, radios, desks and chairs, binoculars, and microcomputers may be included in the operating budget under the heading of "Capital Item," "Capital Outlay," or just simply "Capital." Table 13-1 illustrates a capital budget for a police department.

Operating and capital improvement budgets are normally acted upon separately by the legislative body to which they are presented for consideration. Moreover, in some places such as Tucson, Arizona, the distinction between operating and capital budgets is reflected, as shown in Figure 13-2, in organizational specialists to deal with each of these two different types of budgets.

The Budget Cycle and Roles

Some governments require all their departments to budget for a two-year period called a biennium. The Kentucky State Police represents an agency that practices biennium budgeting. Most governments, however, budget for a shorter time, called a fiscal year (FY). A fiscal year is a twelve-month period that may coincide with a calendar year, although commonly its duration is from July 1 of one year until June 30 of the next; in the federal government, it is from October 1 of one year until

TABLE 13-1. The Las Vegas Metropolitan Police Department's 1985–1986 Approved Capital Budget

Acct. no.	Bureau/section	Office furniture	Office equipment	Radio equipment	Vehicles	Other equipment	Other	Total
3111	Staff	1,217	0	0	0	2,340	0	3,557
3112	Planning	1,907	0	0	9,000	0	0	10,907
3113	Internal Affairs	400	1,000	0	11,000	0	0	12,400
3114	Fiscal Affairs	7,230	0	0	0	2,685	0	9,915
3116	Community Services	262	0	0	0	0	0	262
3131	Intelligence	0	1,974	0	35,200	0	0	37,174
3132	Special/Private Investigations	0	957	0	11,000	0	0	11,957
3141	Patrol	3,433	12,457	3,570	755,305	25,000	6,788	806,553
3142	Traffic	1,540	1,057	1,100	132,890	583	0	137,170
3143	Search & Rescue	975	0	0	13,000	0	0	13,975
3144	S.W.A.T./K-9	0	0	0	72,400	2,875	0	75,275
3145	Airport	0	0	0	24,750	2,300	0	27,050
3146	Resident Officer	0	0	0	80,000	0	0	80,000
3147	Special Events/Reserve	0	0	0	0	0	0	0
3148	S.C.A.T.	2,668	0	0	11,000	0	0	13,668
3151	Detective	100	495	0	216,400	0	0	216,995
3152	Vice	4,050	3,302	8,825	23,200	0	0	39,377
3153	Narcotics	2,970	185	0	16,000	5,164	0	24,319
3161	Personnel	1,216	185	0	11,000	0	0	12,401
3162	Training	0	0	0	0	13,920	10,000	23,920
3163	Crime Prevention	890	957	0	9,000	7,600	0	18,447
3164	Supply	1,648	0	0	9,500	21,242	0	32,390
3171	Records	6,449	27,748	0	0	0	0	34,197
3172	Information Services	0	0	0	0	0	0	0
3173	Communications	0	800	0	0	0	0	800
3174	Fingerprint	1,496	0	0	0	0	0	1,496
3175	Criminalistics	2,800	8,000	0	31,800	0	0	42,600
	Total	$41,251	$59,117	$13,495	$1,472,445	$83,709	$16,788	$1,686,805

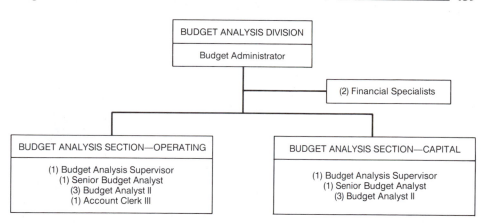

FIGURE 13-2. Organization of the City of Tucson, Arizona, Budget Analysis Division.

September 30 of the following year. A budget that took effect on July 1, 1987, and terminated on June 30, 1988, would be described as the FY '88 budget. Both biennium and annual or fiscal year budgeting systems have fundamental strengths and weaknesses. The biennium approach fosters long-range planning and analysis, but it is more likely to be affected by unforeseen contingencies because of its longer time horizon. Fiscal year budgets provide for a more frequent scrutiny of programs, but they may be costly in that they emphasize thinking in small increments of time to the neglect of more sweeping considerations such as economic trends.

The budget cycle consists of four sequential steps that are repeated every year at about the same time in a well-organized government: (1) budget preparation (2) budget approval, (3) budget execution, and (4) the audit. Fiscal years and the budget cycle overlap. For example, while a police department is executing this year's budget, it will at various times be faced with an audit of last year's and the preparation of next year's. Within each of the steps, a number of things occur that affect the dynamics of budgeting and with which the police manager must be familiar to be effective.

Budget Preparation

Given that the executive budget predominates, whether in the form of the president's, a governor's, a strong mayor's, or a city manager's, this discussion of the elements of the budget cycle will assume for purposes of illustration a city manager form of government.

Long before the police department or any other unit of city government begins the preparation of its annual submission, a great deal of effort has gone on, principally within the Department of Finance or other similarly titled unit. Figure 13-3 depicts the general and detailed organization of such a body.

Included in this preliminary effort are revenue forecasts, determinations of how much money from existing departmental budgets will not be expended, analyses of how population shifts will affect demands for various types of public services, and the development of the city's budget preparation manual. Budget preparation manuals tend to focus on the technical aspects of budget, such as responsibilities, definitions, and instructions on completing forms.

Ordinarily accompanying the budget preparation manual is a memorandum from the city manager that discusses the general fiscal guidelines to be followed by the

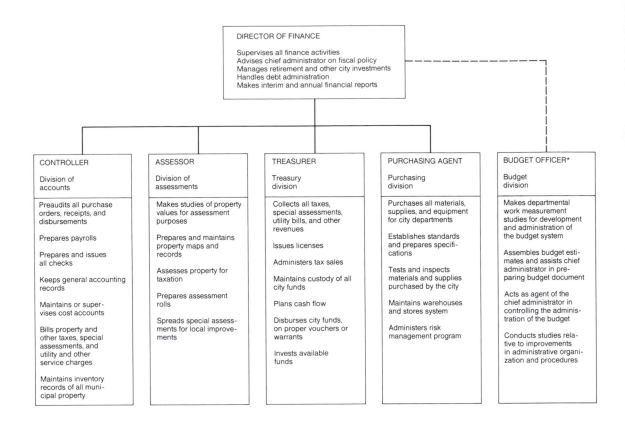

*The dotted line between the director of finance and the budget officer indicates that the latter is often primarily responsible to the chief administrator, being physically located in the finance department to prevent the duplication of records. In many cities the finance director handles the budget.

FIGURE 13-3. A functional organizational chart of a municipal department of finance. [Source: Leonard I. Ruchelman, ''The Finance Function in Local Government,'' in *Management Policies in Local Government,* J. Richard Aronson and Eli Schwartz, eds. (Washington, D.C.: International City Management Association, 1981), Figure 1-1, p. 17.]

departments in preparing their budget requests. The content of this memorandum essentially reflects the data generated by the preliminary effort discussed previously, supplemented by whatever special information or priorities that the city manager may have.

In some jurisdictions the city manager will formally or informally go before the city council to get members' views as to their priorities in terms of spending levels, pay raises, new hirings, and programs. This does not constitute a contract between the city manager and the council; rather, it is an exchange of information that is binding on neither but that can eliminate time-consuming and costly skirmishes later. In other jurisdictions, the council may unilaterally issue a statement of their expectations, or the city manager and department heads may have to try to establish the council's expectations through reading their statements to newspapers or informal contacts with individual council members.

An important element of the budget preparation manual is the budget preparation calendar, which is the time schedule a city follows from the time it begins to prepare a budget until the budget is approved. From the standpoint of a chief of police, there are actually two budget preparation calendars: the one established by the Department of Finance's budget officer and the one the police department develops that duplicates the timetable of the city's overall budget preparation but that also establishes a timetable and set of responsibilities within the police department. Table 13-2 shows an internal budget preparation calendar for a large police department.

Upon receipt of the city's budget preparation manual and the city administrator's fiscal policy memorandum, the chief of police will have the planning and research unit, assuming that this is where the department's fiscal responsibility is located since budgeting is most fundamentally a planning process, prepare the internal budget calendar and an internal fiscal policy memorandum, which, just as the city manager's

TABLE 13-2.   A Budget Preparation Calendar for a Large Police Department

What should be done	By whom	On these dates
Issue budget instructions and applicable forms	City administrator	November 1
Prepare and issue budget message, with instructions and applicable forms, to unit commanders	Chief of police	November 15
Develop unit budgets with appropriate justification and forward recommended budgets to planning and research unit	Unit commanders	February 1
Review of unit budget	Planning and research staff with unit commanders	March 1
Consolidation of unit budgets for presentation to chief of police	Planning and research unit	March 15
Review of consolidated recommended budget	Chief of police, planning and research staff, and unit commanders	March 30
Department approval of budget	Chief of police	April 15
Recommended budget forwarded to city administrator	Chief of police	April 20
Administrative review of recommended budget	City administrator and chief of police	April 30
Revised budget approval	City administrator	May 5
Budget document forwarded to city council	City administrator	May 10
Review of budget	Budget officer of city council	May 20
Presentation to council	City administrator and chief of police	June 1
Reported back to city administrator	City council	June 5
Review and resubmission to city council	City administrator and chief of police	June 10
Final action on police budget	City council	June 20

From National Advisory Commission on Criminal Justice Standards and Goals, *Police* (Washington, D.C.: U.S. Government Printing Office, 1973), p. 137.

fiscal policy memorandum did for the city, establishes the chief's priorities within the context of the directions he has been given. This material—the budget preparation manual with the city manager's and chief's cover memorandums attached—are distributed to the police department's major units where the budget building actually takes place.

Just how far down the organizational hierarchy involvement in this process goes is related somewhat to the size of the police department. In small departments where there is little or no functional specialization, the chief may actually prepare the budget alone or with minimal input from his watch commanders. In some instances, most often when the city manager has a high need for control, small department chiefs may have little or no input into preparing the budget request for their departments and may never actually see the budget under which their departments operate. In police departments sufficiently large for functional specialization, the lowest supervisory ranks in the smallest organizational entities should be involved in preparing the budget request for their own operation; when their request is completed, it is submitted to the next largest organizational entity in the police department's structure, where it is reviewed, returned for any adjustments, resubmitted, and becomes part of the request initiated by that next largest organizational entity. This process if repeated until each of the largest organizational entities, normally designated as bureaus, has a budget request that covers its entire operations for the forthcoming fiscal year.

The planning and research unit will then review the bureau budget requests for compliance with technical budgeting instructions and the priorities of the chief and the city manager. Here and elsewhere, there is often a great deal of communication between the police department's designated liaison with the city budget officer regarding waivers from certain requirements, clarification of guidelines, and other related matters. After any necessary adjustments are made by the bureaus, the planning and research unit will prepare a consolidated budget for the entire police department and submit it to the chief with its recommendations. Following this, the chief will have a series of meetings with the staff of the planning and research unit and the bureau commanders to discuss the department's budget.

In these meetings, the interplay of the stakes, the issues, personalities involved, internal politics, value differences, personal agendas, and other variables create an atmosphere that is tense and sometimes heated. The chief both mediates and contributes to conflicts. One key way in which the chief contributes to mediating and promoting conflict is by using the budget as a means of rewarding "the faithful" and disciplining "the disloyal." In a very real sense, a chief can harm a subordinate's interests more than he can help them; programs can be cut back, assigned low priorities, and eliminated with a greater likelihood of success than can initiating requests for additional personnel, special equipment, and funds to support travel to conferences.

Also considered during these meetings between the chief and his key staff members are questions of overall budget strategy. Such questions include what priorities to assign different programs, how to best justify requests, and how large a request to make. Police administrators must be able to justify the contents of their department's budget proposal. Any portion of a request for which a persuasive defense cannot be made fosters the belief in budget analysts that more, perhaps much more, of the request can be cut. This, in turn, invites even closer scrutiny and some cuts that go beyond "trimming the fat" and go to "cutting muscle and bone." However, if the city's central budget office operates in the role of "cutters" and "defenders of the public treasury" to some extent the practical question is not whether to "pad the budget,'' but rather where and how. This may take the form of requesting funding for one or a few programs that are justifiable, but can essentially serve as ''sacrificial lambs'' while at the same time not endangering the rest of the request. The alternative is to present a budget from which the chief can tolerate no cuts and hope that at some other point of consideration the essential funds cut will be restored. There is a fine point involved here; if the chief is seen as someone who simply routinely pads the budget, he or she will lose the respect and confidence of those with whom they deal in the budgetary process. If, however, the chief is skillful in these maneuvers, his reputation may be enhanced as being an effective advocate for his department, a programmatic innovator, and a realist who can be flexible in budget negotiations. Based upon such considerations and input, the chief makes his decisions and directs the planning and research unit to develop the police department's budget request that is going to be submitted to the city manager. This document is then forwarded to the city manager with a cover letter from the chief of police. This cover letter (one appears in the appendix to this chapter) highlights the detailed budget request, calls attention to new initiatives and past successes, and may warn of consequences if funds are not forthcoming or appropriated.

The city manager will, in turn, treat the police department's budget in the same manner as the unit budgets were treated within the police department. The city manager's budget office will consolidate the requests from the various departments, the heads of which will meet with the city manager and his budget officer to discuss their requests. Subsequently, the city manager will direct the city's budget officer to make certain changes, often ''cuts,'' and prepare a draft of the citywide budget that the city manager will recommend to the council. This recommended budget will then be sent to the council with a cover letter not unlike the one the chief sent the city manager, except that it will be in the broader perspective for the city's needs and may call attention to such variables as the legal requirement for a balanced budget, that is, one in which expenditures do not exceed revenues.

Budget Approval

Having received the city manager's recommended budget, the city council will commence its consideration, which begins with an analysis of the budget by the council's budget officer, if it has one. Subsequently, the city manager will appear before the council to answer whatever questions the members have. At some point, the heads of each department and their key staff members may appear before the council as the budget request for their department is being considered. The appearance of representatives of the individual departments may be opposed by the city manager who sees such appearances as a threat to his power, fiscal policies, or other matters, because it presents the opportunity for department heads to get cuts made by the city manager restored to the police budget.

For example, in San Jose, California, the police department's budget requested no new personnel in accordance with the city administrator's restrictions.[21] However, when presenting the budget request to the council, police officials included a frank description of conditions, using simple and carefully selected graphics. Immediately subsequent to this presentation, the San Jose City Council added ninety new positions to the police department's budget. This incident also gives rise to considering how a police administrator can be effective in obtaining funds from appropriators. In the case of San Jose, the positions given to the police department required reducing the budgets of several other departments. The following represent some things believed to be important to being successful in getting appropriations:[22]

1. Have a budget that is carefully justified.
2. Anticipate the environment of the budget hearing; find out by examining news reports and through conversations the priorities of the council members. Talk to department heads who have already presented their budgets to learn what types of questions are being asked. Analyze local, regional, and national papers to identify criticisms being made of the police and current issues and innovations. For example, reports that the Savannah, Georgia, Police Department modified twenty-five cars to operate on propane might lead city council members in other localities to ask "What are the advantages and disadvantages of using propane as a fuel in police vehicles?"[23]
3. Determine which "public" will be at the police department's budget hearing and prepare accordingly. As the issues change from year to year, so will the portion of the community that is sufficiently aroused to participate in these proceedings. A child killed by a vehicle while crossing an unguarded intersection, a series of violent robberies in the downtown area, and the rapes of several elderly women are likely to mobilize such groups as the parents-teachers association, the chamber of commerce and the merchants association, and the Grey Panthers.
4. Help shape the environment by planting questions with sympathetic council members, the answers to which put the police department in a favorable light.
5. Make good use of graphics in the form of pie charts (Figure 13-4) and bar graphs (Figure 13-5). In Figure 13-5 note how dramatically the increase in vehicle trade-in mileage is displayed, particularly the increase between FY 1979 and FY 1986. In budget presentations the use of carefully selected colors adds to the impact of graphics. In using graphics it is important to be selective and not "go overboard"; short case histories of police successes are natural and potent adjuncts to graphics.

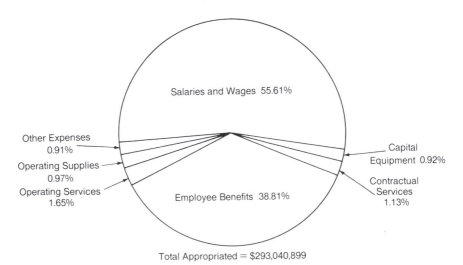

Total Appropriated = $293,040,899

FIGURE 13-4. Pie chart for Detroit Police Department 1985–1986 budget appropriations by major object.

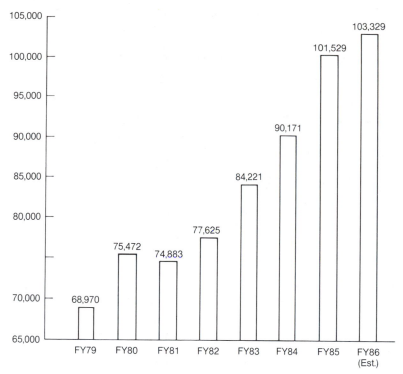

FIGURE 13-5. Bar chart for Illinois Department of State Police average vehicle trade-in mileage—FY79-FY86.

6. Rehearse and critique the presentation several times using role playing; the use of videotaping is especially helpful in this regard.

7. Have the physical layout checked before the presentation so it is known where electrical outlets are, where the screen should be situated, and if an extension cord is needed for any audiovisual equipment.

8. The chief of police must have, or develop, a reputation for being an able and economical administrator.

9. Take advantage of unusual situations to dramatize the need for special police equipment or additional personnel.

10. Be a political realist.

After the police and all other departments have appeared before it, the city council will give directions to the city manager. These directions may take any of several forms, such as cutting the overall city budget request by $1,500,000 with, or without, any guidance as to where the cuts are to be made or directing that certain programs cut by the manager to be reinstated, again with or without guidance in where to find the funds. When all adjustments are made to the satisfaction of the city council, the budget is adopted by the passage of an ordinance by a simple majority vote.

Table 13-3 shows the budget approval process for the Fayetteville, North Carolina, Police Department's FY '86 budget as it relates to major expenditure categories and staffing levels. The "1984–1985 Budget" column indicates the approved totals for FY '85. "The 1984–1985 Actual 12/31/84" column reports actual expenditures through

TABLE 13-3. The Budget Approval Process for the Fayetteville, North Carolina, Police Department Fiscal Year (FY) '86

Service Description

The Police Department is an organization of sworn officers, civilians, and school guards. The Police Department is responsible for enforcing the City and State criminal codes. The Chief of Police directs the department's activities through the Field Bureau and the Service Bureau. The I.D. Bureau is a joint city-county department responsible for providing support detection services to the Police Department and County Sheriff's Department. The I.D. Bureau is organized into two divisions: Criminal Records, which maintains criminal records for the City and County; and the Crime Scene Division, which provides technical services in photography, crime scene searches and evidence collection and perservation.

Expenditure Category	1984–1985 Budget	1984–1985 Actual 12/31/84	1984–1985 12 Months Estimated Actual	1985–1986 Proposed by Department	1985–1986 Recommended City Manager	1985–1986 Approved City Council
Personnel Salaries and Wages	3,709,246	1,766,965	3,619,000	4,245,162	4,030,095	4,030,095
Services Fringe Benefits	678,950	350,413	628,960	805,412	747,199	747,199
Operating Expenses	781,161	312,240	800,070	1,008,730	822,572	822,572
Capital Outlay	240,102	7,190	239,970	514,240	198,435	198,435
DEPARTMENT TOTAL	5,409,459	2,436,808	5,288,000	6,573,544	5,798,301	5,798,301
Authorized Positions						
Temporary Part-Time	–0–	–0–	–0–	–0–	–0–	–0–
Temporary Full-Time	2	2	2	2	2	2
Permanent Part-Time	22	22	22	22	22	22
Permanent Full-Time	221	221	221	242	228	228
Capital Projects						
ASSOCIATED REVENUES						

Budget Comments

ALL-AMERICA CITY

the first six months of their FY '85 budget. The "1984–1985 12 Months Estimated Actual" column is a projection of expenses through the end of their FY '85 budget, and the remaining three columns are self-explanatory. With reference to Table 13-3, each of the expenditure categories are summaries of subcategories. For example, "Salaries and Wages" is comprised of salaries, the city's Social Security contribution for each employee, employee insurance programs, contributions to the employee retirement program, worker's compensation coverage, and the cost of uniforms. Later in this chapter budget formats receive further treatment, but for present purposes it is sufficient to note that Fayetteville uses an object of expenditure budget format.

Budget Execution

The budget execution function had four objectives:

1. To provide for an orderly manner in which the police department's approved objectives for the fiscal year are to be achieved.
2. To ensure that no commitments or expenditures by the police department are undertaken, except in pursuance of authorizations made by the city council.
3. To conserve the resources of the police department that are not legitimately required to achieve the approved objectives.
4. To provide for a suitable accounting, at appropriate intervals, of the manner in which the chief's stewardship over entrusted resources have been discharged.[24]

These objectives are supported by three different mechanisms: (1) a system of allotment, (2) accounting controls, and (3) management controls.[25]

THE ALLOTMENT SYSTEM

Once an appropriations ordinance has been enacted by the city council, money can be expended legally by that unit of government. Once this has happened, it is theoretically the responsibility of the city's finance office to break each department's approved budget up into allocations for specific periods of time. When actually used, this procedure—referred to ordinarily as the allotment system—usually employs a three-month period known as a quarter. However, because the spending patterns of the various departments do not fall into neat "quarters" and vary widely, establishing the actual needs of each department is a time-consuming process. Therefore, despite the attention that allotment systems receive in the literature, many units of government have elected to rely on other mechanisms, such as budget status reports, as a means of monitoring spending and exercising control.

ACCOUNTING CONTROLS

A police department's budget officer, acting on behalf of the chief, will have a system of accounts to ensure that expenditures do not exceed the available resources. Separate budget ledgers are established for the major cost centers involved. Figure 13-6 illustrates the use of cost centers. Expenditures must be authorized by means of appropriate forms and supporting documents. The police department's budget officer wields considerable power in this regard, and occasionally his decisions will be appealed to the chief.

Here a certain dilemma exists that must be dealt with on a case-by-case basis:

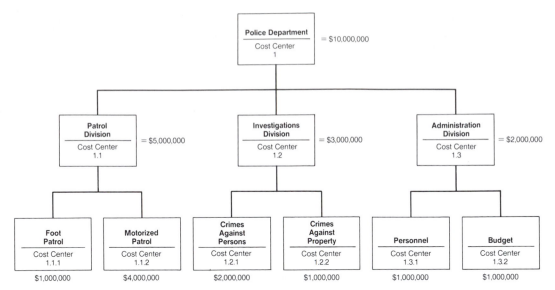

FIGURE 13-6. Illustration of the use of cost centers in a police department. [Source: Kent John Chabotar, *Measuring the Costs of Police Services* (Washington, D.C.: U.S. Department of Justice, National Insitute of Justice, 1982), p. 25.]

if the chief supports too many appeals, his budget officer loses some effectiveness and the chief may find himself deluged with appeals; if no appeals are supported, the police department may lose some effectiveness because of the lack of equipment or may lose the chance to capitalize on some unusual opportunity.

Periodic reports on accounts are an important element of control in that they serve to reduce the likelihood of overspending. Additionally, they identify areas in which deficits are likely to occur. Although police agencies budget for unusual contingencies, deficits may occur because of rises in gasoline prices, extensive overtime, natural disasters, or other causes. Table 13-4 is a budget status report; from the standpoint of managerial use, it incorporates several deficiencies:

1. The "% Used" column reflects only the total in the "Expenses to Date" column without consideration of the amount obligated, but for which no disbursements have been made. This leads to a misimpression as to the amount of funds actually available for use.
2. There is no provision for comparing the percentage of the budget used with the percentage of the budget year that has lapsed to make some judgment about the coinciding of expenditures with the passage of time.

The advent of electronic data processing has facilitated the accounting control function by making information available to police managers on a more timely basis.

MANAGEMENT CONTROLS

The last element of budget execution is management controls, without which financial controls are incomplete. Management controls reach down and throughout a police department to regulate the use of resources. Often, the character of these controls is prospective in that they prevent financial obligations from being incurred. Examples include a chief placing a "freeze" on hiring or requiring that, when a

TABLE 13-4.   A Police Department's Budget Status Report, December 31, 1986

Line item	Amount budgeted	Expenses to date	Amount obligated	Balance to date	% used
Salaries	$1,710,788	$848,161.05	$0.00	$862,626.95	49.58%
Training	15,000	5,374.47	6,098.00	3,527.53	35.83
Professional services	1,000	828.40	115.00	56.60	82.84
Travel	4,500	2,077.55	834.06	1,588.39	46.17
Dues and subscription	1,021	383.83	164.11	473.06	37.59
Communications	19,557	8,669.28	1,273.01	9,614.71	44.33
Utilities	35,000	17,213.81	1,420.36	16,365.83	49.18
Office supplies	21,000	7,988.76	3,274.99	9,736.25	38.04
Printing	7,000	3,725.43	1,854.75	1,419.82	53.22
Repairs to equipment	55,129	25,979.00	3,363.11	25,786.89	47.12
Real property maintenance	4,500	2,946.50	374.28	1,179.22	65.48
Equipment leasing	2,600	1,438.71	352.39	808.90	55.34
Riot agents	1,000	0.00	0.00	1,000.00	0.00
Ammunition	2,500	524.07	745.00	1,230.93	20.96
Investigation fee	4,000	2,057.46	538.00	1,404.54	51.44
Xerox	7,000	2,370.36	625.60	4,204.04	33.86
Fuel and lubricants	108,000	42,103.88	10,000.00	55,896.12	38.99
Janitorial supplies	4,000	1,082.73	808.46	2,308.81	27.07
Uniforms	31,500	10,004.56	3,955.75	17,539.69	31.76
Protective equipment	6,530	1,007.18	1,118.31	4,404.51	15.42
Intoximeter	800	220.53	82.60	496.87	27.57
Cash match	812	0.00	0.00	0.00	0.00
Pistol team	1,500	803.96	681.10	14.94	53.60
Swat team	3,000	66.74	600.00	2,333.26	2.22
Capital teams	84,173	13,713.62	63,685.82	6,773.56	16.29

specific percentage of expenditures in budget categories is reached, his approval is required for any additional expenditures or obligations. Management controls are also retrospective in that a chief may have to initiate corrective action.

Illustrative of this would be preparing a budget amendment request to take surplus funds from one account to cover an account in which a deficit exists. Transfer of funds requests go from the police department to the city's budget officer, through the city manager, and to the city council for their approval if they exceed any latitude given to the city manager by the council for budget administration.

Management controls may also be both retrospective and prospective; the midyear review affords the chief and his command staff the opportunity to examine financial performance and progress toward departmental objectives during the first half of the fiscal year and to plan and take any necessary corrective action for the remaining period. Monitoring actions will occur on a more frequent basis, such as monthly or quarterly, but the midyear review represents a major milestone.

The Audit

The term *audit* refers to the act of verifying something independently.[26] The basic rationale for an audit has been expressed in the following way:

> A fundamental tenet of a democratic society holds that governments and agencies entrusted with public resources and the authority for applying them have a responsibility to render

a full accounting of their activities. This accountability is inherent in the governmental process and is not always specifically identified by legislative provision. This governmental accountability should identify not only the object for which the public resources have been devoted but also the manner and effect of their application.[27]

Audits are concerned with three broad areas of accountability: (1) financial, which focuses on determining whether the financial operations of the police department are conducted properly, whether its reports are presented accurately, and whether it has complied with the applicable laws and regulations; (2) management, which concerns whether the police chief and his subordinate managers are utilizing resources in an efficient and economical manner, along with the identification of any causes of inadequate, inefficient, or uneconomical practices; and (3) program, which determines whether the benefits and objectives that the city council intended to arise and achieve from the operation of the police department during the fiscal year were actually created and attained, along with the causes of any nonperformance.[28]

Figure 13-7 depicts the participants in the audit process; those in the role of auditors vary—for example, they may be part of a state's system of monitoring local finances or, if that provision does not exist, they may be representatives of private sector firms that complement the city's internal audit function. Auditors look for:

1. unauthorized transfers of funds between accounts;
2. failure to compile and submit financial reports punctually;
3. year-end accounting manipulations that move liabilities from one fiscal year to the next;
4. the use of commingled accounts to disguise the use of grant funds for unauthorized purposes;
5. improper computations;
6. the disbursements of funds without adequate documentation;
7. the use of bond proceeds for projects other than those authorized;
8. expenditures in excess of appropriations; and
9. the lack of compliance with established bidding procedures.[29]

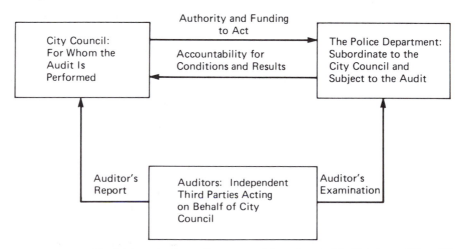

FIGURE 13-7. Participants in the audit process. [From Lennis M. Knighton, ''Four Ways to Audit Effectivenss,'' *Governmental Finance*, 8 (September 1979), p. 9, with modification.]

Before the audit report is submitted, it will be discussed with the chief of police, and any errors of fact or representation in the report will be adjusted. Matters relating to differences of opinion or judgment between the auditors and the chief are usually the subject of a letter from the chief to the city council. After reviewing the auditor's report, the city council may request the formal appearance of the chief to discuss the report or direct the city manager to cause any corrective action required to be initiated.

Although audits may reveal weaknesses and thus are a source of potential professional embarrassment, police managers should welcome them because of the advantages they hold for improved information for decision making, the potential to increase the police department's effectiveness and efficiency, and the opportunity to correct deficiencies that might otherwise lead to the loss of grant funds or other negative consequences.

Budget Formats

At the turn of this century, there was nothing that resembled the budget cycle just described. The situation in California was portrayed by Governor Young as follows:

> When I first entered the legislature in 1909 there was little short of chaos as far as any orderly provisions for state expenditures were concerned. There had been no audit of state finances for over twenty years. The finance committees of the two houses were scenes of a blind scramble on the part of the various institutions and departments of the state in an endeavor to secure as large a portion as possible of whatever money might happen to be in the treasury. Heads of institutions encamped night after night in the committee rooms, each alert for his own interest regardless of the interests of other institutions.[30]

Not only were other states similarly situated, but conditions were not any better in local governments at that time; cities had not yet recovered from the havoc wrought by political rings stealing and squandering enormous sums of public money in earlier years, and waste and extravagance flourished.[31] There were no systematic procedures for handling fiscal matters, there was no comprehensive or long-term financial planning, the total cost of operating a city's government was often unknown or suspect, and one could not tell in advance if the year would end with a surplus or deficit.[32] The practices of the federal government were not sharply differentiated from those of the state and local governments of that time. In 1885, eight committees of the House of Representatives had authority to recommend appropriations; later, this was increased to ten. The Senate was not far behind with appropriating authority given to eight of its standing committees.[33] The assertion of Senator Aldrich in 1909 that the Congress had enacted $50,000,000 of wasteful appropriations gave dramatic publicity for the need for reform.[34]

The center of power in budgeting at the turn of the century was with the legislative body; the following factors characterize legislative budgeting at that time:

1. There was no central official who was empowered to review or revise departmental estimates or to make recommendations to the legislature.
2. Most frequently each department's requests were submitted separately, often at different times.

3. Each agency classified accounts in its own way.
4. Departmental requests were often presented as a lump sum without supporting detail.
5. Requests were not related in any way to revenues anticipated.
6. Each department bargained separately with the appropriations committees.
7. There was little or no supervision of department spending.[35]

Illustrative of several of these points is that, when President Taft prepared a budget for the national government for the 1914 fiscal year and submitted it to Congress, it was coldly received and practically ignored.[36] However, strong forces were at work that led to budgeting reforms at all levels of government. The most significant development was the advent of the executive budget, in which every department submits its estimates to the chief executive of the unit of government involved or his designated representative, which created centralized control. Centralized control hastened, if not made possible, standardized budget cycles, budget formats, and other tools.

The forces that contributed to budgeting reforms include the writings about municipal corruption by such "muckrakers" as Ida Tarbell, Ray Baker, and Lincoln Steffens;[37] the 1899 Model Municipal Corporation Act, which proposed a budget system under the direct supervision of the mayor; the influence of the scientific management movement; the formation of the New York Bureau of Municipal Research in 1906, which brought together such luminaries as Frederick Cleveland, William Allen, and Henry Bruère, who undertook an immediate study of New York City's budgeting and published in 1907 the influential *Making a Municipal Budget;*[38] the good government and city manager movements during the second decade of the century; and the 1916 issuance of a model city charter by the National Municipal League. It is interesting to note that the rise of the executive budget, with its centralized control and standardized budget cycles and formats developed in the cities, spread to the states during 1915–1925,[39] and only appeared in the federal government in 1921 with the passage of the Budget and Accounting Act.

The flow of these events is important from two key perspectives: first, it accounts for the control orientation of the first budget format widely adopted; second, it underpins the notion that each prevailing budget format is understood and appreciated best as a product of the period in which it evolved.

Six different budget formats are covered in the sections that follow. Some have enjoyed a period of dominance, but these periods are difficult to identify precisely because the rhetoric of the budget literature and actual practices do not always coincide. The *line-item budget* remains the single most commonly employed budget format and is associated generally with the period 1915 to just after World War II. *Performance budgets* came into vogue following World War II until about 1960. The *planning-programming budget system* was a dominant theme in the literature from 1960 to 1971, but it was never practiced widely outside of the federal government. *Programmatic budgets* evolved during the early 1970's and variants of it presently abound. *Zero-based budgets* gained attention in the literature in the early 1970s, but they have not been adopted widely by state and local governments. *Hybrid budgets* have always existed, and in actual practice most budgets incorporate features of several different formats.

When attempting to decide what type of a budget a police department uses, the test is not which label is applied—since labels are often used almost indiscriminately—but rather what the emphasis of the format is.

The Line-Item or Object-of-Expenditure Budget

The line-item or object-of-expenditure budget[40] is the oldest and simplest of budget types. It is the basic system upon which all other budget types rely because of its excellence as a control device. As suggested by Table 13-5, the line-item budget derives its identity from its character; every amount requested, recommended, appropriated, and expended is associated with a particular item or class of items; it is therefore described as an input-oriented budget. A budgetary format keyed to objects of expenditure fosters control in a number of ways:

1. Control is comprehensive because no item escapes scrutiny.
2. There are multiple points at which control can be exercised.
3. Control is exact in that expenditures for very specific items can be regulated.[41]

The structure of a line-item budget typically involves the use of about four major categories, each of which has a number of standardly defined categories that are used throughout city government. In police departments large enough for functional specialization, there will be an overall budget and the budget will be broken down into smaller line-item budgets for the various organizational entities such as patrol, investigation, and crime prevention. These smaller budgets serve further to facilitate control and serve as the basis of allocations within the police department. Work load indicators for past years and the forthcoming budget year may also be included as part of a line-item budget. Typically such things as numbers of (1) arrests by various categories, (2) calls for service, (3) traffic and parking citations, (4) accident investigations, and (5) criminal investigations, along with other indicators, such as miles patrolled, will be included.

The line-item budget has five rather straightforward advantages: (1) it is easy to construct; (2) because incremental changes in the appropriations are made annually on the basis of the history of expenditures, the likelihood of the police department having a budget that is grossly inadequate is reduced; (3) it is easy to understand; (4) it is easy to administer; and (5) control is comprehensive. On balance, there are also some clear disadvantages to this budget format: (1) the emphasis on control results in an orientation toward the input to the detriment of managing toward results; (2) long-range planning is neglected; (3) any correlations between the input and results occur at only a very gross level, such as numbers of arrests made; and (4) it has limited utility with respect to evaluating performance.

As a final note, the line-item budget format tends to favor continuation of the police department's status quo—a disadvantage to the reform chief but an advantage to one who has less energy and drive.

The Performance Budget

The key characteristic of a performance budget is that it relates the types and volume of work to be done to the amount of money spent.[42] As an efficiency-oriented tool, the performance budget can be described as input-output centered. The single most important consequence of performance budgeting is that it increases the responsibility and accountability of police managers for output as opposed to input.[43] As a management-oriented system, the performance budget incorporates the following features:

TABLE 13-5. The Object of Expenditure Budget for The Houston, Texas, Police Department[a]

FISCAL YEAR 1986 BUDGET

DEPARTMENT: POLICE
FUND NUMBER: 111000/3000
DIVISION: ALL

Acct.	Acct. description	1984 Actual	1985 Budget	1985 Estimate	1986 Proposed
1101	Salaries & Wages	20,773,305	23,387,035	23,388,561	23,928,034
1102	Overtime	294,465	351,600	343,000	353,000
1103	Classified Salaries	102,966,294	115,940,110	115,939,428	126,137,032
1104	Classified Overtime	6,156,192	8,842,903	8,842,903	7,094,500
1000	Subtotal—Personnel	130,190,256	148,521,648	148,513,892	157,512,566
2110	Postage	109,764	136,000	110,000	120,000
2120	Printing	21,459	57,500	46,000	50,300
2122	Photographic	75,903	120,000	110,000	120,000
2125	Graphic Arts Supplies	4,548	6,100	5,200	5,200
2130	Computer Supplies	26,186	55,775	45,775	33,740
2140	Books Reports & Publicats	28,133	48,853	42,730	48,870
2150	General Office Supplies	237,163	378,081	300,000	380,000
2210	Vehicle Fuel	3,675,005	3,374,038	3,327,435	3,009,500
2230	Clng & Sanitary Supplies	76,391	83,925	81,000	91,600
2240	Chemicals	9,240	12,441	7,003	9,200
2245	Ordinance and Chemicals	102,710	114,150	130,700	114,150
2250	Food	150,437	183,422	175,000	185,000
2252	Clothing	639,963	1,330,515	1,083,000	1,310,000
2255	Clothing Allowance	330,505	341,000	340,815	356,000
2260	Animal Supplies	6,931	9,400	9,400	30,300
2265	Apparatus/Meas Device	2,238	16,860	10,700	13,300
2270	Small Tools and Utensils	36,819	67,800	63,500	36,250
2275	Small Office Instr Equip	10,351	16,400	11,900	16,500
2290	Misc Operating Supplies	77,056	117,695	109,590	146,110
2410	Drugs and Chemicals	4,038	4,959	3,000	6,250
2430	Surgical Supplies	2,183	2,400	2,500	5,750
2440	Laboratory Supplies	21,404	34,519	22,000	36,600
2490	Misc Medical Supplies	186	13,730	11,900	15,750
2000	Subtotal—Gen Supplies	5,648,613	6,525,563	6,049,148	6,140,370
2505	Vehicle & Mtr Equip PMS	1,146,563	1,356,660	1,156,060	1,267,200
2510	Vehicle & Mtr Equip TBA	416,409	427,799	364,952	350,250
2515	Vehicle Oil & Lubricants	89,908	76,744	55,930	67,550
2520	Machinery & Tools PMS	1,878	7,150	5,000	7,150
2525	Inst and Apparatus PMS	8,360	21,817	14,500	19,100
2530	Measuring Devices PMS	0	600	520	930
2540	Furniture & Fixtures PMS	372	0	0	1,000
2544	Computer Equipment	444	1,600	1,600	1,600
2545	Office & Repro Equip PMS	3,000	3,041	3,000	3,000
2550	Elec & Commun Equip PMS	304,247	427,050	427,050	400,000
2555	Land & Building PMS	113,047	129,836	119,400	160,000
2561	Traffic Sign PMS	822	1,000	1,000	1,000
2575	Sanitary Sewer PMS	458	600	600	600
2590	Misc PMS/Maint Contracts	5,179	17,000	13,600	15,000
2500	Subtotal—Maint Supplies	2,090,687	2,470,897	2,163,212	2,294,380

TABLE 13-5 (*Continued*)

Acct.	Acct. description	1984 Actual	1985 Budget	1985 Estimate	1985 Proposed
3110	Car Allowance	94,830	89,100	111,600	111,000
3115	Communications	(244)	0	0	0
3120	Telephone	1,085,631	1,189,100	1,200,000	1,250,000
3125	Electric	1,211,201	1,190,000	1,240,000	1,300,000
3130	Natural Gas	199,007	165,000	215,000	200,000
3135	Water and Sewer	81,655	134,398	115,000	100,000
3150	Office Space—Rent/Lease	252,288	409,784	298,000	500,000
3160	Equipment Rental—Vehicles	22,584	107,144	90,200	107,200
3175	Equip Rental—Office Repro	462,686	590,000	525,000	500,000
3180	Other Rentals	92,112	91,960	89,802	94,310
3190	Misc Operations Services	174,247	335,891	249,291	336,440
3191	Special Services—Grants	0	0	0	22,000
3192	Contract Janitorial Servs	128,588	151,041	151,041	192,000
3210	Legal	810	0	0	0
3215	Advertising	3,684	37,900	26,000	30,000
3220	Medical and Dental	121,329	175,500	134,500	204,700
3225	Computer Services	127,050	189,300	125,700	420,000
3230	Consultant	(95)	101,480	57,427	64,800
3233	Security Service Guards	43,618	66,130	66,130	66,130
3235	Publication-Reproduction	72,986	115,113	104,713	115,100
3290	Misc Support Services	46,298	71,175	60,758	77,130
3291	Demolition—Non Federal	0	0	0	3,200
3000	Subtotal—Gen Services	4,220,265	5,210,016	4,860,162	5,694,020
3510	Veh & Motorized Equip Serv	692,828	771,199	682,605	715,650
3520	Machinery and Tools Serv	1,046	1,050	500	1,050
3525	Inst and Apparatus Serv	36,262	49,198	46,624	52,100
3530	Measuring Devices Serv	2,132	3,326	3,301	3,300
3540	Furn and Fixt Serv	370	4,500	0	3,500
3544	Computer Equipment Serv	32	0	500	2,000
3545	Office & Repro Equip Serv	32,591	119,527	81,000	119,530
3550	Communications Equip Serv	22,041	23,295	18,000	23,300
3555	Land & Buildings Service	88,421	137,535	198,350	237,580
3570	Conduits and Connect Serv	11,628	27,800	16,811	27,000
3590	Misc Maintenance Service	31,279	71,400	46,809	62,000
3500	Subtotal—Maint Services	918,630	1,208,830	1,094,500	1,247,010
4120	Memberships & Dues	1,651	2,220	3,000	4,000
4130	Ins—Prop and Liability	6,272	0	0	0
4135	Surpl Prop and Supplies	2,671	471	471	470
4150	Criminal Intelligence	176,699	185,200	185,200	185,200
4190	Miscellaneous Expenses	69,392	100	0	25,000
4245	Travel/Training	182,967	212,164	198,049	217,450
4250	Local Travel Reimb	133	0	0	0
4255	Education and Training	102,924	421,380	465,380	500,000
4000	Subtotal—Other Charges	542,709	821,535	852,100	932,120
4515	Land Improvements	1,795	150,565	78,647	113,900
4525	Buildings—Struct & Imprvt	1,424	109,900	48,600	162,800
4539	Other Capital Proj Costs	1,600	0	0	95,000
4550	Office & Repro Equip	41,079	382,242	148,340	308,310
4551	Machinery & Tools	1,794	149,015	148,965	30,750

(*cont.*)

TABLE 13-5 (*Conclusion*)

Acct.	Acct. description	1984 Actual	1985 Budget	1985 Estimate	1986 Proposed
4555	Computer Equipment	3,963	46,800	45,000	37,000
4556	Radio Communication Equip	5,535	404,121	129,360	310,770
4557	Instruments & Apparatus	1,135	125,686	46,131	183,220
4558	Other Equipment	7,593	185,144	107,400	213,400
4560	Vehicles	303,369	74,300	60,496	0
4566	Other Vehicles	0	5,000	5,000	0
4570	Motorized Equipment	0	20,000	20,000	0
4571	Misc Equip Attachments	0	0	0	1,100
4580	Audiovisual Equipment	2,056	75,856	62,000	36,150
4585	Photo and Film Equip	3,132	22,250	2,000	31,000
4500	Subtotal—Capital Outlay	374,475	1,750,879	901,939	1,523,400
	Total M&O Expenditures	143,985,635	166,509,368	164,434,953	175,343,966

[a] The Houston Police Department actually employs a programmatic budget; this table merely reflects the line-item portion of it, illustrating that this is the basic format upon which all other budget types depend.

1. A cost structure consisting of the various programs under each of which related functions or activities are clustered.
2. A detailed system of work load and unit cost measures.
3. A line-item component for fiscal control.

While the origin of the performance budget is not universally agreed upon, public sector milestones in the advocacy of its elements and its use and places of adoption are identifiable. This lack of agreement is perhaps best accounted for by the fact that performance budgeting did not spring into use fully developed but rather, evolved over time.

In 1912 the Taft Commission on Economy and Efficiency, which opposed the line-item format, recommended one element associated with performance budgeting— the organization of expenditures around the types of work being done. From 1913 to 1915, the Borough of Richmond, New York City, experimented with a cost data budget,[44] and during the 1920s, periodic mention of this type of budget appeared in the literature.[45] As early as 1939, the Municipal Finance Officers Association advocated a model emphasizing activities grouped under functions. The U.S. Department of Agriculture worked with project and activity budgeting in 1934, and about the same time the Tennessee Valley Authority employed a budget classification of programs and accomplishments.[46] Shortly following the adoption of the city manager form of government in Richmond, Virginia, in 1948, a performance-type budget was implemented.[47]

These various developments received both attention and impetus with the report of the first Hoover Commission in 1949, which called for adoption of a format referred to specifically as a "performance budget." This recommendation was reinforced by the report of the second Hoover Commission in 1955, which applauded the progress made and called for even greater use. In 1950, the federal Budget and Accounting Procedures Act, although not specifically using the term *performance budgeting,* gave further encouragement to its use. Cincinnati began experiments with performance budgeting in about 1950,[48] Maryland adopted it in 1952,[49] and Boston followed in 1955.[50] During the 1950s and very early 1960s, a number of cities experi-

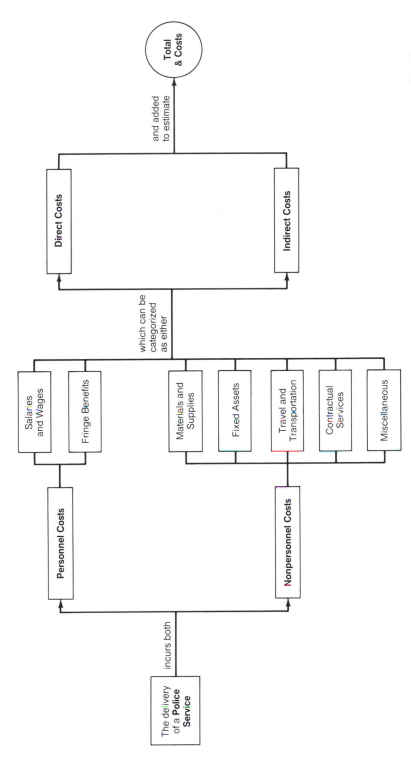

FIGURE 13-8. Elements of total costs for police services. [Source: Kent John Chabotar, *Measuring the Costs of Police Services* (Washington, D.C.: U.S. Department of Justice, National Institute of Justice, 1982), p. 20).]

mented with it, including San Diego, Cleveland, Phoenix, Rochester, and Los Angeles.[51]

The advantages of the performance budget include (1) a consideration of outputs, (2) the establishment of the costs of various police efforts, (3) an improvement in the evaluation of programs and key managers, (4) an emphasis on the responsibility of police managers for output, (5) an emphasis on efficiency, (6) the increased availability of information for managerial decision making, (7) the enhancement of budget justification and explanation and (8) an increased responsibility of police managers, which leads to some decentralization and thus greater participation.

The disadvantages of the performance budget include (1) its expense to develop, implement, and operate given the extensive use of cost accounting techniques and the need for additional staff; Figure 13-8 shows the complexity of using cost accounting to determine total costs; (2) the difficulty and controversies surrounding choosing appropriate work load and unit cost measures; (3) the tendency to generate data more suitable for police managers than for policymakers; (4) its emphasis on efficiency rather than effectiveness; (5) its failure to lend itself to long-range planning; (6) the questionable need, according to police managers, for much of the data; and (7) often the inability to relate community needs systematically to police work load and unit cost measures.

The Planning-Programming Budgeting System (PPBS)

In principle, PPBS or PPB was born and died in the federal government, and its use in state and local government was always negligible. Understanding of it is, however, important in that it is a significant segment of the literature of budgeting and represents part of the stream of thinking and practice devoted to improving budgeting.

To some extent every budget system incorporates planning, management, and control processes.[52] However, only one of these processes can predominate. While PPBS treated the three basic budget processes as compatible and complementary, they were not regarded as co-equal: PPBS was predicated on the primacy of planning.[53] This future orientation of PPBS was to transform budgeting from an "annual ritual" into "formulation of future goals and policies"[54] on a long-range basis. Thus, the singularly unique function of PPBS was to implement policy choices by allocating the resources necessary for their accomplishment. The characteristics of a classical PPBS system include:

1. A program structure.
2. Zero-based budgeting; to be discussed in detail later in this chapter.
3. The use of cost-benefit analysis to distinguish between alternatives.
4. The use of a budgetary time horizon, often five years.
5. The systematic relating of the three basic budgetary processes by a crosswalk system to provide a diversified and comprehensive information base.

General Motors documents reveal that in 1924 it was using a basic PPBS method to identify major objectives, to define programs essential to these goals, and to allocate resources accordingly.[55] The Rand Corporation was a major contributor to the development of PPBS in a series of studies dating from 1949.[56] By the mid-1950s a few states, such as California, Illinois, Kentucky, Washington, North Carolina, and Pennsylvania, were utilizing elements of a PPB system. It remained, however, for Secretary Robert McNamara to introduce PPBS into the Department of Defense for the system to emerge fully in government. In 1965 President Johnson issued a directive calling for its use in the federal government. The "Five-Five-Five" project, fully operational in 1967, sought to test a "true" PPB system in five states, counties, and cities.[57]

A 1971 survey revealed that only 28 percent of the cities and 21 percent of the counties contacted had implemented a PPB system or significant elements of it.[58] Also in 1971, the "death" of PPBS was announced in the federal government by a memorandum from the Office of Management and Budget. The general interest in PPBS faded rapidly as did its practice in the few states and local governments that had adopted it.

Implied and partial explanations of the demise of PPBS are sprinkled throughout the literature and include "fantastic terminological tangles used with a false sophistication" and the absence of a precise definition of PPBS.[59] Since PPBS was born and died in the federal government, analysis of its demise there is most appropriate. The most lucid and complete dissection of PPBS becoming an "unthing" in federal agencies is provided by Schick, who attributes the following factors as leading to its death:[60]

1. PPBS failed because it did penetrate the vital routines of putting together and justifying a budget. Always separate, but never equal, the analysts had little influence over the form or content of the budget.

2. Many analysts failed to comprehend the connection between their work and budgeting. Because they came to PPBS with little administrative or budgetary experience, they did not recognize that the fate of analysis hinges on its use in budgeting.

3. The government-wide application of the Department of Defense's PPBS gave little consideration to the preferences or problems of individual departments.

4. For all its talk about an integrated planning and budgetary system, the Bureau of the Budget kept the two apart, quarantining its tiny PPBS operation from the powerful budget review staffs and promulgating separate PPB and budget instructions.

5. PPBS had become a threat to budgeters and an embarrassment to reformers, reminding the latter of their failure to deliver and the former of the inadequacies of their process.

6. PPBS was introduced without much preparation, inadequate support, and a leadership with too few resources to invest in its behalf.

7. There was neither an adequate number of analysts nor sufficient data, and PPBS did not have enough time to make up the deficit.

8. The implementors of PPBS were arrogantly insensitive to budgetary traditions, institutional loyalties, and personal relationships.

9. PPBS was conceived almost exclusively from an executive perspective, as if Congress did not exist.

10. PPBS failed to penetrate because budgeters did not let it in and PPBS'ers did not know how to break down the resistance.

The explanation that PPB failed because of agency subversion is rejected by Schick, who feels that most departments gave it a try.[61] Another explanation rejected by Schick is that offered by Thompson, who contends that the emphasis on rationality and analysis is at odds with the American political process.[62]

Among the police departments that employed a PPBS at one time are those in Phoenix, Arizona; Dayton, Ohio; Dade County, Florida; and San Diego, California.

The Programmatic or Results Budget

Programmatic or program budget is a term that has been used to describe a variety of practices. In the 1950s and 1960s, it referred to, along with functional or activity budgets, simply using programs as cost centers with little additional data. During the 1960s and early 1970s, it was a popular shorthand used to refer to a PPB system. In the contemporary sense, it refers to budgets that emphasize the results achieved or outcomes produced.

While the literature of budgeting and the practice of federal budgeting was being dominated by PPBS during 1960–1971, the practice of local governmental budgeting was quietly undergoing change. Performance budgeting, with its emphasis upon work load and cost measures, did not disappear entirely, and there was considerable interest in the achievement of policy aspects of PPBS. The result was the evolution of a budget type that incorporated features from the performance and PPBS formats and is referred to as a results, outcomes, objectives, or programmatic—in the contemporary sense—budget. In general, a programmatic budget typically includes

1. A statement of need as established by legal mandates, executive orders, the population to be served, or other related indicators.
2. A program structure.
3. The identification of objectives to be achieved within each of the programs identified.
4. A brief work plan.
5. Limited and carefully selected work load and cost measures for each of the programs identified.
6. A line-item component for fiscal control.

Additionally, multiyear projections may be included, although the practice is probably more honored in its breach than in its observance.

Table 13-6 illustrates a portion of a programmatic budget for a sheriff's office. A review of the six elements identified previously as typically being included as part of the structure of the programmatic format and of Table 13-6 reveals that all six elements are present. Note, however, that, whereas some of the elements are clearly immediately identifiable, (e.g., there are work load and cost measures and a line-item component for fiscal control), other elements, although present, are less immediately identifiable. For example, no overall program structure is presented, but it can be properly inferred from the designation of the portion of the budget presented as being the Northern Field Operations Program that there is a larger structure that encompasses other programs such as detention and investigations.

The advantages of the program budget include (1) an emphasis upon the social utility of programs conducted by the police department; (2) a clear relationship between policy objectives and expenditures; (3) organizational behavior that is directed at the attainment of specific objectives; (4) its ability to provide a good basis for justifying and explaining the budget; (5) its facilitating citizen understanding of police programs

TABLE 13-6   A Portion of the San Diego County Sheriff's Department's Programatic Budget

Program: Northern Field Operations   # 12001   **Manager:** B. R. Oldham, Inspector

Department: Sheriff   # 2400   Ref: Pr. Yr. Bud. Volume, pg. I-268

Function: Public Protection   # 10000   Service: Police Protection   # 11000

Authority: The county charter (section 605) requires the sheriff to provide the county efficient and effective police protection and to perform all the duties required by law. The government code (sections 26600–26602) requires the sheriff to preserve the peace, to make arrests, to prevent unlawful disturbances that come to his attention and to investigate public offenses that have been committed.

	Actual 1976–77	Actual 1977–78	Budget 1978–79	Adopted 1979–80	% Change from 1978–79 budget
Costs					
Direct					
Salaries and benefits	$1,798,375	$2,096,835	$2,102,757	$2,408,949	15%
Services and supplies	40,613	96,263	55,833	78,923	41
Direct costs	$1,838,988	$2,193,098	$2,158,590	$2,487,872	15
Indirect					
Dept. overhead	25,983	34,524	33,122	35,252	6
Ext. support/overhead	787,628	866,280	940,809	938,845	1
Capital Outlay Fund	—	—	—	—	—
Total costs	$2,652,599	$3,093,902	$3,132,521	$3,582,722	14
Funding					
Charges, fees, etc.	29,118	36,166	36,650	36,600	(1)
Subventions	—	—	—	—	—
Grants	—	—	—	—	—
CETA	—	50,000	20,000	15,000	(25)
Interfund charges	—	—	—	—	—
Total Funding	29,118	86,166	56,650	51,600	(9)
Net County Costs	$2,623,481	$3,007,736	$3,075,871	$3,531,122	15
Capital Program					
Capital outlay	$ 71,082	—	—	—	—
Fixed assets	3,317	$ 25,740	$ 4,660	$ 3,600	(23)
Vehicles/communications	60,552	18,069	20,242	35,581	76
Revenue	—	—	—	—	—
Net cost	$ 134,951	$ 43,809	$ 24,902	$ 39,181	57
Staff Years					
Direct program	94.60	107.06	101.68	112.98	11
CETA	—	5.00	2.00	2.00	—
Dept. overhead	.882	.91	1.00	1.03	3

Program Statement

Need: The citizens of northern San Diego County have unique and varied needs as a result of the heterogeneous characteristics of the area. With a densely populated coastal belt, sparsely populated agricultural areas, miles of recreational beaches, and the forests of Palomar Mountain, the rapidly growing North County consists of 539 square miles with a resident population of 186,000 persons. The sheriff's jurisdiciton also includes the cities of Del Mar, San Marcos, and Vista, which contract for police services. The coastal communities, with high tourist volumes and sizable transient population, also have one of the highest property crime rates in the county.

Description: Law enforcement services in the unincorporated North County and contract cities are provided by resources deployed from the Vista and Encinitas stations and officers located in Valley Center and Fallbrook. Sheriff's personnel respond to citizen requests for service, investigate reported crimes, and serve civil process. Officers are specifically responsible for protecting lives and property, effecting arrests, preserving the peace, and preventing crime through the maintenance of a visible posture. Specialized resources are available to North County residents, in the form of air support, reserves, and selective enforcement teams.

TABLE 13-6 *(Continued)*

Need and performance indicators	Actual 1976–77	Actual 1977–78	Budget 1978–79	Actual 1978–79	Adopted 1979–80
Vista Patrol (56%)					
Need					
Population	63,320	64,000	74,750	74,750	81,650
Effective square miles	361	361	361	361	361
Population per effective square mile	175	177	207	207	226
Workload					
Calls for service per 1,000 population	193	194	210	199	208
Thefts per 1,000 population	22	25	20	23	24
Reports taken	2,302	2,168	2,076	2,923	3,332
Total arrests	838	810	815	896	940
Citations	945	791	691	837	878
Efficiency					
Cost to respond to each call for service	84.00	97.00	77.00	81.00	82.00
Productivity index					
Calls per unit	1,373	1,093	1,540	1,460	1,705
Effectiveness					
Average response time to priority calls	15.3	14.0	14.0	8.5	8.5
Auth. patrol units per 10,000 population	0.70	0.77	0.77	0.73	0.80
Encinitas Patrol (44%)					
Need					
Population	54,130	55,000	58,950	58,950	60,350
Effective square miles	46.4	46.4	46.4	46.4	46.4
Population per effective square mile	1,160	1,185	1,270	1,270	1,300
Work load					
Calls for service per 1,000 population	304	316	327	342	359
Thefts per 1,000 population	38	38	40	47	51
Reports taken	3,574	3,300	3,000	3,986	4,185
Total arrests	1,329	1,558	1,656	1,683	1,884
Citations	1,319	1,870	2,132	1,320	1,399
Efficiency					
Cost to respond to each call for service	51.00	55.00	48.00	41.00	56.00
Productivity index					
Calls per unit	1,096	1,271	1,285	1,344	1,444
Effectiveness					
Average response time to priority calls	6.9	7.3	6.9	7.3	7.3
Auth. patrol units per 10,000 population	1.03	0.93	0.93	0.83	0.93

Unit cost Defined: $\dfrac{\text{Total direct cost per activity.}}{\text{Calls for service per Activity}}$ Productivity index Defined: $\dfrac{\text{Total calls per Activity.}}{\text{Number of units per activity.}}$

Comments on degree of achievement of 1978–79 objectives:

1. Crime prevention programs and training programs continued at the station level (Encinitas and Vista).

2. Average response time for priority calls decreased to 8.5 minutes in Vista while Encinitas increased average response time to 7.3 minutes.

1979–80 proposed objectives:

1. To continue community-based crime prevention and training programs at the station level (Encinitas and Vista).

2. To maintain the average priority response time within the Vista command at 8.5 minutes and within the Encinitas command at 7.3 minutes.

TABLE 13-6 (*Continued*)

| | Staffing schedule | | | |
| | Staff years | | Salary and benefit costs | |
Classification	Budgeted 1978–79	Adopted 1979–80	Budgeted ($) 1978–79	Adopted ($) 1979–80
Sheriff's inspector	1.00	1.00	$ 38,060	$ 38,943
Sheriff's captain	2.00	2.00	63,077	64,326
Sheriff's lieutenant	3.00	3.00	81,711	79,522
Sheriff's sergeant	11.56	12.56	269,295	298,044
Deputy sheriff	71.12	79.12	1,470,366	1,636,192
Senior stenographer	1.00	1.00	12,617	14,276
Senior clerk typist	2.00	2.00	27,129	27,943
Intermediate stenographer	5.00	5.00	63,150	60,695
Intermediate clerk typist	2.00	6.00	24,158	65,751
Country deputy sheriff	1.00	1.00	8,880	9,683
Extra help	2.00	2.00	17,559	19,958
CETA	2.00	2.00	21,627	17,453
	—	—	—	—
Adjustments			5,088	157,468
Additional salary savings	—	(1.70)	—	(81,305)
Total direct program	103.68	114.98	$2,102,757	$2,408,949
Department overhead	1.00	1.03	23,613	27,967
Program totals	104.68	116.01	$2,126,370	$2,436,916

Courtesy of San Diego County Sheriff's Office.

and objectives; (6) its establishing a high degree of accountability; and (7) its format and the wide involvement in formulating objectives, which leads to police officers at all levels of the department understanding more thoroughly the importance of their role and actions.

The disadvantages of this budget type include (1) its cost in terms of time and dollars to develop, implement, and administer; (2) the fact that police managers may be resistant to increased accountability; (3) difficulties associated with developing appropriate objectives and performance measures; (4) the fact that the city council may rely on the line-item portion of the budget to make adjustments in appropriations, negating the policy value of this format and causing serious problems in the execution of programs; and (5) the fact that police managers responsible for the various programs may not have been or may not be interested in developing the skills necessary for directing large-scale and complex programs.

Zero-Based Budgets

The concept of a zero base is not new. It is one of the elements associated with PPBS, and the FY '64 budget submitted by the U.S. Department of Agriculture was a zero-based budget. An analysis of that experience revealed that it produced only $200,000 in changes in the department's budget while consuming at least 180,000 person-hours of effort.[63]

Based on Peter Phyrr's use of a zero-based budget (ZBB) at the Texas Instruments Company, Jimmy Carter, then Governor of Georgia, implemented it in that state during the early 1970s. After election to national office, Carter announced that ZBB would be implemented in the federal government for FY '79. Other governmental adopters have included New Mexico, Montana; New Jersey; Texas; Arlington County, Virginia; Wilmington, Delaware; and Orange County, Florida. Some agencies, such as the Portland, Oregon, Police Bureau, at one time used variants that incorporate many of the features of a ZBB.

As popularly understood and in the most literal sense, ZBB implies preparing a budget without any reference to what was done before.[64] This interpretation has been widely condemned as naïve and impractical;[65] such an application would unproductively utilize enormous amounts of energy, and the product would be likely to confuse, if not overwhelm, decision makers. As actually practiced, ZBB involves the use of marginal analysis techniques to see how various levels of funding affect the delivery of services. The heart of ZBB is a four-step analytical process:

1. *Establishment of budget decision units.* The decision unit (DU) represents the smallest entity for which a budget is prepared in the police department. Every DU has an identified manager empowered to make all decisions regarding the budget submission. As a practical matter, DUs tend to coincide with the police department's organizational structure.

2. *Budget unit analysis.* The police manager responsible for the DU must conduct a detailed appraisal of the purpose and operations of the unit prior to any consideration of costs. This critical examination includes asking the zero-base question of what consequences would there be if this DU were eliminated, clarifying objectives, describing current operations, analyzing for potential productivity improvements, and specifying the measures that can be used best to justify and monitor the DUs work load and performance.[66]

3. *Service level analysis.* The manager responsible for the DU must next define the service priorities and structure them into a series of incremental packages of activities, resources, and projected performances. Called ''decision packages'' in some ZBB systems and ''service levels'' in others, these incremental packages are the building blocks for the budget request ultimately submitted by the police department. The first package is designated as the base, the minimum service level, and is the deepest possible programmatic and economic reduction short of the total elimination of the DU. The second package provides an additional level of service above the base; the third package provides an increment of service above the second package; and so forth.

4. *Ranking.* After the lower-level DU managers in the police department have prepared the decision packages, they are placed in a priority ranking by the department's command staff in a group session. Table 13-7 reflects the priority ordering for thirty-seven packages used by the Portland Police Bureau in developing its fiscal 1981 request. Note that the first five choices represent the base for certain key areas of the organization but that the sixth choice, an incremental increase in precinct operations services, was given a slightly higher priority than the base for special operations. The priority list, also referred to as a ranking table, is important because once a level of funding is selected, the ''line is drawn,'' meaning that lower-priority packages are not funded. In the case of the Portland Police Bureau's fiscal 1981 requests, packages 23 to 37 fell below the line.

The advantages of a ZBB include (1) a fresh approach to planning by requiring police managers to ask the question, ''Why are we doing this?''; (2) the duplication of effort is identified and eliminated; (3) emphasis can be given to priority programs;

(4) marginally effective and nonproductive programs can be rationally eliminated; (5) there is better information for managerial decision making;[67] (6) the evaluation of the police department's performance and that of its subordinate managers is strengthened; (7) it improves communications between different levels of the police department; (8) budget information and justification is improved; (9) it fosters better linkages between police operational planning and budgeting; and (10) police managers are involved in budgeting in a more substantive way.[68] The disadvantages include (1) the number of decision packages may become overwhelming—the fiscal 1973 use of ZBB in state government in Georgia, for example, contained an estimated 10,000 of them; (2) the process of developing the system and each annual budget request requires the use of considerable resources; (3) the process is weakened considerably by poorly prepared decision packages; (4) police managers may not be very motivated to undertake critical self-examinations; and (5) the system may implicitly foster a belief that increased funds are the only way in which to increase services, causing police managers to neglect other means of improving productivity.

The zero-based budget (ZBB) represents the last major innovation designed to improve budgeting. In 1980, some knowledgeable observers of the budgetary scene predicted that ZBB would experience the same sort of mercurial fall that PPBS did. Although ZBB has not been officially pronounced as deceased, by 1986 it was infrequently practiced as described herein. Moreover, the Portland, Oregon, Police Department no longer practices it as shown in Table 13-7. Portland adopted ZBB during a time of financial pressure; as these pressures declined there was more resistance from managers throughout the city who did not want to go through the ZBB process. As a consequence, Portland moved to a budget with a program structure and no performance indicators. Subsequently, police managers found that they did not have the data to resist budget cuts—one estimate is that as a result of budget cuts after abandoning ZBB, the police department's response time to calls gradually increased by approximately two minutes. The legacy of ZBB is that many departments that use a line-item or some other format have incorporated the use of decision packages into the budget request process. For example, in Fort Worth, Texas, a decision package (DP) is a narrative and financial description of a service or a program that is part of the police department's budget request. In Fort Worth there are four types of DPs:

1. reduction or elimination of an existing service or program;
2. continuation of an existing service or program;
3. expansion of an existing service or program; and
4. addition of a new service or program.

Thus, although increasingly less practiced, ZBB has contributed to the evolution of budgetary practices and the decision package continues to be part of the language and practice of financial management.

Hybrid Budgets

Although it is important to understand the orientations of different budgeting systems, their emphases, and their relative advantages and disadvantages, budget systems can be discussed with a great deal more purity than they exist in actual practice. Most police budget systems are a hybrid of several approaches that are blended together

TABLE 13-7. Portland, Oregon, Police Bureau Package Ranking and Summary[a]

(1)		(2)	(3)	(4)	(5)	(6)
Rank		Package name/Number/Description	Full-time positions 1980–81	Approved budget 1979–80	Discretionary request 1980–81	Total request 1980–81
1	PO-1	Precinct Operations Base	372.38	$10,735,358	$12,112,450	$12,150,118
2	SER-1	Services Base	17.38	819,008	757,399	807,116
3	INV-1	Investigations base	204.76	5,862,717	6,307,822	6,356,935
4	REC-1	Records base	76.06	1,459,476	1,461,595	1,595,200
5	MGT-1	Management base	20.93	545,964	740,111	740,527
6	PO-2	Current service level	28.84	663,261	713,371	713,371
7	SO-1	Special operations base	11.27	445,500	427,424	447,676
8	TRA-1	Traffic base	65.90	2,397,426	2,663,063	2,664,588
9	CPD-2A	Locks project	6.06	234,282	2,406	231,351
10	SER-2	Current service level	13.08	324,770	359,831	371,775
11	REC-2	Current service level	8.14	128,795	137,645	137,645
12	REC-3	CRISS conversion	4.00	—	86,447	86,447
13	INV-2	Current service level	7.50	218,586	217,212	220,467
14	CPD-1	Crime prevention base, target level	11.32	804,371	392,396	571,179
15	TRA-2	Current service level	10.22	318,810	317,638	317,638
16	SER-3	Affirmative action, court coordinator, word processor	5.00	—	83,988	83,988
17	MGT-2	Current service level (word processor)	1.16	—	32,144	32,144
18	MGT-3	Legal advisor	1.00	—	16,508	16,508
19	PO-4	Horses, horse patrol(6)	7.00	—	225,853	225,853
20	REC-4	Shelving	—	—	127,000	127,000
21	PO-6	Reserves	—	—	9,154	9,154
22	INV-5	Cameras, bureau request	—	—	2,004	2,004
		Total request	872.00		$27,079,161	$27,794,384

23	PO-3	Annexation	12.00	270,240	270,240
24	INV-3	CJO	2.00	53,333	53,333
25	CPD-2B	GF transition	—	175,844	175,844
26	REC-5	Property room	—	5,000	5,000
27	INV-4	Paraprofessional	2.00	34,551	34,551
28	TRA-3	Prior current service level	10.00	251,211	251,211
29	REC-6	Current years planned service level	8.00	105,903	105,903
30	SER-4	Evaluation system, background checks	2.00	76,159	76,159
31	SER-5	LET, instructors	8.00	151,889	151,889
32	REC-7	Purge record files	6.00	83,495	83,495
33	INV-7	Prior current service level	7.00	159,508	159,508
34	INV-6	New ID technicians	4.00	66,034	66,034
35	MGT-4	Command coordinator	1.00	32,921	32,921
36	REC-8	New files	—	24,000	24,000
37	PO-5	Horses, horse patrol(2)	2.00	49,187	49,187
		Total all packages	936.00	$28,618,436	$29,333,659

[a] The Portland Police Bureau no longer uses ZBB, but for illustration purposes its FY '81 ZBB Format is shown.

[Courtesy of Portland, Oregon, Police Bureau.]

to meet the particular needs of a unit of government. Given the different approaches, the relative emphasis that can be placed on them, and the sheer frequency of hybrid budget systems, one should not be startled when examining a police department's budget to find that it is not clearly one type or another. Nor should judgments be made too quickly about the "rightness" of what has been done. To understand and appreciate it in context, one must understand the needs, resources, and priorities that led to its implementation, another manifestation of the political nature of financial management.

Strategies for Supplementing the Police Budget

Police departments can employ a variety of tactics to reduce the cost of delivering services such as using volunteers and replacing officers with less costly civilian positions whenever possible. This section focuses on strategies for supplementing the department's budget by: (1) obtaining grants from federal agencies and general foundations; (2) implementing donation programs; (3) taking advantage of forfeiture laws; (4) initiating user fees; (5) enacting police tax legislation; and (6) applying for Internal Revenue Service rewards.[69]

Federal and General Foundation Grants

Over the past twenty years, grant-awarding organizations—such as the now defunct Law Enforcement Assistance Administration, the Highway Traffic Safety Administration, and to a lesser extent general foundations—have been important sources of funding external to the normal budgeting process of police departments. Some recipients of grants, despite provisions to prohibit such employment, have substituted the money for resources that otherwise would have been appropriated or expended by the unit of government involved.

Grants have been used for a variety of endeavors, including the purchase of vehicles, riot equipment, and communications centers; for training; to create regional crime laboratories, frequently emphasizing the examination of narcotics evidence; and to develop special efforts in such areas as crime prevention, alcohol safety-accident prevention, family crisis intervention, and programs for rape victims and the elderly. Many police agencies became adept at getting grants by locating potential grantors in the *Federal Directory of Domestic Aid Programs* and elsewhere and by preparing well-conceived, responsive proposals.

The reasons for pursuing grants have been varied. Occasionally, it was done simply to get the city manager "off the back" of the chief or to provide "evidence" that the chief was a "good administrator." In other instances, law enforcement agencies accepted grants urged on them by the funding source for experimental or demonstration projects. In such cases, at least some police agencies had little commitment to the "pet project" of the grantor but accepted the grant in the belief that it would create goodwill at the time when the grantor was considering some future proposal from that police department or in the belief that enough equipment or other resources would remain as a useful residue from the project, regardless of its other merits. Often missing in the various machinations involved in "getting the money" was a strong management analysis of certain factors:

1. What problem or need, if any, will go unmet in the absence of the grant funds?
2. What would be the probable qualitative and quantitative impact of not meeting the problem or need?
3. What would be the qualitative and quantitative impact on police services of using the grant funds?
4. If a multiyear grant, what are the consequences and probabilities of midproject termination or reduced funding?
5. How many sworn and civilian employees will be added to the total personnel complement who may have to be continued on the payroll at the end of the project?
6. Will any equipment or facilities be acquired that nongrant funds ultimately will have to maintain?
7. What obligations are incurred with respect to continuing the effort initiated following the termination of the grant period?
8. Must the police department provide some matching contribution to the project? If so, how much? Can it be an in-kind match, such as providing space, or must the match be in actual funds? If actual funds are required, will it come from the police department's budget or from a special municipal fund established for just such purposes?
9. What operational or financial procedures have to be changed to meet grant requirements?
10. What ongoing programs will be brought under new state or federal regulations as a result of receiving the grant, in what way, and at what costs?
11. What will be the cost of the administrative overhead outside of the police agency necessary to support the administration of the grant?[70]

None of this is intended to ignore the existence of many exemplary projects that have improved the delivery of police services to the public. However, even in some number of excellent projects, there have been side costs, and the potential for these "hidden" side costs increases inversely with the amount of management planning done when considering whether to take grant funds offered or whether to apply for grant funds. It is also important to note that some police chiefs have deliberately chosen not to raise certain of the issues identified—to the chagrin of their city managers and sometimes at risk of their own jobs—to initiate badly needed programs that could not be funded through the normal budget process.

Donation Programs

Police donation programs may be characterized as single issue or ongoing. Single-issue programs seek to obtain funds for a particular purpose and may be fairly small or large in the level of support they are seeking. Illustratively, the Erie County, New York, sheriff's office got $5,000 from a local bank to renovate an old van for use in a crime-prevention program. More expansive was the raising of $1,500,000 in Chicago over a period of 18 months to buy bulletproof vests for officers. In terms of ongoing donations, in 1971 the New York City Police Foundation was formed as a nonprofit, tax-exempt organization independent of the city with the following goals:

1. enhancement of police-community relations
2. improvement of police service

3. funding of police projects
4. combating police corruption

The projects undertaken by the New York City Police Foundation have been diverse and include providing police scholarships, creating a program to reduce officer hypertension, and establishing a bomb squad. In one recent year this foundation raised $1,300,000 for worthy initiatives. In 1979, the Baltimore County Police Foundation was established for similar efforts.

Forfeiture Laws

There is a wide variety of statutes among the various states regarding forfeitures, but they generally cover cash and property from four categories of crime:

1. narcotics
2. transportation of any contraband goods
3. organized crime, racketeering, and unlawful gambling
4. targeted crimes, e.g., in North Carolina vehicles used in serious drunk-driving cases may be forfeited

Upon seizing airplanes, cash, cars, boats, guns, or other property subject to their state's forfeiture law, law enforcement officers may initiate forfeiture proceedings by making a request to the prosecutor or by retaining a lawyer for that purpose. Care is taken to protect the rights of others who were not involved in the crime and who have a financial interest in the forfeited property, such as a lender who has a lien on an airplane. Four patterns exist regarding how forfeited property is handled:

1. all benefits from the forfeiture go to the unit of government's general fund;
2. the police may keep all property, typically using cars for undercover operations and aircraft for surveillance, but if the property is later sold, the proceeds of the sale go to the unit of government's general fund;
3. the police may keep or sell the property, but if it is sold, the police can keep up to only some ceiling amount, such as $20,000, and any excess goes into a trust fund to which the department can apply for specific uses;
4. all property and cash can be kept by the police department.

Between 1980 and 1983, the Fort Lauderdale Police Department realized forfeitures totaling $5,500,000; Florida law forbids reducing a police department budget because of money acquired through forfeitures, placing the police department in a very advantageous position.

User Fees

User fees can be very controversial when used by police departments. The public accepts being charged a nominal fee to obtain a copy of an accident report and the cost of police permits for parades and special events such as rock concerts. However, cities that have tried to charge for such public services as unlocking car doors to get keys accidentally left inside the vehicle have often had to retreat in face of public outcry. Perhaps the largest and yet least controversial sources of user fees have been charges to hook up alarms to the police monitor or to a computer-aided dispatch (CAD) system, as well as charges to monitor the alarms and the cost of responding to false alarms. In one year, Miami, Florida, collected $270,000 in alarm permit and false alarm fees. Typically user fees end up in the unit of government's general fund, but although not directly strengthening the police budget, they do put managers in a more advantageous position during the budget review process.

Police Taxes

As a reaction to "Proposition 13" limitations some jurisdictions—Palos Verdes, California, for example—have adopted referendums to institute a special police tax. In Palos Verde "Referendum A" allowed a tax of up to $300 per year based on property value to support police services.

Internal Revenue Service Rewards

Realizing that it often arrested racketeers who had not properly reported their income to the Internal Revenue Service, the Atlanta Police Department approached the IRS about collecting the 10 percent informer's fee on unpaid taxes. Subsequently, the city council passed an ordinance allowing the Atlanta Department of Public Safety to apply for rewards on behalf of the city, to be deposited in a special account earmarked for law enforcement activities. Atlanta has already filed thirty-one claims that are pending.

Summary

Some police executives view financial management as an unattractive responsibility. Successful police executives know that money is the fuel upon which police programs operate. The unwillingness to invest a high level of energy in acquiring and managing financial resources is to pre-establish the conditions for mediocre or worse performance by the police department.

Government activities inherently involve public funds; thus financial management is a political process. Illustrative of the entwining of politics and financial administration are state provisions for monitoring and controlling certain aspects of local government finance; the budget preparation instructions given to the various departments by the mayor, city manager, or finance director; the internal dialogue within a police department when deciding how much to request; the development of the city's consolidated budget; the appropriations decision by the city council; and decisions made in the course of executing the budget.

Typically, local government budgets for a twelve-month period are referred to as a fiscal year. In properly administered governments, there is a sequence of four steps that are termed the budget cycle and that are repeated at approximately the same time each year: (1) budget preparation, (2) budget approval, (3) budget execution, and (4) the audit.

Numbers are the basic language in which budgets are expressed; the way in which those numbers and any accompanying narrative are organized is termed the budget format. The oldest, simplest, and most universally employed budget is the line item, because of its ease of construction and the potential for control that it offers. In fact, because of its control feature, it is the base upon which all other formats rest. Each budget format can be associated loosely with a time in which it was the dominant force; sometimes this domination was far greater in the literature than in actual practice. Nonetheless, from the line item forward, each format can be viewed as an attempt to improve and reform the practice of financial management.

In addition to the use of volunteers and the substitution of less costly civilian positions for sworn positions whenever feasible, police executives can strengthen their budgets by (1) federal and general foundation grants, (2) donation programs, (3) forfeitures, (4) user fees, and (5) IRS rewards.

Discussion Questions

1. How can politics and financial management be related usefully?

2. What is the budget cycle and what are the major steps in it?

3. How do the federal and state governments shape the practice of local financial management?

4. What is a fiscal year? What are some examples of different fiscal years?

5. Are there some things that police managers can do to enhance the likelihood of getting their department's budget enacted? If so, what are they?

6. If you were a police manager undergoing an audit of the department's last fiscal year budget, what are some things you would expect to see examined?

7. What are the advantages and disadvantages of the following budget formats?
   a. Line item
   b. Performance
   c. PPBS
   d. Programmatic
   e. ZBB

8. What is the significance of hybrid budgets?

9. You are the recently appointed director of planning and research for the department, and the chief of police has just called you into his office. The chief tells you that he is considering applying for a grant from a federal agency. The chief is seeking your advice as to whether or not to apply. What kinds of perspectives would you encourage the chief to consider?

10. Identify and discuss three strategies for supplementing the police budget.

Notes

1. This idea and several of the examples in the next sentence are taken from Felix A. Nigro and Lloyd G. Nigro, *Modern Public Administration*, 5th ed. (New York: Harper & Row, 1980), p. 337.
2. See National Highway Traffic Safety Administration, "The Impact of Fuel Costs on Law Enforcement," (Washington, D.C.: Mimeographed, February 1, 1980), 11 pp. For a view of some models on police financial stress, see Charles H. Levine, "Police Management in the 1980s: From Decrementalism to Strategic Thinking," *Public Administration Review*, 45 (November 1985), pp. 691–700.
3. Mary Jo Patterson and Arthur K. Lenehan, "Newark Police Accused of Vandalism After Layoff Announcement," *Police* (January 1979), p. 67.

4. San Jose Peace Officers Association, *Vanguard,* 1:6 (September 1979), p. 1.

5. Roland N. McKean, *Public Spending* (New York: McGraw-Hill, 1968), p. 1.

6. Aaron Wildavsky, *The Politics of the Budgetary Process,* 2nd ed. (Boston: Little, Brown, 1974), p. 4.

7. S. Kenneth Howard, *Changing State Budgeting* (Lexington, Ky.: Council of State Governments, 1973), p. 13.

8. Harold F. Gortner, *Administration in the Public Sector* (New York: John Wiley, 1977), p. 315.

9. Advisory Commission on Intergovernmental Relations, *City Financial Emergencies* (Washington, D.C.: U.S. Government Printing Office, 1973), from Table 2-1, p. 10.

10. Advisory Commission on Intergovernmental Relations, *State Mandating of Local Expenditures* (Washington, D.C.: U.S. Government Printing Office, 1978), from Table IV-4, p. 55.

11. No author, "Inflation, Limits, Mandates, Strain Budgets," *Iowa Municipalities,* 34:7 (January 1979), p. 3. Also, see George E. Hale and Marian Lief Palley, "The Impact of Federal Funds on the State Budgetary Process," *National Civic Review,* 67:10 (November 1978), pp. 461–464 and 473.

12. The information in this paragraph is taken from John E. Peterson, C. Wayne Stallings, and Catherine Lavigne Spain, *State Roles in Local Government Financial Management: A Comparative Analysis* (Washington, D.C.: Government Finance Research Center, 1979), pp. 1, 5. The Government Finance Research Center is a nonprofit professional service organization that serves as the research arm of the Municipal Finance Officers Association.

13. The rule is described in ibid., p. 4 as follows: "Dillion's Rule, first espoused by John F. Dillion, a justice of the Supreme Court of Iowa, from 1862 to 1869, and later accepted by courts in many other states and the U.S. Supreme Court, establishes the full legal superiority of the state over local governments." Dillion, himself, stated the rule as follows: "It is a general and undisputed proposition of law that a municipal corporation possess and can exercise the following powers, and no others: First, those granted in express words; second, those necessarily or fairly implied in or incident to the powers expressly granted; third, those essential to the accomplishment of the declared objects and purposes of the corporation—not simply convenient, but indispensable. Any fair, reasonable, substantial doubt concerning the existence of power is resolved by the courts against the corporation, and the power is denied." In states that have a constitutional provision conferring home rule powers on cities, Dillion's Rule is used by the courts in interpreting the scope of home rule powers.

14. Paul Moore and Alan G. Billingsley, "Financial Monitoring of Local Governments," *State Government,* 52 (Autumn 1979), p. 155.

15. A. E. Buck, *The Budgets in Governments of Today* (New York: Macmillan, 1934), p. 5.

16. See James C. Snyder, "Financial Management and Planning in Local Government," *Atlanta Economic Review* (November–December, 1973), pp. 43–47.

17. Wildavsky, *The Politics of the Budgetary Process,* pp. 1–4.

18. Orin K. Cope, "Operation Analysis—The Basis for Performance Budgeting," in *Performance Budgeting and Unit Cost Accounting for Governmental Units* (Chicago: Municipal Finance Officers Association, 1954), p. 8.

19. James W. Martin, "An Economic Criteria for State and City Budget Making," *Public Administration Review,* 24 (March 1964), p. 1.

20. Fritz Morstein Marx, "The Bureau of the Budget: Its Evolution and Present Role, II," *The American Political Science Review,* 39 (August 1945), p. 871.

21. This case is taken from William P. Gloege, "Successful Police Department Budgeting," *Police Chief,* 44:5 (May 1977), pp. 58–59.

22. These strategies, with some change, are essentially those identified by Wildavsky, *The Politics of the Budgetary Process,* pp. 63–123.

23. Margret Minis, "Savannah Will Modify Police Cars for Propane," *The Atlanta Journal and Constitution,* June 1, 1980, p. 4-B.

24. Lennox L. Moak and Kathryn W. Killian, *A Manual of Techniques for the Preparation, Consideration, Adoption, and Administration of Operating Budgets* (Chicago: Municipal Finance Officers Association, 1973), p. 5, with changes.

25. These three types of controls are identified in J. Richard Aronson and Eli Schwartz, eds. *Management Policies in Local Government Finance* (Washington, D.C.: International City Management Association, 1975), pp. 86–87, and are drawn upon with changes here.

26. Lennis M. Knighton, "Four Keys to Audit Effectiveness," *Governmental Finance,* 8 (September 1979), p. 3. Also, see Kenneth S. Caldwell, "Operational Auditing in State and Local Government," *Governmental Finance,* 3–4 (May 1974–1975), pp. 36–43.

27. The Comptroller General of the United States, *Standards for Audit of Governmental Organizations, Programs, Activities, and Functions* (Washington, D.C.: General Accounting Office, 1972), p. 1.

28. These three types of accountability are drawn, with modification, from ibid.

29. Peter F. Rousmaniere, ed., *Local Government Auditing* (New York: Council on Municipal Performance, 1979), from Tables 1 and 2, pp. 10 and 14.

30. A. E. Buck, *Public Budgeting* (New York: Harper and Brothers, 1929), p. 12.

31. Ibid., p. 12.

32. Ibid., p. 12.

33. Jesse Burkhead, *Government Budgeting* (New York: John Wiley, 1956), p. 11.

34. Ibid., p. 17.

35. Allen Schick, *Budget Innovation in the States* (Washington, D.C.: Brookings Institution, 1971), pp. 14–15.

36. Buck, *The Budgets in Governments of Today,* p. 40.

37. Burkhead, *Government Budgeting,* p. 13.

38. Ibid., p. 13.

39. In 1913, Ohio became the first state to adopt the executive budget.

40. Budget purists would argue that there are technical differences between line-item and object-of-expenditure budgets. In common usage and practice, however, they are synonymous.

41. Schick, *Budget Innovation in the States,* p. 23; Schick lists a total of ten ways in which the line-item budget fosters control, but these three sum them up adequately.

42. Malchus L. Watlington and Susan G. Dankel, "New Approaches to Budgeting: Are They Worth the Cost?" *Popular Government,* 43 (Spring 1978), p. 1.

43. Burkhead, *Government Budgeting,* p. 155, with change.

44. Herbert Emmerich, chairman, "Symposium on Budget Theory," *Public Administration Review,* 213 (Winter 1950), p. 26.

45. See, for example, A. E. Buck, "Measuring the Results of Government," *National Municipal Review,* (March 1924), pp. 152–157.

46. Burkhead, *Government Budgeting,* p. 134.

47. Robert B. Elmore, "Performance Budgeting in Richmond, Virginia," *Municipal Finance,* 28:2 (November 1955), p. 77.

48. Vernon E. Koch, "Cincinnati's Budget Developments," *Public Administration Review,* 20:20 (Spring 1960), p. 79.

49. John A. Donaho, "Performance Budgeting in Maryland," *Municipal Finance,* 28:12 (November 1955), p. 69.

50. Joseph P. Lally, "Performance Budgeting in Boston," *Municipal Finance,* 28:2 (November 1955), p. 80.

51. Burkhead, *Government Budgeting,* p. 137.

52. Allen Schick, "The Road to PPB: The Stages of Budget Reform," *Public Administration Review,* 26 (December 1966), p. 244.

53. Ibid., pp. 245–246.

54. Ibid., p. 244.

55. David Novick, ed. *Program Budgeting* (New York: Holt, Rinehart and Winston, 1969), p. xxvi.
56. Ibid., p. xxiv.
57. For information on this project, see Council of State Governments, *State Reports on Five-Five-Five* (Chicago: Council of State Governments, 1968). The states involved were California, Michigan, New York, Vermont, and Wisconsin; the counties were Dade (Florida), Davidson (Tennessee), Los Angeles (California), Nassau (New York), and Wayne (Michigan); and the cities were Dayton, Denver, Detroit, New Haven, and San Diego.
58. International City Management Association, *Local Government Budgeting, Program Planning and Evaluation* (Urban Data Service Report, May 1972), p. 7. Also see Selma J. Mushkin, "PPB in Cities," *Public Administration Review,* 29:2 (March–April 1969), pp. 167–177.
59. These two examples are drawn from Roger H. Jones's "Program Budgeting: Fiscal Facts and Federal Fancy," *Quarterly Review of Economics and Business,* (Summer 1969), p. 45.
60. Allen Schick, "A Death in the Bureaucracy: The Demise of Federal PPB," *Public Administration Review,* 33 (March–April 1973), pp. 146–156.
61. Ibid., p. 148.
62. Ibid., p. 149.
63. Joseph S. Wholey, *Zero-Base Budgeting and Program Evaluation* (Lexington, Mass.: Lexington Books, 1978), p. 8.
64. Graeme M. Taylor, "Introduction to Zero-Base Budgeting," in *Experiences in Zero-Based Budgeting,* ed. Joseph L. Herbert (New York: A Petrocelli Book, 1977), p. 3.
65. Ibid., p. 3.
66. The descriptions of budget unit and service-level analysis is drawn with some changes from J. Robert Krebill and Ronald F. Mosher, "Delaware Budgets for Productivity," *State Government,* 53 (Winter 1980), pp. 20–21.
67. Robert F. Littlejohn, "Zero-Base Budgeting," *Police Chief,* 45 (December 1978), p. 35.
68. Points 6 through 9 are restatements of matter found in Taylor "Introduction to Zero-Base Budgeting"; the article also appeared in *The Bureaucrat,* 6 (Spring 1977), pp. 33–55.
69. The information on donation programs, forfeitures, user fees, police taxes, and IRS rewards is drawn from Lindsey D. Stellwagen and Kimberly A. Wylie, *Strategies for Supplementing the Police Budget* (Washington, D.C.: U.S. Department of Justice, National Institute of Justice, 1985), with some restatement.
70. Some of these eleven points are identified by Wayne Stallings, in "Improving Budget Communications in Smaller Local Governments," *Governmental Finance,* (August 1978), p. 24.

A Budget Transmittal Letter

OCALA   POLICE   DEPARTMENT

P. O. BOX 1270, OCALA, FLORIDA 32678

July 30, 1985

Mayor Wayne L. Rubinas
City of Ocala
Post Office Box 1270
Ocala, Florida 32678

Dear Mayor Rubinas:

Our 1985-86 budget is $4,757,285, an increase of $720,244 or 18 percent over this current fiscal year.

I have listed below our major priorities for the coming year. We are not requesting any additional sworn officers. As you remember, City Council approved four patrol officer positions in this year's budget as of July 1985 if funds were available.

Due to vacancies there were unencumbered funds and four new officers are being hired. Since I don't know the impact they will have on our workload this early, I have refrained from asking for more sworn officers.

Our budget needs this year are staff and support personnel. I must commend every secretary and communications officer in the Police Department. We have added responsibilites, increased our workload rapidly, and placed heavier demands on a small, overworked but very dedicated staff.

But we can no longer maintain our administrative functions without some increase in support personnel.

BUDGET PRIORITY #1 - THREE COMMUNICATIONS OFFICERS

Our most critical, present need is to increase the number of Communications Center personnel. I have asked for three additional positions (one per shift).

Our Computer-Aided Dispatch Communications Center was opened in 1981. At that time, our total calls for service in 1981 was 36,698. The Center was designed for three on-duty personnel, but could operate with only two people.

To date this year, our calls total 37,244. We operate the Communications Center with two people about 60% of the time.

During these years, we have placed more responsibility on the Center by requiring them to receive certain minor calls over the telephone. This program allowed the patrol officers to devote more time to more serious complaints.

During this period also, we have established a five officer Motorcycle Traffic Enforcement Unit, increased the number of patrol officers, and seen the heavy increase in workload.

We must increase our Communications personnel so that we can operate with three on-duty people. This increase would allow:

1. One person to handle the Information Channel, State and FBI Computer and Walk-in Complaints

2. Another person to receive all telephone calls for

assistance, take information over the telephone, answer questions, and follow-up on telephone call-backs, and

3. Allow the third person to devote full time to dispatch responsibilities

BUDGET PRIORITY #2 - PATROL DIVISION SECRETARY

The Patrol Division has the largest number of Departmental employees and its responsibilites are the most varied and complex within the Department. For the past 10 years there has been only one Senior Secretary to handle the workload of the Division Commander, Administrative Sergeant, three Lieutenants, and nine sergeants. There is no way she can maintain this demand.

I have requested a Secretary who would be assigned the responsibilities of handling the work for the three Lieutenants, the press release typing for the Administrative Sergeant, assist with the Field Training Officer program, and assume many of the receptionist duties of Mrs. Bray.

BUDGET PRIORITY #3 - CRIMINAL INVESTIGATION CLERK

There is only one Secretary assigned to CID to handle the typing of all investigative reports. In addition she must answer all telephone calls into the office and serve as receptionist.

The demands of more indepth investigations, added responsibilities from the State Attorney's Office on case intake and victim/witness responsibilities, and handling the clerical duties for the Crime Prevention Section are demanding more than one person.

This requested position would assist in typing continuing investigations and handle Crime Prevention's needs.

BUDGET PRIORITY #4 - MANAGEMENT ANALYSIS SECRETARY

There is one Secretary handling all the responsibilities for three administrative units: Management Analysis (Inspector Whiteacre and all the computer functions); Training (Inspector Welch with all departmental inspections and internal investigations), and Planning and Research (Mr. Adams with numerous research studies).

This requested position will be assigned to Inspector Whiteacre. It will allow us to reinstitute our Crime Analysis program which has been reduced because of workload, plus handle all the secretarial duties involved with our Computerized Police Information System.

BUDGET PRIORITY #5 - STREET CRIME UNIT SECRETARY

This unit, whose mission is to target major criminal offenders, including the drug trafficking, operates without any clerical help.

They are relying on either the CID Secretary or the Patrol Division Secretary, neither of whom can handle their present duties.

Consequently, members of this unit spend excessive time typing their own reports instead of being on the street.

This position would allow better use of this valuable investigative unit.

BUDGET PRIORITY #6 - BUILDING MAINTENANCE COORDINATOR

This Police Department's maintenance responsibilities include:

*   Vehicle Maintenance - requiring almost one person dedicated to shuffling cars back and forth to the garage (we average 8-9 vehicles a day to the garage).

* Radio Maintenance - coordinating installations and repairs of our base station, portables, and vehicle radios.

* Building Maintenance - the use of the building 24 hours a day, 7 days a week, places considerable pressure on our cleaning employees to maintain the building.

* Miscellaneous Maintenance - the type of specialized equipment used in law enforcement, from radar units to cameras to microcomputers, requires someone to see that they are delivered to repair agencies and returned.

This position will provide supervision and coordination on all our maintenance functions and maintain constant liaison with other city departments who provide maintenance work.

BUDGET PRIORITY #7 - CONVERT PART-TIME RECORDS CLERK TO FULL-TIME

The Police Department has been authorized one part-time Records Clerk for several years. Due to the increasing workload and demands of the Court system, we are requesting that this position be converted to full-time.

This request, when approved, will allow the Records Section to remain open for the public and the officers for a longer period of time. (We plan on keeping Records open until 10:00 PM). We feel that this change will better serve the citizens while allowing us to maintain a rapidly increasing workload.

In addition to these personnel priorities, we have addressed other critical areas in the 1985-86 budget. The following summary highlights these areas.

PATROL VEHICLE PROGRAM

The Patrol Division has requested that City Council consider establishing a patrol vehicle program which would allow each officer to be assigned a vehicle.

Our experience with the "Personal Vehicle Program" (where officers residing inside the City are assigned a vehicle to take home) has shown it to be a major cost saving to the City.

We have found that the average cost of a personally assigned vehicle is $3,905 **LESS** than a vehicle in the fleet (shared by several officers).

We have found also intangible benefits. The officers take more pride in a personally assigned vehicle.

We have requested 14 additional patrol vehicles. These cars combined with keeping all existing vehicles would allow us to implement the proposed program.

EMERGENCY SERVICE UNIT

We are requesting 14 multi-channel radios and 10 heavy protective vests for our Unit.

As you remember from the critique of the recent shooting involving the Sheriff's SWAT, our most critical need was the ability for our ESU officers to have communications.

A further critical need was to provide vests more protective than the normal ones worn on general patrol.

CRIMINAL INVESTIGATORS DIFFERENTIAL PAY

Our Patrol Division personnel receive a pay differential for working either the evening or midnight shifts.

The CID investigators receive no compensation for being on-call at night or weekends. Yet, this on-call status requires them to remain in contact with the department and limits their activity to the proximity of the City.

Neither do the Investigators receive a differential for working the evening shift, which each must do in rotation.

We are requesting that a six percent differential be established for CID investigators and paid to them when they work evenings or are on call. They will not be paid the differential automatically, only when they meet those conditions.

MISCELLANEOUS REQUESTS

The remaining budget areas are requests to either maintain our present level of effectiveness or, in limited areas, to improve our ability to provide service. These areas are addressed in each of the Sub Program Productivity Summary Sheets provided with this letter.

Yours truly,

Lee McGehee
Chief of Police

*We have no choice but to learn
to manage the service institutions
(such as the police) for
performance and productivity.*

PETER F. DRUCKER

Productivity
and Evaluation of
Police Services

Introduction

Productivity and evaluation of police services research are rational enterprises.[1] Productivity seeks to specify the relationship between inputs to the police organization (such as money allocated in the department's budget) to outputs (such as number of traffic accidents investigated and other such indicators). In contrast, program evaluation seeks to assess the extent to which goals are realized (for example, has the number of violent crimes reported to the police decreased in the past year?). The assumption is that by providing "the facts," productivity measures and program evaluations assist decision makers. However, evaluation is a rational enterprise that takes place in a political context. This chapter explores this area and provides various perspectives on the interrelatedness of productivity and program evaluation within police administration.

Productivity

There are three basic reasons why all of us should be concerned about productivity:

1. Our *real* wages go up, over the long run, as fast as our productivity increases. And real wages are the dollars left in our pay envelopes after deducting what inflation eats up. Only real wages give us more purchasing power.
2. We can get more leisure time only as our productivity improves. By increasing output per man-hour, we can get more of the goods and services we want while working the same or less.
3. Productivity gains give us, as a nation, choices we may not have had before. As productivity goes up, we can spend the increased output in a variety of ways. We can pay for a cleaner environment, for more education, earlier retirement, improved health or government services, or any combination of these. The United States has been fortunate over the past 200 years in that the choices we could make to improve our lives have constantly expanded. By increasing our productivity, we can assure that this will continue to be the case for ourselves and for future generations.[2]

Although the costs of operating local government have increased, there has not been a proportional rise in the resources available to pay for those increases.[3] Citizens have resisted higher taxes and are defeating badly needed bond issue proposals. When bond issues are defeated, new schools, hospitals, jails, courthouses, fire stations, and police buildings go unbuilt, leaving the professionals who work in these settings to labor under increasingly crowded conditions with old and dated equipment. At least nine states have imposed tax ceilings on their localities because of continued citizen pressure for tax relief.[4] In California, this was done in 1978 through the adoption of Proposition 13 by voters.[5] Local governments across the country have also seen Proposition 13 type referenda enacted since 1978. When voters in California approved Proposition 13, the assessed values on commercial and residential property were rolled back to the 1975–1976 level and increases in their assessed valuation were limited to a 2 percent increase per year.[6] One California chief commented afterward that:

> Police officers are being laid off and services are being cut. This includes juvenile, crime prevention, community relations, investigative functions, and training. Budget cuts at the county level will reduce sheriff's department functions, including all those cut at the local level, plus substations and regional laboratory services, SWAT teams, jeep and horse patrols, and helicopter services. Also threatened are regional narcotics and vice squads, bomb squads, K-9 patrols, and hostage negotiation teams.
>
> In addition to layoffs, other proposals include a freeze on hiring, reduction of salaries, reduction in rank, shared jobs, consolidation of departmental functions to be handled by one staff member, where two handled these functions previously, and elimination of overtime. These actions must result in longer hours and reduced efficiency and morale. Militant employee unionism is around the corner in the case of those public servants who are being forced to pay from their salaries for the property tax cuts of their neighbors.
>
> Line officers can expect to be affected drastically. Pay cuts may ensue as well as a freeze on pay increases. This will lead to the loss to private industry of first-rate officers, and the recruitment of first-rate individuals into the police service will suffer when pay and benefit incentives fall further below those offered by the private sector. This could

lead to the recruitment and retention of less than satisfactory individuals who might be tempted to accept gratuities or enter into corrupt activities to supplement their income. Monies for training will be trimmed from local budgets, further negating the professionalism that law enforcement has striven to achieve. My personal assessment is that law enforcement will be set back many years because we will not be able to afford the type of individual we need to employ.[7]

On the East Coast, Michael Codd, former commissioner of the New York City Police Department, also spoke to the issue of constrained resources:

When budget cuts have to be made in the police department it means manpower cuts because the bulk of our budget costs goes for personnel services. We lost 2,864 officers, all the School Crossing Guards (2,247) and about 100 civilians in the layoffs thus far, and 1,088 more layoffs or attritional reductions, including 205 civilians, are projected for the near future. We strongly hope that attrition will make layoffs unnecessary. . . . Relatively speaking our women officers suffered the greatest losses. Of the 2,864 layoffs, 399 were women. This was more than 56 percent of our entire women's complement. Their loss put a serious dent in our women-on-patrol program because most of these women had been assigned to patrol. . . . The blacks and Hispanics also suffered heavy losses. Of the 2,488 black officers, 413 were laid off; of the 1,014 Hispanic officers, 202 were laid off. In percentages, the blacks in the department decreased from 8 to 7.4 percent; the Hispanics from 3.4 to 2.8 percent. . . . All told, the picture I've just painted is pretty grim, and if more layoffs are made, it will be even grimmer. But there is no point in being unrealistic or in deluding ourselves. We are in for hard times, and for a long time to come.[8]

Although Codd's statement was made in 1975, his judgment that "we are in for hard times; and for a long time to come" has been proven correct. Illustrative, in 1980, was Philadelphia's laying off of 748 police department employees, creating what one veteran described as the "lowest morale in 25 years," and the massive layoffs in Detroit.[9] In 1979, Detroit had also experienced layoffs of police officers that appear to be affecting organizational performance; by July 1980, records indicated that almost 4,000 of the 31,000 emergency calls for police service resulted in no police action.[10]

Although the mid-1980s appear to show a decrease in police layoffs, departments still have not regained their previously held personnel strengths. A survey of law enforcement agencies found that 44 percent of police and sheriff's departments reported the same or fewer personnel in 1984 as they had five years earlier.[11] The primary reasons for reductions in police personnel included hiring freezes and the "economic realities" that force police to seek ways to reduce work load.[12]

A major shift in crime protection appears to parallel decreasing police resources. Figures 14-1 and 14-2 reflect the recent increases in private police service within our society. Private protection resources have recently and drastically exceeded those of public law enforcement. Further, private security personnel also significantly out-number sworn law enforcement personnel by nearly 2 to 1.[13] The Bureau of Labor Statistics forecast that about 215,000 new operating personnel will join private security employment by 1990. The "Hallcrest Systems Study" suggests even further changes in future law enforcement service. James K. Stewart, director of the National Institute of Justice, may have best summed the challenge facing managers concerned with police productivity:

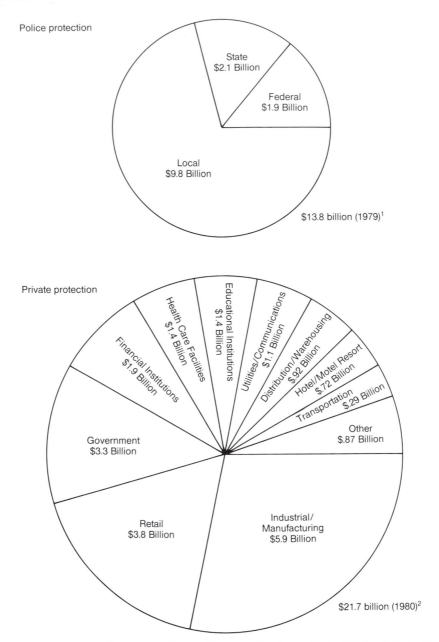

FIGURE 14-1. Gross expenditures for protection in the United States Private Versus Public Protection [Source: *Sourcebook of Criminal Justice Statistics*, 1981. *Bureau of Justice Statistics*, 1982; *Key Market Coverage, Security World*, 1981; *The Growing Role of Private Security*, NIJ Research in Brief, 1984.]

The National Institute of Justice funded the private security study (Hallcrest Systems Study) as part of its *priority* research on effective use and deployment of police resources. Smaller local budgets and fewer police personnel require law enforcement agencies to make more efficient use of what they have. Cooperative programs with private security could provide a way to do more with less.[14]

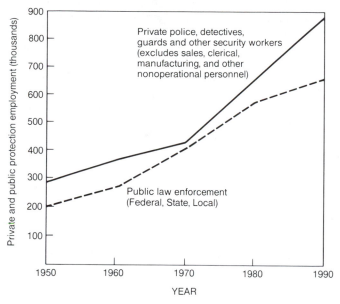

FIGURE 14-2. Trends in private and public protection employment [Source: Bureau of Census and Bureau of Labor Statistics; *The Growing Role of Private Security,* NIJ *Research in Brief,* 1984.]

The Hallcrest Systems Study reflects a thirty-month investigation undertaken by Hallcrest Systems, Inc. It provides the first comprehensive look at private security in more than a decade and outlines specific strategies to better utilize the joint resource of law enforcement and private security in an effort to improve efficiency and productivity.

Defining Productivity

Specialists have not always agreed on the precise definition of productivity, but it is generally assumed to be a ratio of "output" to "input." A somewhat longer definition is that:

> Productivity improvement is among the practical approaches government is taking to achieve its objectives of effectiveness, efficiency and economy. The concept of productivity improvement focuses on whether the right things are being done and whether they are being done without wasting valuable resources.[15]

The National Commission on Productivity has determined that police productivity can be improved in the following four ways:

1. Improve current police practice to its optimum level; to achieve better performance without causing a proportionate increase in cost. Put simply, this means doing the necessary tasks of police work, but doing them as efficiently as possible.
2. Allocate the resources to those activities which give the highest return for each additional dollar that is spent. This involves a number of decisions

focusing on police services. Are the police not only doing things right, but are they also doing the right thing?

3. Increase the probability that a given objective will be met. For instance, the most successful criminal apprehension programs assign police personnel when and where crime is the highest or calls for police service are the heaviest. This can be achieved through careful analysis of data to pinpoint the likely times and places of crime occurrence, thereby increasing the probability that a suspect will be apprehended.

4. Make the most of personnel talents. Many times the individual talents of police officers are overlooked by rigid organizational procedures. This not only squanders public resources but also suffocates individual potentials and desires.[16]

Efficiency and Effectiveness

In its application to the public sector (especially police), the notions of productivity have centered largely on two basic concepts: efficiency and effectiveness.

> Efficiency measures determine the level of resources—human, financial, and environmental—that are required to provide a given level of service; effectiveness measures determine the impact and quality of the service being provided. Efficiency measures describe how much of a given service is being provided and the costs associated with that service level; effectiveness measures describe the results—both positive and negative—that the provision of the service has on the client or community.[17]

In this definition, the qualitative dimension of service is considered as part of the measures of effectiveness, although another perspective is that quality is itself a separate dimension. Stated more simply, effectiveness is the ability to get a job done, including meeting the standards set for quality control. Efficiency, on the other hand, is determined by what resources (inputs) are needed in producing outputs.

Effectiveness and efficiency must both be present if there is to be an improvement in productivity. Measurements such as man hours of work, individual response time to calls, and number of arrests, are necessary to *monitor* effectiveness and efficiency. Measurements comparing specific time periods, such as last calendar year versus the present calendar year, are essential to indicate whether improvement has been achieved.

Implementing a Productivity Program

Whether a police productivity improvement program is large or small, simple or complex, experience has demonstrated that there is a basic checklist of conditions that must be satisfied for it to be developed and implemented successfully. Police leaders must have:

1. The courage and determination to initiate and sustain the program.
2. The analytical capacity to determine what needs to be done, what can be done, and how to do it.
3. The active support or, failing that, at least the neutrality of relevant others, such as the city or county manager, the legislative body, the interested public, and the union.

4. The ability to overcome resistance from other departments of government, such as personnel or central purchasing who may resist the writing of new job and equipment specifications because they impinge upon established control practices.

5. Overall, the cooperation of the people within the police department. Even if large numbers of personnel are committed, lesser numbers of well-situated people opposing the program can mean failure. As we discuss later in this chapter, the opposition of middle managers in some departments to team policing led to its failure.

6. The organizational control system and controls to facilitate and reinforce the changes to be made.

7. Competent persons responsible for the changes.[18]

A key and positive way of reinforcing the changes to be made is a widespread system of incentives that makes efforts to improve productivity have some "payoff" to those involved. Police administrators may be guaranteed that some portion of the savings that will be generated by productivity improvements will be made available to them for new or expanded programs.[19] For example, in Plainville, Connecticut, police officers with perfect attendance for ninety days are given an extra day off, a measure that has reduced the use of sick days considerably.

Basically, productivity improvements can be made in two ways: (1) increasing the level of output while holding the level of resources used constant, or (2) maintaining or increasing the level of output with a decrease in the level of resources used. Productivity improvement does not mean working harder; it means working "smarter." The efforts to do so show rich diversity as in the following cases:

> Cottage Grove, Oregon, has used volunteer senior citizens trained in crime prevention to go from door to door marking personal property and recommending security improvements.[20]
>
> Holmdel Township, New Jersey, contracted with a private firm to do routine maintenance on police cars and produced a 50 percent savings over prior auto maintenance costs.[21]
>
> The New York City Police Department studied court appearances by officers and found that 45 percent of those scheduled were not actually needed. A new court scheduling system eliminated 28,000 police appearances and saved $4,000,000 annually.[22]
>
> Jurisdictions such as Elk Grove, Illinois; Richmond, Virginia; and Tempe, Arizona; have reduced the costs of directing traffic, investigating accidents, and dispatching by the use of paraprofessionals. In Scottsdale, Arizona, "police assistants" have been used in certain types of preliminary investigations, follow-up investigations on runaway juveniles, bicycle thefts and malicious mischief, and traffic control and accident investigation. In the first four years of operation, savings of 9,000 patrol officer days and $188,000 in salaries were obtained.[23]
>
> Mount Morris, Minnesota; Wheaton, Illinois; and White Fish Bay, Wisconsin; have equipped officers with portable dictating units, reducing the time necessary to complete reports.[24]
>
> The Police Executive Research Forum (PERF) has replicated the Stanford Research Institute burglary case-screening model. The replication involved 12,001 cases from twenty-six different police departments and proved 85 percent accurate in determining which cases would benefit from follow-up investigations. From it, two implicit findings emerge: (1) the success or failure of the follow-up investigation is more a function of the characteristics of the case than the follow-up investigation itself, and (2) the application of the model eliminates a great deal of nonproductive investigative effort.[25]

The first major audit of the Philadelphia Police Department in fourteen years found that the police averaged 16.8 sick days per year and that a strictly enforced sick leave policy (one which required a doctor's note for absences) could save the city $6,000,000 annually.[26]

Flint, Michigan; Orange, California; and New York City represent a few of the jurisdictions that have tied productivity to the collective bargaining process. In general, such efforts offer incentives for improvements or seek to renegotiate contractual provisions—such as a requirement that all cars be manned by two officers—that may be blocks to increased productivity.

From these illustrations, it can be seen that productivity improvement efforts are possible in both large and small police departments and that they may involve a variety of strategies. As suggested by the National Commission on Productivity and Work Quality, a shift in the style of management employed by a police department may itself be a productivity improvement measure. In terms of sequential steps, the implementation of a productivity improvement effort involves:

1. Selecting a program, subprogram, or activity for concentrated study, such as a neighborhood crime watch program.
2. Determining the true objectives of the program; to increase crime prevention awareness within specific neighborhoods and thereby reduce reported street crime.
3. Choosing the appropriate analytical procedures for eliciting information, such as interviewing victims or surveying officers.
4. Designing several program improvement options; for example, new technology, improved procedures, increasing employee motivation, contracting out service, and so on.
5. Forecasting direct and indirect impacts of program options, such as decreased fear of crime and safer and more secure public feeling.
6. Implementing the program—putting the selected program option into effect. This includes developing strategies for overcoming individual, organizational, and institutional barriers.
7. Evaluating the program—determining how well the new or adjusted program works when compared with the original program.[27]

Management Style and Productivity

The overall strategy involved in implementing a productivity improvement program may take one of three forms: (1) centralized (2) nondirective, and (3) decentralized.[28] Phoenix, Arizona; Milwaukee, Wisconsin; and San Diego, California;[29] all operate from a centralized perspective with their, respectively, Department of Budget and Research, Bureau of Budget and Management, and Financial Management Department taking the lead role. In a highly centralized system, the productivity staff might have responsibility for:

1. Establishing and imposing performance targets and timetables on the operating agencies.
2. Identifying the programs or activities for which productivity improvements will be developed.
3. Analyzing programs and activities.
4. Designing and scheduling productivity improvement projects.

5. Managing the implementation of productivity improvement projects.
6. Operating a central information and control system on all productivity improvements.
7. Negotiating or controlling negotiations with employee unions on productivity improvements.[30]

The case for a centralized system is that it unites trained analysts with elected officials and ties productivity improvements to the power of the budget. Against it is the inherent danger of resistance from the police or other departments when change is experienced or perceived as being imposed. Tacoma, Washington, represents a nondirective approach in that, although the city manager "made no bones" about his interest in productivity improvements, he left it to the department heads to decide a course of action. For those who sought improvements, he provided substantial assistance in eliminating bureaucratic obstacles, obtained expert help, and was otherwise actively supportive. No pressure was placed on the "laggards" save the example set by the city manager and the responsive department heads; over time, increasingly more departments joined the effort. Decentralization places responsibility for improvements with the heads of operating agencies, and although there is a reduction in central control, there is also less tension from imposed change and a closer linkage between the analysts and operations—improving both—since they are housed within each department of government.

Total Performance Management

Total performance management (TPM) is a comprehensive approach to improving productivity. Its underpinnings reaffirm from yet another perspective Douglas McGregor's observation that theory and practice are inseparable. Figure 14-3 summarizes TPM, which combines elements of industrial engineering—with roots back to scientific management—and the use of behavioral science techniques, such as survey research feedback. The use of TPM requires:

1. The collection of data from customers and employees to provide information about both positive and negative aspects of performances, along with data about productivity.
2. "Playing back" the data in summarized forms to both managers and employees.
3. Managers and employees who develop action plans to build on strengths and eliminate or reduce weaknesses.

From the types of data gathered and how they are used, certain key aspects of TPM can be seen: it assumes that customers can and will provide valuable information about services received; employees are an important source of data and creativity; and at the core of any productivity improvement program is some amount of relevant data upon which decisions can be made.

TPM was developed by the General Accounting Office of the United States in cooperation with the National Center for Productivity and Quality of Working Life. The first application of TPM was in a small editorial unit of a federal agency, about whose "sloppy" work and missed deadlines other units of the agency had been complaining.[31] Impressive results were obtained from this first small-scale initial experimentation, including a 45 percent decline in the time required to respond to requests

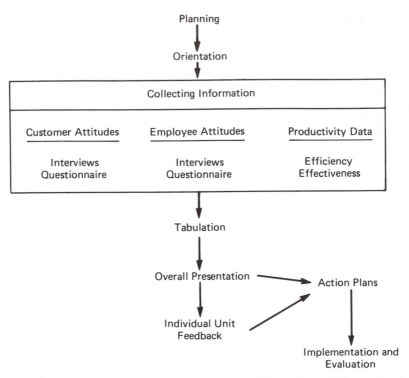

FIGURE 14-3. Total Performance Management. [From National Center for Productivity and Quality of Working Life, "Total Performance Management: Some Pointers for Action" (Washington, D.C.: U.S. Government Printing Office, 1978), p. 6.]

for services, higher quality, higher work force morale, and increased customer satisfaction.[32] Several California jurisdictions, including Sunnyvale, San Diego, Los Angeles County, and Manhattan Beach, have experimented with TPM.[33] For the most part, these initial experiments with TPM have been encouraging, reflecting similar results in increased productivity and morale.

Conditions that suggest the wider use of TPM in the future include (1) the fact that TPM lends itself to a centralized implementation strategy, which many city leaders may prefer; (2) it is systems oriented; (3) it provides an opportunity for employees to participate in defining and shaping the solutions to problems; and (4) elements of it are already being practiced in many places—the city of Charlotte, for example, has surveyed citizens on their perception of police performance at least since 1976.[34]

Management by Objectives

A management approach that is a natural adjunct to productivity programs and that enhances them is management by objectives (MBO) or some alternative designation of it, such as policing by objectives (PBO).[35] The concept of MBO is widely attributed to Peter Drucker in *The Practice of Management* (1954). In general, the use of MBO in government can be described as a late-1960s early- 1970s movement. Its adoption has not been universal, and as late as 1978, some major police departments were only beginning its implementation.[36]

MBO can be defined as having a result- as opposed to an activity-orientation to managing whose underlying philosophical bias is participative management. Drucker elaborates on this philosophical bias by describing MBO as a common and explicit understanding between managers and their subordinates regarding what their contributions to the organization will be over a definite period of time.[37] Where MBO has been tried by police departments and has "failed," its lack of success most often has been caused by using it as a purely technical management system implemented without a shift from reliance on traditional organizational theory precepts to the use of bridging or open systems theories, which stress the importance and worth of officers at all levels of the department. Stated in terms of leadership orientations, the MBO system implemented under a 9,1 (authority obedience) orientation incurs a greater risk of failure than under the 5,5 (organization man management) or 9,9 (team management) approaches.

The underlying rationale of MBO has been stated as, "the better a manager understands what he hopes to accomplish (the better he knows his objectives), the greater will be his chances for success."[38] In a sense, MBO provides the manager with a blueprint that guides him or her toward the objective he or she has set. Others suggests, "if one knows where he is going, he finds it easier to get there, he can get there faster, and he will know when he arrives."[39]

Figure 14-4 summarizes the major steps commonly involved in the MBO process. The formulation of long-range goals and strategic plans is preceded by the development of the police department's *mission statement,* which is the broadest, most comprehensive statement that can be made about the overall purpose of the police department.[40] The mission statement recognizes either explicitly or implicitly legislatively mandated roles, professional tenets, community preferences, and related sources.

Goals are end states or conditions which take one or more years to achieve. Complex goals, e.g., designing, obtaining approval for, procuring, and placing a new jail communications system into operation, may take three to five years. Goals may also be stated in such a fashion that the pursuit of them is continuous (e.g., "to promote officer safety and performance by providing a variety of basic and in-service training experiences"). Because of the time-horizon associated with goals, they are supported by more immediately achievable (and subsequently measurable) objectives.

Objectives are end states that can be achieved in one year or less. Well-stated objectives have three characteristics:

- target specific
- quantified
- identified time frame

The following statement of an objective illustrates the use of these three characteristics: Objective One: "to have at least 90 percent of all police officers complete a 400 hour basic officer training program in FY '88." These characteristics are important because they provide a basis for determining whether or not the organization accomplished what it set out to do. These characteristics also help explain one underlying cause why there is often resistance to planning in general and goal and objective setting in particular; formal statements of expectation are generated, impacting upon *responsibility* and *accountability,* the very essence of program evaluation.

The achievement of the objectives identified is then reinforced by the development

Key Elements in the MBO Process

1. Goal and objective setting: establishing tangible, measurable, and verifiable objectives in major areas of performance.

2. Action planning: developing plans intended to determine what, who, when, where, and how much is needed to achieve a given objective.

3. Implementation and self-control: permitting participation in the goal-setting and action-planning process and providing feedback and information needed to assess progress and to take corrective action.

4. Reviews and evaluations: providing reviews designed to evaluate progress and performance in terms of the established objectives and to identify and to remove problem areas.

Major Steps in the MBO Process

1. Formulate long-range goals and strategic plans.

2. Develop the specific objectives to be achieved within the given time period.

3. Establish derivative objectives and subobjectives for major bureaus and subunits of the police department.

4. Set realistic and challenging objectives and standards of performance for members of the police department.

5. Formulate action plans for achieving the stated objectives.

6. Implement and take corrective action when required to ensure the attainment of objectives.

7. Review individual and organizational performance in terms of established goals and objectives.

8. Evaluate overall performance, reinforce behavior, and strengthen motivation.

FIGURE 14-4. The MBO process. [From Anthony P. Raia, *Managing by Objectives*. (Glenview, Ill.: Scott, Foresman, 1974), p. 16. Copyright 1974 Scott, Foresman Co. Reprinted by permission].

GOAL	To provide a management environment that facilitates achieving department goals while providing for the career needs of its employees.	
OBJECTIVE	To develop and place into operation by August 4, 1986 a new telecommunications center.	TARGET DATE August 4, 1986

DIVISION		PERSON RESPONSIBLE
	Administration	M. E. Deen

ACTION PLAN	TARGET DATE
Development and Construction of Ocala Police Department Communications Center to Be Operational by August 4, 1986.	
A. Equipment selection to include equipment options	Jan. 31, 1986
B. Develop equipment specifications	Feb. 25, 1986
C. Site plan and specifications completed	Feb. 25, 1986
D. Bids released on communications equipment and construction	March 3, 1986
E. Bids received by city of Ocala purchasing office	Mar. 28, 1986
F. Bids awarded for equipment and construction by city council	Apr. 1, 1986
G. Communications equipment ordered from successful bidder	Apr. 2, 1986
H. Construction begins on communication center	Apr. 14, 1986
I. Delivery and installation of communications equipment	Jul. 23, 1986
J. Construction work in center completed	Aug. 1, 1986
K. Communications center operational	Aug. 4, 1986

PREPARED BY M. E. Deen	DATE PREPARED Jan. 31, 1986
APPROVED BY	DATE APPROVED

FIGURE 14-5. An Action Plan. [Source: The Ocala, Florida Police Department, 1986].

of an action plan, as shown in Figure 14-5. The specificity of the action plan allows for (1) monitoring, (2) taking corrective action as needed, as the basis of evaluating, and (3) improved planning and decision making. In Ocala, Florida, a zone awareness program allows the individual officer assigned to each geographic area to develop, in cooperation with his or her supervisor, objectives for policing the area.[41] Progress toward achieving the objectives is monitored, adjustments are made as needed, and in bimonthly meetings the officer's performance is evaluated and new objectives are prepared. Thus, MBO can be a tool not only for evaluating programs but also individual performance.

Obstacles and Benefits

Management by objective systems can fail for a variety of reasons. Stein[42] conducted a study in which the attitudes of lower-level and midlevel management personnel using MBO were examined. The results of the study revealed a number of problems associated with the MBO system. The three most critical problems were:

1. Difficulty in defining objectives that were both meaningful and measurable.
2. Insufficient follow-up, monitoring, and updating of the program.
3. Lack of commitment by management to the purposes and concepts of MBO.[43]

Further, it should be remembered that the implementation of MBO requires large-scale organizational change. However, a fully developed and properly implemented MBO system may require two to five years of sustained effort in large organizations before it takes hold. A review of the research on MBO reveals that it has the potential to:

1. Increase goal specificity.
2. Increase awareness of goals.
3. Contribute to improved planning.
4. Result in greater specificity in identifying and defining problems.
5. Produce better resource allocation.
6. Have a favorable effect on productivity.
7. Improve superior-subordinate relationships.
8. Increase the receptivity of superiors to new ideas and suggestions.
9. Make greater use of subordinates' ability and experiences.
10. Improve interpersonal and organizational communications.
11. Increase motivation and job satisfaction among employees.
12. Increase objectivity in evaluating performances.[44]

From these points, one could conclude, as one chief wryly did, "that MBO will do everything but take out the garbage." Given its potential utility, why aren't fully developed MBO systems being used in every police department? There may be no single answer, but from experience some observed reasons are that (1) it is easier to maintain the status quo than to enter into the change process; (2) some police leaders are unable or unwilling to part with highly centralized control; (3) MBO has been oversold in that, as compared with its benefits, not as much attention has been given to the reality that it takes sustained hard work to achieve changes; it cannot simply be dropped into the police department like a set of spark plugs into a car; (4) some managers do not really want to know the answer to the question, "how well am I (or we) doing?"; (5) reports of "failures" in the use of MBO have discouraged some potential adopters; and (6) the costs involved in developing the system and training personnel in both the technical and behavioral aspects of it are high.

Additionally, research also suggests that MBO may have certain dysfunctional consequences if not implemented properly: (1) over time, officers may become indifferent to it as "just another management procedure"; (2) when participation in objective setting does not reach the lower levels of the organization, it is likely to fail, making future innovations more difficult to implement; (3) it can create excessive paperwork with an emphasis more on building a paper record than on achieving results; and (4) easily quantifiable objectives may be substituted for more important, but more difficult to measure, ones.[45] Despite such barriers, the use of MBO should, and is likely to, increase within police departments.

Productivity Measurement

Whereas the concept of productivity is deceptively simple, trying to employ it meaningfully in policing presents challenges. The fact that such challenges exist does not, however, mean that productivity improvement efforts (PIEs) should not be undertaken. At present, productivity measurement in policing is still in a relatively early stage; some number of performance measures (PMs) are crude because the technology is developing. However, the legacy of the resource scarcity over the past decade has been a heightened concern for "getting the most for the buck," resulting in a continued movement toward the use of more formal PIEs and PMs. Relatedly, the most fundamental obligation that managers seeking public appropriations have is to demonstrate that they have exercised careful stewardship over the resources previously entrusted to them. Failing a demonstration of that, on what grounds can police managers reasonably expect effectively to advance a case for any additional funding?

A key issue in using PMs is developing a definition of output. If part of the role of the police is preventing crime, how, for example, do you measure how many crimes the police prevented? A related problem is establishing that there is some relationship between police effort and the outcome. To illustrate, if reported crime decreases or increases, it may be the result of a reduction in, or an increase in, public confidence that the police cannot or can do something about crime. This shift in public confidence may occur quite independently of anything that the police may or may not do; such a shift may be caused by rumors, statements by political candidates, or the errors in news reports that occasionally happen under the pressure of deadlines. Additionally, if specific police programs aimed at particular crime problems do not yield results, the police may be tempted to discourage the filing of complaints or assign the complaints to another crime category. In a city with a rash of robberies, the uniformed officers may be told at roll call to "make sure you really have a robbery; some of those reports coming in as robberies are actually larcenies, and it's causing extra paperwork in getting them classified properly." The words spoken notwithstanding, the real message is "we're taking a lot of heat about these robberies and one way or another we've got to reduce them."

Other problems relating to measuring productivity include the following: (1) an increase in police productivity may be accompanied by a reduction in the quality of output; (2) the achievement of a given productivity level does not mean that the level of services being provided is consistent with community desires or needs; (3) there is difficulty in developing adequate and appropriate measures for staff functions such as personnel and training; and (4) achieving the desired level of productivity in one area may make it difficult to achieve the desired level in another.

In some cases, the crime control and community relations functions may come into conflict. For example, assume that a police department assigns officers in teams to various high-crime neighborhoods. All members of the team are dressed to blend into the street life where they are assigned and one or more serve as decoys. When offenders attempt to victimize the decoys, the other team members close in and make an arrest. After seven months, the arrest and conviction rates for serious offenses are five times higher among team officers as compared with the rates for conventionally deployed officers. However, in the course of these special operations, six minority citizens have been shot to death and two others wounded as they attempted to commit violent felonies involving the decoys as victims. As a result, the minority community is aroused, and their relations with the police are reaching new lows. Thus we have two desirable goals that are in conflict, namely improved community relations and the reduction of violent street crime.

MBO and Productivity Improvement Efforts

Figure 14-6 depicts the integration of an MBO system and a productivity improvement effort. Although an MBO system and a PIE effort have some overlapping features—which is why MBO is a natural adjunct to a productivity program—there are some

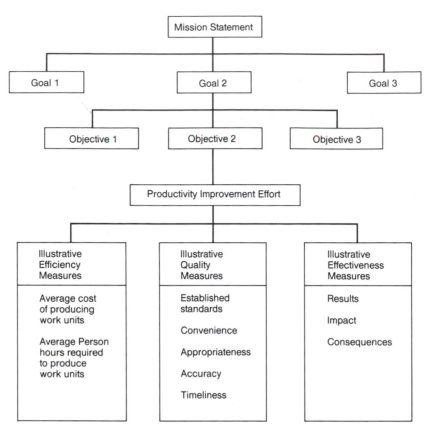

FIGURE 14-6. The integration of an MBO system and a productivity improvement effort. [Portions of this figure are drawn and modified from Brian Usilaner and Edwin Scott, "Productivity Measurement," in *Productivity Improvement Handbook for State and Local Government*, ed. George J. Washnis (New York: John Wiley, 1980), p. 93.]

differences. The starting place for an MBO system is the mission statement, which is a global orientation, whereas the starting place for a PIE is selecting a program, a subprogram, or an activity for concentrated study.

Three separate types of performance measures are identified in Figure 14-6. (1) efficiency, used to denote the efficiency of the service delivery system rather than the individual worker; (2) quality; and (3) effectiveness. Typically, when a productivity system is introduced, the measures of efficiency and effectiveness draw the early attention. Subsequently, concern for what will happen or what is happening to the quality of service delivery emerges and measures are adopted or developed to deal with this concern.

Figure 14-7 illustrates the relationship of objectives and PMs. Naturally, in a productivity context, intervening between the objectives and the PMs would be whatever PIEs had been determined to be needed. Figure 14-7 also illustrates the need for a productivity system to define the terms it uses; for example, in the first objective, does the "average cost" include vehicle costs and travel time or only the cost of actual person-hours spent at the call's location? Too, it should be observed that some of the objectives identified in Figure 14-7 might be considered subobjectives

---

Objective: To reduce the average cost of uniformed officers responding to domestic disturbance calls by 10 percent in fiscal 1986 as compared with Fiscal 1985

Performance Measure:

$$\frac{\text{Average cost of sample FY '85 calls} - \text{Average cost of sample FY '86 calls}}{\text{Average cost of sample FY '85 calls}} \times 100 = \underline{\hspace{1cm}} \%$$

Objective: To provide a minimum of 40 hours of appropriate training to not less than 80 percent of sworn personnel during fiscal 1986

Performance Measure:

$$\frac{\text{Number of officers receiving at least 40 hours training}}{\text{Number of total actual strength officers}} \times 100 = \underline{\hspace{1cm}} \%$$

Objective: To maintain the accuracy of data entered into the computer system at 95 percent during fiscal 1986

Performance Measure:

$$\frac{\text{Total number of entries made in sample period without error}}{\text{Total number of entries made in sample period}} \times 100 = \underline{\hspace{1cm}} \%$$

Objective: To ensure that in fiscal 1986 all cases investigated, prepared, and submitted to the judicial system by the Investigation Division are of sufficient quality that 65 percent of those cases pass the first judicial screening.

Performance Measure:

$$\frac{\text{Number of cases that pass first judicial screening}}{\text{Total number of cases submitted}} \times 100 = \underline{\hspace{1cm}} \%$$

Objective: To decrease the fiscal 1986 accident-related police vehicle collision repair costs by 10 percent as compared with fiscal 1985

Performance Measure:

$$\frac{\text{Collision repair costs for FY '85} - \text{collision repair cost for FY '86}}{\text{Collision repair costs for FY '85}} \times 100 = \underline{\hspace{1cm}} \%$$

Most of these illustrations are taken, with modification, from the Portland, Oregon, Police Bureau's 1980–1981 Alternative Service Level Budget Submission.

FIGURE 14-7. Illustrative Objectives and Performance Measures.

of objectives, even as objectives are subdivisions of goals. If an objective is written fairly broadly, it is likely to incorporate a number of subobjectives, roughly three to five. These subobjectives may separately or in some combination deal with the three measures of service delivery: efficiency, quality, and effectiveness. However, one should not expect all objectives or subobjectives to be accompanied routinely by all three types of PMs.

Program Evaluation

As in the case of many other basic concepts, evaluation is one that everybody seems to understand and agree upon until they begin to define it.[46] Then, a great deal of difference begins to emerge. Most definitions seem to look at evaluation from one or more of three perspectives:

1. As a process, which focuses on how evaluation is done, the steps and procedures involved in designing and conducting an evaluation.

2. As a product, meaning the findings or judgments that are made as a result of doing an evaluation.
3. In terms of its purpose, the end use of evaluation, such as for planning, policymaking, and decision making.[47]

These three perspectives can be grouped together logically to form a view of evaluation as a process, which results in a product, which has a purpose.[48] This section is not intended to provide information about how to do evaluation, on which there is ample literature, but rather about how to examine evaluation from an administrative point of view.

Types of Program Evaluation

In its broadest context, "program" refers to an activity or group of related activities undertaken by a unit of government to provide a service to the public.[49] A program may be contained in a single agency, such as the police department, or spread among several agencies, such as emergency medical services. Again in the broadest context, "program evaluation" refers to the systematic assessment of an activity or group of related activities. Under the umbrella heading of program evaluation, three different types are recognizable:[50]

1. Process evaluation. This type of evaluation is not concerned with the ultimate usefulness or appropriateness of the program activities but, rather, with only how well they are being performed. It looks at, for example, whether intermediate hiring quotas are being reached or if the police department's budget is being expended at the projected rate. Process evaluation goes beyond program monitoring in that, in addition to describing what is happening, it determines, "why or why not" these things are happening. Although often not recognized as such, process evaluation is an ongoing activity in police departments and is part of the way in which organizations are controlled. Illustrative are the periodic receipt and analysis of budget status reports and the system of administrative inspections that are conducted to determine if established policies and procedures are being followed, to identify deviations, and to recommend any needed corrective actions.
2. Program Evaluation. This type of evaluation asks whether or not a program has met its ultimate objectives. It is concerned with the intended consequences of a police department's various programs. Police departments, although often not recognizing it, do more program evaluation than they realize. For example, the one-group pretest versus posttest design is represented in the following way:

$$O_1 \quad X \quad O_2$$

This design consists of a first observation (O_1), where a measurement is made, a treatment (X), such as a productivity improvement program; and a second observation (O_2). The difference between the two measurements is then considered to be a function of the treatment. However, this design is methodologically simple and subject to influences other than the treatment. To use an earlier example, a reduction in reported crime may not be due to anything that the police are doing but, instead, be a function of some event that occurred between O_1 and O_2, such as rumors sweeping the community that reduce confidence in the ability of the police to deal with crime, leading to a reduction in reported crime. The issue is not what the limitations of the one-group pretest versus posttest design are; rather, it is what forms of program evaluation the police should be and are engaged in.

3. Impact Evaluation. This type of evaluation is the most difficult and costly to perform. It goes beyond the issue of how well the program was operated and whether it met its objectives to ask the question, "In both a positive and negative sense, what differences did the operation of this program make?" Of the three types of evaluation, impact is used least by police departments. The importance of impact evaluation is established easily, however, by returning to the example of the decoy teams discussed in the productivity section. Assume that the process evaluation of that program was positive and that the program evaluation revealed that it was exceeding its stated objectives. The use of an impact evaluation could, however, provide a measure of the discontent and anger existing in the minority community. These data could then serve as a basis to eliminate or modify the program, be helpful in reducing the level of tension by giving minorities a formal means of expressing their views, and provide a priority focus for community relations efforts.

FIGURE 14-8. Neighborhood Crime Watch is a good example of a police program that has significantly reduced overall crime rates in a number of urban communities. [Courtesy of the San Diego Police Department.]

The Police Administrator and Evaluation

There is an old saw that says, "Regardless what patients do regarding their appointment with a psychiatrist, some useful meaning can be gained by the psychiatrist." If patients are early, they are anxious; if they are on time, they are compulsive; if they are late, they are resistant. In a similar vein, historically police administrators have relied, to their own advantage, on reported crime as the evaluative measure of their department's performance. If crime was falling, cuts in personnel were resisted so that the "favorable position" could be maintained; if crime was increasing, additional officers were "required" to "turn the situation around." There is a sense in which program failure is essential for many organizations in that the effective solution of the problems they address would eliminate the purpose and, therefore, the very need for the organizations.[51] Recognizing this, the appropriators of funds and others began raising the question as to whether they should continue to support organizations that benefit from their own failure.[52]

Crime is a complex social issue on which the police have a negligible or marginal impact at best; the elimination of crime and consequently the need for the police are unlikely to happen. However, between the late 1960s and early 1970s, city managers, directors of departments of finance and management, and city councils became increasingly disinclined to accept the self-serving manipulations of some police chiefs to justify their budgets and characterize the performance of their departments. Consequently, there was an increasing use of some sort of performance standard or MBO system as a measure of program evaluation. Impetus was given to developing more sophisticated evaluation measures during 1970–1975 as productivity emerged as a national issue, a movement reinforced by the requirement for an evaluation component in the numerous Law Enforcement Assistance Administration grants that were awarded to the police.[53]

Despite these and related pressures, some chiefs resisted using—where they existed—their planning and research units for much more than tabulating statistics for the annual report and performing crime analysis for the line bureaus. Among the reasons for this posture were the following:

1. Police administrators did not understand, or would not acknowledge, the advantages to be gained from comprehensive program evaluation.
2. The policy preferences and positions of police administrators are translated into programs, and they were not very motivated to do anything that could discredit their stances.
3. The allocation of resources to the staff function of program evaluation was often viewed as a lower priority than the allocation of resources to line functions.
4. A distrust of evaluation existed that was coupled with a preference for relying upon subjective judgments gained through years of experience.
5. Disfavorable evaluations were feared as a powerful tool for "outsiders" to criticize the administrator personally or the department, whereas favorable evaluations would not be accorded very much weight.
6. Initiating evaluation and then using the results involves a commitment to being change-oriented, and sheer organizational inertia was a frequent barrier.

The resistance of some chiefs notwithstanding, by the mid-1970s there was widespread acknowledgment in more forward-thinking police departments that, whatever the merits of MBO as a decentralized, but coordinated, means of evaluation, it was not an adequate means for answering such questions as:

1. Does aggressive preventive patrol prevent crime?[54]
2. What are the consequences of training police officers as family crisis intervention specialists?
3. How much do detectives really contribute to the solution of crimes?[55]
4. In comparison with men, how do women perform in generalized police assignments?

Two of these questions have been the subject of extensive social science research. They are offered as examples of controversial evaluation findings.

The Kansas City Patrol Experiment

From October 1, 1972, to September 30, 1973, the Kansas City Police Department, along with the support of the Police Foundation, conducted a study to determine if routine patrol using conspicuously marked vehicles had any measurable impact on crime or the public's sense of security.[56] As noted in a report on the study, "police patrol strategies have always been based on two unproven but widely accepted hypotheses: first, that visible police presence prevents potential offenders; second, that the public's fear of crime is dimished by such police presence."[57]

The Kansas City experiment was conducted within fifteen beats in a thirty-two square mile area with a resident population of 148,395 (refer to Figure 14-9). The beats were designated as reactive, proactive, and control areas. Reactive beats did not have preventive patrols; officers entered these areas only when a citizen called and requested service. When the officers were not responding to calls, they patrolled adjacent proactive beats on the boundaries of their own beats. With proactive beats, the routine preventive patrol was intensified to two to three times its usual level, whereas in control beats, the normal (usual) amount of patrolling was conducted. The following were noted in the evaluation of this experiment:

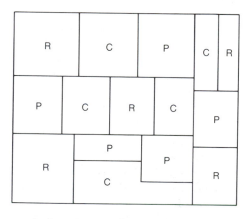

P Proactive   C Control   R Reactive

FIGURE 14-9. Schematic representation of the fifteen-beat experimental area of the Kansas City Patrol Experiment. [From George L. Kelling et al., *The Kansas City Patrol Experiment* (Washington, D.C.: Police Foundation, 1974), p. 9.]

1. The amount of reported crime in the reactive, control, and proactive beats revealed only one significant statistical variation: The number of incidents under the category of "other sex crimes," including such offenses as exhibitionism and molestation (excluding rape), was higher in reactive areas than in control areas, but project evaluators felt this significance was most likely random.

2. There were no statistically significant differences found in regard to fluctuations in crimes that were not officially reported to the police.

3. No statistically significant differences in arrests among the three types of beats were found.

4. Security measures taken by citizens and businesses were not significantly altered with the variations in the level of patrolling.

5. There was little correlation found between the level of patrol and the citizens' and business persons' attitude toward the policing.

6. The citizens' fear of crime was not significantly changed by the alterations in the level of routine preventive patrol.

7. The response time taken for police to answer calls was not significantly changed by variations in the level of routine preventive patrol.

8. The level of patrol had no significant effect on the incidence of traffic accidents.

The interpretations and findings of the Kansas City Patrol Experiment are highly controversial. Upon learning of the study, some local leaders felt that further increases in police manpower were not warranted and that decreases might even be justified. However, these persons failed to realize that a random moving patrol is not the only strategy of prevention available to police. The findings do suggest that administrators might be able to move into team policing—diverting significant person hours from routine patrol to community interface—without increasing the crime rate. This linkage, however, between the Kansas City Patrol Experiment and team policing is tenuous.

The RAND Criminal Investigation Study

In 1973, the RAND Corporation was awarded a grant by the National Institute of Law Enforcement and Criminal Justice to undertake a nationwide study of criminal investigations in major metropolitan police agencies.[58] The purposes of the study were to describe how police investigations were organized and managed and to assess the contribution of various activities to overall police effectiveness. Prior to the RAND study, police investigators had not been subject to the type of scrutiny that was being focused on other types of police activity. Most police administrators knew little about the effectiveness of the day-to-day activities of their investigative units, and even less about the practice of other departments.

The RAND study focused on the investigation of serious crimes against unwilling victims (index offenses), as opposed to vice, gambling, and narcotics. The information on current practice was obtained by a national survey of municipal and county police agencies who employed more than 150 officers or jurisdictions with a population over 100,000. In order to obtain a representative sample, interviews and observations were conducted in over twenty-five departments. Data on the outcome of investigations were obtained from the FBI Uniform Crime Report tapes, from internal evaluations, and from samples of completed cases. In addition, data on the allocation of investigative efforts were obtained from a computerized work-load file maintained by the Kansas City Police Department.

The data from the national survey and the Uniform Crime Reports were then combined in order to analyze the relationships between departmental characteristics and apprehension effectiveness. In turn, case samples were analyzed to determine how specific cases were solved.

Policy Recommendations

1. The RAND study strongly suggests that post-arrest investigation activities be coordinated more directly with the prosecutors, either by allowing prosecutors to exert more guidance over the practices and policies of investigators, or by assigning investigators to the prosecutor's office. The purpose of this recommendation was to attempt to increase the percentage of cases that could be prosecuted.

2. Patrol officers should be given a larger role in conducting preliminary investigations—to provide an adequate basis for case screening and to reduce or attempt to eliminate redundant efforts by an investigator.

3. Additional and improved resources should be devoted to the processing of latent prints and improved systems should be developed for the organizing and searching of print files.

4. The study recommended that with regard to follow-up investigations for the cases a department selected to pursue, a distinction should be drawn between cases that merely require routine clerical processing and those that require legal skills or those of a special investigative nature.

The RAND study is still a subject of controversy within the police profession. Many police officials, especially those without detective experience, were sympathetic to the study in that it supported their own impressions of how investigators functioned. Others criticized the study for "telling us what we already knew." Some police chiefs became resentful because the study was used by city officials as an excuse to cut police budgets, and others refused to accept the findings because of the limited number of departments that were studied.[59]

There have not been any major attempts to extend or replicate the findings in the RAND study; a number of reports have been published with consistent findings. Bloch and Weidman's[60] analysis of the investigative practices of the Rochester, New York, Police Department and Greenberg's[61] efforts to develop a felony investigation decision model both resulted in findings that support the idea that preliminary investigations, which are carried out in a majority of arrests, can provide adequate information for screening cases. A report by the Vera Institute on felony arrests in New York City indicated that a substantial portion of felony arrests for street crimes involve offenders who are known to their victims,[62] and a report by Forst on the disposition of felony arrests in Washington, D.C., demonstrates the importance of physical evidence and multiple witnesses in securing convictions for felony street crimes.[63] In general these studies suggest that often much of the information needed to solve a case is supplied by the uniformed officer who does the original investigation as opposed to cases which are solved by a detective's followup investigation.

Making Evaluation Work

The previously cited projects have yielded considerable debate similiar to other controversial studies focusing on the impact of computerization on the police, the effectiveness of women officers, and the general role or function of uniformed police. It has become apparent that with respect to evaluations, there are two types of police administrators:

1. "Trapped" administrators believe in the efficiency, rightness, or perhaps the inevitability of their programs. If evaluations demonstrate a lack of effectiveness in the programs advocated by these administrators, they are likely to dismiss the evaluations as "irrelevant," "too academic," or "invalid," or to simply shelve and ignore them. This posture creates problems for evaluation staffs and inhibits the intelligent development and execution of police programs.

2. "Experimental" administrators are not committed to a particular program, but to the concept of improving individual programs and the police department as a whole. If new or old programs are found by experimental administrators to be lacking, they are shelved or modified in attempts to find more successful ways. Experimental police administrators might be disappointed if evaluations showed ineffectiveness, but unlike the trapped administrators they are not disorganized nor do they fail to act upon the results. The experimental administrators are pragmatic and more interested in finding solutions than in justifying a particular course of action.[64]

Returning to the material covered in Chapter 5 on leadership, many of the attributes of the experimental administrator can be associated with the reform-oriented and nontraditional leadership styles. Additionally, by comparing the attributes of trapped and experimental police administrators, it is seen that the administrator is the key to whether evaluation will be a useful management tool. In order to make evaluation "pay off" police administrators must:

1. Adopt a genuinely supportive stance toward evaluation. Such a stance is reflected in the quality of staff selected for assignment to the evaluation function; in the resources made available to the evaluation effort; in according evaluation a place in the police organizational structure, which suggests its importance to the administrator; in the willingness to be involved in the evaluation process; and in ensuring a good relationship between the evaluation unit and the line bureaus.

2. Be willing to learn the key concepts in evaluation. There is considerable amount of informative, but not overly technical, written material for police administrators, and they must avail themselves of it and other opportunities to learn, including attendance at workshops.[65]

3. Require informative evaluation. To "inform" means that the "information" being transmitted is understood. This requires not only that police administrators learn something of the key concepts and language of evaluation but that they require evaluators to learn the key concepts and language of management.

4. Be assertive when dealing with researchers. The expectations and informational needs to administrators must be made known specifically to the evaluators. When evaluators present concepts or procedures with which administrators are unfamiliar, they should require an explanation in terms that can be understood by the administrators. Nothing should be accepted "on faith."

5. Remember George Bernard Shaw's observation that every profession has its "conspiracy against the laity." Evaluation reports are often laced with dozens of complex statistical tables that are easily understood by evaluators but not by administrators. Evaluation, however, is a logical and not a statistical process. Complex statistical notations should be eliminated altogether, except perhaps as appendices, and the results stated in straightforward language. Reports that do not do so should be returned to the evaluators for redrafting.

6. Be able to describe the evaluation procedures and results to other nonresearchers, such as city managers, budget analysts, civic club members, and city councils or county commissions. Although administrators may have gained some sophistication in evaluation, they must guard against the use of "research jargon." Their purpose is not to display mastery but to win supporters for police programs.

7. Lose no chance internally or externally to praise the evaluation staff, their products, and their contributions.

8. Personally adopt and foster an environment supportive of experimentation.

9. Understand that much evaluative research is flawed and can be criticized but that the defects are seldom so great that all the information is useless. This means that police administrators must be willing to accept a certain element of risk in making policy and program decisions.[66]

The Insider-Outsider Evaluator Question

Police administrators have several options with respect to who conducts the evaluation of experimental programs: (1) the police units conducting the activity may also perform the evaluation; (2) the evaluation may be done by the police department's planning and research unit; (3) another department of government, such as Finance and Management, may take responsibility; or (4) a contract may be executed with a research institute, a consultant, or some other related independent provider of services. These various possibilities raise certain questions, such as "Is it appropriate for the police unit conducting an experimental program to evaluate itself?" Whereas the need to separate those who are carrying out an experimental program and those who evaluate it is apparent, the question of how much separation there should be gives rise to the "insider-outsider" evaluator question.

Among the views that should be considered when a police administrator is trying to decide whether to use the department's planning and research unit or an "outsider" to evaluate an experimental program are:

1. The public and public officials may have more confidence in an autonomous "outsider."

2. The "outsider" may have greater competence.

3. "Outsiders" may be perceived as being more objective.

4. An "outsider" may have a prestigious name that can be an asset in promoting the experimental program.

5. "Outsiders" may "sweeten" the results obtained by the program to gain favor and possible future business.

6. "Insiders" have greater knowledge of the operation of their particular department.

7. "Insiders" may see more practical ramifications to the results of the program than "outsiders."

8. "Insiders" may suppress negative findings out of departmental loyalty or fear of personal and professional consequences to them.

9. "Insiders" may be more responsive to the legitimate directives of police administrators.

10. "Insiders" may have a "special axe to grind" and withhold or distort findings that reflect favorably on the program or on particular individuals.[67]

When such factors as cost, departmental staff capacity, and the availability of competent outsiders are added, the most advantageous way in which to proceed may still not be clear. In such matters, the identification of the issues is often a great deal easier to come by than is the answer. In other cases, there may be no decision to make other than who the external evaluator will be, since some grants are conditioned by the requirement of—and money is provided for—an independent evaluator who is external to the unit of government being used.

Summary

Productivity has two fundamental components: effectiveness and efficiency. Stated simply, effectiveness means that the police reached the objective they sought to achieve. In considering efficiency the question is, "How much of our resources were required to achieve this objective?" More recently, considerations of productivity have also included the dimension of quality. Successful productivity improvement programs are generally found to have met a basic checklist of conditions that include such variables as some analytical capacity and the ability to overcome any resistance.

Productivity programs may be—in terms of implementation—centralized, decentralized, or nondirective. Regardless of the implementation strategy, productivity programs require (1) doing more with current resources or (2) maintaining or increasing output in the face of decreased resources. Total performance management is a comprehensive approach to productivity improvement that combines the features of industrial engineering and behavioral science techniques. A natural adjunct to a productivity improvement program is an MBO system. The measurement of productivity raises difficult challenges such as establishing some relationship between what the police do and any changes, and how to ensure that an increase in productivity does not have the unintended consequences of reducing the quality of service.

The evaluation of police programs is an absolute necessity. Three types of evaluation can be employed: (1) process, (2) program, and (3) impact. The police routinely, often without recognizing it, do process evaluation, and performance measures are often nothing more than a variant on some type of program evaluation design such as the one-group pretest versus post-test comparison. Police administrators can and must take certain steps to ensure useful evaluations. The issue of inside versus outside program evaluators raises a number of questions that must be considered in light of the specifics of the situation involved, as does the issue of "insiders versus outsiders" in organizational change, discussed in the next chapter.

Discussion Questions

1. Discuss the growing relationship between private security and public law enforcement.
2. For what three reasons should all of us be concerned about productivity?
3. What four ways can police productivity be imposed according to the National Commission on Productivity?
4. Define the words *efficiency* and *effectiveness*.
5. You have been assigned the responsibility for developing a productivity improve-

ment effort. What sequential steps will you follow in developing and implementing it?

6. What is TPM?

7. Discuss the key elements of MBO.

8. What are the three major obstacles in implementing an MBO program?

9. Describe the three types of program evaluation.

10. Explain the Kansas City Preventative Patrol Experiment and the RAND Criminal Investigation study in terms of evaluation.

11. Distinguish between "trapped" and "experimental" administrators.

12. What measures must a police manager take to make program evaluation meaningful?

13. What issues arise when attempting to decide whether to use the police department's internal unit or an "outsider" to evaluate an experimental program?

Notes

1. Much of this section has been modified from Carol H. Weiss, "Evaluation Research in the Political Context," in E. Struening and M. Guttentag, *Handbook of Evaluation Research*, vol. 1 (Beverly Hills, Calif.: Sage, 1975), pp. 13–25.

2. U.S. Civil Service Commission, *Ten Questions and Answers on Productivity* (Washington, D.C.: U.S. Civil Service Commission, 1977), p. 3. Also, see Daniel A. Blumberg, "Higher Productivity: The Only Lasting Answer to Spiraling Inflation," *Financial Planning Today*, 4 (July 1980), pp. 159–165.

3. Mark E. Keane, "Why Productivity Improvement?" in *Productivity Improvement Handbook for State and Local Government*, ed. George J. Washnis (New York: John Wiley, 1980), p. 10.

4. Ibid., p. 10.

5. Ibid., p. 10.

6. John J. Norton, "Proposition 13: Law Enforcement's Unlucky Number," *Police Chief*, 45:9 (September 1978), p. 22.

7. Ibid., p. 22.

8. Michael Codd, a 1974 address at a John Jay College of Criminal Justice alumni luncheon, New York City, as reported by James M. Erikson, "When the Buck Stops," *Police Chief*, 43:4 (April 1976), p. 15.

9. "Layoffs Lay Police Spirit Low," *Law Enforcement News*, 6:7 (April 7, 1980), p. 1, and "911 Calls Ring Off the Hook as Detroit Sings Layoff Blues," *Law Enforcement News*, 6:15 (September 8, 1980), p. 2.

10. "911 Calls Ring Off the Hook," p. 2.

11. W. C. Cunningham and T. H. Taylor, "The Growing Role of Private Security," *National Institute of Justice Research in Brief* (Washington, D.C.: U.S. Government Printing Office, October 1984), p. 3.

12. Ibid., p. 4.

13. Ibid., p. 3.

14. Ibid., p. 1.

15. *Personnel News*, 40 (September 1974), p. 1.

16. National Commission on Productivity. *Report of the Advisory Group on Productivity in Law Enforcement on Opportunities for Improving Productivity in Police Services* (Washington, D.C.: U.S. Government Printing Office, 1973).

17. Keane, "Why Productivity Improvement?", p. 8.

18. Frederick O'R. Hayes, "Leadership and Politics of the Productivity Process," in *Productivity Handbook for State and Local Government*, pp. 19–23, with some changes and additions.

19. Edgar G. Crane, Jr., "Productivity in State Government," *Productivity Handbook for State and Local Government*, p. 55.

20. National Center for Productivity and Quality of Working Life, in *Guide to Productivity Projects*, 3d ed. (Washington, D.C.: U.S. Government Planning Office, July 1976), p. 46.

21. Ibid., p. 44.

22. James P. Morgan, "Planning and Implementing a Productivity Program," in *Readings on Productivity in Policing*, eds. Joan L. Wolfe and John F. Heapy (Washington, D.C.: Police Foundation, 1975), p. 130.

23. The Scottsdale, Arizona, case is taken from George P. Barbour, Jr., "Law Enforcement," in *Productivity Handbook for State and Local Government*, p. 938.

24. National Commission on Productivity and Work Quality, *Jurisdictional Guide to Productivity Improvement Projects* (Washington, D.C.: U.S. Government Printing Office, November 1975).

25. "SRI Model Gets High Marks as a Solvability Predictor," *Law Enforcement News*, 6:3 (February 11, 1980), pp. 1 and 6.

26. "First Audit of Philly Police in 14 Years Shows Abuse of Sick Leave, Areas to Trim," *Crime Control Digest*, 14:11 (March 17, 1980), pp. 4–5.

27. Keane, "Why Productivity Improvement?" pp. 9–10.

28. The discussion of these three strategies is drawn from Frederick O'R. Hayes, "Implementation Strategies to Improve Productivity," in *Productivity Improvement Handbook for State and Local Government*, pp. 26–27.

29. For information on San Diego's Financial Management Department's work on police productivity, see *Productivity Improvement Program: Police Investigations Bureau* (San Diego, Calif.: Financial Management Department, 1979).

30. Hayes, "Implementation Strategies to Improve Productivity," p. 26.

31. National Center for Productivity and Quality of Working Life, *Total Performance Management: Some Pointers for Action* (Washington, D.C.: U.S. Government Printing Office, 1978), p. 2.

32. Ibid., p. 3.

33. "Performance Management Yields Morale Benefits," *Public Administration Times*, 2:7 (April 1, 1979), p. 10; Sherry A. Suttles, "TPM: Long Beach Tackler Performance," *Western City* (February 1979), p. 1.

34. See Budget and Evaluation Department, *Police Field Patrol Activities: An Evaluation* (Charlotte, N.C.: Budget and Evaluation Department, August 6, 1976).

35. Other terms that describe an MBO-type system include "cohesive management system" and "priority program planning system," both of which were used by the New York City Police Department in 1974 and 1975.

36. Drucker is commonly credited with coining the term and probably should be accorded recognition more for publicizing than innovating the operations involved.

37. Peter Drucker, *Management: Tasks, Responsibilities, Practices* (New York: Harper & Row, 1973, p. 438). Also, see George S. Odiorne, *Management by Objectives* (New York: Pittman, 1965), pp. 55–56. For an excellent synopsis on the empirical evidence on MBO, see Mark L. McConkie, "Classifying and Reviewing the Empirical Work on MBO: Some Implications," *Group Organization Studies*, 4:4 (December 1979), pp. 461–475.

38. Charles D. Hale, *Fundamentals of Police Administration* (Boston, Mass: Holbrook Press, 1977), p. 333.

39. Rodney H. Brady, "MBO Goes to Work in the Public Sector," *Harvard Business Review*, 51 (March-April, 1973), pp. 65–74.

40. Ronald G. Lynch, *The Police Manager,* 2d ed. (Boston, Mass: Holbrook, 1978), p. 154.

41. The Ocala Police Department, "Zone Awareness Program" (Ocala, Fla.: Mimeographed), 10.

42. C. D. Stein, "Objective Management Systems: Two to Five Years After Implementation," *Personnel Journal,* 54 (October 1975), p. 525.

43. Ibid., p. 525.

44. Mark L. McConkie, "Classifying and Reviewing the Empirical Work on MBO: Some Implications," *Group and Organization Studies,* 4 (December 1979), pp. 467–471.

45. Ibid., pp. 471–472.

46. Jack Reynolds, *Management-Oriented Corrections Evaluation Guidelines* (Washington, D.C.: U.S. Government Printing Office, 1979), p. 3.

47. Ibid., p. 3.

48. Ibid., p. 3.

49. Harry P. Hatry, Richard E. Winnie, and Donald M. Fisk, *Practical Program Evaluation for State and Local Government Officials* (Washington, D.C.: Urban Institute, 1973), p. 8.

50. U.S. Department of Housing and Urban Development, *A Guide for Local Evaluation* (Washington, D.C.: U.S. Government Printing Office, 1976), pp. 1–2, with minor modification.

51. James F. Rooney, "Organizational Success Through Program Failure: Skid Row Rescue Missions," *Social Forces,* 58 (March 1980), p. 904.

52. Ibid., p. 904.

53. This is not to suggest that the evaluations were done very well. In a sample for forty-two completed evaluations done in four states between 1973 and 1975, one study found serious deficiencies. For example, only 19 percent of the projects adequately set forth the evaluation research design and methodology used, and 55 percent did not present the projects' hypotheses or relate them to the projects' intended goals and objectives. See U.S. Comptroller General, *Evaluation Needs of Crime Control Planners, Decision-Makers, and Policy Makers* (Washington, D.C.: U.S. Government Printing Office, 1978), p. 49. Illustrative of other evidence regarding the need for improved police program evaluation was a major 1974 study funded by the National Science Foundation, which was generally critical of what existed. See Saul I. Gass and John M. Dawson, *An Evaluation of Policy Related Research: Reviews and Critical Discussions of Policy Related Research in the Field of Police Protection* (Bethesda, Md.: Mathematica, 1974).

54. See George L. Kelling et al., *The Kansas City Preventive Patrol Experiment* (Washington, D.C.: Police Foundation, 1974); Richard C. Larson, "What Happened to Patrol Operations in Kansas City: A Review of the Kansas City Preventive Patrol Experiment," *Journal of Criminal Justice,* 3 (Winter 1975), pp. 267–297; Stephen E. Feinberg, Kinley Larntz, and Albert J. Reiss, Jr., "Redesigning the Kansas City Preventive Patrol Experiment," *Evaluation,* 3:1–2 (1976), pp. 124, 131.

55. See William B. Sanders, *Detective Work: A Study of Criminal Behavior* (New York: Free Press, 1977); Peter W. Greenwood, Jan. M. Chaiken, and Joan Persilia, *The Criminal Investigation Process* (Lexington, Mass: D. C. Heath, 1977).

56. This section is a synopsis of the Kansas City Patrol Experiment as reported by G. L. Kelling et al., *The Kansas City Preventive Patrol Experiment* (Washington, D.C.: Police Foundation, 1974), and H. J. Vetter and L. Territo, *Crime and Justice in America* (St. Paul, Minn.: West Publishing, 1984), pp. 161–163.

57. George L. Kelling et al., *The Kansas City Preventive Patrol Experiment,* (Washington, D.C.: Police Foundation, 1974), p. 42.

58. This section is a synopsis of the RAND Criminal Investigator Study as reported by Peter W. Greenwood, *The RAND Criminal Investigation Study: Its Findings and Impacts to*

Date (Santa Monica, Calif.: The RAND Corporation, July 1979), pp. 3–7 and H. J. Vetter and L. Territo, _Crime and Justice in America_ (St. Paul, Minn.: West, 1984), pp. 176–178.

59. Daryl F. Gates, and Lyle Knowles, "An Evaluation of the RAND Corporation Analyses," _The Police Chief_ (July 1976), pp. 20–24, 74, 77.

60. P. Bloch and D. Weidman, _Managing Criminal Investigations: Prescriptive Package_ (Washington, D.C.: U.S. Government Printing Office, 1975).

61. B. Greenberg et al., _Felony Investigation Decision Model: An Analysis of Investigative Elements of Information_ (Washington D.C.: U.S. Government Printing Office, 1977).

62. The Vera researchers noted that in 56 percent of all felony arrests for crimes against the person, the victim had a prior relationship with the offender. In turn, 87 percent of these cases—as compared with only 29 percent of cases involving strangers—resulted in dismissals because the complainant refused to cooperate with the prosecutor. Once complainants "cool off," they are not interested in seeing the defendants prosecuted. Consequently, the Vera report recommends the use of neighborhood justice centers, rather than the courts, as the appropriate place to deal with most cases that involve prior relationships between victims and perpetrators.

63. B. Forst, _What Happens After Arrest_ (Washington, D.C.: U.S. Government Printing Office, 1978).

64. For a description of the trapped and experimental administrators, see Donald T. Campbell, "Reforms as Experiments," in _Quasi-Experimental Approaches,_ eds. James A. Caporaso and Leslie L. Rose, Jr. (Evanston, Ill: Northwestern University Press, 1973), p. 224; Stuart Adams, _Evaluative Research in Corrections_ (Washington, D.C.: U.S. Government Printing Office, 1975), pp. 19–20.

65. For example, see Lawrence P. Clark, _Designs for Evaluating Social Programs_ (Croton-on-Hudson, N.Y.: Policy Studies Associates, 1979); Guy D. Boston, _Techniques for Project Evaluation_ (Washington, D.C.: U.S. Government Printing Office, 1977); Weiss, _Evaluation Research,_ pp. 6–9, on the differences and similarities between evaluation and other types of research; Douglas K. Stewart, _Evaluation for Criminal Justice Agencies: Problem-Oriented Discussion_ (Washington, D.C.: U.S. Government Printing Office, 1978); National Criminal Justice Reference Service, _How Well Does It Work: Review of Criminal Justice Evaluation_ (Washington, D.C.: U.S. Government Printing Office, 1978); Donald T. Campbell and Julian C. Stanley, _Experimental and Quasi-Experimental Designs for Research_ (Chicago: Rand McNally, 1963).

66. These points are restatements, with some additions, of material found in Michael P. Kirby, _The Role of the Administrator in Evaluation_ (Washington, D.C.: Pretrial Services Resource Center, 1979), pp. 11–12.

67. On these points, see Weiss, _Evaluation Research,_ pp. 20–21; Charles S. Bullock, III, and Harrell R. Rodgers, Jr., "Impediments to Policy Evaluation: Perceptual Distortion and Agency Loyalty," _Social Science Quarterly, 57_ (December 1976–1977), pp. 506–519.

*Each progressive spirit is opposed
by a thousand men appointed to
guard the past.*

MAETERLINCK

Organizational Change

Introduction

In the dynamic society surrounding law enforcement agencies today, the question of whether change will occur is not relevant. Instead, the issue relates to how do police executives cope with the barrages of changes that confront daily those who attempt to keep their agencies viable, current, and responsive to community needs. Although change is a fact of life, police executives cannot be content to let change occur as it will. They must be able to develop strategies to plan, direct, and control change.[1]

To be effective in the change process, police executives must have more than good diagnostic skills. Once they have analyzed the demands of their environment, they must be able to adapt their leadership style to fit the demands and develop the means to change some or all of the other situational variables.[2]

This chapter has been organized to facilitate an examination of some of the critical dimensions of planned change. A police executive contemplating the implementation of change, especially on a large scale, will increase the likelihood of success if certain fundamental principles, discussed here, are followed.

Why Change Occurs

The initiation of large-scale organizational change in American law enforcement tends to follow similar patterns. Often, a new police chief will be appointed either from within or from outside of the law enforcement agency as a prelude to a planned, large-scale reorganization desired by a city manager, mayor, or some other influential person or groups in the community. Prior to the appointment of the police chief, it is likely that one or more of the following events transpired and gave impetus to the plan changes:

1. A new mayor is elected or a new city manager appointed who wants to replace the current chief with a new chief of his own choice.
2. The police department has been judged to be generally deficient in its crime-fighting capabilities by a study, the local media, by interest groups within the community, or by a commission of citizens created specifically to make a careful assessment of the capabilities of the department.
3. Police minority relations are at an all-time low, in part because of repeated alleged acts and misconduct by the police in dealing with members of the minority community.
4. The police department has a poor public image because of its low recruiting standards and failure to provide adequate training for its officers.
5. The previous police chief and or other high-ranking police officials have been indicted for accepting payoffs related to gambling, prostitution, liquor violations, or narcotics violations.
6. The former police chief, who was an elderly person and who had served for many years as the bulwark of traditionalism, recently retired.
7. The ranks of the police department and the community agree that morale among the police officers is dangerously low, as reflected in an abnormally high attrition rate, excessive use of sick time, incidence of injury to prisoners, high numbers of resisted arrests, increasing citizen complaints of officer misconduct, poor supervisory ratings, and generally poor performance of personnel throughout the organization.

The newly appointed police chief has likely been given a mandate to move forward with speed to rectify the difficulties in the department and is, more often than not, excited and enthusiastic about the prospect of implementing ideas formulated through years of professional growth and experience. It may appear that the chief is operating from a position of considerable strength and need not be too concerned with those who might try to thwart the change process. However, such an assumption could be very risky, although there will be factions in the department and in the community that fully support the change effort, there will be powerful factions within the police department and within the community that will attempt to block any changes that appear to endanger their interests.

No chief can afford to overlook the impact that each type of group can have upon the planned changes. In developing a strategy for change, certain elements must be built into the plan to identify and enhance the cooperation and support a group that desires change and enhance the possibility of winning over the groups that may be neutral or only moderately opposed to the planned changes. Also, the plan must have a number of highly developed strategies to counteract or neutralize

BOX 15–1.

Study Hits Gardner Police

By STEVE MARANTZ, *Globe Staff*

GARDNER—The 173-page Gardner "Police Management Study" took two months and 686 hours to prepare. When it was released last Monday, Capt. R. P. Bernard summarized it in a few seconds, his descriptions apt for a supermarket tabloid.

"This report makes us out to be sex maniacs who sleep on duty and act rude to the public, and it makes the city sound like it's wide open to gambling and drugs," said Bernard.

"Did I leave anything out?"

Only a few things. The study, prepared by Northeastern professor Robert Sheehan, also noted that equipment is obsolete, the station is run down, morale is low, public image is bad, management is backward, the union is too strong, officers abuse sick time and make minor arrests to ensure paid court time, and job stress is so severe it could result in violence.

The study concluded that "police officers function in a milieu of near anarchy with little or no supervision, behave like spoiled children, relate to the public poorly, and go about what little work they do in a self-serving manner."

On Tuesday, officials in this north-central town of 17,000 reacted. City Councilor Rosaire St. Jean, referring to the study's mention of an unspecified location where in the past on-duty officers allegedly trysted with females, said, "This reminds me of the book 'The Choir Boys.' "

"Take two steps back"

Wednesday, Mayor Charles P. McKean, who commissioned the study at the urging of the 25-member officers' union, called for the resignation of Chief Richard L. Gemborys, saying, "Sometimes you've got to take two steps back and one forward." Officer Bernard DiPasquale, president of the union, also called for Gemborys' resignation, saying "This department is a mess."

Thursday Gemborys returned from a deer-hunting vacation, during which he had sighted two bucks and missed both, and said of the study, "To paraphrase Clint Eastwood, it didn't make my day."

Gemborys, saying he will not resign, minimized the study, and said Sheehan has produced "hatchet" studies of at least two other police departments. "When this guy gets done, there's nothing but dead bodies around," said Gemborys.

Sheehan could not be reached for comment.

Gemborys also downplayed the importance of rank-and-file criticism cited in the study.

"I have one officer who called me a dictator," said Gemborys. "He's the one charged with rape. He's got a district court hearing coming up." (All charges against the officer were dropped Friday.)

A rift is acknowledged

Gemborys does not deny that a labor-management rift exists.

"You know the old theory about how prisoners should run the prison because they spend the most time there?" said Gemborys, 48, and chief for the last eight years. "No way. You can't have the inmates running the prison.

"To be perfectly frank, the majority of these guys bitching and moaning can't pass the promotional exam. We recently had six officers take the sergeants promotional exam. One passed. One of the guys who failed is the union president."

Some officers claim Gemborys administers arbitrary and vindictive punishment for minor rule infractions. "It got so bad one guy was afraid to go inside a department store to warm up," said an officer. "The poor guy had icicles on his eyebrows."

Almost everybody deplores the condition of the station; DiPasquale complained of an ant infestation.

McKean said he has made improvements, among them the removal of a worn rug in the front corridor.

"We took up the rug and there was a hole in the floor, which we fixed," said McKean. "So what do they do? They lay down orange linoleum. I could have killed them."

A relaxed atmosphere

The study cites the "clubhouse" atmosphere of the station as a place where officers congregate to watch television and drink coffee. In fact, the desk officer early Wednesday evening was watching "Hawaii Five-O" on a shelf-mounted color television. "We condone the television so that officers can keep up with what's happening," said Bernard. "We brought in a coffee machine because we'd rather see them drink coffee in here than some coffee shop. We did it as a public relations thing. Plus, I like coffee myself."

As a result of the chaotic and demoralized force, the study suggests, illegal gaming and drug trafficking are flourishing in Gardner. Bernard said that a recent arrest of three persons on gaming charges put a crimp in the city's gambling activity. He said that robbery and burglary have declined steadily for the last five years.

Source: The Boston Sunday Globe, December 22, 1985, p. 47.

those individuals or groups that will make every effort possible to reduce the success of the planned changes.

The risks involved in implementing large-scale changes are considerable, but, surprisingly, many police executives either fail to take notice of these risks in their preplanning strategies or grossly underestimate them. This phenomenon has too often resulted in both goals and objectives falling far below expectations or failing to come to fruition at all. In other instances, the change effort encounters so many difficulties, obstacles, and opposition that the chief is eventually forced to resign or is fired.

The Change Agent

Throughout this chapter, the term *change agent* will be used to describe an individual or group from within or outside the police department whose role involves the stimulation, guidance, and stabilization of change. Within the context of planned organizational change, the role of the change agent is to assist in resolving organizational problems.[3] The specific person or group playing the role of change agent will vary. In some cases, the change agent will be the police chief or some person within the agency designated by the chief to assume responsibility for implementing change. In other cases, the change agent may be some individual or group of consultants hired from outside the organization to conduct a comprehensive study of all or certain segments of the organization and to produce a comprehensive report with specific recommendations for enhancing the operation of the police department. On occasion, outside consultants will also assist in implementing the recommended changes.

When a police agency does seek outside assistance, it frequently contracts with a private firm whose members possess high levels of experience, skills, techniques, and knowledge about how to improve the level of performance of law enforcement agencies.[4] Such consultants often possess academic credentials at the graduate level and considerable prior experience as law enforcement practitioners, administrators, or educators.

Framework for Change Agent's Role

The change agent's organization model determines what information is collected for diagnosing an organization's problems.[5] The most important things examined during diagnosis also tend to be the things that are worked on most often to create change in the organization. The relationship between diagnosis and change approaches has been proposed by Noel Tichy, who studied ninety-one types of change agents.[6] Figure 15-1 is a model designed by Tichy for studying the role of change agents.

There are five basic components to the model, all of which interact with one another. First are the *background characteristics* of the change agent. These typically include the agent's educational training, income, religion, age, sex, relationships to clients, and so forth. Second is the *value component*. This is the agent's evaluative orientation toward change, such as attitudes toward important social changes, political orientation (liberal, moderate, conservative), social-change goals (increased range of individual freedom and choice, improved satisfaction of members, equalization of power between organization members, and so forth), and the goals that he or she feels change agents should have. This component represents behavior expected of a change agent. The third basic component is the agent's *cognitive component*—concepts about means of affecting change. The fourth is the agent's *technology component*. This refers to the tools and skills the change agent has used to effect social change. To make use of his or her knowledge (cognitive component) and to act on his or her other values (value component), each change agent has a set of techniques, such as sensitivity training, operations research, survey feedback, and team development that can be applied to a situation. Finally, the *concurrent characteristics* refer to the actual behavior of the change agent. The relationship among the five components of the model assumes that stress exists in the change agent when the value component and concurrent characteristics or the cognitive component and actions are not in agreement with each other.

Types of Change Agents

Based on consistent differences in the patterns of these five components of the model in Figure 15-1, four different types of change agents have been identified. These are (1) people change technology (PCT), (2) analysis from the top (AFT), (3) organization development (OD), and (4) outside pressure (OP). Since the outside pressure type (e.g., Ralph Nader, Betty Furness) is rarely used by managers to bring about changes, only the three other types of change agents will be discussed.

People Change Technology (PCT). Change agents who use people change technology work to achieve change in the ways in which employees behave. These agents are concerned with improving motivation, job satisfaction, and productivity. One PCT agent described her role as being

> to help individuals and organizations focus on goals, obstacles that stand in the way of goal attainment, individual motivation patterns and requirements of the task, organizational goal attainment, emphasis on individual, and organizational self-development.

Tactics favored by the PCT change agent are role clarification, change in reward structure, change in decision-making structure, technological innovation, job training,

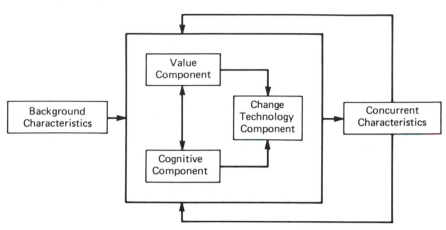

FIGURE 15-1. Framework for change agent's role. [From Noel M. Tichy, ''Agents of Planned Social Change: Congruence of Values, Cognitions, and Actions,'' *Administrative Science Quarterly,* 19 (1974), p. 165.]

and team development. Use of these tactics should lead to job enrichment, behavioral modification, need achievement training, management by objectives, and the like. The basic assumption of PCT change agents is that, if individuals change their behaviors, the organization, too, will change, especially if enough (or the right) individuals in the organization change.

Data gathered by Tichy indicate that PCT change agents usually hold academic positions with doctorates, range in age from thirty-five to forty, and have median incomes of $20,000 to $30,000. Their political orientation is liberal, and they express a moderate degree of social criticism. The linkage between political orientation and values indicates that their primary value is to improve system efficiency, increase output, and equalize the power and responsibility with the organization.

ANALYSIS FROM THE TOP (AFT)

Change agents who use the analysis-from-the-top approach rely primarily on the operations research model. These agents work on improving decision making and maintaining and controlling employee performance. One AFT agent described his role as being

> to work with groups concerned with problems of design and operation of system, to aid in resolving their problems. Normally, the work involves technological remodeling and analysis.

Tactics favored by the AFT change agent are changes in the decision-making structure, role clarification, technological innovation, job training, and changes in the reward structure. Use of these tactics should lead to changes in the decision-making structure of the organization, technological innovations, and job training in areas such as computerized information processing systems and development of new tasks. AFT change agents assume that, if the organization's impersonal technical and structural processes are changed, the organization's efficiency will increase.

AFT change agents are likely to be older than PCT change agents (ranging in age from forty to fifty), have a median income over $40,000, are not associated with an academic institution, and do not have a doctorate. They are moderates in political orientation and are not critical of society.

ORGANIZATION DEVELOPMENT (OD)

Change agents who use organization development techniques work to improve the organization's problem-solving capabilities by helping people learn to help themselves. This involves assisting members of the organization to work out their interpersonal problems and communications, conflicts of interest, career plans, and the like. OD change agents rely on team development, role clarification, confrontation meetings, change in decision-making structure, and sensitivity training to achieve their goals. A basic goal of the OD change agent is to increase democratic participation in decision making by all members. In this way, the organization can develop problem-solving mechanisms so that key executives can work with each other.

The background characteristics of the OD change agents include a median age of forty to fifty, primarily Protestant religious beliefs, a high proportion holding degrees, and a median income of $30,000 to $40,000. Their political affiliation tends to be liberal to moderate. They do not advocate radical changes in organizations to achieve their objectives.

Basic Qualifications of Change Agents

The selection of change agents and or leaders for teams is a crucial element in the process of organizing for change. The capabilities and performances of the team leader have often been the critical factors in the success or failure of many programs of planned change.[7]

There are a number of qualities and qualifications that the change agent must possess to be successful, the single most important one being technical competence in the specific tasks of the change project. Dangers exist in bringing in persons from an unrelated or marginally related field.[8]

Another factor related to technological qualifications is the ability of the agent to develop solutions and recommendations for change that can be applied realistically within the framework of the skills and resources available within the organization. Thus, an understanding of the way in which police departments operate and are organized is essential to persons involved as change agents.

Planning skill is another important capability a change agent should possess. Particularly important is the ability to plan for the unexpected by allowing flexibility through alternative or contingency planning and the maintenance of reserved resources. Although the change agent should be able to function well in a crisis, efforts should be made to avoid crisis management as a characteristic mode of management.[9]

The ability of the change agent to work well with members of the organization who are not involved directly in the change plan is crucial. Indifference to persons and organizations outside the change team can create major problems.[10] Empathy with members of the larger organization can sensitize change agents to delicate areas in which extra caution is necessary; if an intervention in those areas is under consideration, it will increase the likelihood that change will be well received.[11]

Change Agent Errors

Just as change agents can enhance the effectiveness of change programs by developing certain traits, they can limit the effectiveness of the program or team by committing certain errors.

One serious error that a change agent can make is to become tied prematurely to a particular set of strategies and tactics. This problem is more severe when the commitment is made publicly and is compounded when individuals critical of the change process were not consulted prior to making the public statement about a change that will directly affect them or their areas of responsibility.

Planning for change should involve the identification of relevant groups affected by the change teams efforts, their interdependencies, and their need to feel involved in goal-setting and strategy design processes. Typically, the importance of cooperation is overlooked because a change agent may underestimate the value of the contribution that members of the organization can make in helping to structure and focus the change process. Sometimes the change agent is under the mistaken assumption that members of the police department do not want to participate actively in various aspects of change programs directed at them and/or they are unable to provide useful information through participation.[12]

Another error is inadequate planning for the initiation of the change process. The sudden creation of a formal commission, the quick institutionalization of a change team, the hasty hiring of a consultant, or some other rapid implementation of a formal change program may create immediate resistance. The change agent must not overlook the informal system, a problem likely to occur when the change agent is overly confident of his or her perception of the changes needed.

The change agent must also consider the roles played by individuals and groups outside the police department. This may include members of the local political community, citizen action groups, unions, and even spouses. The change agent must consider how the advocated change will affect these groups and what their perceived needs for change are, as well as what their expectations may be regarding the behavior of the change team and the consequences of the intervention.[13]

Change agents sometimes fail to identify or even recognize influential individuals or groups that may be willing to provide support for the change effort. Such persons or groups may be developed into strong advocates of the change if provided with adequate information in the appropriate manner. If an influential person or group is favorably disposed toward innovation, reinforcing information should be provided routinely, particularly if the advocated change is controversial and resisting groups are trying to alter the influential party's feelings and beliefs.[14]

Internal versus External Change Agents

When a decision has been made to reorganize a police department, one of the most important concerns is determining who will undertake the task. Should personnel from within the organization be selected? Should outside consultants be employed? Should a combination of sources from both groups be pooled in a cooperative effort? A number of useful guidelines can help to answer these questions.

Internal Change Agent: Pros and Cons

Certain positive features associated with selecting a change agent from within an agency make this an attractive alternative. The internal change agent will have valuable insights into both the formal and informal organization and will be aware of the potential sources of support for certain types of change as well as from which segments of the organization resistance is most likely to come. Such knowledge can prove quite useful in developing strategies for planned change. Because the change agent is a part of the organization, he or she will likely share certain values and attitudes with members of the organization with whom the agent will be working that will facilitate communications in all directions.[15] If the internal change agent has a reputation within the organization as a competent professional with unquestioned integrity, this, too, will enhance the change effort.

One drawback to using an internal agent is the possible lack of acceptance of the person by the organization as an "expert." Colleagues who remember when the change agent was "just a wet-behind-the-ears rookie" or who have personal jealousies or animosities directed at the agent will make it difficult for the internal agent to establish credibility. Some important questions may be raised when internal change agents are used. For example, what possible personal or professional gain does the individual hope to acquire? Is the change agent overly concerned about the ways in which the changes will negatively impact upon agency personnel that he or she knows personally? Does the internal change agent have some preconceived notions about the direction the change should take, thus limiting the range of viable alternatives that might be considered realistically?

Finally, individuals from within the agency acting as change agents will possibly have to be relieved of their present responsibilities, thus shifting the burden of their work to someone else. The extent to which this will impact upon the organization depends upon the amount of time involved in the change process, the amount of work to be shifted to subordinates, and the abilities of the subordinates.

External Change Agent: Pros and Cons

The externally selected change agent has from the outset certain important advantages over the internal change agent. Individuals from outside the organization employed as change agents are selected because of their knowledge, experience, and professional reputation. Thus, when entering the police agency, they already enjoy considerable credibility as "experts" in their field. This legitimacy tends to bestow upon the change agent a high degree of respect and deference. This, in turn, facilitates cooperation from key members of the organization, at least in the early stages of the change process. The external change agent has, more often than not, a broad range of experience with planned change and can complete the task both effectively and expeditiously.

One of the important disadvantages faced by the external change agent is the absence of knowledge to identify with accuracy the major forces within the organization that can help or hinder the change process. For example, is a group of police officers within the agency fearful of certain changes and are these officers prepared to mobilize support in the community to resist such changes? Is the police union potentially supportive of some changes but opposed to others? Who are the informal leaders in the organization? Is the reorganization effort just a ploy by a city manager, mayor, or city council to embarrass the police chief into a forced resignation or dismissal?

Since external change agents rarely have to actually implement the changes they recommend, have no long-term commitment to any single agency, and may be unfamiliar with the factors outside their designated realm, they may make recommendations that are difficult or impossible for the agency to implement. It is not unheard of for a consulting firm to make some recommendations that cannot be implemented legally, especially if the consulting firm representatives are not familiar with the state laws, local ordinances, civil service regulations, or state-mandated police officers' standards. Other recommendations may be impossible to implement because of serious budgetary limitations related to a community's tax base or because agency personnel lack the experience or expertise to do so.

It could be argued that it is precisely because the external change agent does not have to be concerned about certain extraneous elements that the external change agent can make a fair and objective assessment. However, the external change agent, to be of maximum benefit to the police department, must be able to assist in improving the organization within the framework of its ability to change. There are those who would suggest that the closer someone comes to actually having to be responsible for implementing change, the less idealistic and more realistic that person becomes. Thus, some police departments actually require as a part of the contractual agreement with a consulting firm that the representatives of the firm remain with the agency for some reasonable period of time to implement the more difficult changes.

Locating External Change Agents

The police chief or city manager contemplating the possibility of seeking outside assistance to provide an in-depth study of the police department is frequently faced with the dilemma of locating and then selecting the individual or firm that will provide this service. Although there is no central directory containing the names of individuals or firms providing this type of service, contact with the State Criminal Justice Planning Agency is a good starting point, as this agency often underwrites grants to fund such projects. The state planning agency will be able to provide information relating to police departments that have used consulting services and the names of firms providing such services. Police agencies using a particular consultant can then be contacted and their assessments of the consultants solicited. The consultant's final report to each police department should, if possible, be reviewed. Contacts should be made with the firm providing the service and a request made for a list of their former law enforcement clients. These departments, too, may be contacted and an assessment of the firm requested. After these contacts are made, a reasonably accurate picture of the quality and cost of services a consulting firm can deliver will emerge.

Methods of Organizational Change

Organizational change can be initiated in numerous ways, but approaches can be grouped into two broad categories: (1) those that focus on changing the individuals working in the organization and (2) those that focus on changing specific organizational structures. Effective programs of organizational change usually involve the simultaneous use of both approaches and a variety of intervention techniques.[16]

Changing Individuals

In general, future behavior is predicted by past behavior; that is, circumstances being equal, people will go on doing what they have always done. If an individual has been compliant, that person will continue to be compliant; if self-seeking, the individual will continue to be self-seeking. This picture is neither cynical nor pessimistic, it is simply realistic.[17]

Of course, individuals can change their attitudes and their behaviors. Certain conditions typically are associated with such change, and, by knowing what these conditions are, a person can increase the likelihood of effecting a desired change in behavior.[18]

Lewin suggests that change occurs in three phrases: (1) the unfreezing of an old pattern of relationships, (2) the changing to a new pattern through change induced by a change agent, and (3) the refreezing of a new pattern of relationships.[19]

UNFREEZING

A key motivator in the unfreezing phase of change is a feeling of discomfort with old behavior.[20] If a person feels no discomfort, no logic or force or threats will motivate the person to change. Certain techniques, however, can be employed to induce an individual to change.

The first step in a change program is to "unfreeze" or rearrange the environmental context that supports the individual's current behavior. Some of the mechanisms that might be used include removing reinforcement for the current behavior, inducing guilt or anxiety about the current behavior, making the individual feel more secure about change by reducing threats or barriers to change, removing the individual from the environment that supports current behavior, or physically changing the environment in which the person is behaving.

The following is an example provided by Reitz:

> a program designed to change a manager's leadership style could provide him with feedback that his current style is ineffective and inappropriate. It could involve changing his office location to make him more or less accessible to his employees. It could remove him from the situation and provide a "safe" climate in which he can experiment with alternative behaviors by sending him to a training program conducted away from the premises.[21]

CHANGING TO A NEW BEHAVIOR PATTERN

After the unfreezing of old behaviors, individuals seeking change must try an alternative behavior and determine its consequences.[22] There are two important elements necessary in this phase of the process. First, the change agent must be sensitive to the fact that experiences of success with a new behavior are so important that the behavior in the beginning should take place under controlled conditions. A change agent who wishes to establish problem-solving behavior, for example, should have individuals or groups participate in simulations or experiential learning situations that have predictable outcomes. By knowing that an exercise will demonstrate successful utilization of problem-solving skills, the change agent reinforces the knowledge, attitudes, and skills necessary to deal with more complicated, nonexperiential situations; success in an initially controlled training environment begets success in real-life situations.

Second, if an individual's regular environment is antithetical to the successful trial of a new behavior, the individual should, if it is practical, be removed from the existing environment until the new behavior is learned.[23]

REFREEZING

Refreezing is the stabilization and integration of the changed behavior. It is accomplished most effectively by providing the individual with a social and physical environment that will support the changed behavior.[24]

One authority has identified a number of subprocesses for the refreezing phase:

> If the new attitude has been internalized while being learned, this has automatically facilitated refreezing because it has been fitted naturally to the individual's personality. If it has been learned through identification, it will persist only so long as the target relationship with the original influence model persists unless new surrogated models are found or social support and reinforcement is obtained for expression of the new attitude.[25]

Changing Organizational Structures and Systems

An alternative to attempting to change people who make up an organization is to change the structure of the organization itself or the systems and practices that guide its activities. Sometimes, the organizational change simply amounts to somebody pushing boxes around in an organization chart, with nobody else knowing or caring much about it. In other instances, this approach to change can profoundly influence the patterns of activity that take place within organization boundaries, with important consequences for the long-term growth and health of the organization.[26]

In law enforcement agencies, changing organizational structures is not an unusual way in which to implement change. Naturally, the extent of any reorganization will be affected by a number of variables, including the availability of funds to create new positions; the support for change from the city manager, mayor, or other local officials; and the reasons for the reorganization in the first place.

A reorganization can be a very powerful tool for implementing change. It can be used to designate new priorities in the areas of enforcement, improve the quality and quantity of police service, or improve police minority relations.

Radical versus Gradual Change

The objectives for any police chief contemplating change should be to do so in a manner that offers the greatest possibility of success; does not result in a reduction of the quality or quantity of service to the public; does not polarize the organization into warring factions; and does not result in the police chief being forced to resign or being fired. To achieve these goals, gradual changes are sometimes more effective than radical changes.

Conventional wisdom about change states that the way in which to change an organization is to bring in a new top executive, give the individual his or her head (and maybe a hatchet as well), and let the individual make the changes that he or she deems necessary. And, in fact, organizations (especially in times of crises) often use exactly that strategy to achieve change—sometimes unwittingly, sometimes not. What the conventional wisdom overlooks are the long-term consequences of unilateral,

top-down change. It may often be the case, for example, that short-term problems are solved quickly, radically, and dramatically by executive action but that the "human problems" of the organization, which very well may have been causal in generating the short-term problem in the first place, are substantially worsened in the process.[27]

The problem with radical and unilateral change, then, is the possibility of creating a negative balance of the human resources of the organization, which can result in a severe backlash in the organization over the long term. The complementary problem for changes that are made very gradually and participatively is that, after years of meetings and planning sessions and endless questions, nothing very striking or interesting has actually happened in the organization, and in a spirit of resignation, organization members slowly abandoned their change activities and settled back into their old ways.[28]

Finding an appropriate pace for change to take place—neither too quickly and radically nor too slowly and gradually—is one of the most critical problems of planned organizational change. Trying to set the right pace often poses special problems for organizational consultants—especially those who are based outside the organization. On the one hand, if they suggest or introduce change that moves too quickly or radically vis-à-vis a given organization, they risk losing their association with the organization and, therefore, any chance they might have to influence the effectiveness of the organization.[29] As one experienced observer notes in a list of "rules of thumb for consultants," the first task of the consultant is to "stay alive," one means of which is to take the level and pace of one's consulting activities in reasonable congruence with the current state of the organization.[30] Similarly, others[31,32] counsel consultants explicitly about being careful not to introduce interventions that are too intense or deep for the change organization to handle.

The other side of the issue is, of course, that the consultant or change expert can be "seduced" by the existing values in the client system and ultimately find himself or herself co-opted by that system or even implicitly colluding with it in activities that restrict genuine change. For this reason, it is often useful for consultants to work in groups, so that they can maintain an independent point of reference that contrasts to that of the client organization. By this means, additional insurance is provided that the consultant will be more likely to adhere to professional values concerning change recommendations.

In summary, the tension between the readiness of (and capabilities of) the organization for change and the values and aspirations of the professional change consultant is a continuing problem for which no easy resolutions are available or appropriate. Somehow, the consultant must introduce material to the organization that is sufficiently discrepant from the status quo to provide impetus for change—but not so deviant as to be rejected out of hand by the organizational managers. That, as most practicing organizational interventionists know very well indeed, is a fine line to walk.[33]

As suggested earlier in this chapter, a police chief is sometimes appointed specifically to effect reform and thus may be under pressure to make changes (sometimes radical ones) quickly. Drastic changes, whether implemented or only planned, however, make the chief vulnerable to attack.

Resistance to Change

Over and above the general predisposition against change in the social climate of most organizations, specific proposals for change are almost certain to encounter

rigorous obstacles in the form of organized resistance from individuals and groups both within and external to the organization.[34] Rather than being attributable to personality characteristics, the causes of resistance may be rooted in a past experience or past reinforcement history of those facing change. Lower-level members of organizations in particular may have had direct experience that has led them to associate change with negative consequences.[35] If, for example, the last organizational change undertaken by a police department resulted in patrol officers having to work more evening hours to accommodate increased calls for service and increased crimes, and if this change disrupted the officers' off-duty personal lives and also failed to provide salary or other compensating differentials, then some officers will very likely be predisposed to believe that change, although perhaps beneficial to the organization, is not beneficial to them.

Most people who perceive, rightly or wrongly, that a proposed change will adversely affect them can usually be counted on to resist the change as mightily as they can.[36] In any case, most members of an organization have a vested interest in the status quo. They have adapted to the organization's environment and know how to cope with it; they have developed behavioral patterns that enable them to obtain satisfactory outcomes and to avoid unpleasant outcomes. Change means uncertainty; there is no assurance that a new scheme will be as satisfactory as the old one, even though the old one may have been flawed.[37] Thus, people sometimes resist innovations even when they cannot identify any results harmful to them simply because they grow anxious about consequences they cannot foresee that might injure their interests.

Occasionally, resistance to change is presented by individuals or groups even when it is known that their interests will not be compromised. These people may be obstructionists in the hope of exacting concessions or other advantages in return for their support or acquiescence.[38]

Some individuals may resist change because of the heavy psychic costs associated with change. According to Kaufman,

> The advocates of change naturally concentrate so heavily on the benefits to be derived from their recommendations that they sometimes lose sight of the personal effort and agony of people who have to accommodate the new patterns. Over and above advantages lost and penalties inflicted by opponents, beyond the humiliation of becoming a raw novice at a new trade after having been a master craftsman at an old one, and in addition to the expensive retraining and retooling, is the deep crisis caused by the need to supress ancient prejudicies, to put aside the comfort of the familiar, to relinquish the security of what one knows well. Put aside the social and financial incentives to stand fast: after those are excluded, it is still hard for most of us to alter our ways. The psychic costs of change can be very high, and therefore go into the balance sheet on the side of keeping things as they are. In addition, the psychic cost of pressing for an innovation are substantial. If the change is adopted and fails, the embarrassment and loss of stature and influence can be chilling to contemplate; the costs and benefits of the old ways are at least known. If battle is joined on behalf of change the proponents are likely to be opposed from all sides. Some critics will accuse the advocates of being too timid in the struggle, while others will portray the campaign as evidence of hunger for power; some will call them tools of vested interest, while others will depict them as running amok; some will complain of the innovator's readiness to experiment wildly at the expense of those they serve, while others ridicule them for unwillingness to try something more daring than marginal adjustments. To win allies the proposed reforms must be amended and weakened and compromised until the expenditure of efforts seems hardly worthwhile. Meanwhile the drama of the struggle often arouses expectations among the beneficiaries out of all proportion

to the realities of the improvement; instead of winning the applause and gratitude, the innovators often reap denunciation from those they thought they were helping as well as from their adversaries in the controversy. And anyone with experience in such a contest is aware that he or she may end up with obligations to supporters whose purposes he or she does not share and with fleeting credit but lasting enmities. On balance, then, the members or contributors to an organization are presented with much stronger incentives to act warily than daringly. Precedent serves as a valuable guide because it clearly defines the safe path; in a mine field wise men step exactly in the footprints of predecessors who have successfully traversed the hazardous area.

The collective benefits of stability and the calculated opposition to change thus weigh heavily against innovation even when the dangers of inflexibility mount.[39]

Finally, it is often overlooked that police departments have a number of features that make them quite resistant to change. For example, the behavioral expectations for police officers, especially of those in medium-sized and larger agencies, are usually specified in great detail and are divided very specifically. Every component must perform according to a set pattern, or there is a danger that the entire operation will be disrupted. Officers are therefore screened and groomed for the positions they will occupy; they are socialized and fitted into the ongoing system. Officers are chosen not only for skills and aptitudes but also for attitudes and personality traits. Their values and perceptions are then shaped by the organization. Officers learn their training manual, master the methods of their department, and forge understandings with their fellow officers until the whole system becomes second nature to them. Directives, orders, commands, instructions, inspections, reports, and all other means of organizational control, however irksome they may once have been, are gradually accepted as each officer's own premise of thought and action, until compliance with them is no longer reluctant or indifferent obedience, but an expression of personal preference and will.[40] Change after such indoctrination can be traumatic indeed.

Success and Failure Patterns in a Planned Change

A great deal can sometimes be learned by studying the success and failure patterns of organizations that have undertaken planned change. To discover whether there were certain dimensions of organizational change that might stand out against the background of characteristics unique to one organization, Greiner and others conducted a survey of eighteen studies of organizational change. Their findings were as follows:

Specifically, we were looking for the existence of dominant patterns of similarity and/or difference running across all of these studies. As we went along, relevant information was written down and compared with the other studies in regard to (a) the conditions leading up to an attempted change, (b) the manner in which the change was introduced, (c) the critical blocks and/or facilitators encountered during implementation, and (d) the more lasting results which appeared over a period of time.

The survey of findings shows some intriguing similarities and differences between those studies reporting ''successful'' change patterns and those disclosing ''less successful'' changes—i.e., failure to achieve the desired results. The successful changes generally appear as those which:

Spread throughout the organization to include and affect many people.

Produce positive changes in line and staff attitudes.

Prompt people to behave more effectively in solving problems and in relating to others.

Result in improved organization performance.

Significantly, the less successful changes fall short of all of these dimensions.

Success Patterns. Using the category breakdown just cited as the baseline for "success," the survey reveals some very distinct patterns in the evolution of change. In all, eight major patterns are identifiable in five studies reporting successful change, and six other success studies show quite similar characteristics, although the information contained in each is somewhat less complete. Consider:

1. The organization, and especially top management, is under considerable external and internal pressure for improvement long before an explicit organization change is contemplated. Performance and/or morale are low. Top management seems to be groping for a solution to its problems.
2. A new man, known for his ability to introduce improvements, enters the organization, either as the official head of the organization, or as a consultant who deals directly with the head of the organization.
3. An initial act of the new man is to encourage a reexamination of past practices and current problems within the organization.
4. The head of the organization and his immediate subordinates assume a direct and highly involved role in conducting this reexamination.
5. The new man, with top management support, engages several levels of the organization in collaborative, fact-finding, problem-solving discussions to identify and diagnose current organization problems.
6. The new man provides others with new ideas and methods for developing solutions to problems, again at many levels of the organization.
7. The solutions and decisions are developed, tested, and found creditable for solving problems on a small scale before an attempt is made to widen the scope of change to larger problems and the entire organization.
8. The change effort spreads with each success experience, and as management support grows, it is gradually absorbed permanently into the organization's way of life.

The likely significance of these similarities becomes more apparent when we consider the patterns found in the less successful organization changes. Let us briefly make this contrast before speculating further about why the successful changes seem to unfold as they do.

FAILURE FORMS

Apart from their common "failure" to achieve the desired results, the most striking overall characteristic of seven less successful change studies is a singular lack of consistency—not just between studies, but within studies. Where each of the successful changes follows a similar and highly consistent route of one step building on another, the less successful changes are much less orderly.

There are three interesting patterns of inconsistency:

1. The less successful changes begin from a variety of starting points. This is in contrast to the successful changes, which begin from a common point—i.e., strong pressure

both externally and internally. Only one less successful change, for example, began with outside pressure on the organization; another originated with the hiring of a consultant; and a third started with the presence of internal pressure, but without outside pressure.

2. Another pattern of inconsistency is found in the sequence of change steps. In the successful change patterns, we observe some degree of logical consistency between steps, as each seems to make possible the next. But in the less successful changes, there are wide and seemingly illogical gaps in sequence. One study, for instance, described a big jump from the reaction to outside pressure to the installation of an unskilled newcomer who immediately attempted large-scale changes. In another case, the company lacked the presence of a newcomer to provide new methods and ideas to the organization. A third failed to achieve the cooperation and involvement of top management. And a fourth missed the step of obtaining early successes while experimenting with new change methods.

3. A final pattern of inconsistency is evident in the major approaches used to introduce change. In the successful cases, it seems fairly clear that *shared* approaches are used— i.e., authority figures seek the participation of subordinates in joint decision making. In the less successful attempts, however, the approaches used lie closer to the extreme ends of the power distribution continuum. Thus, in five less successful change studies, a *unilateral* approach (decree, replacement, structural) was used, while in two other studies a *delegated* approach (data discussion, T-group) was applied. None of the less successful change studies reported the use of a *shared* approach.[41]

Summary

The objectives of any police executive contemplating change should be to do so in a manner that offers the greatest possibility of success, does not result in a reduction of the quality and quantity of service to the public, and does not polarize the organization and the community into warring factions. In this chapter, we have examined some of the major components of the change process to accomplish these objectives.

We started by examining some of the most common reasons for initiating change within a law enforcement agency. They tend to evolve from issues related to the crime fighting capabilities of a police department, poor police-minority relations, poor public image, corruption, retirement of a long-tenured police chief, and poor morale.

The person or persons who actually assume the role of change agent will vary. In some cases, it may be the police chief or some other person designated by the chief from within the organization. In other cases, the change agent may be some individual or group of consultants hired from outside the organization.

To better understand planned organization change, Tichy has created a model that is comprised of five major components: (1) the background characteristics of the change agent, such as education, income, religion, and service; (2) the value component, which includes the change agent's attitude toward important social changes, political orientation, and own special goals; (3) the agent's cognitive component, that is, concepts about means of effecting change; (4) the agent's technological component, such as the tools and skills used to effect change; and (5) the concurrent characteristics, that is, the actual behavior of the change agent. Based upon this model, four types of change agents have been identified: (1) people change technology (PCT), which works to achieve change in the way employees behave; (2) analysis from the top (AFT), which relies primarily on the operations research model and works on improving decision making and maintaining and controlling employee performance; (3) organization development (OD), which works to improve the organization problem-solving capabilities by helping people to learn to help themselves and involves assisting members of the organization to work out their interpersonal problems and communication, conflict of interest, and career plans; and (4) outside pressure (OP), which is rarely used by managers to bring about change.

Change agents must possess a number of basic qualifications: technical competence, ability to develop realistic solutions, planning skills, and the ability to work well with members of the organization.

The most common change agent errors are becoming tied prematurely to a particular set of strategies and tactics; failing to identify relevant groups affected by the change team's efforts; failing to recognize the relevant groups' interdependence; failing to fulfill their need to be involved in goal setting and the strategy design process; planning inadequately for the initiation of the change process; failing to plan adequately for the initiation of the change process; and failing to consider the roles played by individuals and groups outside the police department.

Once the decision is made to implement change within the law enforcement agency, consideration must be given to using internal change agents, external change agents, or a combination of both types. Internal change agents have the benefit of valuable insights into both the formal and informal organization as well as the potential sources of support or opposition. However, internal change agents sometimes experience difficulty in establishing credibility. Further, their motives may be questioned, and, if the change process is a lengthy one, someone will have to assume their regular duties.

External change agents frequently have the advantage of considerable knowledge and experience, which provides assurance that the planned change will be completed effectively and expeditiously. In addition, they also enjoy considerable credibility as experts in the field. The one important disadvantage faced by external change agents is their lack of knowledge to identify accurately the major forces within the organization that can help or hinder the change process.

The actual methods by which organizational change can be initiated may vary, but generally they can be grouped into two broad categories: (1) those that focus on changing the individuals working within the organization and (2) those that focus on changing specific organizational structures.

One major problem faced in implementing change is that of determining a pace that is neither too quick nor radical nor too slow and gradual. Setting the right pace often poses special problems, especially for outside consultants. On the one hand, if outside consultants suggest or introduce change too quickly or radically, they risk losing their association and therefore any chance they might have had to influence the effectiveness of the organization; on the other hand, the consultant or change expert can be "seduced" by existing values in the client system and ultimately find himself or herself co-opted by the system or even implicitly colluding with it in activities that restrict genuine change.

An understanding of why people resist change is absolutely essential to the successful accomplishment of a change process. Over and above the predisposition against change in the social climate of most organizations, specific proposals for change are almost certain to encounter rigorous obstacles in the form of organized resistance from individuals and groups both within and external to the organization. This resistance by individuals may be attributable to certain personality characteristics, but it is more likely to be rooted in some unfavorable past experience with the change process. Most people who perceive that change will affect them adversely can be counted on to resist it. Also, police departments frequently have a number of features that make them quite resistant to change. These include highly defined behavioral expectations that are uniform in the training and supervision of officers and a host of rules, regulations, policies, and procedures that are viewed as the organizational gospel. Thus, the officers' values and perceptions may be shaped by all these factors for many years, and sudden change can be perceived as being threatening.

Although there are no guarantees that any particular pattern of planned change will succeed or fail, a great deal can be learned from the experience of organizations that have undergone change. Greiner and others conducted a survey of eighteen organizations that had undertaken planned change and noted the following success and failure patterns. Success patterns were spread throughout the organization to include and affect many people, produce positive changes in line and staff attitudes, prompt people to behave more effectively in solving problems, and result in improved organization performance. The failure patterns included a lack of consistency in the planned change, wide and seemingly illogical gaps in the sequence of planned change, failure to achieve cooperation and involvement of top management, and failure to use a shared approach.

The likelihood of implementing successful organizational change will be enhanced considerably if certain aspects of the change process are handled appropriately. Failure to consider many of the factors discussed in this chapter will likely result in both the goals and the objectives of police executives falling far below their expectations or perhaps failing to come to fruition at all. In addition, a poorly planned and poorly timed change effort could result in the mobilization of certain powerful groups within the police agency and in the community joining together to force the police executive's resignation or dismissal.

Thus, an understanding of the change process will facilitate maximum goal achievement while minimizing the risk of failure.

Discussion Questions

1. What types of events frequently give impetus to planned change within a police department?

2. Briefly discuss the four different types of change agents that have been identified.

3. What are the basic qualifications of a change agent?

4. What are some of the most serious change agent errors?

5. What are the pros and cons of internal change agents?

6. What are the pros and cons of external change agents?

7. According to Lewin, change in individuals occurs in three phases. What are they?

8. If changing the organizational structure of a law enforcement agency is determined to be the means employed to change the organization, certain factors must be considered. What are they?

9. Successful change patterns in organizations generally achieve certain results. What are they?

10. There are a number of interrelating patterns of inconsistency among those organizations experiencing less successful changes. What are they?

Notes

1. P. Hersey and K. H. Blanchard, *Management of Organizational Behavior: Utilizing Human Resources,* 3d ed. (Englewood Cliffs, N.J.: Prentice-Hall, 1977), p. 273.
2. Ibid., p. 273.
3. G. N. Jones, *Planned Organizational Change* (New York: Praeger, 1969), p. 19.
4. Ibid., pp. 19–20.
5. D. Hellriegel and J. S. Slocum, *Organizational Behavior,* 2d ed. (New York: West, 1979), pp. 564–568. Much of this discussion on the topic framework for change agents' role and accompanying references were taken from this source.
6. N. Tichy, "How Different Types of Change Agents Diagnose Organizations," *Human Relations* (November 9, 1975), pp. 771–779; N. Tichy and J. Nisberg, "Change Agent Bias: What They View Determines What They Do," *Group and Organization Studies,* 1:3 (September 1976), pp. 286–301.
7. G. Zaltman and R. Duncan, *Strategies for Planned Change* (New York: John Wiley, 1977), p. 190.
8. Ibid., p. 190.
9. Ibid., p. 191.
10. Ibid., pp. 192–193.
11. Ibid., p. 193.
12. Zaltman and Duncan, *Strategies for Planned Change,* pp. 204–205.
13. Ibid., pp. 205–206.
14. Ibid., pp. 206–207.
15. E. M. Rogers and D. K. Bhowmik, "Homophily-Heterophily: Relational Concepts for Communications Research," *Public Opinion Quarterly,* 34:4 (Winter 1970–1971), p. 529.
16. L. W. Porter, E. L. Lawler, III, and J. R. Hackman, *Behavior in Organizations* (New York: McGraw-Hill, 1975), p. 439.
17. A. C. Filley, *Interpersonal Conflict Resolution* (Glenview, Ill.: Scott, Foresman, 1975), p. 126.
18. Ibid., p. 126.
19. K. Lewin, "Group Decision and Social Change," in *Readings in Social Psychology,* eds., E. E. Maccoby, T. M. Newcomb, and E. C. Hartley (New York: Holt, Rinehart and Winston, 1958), pp. 197–212.
20. H. J. Reitz, *Behavior in Organizations* (Homewood, Ill.: Richard Irwin, 1977), pp. 546–547.
21. Ibid., p. 547.
22. Filley, *Interpersonal Conflict Resolution,* p. 133.
23. Ibid., pp. 133–134.
24. W. G. Bennis, E. H. Schein, F. I. Steele, and D. E. Berlew, *Interpersonal Dynamics* (Homewood, Ill.: Dorsey Press, 1968), pp. 338–366.
25. E. H. Schein, "Management Development as a Process of Influence," *Industrial Management Review,* 2:11 (November 1961), p. 10.
26. Porter et al., *Behavior in Organizations,* p. 446.
27. R. R. Blake and J. S. Mouton, *Building a Dynamic Corporation Through Grid Organization Development* (Reading, Mass.: Addison-Wesley, 1969), pp. 8–9.
28. Porter et al., *Behavior in Organizations,* p. 479.
29. Ibid., p. 479.
30. H. A. Sheppard, "Changing Relations in Organizations," in *Handbook of Organizations,*

ed. J. G. March (Chicago: Rand-McNally, 1965), as cited in Porter et al., *Behavior in Organizations,* p. 479.

31. R. Harrison, "Choosing the Depth of Organization Intervention," *Journal of Applied Behavioral Science,* 6 (November 1970), pp. 181–202.

32. E. H. Shein, *Process Consultation: Its Role in Organizational Development* (Reading, Mass.: Addison-Wesley, 1969), as cited in Porter et al., *Behavior in Organizations,* p. 479.

33. Porter et al., *Behavior in Organizations,* p. 480.

34. H. Kaufman, *The Limits of Organizational Change* (University of Alabama Press, 1971), p. 10.

35. H. J. Reitz, *Behavior in Organizations,* p. 545.

36. Kaufman, *The Limits of Organizational Change,* p. 11.

37. Rietz, *Behavior in Organizations,* p. 545.

38. Kaufman, *The Limits of Organizational Change,* p. 11.

39. Ibid., pp. 13–15.

40. Ibid., pp. 16–18.

41. L. E. Greiner, "Patterns of Organization Change," *Harvard Business Review,* 45:3 (May and June 1967), pp. 124–125. This article is part of a larger study on organizational development involving Greiner and his colleagues, L. B. Barnes and D. P. Leitch, that was supported by the Division of Research, Harvard Business School.

Index